STRANGE RICHES

Bengal in the Mercantile Map of South Asia

Rila Mukherjee

FOUNDATION
BOOKS

Delhi • Bangalore • Mumbai • Kolkata • Chennai • Hyderabad

Published by
Foundation Books Pvt. Ltd.
Cambridge House, 4381/4 Ansari Road, Daryaganj, **New Delhi** 110 002

FOUNDATION BOOKS PVT. LTD.
C-22, C-Block, Brigade M.M., K.R. Road, Jayanagar, **Bangalore** 560 070
Plot No. 80, Service Industries, Shirvane, Sector-1, Nerul, **Navi Mumbai** 400 706
60, Dr. Sundari Mohan Avenue, 1st Floor, **Kolkata** 700 014
21/1 (New No. 49) 1st Floor, Model School Road, Thousand Lights, **Chennai** 600 006
House No. 3–5–874/6/4, (Near Apollo Hospital), Hyderguda, **Hyderabad** 500 029

First Published 2006

ISBN 81-7596-324-7

Published by Manas Saikia for Foundation Books Pvt. Ltd. and printed at Print Perfect, New Delhi - 64.

For my father Professor Ramkrishna Mukherjee and my mother Dr Prabhati Mukherjee who comes from Southeast Bengal

Contents

'Maya faced the river, which was almost an ocean. She felt that just as there was a city on land so was there a city on water. As far as she could see, boats crowded the river. So many people lived and worked on these boats; work continued day and night. (When) the boats sailed away Maya thought: Strange! Just a while ago there was this great city on water, now there is only water! One can barely see land on the other side. There is nothing, just the sky above and water below.' Attributed to the eleventh century. (Haraprasad Sastri, *Bener Meye*, *Collected Works*, V.1, Ed. Sukumar Sen, 1980, Paschim Banga Rajya Pustak Parishad: 322–324). [In Bengali, my translation].

'The river is approximately as wide as the Tagus between Almada and Lisbon' (*Voyage dans les Deltas du Ganges et de l' lrraouaddy, 1521*, Presenté et edité Par Genevieve Bouchon et Luis Fi'pe Thomaz, Fondation Calouste Gulbenkian, Paris, 1988:318).

'...the great Bay of Bengala, and Pegu, where ... we once had great settlements of Portuguese ... all of them came to an end with great destruction and devastation, and hence today one only navigates to the port of Orixa in the kingdom of Bengala (Pipli), where there is a Portuguese captain appointed by the viceroy only in order to treat with the Moorish vassals of the Mogor, to whom the port belongs...but he has nothing else there, not even a house, save some made of straw... .' (Bocarro's lament for the Bay trade in the *Livro das Plantas*, in the 1630s, from Sanjay Subrahmanyam, *Improvising Empire: Portuguese Trade and Settlement in the Bay of Bengal 1500–1700*, New Delhi, Oxford University Press, 1990: 262).

'It (Bengal) is one of the largest and most Potent Kingdomes of Hindostan...blessed with many fine Rivers that issue out into the sea of Gulph of Bengala vizt. below Point Palmirs...and the Arackan Shore...some of which are navigable both for great and small ships... This Kingdome is now become the most famous and Flourishinge' (Thomas Bowrey, *A Geographical Account of the Countries Around the Bay of Bengal 1669–1679*, R.C.Temple (Ed)., Cambridge, Hakluyt Society, M D CCCCV: 131).

'Adieu to ye Bay of Bengal ye best flower in ye Company's Garden and all India...' (William Hedges, *Diary of, During His Agency in Bengal 1681–87*, R.Barlow and H.Yule (eds). London, Hakluyt Society, 2 vols. M D CCC LXXX, V .1: 117).

Preface

I

Strange Riches was originally the introductory draft of the work that emerges from the thesis I presented at the E.H.E.S.S., Paris, in the summer of 1985. The introduction formed a composite whole by itself; and it developed further as my interest in Bengal's early commercial history grew.

The time span from the tenth century to the eighteenth century has been highlighted in this look. This covers both of what are termed conventionally the 'ancient' and the 'early medieval' in Bengal's history and the book thus talks of Bengal's mercantile history for three hundred years before the Turko Afghans came to Bengal and continues through the Ilyas Shahi, Abyssinian, Husain Shahi, Afghan, Mughal and Nawabi periods in Bengal's history. However, this volume does not take the thirteenth century (the coming of Islam etcetera) as the starting point for a discussion of Bengal's mercantile history in medieval times as has been the conventional practice. The arguments presented here range from as early as the fourth century of the Christian Era; and the conclusion presents data as recently as 2003.

The area covered in the book is the whole of 'Bengal' during these periods; however the east and the north east of the region have been emphasised, for reasons that will become clear as the reader progresses through the book. If you consider the geographic space from Dhaka and deltaic Sunderbans in the centre and the south (most now in present day Bangladesh), Comilla in the centre, Tripura, Kamrup and Assam in the north east and Chattagram and Arakan in the south east you get a good idea of a real emphasis of *Strange Riches*. This space forms an area of darkness in Bengal's history. It was deemed unrefined to successive generations of historians. Sarkar commented that 'The civilising of East Bengal (if I may be permitted the expression) began with Islam Khan's conquests from Dacca as his base, and the process was completed when the later Viceroys made that city the seat of their government'[1]. The early history of this area was ignored. The one exception was R.C.Majumdar, but understandably, he was more preoccupied with establishing the political history of the region in early times[2].

II

It is difficult to write a mercantile history of Bengal keeping a dynastic and territorial space in mind. Information about mercantile activity come up very frequently from spatially liminal zones in Bengal that are difficult to fit in either into a chronological (in this case dynastic time) or territorial (hazy frontiers during the late ancient and the early medieval periods in Bengal do not help in advancing our knowledge) frames. For example, the geographical area studied in *Strange Riches* abounds with references to Pundravardhana and Kamrup. None of these existed as political units for most of the period studied here, but both achieved such allegoric status in Bengal's history for the ancient and medieval periods respectively that areas were designated as belonging to these geographical units long after they ceased to exist as coherent political forces. Similarly, the period from the ninth to the thirteenth century in Bengal has been studied conventionally as the Pala-Sena-Turko Afghan period. But this dynastic frame does not explain adequately political developments in the south east. The south east and the north east (called the 'far east' in this volume for reasons of convenience) were home to so called 'minor' dynasties: the Khadgas, Chandras, Pala-Khamboj, Varmans and Devas who have been highlighted here, who ruled in the area known as Pundravardhana, and who continued to rule long after the Turko-Afghan conquest of western Bengal. For 'minor' although they may have been from the political point of view, mercantile activity during their reigns paints a different picture. This volume on Bengal's commercial history attempts to reconstruct a picture of Bengal's trade during their reigns.

The period from the tenth to the thirteenth centuries is truly a period of darkness in Bengal's history. Moreover, this time slice occupies an unfortunate place in conventional chronology for the overall history of South Asia. This period is regarded as neither ancient nor medieval; and

---

[1] Sarkar, Jadunath, 1973, *The History of Bengal: Muslim Period 1200–1757*, Patna, Academica Asiatica: 228.

[2] Majumdar, R.C. ed. 1943, *The History of Bengal*. V.1 Hindu Period, Dacca, The University of Dacca.

thus it is ignored by the practitioners of the first and forsaken by those of the second. Understandably so, for the period fits in neither with the 'ancient' nor with the 'medieval' (or 'Islamic period') on land.

But the perspective from the sea yields a different slant. This period saw a veritable revolution in commerce in the Bay of Bengal. The eleventh century witnessed a 'trade revolution' in the Indian Ocean. This fact was first articulated by K.N.Chaudhuri[3] and later developed by Hermann Kulke[4], Denys Lombard[5] and Jan Wisseman Christie[6] to encompass the entire period from the tenth to the thirteenth centuries. This revolution impacted on Bengal's shores and a sub sector trade sprang up in the northern Bay of Bengal between eastern Bengal and her immediate neighbours. The political units in Bengal that saw this small sector trade emerge were the shadowy Khadga, Chandra and Pattikera kingdoms in east Bengal, in the Comilla-Dhaka Vikrampur area. The Khadgas were Buddhist and maintained close relations with their Buddhist neighbours in the north Bay. Similarly the Buddhist Chandras interacted, not only with their Pala contemporaries in western Bengal, but with the kingdom of Pagan to their east. They also traded, mainly in aloes wood, an item in great demand in the medieval world, from Srihatta, Kamrup and Assam and exported them to the greater Buddhist world in the Bay. We have no definite indications that they traded with the Ganga Valley and north India, although they must have done so. The Pattikera kings continued the Chandra tradition and interacted with Arakan which was nominally under the suzerainty of Pagan until the latter's collapse in the thirteenth century. However, Arakan maintained an independent stance in its relations with eastern Bengal from as early as the eleventh century as is clear from Tilman Frasch's account that I have used later on in this volume.

---

3 Chaudhuri, K.N., 1985, *Trade and Civilisation in the Indian Ocean: An Economic History from the Rise of Islam to 1750*, Cambridge University Press.

4 Kulke, Hermann, 1999, 'Rivalry and Competition in the Bay of Bengal in the Eleventh Century and its bearing on Indian Ocean Studies', in Om Prakash and Denys Lombard eds. *Commerce and Culture in the Bay of Bengal 1500–1800*, New Delhi, Manohar/ ICHR: 17–35.

5 Lombard, Denys, 1990, *Le Carrefour Javanạis: Essai d'histoire Globale*, III, *L'Heritage des Royaumes Concentriques*, Paris, Editions E.H.E.S.S.

6 Christie, Jan Wisseman, 1999, 'Asian Sea Trade between the Tenth and Thirteenth Centuries and Its Impact on the States of Java and Bali' in Himanshu Prabha Ray ed. *Archaeology of Seafaring: The Indian Ocean in the Ancient Period*, ICHR Monograph Series 1, New Delhi, Pragati: 221–270.

III

After the thirteenth century there is a gap in the mercantile history of Bengal. The history of the sixteenth to the eighteenth centuries is undoubtedly the 'history of the west', both locationally and conceptually. Historical events on the western side of the province now dominate the scene. The history of Bengal was seen (and written) from the point of view of 'renaissances'. J.N. Das Gupta went so far as to call the Husain Shahi period a renaissance: 'The phenomena with which we are familiar in Europe during the Renaissance meet us everywhere in Bengal in the sixteenth century'[7]. Echoing Burckhardt, Das Gupta went on: 'In Europe, with the Renaissance, we are told, man discovered himself and became a spiritual individual…As in Europe, so in Bengal, after years of groping in the dark, in Green's picturesque phrase, men opened their eyes and saw'[8].

Jadunath Sarkar closed the medieval in Bengal's history and hailed the modern as yet another 'renaissance'[9]:

> When the sun dipped into the Ganges behind the blood red field of Plassey, on that fateful evening of June, did it symbolise the curtain dropping on the last scene of a tragic drama?...Today the historian…knows that it was the beginning, slow and unperceived, of a glorious dawn, the like of which the history of the world has not seen elsewhere. On 23rd June 1757, the middle ages of India ended and her modern age began….It was truly a Renaissance, wider, deeper and more revolutionary than that of Europe after the fall of Constantinople.

While the the sixteenth and the eighteenth centuries are signalled by two 'renaissances' the period immediately preceding these centuries received no such accolades. There has been little work on Bengal's commercial and social history for the early medieval period. The thirteenth to the fifteenth centuries form a void in Bengal's history. Understandably, most authors restrict themselves mainly to the sixteenth century for which sources are available. M.R.Tarafdar and Aniruddha Ray worked on the Husain Shahi

---

7 Das Gupta, J.N. 1914, *Bengal in the Sixteenth Century* A.D., Calcutta, Calcutta University: 25.

8 *Ibid.*: 24.

9 Sarkar, Jadunath, 1973,: 497–99.

period and on Gaur[10] respectively. Hitesranjan Sanyal worked on social mobility in Vaishnav Bengal in Husain Shahi times[11]. The Husain Shahi period was singled out for special attention and Tarafdar extolled Husain Shahi rule as the one inaugurating the 'early modern' in Bengal[12].

IV

Unlike the Husain Shahi period the period immediately preceding it, the Ilyas Shahi period in Bengal's history, has received little or no attention in historical scholarship. Yet, it had witnessed intense political, cultural and mercantile activity in medieval Bengal. The Ilyas Shahis ruled Bengal from 1342 to 1487, that is for almost a hundred and fifty years, except for a short interregnum between 1410 to 1435. One exception to this trend is the work of Haraprased Ray. His work on fifteenth century trade, routes and China-Bengal diplomacy has proved invaluable for reconstructing the commerce of the period[13].

Atul Chandra Roy placed the Ilyas Shahis in their rightful context when he claimed in his *History of Bengal: Turko-Afghan Period*[14]:

> The Ilyas Shahi dynasty occupies a distinct place in the history of Bengal. This dynasty preserved remarkable political consistency and produced a chain of able rulers who ruled over a vast kingdom like Bengal for such a long time at a stretch with a short interregnum…The greatest political contribution of this dynasty lies in the fact that it not only recovered Bengal's political independence (from Delhi) but also preserved the same against Delhi's repeated aggressions…It was Ilyas Shah who restored Bengal's political and administrative unity under one authority (by introducing) some sort of a central government...The Ilyas Shahi rulers were also great conquerors…Bengal witnessed a large territorial expansion under the rule of the Ilyas Shahis. The Ilyas Shahis were tolerant,

10 With the exception of Ray's (2004) *The Merchant and the State: The French in India 1666–1739*, New Delhi, Munshiram Manoharlal. See Ray's Introduction to Abid Ali Khan's *Memoirs of Gaur and Pandua*, Calcutta, West Bengal Directorate of Archaeology, 1986, where he discusses the location of the City of Bengalla and whether this can be identified as Gaur.

11 Sanyal, Hitesranjan, 1981, *Social Mobility in Bengal*, Calcutta, Papyrus.

12 *Husain Shahi Bengal: A Socio Political Study*, Dacca, 1965.

13 See the section on sources later on in this volume.

14 1986, New Delhi/Ludhiana, Kalyani Publishers: 245–6.

enlightened and great builders too....(They) were patrons of art and architecture and built numerous mosques and public buildings.

Not only were the Ilyas Shahis all of the above; they also motored an immense commercial boom in Bengal. In most part, this was the same mercantile space in the east and the north east that was occupied previously by the 'minor' dynasties of Bengal in *samatata*, *harikela* and parts of Pundravardhana. There was no decisive waning of the Buddhist world of commerce at the time of its replacement by an Islamic one in the thirteenth century initially.

But now, by way of commerce, the Ilyas Shahis moved far beyond the confines of the Buddhist world and they placed Bengal within an expanding network of Islamic states that radiated from east Africa through southern Europe, Mecca, Central Asia and China through a mixture of religious (charitable works such as the foundation of mosques and madrassas at Mecca), diplomatic (mission to Herat), trade (between East Africa and China; at least one giraffe from Africa was sent by the Bengal sultan to China) and tribute (voyages to China)[15] missions. The Ilyas Shahis therefore negotiated a vast physical space: from China to Central Asia and Africa. Their rule was truly international.

How was this changeover possible? It was possible because the Ilyas Shahis insinuated themselves into two favourable conjunctures for Bengal's commerce. On the one hand the Islamic conquest of Bengal inserted the region into a vast maritime network stretching from Spain, Persia, West Asia and East Africa up until the China coast. On the other hand, Mongol invasions on the northern Chinese border made the Chinese abandon the traditional overland silk route through Herat and Mashad and look southwards through the port of Ch'uan Chou or Zaitun for tribute and trade. This gave a great boost to oceanic trade in the eastern Indian Ocean. Zaitun became the premier mercantile city in the eastern Indian Ocean by the thirteenth century.

V

The Chinese diversion from the Mongol overland trade route and the drive southwards to the sea had repercussions on Bengal's northern frontiers as well. By the thirteenth century a renewed urbanisation was seen in the

[15] Church , Sally, K., 2004, 'The Giraffe of Bengal: A Medieval Encounter in Ming China', *Medieval History Journal*, 7,1: 1–37 and 'Teobaldo Filei', 1972, *China and Africa in the Middle Ages*, London.

region of Assam, Kamrup, Little Tibet and Chinese Turkestan. New towns such as Karampatan, famed for the horse trade with both China and Lakhnauti, Mardhan Kot in Kamrup on the Brahmaputra built on the model of towns in Mongol China by Gurhasp Shah on his return from China, and Ku'lam, known for its Chinese style ceramics and famed for its trade in aloes, became important off shoots of the new silk route. These towns on the northern frontier of Bengal, running through Kamrup and Ava into Chinese Turkestan and Tibet, may have furthered the old Buddhist network. They certainly introduced a new pattern of trade into Bengal by the end of the thirteenth century. Bengal's ports now began to connect with these caravan trading towns through its intricate fluvial system. Rivers that were important for commerce were the Karatoya, the Tista and the Brahmaputra. Bengal's ports prospered from this time. The area stretching through Bengal into south China and encompassing Kamrup, Ava, Arakan and much of Assam-formed an independent and unified economic realm by the fourteenth century. Chinese tea and porcelain was exchanged for Bengal cotton and Kamrup/Srihatta aloes. Trade in the sturdy hill horses from Turkestan and Tibet mediated this process.

The thirteenth century was therefore significant for events on both land and sea. On land, there was the Islamic conquest of Bengal and the Mongol putsch from Central Asia eastward and southward. The effects of these landward putsches have been much studied in history but what is often forgotten is that the eastern seas saw the end of two empires in the same century. One, the Pagan empire that was a dynamic neighbour of Bengal was overthrown by the Mongols between 1280 and 1300, and two, the Sailendras Srivijaya who had held a quasi monopoly of the eastern Indian Ocean trade in the eleventh and twelve centuries, were overthrown also by the Mongols in 1293.

The Mongol invasions, while not touching Bengal's territory directly, were therefore of great significance for Bengal's overseas connections. Between the thirteenth and fourteenth centuries their conquests radically altered the political life of the Bay of Bengal. The fall of the Sailendras led to the rise of the kingdom of Majapahit in Java in 1293, the fall of Pagan in the same century led to the empire splitting up into that of the Shans in Ava and the Mons in Pegu. The Irrawady basin broke up. Arakan now became quasi-independent. This had great implications for the trade of Bengal as we shall see in subsequent pages. Finally, the Mongol invasions resulted in Chinese revolts that brought the Mings to power in 1368. This was significant, again for Bengal, because from the fifteenth century a direct Bengal-China trade developed by sea.

There were thus three trade cycles that were favourable for medieval Bengal. The first was in the tenth-eleventh centuries. This was powered from the southeast. The second was in the thirteenth century; its effects were seen largely in the north east. And the third was in the fifteenth century. This was powered from the political capital of Lakhnawati/Pandua in the west, but mercantile activities were geared towards the east. So yet another argument of *Strange Riches* is that the Ilyas Shahi period, and not the Husain Shahi period, is crucial for understanding the peculiar mercantile history of Bengal.

VI

The fifteenth century was decisive in expanding Bengal's commercial links with the medieval world of Asia. As just noted, the Ilyas Shahis promoted commercial activities in both the eastern and western Indian Ocean. In 1404, the Ilyas Shahis sent the first diplomatic mission to China, in 1406/7 they offered refuge to the Arakan king Min Sowa Mun (Narameikhla) at Gaur, and in 1432 they helped Narameikhla regain his throne in Arakan[16]. Thereby, the Ilyas Shahis established their hegemony not only on land; they attempted the same for the maritime space of the Bay of Bengal.

To reiterate, the Ilyas Shahis occupied the first Islamic network and it was indeed an era of cosmopolitanism for Bengal. Yet we saw that this period is largely ignored when we discuss the mercantile history of Bengal. I argue that we should see Bengal as part of the first Islamic-Mongol network that stretched from North Africa into China of which Ibn Khurdadbih, al Idrisi, Ibn Haukal, Ibn Batuta, Ibn Khaldun and the Chinese have left us their impressions. One author who takes account of the vast physical space of Ilyas Shahi activities (albeit only to the East) is Haraprasad Ray whose data on fifteenth century trade has proved invaluable in reconstructing much of the mercantile history of Bengal in the pre Husain Shahi period[17].

VII

This book attempts to look at Bengal's commercial history as one somewhat apart from mercantile developments in the middle Gangetic

---

[16] This was Jalal ud Din, son of Kans or Raja Ganesh.

[17] Ray, Haraprasad, 2003, *Trade and Trade Routes between India and China*, Calcutta, Progressive Publishers. Ray, Haraprasad, 1993, *Trade and Diplomacy in India-China Relations-a Study of Bengal During the Fifteenth Century*, New Delhi, Radiant.

plain. Yet another attempt of this volume has been to understand Bengal's commercial and social history in terms of its links with neighbouring countries in the north Bay. One such fluid political unit was Arakan-nominally under Pagan suzerainty–which was an ally of the Chandras in the eleventh century. This argument was difficult to flesh out, since source material on the early history of Arakan is scant. Even those from the eleventh until the sixteenth centuries are few and far between; frequently Arakan's history has had to be imagined from accounts of Tripura and the history of Chattagram. Source material for Arakan between the sixteenth and eighteenth centuries are more plentiful; although they are mainly travel accounts written by the Portuguese, the Dutch, the French and the English.

Unfortunately there have been also only a few secondary works published on Arakan in recent years. Exceptions are Tilman Frasch's 'A Buddhist Network in the Bay of Bengal: Relations Between Bodhgaya, Burma and Sri Lanka, c.300–1300' in Guillot, Lombard and Ptak (eds). *From the Medietrranean to the China Sea: Miscellaneous Notes*, Wiesbaden, 1998, Frasch again and others in Gommans and Leider (eds). The Maritime *Frontier of Burma: Exploring Political, Cultural and Commercial Interaction in the Indian Ocean World, 1200–1800*, Leiden, 2002, Pamela Gutman's *Burma's Lost Kingdoms: Splendours of Arakan*, Weatherhill CT and Orchid Press, Bangkok, 2001, Michael W.Charney's 'Crisis and Reformation in a Maritime Kingdom of Southeast Asia: Forces of Instability and Political Disintegration in Western Burma (Arakan), 1603–1701, *Journal of the Economic and Social History of the Orient*, V.41: 185–219 in 1998, Sanjay Subrahmanyam's 'Dutch Tribulations in Seventeenth Century Mrauk-U' in *Explorations in Connected History: From the Tagus to the Ganges*, Oxford University Press, New Delhi, 2005: 200–247, and finally, M.A.Chowdhury's *Bengal-Arakan Relations*, Calcutta, Firma KLM, 2004. In contrast to the limited corpus of secondary works on early Arakanese history, there has been considerable work on Bengal-Arakan coinage, some of which has been used in this volume.

VIII

By the sixteenth century however, the Mongol challenge was exhausted. The Ottomans, Persians, Uzbegs and Mughals occupied their political space. New trade networks rose in their turn and also a second Islamic commercial world in Asia and Europe.

To investigate what, if any, made this new world different from the earlier one, I tried to develop a section on Mughal attitudes to trade and mercantilism. Unfortunately, material on these themes is yet to be worked upon; notable exceptions are the *Da'a'im al-Islam* of al-Qadi al-Nu'man[18], composed around 960 AD, the official code of the Fatimid state (often taken as a model for the Islamic states in India) , Anthony Black's *The History of Islamic Political Thought* (From the Prophet to the Present)[19], which I found very useful indeed, R.Stephen Humphreys' immensely stimulating *Islamic History: A Framework for Inquiry*[20], Muzaffar Alam's *The Languages of Political Islam in India c.1200–1800*[21] and Harbans Mukhia *The Mughals of India*, Blackwell Publishing, 2004. As is evident from the titles these do not address trade and mercantilism directly and, for the most part, I have had to draw conclusions (always speculative!) from the material presented in these volumes.

In writing this book I have touched upon key issues in both maritime and territorial histories such as the early medieval trade revolution which has been attributed to the eleventh century, the thirteenth century 'rupture' and its impact on Bengal's borders, a further maritime trade revolution in the thirteenth century in the eastern Indian ocean, the very notion of an 'Asian trade", the fissures in the historiographic exercise on Bengal and the debates surrounding the 'primacy of Bengal' in the eighteenth century. I hope the reader will find these of interest. As regards sources much of this volume, by reason of paucity of source material, remains speculative–especially as regards the fifteenth century–and I hope that some day this gap in Bengal's commercial history will be filled in.

The focus of this volume is on Bengal's south east, the area I call the 'far east' of Bengal. As I have said, one of the main thrusts of this book is that it was this area that was probably the first in the region to throw up the first states in coastal (eastern) South Asia. It was also the first area to exhibit commercial dynamism after the (debated) participation in Roman trade died out in eastern India. This was economically the most developed area in Bengal; in terms of transport networks, agricultural and artisanal production and trade. Most of this area underwent two transformations in the twentieth century; once as East Pakistan in 1947 and once again as the independent nation of Bangladesh in 1971. The volume thus ends with the 'big issues' between India and Bangladesh at

---

18 Translated by Asaf A.A. Fyzee and completely revised and annotated by Ismail Kurban Husein Poonawala, 2 vols., Oxford, India, 2004.

19 Oxford, Pakistan, 2004.

20 Revised Edition, Oxford, Pakistan, 2003.

21 New Delhi, Permanent Black, 2004.

the turn of the twenty-first century. A reading of this section will show that the lines of inequality between east and west Bengal were laid in the seventeenth century, when the 'far east' became a marginal land.

Finally, a few words about spellings and transliteration. I have retained Arabic and Persian words in the English form. As regards place names such as Dhaka, Pegu and Chattagram (and others) I have retained both contemporary usages as well as the names under which they are known today. Different editions for the same text I have used, such as the *Suma Oriental*, or the *Ain-i-Akbari*, or Elliot and Dowson's *History of India as Told By its Own Historians*, or for Bernier's *Travels*, have been indicated in the footnotes. If the text is in a language other than English this too has been indicated in the footnote. A separate bibliography has been included in this volume.

I am grateful to Foundation Books for the publication of this volume. Errors and inadequacies of this book remain, needless to say, my responsibility.

Rila Mukherjee
Kolkata
2006.

Acknowledgements

The preliminary foraging for material for this volume was done at the Archives Nationales, the Bibliotheque Nationale as well at the Archives Nationales Section Outre Mer (Oudinot), in Paris. With the exception of the collections at the B.N., and those of the Ministry of the Marine, all the South Asia holdings are now available at Aix-en-Provence. References of documents used are given citing their original provenance[22].

Background material was gleaned from Lisbon, notably from the Arquivo Nacional da Torre de Tombo and from the archives of the India Office Library and Records, London. To the staff of the libraries and archives mentioned above, and especially to the staff at the library of the Maison des Sciences de l'Homme, and the Archives Nationales, Paris and Aix-en-Provence, a big thank you.

I owe thanks to my tutors at the Ecôle des Hautes Etudes en Sciences Sociales, Paris, most notably to my supervisor the late Professor Denys Lombard who patiently guided me through the intricacies of research. Denys Lombard also opened my eyes to the 'other' side of Bengal, that is, to the common yet often neglected heritage shared together by Bengal and South East Asia. Therefore a substantial section of this book has been devoted to exploring Bengal's affinities–topographical and cultural–with its eastern neighbours. Understandably , my pleas for help to Burma went unanswered! Therefore I have attempted to reconstruct the commerce of Bengal with her eastern neighbours from Portuguese and French sources as well as recent publications from Bangladesh.

I also owe a debt to my French tutors of the Diplome d'Etudes Approfondis or D.E.A (M.Phil) course (Mme. Genevieve Bouchon and the late Prof. Jean Aubin, as well as the late Denys Lombard) at the little study group at the Rue de Passy who taught me that structures of everyday life and material culture in a civilization can have a bearing on polity and economy. The lectures of the late Jean Aubin on the Persian Gulf and those of Mme. Genevieve Bouchon and Dr. Luis Filipe Thomaz on the

[22] See abbreviations used in the following section.

Portuguese presence in the Bay of Bengal clarified ideas further. I accordingly situated the discussion in this book from the eighth century when a discernible economic order emerged around the Bay of Bengal. The thirteenth century is also emphasised for that is when a new commercial order emerged in Bengal. I attempted thereby to investigate the rhythms of commerce in ancient Bengal; and to establish linkages and ruptures between it and Sultani (thirteenth to sixteenth centuries), Afghan (sixteenth century), Mughal (seventeenth and eighteenth centuries) and Nawabi (eighteenth century) Bengal.

Further clarification and elaboration of the original thesis was made possible by a three year period (1986–89) as Fellow in History at the Centre for Studies in Social Sciences, Calcutta which made possible a trip to Pondichery to consult the various libraries and archives dotted around that city, mainly the collections of the Institut Francais and the Ecole Francaise d'Extreme Orient, the Bibliotheque Romain Rolland and the Bibliotheque de l'Institut Historique there.

Likewise grants and invitations between 1998 and 2000 made it possible to gather further material from the libraries of the Centre de Sciences Humaines, New Delhi, the Maison des Sciences de l'Homme, Paris, the Italian Institute of Africa and the Orient, Rome, the Sud Asien Institut, Heidelberg, and the French archives at Aix-en-Provence. A stint at the National Institute of Advanced Studies, Bangalore and successive stays at the Indian Institute of Advanced Study, Shimla with its wonderful library, contributed greatly to the maturing of the ideas presented in this volume.

This book took a long time to write. I am gratified at the help that the academic community extended to me while writing this volume. I wish to express my gratitude to those who took the trouble to read drafts of this book and comment on them. Professors Michael Pearson and Teotonio R. de Souza undertook to read the draft by email and comment incisively on all the sections, as did Professor S. Jeyseela Stephen. Professor Jean Marie Lafont, a good friend over the years, encouraged me throughout its writing.

A section from this book on the nature of the mercantile and war economy economy in eighteenth century Bengal was presented at the conference 'India in the Eighteenth Century: Claude Martin and the Age of Enlightenment' orgainsed by Jean Marie Lafont and Jean Francois Salles at Lyon in 2000. Comments and suggestions from Professors Peter Marshall and Jean Marie Lafont at Lyon have enriched the section on the eighteenth century. Another section from this volume–the notion of the primacy of Bengal in the eighteenth century-was presented at the conference organised by Dr. Himanshu Prabha Ray called 'Narratives of the Sea' at the Nehru Memorial Museum and Library, New Delhi in 2003. I benefitted enormously from the comments of the participants, notably Professors M.N.Pearson and Teotonio R. de Souza.

A section of the book was published as a pre-publication essay titled 'Rice Culture of Divine Right in a Celestially Ordered Commercial Zone: Bengal Until 1700' in *Campus Social*, 2004 under the editorship of Teotonio R. de Souza. The section on Asian Trade was published in 2002 in Jadavpur University's *Journal of History*, vol. XIX as 'Ideologies in Conflict: The Precolonial South Asian Economy', Jadavpur University, 2001–2002. The section on markets was included as 'The Nawab's Business: Agricultural and Commercial Practices in Eighteenth Century Bengal', in the Bhattacharyya and Palit edited proceedings of the Business History conference organised by the Department of History, Jadavpur University in 2002 (forthcoming).The mystery of the port of Samandar was included, with the title 'An Elusive Port in Early Medieval Bengal: The Mystery of Samandar', in a forthcoming volume on trade edited by S. Jeyaseela Stephen.

I would like to register my deep gratitude to Dr. Gautam Sen Gupta, Director of the Centre for Archaelogical Studies and Training, Eastern India (henceforth CASTEI), Calcutta, who not only listened patiently when I elaborated my ideas, who not only sourced rare books when needed but who was also kind enough to put the resources of CASTEI at my disposal. Sri Pratip Kumar Mitra, Keeper, State Archaeological Museum, Kolkata, was extremely helpful when I was writing the sections on late ancient and early medieval Bengal.

The story of medieval Bengal's tryst with her north-eastern neighbour Arakan owes much to the Arakan studies pioneered at the Sud Asien Institut, Heidelberg University. I am extremely grateful to Dr.Tilman Frasch formerly of the South Asia Institute, Heidelberg, and now of Manschester Metroplitan University, U.K., who supplied me with much of the material on medieval Arakan's trade and religion. Dr.Schmidt-Vogt opened my eye to Siam's history and the geo-body of a state that was a former commercial partner of Bengal. For Professor Dietmar Rothermund, former Director of the SAI, Heidelberg, who was gracious enough to comment extensively on this book, I reserve my deepest thanks.

Professor Maurice Aymard, Director of the Maison des Sciences de l'Homme, Paris, took time off from his busy schedule to discuss with me the possible implications of slave raiding and piracy off the Bengal coast. As successive chapters will show, piracy and slave trading formed significant economic activities in medieval coastal Bengal, and I must record my gratitude to Prof. Aymard for having opened this 'window' for me.

I would like to express again my deep gratitude to Professor M.N. Pearson who was kind enough to send me a copy of his essay on littoral societies, an essay which is responsible in no small measure for many of the ideas on Bengal that I have presented in the beginning of this book (although I alone remain responsible for any errors that may have crept in while reformulating it in the context of Bengal!).

Thanks are also due to Dr. Bhaskar Mukhopadhyay in Calcutta who helped me with books when needed as well as others too numerous to mention here but whose kindness enabled me to complete this book.

A Visiting Professorship to France in the summer of 2004, under the aegis of the Indo-French Agreement, enabled me to visit once again the archives at Paris and Aix and fill in the gaps in the story of Bengal's encounter with Arakan. My thanks to Professors Maurice Aymard and Gilles Tarabout of the Maison des Sciences de l'Homme, Paris, who made this possible.

An invitation by the East china Normal University, Shanghai, to spend two weeks in China as visiting Scholar in 2006 made it possible for me to visit a country which had substantial commercial interests in medieval Bengal. My thanks to Dr. Biao Yang of the Department of History at ECNU who arranged this as well as a visit to the port of Taichang from where Cheng He launched his voyages.

Finally, a grant from the French Ministry of Culture for a project on Chandernagore made it possible to visit once again the old haunts of the French in Chandernagore and Pondichery. My thanks to M.Jean Claude Tribolet, Conseiller Culturel, Embassy of France in India, New Delhi, India, who provided the initial funds to kickstart the project on Chandernagore, and which has, in many ways, supplemented the arguments presented in this volume.

Rila Mukherjee
Kolkata
2006.

Abbreviations

Archives Nationales, Paris.	A.N. Paris.
Archives Nationales Section Outre Mer, Oudinot, Paris.	A.N.S.O.M. Paris.
Ecole Francaise d'Extreme Orient.	E.F.E.O.
Asia holdings at Aix-en-Provence (previously at A.N.S.O.M.) Now called Centre des Archives Outre Mer.	C.A.O.M., Aix.
India Office Library and Records, London now British Library, King's Cross.	I.O.L.R. London.
Factory Records.	F.R.(with the name of the factory at the beginning. For example K.F.R. refers to Kasimbazar Factory Records and D.F.R. Dacca Factory Records).
Home Miscellanous Series.	HMS.
Bengal Public Consultations.	BPC.
Bibliotheque Nationale, Paris.	B.N. Paris.
Bibliotheque Romain Rolland, Pondicherry.	R.R.
Affaires Etrangères.	A.E.
English East India Company	EEIC.
French East India Company	FEIC.
East India Companies in general	EICs.
the term 'companies' denotes	European companies in general.
Company	English East India Company.

Ecole des Hautes Etudes en Sciences Sociales, Paris.	E.H.E.S.S., Paris.
Cambridge Economic History of India	CEHI.
New Cambridge History of India	NCHI.
Modern Asian Studies	MAS.
Journal of Asian Studies	JAS.
Medieval History Journal	MHJ.
Journal of the Economic and Social History of the Orient	JESHO.

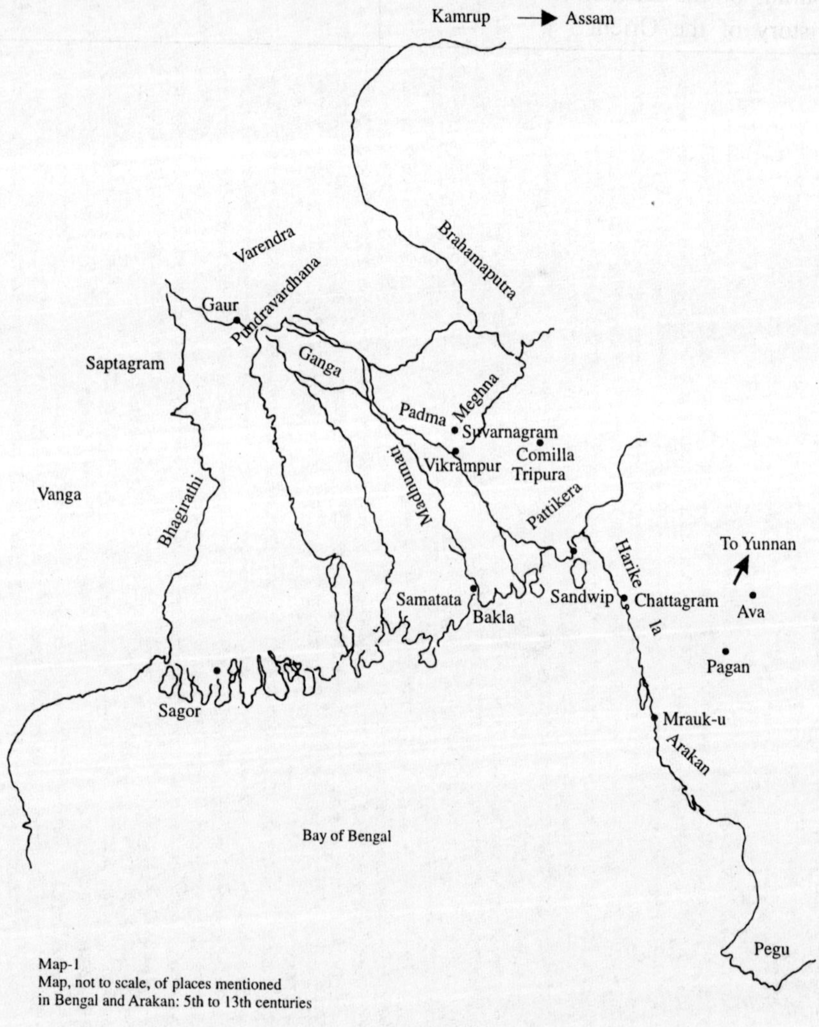

Map-1
Map, not to scale, of places mentioned in Bengal and Arakan: 5th to 13th centuries

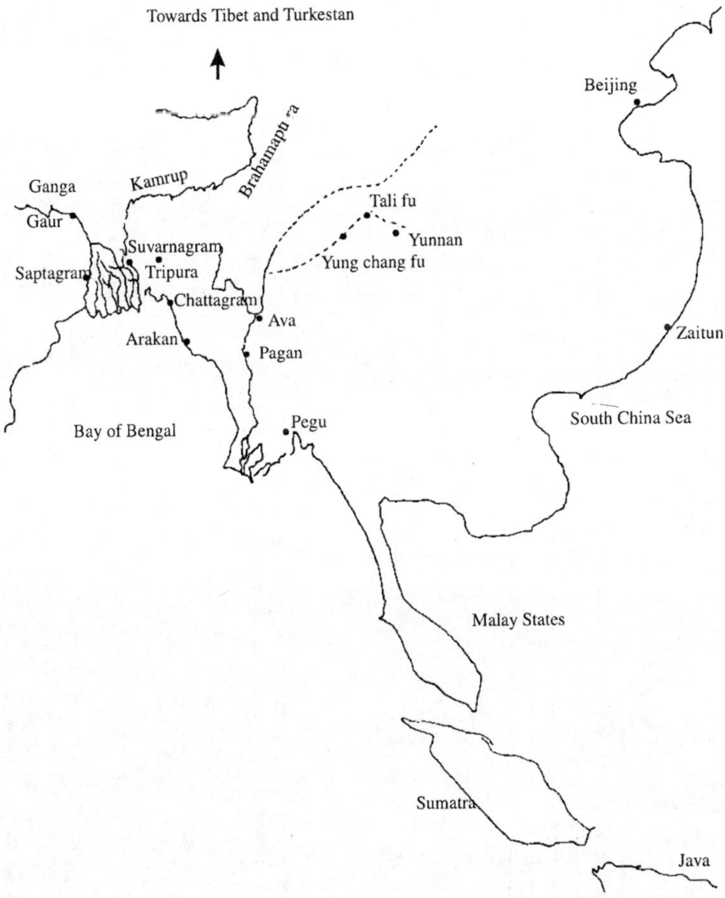

Map-2
Map, not to scale, of the land and sea routes of the
Eastern Indian Ocean: 13th to 15th centuries

1

Introduction

Bengala, a most spacious and fruitful province, but more properly to be called a kingdom, which hath two very large powers in it, Purb and Patan, the one lying in the east, the other on the west side of the river Ganges ... the chief cities in it are Ragamahat and Dakaka. It hath many havens and ports belonging unto it, which are places of very great trade. (Edward Terry, *Voyage to East India,* London, T.Wilkes, MDCC LXXVIII: 84–5)

I

My interest in Bengal's commercial history from the early to the late medieval period is a by product of the doctoral thesis on trade and merchants in eighteenth century Kasimbazar that I did under the supervision of the late Professor Denys Lombard at the Ecole des Hautes Etudes en Sciences Sociales, Paris; a work that was made possible through a French Government doctoral grant from 1981-1985. This was published in 2006 as *Merchants and Companies in Bengal: Kasimbazar and Jugdia in the Eighteenth Century,* New Delhi, Pragati Publications. At the time, notions of 'Asian Trade' and 'successor states' dominated academic studies on eighteenth century South Asian history. Both notions displayed a deliberate and genuine attempt to understand the pre-colonial period and the nature of transformations in the colonial period. A debate that held centrestage at this time was whether (or not, as the case may be) the seeds of capitalism were present in seventeenth century South Asia.

But there was an inherent drawback in this formulation. This has been named the 'characteristic counterfactual proposition'. Subrahmanyam writes[23]:

[23] Sanjay Subrahmanyam, 2005, *'Dreaming an Indo-Persian Empire in South Asia: 1740–1800'*, *Explorations in Connected History: Mughals and Franks,* New Delhi, Oxford University Press: 173–209. See 173–4. As controversial as his writings may be, one cannot ignore his reading of historiographic trends in India after independence.

> Through much of the 1960s and 1970s, students of economic history in the University of Delhi were routinely confronted in their examinations with a characteristic counterfactual proposition: what form would Indian industrialization have taken in the absence of the British colonial state. Answers ranged typically within a rather limited set of possibilities. One tendency was to argue that an independent India (which it was tacitly assumed would be politically coherent and a unitary state) would have developed economically...along the lines of Japan. To this scenario...was contrasted a rather more pessimistic view, sustained by writers such as Morris David Morris, who argued that India by 1750 was already sufficiently 'backward' in terms of infrastructure and markets...If one were to take the first of these tacks, a subsidiary question was then inevitable. Under what conditions would one be authorised to imagine the absence of the colonial state? (such) conceptions have their 'share of illusion...but in the final analysis making a counterfactual is something of a conjuring act.

Problems in such formulations rise largely because notions of 'asian trade', 'successor states' and whether (or not!) there were potentialities for capitalist development in the pre colonial period stem from notions of comparative history. The idea of linear progress that is the motor force of western history underscored this style of history writing.

Independent India's historians believed in the grand emancipatory project that was the rewriting of the history of South Asia–that of a single history and a single voice for a single nation. This meta-history was further classified into the meta-narratives of economy and state. Economy was further classified into agrarian and mercantile economies. The result was a strangely dislocated history; and one that justified all reconstructions of the past from a single originary moment: the imposition of colonial rule in Bengal. My intention is not to minimise the effects of colonialism here; nor to deny that this occurred first in Bengal. But, one of the purposes of writing this book is to demonstrate that the 'balkanisation' of the history of Bengal that we note today is the inevitable outcome of this particular fashion of history written on pre-colonial South Asian polity and economy that emerged after Indian independence.

Pre-colonial trade–both inland and maritime–has really not received the attention it deserves by Indian historians of the Mughal Empire. This was natural given the conventional assumption that the Mughals' interest in trade was minimal at best. However it was evident that from the middle of the seventeenth century a thriving overland and maritime trade had commenced under the aegis of European capital. Further investigation revealed that far from being introduced by Europeans as an economic activity, trade had always been a sustaining feature of the South Asian economy and stretched over a long network of first Buddhist states around the Bay of Bengal and the China Sea, and then of Islamic states from East Asia into Europe and Africa. Bull and Watson comment[24] :

> In the centuries immediately preceding Europe's expansion, the most important regional international systems, alongside medieval Latin Christendom from which the modern European states-system developed were: the Arab-Islamic system, which stretched from Spain to Persia; the international system of the Indian subcontinent and its extensions eastward...the Mongol-Tatar domination of the Eurasian steppes, which had also become Muslim; and the Chinese system, long under Mongol domination. [Elsewhere] ...there was nothing that could plausibly be called an international system, such as had existed for millennia in the Middle East, India and China.

For millennia trade had been an indispensable part of the sub continent. The coastal regions of India–little maritime states–were dependent much more on revenue generated from trade than from agriculture[25]. We have seen that little mercantile states at the mouth of deltaic Bengal–such as Pattikera in ancient Bengal or Sripur and Bakla in medieval Bengal–traded with Arakan and beyond. They based their fortunes on trade. This was however an unstable trade at best; unstable because of the very nature of this deltaic area where rivers changed courses rapidly and new ports and villages disappeared overnight.

These feeder routes converged on the greater Bay of Bengal routes. Part of this latter trade–centering on the Indian Ocean, the Indonesian archipelago and the South China Seas–was dominated by Asian and Indian merchants. This overturned earlier assumptions. How best to classify this trade given the previous marginalisation of it by historians of India: colonial, nationalist and Marxist?

---

24 Bull, Hedley and Watson, Adam (eds). 1984–85, *The Expansion of International Society,*Oxford, Clarendon: 2–3.

25 Heesterman emphasises this particularly when he talks of littoral economies. See Heesterman, J.C. 1980, 'Littoral et interieur de l'Inde', *Itinerario*, I : 89

From the nineteen seventies therefore a category of merchant capitalism called Asian Trade became fashionable among historians[26]. Why Asian mercantilism needed to be singled out from its others was never made clear. Its unconscious originator was the pioneering work of Van Leur, who sought to record the distinctiveness of asian commerce, and this was subsequently developed by Meilink-Roelofz, Glamann and Steensgaard[27]. This all encompassing term 'Asian Trade' sought to deny to Asian commerce that momentum ascribed to European capital and trade. By classing all 'pre company' trade as 'asian' European scholars deliberately ignored the different phases (late ancient, early medieval and medieval) and various networks ('Hindu', 'Buddhist', 'Mongol' 'Islamic'). Consequently, changes over time (and vitality/decline) visible in trading networks in Asia were ignored. By inference such a position also obscured the processes that made specific regions within pre colonial commercial networks (such as Bengal) more or less significant than others.

Also it was never made clear where 'western' trade ended and 'asian trade' began–its spatial scope was stretched constantly along with European 'expansion' in eastern waters.[28] 'Asian' therefore was symbolic; this symbolic space in a metahistorical frame produced economic identity as a historiality–that is it worked on an atemporal surface. This territorial imaginary then produced studies that were essentially out of touch, out of time, out of history. In short Asian commerce was historialised.

---

[26] It is noteworthy that Sinappah Arasaratnam uses this term as late as in 1998. See Arasaratnam 1998 in Mukherjee and Subramanian eds. *Politics and Trade in the Indian Ocean World : Essays in Honour of Ashin Das Gupta* Delhi, Oxford University Press.

[27] Van Leur, J.C., 1955, *Indonesian Trade and Society: Essays in Social and Economic History,* The Hague and Bandung, W.van Hoeve. Meilink-Roelofz, M.A.P., 1962, *Asian Trade and European Influence in the Indonesian Archipelago Between 1500 and about 1630,* The Hague, Martinus Njihoff. Glamann, K., 1981, *Dutch-Asiatic Trade 1620-1740,* The Hague, Martinus Njihoff, 2nd ed., Steensgaard, N., 1974, *The Asian Trade Revolution of the Seventeenth Century, Chicago.* See also Tracy, J.D. (ed). , 1990, *The Rise of the Merchant Empires: Long Distance Trade in the Early Modern World 1350–1750,* and 1991 *The Political Economy of Merchant Empires,* Cambridge University Press for a different perspective.

[28] It is interesting to note that no such attempts were made to fashion a particular 'mediterranean' trade–despite Braudel's insistence that the mediterranean space signified a distinct 'social space' and that the 16th century was not the twilight era of the Mediterranean. See his *La Mediterranee et Le Monde Mediterraneen* (1949), Paris, Armand Colin, the 3 volume *Civilization and Capitalism,* (1979, 1981, 1984), Paris, Armand Colin and especially his inedited mss.published as *Autour de la Mediterranee,* (1996), Paris, Fallois where the emphasis on the multiplicity of layers (and not the mechanical duree) is more pronounced.

Subsequently the frontiers of 'Asian Trade' were pushed ahead by the provocative works of Ashin Das Gupta and Sanjay Subrahmanyam on Bengal as also Om Prakash and Sushil Chaudhuri on Bengal's financial fortunes[29]. Towards the end of his life Das Gupta conducted studies on Bengal–studies in which the particularity of Bengal was very clearly underlined. But 'Asian Trade' offered no intellectual egress; practitioneers increasingly found themselves in the 'huis clos' of a zero sum game where the old adage–the more it changes the more it remains the same–held good.

Four studies that attempted to go beyond the received historiography and unite trade, markets, the state and the social and political realm of the merchant, were those of Sanjay Subrahmanyam (1990)[30], Kumkum Chatterjee (1996)[31], Anand Yang (1998)[32] and Rajat Datta (2000)[33]. Subrahmanyam sought to move away from 'tyranny' of the potentialities

---

[29] Good overviews of the subject, and the issues and debates therein, can be found in Furber, Holden 1951, *John Company at Work, A Study of European Expansion in India in the Eighteenth Century.* Cambridge: Harvard Press, Chaudhuri, K.N. 1978, *The Trading World of Asia and the English East India Company 1660–1760.* Cambridge: University Press and in Das Gupta, A. and Pearson, M.N. ,eds., 1987 *India and the Indian Ocean 1500–1800.* Calcutta: Oxford. For specific area studies see Das Gupta, Ashin 1967, *Malabar in Asian Trade.* Cambridge: University Press and 1979, *Indian Merchants and The Decline of Surat,1700–1750,* Wiesbaden, Steiner Verlag; Chaudhuri, Sushil 1975, *Trade and Commercial Organisation in Bengal, 1650–1720.* Calcutta: Firma KL; Om Prakash 1986. *The Dutch East India Company and the Economy of Bengal, 1640–1720.* Princeton: University Press; Subrahmanyam, Sanjay 1990 *Inprovising Empire, Portuguese Trade and Settlement in the Bay of Bengal, 1500–1700.* Delhi: Oxford Press; Arasaratnam, Sinappah 1986 *Merchants, Companies and Commerce on the Coromandel Coast, 1650–1740.* Delhi: Oxford Press. Marshall, P.J.'s early work *East Indian Fortunes* 1976 Oxford: University Press and more recently Om Prakash and Lombard (eds). 1999 *Commerce and Culture in The Bay of Bengal 1500–1800,* Delhi, ICHR/Manohar and Sushil Chaudhuri and Michel Morineau (eds). 1999 *Merchants, Companies and Trade–Europe and Asia in the Early Modern Era,* Cambridge.

[30] Subrahmanyam Sanjay 1990 *The Political Economy of Commerce : Southern India 1500–1650.* S.Asian Studies #45, Cambridge.

[31] Chatterjee K., 1996 *Merchants, Politics and Society in Early Modern India: Bihar 1733–1820,* E.J.Brill, Leiden.

[32] Yang, Anand A., 1998, *Bazaar India: Markets, Society and the Colonial State in Bihar,* Berkeley and L.A., California Press.

[33] *Society, Economy and the Market: Commercialisation in Rural Bengal c. 1760–1800,* Manohar, Delhi, 2000.

thesis[34] (the straitjacket of the 'prosperity to decline' issue[35]). Chatterjee commented:[36]

> First the question of the political connections of the merchant....cannot prosper our understanding much further unless such analysis is grounded in an analysis of the different levels of the political system together with an attempt to show how and why commercial interests were aligned to it at different levels. Second the social nexus of mercantile activity can never be fully explored...without a conscious effort to delineate how wealth accummulated through trade or banking translated into actual social status, power and cultural leadership as well as the forms and modes through which these were expressed. This approach to analysing the social nexus of trade becomes even more important when the subject of the merchant....caught up in the throes of political transition comes up.

Once the concept of the social nexus trade was fully explored it was agreed that the pre-colonial economy could not be seen merely in terms of economic and political histories; it was equally important to take cognizance of new cultural forms emanating from outside such as exposure to new technologies, military reorganisation, science (cartography and military engineering) and art (perspective) long before actual conquest,[37] as well as changing attitudes to knowledge, visible in a new commercial language and new commercial practices as emerged in the commercial manuals of the eighteenth century, written mostly in Bengali[38].

II

Studies of the state in pre-colonial South Asia suffered from a curious ambivalence after independence in India, as well. Studies of the Sultanate

---

34 Subrahmanyam Sanjay, 1990: 3.

35 Chaudhuri Sushil, 1995, *From Prosperity to Decline: Bengal in the Eighteenth Century,* New Delhi, Manohar.

36 Chatterjee K., 1996: 9–10.

37 Alam, Delvoye and Gaborieau eds. (2000) *The Making of Indo-Persian Culture.* New Delhi, Manohar and CSH.

38 Mukherjee, Rila, 2005, *'Eighteenth Century Bengali Letters in the French Archives'* (In Bengali), *Itihas Sansad* at Tamluk, January. In Mukherjee, Rila, 2006, *Merchants and Companies in Bengal: Kasimbazar and Jugdia in the Eighteenth Century,* New Delhi, Pragati Publications.

and Mughal behemoths comprised a kind of master narrative in which the location was always the upper/middle Gangetic plain and where economy was primarily land based. The margins of these behemoths were not studied. State forms prior to the eighteenth century shift: the Bengal and Gujarat sultanates, the Vijayanagar and *dakhini* states received little or no attention and have been incorporated into the history syllabus only recently (and likewise into textbooks). Despite the attempts of individual scholars in the field there has been no attempt to provide a composite explanation of the changes in regional economies. This 'regnal' model or what Stein termed the Mughal 'orientalist' model is today challenged, for it provides little explanation for activities outside the scope of this model. Yet such activities clearly manifested themselves from the last years of the seventeenth century[39]. This omission became patently obvious by the late seventies and post graduates in Indian universities in the heady seventies wondered whether this limited engagement was all that the rich history of pre-colonial south Asia deserved?

In the light of new research, and to redress the balance somewhat, a new formulation for studying post Mughal South Asia was therefore introduced. Moving away both from the theme of decline so beloved of late colonial historians and the Delhi-Agra centred model discussed here, the idea of the vigorous *riyasat* or the 'successor state' (as supplanting the Mughal in South Asia) was floated from the seventies of the last century. Following in the path of imperial formations–and in the search for the perfect state in the shadow area of the eighteenth century–it was but natural that the shift of focus away from the Vijaynagar and Mughal goliaths resulted in the concept of the successor state (with elaborate bureaucracies and a high degree of centralism) as perpetrator of older structures of taxation and coercion.

But as Cohn (1962) in Political Systems in Eighteenth Century India pointed out, the successor state formulation was inadequate for studying the almost incessant process of state formation in the wake of the Mughal collapse. New typologies of the various new state forms such as imperial (Mughal), secondary (Bengal/Awadh), regional (Marathas) and local (Pindari, Koli, Banjara 'states' as well as the little areas dominated by a combination of trading/marauding peoples that sprang up over north India

[39] 'Eighteenth Century India: Another View', 1989, *Studies In History,* v. in Marshall, 2003, (Ed). *The Eighteenth Century in Indian History: Evolution or Revolution?* Oxford : 62–89.

following the imperial decline) were necessary. Menon pointed out that the *riyasat* argument actually permitted a glossing over of differences between the pre colonial and colonial state and between the various types of state forms that proliferated over the sub continent in the wake of the Mughal/Vijayanagar collapse.[40]

More important, the idea of the *riyasat* (or inland state) actually worked in tandem with the idea of Asian Trade (concerning maritime states) by creating an artificial divide. Economy was taken to be land based for the Sultanate, Vijayanagar and Mughal behemoths. Those that did not fit this model, and naturally most of these were coastal political formations, were thought to be subscribing to 'Asian Trade'. Pre-colonial South Asian history was therefore artificially truncated–the two blocs were seen as being ruled by separate sets of references.[41] Both arguments successfully eliminated any element of dynamism inherent within the two structures. Both formulations stemmed from distinct ideological camps yet both fell into the same trap : in their attempts to rewrite Asian history (and clarify old unresolved issues) they made it all the more obscure.

But not for too long. The eighteenth century, and of late the entire history of pre-colonial South Asia has been subjected to intense scrutiny once again[42]; this has indeed become an ideological battleground for historians of divergent formations and inclinations so much so that over the last twenty years distinct camps have hardened into 'schools' which consciously negate the claims of the others to write a 'true' history. This is shown in the politics of footnoting, in rehearsed silences regarding 'other' writings, and in the well orchestrated power play of the custodians

---

40 See Menon, Dilip, 2000, *'Houses by the Sea : State Experimenation in Malabar 1760–1800'* in Chandoke, N. (ed). *Mapping History: Essays Presented to Ravinder Kumar,* Delhi: 161–86.

41 It was generally recognised that the Mughal had little interest in the profits of maritime states. Recent research however proves that the South Asian littoral had a long and distinguished tradition of maritime polity and warfare. Whether we can apply this formulation to the whole of South Asia awaits further research. A good start has been made in Dilip M. (2000) where he argues that we can look at 'state experimentation' rather than 'state formation' in our search for the state between the pre colonial and colonial . Many of his other suggestions are yet to be substantiated, however.

42 For the latest offerings on the eighteenth century debate see Marshall, Peter J. (Ed). 2003, *The Eighteenth Century in Indian History: Evolution or Revolution?* Delhi, Oxford University Press, Alavi, S., 2002, *The Eighteenth Century in India,* Delhi, Oxford University Press, and Barnett, R., 2002, *Rethinking Early Modern India,* Manohar. For the earlier period see Subrahmanyam, Sanjay and Alam, Muzaffar, 1998, *The Mughal State* 1526–1750, New Delhi, Oxford University Press.

of our archives. We have therefore come to historialise the debate on the nature of the economy in south Asia; we have in a word 'orientalised' our own history once again.

The consequences of a tunnel vision of south Asian history is that the new generation of south Asian scholars have to grapple with a massive gap in historical knowledge in fringe areas even today–colonial ethnography from the late eighteenth century has naturally, for reasons of empire, focussed on the heartland of South Asia with the result that we know almost nothing of indigenous technology, social organisation, knowledge systems, indigenous maritime histories and so on outside the heartland of empire.[43] History after all is always written by the victors.

III

The relationship between 'Asian Trade' and the 'successor state' was sought through an examination of the merchants' links with the court. The merchant-at-court thesis was initially formulated in European history writing and the mercantile-political nexus was deemed to be the one valid indicator of potentialities for transition to a capitalist economy. The assumption was that strong links would indicate a vibrant mercantile economy that functioned with state support; weak links would naturally indicate otherwise. Therefore, studies of commerce in pre-modern Asian societies displayed an engagement with studies that dealt with the coming of capitalism in the west-specially in England, from the 1980s. Comaparative history was fashionable among South Asian historians till late.

Favoured themes of comparative history are, still today, the commercialisation of agriculture and the political links of the early modern merchant that was evident in Europe. That both were visible in certain regions of South Asia by the seventeenth century lent impetus to such comparative studies. It is however important to bear in mind that such events occurred in a specific social context in Europe-the coming of capitalism and by way of an agency-mercantilism. The second was not present in Mughal India. Works dealing with 'capitalist potentialities' in South Asia were plenty in the 1970s and 1980s[44]. It was however never

[43] Ray, Himangshu Prabha, 1996, 'Sea Faring and Maritime Contacts: An Agenda for Historical Analysis', *JESHO,* 39,4.

[44] For example, Irfan Habib's'Potentialities of Capitalist Development in the Economy of Mughal India'in Habib, *Essays in Indian History: Towards a Marxist Perception,* 180–232, New Delhi, 1995.

made clear what type of social formation could translate into a 'successful' capitalist enterprise[45]. Moreover the birth of capitalism in Europe displays neither a unilinear path nor a synchronicity between regions. France and Spain made the transition much after The Netherlands or Britain.

Likewise South Asian economic formations display no unilinearity. Irfan Habib noted the extractive character of the Mughal state and the cracks in the agricultural base that were visible by the end of the seventeenth century[46]. Bayly pointed to the commercialisation of agriculture and the booming of cash crops in northern India soon after[47]. Although we have here two visions of the pre-colonial agrarian economy, beliefs in the unilinearity and synchronicity of capitalist development continued to persist in academic works in South Asia.

Studies in the development of capitalism in the west have also made much of mercantile links at the courts of Europe, for the reasons described earlier. Visible from the Middle Ages in Europe, such links took off in the era of mercantilism. That these did not happen in all cases can be illustrated by a comparison of the Fuggers with the Medicis. The Fuggers of Augsburg could finance Charles V in the sixteenth century and underwrite the Seville-Atlantic trade because of their links with the Spanish Court. At the same time the Medicis of Florence, who had been active in energising the Mediterranean trade with Flanders in the fourteenth and fifteenth centuries, could not make the transition to trade in early modern Europe. They remained essentially medieval merchants, and by the middle of the fifteenth century they translated into French royal bankers at the court at Lyon.

So Chatterjee rightly comments, as we noted before:[48]

> First the question of the political connections of the merchant...cannot prosper our understanding much further unless such analysis is grounded in an analysis of the different levels of the political system together with an attempt to show how and why commercial interests were aligned to it at different levels.

---

[45] Supple, Barry B. 1970, *Commercial Crisis and Change in England 1600–1642: A Study in the Instability of a Mercantile Economy,* Cambridge University Press.

[46] *The Agrarian Crisis of the Mughal Empire 1556–1707,* Bombay, 1963.

[47] *Rulers, Townsmen and Bazaars,* etc. Oxford University Press, 1983.

[48] Chatterjee K., 1996 : 9–10.

> Second the social nexus of mercantile activity can never be fully explored...without a conscious effort to delineate how wealth accummulated through trade or banking translated into actual social status, power and cultural leadership as well as the forms and modes through which these were expressed. This approach to analysing the social nexus of trade becomes even more important when the subject of the merchant...caught up in the throes of political transition comes up.

Chatterjee thus opened an intriguing window for South Asian trade historians. In her book Chatterjee did not engage with eighteenth century commerce in Bengal *per se*; instead she isolated a significant slice of time–the 1740s–when the commerce at Patna, Bengal's gateway to Upper India, became crucial to the commerce of Bengal, and when new political and fiscal alignments were visible on the political map of Bengal after the capture of political power by Alivardi Khan and his coterie in Bengal in 1740. Bihar, from where Alivardi came, gained prominence in Bengal affairs from this time. Chatterjee's volume deals with Bihar merchants at this crucial transitional time that some have held to be mercantilist in nature.

But was the *nawabi* state in the Bengal of the 1740s mercantilist? Mercantilism, as it developed in Europe, was full of contradictions in its initial phase as Rothermund pointed out[49]. France and England developed a body of mercantlist literature when the Dutch Republic did not; this is striking when we remember that Holland became one of the leading trading nations while France never shook off the image of its trade as a 'royal enterprise'.

Rothermund's typology of 'captive trade' as one where the merchant is assured of a stable supply and demand under all conditions is useful in this context[50]. Such a merchant would 'ward off competitors as far as possible and establish relationships with the suppliers which attach them to his interest...European rulers were potentially interested in extending external support to this captive trade'[51]. By contrast Asian rulers were not interested in providing support to captive trade; their interest in sea borne trade was marginal on the whole and there was never any maritime policy

---

[49] Rothermund, Dietmar, 1981, *Asian Trade and European Expansion in The Age of Mercantilism,* Delhi, Manohar : 1–5.

[50] *Ibid.*: 9.

[51] *Ibid.*: 9,11.

framed by the Mughals. Trade was beneficial as long as precious metals flowed in, this enabled the circulation of money which in turn facilitated the collection of land revenue. In short, European rulers afforded special privileges to their leading merchants, because their interests and their merchants' interests coincided. Both searched for markets beyond their nations' borders. For the South Asian rulers there was no concept of a 'national' merchant class simply because Asian states did not have borders in the sense that the European early modern states did, and their rulers were not interested in searching for markets beyond national borders. And because there was no concept of a 'national', 'Indian' merchant as opposed to say 'Arab', 'Armenian', 'Mughal', 'Persian' and so on, there was absolutely no question of the court favouring one group of merchants over others. Therefore, determined through specific social conditions, and governed by the very virtue of his national affiliation and citizenship, the political linkages of the European merchant were very different from his Asian counterpart and it is important to bear this in mind when scholars search for the political-commercial nexus in South Asia even today. This is particularly true for Bengal.

IV

During the seventies and eighties, the idea of 'the primacy of Bengal' within the commercial history of eighteenth century South Asia was a well-established canon in academic studies; and while conducting research into mercantile activity in the silk trade at Kasimbazar I took it as a given that Bengal in the eighteenth century was the foremost mercantile area in South Asia.

Yet in the process of writing my dissertation titled *Commerce et Marchands Autour de Kasimbazar 1704–1757*[52] I was struck by the curious fact that Bengal seemed to display no *independent* commercial momentum of her own in the eighteenth century; while the second half of the eighteenth century is definitely a period of overall commercial decline for South Asia, the non-existence of a historically vibrant merchant community in eighteenth century Bengal was particularly glaring. Instead of merchants and ship owners emerging on their own intitative, controlling the home market and moving on to conquer others (as was attempted by the Gujarat merchants) trade in Bengal at least had always been of something of a 'protected domain' and of a 'royal' nature. This did not mean that all

---

[52] Mukherjee, Rila, 2006, *Merchants and Companies in Bengal: Kasimbazar and Jugdia in the Eighteenth Century,* New Delhi, Pragati Publications op. cit.

rulers participated in trade in their official capacity, what it did mean is that rulers granted farms, monopolies and other favours to a clique of a few courtiers. This was hardly a commercial-political nexus except in a very loose sense of the term. In eighteenth century Bengal therefore we frequently find references to merchants such as Umichand and Ramkrishna Babu who had 'powerful friends' in court[53]. But this did not imply a strong mercantile influence on the court; on the contrary. Merchants worked as the proteges of courtiers. Traders did not venture out of the state to control networks emanating from other ports along the eastern seaboard.

The absence of a vibrant commercial culture manifested itself by the fact that there was hardly an organised indigenous and vocal mercantile community worth its name as in Surat, the Malabar or the Coromandel in the same period. The energetic Chintaman Shahs and Khemchands of the seventeenth century[54] translated into the politically active Katmas[55] who acted as suppliers (known as *dadni* merchants) to the EEIC. By mid-century we find them withdrawing from active trade and functioning as Chief Brokers to the EEIC[56]. In 1772 they financed the FEIC as well[57]. In other words, instead of the courtier becoming merchant, the merchant became the courtier. This reinforces our impression that an independent and energetic mercantile community was on the wane in Bengal.

Instead of the merchant with links at court the inverse was usually the case in South Asia and certainly in Bengal. Many merchants were in actual fact courtier-merchants. Mathuradas (the "Muttradass' of the 1670s and 80s) was actually a 'servant' (this usually meant protégé as well) of Bal Chand, the governor of Murshidabad[58]. Similarly, in the eighteenth century, one 'mighty' merchant combine which dominated the Investment Lists of the EEIC at Kasimbazar was that of Alam Chand[59]. Closer inspection tells us that far from being merely a merchant Alam Chand was first the *Diwan* (or Finance Minister) and then *Rai Rayan* (or the Chief

[53] *K.F.R.*, London

[54] Chaudhuri, Sushil, *Trade and Commercial Organisation*, etc., op. cit

[55] The Katmas are designated as Cotma in the K.F.R.

[56] KFR in *Merchants and Companies*, op. cit.

[57] Entry of September 16 1772 at Chandernagore, *No.2530, 22MI41* at CAOM, Aix. Here they are referred to correctly as Katma. The names mentioned are Baburam, Boubon, Panchou and Poran.

[58] See The Structure of Trade in Medieval Bengal later.

[59] KFR, May 1 and 20, 1755 named the combine of Alamchand Gainchand as 'substantial merchants" in Mukherjee, Rila, 1994, 'The Story of Kasimbazar: Silk Merchants and Commerce in Eighteenth Century India', 499–554 : 541, *Review,* XVII, 4, Fall Issue.

Minister) in the 1730s in Bengal. Alam Chand was the most powerful financial figure in Shuja's Murshidabad in the 1730s, his son Raja Kirti or Kriti Chand ('Krittichund' in the KFR) had considerable financial interests in Patna. As *Diwan* and then *Rai Rayan* Alam Chand had so many fingers in every financial pie that Alivardi, when he came to power, did not risk antagonising him. His protégé Chain Ray · was made *Rai Rayan* and the various firms of Alamchand Gainchand and Alamchand Nimchand then ran successful banking firms at Kasimbazar, Dhaka and Patna[60].

Because of the presence of merchant-courtiers in Bengal there was little need for sustained state promotion (or sponsorship) of trade in Bengal as in the Malabar. Rulers, by and large, seemed disinterested in trade. In the 1660s the ruler of the Maldives, with which island ports on the Bengal and Orissa coasts had a very profitable trade in *cauris*, wrote to the Mughal governor of Balasore (Malik Beg?) complaining against Dutch and English ships which came seeking trade opportunities there. The Maldives ruler asked further that Aurangzeb be informed of this and that Aurangzeb should prohibit the EEIC and the DEIC to sail on this profitable route. The reply was that Aurangzeb was a ruler of land and not of the sea[61]. This attitude of the central authorities seems strange when we condsider that the Bengal-Orissa-Maldives route was a very profitable run at this time[62]. More of these different perceptions later.

However it is necessary here to distinguish between attitudes towards trade at the centre and at the actual ports themselves. Throughout South Asian history, even at times of inland commercial decline, as after the Guptas, ports and coastal cities continued to flourish. It is certainly inexplicable that maritime and coastal trade continued to flourish at a time when inland regional economies showed decline in trade, visible in the shrinking of towns, shortage of coinage in circulation and declining mart towns. The flow of matitime trade showed a resistance to the shrinking effects of capital further inland.

We will see later that port officials and governors were pro-active and certainly aware of the immense possibilities of commerce; indeed from the careers of Malik Beg, Malik Kasim and Malik Zindi in pre-colonial Bengal, there are indications that the post of Faujdar of Hugly

[60] KFR as before and DFR 1750 12 November in Mukherjee, Rila, *Merchants and Companies*, etc.

[61] Rothermund, 1981:69.

[62] Bowrey op. cit.: 179–80.

was confined to a small clique of courtiers with trading interests and was well on the way to becoming hereditary from the middle of the seventeenth century[63].

But at courts inland the merchant was frustrated at every step by the courtier-as-merchant and was not in a position to 'capture' the state in Bengal. The absence of an energetic and spontaneous mercantile culture was further visible in the fact that merchant-shipowners of Bengal (including the *subahdars*) withdrew from trade in the eighteenth century. Many functioned as middlemen to other merchants who came into Bengal. Boats now left the seas and plied the inland waters of Bengal. Merchant capital, instead of consolidating itself and crystallising into a strong merchant class, became fragmented. The 'big' trade of Bengal was conducted by 'up country' merchants. Smaller categories of merchants who provisioned mart-towns from remote inland areas now came into being; these were mainly native Bengalis.

Even as middlemen the merchants were not too successful; this reaffirms our view that the entire commercial network was, by then, in the hands of 'up country' merchants[64]. It is necessary here to precise what exactly we mean by the term 'up country' merchants.

Until the eighteenth century there were at least four mercantile networks in Bengal. The first was the caravan trade nework; its provisioning was looked after by the 'Mughal' or Central Asian, Persian, Armenian and Arab merchants who were settled at Kasimbazar, Hugli, Dhaka and Patna with their chain of Bengali subordinate merchants and officials.

The second was the maritime network run by Persian and Arab merchants from Chattagram and Hugli. The third was the inter-regional trade, mainly the Surat-Bengal trade, controlled by Gujarati-Muslims, the Gujarati banias and merchants from the middle Gangetic plain. These were the 'up country' merchants, some settled permanently in Bengal and this was the group that exerted the most influence on its economy. If 'Gujarati' merchants bought up silk filaments (*putney*) early on in the season, a correspondingly high price for raw silk resulted and the EEIC investments suffered[65]. Therefore this was the group the EEICs attempted to wage war against through their *dadni* merchants. This 'Gujarati' merchant

---

63 The Structure of Trade in Medieval Bengal further on.

64 The *dadni* lists for K.F.R. in the eighteenth century feature only a few Bengali names. See Mukherjee, Rila, 2006, *Merchants and Companies* etc., New Delhi, Pragati Publications.

65 *Ibid.*

group had close links with the court. This was the group on whom the Mughal *subahdars* and then the Bengal Nawabs relied the most since it was through them that remittances to Delhi were transmitted. Other than the Gujaratis the Biharis were another prominent 'up country' group.

Last of all came the independent Bengali merchants who were slow in coming into their own in the eighteenth century; this category operated at the bottom of the commercial chain but was indispensable to Bengal's economy by ensuring a) that production satisfied demand at mart-towns and ports and b) that taxation encouraged trade and vice versa. Capitalist agriculture was the agency through which this commercial nexus functioned.

Calitalist agriculture arrived in South Asia in the seventeenth century. But this commercialisation operated within a semi-feudal semi-peasant framework. Most of inland Bengal was involved in 'small' petty agriculture. However, all sections of society depended on the agrarian base. The merchants were not urban creatures; and in Bengal particularly, the merchant rested on an uncertain agrarian base. The peasant was also the weaver or spinner. Washers and dyers supplemented their income from small peasant land holdings. The production sector was not dynamic; in fact little innovation in production is noticed for Bengal. A large population, whose needs were partly met through agriculture, meant that a large labour force was available. The reliance on agriculture also meant that industrial wages were low. A large labour force and low wages impeded the introduction of new technologies in production. In Surat production was not rural; it was gradually getting urbanised. Artisans were moving to the towns. The production process, too, was getting fragmented. This did not happen much in Bengal. Do these factors not mitigate against the notion of Bengal as a prime mercantile zone in the eighteenth century?

Records tell us that the middlemen seem to have structured themselves only towards the middle of the eighteenth century when it was, alas, too late; until then markets were 'unregulated', routes short-lived, ports transient and merchant communities and organisations (such as *dadni*, or *dalal*) weak. Late seventeenth century trading practices seem to have been largely a hit-or-miss affair; a matter of being at the right place at the right time (a factor that contributed to the understandable ire of European company servants on whose records we rely for this period!). Something impeded the growth and maturity of the strong commercial potential of Bengal; the low prices and low cost of living and the prodigious manufactures that made Bengal's products a strong player on the world commercial stage did not translate into a correspondingly strong position for Bengal's merchants.

Bengal's prominent place in writings on eighteenth century trade and politics in South Asia–in light of the eighteenth century debate whose three chief markers were visible in Bengal: decline of Mughal power [contested since there was hardly a strong Mughal presence there that sustained and reproduced itself for a long period], the rise of a regional power [uncontested yet ephemeral], and European ascendancy in trade and politics [uncontested])–is hardly borne out by its previous history which was fairly marginal to developments in South Asia.

V

Part of the reason for this confusion rests on the fact that Bengal was the first area of the sub-continent to be studied in terms of political, and then economic, history; for no other province in India do we have so many writings from so many 'schools'; the colonial, the nationalist, the Marxist, the subaltern, the revisionist and so on and so forth. This rich historiography on Bengal owes its lineage to the massive corpus of works dealing with the political and economic history of Bengal. The process of 'writing a history of Bengal' and of deliberating on the 'political economy' of Bengal started from the eighteenth century itself. Mir Golam Hussain, Salim Ullah Munshi, Ghulam Husain Salim, Orme, Abbe Raynal, Holwell, Scrafton, Stewart, Hill, and countless others, wrote on the 'revolution' of 1757 in Bengal and in the process digressed on Bengal's prodigious riches; this legacy has had the unfortunate effect of giving Bengal undue prominence as regards eighteenth century political, commercial and agrarian studies of South Asia[66].

These authors who compiled 'a history of Bengal' unconsciously trivialised the history of the region by focussing on the western part of Bengal-naturally enough, since the court of Murshidabad was located there-and by tracing the history of Bengal from an originary event: the English takeover in 1757.

In their attempts to understand–or justify–the 'revolution' of 1757 they were obsessed with political events that culminated in the EEIC domination in Bengal. Most narratives started with the death of Aurangzeb in 1707. A political narrative was thus fabricated, one that attempted the

[66] 'Bengal the most Eastern province of the Empire, and the only one which is entirely under the management of the Qhalissah or Exchequer-office, produces the greatest revenue to the Emperor', *Seir Mutaqherin or View of Modern Times,* Seid Gholam Hossein Khan, Tr. Nota Manus, Calcutta, T.D.Chatterjee, V.1 :40.

story of 'Muhammadan' dynasties in terms of their rise and fall from 1204 to 1707. Onto this atemporal surface of the telling of the story of 'Islamic' Bengal no one decisive moment was inserted; so there was no one history in terms of unities, relations and series from 1204 to 1757 that was attempted for Bengal.

Thus there was no effort to understand the different impulses that shaped the forces of Bengal's history under the all encompassing umbrella of 'Muslim'; there was, consequently, no attempt to differentiate between Sultani, Mughal and Nawabi Bengal. The story of 'Muslim' Bengal started and ended in the eighteenth century and a certain historiographic trend for Bengal was created where the past had little relevance[67]. This narrative style was followed by the English when attempting the 'history of Bengal'.

Bengal's prominent place in eighteenth century commercial annals was also determined by contemporary English records. From the 1670s itself, that is almost a century before the 'revolution' of 1757, the EEIC decided that Bengal was to be their theatre of operations. As K.N.Chaudhuri notes[68] :

> In the 1680s with the expansion in the Company's textile trade, the Court of Committees began to refer to Bengal as the rising investment area in India. Although factories had been established at Balasore, Hugli, Kasimbazar and Dacca over the previous three decades, the productive capacity of the province, as seen in the lower prices of export goods, convinced the Company that *here was an area the full potential of which was not yet properly utilised* (*my emphasis*).

Master and then Hedges were sent to organise the Bengal trade as an independent category in the seventies and the eighties of the seventeenth century and place it on equal footing with that of the Coromandel. Master's instructions were to move the administration of the Bengal trade away

---

[67] The title of the Syer Mutaqherin is revealing. The full title runs thus: *Seir Mutaqherin or View of Modern Times being an History of India from the Year 1118 (1707–8) to the Year 1194 (1781–2) of the Hedgirah: Containing, in General The Reigns of the seven Last Emperors of Hindostan and Particularly an account of the English Wars in Bengal, With a Circumstantial Detail of the Rise and Fall of the Families of Seraj-ed-Dowlah and Shudjah-Ed-Dowlah, the Last Sovereigns of Bengal and Oud; To Which the Author has added A Critical Examination of the English Government and Policy in Those Countries Down to the Year 1783.*

[68] Chaudhuri, K.N., 1978, *The Trading World of Asia and the English East India Company 1660–1760,* Cambridge University Press: 52.

from the control of the Coromandel factors and thereby remove the restrictions it had previously been subject to.

Cheap prices and its vast production were not the only reason for concentrating on Bengal. Bengal was a province that was free of the wars which were devastating the Deccan and affecting the Coromandel at this time[69]. Moreover the losses incurred through heavy borrowings at Surat (Rs. 523501 was owed to Surat shroffs and bankers by 1670) could be offset by the high quality yet cheap goods from Bengal[70].

This new policy towards Bengal was soon expressed in the percentage of total exports of Indian goods into Britain. In 1664 Surat provided 50% of the total quantities and 35% of the total value of textile imports, Madras accounted for 41% of the total quantity and 48% of the value, and Bengal accounted for 9% of the volume and 17% of the value. But from the 1680s the share of Bengal goods in total trade rose[71]. Until 1700 Surat and Madras between them had supplied 60-80% of the total imports; in 1700 the share of Bengal goods reached 47%, and after 1726 it was not less than 50–60%[72].

It is therefore obvious that from the last decades of the seventeenth century EEIC records 'primed' Bengal as the chief seat of commerce in India. As Bowrey wrote in the 1670s[73] :

> Upon the banks (of the great river Ganges and the many large and faire arms thereof) are seated many faire villages, delicate groves and Fruitefull lands (offering)...cottons, lac, honey, beeswax, butter, oil, rice and grain...great commerce goeth on into most parts of accompt in India, Persia, Arabia, China and the South Seas...

Brand Bengal, if I may use a current term, was thus born. If we then accept the fact that imperatives of Company trade led to the conquests from 1757 to 1765, and this in turn facilitated the entry of Bengal onto the world stage in eighteenth century annals, our misconceptions regarding Bengal's actual place in South Asian trade history soon disappear. Colonial India started in Bengal. Company records–derived from contemporary

---

69 *Ibid.*: 62.

70 *Ibid.*: 67.

71 *Ibid.*: 290.

72 *Ibid.*: 98.

73 Bowrey: 132-133.

Muslim accounts–underscored the importance of Bengal in Company affairs. We forget that this centrality was possible because of Bengal's comparative marginality in South Asian affairs previously.

The very fact of this historical marginality from events forged in the middle Gangetic plain enabled the entry of Europeans into Bengal. The Mughals were always more concerned about Lahore and Agra; they bothered hardly about Dhaka (or Rajmahal). This marginality, forged in history, was reflected in contemporary Muslim accounts of Bengal when learned men attempted to write a history of the province. Owing to the obsession with the originary year of 1757 the marginalisation operated on two levels: (1) the entire past prior to 1757 was deemed of little relevance. Thus there was no attempt to understand the history of Bengal as part of a wider history, and (2) only the western part of the province featured in these narratives. The east was completely neglected in the early historical accounts since the EEIC takeover happened in the west. Contemporary accounts thus presented a fractured history of Bengal; such a history obscures dynamic moments in Bengal's history and gives rise to a plethora of misconceptions.

One of the main arguments of this book is that the roots of Bengal's strange riches–its peculiar mercantile history-have to be sought in the history of its interactions with its eastern neighbours rather than with those in Gangetic South Asia. These interactions took place in the very easternmost parts of Bengal. This eastern focus was destroyed in the sixteenth century once Bengal became a part of the Mughal Empire. Therefore the crucial turning point of her commercial past lay in the events of the late sixteenth and seventeenth centuries. And her so called 'primacy' did not stem from commercial advantage, but from low prices and abundant raw material.

Our dissatisfaction with the state of commercial studies of Bengal arises from the two assumptions–the so called primacy of Bengal and the importance of the western part–that we just discussed. These assumptions will form the basis of my arguments and counter-arguments in subsequent pages.

2

Conceptual Formulations

The river Ganges is of very unequal breadth, being in some places a League, in others a League and a half wide; so that when the wind is high this River abounds with Waves and Billows, no ways inferior to those of the sea (Glanius, *A Relation of An Unfortunate Voyage to the Kingdom of Bengala*, 1682, London, Henry Bonwick: 151–2).

States, Religious Networks and Maritime Societies

This book is about Bengal. Bengal is a land of rivers. Its coastal (or littoral) history is marked by centuries old interactions with other lands, peoples and cultures. The history of its coastal commerce and sea trade betrays a continuous negotiation between placid upland rivers coming from the Gangetic plain, swift rivers coming down from the north eastern India, sluggish deltaic zones that house many of Bengal's ports, and the open sea. Such a landscape has rendered Bengal's littoral space unique. The discovery of pre-historic stone figures from eastern India–mainly of snakes, monitor lizards, ducks, birds, toads and frogs–affirm the existence of this distinctive zone from very early times[74]. No work on the commercial history of Bengal can afford to ignore this distinctive waterscape.

Sailing in Bengal is a combination of riverine (upcountry), coastal and sea navigation. Sailing is an integral part of this landscape. Ballads have been composed around boats, poems and novellas have been written about ships at sea, and customs, rituals and festivities have grown around sailing practices and passed into the stuff of legend. Sailing practices have

[74] Bhattacharya, R.N., 2003, 'Pre Historic Stone Figurines in Eastern India', *Journal of the Asiatic Society*, XLV, 2, Calcutta: 1–52.

complemented three types of trade: riverine, coastal and long distance. Rather than viewing them as unconnected and dissimilar activities, it may be more fruitful to see them in entirety–within the context of what historians call a maritime society.

In his story of the tenth century merchant princess Maya, Haraprasad Sastri describes Maya as standing on the covered balcony (*jharoka*) over her warehouse at the port of Saptagram. She sees the great river [which is fed by a *khari* (inlet) which brings in the waters of the Bay of Bengal] crammed full of vessels of every kind. Just as there was a city on land, so was there a city on water. This maritime city disappeared as the boats vanished[75]. Sastri's description of Saptagram sums up the vibrant but ephemeral atrributes of a maritime city.

While *Bener Meye* describes the commercial vitality of early medieval Saptagram, an anonymous Portuguese travel account of 1521 describes the naval might of Nasir al Din Nusrat Shah. In 1521, when a Portguese mission visited Gaur, they noted[76]:

> We arrived at Gaur at sunset. We saw many *paraos* of varied shapes on the river. Amongst them, (we) saw one hundred and thirty with gilt stitching, and when (we) asked who owned these *paraos*, I was told that they belonged to the Sultan[77] for his private use. We saw there a ship brought by the Governor of Sonargaon for the service of the Sultan. The stern was round and had cabins embroidered in gold. In the centre was a pinnacle which had a thousand gilt and blue figures carved into it. The entire ship was adorned with gilt galleries…the prow looked like that of a caravel. Any part of the body work which was not gilded was painted in various colours.

The wealth and opulence of the maritime society of Bengal is evident from these two passages. But there are conflicting views as to what comprises a maritime society. Chaudhuri feels that the lowly status of fishing and sailing communities in South Asia meant that they could not evolve a single national maritime tradition to be used as

---

75 *Bener Meye*, *Collected Works*, V.1 op.cit : 322–3.

76 'Voyage dans les Deltas du Gange et l'Irraouaddy', *1521*, Anon. Presented and Edited by Genevieve Bouchon and Luis Filipe Thomaz, Fondation Calouste Gulbenkian, Paris, 1988 : 318.

77 Nasir-al-Din Nusrat Shah, son of Husain Shah.

an arm of the state. Therefore, he says, very often piracy ruled the Asian seas[78]. By inference, such maritime socieities were limited in their scope.

Piracy is seen here as the other of organised trade, as is the slave trade; however our reading will show that, far from being antithetical to trade, piracy and slave trade often supplemented official trade. Also, lower orders such as Kaivartas and Bagdis often attained political power in ancient Bengal; there are references to Kaivartas capturing state power in Bengal in 1075 AD. and establishing a dynasty of which we have the names of three kings. These ruled over the area known as varendri or northern Bengal–the original Pundravardhana referred to earlier. In their expansion of the state the Kaivartas clashed with the Varmans in the east. The last Kaivarta ruler was ultimately defeated by Ramapala[79]. Such incidents were probably not isolated because they find their echoes in literature. In literature Bagdis too attained political power[80].

If Chaudhuri talks of lowly status impeding the growth of a maritime tradition; Wink shows that a maritime tradition had emerged in the Islamic states. Wink tells us that by the ninth century the Indian Ocean integrated the Arabic speaking world. An uniform currency based on the gold dinar and the silver dirham created a cultural and financial unity in a vast area stretching from Asia and the Middle East into Europe[81]. In other words, Wink suggests that a strong maritime state tradition (a national tradition ?) had emerged in the Islamic world. Since Islam expanded through conversion; and since it was frequently those of lowly status who converted, at least in South Asia, how can we reconcile the two viewpoints? It is difficult to incline to Chaudhuri's view of lowly status impeding the development of a maritime tradition in Asia, for then the Islamic maritime tradition centreing on South Asia-and surely Bengal-would be unthinkable.

So we have here two conflicting visions of a maritime society in South Asia. One presupposes that the cultural context of trade-the maritime tradition-evolved within 'low' castes and communities and could not become

---

[78] *Trade and Civilisation in the Indian Ocean: An Economic History from the Rise of Islam to 1750*, Cambridge, 1985: 15, 121–2.

[79] There are references in history to the Kaivarta rebellion in Bengal. See Majumdar, R.C., 1943 op.cit: 152–5, 159.

[80] For the Bagdis see Sastri's depiction of Rupa Bagdi as the raja of Saptagram in the tenth century in *Bener Meye* op.cit.

[81] Wink, Andre, 1990, *Al Hind*, V.1. New Delhi, Oxford University Press.

a 'great' tradition, while the other view suggests that trade incorporated indigenous elites into the system. Why is this so?

These contrasting visions result from different notions of the 'coming of trade' in South Asia. For Chaudhuri trade is a material practice and, largely, an indigenous tradition that was *boosted* by the entry of Islam into Asian waters; for Wink it is a practice that *rose* with the advent of Islam into South Asia.

Humphreys notes[82]:

> The Arab Conquests irrupted into two highly monetized economies–the Roman-Byzantine and the Sassanian–and from the outset the new rulers attempted to integrate the established monetary systems into their own emerging fiscal and economic framework. In this effort they succeeded, and one of the salient features of Islamic history, in almost every period and region, is the primary role of coined metal (gold, silver and copper) within its several monetary systems.

In other words, Islam did not bring trade into the countries it conquered; rather the Islamic trading network inserted itself into previously existing networks and then augmented them. While not a part of either of these two monetised economies, nevertheless, Bengal and South Asia participated historically in the trade emanating from these two areas, viz. the Roman-Byzantine and the Sassanid[83].

Religion and Trade

We saw that the expansion of Islam did not bring trade to South Asia; other religious traditions such as Hinduism, Jainism and Buddhism greatly facilitated trade in the early history of South Asia[84]. Indeed Buddhism integrated much of eastern and northern India into a vast trading network. Moreover, it created its own maritime space stretching from

---

[82] *Islamic History: A Framework for Inquiry*, Revised Ed., Pakistan, Oxford University Press: 49.

[83] See later.

[84] Ray, Himanshu Prabha, 2003, *The Archaeology Of Seafaring in Ancient South Asia*, Cambridge World Archaeology Series, Cambridge University Press, notes that in Buddhist maritime activity there was the added innovation of the notion of a saviour from the dangers of the sea.The Bodhisattva in the form of a horse saved shipwrecked sailors from a group of hungry yakshis or demonesses. There was also the notion of sea monsters that threatened to swallow boats. Yet another innovation was the cult of Bodhisattva Avalokitesvara as saviour of mariners and travelers in distress: 258.

Ceylon in the south, through the Coromandel and Bengal coasts, up until Arakan, Burma and beyond to China and Japan. The rise of Islam did not stop the commercial development of this maritime space, although Wink suggests otherwise[85]. Wink asserts that between the seventh and thirteenth centuries Islam replaced Buddhism as a great cosmopolitan trading religion. Muslims were certainly there in South Asia from the eighth century (and in Bengal[86]), and certainly in no small number. Tajiks (*tajikas*) and Turks (*turuskas*) were present in coastal South Asia from the seventh century. From the Gahadavala inscription of the Ganga basin it seems that a tax was imposed on their settlements[87]. We can infer that these settlements were not small either in terms of size or in number. Moreover, such settlements must have been wealthy.

But Wink's argument about Islam outpacing Buddhism in creating a maritime space between the seventh and the thirteenth centuries is clearly not tenable as our subsequent reading will show. The earlier sailings to Buddhist lands continued[88]. Bengal cotton seeds were taken to Japan by a pilgrim from South Asia at the end of the eight century of the Christian era[89]. Inscriptions at the Horiuzi temple in Japan were found to be written in the Bengali script of the eleventh century[90]. One can find evidence of similar pilgrimage-commercial activities in Sri Lanka in the twelfth century The Buddhist site of Ratnagiri experienced phenomenal growth during this period. The fifteenth century Kalyani inscription of King Dhammaceti of Pegu (1472–1492) refers to pilgrim mobility: Anandathera (d.1245) went to Pagan in Burma. There is also a reference to shipwrecked *theras* (devotees) at Nagapattinam who, being shipwrecked on the way to Sri Lanka, prayed at a Buddhist shrine there. This shrine was erected, significantly, on the orders of the King of China.[91] The evidence presented by Frasch later in this volume also corroborates this view. The eastern Indian Ocean, at least, was not totally an Islamic sea as late as in the fifteenth century. Pilgrimage as trade continued throughout this period.

---

85 Wink, 1999, *Al-Hind,* v.2, New Delhi, Oxford University Press: 349.

86 See the evidence from M.M. Ali later.

87 Ray, Himanshu Prabha, 2003, : 289.

88 Mookerji, Radha Kumud, 1962 (Reprint), *Indian Shipping, A History of the Sea Borne Trade and Maritime Activity of the Indians from the Earliest Times*, Allahabad, Kitab Mahal : 48–54.

89 *Ibid.* : 122–123.

90 *Ibid* : 108.

91 Ray, Himanshu Prabha, 2003: 287.

Things changed in the sixteenth century. Islam integrated the coastal areas of South Asia into a vast trading network that spanned Europe and Africa in the west and China in the East. This success was partly due to the Chinese withdrawal from the eastern Indian Ocean, as we shall see later.

Coastal Communities

Most historians do not refer to coastal communities as such for that is not their concern when doing maritime history. Yet the ocean is not an empty space. It is inscribed by the practices, behaviour and actions of the people living along it. Kenneth McPherson was one of the first to note the response of coastal communities to the resources of the seas[92]. The Indian Ocean cannot be studied without referring to the people who live along its shores and work in the sea.

A proper maritime history should include histories of traditional fishing and sailing communities and nature of craft used. In historical tradition trade was an important part of material culture for the peoples of South Asia. Trade in ancient India was not just in luxury goods-'a regular sailing and maritime network was sustained historically in the Indian Ocean by traffic in timber, cloth, metal, dried fish and so on'[93]. If we regard maritime history in this fashion then trade is not merely an offshoot of elite activity and agricultural expansion as is conventionally supposed (Ray 2003: 6), nor are sailing and fishing 'lowly' occupations. Instead of viewing maritime activites in terms of 'high' and 'low' culture it may be more useful to regard trade, political consolidation, social mobility and religious expansion as competing loci of power (Ray 2003: 2).

So what denotes this maritime cultural landscape? It consists of material and cultural practices visible in the demarcation and utilisation of the maritime space by different communities for fishing, sailing, shipping, boat building and repairing and so on. Most significant in such a waterscape is the sensitive interface between the riverine and maritime zones. By maritime is meant both coastal as well as deep sea trade.

This interface is particularly valid for Bengal where ports were situated at the mouth of rivers and not on the open seas. As elsewhere in South Asia riverine ports, close to the open seas, were the norm and not deep sea ports. Silting was a common problem, and this explains why deltaic

---

92 *The Indian Ocean: A History of the People and the Sea,* 1993, New Delhi, Oxford University Press.

93 Ray, Himanshu Prabha, 2003: 5–6.

Bengal contained numerous ports whose fortunes varied over time. These ports contained a common hinterland area which expanded or decreased in concentric circles as ports came up and disappeared on the Bengal coast. The coast, in the case of Bengal, was constantly in flux. Coastal communities in Bengal too were constantly under pressure from such changes.

Coastal communities form a significant part of what we term a 'maritime' society. A maritime society is built upon maritime activity and in its functions it is guided by the knowledge generated throughout the theatre of its activities; be it the East African coast, the Gujarat /Malabar coastline, or, what concerns us here, the northern Bay of Bengal coastline. A maritime society contains ports, port towns, caravan trade routes converging onto ports, transport networks continuing into the interior, as well as a multitude of peoples: traders, sailors, moneychangers, accountants, insurance agents and lawyers, as well as the communities of the defined coastal area. Various communities make up a maritime society; of these coastal communities form only a part.

Littoral Societies

Coastal communities can, and frequently do, form a littoral society. A littoral society is not the whole of the maritime or coastal society in spatial terms; for it is limited to that peculiar strip of land between land and sea. In physical spatial terms, a littoral society denotes the *limits* of the coastal area. Littoral societies form a no-man's land-or a boundary if you like-between inland regions and sea. A littoral society is distinct from a maritime society in that it forms a sub sector within it. Although geaographically somewhat of a fuzzy zone; it has a distinct physical and topographical character, made up not only of beaches, but of lagoons, backwaters, deltas and marshes. Naturally, a littoral society contains also distinctive material practices.

In the last ten years or so, a definite notion of a littoral society has emerged in academic circles; distinct from a maritime society, being a blend of the maritime and the terrestrial. Pearson, who was one of the first to develop the notion of a littoral society on the Indian Ocean rim, noted in *'Littoral Society: The Concept and the Problems'*[94]:

[94] Unpublished keynote address to the conference *'Seascapes, Littoral Cultures and Trans-oceanic Exchanges,'* sponsored by the American Historical Association, Washington DC, February 12–15, 2003. Sent by Prof. Michael N. Pearson on February 8, 2005.

> If I look out from my front balcony at the seashore, 30 meters away, I can extend my gaze over the Pacific Ocean, where the nearest land is Chile, some 12,000 kms away. I am located on the land, yet frequently walk on the beach, or fish or swim, cautiously in water only up to my waist. Does this make me littoral? Not really: if we look at three criteria, I am located on the littoral, or near enough, but my occupation has nothing to do with the marge (except perhaps that I am retired, and retired Australians often head for the coast), and nor does my culture. These three distinctions will underlie my discussion of littoral society. To anticipate the conclusion, location is an obvious matter. However, both occupation and culture are more difficult. Many aspects of both do indeed show the classic characteristics of littoral society, that is a symbiosis between land and sea; but other parts do not. It is this mixture of maritime and terrestrial influences which distinguishes a study of littoral society from maritime history.

Pearson claims that 'In any study of seascapes an investigation of the littoral must be central, for it is here that land and sea meet. Yet how difficult it is to locate and specify this place and the societies located there! ….'. He then asks what distinguishes a littoral society:

> Most basically, is there such a thing as littoral society, that is can we go around the shores of an ocean, or a sea, or indeed the whole world, and identify societies which have more in common with other littoral societies than they do with their inland neighbors? Does location on the shore transcend differing influences from an inland which is very diverse, both in geographic and cultural terms, so that the shorefolk have more in common with other shorefolk thousands of kilometers away on some other shore of the ocean, than they do with those in their immediate hinterland? Do these societies draw more on their forelands, that is maritime connections, than on their hinterlands? Certainly there are important gradations along the strand, from wholly aquatic people to those who move easily between land and sea, and indeed may, despite their physical location, draw much more from the land than the sea both in terms of livelihood and of culture.

Traditionally, sea and land have been seen as binary opposites. Pearson notes[95]:

> Lencek put it rather melodramatically: "it was on the borders of continents and islands that the first living creatures crawled out from the sea to begin their inexorable march toward conquest of terra firma." One "cannot help being intrigued by the face-off between land and water . . . Here, two titanic forces – one stationary and one in motion – engage in eternal dispute."

David Sopher's classic study[96] introduces the subject of plants and people who live on the littoral or, as he calls it, the strand. The environment of the strand begins where the land meets the sea and extends landwards and seaward from this line. The strand is best regarded as a zone of transition between the sea and terra firma; as such it is very often characterised by its own special land forms and life forms. . . people who live on the strand or make use of it generally have a habitat that extends well beyond its limits. The extent of the habitat of strand folk varies greatly, in part depending on the complexity of their society. Other than strand or littoral such an area may well be a beach, the seashore, the coast, the marge, the coastal zone, the limicole [or limicoline] realm.

Seen this way, the littoral is a transitional area. Littoral people are very various. Jan Heesterman stressed that "The littoral forms a frontier zone that is not there to separate or enclose, but which rather finds its meaning in its permeability". Braudel wrote evocatively about coastal society, stressing that it was as much land as sea oriented. The life of the coast of the Mediterranean "is linked to the land, its poetry more than half-rural, its sailors may turn peasant with the seasons; it is the sea of vineyards and olive trees just as much as the sea of the long-oared galleys and the round-ships of merchants, and its history can no more be separated from that of the lands surrounding it than the clay can be separated from the hands of the potter who shapes it".[97]

If the littoral is *permeable*, continues Pearson, then the description of it must be *amphibious*, moving easily between land and sea. A complementary way to conceptualize land/sea relation and connections is

---

[95] Pearson, unpublished, 2003.

[96] In *Ibid.*

[97] Quoted in *Ibid.*

Jean-Claude Penrad's notion of *ressac*, the three-fold violent movement of the waves, turning back on themselves as they crash against the shore. Penrad uses this image to elucidate the way in which the to-and-fro movements of the Indian Ocean mirror coastal and inland influences which keep coming back at each other just as do waves.

Historically speaking, did the shores of the Indian Ocean nurture a littoral society in Africa and Asia? It certainly seems so. Pearson quotes Middleton and Pouwels in this context. Middleton focused on the east African coast and claimed "Part of the coast is the sea: the two cannot be separated. The Swahili are a maritime people and the stretches of lagoon, creek, and open sea beyond the reefs are as much part of their environment as are the coastlands. The sea, rivers, and lagoons are not merely stretches of water but highly productive food resources, divided into territories that are owned by families and protected by spirits just as are stretches of land. The Swahili use the sea as though it were a network of roads". The very term "Swahili" means "shore folk," those who live on the edge of the ocean. As Pouwels has it, Swahili culture was "a child of its human and physical environment, being neither wholly African nor 'Arab,' but distinctly 'coastal,' the whole being greater than the sum of its parts".

Not all coastal areas are beaches. Bengal is a case in point. Its coast is mostly deltaic, carved out by fast flowing rivers on their way to the Bay of Bengal. In such a case distinction between land and sea becomes even more fuzzy. The permeability is accentuated.

Pearson continues[98]:

> "In delta areas we find ambiguity, lack of definition and boundaries, a zone where land and sea intertwine and merge, really the fungibility, the interchangeability, of land and sea. Emily Eden looked at the Sunderbans down from Kolkata in 1837 when she was traveling on a "flat" or large barge towed by a steamer. The scene she saw was "a composition of low stunted trees, marsh, tigers and snakes, with a stream that sometimes looks like a very wide lake and then becomes so narrow that the jungle wood scrapes against the sides of the flat . . . . Then she reflected, very acutely, that "It looks as if this bit of world had been left unfinished when land and sea were originally parted".

[98] As before.

In *The Hungry Tide* Amitav Ghosh makes the same point (when he says that at night the Sunderban landscape is inverted; there is the illusion that the water is the land and the islands dark seas): 'the landscape, in its epic mutability, had undergone yet another transformation: the moonlight had turned it into a silvery negative of its daytime image. Now it was the darkened islands that looked like lakes of liquid, while the water lay spread across the earth like a vast slick of solid metal'[99] and Alan Villiers' classic account of the Rufiji delta finds a similar, and hostile, merging.

Who are the people who live on or near the beach, those who inhabit the coastal zone, not just the coast? They have been called the shore folk, or sea nomads, or members of a littoral society. Pearson calls the inhabitants of the port cities ...'more cosmopolitan than in towns in the interior, yet even so I prefer to see port cities as nodes along the coast, or up an estuary or river. They have been much described both in historical and modern literature; few comment on the littoral between them...These folk live on shore, but work on the sea: they are very precisely littoral.'

Several modern scholars have ruminated on the nature of the shore folk of the Indian Ocean, and islands are perhaps where we are most likely to find littoral societies. Indeed, on smaller ones there would be nothing but coastal people, for the sea permeates the whole area. The Andaman and Nicobar islands, tiny fragments of land in the ocean, are purely littoral. The Nicobars, today an 'undeveloped', indeed 'primitive', island chain south east of Bengal was an important port of call for ships sailing from Bengal to points east and vice versa until the seventeenth century. Similarly, islands in the rivers can be seen as making up little littoral societies all their own, even far "inland"-such as the Hugli, the Ganga, the Tigris-Euphrates, the Irrawaddy and so on. Fish, salt, coconuts, sea weed form traditional trade items of littoral societies and it is by way of trade between these societies and inland ones that links are maintained between the two sectors. Littoral societies are distinctive; yet they and inland societies are interdependent. This indeed is *ressac*, mutual dependence, with the mixture varying from time to time. If we were to try to construct a continuum of dependence on the sea, we would have peasants and pastoralists at one end, then maybe various gradations of the inhabitants of the port cities, then fisherfolk as the classic littoral people, and finally aquatic folk.

---

99 India, Harper Collins, 2005: 154.

Because some exceptional peoples are really not littoral at all: they are aquatic. Pearson notes that: They are *not* amphibious: their lives are spent on or in the water. Some such people are simply sailors who sail for a long time, so long that they may lose their land ties. Some of the merchants of the great port of Siraf around 1000 traveled so much that they were away at sea all their lives…The best studied truly aquatic people are the famous Marsh Arabs of the Tigris-Euphrates delta, occupying the vast palustral triangle between An-Nasiriyah, Al-'Amarah, and Basra. Their way of life goes back perhaps 5000 years. …..This was a totally aquatic society. "The ground looked solid but felt very soggy. Actually it consisted of a layer of roots and decomposed vegetation floating on the surface"[100].

This description is particularly apt for the Sunderbans–the mangrove delta-that formed almost a quarter of the land surface of medieval Bengal. Some of the islands in the delta are only a few square yards, others an acre, some tethered, some floating about, as Pearson also notes. The houses are built on reed platforms floating on the water, and all transport is in boats, usually very small. In other places, we find floating markets, extremely venerable, yet today also tourist attractions. The one in Bangkok is a compulsory sight for any visitor. So also for the floating market of Banjarmasin, in southern Borneo, which is like the chaotic markets of large southeast Asian cities, "a flotilla of different types of boats imitating the chaos on the roads"[101]. This could well apply to many towns in medieval deltaic Bengal and Arakan. Dhaka, Noakhali and Mrauk-U had floating markets as well.

What are the occupations of littoral folk? The economic forces which govern their lives move amphibiously from land to sea. This then seems to provide an element of commonality for many, though far from all, folk who live on the shores.

What about their material culture? Is there anything to show that indeed coastal zone people, at least all those around the shores of warm seas and oceans, have more in common with each other than with their inland neighbors? Yes. We can look at food, obviously largely derived from the sea, even if some fisherfolk prefer to trade some of their catch for grain.

Themes such as this have been discussed in succeeding pages. Houses are also usually different from those inland. As one would expect, locally

---

[100] *Ibid.*

[101] *Ibid.*

available materials are usually employed. For much of the tropical coast this means that palm trees are used to provide a housing structure, and a thatched roof along with another quintessential littoral product, mangrove poles. Jacques Cousteau found coral to be of universal utility in the Maldives: it was used to construct the landing strip and the houses, and even the beaches were pulverized coral, not sand. "Everywhere we saw tiny cemeteries under palm clusters. The tombs themselves, crosses and all, were made of coral. Everything here is bound up with the sea, even life and death"[102]. It is the same with the coconut and palm in Bengal and points further east along the coast.

Does the development of language, and the *use* of a language, show a commonality among littoral folk? We are inclined to believe that such was certainly the case for Bengal. Certain languages achieved wide currency, thus providing another commonality around the shores of the Indian Ocean. One such was Arabic in the earlier centuries. Pearson noted that there are some 5,000 words of Arabic influence in Malay, and more than that in Swahili, and about 80% of these are the same, that is in Malay and Swahili, so that we have a "corpus of travelling Arabic words". I do not know if a similar exercise has been attempted for the Bengali language; but my hunch is that we should find similar figures for an Arabo-Bengali mix. Later a sort of nautical Portuguese impacted on Bengali. As it did on many a shore of the Indian Ocean.

Do littoral folk share similar practices? It would seem so. Mookerji mentions the practice of carrying birds to sight land on long sea voyages[103]. There was also the common idea that the moon and stars exerted influence on the humours of mariners, navigators and sailors[104]. In fact, the astronomical works of early India mention various classes of sailors and traders, where lesser sailors (those confined to inland, that is riverine, navigation) are singled out for special reference[105]. Throughout history inland states have made use of their knowledge for maritime administration. The rules and duties laid down for Akbar's admiralty suggest that this department recruited a class of efficient mariners who were well versed in littoral and maritime practices, who knew the nature of tides, the depths of channels, the coasts to be avoided and the character of winds. This department also sought the services of a class of men with even

[102] In *Ibid*.

[103] Mookerji, 1962: 51.

[104] *Ibid*.: 43–4.

[105] *Ibid*.: see p.44.

more specialised knowledge: of soundings at sea, the situation of stars and the technical aspects of navigation[106]. The *Ain-i-Akbari* mentions the following categories of specialised sevices recruited by Akbar's admiralty: *muallim* or captain, *tamdil*, chief of *khalassis* or sailors, *kharwas* also sailors, *sarrang* or mate, *sukkangir* or helmsman, *panjari* or looker out, apart from a series of clerks. Since there was no college for mariners at this time we may safely assume that the Mughals, like the Mauryas, the Guptas, the Cholas, the Chandras, and countless others before them, accessed this specialised knowledge from the folk of littoral societies.

Coastal religion is also distinctive. Material culture forms a significant component of religious practices in coastal areas. Pre historic stone figurines found from eastern India comprise fish, snakes, toads, frogs, owls, ducks, monitor and other lizards, tortoise and ant eaters[107]. Littoral people, living in a more cosmopolitan environment than those inland, are more likely to convert. In the case of the Indian Ocean, the cosmopolitan, international, aspect of Islam has often been cited as a prime motivation for conversion, and while this applied most strongly in the port cities, it also was evident on the coasts between them. Coastal people especially found their indigenous beliefs, localized and very specific, to be inadequate as their world expanded. When they were exposed to a universal faith, Islam as exemplified by visitors from the north, the attraction was obvious, and the results can be seen all over the Indian Ocean world from the early modern period onwards.

Folk religion on the littoral, beneath an Islamic veneer, similarly is to be distinguished from inland manifestations. The concerns of coastal people were usually quite different from those of peasants and pastoralists inland. On the coast religion had to do with customs to ensure safe voyages or a large catch, or a favorable monsoon so that fishing could recommence. Particular gods were propitiated for these purposes. In the Sunderbans Dakhin Rai the demon (frequently in the form of the Royal Bengal Tiger) and Bon Bibi the Islamo-Hindu goddess wage a perpetual war. The forces of good and evil exist in perfect equilibrium in the littoral society of the Sunderbans.

Further inland, but still maritime, regions celebrate their coastal traditions. One rite on the west coast of India celebrates the end of the

[106] *Ibid.*: 148.

[107] Bhattacharya, R.N., 2003, 'Pre Historic Stone Figurines in Eastern India', op. cit.

southwest monsoon and so the beginning of the sailing and fishing year. Dr. John Fryer noted this in Bombay in the 1670s: "After this Full Moon, the Banyans, assisted by their Brachmins, go in Procession to the Sea-shore, and offer Cocoe Nuts to Neptune, that he would restore them their Mare Pacificum; when they make Preparations to go to Sea, and about their Business of Trade"[108]. Dr. Varadarajan's ethnographic work in Gujarat has found rather similar things happening today, though based on very old traditions. Her account makes clear that littoral location, and occupation, transcend religion. On the "narial prunima" day both Hindus and Muslims take part in ceremonies when the forces governing the sea are worshipped, and boats are symbolically taken out to mark the beginning of the season. Rites are conducted by the community rather than the temple priest. "As the ritual is so intimately connected with their vocational life, all seafaring folk come together to celebrate this day coalescing religious heterogeneity through group participation." In general "occupational hazards to which they are exposed cut across religious differences"[109]. A similar religious practice tied to the sea, not to any formal canon of normative belief, governed boat building in south Sulawesi: the whole process of building a *prahu*, from felling the tree to launching the boat, was governed and accompanied by precise ritual ceremonies, and many of them were not purely Islamic either. Among other things, a live black goat was sacrificed by fire just before the launching[110]. In Goa today fishing boats are named after saints, and the owners and crew make offerings to the relevant saint on his or her feast day.

From Littoral Communities to a Maritime State

Bengal was boat country *par excellence*. From very early times we get references to navigation[111]. Terms of marine insurance, inland taxes as well as transit ones were clearly spelt out from Mauryan times until at least the eighteenth century[112]. For inland navigation, *ghats* or landing places were marked *nau-dandakas* or *nau-bandhakas*. There are references to *Nau-ata-kseni* (boat harbour), *Nau-vataka* and *Ardha-nau-vataka* in the Madanpur plate of Srichandra (circa tenth century).

[108] In Pearson 2003.

[109] *Ibid.*

[110] K.N.Chaudhuri, 1985: 143.

[111] See Mookerji, 1962, for references to centralized marine administration under the Mauryas and Guptas.

[112] Mookerji, 1962: 74–5, 148–9, 151.

Merchants had *golas* (warehouses) at port cities that directly fronted the water. Vessels of individual merchants could unload their goods directly at their own warehouses. During the busy season there was frequently a traffic jam on the water! Writing towards the end of the eighteenth century, Rennell commented on the immense inland navigation system of Bengal[113]:

> This inland navigation…gives constant employment to 30000 boatmen…a large proportion of the food, consumed by ten millions of people, are conveyed by water, within the kingdom of Bengal and its dependencies. To these must be added the transport of the commercial exports and imports…the fisheries and the articles of travelling.

This was truly the kind of maritime society evoked by Pearson and Ray, linking littoral to inland in a vast maritime-riverine landscape[114].

The culture of this littoral society was mirrored in its customs. In Bengal the practice of *bera bhasan* (meaning literally putting a boat out to river/sea) developed from older Persian traditions of appeasing sea monsters and was enriched through the incorporation of similarly old Hindu traditions of placating the rain and river gods (such as the Hindu festival of *sedo* held on the last day of *pous* or January when women put out similar rafts adorned with flowers, sweets and lamps). *Bera Bhasan* took place in September, when the rains receded and the state got ready for harvesting. It was celebrated on the last Thurday of the Bengali month of *bhadra*; if the feast for *Ramzan* fell on that day; the ceremony was adjusted accordingly[115].

The first reference we get to the practice of *bera bhasan* is in the seventeenth century, from Dhaka. Mukarram Khan, the Mughal *subahdar* at Dhaka (1626–1627 AD) inititated this practice. Stewart noted:[116]

> The eastern parts of Bengal are intersected with rivers and creeks, navigable at all seasons of the year…the mode of travelling is by water: on which account the governors of Bengal have always kept up a large establishment of boats…the veneration of the inhabitants for the tutelary deities, who are

[113] Rennell, James, 1976, *Memoirs of a Map of Hindoostan or the Mogul Empire*, Reprint, Editions Indian, Calcutta: 382.

[114] See M.N. Pearson and Himanshu Prabha Ray, both 2003, in the preceding pages.

[115] See Ray, B., 1961, *West Bengal District Census Handbook: Murshidabad*, Calcutta . See also O'Malley, L.S.S., and Chakravarti, M., 1914, *Bengal District Gazeteer: Murshidabad*, Calcutta, Bengal Secretariat Book Depot.

[116] Stewart, Charles, 1903, *The History of Bengal*, Calcutta, Bangabashi Press : 268, 461.

> supposed to preside over the rivers and waters is carried to an extreme, both by Hindoos and Mohammedans...even the present governors are obliged to comply with the superstition of their subjects by making, at Dacca, an annual offering to Khwaja Khizer (supposed to be the prophet Elias), to propitiate his good offices in protecting their inland commerce.

After the Mughals, the Bengal Nawabs took over this practice in the eighteenth century to reaffirm the continuum between land and water. But new elements were now added. It also became a harvest festival (*punya*) as well as a festival commemorating the might of the state and for celebrating the loyalty of its subjects. The festival now took place on the Bhagirathi at the royal capital of Murshidabad. The first Nawab, Murshid Quli Khan (1704-27), used the festival as a means of bringing together the diverse communities under his rule[117]. By the time of Siraj-ud-Daulah (1756-7), the last of the independent nawabs of Bengal, this simple festival had been transformed into a political paegantry.

If one looks at the changes in the practice of *bera bhasan* one will realize how the simple customs of a littoral folk were utilized by politics as a tool for governance. *Bera bhasan* started intitally with paper boats with clay lamps being set out to water. This was no doubt the practice of ordinary folk who started the tradition. Murshid Quli Khan kept to this simple practice[118] but by the time of Siraj-ud-Daulah the simple paper boats and clay lamps used earlier had evolved into more permanent rafts with fireworks. The rafts were lit by gold lamps[119]. Indeed the ceremonial was not limited to the actual practice of *bera bhasan* alone but extended over a few days. A few days before the festival the court closed for *punya* (the harvest accounts)[120], and on the day before *bera bhasan* an assembly was held in the nawab's *durbar* where his prominent subjects, both Indian and European, offered him *nazr* (a present or offering from an inferior to a superior in rank) and were entertained by music, dancing and refreshments[121].

---

[117] Salim Allah, 1788, *Tawarikh-i-Bangalah or a Narrative of the Transactions in Bengal* (Tr.Francis Gladwin), Calcutta: 111.

[118] *Ibid.*

[119] Stewart, Charles, 1903: 268 (footnote) and Blochmann, H., 1867, 'Notes on Sirajuddaulah and the Town of Murshidabad, taken from a Persian Manuscript of the Tarikh-i-Mancuri', *Journal of the Asiatic Society*, Part I, no.II.

[120] See K.F.R., London.

[121] See both Stewart and Blochman op.cit.

There was also considerable ceremonial attached to the actual practice of setting the rafts (made of plantain leaves taken from the banana tree) to water. First, there was the royal procession that started from Mahinagar (a suburb of Murshidabad); this majestic procession was swelled along the way by aristocrats, local dignitaries, members of the European trading companies and the common folk. On reaching the river the nawab set off the first raft, lit by a golden lamp, to the accompaniment of a massive display of fireworks. Then the Jagat Seths, bankers to the world, the nawab's Treasurer General and Controller of the Mint of Bengal, set off a similar raft with a silver lamp. After the nobles, the common folk set off their rafts. The grand spectacle was punctutated by the acclamations of people at the splendid sight afforded by so many lights bobbing against the dark carpet of a sultry post monsoon Bengal sky. Throughout the whole time, drums beat, conch shells were blown and the *shehnai* (a kind of clarinet) played[122]. The audio-visuals accompanying the practice were no less impressive and reaffirmed belief in the invincibility of the Nawabi state of Bengal.

Bera Bhasan then was an unique festival connecting folk beliefs towards water (safety from floods, security in navigation) and land (prayer for a good harvest) of both Hindus and Muslims. This custom of an agrarian and riverine economy was then annexed to the political ideology of the (mainly) land based economy of the Bengal Nawabs. This littoral practice became, in the course of the eighteenth century, an ideological rallying point for the articulation of the might of the nawabi state of Bengal. The practice of *bera bhasan* is still carried on today in Murshidabad; as a state sponsored enterprise[123].

A similar exercise was started in medieval Venice and is also still carried on today; albeit as carnival. Built on numerous islands on marshy lagoons opening on the Adriatic, Venice's maritime prosperity since the ninth century was reinforced through a festival on March 24 when the Doge, in the Bucintoro ship, tossed a ring into the water to reaffirm the city's 'marriage with the sea'[124].

Bengal thus offers us an exceptional case study of a maritime society whose littoral zone became an expanding cultural zone that moved further

---

[122] See Stewart, Blochmann op.cit.

[123] Ray, B., 1961. See Ghosh, Ishani, 1998, 'A Folk Ritual and the Emergence of a Regional Polity: Murshid Quli Khan and Local Cults in Bengal', *Journal of History*, Jadavpur University, V. XVI, 1997–8: 49–54.

[124] Mukherjee, Rila, 2003, *The Lost Worlds of Europe*, Calcutta, Progressive Publishers: 71.

inland by incorporating various levels of the population into its customs and practices. Her littoral practices were not liminal–as was suggested by Pearson in other cultures–but became *central* to the nawabi statecraft in the eighteenth century.

Yet another littoral society, crucial to Bengal's existence as an independent maritime power, was Arakan; more specifically at the time of the Mrauk-U dynasty that lasted from the 1430s (King Narameikhla) until 1684 (the reign of King Sandathudhamma, 1652-84). The existence of this littoral state, its preponderant influence in politics, religion and commerce on the states of the northern Bay, continued for an exceptional 250 years; perhaps the longest for any littoral state in the Indian Ocean to hold onto power. More about Arakan later.

Do littoral societies exist today? Yes, but their existence is coming under threat. The complex symbiosis between land and sea which we found to characterize littoral society for most of history is fast being undermined. Land influences, often from far away, are destroying what used to be an important, albeit elusive, segment of human society. Majoritarian politics are destroying many such practices and beliefs. People still live on the coast, but a littoral society which moves easily between land and sea, an amphibious society governed by *ressac*, back and forth, has now been overwhelmed by forces from far inland, and far away.

Maritme Cities, Harbours, and Ports

The port city was the maritime city. The South Asian maritime city, Ashin Das Gupta noted, was both dynamic and ephemeral. Dynamic because of its open society and the cosmopolitan nature of its links, ephemeral because its fortunes fluctutated according to the vicissitudes of trade. It was quite possible to find a maritime city 'dismantling itself and reassembling in a more suitable location'[125]. But however ephemeral, a maritime city was built around certain tangible and intangible structures that promoted its activities. Among the first, the existence of a money market, a mint and a customs house were crucial[126]. In the second category

[125] Das Gupta, Ashin, 1992, 'The Maritime City' in Indu Banga ed. *Ports and Their Hinterlands in India 1700-1950*, New Delhi, Manohar : 359–65. See p.365.

[126] See the Surat mint figures in Moosvi, Shireen, 1992, '*The Gujarat Ports and Their Hinterland : The Economic Relationship*' in Banga ed. op.cit. : 121–9. The link between the emergence of Surat as the premier port on the West Coast and the establishment of a mint is clearly highlighted.

trust, protection and character were important, as well as the presence, quite frequently, of a dominant mercantile community, such as that of Arabs and Persians in Chattagram or Gujaratis and Konkanis in the ports on the west coast.

However the maritime city was not always the port city. Thatta, the famous maritime city on the west coast, was located some thirty miles away from its port at Lahori Bandar. Within the port town there were variations in functions as Arasaratnam (1992) noted. There was a variation in the population of port towns from Masulipatnam and Surat which had upwards of 200000 people to small localised ports which boasted perhaps 50000 inhabitants. The nature of political control was important for the development of both the maritime and port cities and the nature of administration depended upon the specific character of the city in question. How autonomous was the port administration? How far was its administration integrated at two levels: the regional administrative apparatus and the central administration? For example, in the case of the Mughal port of Hugli, we can ask ourselves how far its administration was linked to the overall administration of Mughal Bengal. Or, to take this point further, how far was the political and economic administration of Hugli as royal port linked to the Mughal administrative apparatus at the centre? Arasaratnam asks whether the port was held as a revenue farm by an individual or whether it was administered by the central power. In either case its functions would vary. Was there a civilian arm and a military arm in administration as in the case of Surat? Or was the maritime city in question a city state such as Calicut or Cochin (or Malacca and Achin)?[127]

A maritime city could be located at quite a distance from its port and harbour. Again a port and harbour may not be at the same location. A port is an economic concept, a harbour a physical one. Good harbours do not always attract ports if the coasts on which they lie are not important for trade. Consequenly, many fine harbours attract few ships while most ports have poor harbours.

Ports which are involved in trading in their own commodities are distinct from entrepots which essentially transfer goods from one port to another. In the former case, the port in question has to have a hinterland of its own. Here the question of territorial political linkages between port and hinterland becomes crucial, while for the latter case (the entrepot) a hinterland may even be redundant.

[127] Sinappah Arasaratnam, 1992, '*Pre Colonial and Early-Colonial Port Towns*' in Banga ed. op.cit.: 367–374. See pp. 367, 370–71.

Broeze developed the concept of the hinterland by dividing it into three zones[128]. These are one, the hinterland, two, the foreland, and three, an umland which is part of the foreland. The hinterland is of course the most commonly used and means, in its strictest sense, as that area from which the port obtains the goods for export overseas and to which it distributes the goods it receives as imports. But Broeze introduced the concept of maritime hinterland in this formulation because the distributive and collective functions of a port can equally be exercised over sea space. The maritime hinterland of a port then includes ports in those countries with which it has social (pilgrimage) and economic (trade) linkages. The foreland is that immediate area before the port that is dominated by its shipping, trade and passenger traffic[129].

But Morgan pushed the concept of the hinterland even further. He wrote[130]:

> The concept of hinterlands of ports as a simple parcelling out of the country behind them, with areas of overlap where ports compete...is hardly adequate. A port generally has a different hinterland for each commodity which enters into its trade, and has thus an enormous number of hinterlands... The nature of the structure and the areal extent of hinterlands are subject to variations arising from three main factors: the nature of commodities, the mechanism of sea transport and the influence of political policies. As a result of the interplay of these factors hinterlands show variations...there are orders of hinterlands or a hierarchy.

Morgan thus introduced the concept of different economic hinterlands and a spatial order among them. In a similar vein Norton emphasised the 'mercantile' model of port development as against the central place theory of Christaller when he argued that trade cycles and corresponding economic activities also dictated port evolution and control over the resources of the hinterland. Norton underlined three phases in port evolution in terms of peripheries: a pioneer periphery which saw the beginning of settlement and agriculture, a specialised periphery with dominant urban centres, commercial agriculture and specialisation, and a transitional periphery which saw the hinterland linked to national networks. T

[128] Frank Broeze, 1992, '*The External Dynamics of Port City Morpholo 1815–1914*' in Banga ed. op.cit.: 245–272.

[129] *Ibid.*: 251.

[130] Morgan, F.W., 1952, *Ports and Harbours*, London, Hutch

last phase saw agricultural commercialisation, diversification and manufacturing[131].

Morgan continued with his description of primitive hinterlands[132], a description which is strikingly close to Norton's idea of the pioneer periphery:

> Port hinterlands which are simple in composition and outline may be called 'primitive'. They lie behind ports...along coasts where there is no cheap and easy lateral transport communication with the hinterland of the next port along the coast. Then all goods entering into the trade of each isolated community pass through each port and the hinterland of each port is the entire local inhabited area.

Morgan therefore extends Christaller's central place thesis (or spatial ranking) to include not only ports, but their hinterlands. In Morgan's theory a dominant ranking of a particular port does not automatically evolve a similar reordering of its hinterland, because there is an independent reordering of hinterlands.

To move from hinterland to port it may be useful to see the Rimmer thesis[133]. Rimmer developed his concept of port evolution by using Christaller's central place theory of spatial ordering. He argued that in the first phase there was a dispersed pattern of sea ports with centres scattered along the coast serving limited hinterlands. The only connection between ports were irregular visits of trading vessels. In the second phase, as transport networks developed some ports along a particular coast developed in relation to others. In the third phase one dominant port emerged along the coast in question. This has been labelled 'port piracy', that is, when one port takes over many of the functions of its neighbouring ports. In phases four and five, specialised services were developed by the dominant ports and the marginal ports acted as auxiliary ports. For example Vigarie, in his study of Nantes during the Industrial Revolution, suggested that economic cycles with their corresponding commercial practices now became dominant: the search for depth and more free areas and a corresponding

---

131 Norton, William, 1984, *Historical Analysis in Geography*, U.K., Longman: 155–6.

132 Op.cit: 111.

133 Rimmer, P.S. 1973, 'The Search for Spatial Regularities in the Development of Australian Seaports 1861–1961/2' in B.S. Hoyle ed. *Transport and Development*, London, Macmillan : 63–86.

conflict between the urban economy and the port economy for occupation of land[134].

The foregoing discussion on port cities, ports and hinterlands is significant as far as our reading of Bengal's mercantile history goes. For example, applying Broeze's concept of maritime hinterland and foreland to medieval Bengal's ports, it will immediately be obvious that the deltaic ports of Sripur, Sandwip and Bakla had lesser of both maritime hinterland and foreland. Travellers attest that their trade was essentially a bulk trade along the coast and to neighbouring states. Long sea linkages from these ports were the exception rather than the rule. But Chattagram, and possibly Sagor and Samandar[135], had larger maritime hinterlands and forelands in the same period.

But the lesser ports too tried to attract traders. On April 30, 1559, a treaty was signed between Parmananda Ray, king of Bakla, and the Portuguese Viceroy Constantino de Braganza, at Goa. This treaty, which placed Bakla in the position of a subordinate ally, is important for our understanding of port evolution in medieval Bengal. The king of Bakla undertook to throw open his port to Portuguese trading fleets if the latter discontinued their visits to Chattagram, then under Arakanese control. The king of Bakla made his port more attractive by promising

1 justice and fair treatment at Bakla,

2 low and fixed custom duties and

3 to undertake the provision of a full cargo of *the produce of the entire coast* stretching from Bakla to Paigao (Paigram in Khulna?).

The Portugese, in their turn, promised

1 to discontinue their trading voyages to Chattagram,

2 to pay lawful duties levied at Bakla, and

3 to grant license to four of the raja's ships to visit Goa, Hormuz and Malacca[136].

Arakan, which had developed the port of Mrauk-U by this time, was reportedly furious at this deal.

Around 1600, once again, we find the Portuguese father Fonseca (of the Society of Jesus) stopping at the court of Pratapaditya at Bakla, on

---

[134] In Kidwai, Atiya Habeeb, 1992, 'Conceptual and Methodological Issues: Ports, Port Cities and Port Hinterlands' in Indu Banga ed. op.cit.: 7–43.

[135] Yet to be identified conclusively. See later.

[136] Sarkar, Jadunath, *The History of Bengal*, Muslim Period 1200–1757, Patna, Academia Asiatica, 1973 Reprint: 358–9.

his way to Sagor. Possibly in a bid to outclass the King of Sagor, Pratapaditya granted Fonseca the right to erect churches and carry on missionary work (conversions) at Bakla[137]. The kings of Sagor and Sripur welcomed the Portguese as sailors and employed them as commanders of their navies. Kedar Rai of Sripur took Carvalho into service around 1601. Sebastian Gonsalves was supported in his piracy by the people of Bakla and Sandwip and Gonsalves made himself master of Sandwip in 1609[138]. Piracy complemented 'official' trade!

Thus, through a happy combination of shrewd political moves and economic considerations, did the delta ports invite increased traffic.

The comparatively lesser status of the deltaic ports can be understood by applying Morgan's notion of a primitive hinterland or Norton's notion of the pioneer periphery. The deltaic area saw shifting settlements and agriculture due to frequent changes in courses of rivers in the region. In consequence, Sripur, Bakla and their like served isolated communities. These were of necessity isolated because of the peculiar riverine terrain at whose mouths they lay. Each river course carved out its own community of consumers. Rimmer had stated that a basic dominance ranking of ports took place according to the improvement of internal accessibility[139]. Frequently there was no easy communication with the hinterland of the next port along the coast. Therefore all goods entering into the trade of each isolated community passed through each port. The hinterland of each port was the entire local inhabited area of the river valley.

Moreover the degree and extent of political control that was needed in the area to link it with wider regional and imperial transport networks faltered beyond a point. The resource base of the Chandras, Varmans, Devas and Khadgas-kings of Dhaka-Vikrampur-was limited by nature of their areal extent. Therefore local agricultural produce could not enter martime trade beyond a certain point; and this may have impeded further development of the deltaic ports. By contrast, states in western Bengal may have had larger resource bases and not such hostile terrain, but from all accounts their interest in overseas commerce in the early medieval period was limited at best.

---

137 *Ibid.*: 359–60.

138 *Ibid.*: 361–2.

139 Rimmer, 1973, op.cit.

Finally Angela Scottenhammer's study of medieval Zaitun[140], unarguably the greatest port in the eastern Indian Ocean in the thirteenth and fourteenth centuries, makes two significant points that are relevant to port development. One, that it is necessary for port evolution to move beyond transhipment functions. She tells us that Zaitun was a transhipment port under the T'angs but it transformed itself in the Song period when it became integrated into a wider net of maritime trade relations. This happenned when Zaitun started trading directly with the Arabs in silk and porcelain following the commercial decline of Srivijaya in the twelfth century.

It may be instructive to look into Srivijaya's career as a transhipment centre for Arab commerce to understand port evolution. In the tenth and eleventh centuries the ports in the Srivijaya kingdom were entrepots which exchanged Arab goods against East and South East Asian goods. In the twelfth century Srivijaya's wars with the Cholas and the Javanese in the eastern Indian Ocean led to its loss of control over the Straits of Malacca which commanded the gateway into the East Asian maritime world. Now the eastern Indian Ocean was opened up to more direct commercial contacts and the Songs took advantage of this.

The second point Schottenhammer makes is that once regional production entered maritime networks it was necessary to exercise a proactive administration that integrated hinterland and port. It was similarly vital to implement fiscal measures that were necessary to sustain a growing trade. This was not done beyond a certain point for Zaitun and the port collapsed soon after, despite having made the leap from transhipment port to one that integrated regional produce in its exports. The hinterland, and political and economic administration there, becomes the theatre of contradictory views of maritime commerce between merchants and the state.

Maritime Societies and the State

Thus far we have talked of trade, sectors within a maritime zone and social practices. Let us now see the attributes of a maritime society and study its interactions with the state. Chaudhuri, echoing Braudel, wrote somewhat differently that[141]:

> The relationship between land and sea in human civilisation all through history has been determined at various levels. First of all, there is the geographical factor, largely though

[140] Schottenhammer, Angela, 1999, 'The Maritime Trade of Quanzhou (Zaitun) from the Ninth through the Thirteenth Century' in Himanshu Prabha Ray ed. *Archaeology of Seafaring: The Indian Ocean in The Ancient Period*, New Delhi, Pragati Publications: 271–290.

[141] Chaudhuri, 1985: 160.

not entirely beyond the control of man. Technological knowledge and constraints, closely interwoven with social and cultural habits, constitute the second dimension. Lastly, the random elements of time, wars, famines, and the rise and fall of political empires, added their own imprints on the varying fortunes of ports, cities, merchant communities, and all those who stood to gain from long-distance maritime trade.

What does a maritime society consist of? A maritime society contains ports, port towns, caravan trade routes converging onto ports, transport networks continuing into the interior, as well as a multitude of peoples: traders, sailors, moneychangers, accountants, insurance agents and lawyers, as well as the communities of the defined coastal area, as we have already argued.

How does a maritime society function? What are its practices? We can isolate at least four levels here. First, a maritime society, that is one whose members are involved in long distance trade of some kind or other, must share in a common pool of knowledge about winds, navigational skills, routes and commodities. Second, a maritime society participates in the knowledge that a customary international maritime law (safe conduct for example) exists. Third, a maritime society participates in a vast economic network that fixes, however informally, prices, weights, measures and currency standards. Fourth, a maritime society functions on the basis of trust. This trust, cutting across different political spaces both on sea and land, ensures the dispensation of justice. Fifth, a maritime society is an open society. It is cosmopolitan. Finally a maritime society is one marked by extreme mobility and adaptability.

Are all of these possible without the support of rulers? *No.* Would a strong maritime tradition evolve if the state pursued active maritime interests? *Yes.* Yet, we know that in the case of South Asia, state interest in trade was sporadic and minimal at best. Except brief spurts under kings in various parts of the sub continent trade remained largely an affair of traders. Rajendra Chola in South India and the Chandras in eastern Bengal in the eleventh century, or the rulers of the Malabar in the sixteenth-seventeenth centuries were exceptions; and Jahangir was the first Mughal, despite the Mughals participating in sea trade, to see the sea!

A strong maritime tradition–of course, fluctuating over time-*can* evolve without direct state intervention. One cannot speak of a single 'national'-that is as state enterprise-maritime tradition in history, except under the Mings in China in the fifteenth century. The evidence of the 'trade coins' of Chattagram that facilitated trade between 1538 and 1575, a period when there was no political authority in Chattagram, is testimony to this absence of state regulation.

Does the state function at all in maritime society? Obviously the existence of a strong state apparatus is needed to organise maritime (that is long-distance) trade as also to facilitate transport of goods and people between inland marts and port cities. Yet one is told time and again that there were differences in the perception of trade between inland agarian states and coastal maritime states. The attitude of inland empires towards sea trade was never proactive (in terms of promoting a concerted maritime policy), and largely reflexive. Yet such inland empires also undertook to organise markets, fix prices, standardise weights and measures within their domains. Trust, protection and justice were three key factors. Abd-er-Razzak wrote of fifteenth century Calicut that 'security and justice are so firmly established in this city that the most wealthy merchants bring thither from maritime countries considerable cargoes, which they unload, and unhesitatingly send into the markets and the bazaars, without thinking in the meantime of any necessity of checking the account or of keeping watch over the goods. The officers of the custom house take upon themselves the charge of looking after the merchandise, over which they keep watch day and night'[142]. Jahangir, upon his accession, issued twelve decrees in 1605. In one of them, he assured merchants of every protection when they travelled within his domains[143].

A similar system operated with respect to maritime trade. Nicolas de Graaf who travelled in South Asia from 1639 to 1689, wrote of a highly organised mercantile system in operation at Hugli, then the chief port of western Bengal[144]:

---

[142] Major, R.H., (ed.), 1857, *India in the Fifteenth Century, Being a Collection of Narratives of Voyages to India*, London, Hakluyt Society,: ii, 10, 21, 27.

[143] *The Jahangir Nama*, translated, edited and annotated by Wheeler M. Thackston, Freer Gallery of Art and Sackler Gallery, Washington and Oxford University Press, New York, Oxford, 1999: 26–7.

[144] *Voyages de Nicolas de Graaf aux Indes Orientales* etcetera (1639 1689), Amsterdam, J.F.Bernard, MD CCXIX: 306-7. As soon as the ships anchor at port before the factory, the Fiscal (Darogha?), accompanied by deputies, comes on board..orders are given, on pain of confiscation, that no one, neither officer or sailor, should take out or bring in packets or chests without the permission of the Director (of the Company) or the Fiscal, except in special cases. After the goods are verified and the Fiscal leaves, the Captain, the Pilot, the Book Keeper, the Chaplain, the First Merchant and others take out all their goods from the ships in plain view of all and sundry and transport them to the warehouses rented specially for this, while they do business with those they know and the merchants of the city. It is risky to buy from the Hindu and Muslim merchants without informing the port official (my translation).

> Des que les vaisseaux ont jette l'ancre devant la loge, le Fiscal, accompagne de quelque Deputez, s'y transporte pour faire la visite…on publie un ordre, que personne, de quelque rang qu'il soit Officiers ou Matelots n'entreprenne de porter a terre ou de faire venire a Bord quelque paquet, caisse ou autre chose particuliere, sans la permission du Directeur ou de Fiscal, a peine de confiscation de ces effets, et autre correction selon Exigeance du cas. Apres cela le Fiscal et ses gens s'ent vont a terre le lendemain la Capitaine du vaisseaux, le Pilote, le Teneur des Livres, le Consolateur, le premier Marchand et autres envoient ce qui leur appartient a terre, a la veue de tout le monde, et le font porter dans les maisons qu'ils sont loue pour ce temps la, negotiant tout le jour avec ceux de leur connoissance, ou avec des marchands du Pais…On achete les merchandises des marchands Banyanes et More au risqué de tomber entre les mains du Fiscal, quoiqu'on employe tous les moyens imaginables, pour n'etre pas surpris…

The administration of maritime commerce seems to be very tightly regulated in seventeenth century Bengal and de Graaf compares this to the practice at Japan 'Quoi qu'au Japon il n'ya point de Fiscal de la Compagnie'[145].

Port administration continued to be highly regulated in eighteenth century Bengal; the K.F.R. contain many references to outgoing ships being inspected to check whether they were carrying more grain and sugar than was needed for the number of heads they carried as filed in the manifest. Despite references to this tight port administration Luillier wrote in 1701 'comme Bengale est le lieu des Indes ou le Commerce est plus libre et plus ouvert'[146] (Bengal is the one place in the Indies where trade is most free and open-my translation). Two models of port administration (and commercialisation) thus emerge. The ports on the western Indian Ocean side-Calicut, Cambay for example were highly organised in terms of security and safe conduct; ports on the eastern Indian Ocean were just beginning to catch up.

Salaries too, were less in the eastern Indian Ocean. The *Ain-i-Akbari*[147] tells us that a *nakhoda* (loosely translated as captain-shipowner) in Cambay

---

[145] *Ibid.*: 305. It seems that Japanese ports had no such practice.

[146] *Voyage du Sieur Luillier aux Grandes Indes avec une Instruction Pour le Commerce des Indes Orientales*, Paris, Claude Cellier, MC CC V.

[147] *The Ain-i-Akbari of Abul Fazl Allami*', Translated by Col. H.S. Jarrett and forwarded by Sir Jadunath Sarkar, 1891, 2nd ed. (by J.N. Sarkar) , 1949. Here the first reprint of 1988, New Delhi, Crown Publication, is used.

earned Rs. 800; his counterpart at Saptagram received Rs. 400. In Pegu and Tenasserim the rates were the same as at Hugli. At Achin, a chief trade hub in the sixteenth and seventeenth centuries, the *nakhoda* earned half of that of Cambay. The one exception was *Malacca*, where *nakhodas* earned twice as much (that is, Rs. 1600) as that of Cambay. This was understandable, given Malacca's status as the premier eastern entrepot in the trade of the Indian Ocean.

Salaries of *nakhodas* depended, the *Ain* tells us, on the cost of living at the port concerned and the length of the networks radiating from it. Therefore we can glean an idea of the comparative profitability of commercial networks from the differential wages at ports.

Should we then think of two sectors with parallel economic activities–one territorial and one maritime-but ruled by different imperatives? It seems so but there is however one dynamic in history that militates against this hypothesis. The sea trade of the Indian Ocean was supplemented throughout history by the overland caravan routes that joined China, northern Bengal and Bihar, and north India, Gujarat, Lahore to Afghanistan, Central Asia, Russia, Persia and the Ottoman Empire. In other words, inland and maritme trade converged at some point or the other throughout South Asia. As Chaudhuri puts it[148]:

> Just as the monsoon winds obeyed a global climatic law…so the sea lanes of the Indian Ocean were supplemented all through history by the northern caravan routes with sturdy two-humped camels, horses, and mules as transport.

And South Asia, particularly Bengal, was no exception to this rule. The port towns and their hinterlands were intimately connected through mart towns further inland all the way to the routes themselves, for the selling and buying of goods, as we shall see later. This linkage was neither accidental nor haphazard; it depended upon a fairly centralised state apparatus that could ensure the smooth flow of peoples and goods within and across its frontiers. This emerged in Bengal by the fifteenth century.

The State in the Maritime Network

The state is never a horizontal and uniform system. A state can base itself on a number or types of activities. These determine the political economy of the state in question. Just as a state contains within it physical features such as rivers, valleys, mountains and routes, it contains within

148 Chaudhuri, 1985: 39.

it also a whole range of cultural practices that may be used to articulate the might of the state. We have seen this in the case of *bera bhasan* in Bengal: when a folk ritual was transformed into a state ritual.

Yet, conventionally, the emergence of state has been studied in the following fashion: It is held that a state is normally underpinned by a large scale agricultural system. A large and flourishing agrarian economy leads to urbanisation. This in turn leads to the increased production of goods for trade; and this leads to an increase in maritime trade.

In this scheme the role of agriculture in state formation is emphasised. But we have to ask ourselves the following questions. Does *only* large scale agricultural growth lead to the emergence of the state? This model of agriculture production–emergence of state–rise of towns–increased commodity production–commerce–maritime trade, may need to be revised. The mercantile state of the Chandras in eleventh century Bengal (at Dhaka-Vikrampur) did have some kind of an agrarian base as the land grants suggest; but its area was small and the agrarian resources were nowhere near to those of the Palas who ruled further west (near north Bengal). Yet the Chandras carried on an active maritime commercial policy while the palas did not.

Indeed, Thapar suggests that there was no one model for the emergence of the state in South Asia[149]. The early Islamic trade network that emerged by the ninth century was certainly underpinned by strong states, but it is not quite certain how far an extensive agrarian production played a role in their emergence.

How far did the state succeed in controlling diverse economic activities such as mining, trade, fishing, and craft production? How far did urban settlements, and market centres retain their autonomy? Can we accept the notion of the centrality of the state in economic activities? These are questions that need to be addressed. It is evident that there can be no one model to explain the emergence and consolidation of the state[150]. And we can stretch the question further to ask how central agriculture and politics were to commercial activities.

---

[149] Thapar, Romila, 2002, *The Penguin History of Early India, From the Origins to AD 1300*, India, Penguin Books, See xxvi-xxvii, 31. She notes, significantly, 'In the immediate post-Gupta period commercial activity in some parts of northern India appears to have declined….ports and coastal towns appear to have beeen less affected by commercial decline…' (456). The associations between political disintegration, commercial decline and urban decay are not always linear. See too Thapar, Romila, 2002, *Cultural Pasts*, New Delhi, Oxford University Press : 81–82, 389–390. See too Sharma, R.S. 2001, *Early Medieval Indian Society: A study in Feudalisation*, Orient Longman : 124–29.

[150] See Ray, Himanshu Prabha, 2003: 132. See Thapar, Romila, 2002 : 81, 83, 390.

The South Asian historical experience tells us that centralised territorial states had more interest, naturally, in agriculture and internal trade, while coastal states pursued an active maritime commercial policy. In the case of the latter agrarian surplus was not always a determinant of the state's emergence and functionality. Many states based themselves on the income from ports with entrepot functions.

The different commercial histories of states in the Indian Ocean may elucidate this further. By virtue of geographical factors states in the western part of the Indian Ocean had less of agrarian acitivity and more of commerce; basing themselves in most cases on entrepot functions. We do not know exactly how far states in the eastern Indian Ocean based themselves on commerce. But we do know that states in the eastern Indian Ocean had greater areas of settled agriculture; with the exception of states in the Malay peninsula and the Sumatra-Java area. It is no coincidence then that the latter and Malacca (a city state with no agricultural land) emerged as the trading hubs of the eastern Indian Ocean world. Let us see the links between agriculture and trade in detail.

In the western Indian Ocean we may count states in Egypt, Arab Asia, Turkey, Iran, Libya, Sudan, Tunisia, Algeria and Morocco upto Central Asia and Afghanistan. This area may be divided geographically into two zones with the mid-line running from Antioch to Basra. The north area is marked by the great basins of Anatolia, Iran and Afghanistan. This is an area of great mountains. The rivers that rise in the Hindu Kush, Khurasan, Elburz, Pontus, Sulaiman, Makran, Fars, Zagros and Taurus chains give birth to the rivers that are the source of agriculture in the region. The plains grow poplar, olive, date and citrus. The southern area is somewhat hilly but has mostly plains and deserts. The desert is very important in the landscape of the western Indian Ocean. Southern rivers and streams disappear into the desert. Apart from Yemen this whole area is dependant on winter rains. Total rainfall is around four inches per annum. The area is dry and irrigation is essential.

Agricultural crops are restricted to four main regions. They are

1. coastal north Africa west of Alexandria

2. the Levant and its hinterland

3. the southern highlands of the Arabian peninsula and the Tigris-Euphrates area and

4. the mountains and basins of Anatolia, Armenia, west and north Iran and north and east Afghanistan. From the area east of the Nile and

the south of the Dead Sea to Basra (the actual place where the Tigris and Euphrates meet and a place very important for trade in the Arab world) there is not a single permanent watercourse in the drylands. The streams run into the desert. While most middle eastern rivers enter the Atlantic Ocean, or the Mediterannean, Black, Caspian, and Red Seas, the Persian Gulf or the Indian Ocean, the rivers that rise in the South Atlas disappear into the desert. Therefore all villages in countries around the western Indian Ocean practice mixed farming. They grow a selction of field crops and raise chicken, sheep, goats, donkeys and cattle[151].

Irrigation is therefore vital in countries around the western Indian Ocean. But large scale irrigation is only practicable in the Nile Valley (Egypt), and in the area of the Euphrates, Tigris and Karun lowlands between the Persian Gulf and the foothills of the Taurus, Zagros and Levantine ranges. Outside the oases and the valleys, inhabitants of the dry regions rely on animal husbandry for sustenance.

Rivers are necessary not only for agriculture but for transport. Again, in states around the western Indian Ocean, river transport is restricted along the Nile, Tigris and Euphrates rivers. It is no accident then that these areas feature time and again in the political history of Islam: the well watered Atlas mountain region of Morocco, Tunis and Carthage, the Nile region, Arabia, the Levant, the Tigris-Euphrates valley of Mesopotamia and the mountain basins of Anatolia and Central Asia.

In East Asia on the other hand, irrigation is not a major problem. The area is abundantly blessed with rivers that flow into the Pacific; it is also crisscrossed by mountains, plateaus and basins. The Yangtze and Yellow rivers, the T'ung-t'ing and P'o-Yang lakes saw the birth of settled agriculture in China. The most watered portion of China is the south. Yunnan, an area that we shall have occasion to refer to time and again when talking of the Bengal-Ava-Arakan-China trade, saw settled agriculture first. It has between forty and fifty per cent of rainfall per annum.

South East Asia is geographically separated from China by the hills that run from the Himalayas down to the China Sea; it is separated from South Asia by the low mountain chain that acts as the watershed between

---

[151] Quayle, Robina G., 1966, *Eastern Civilisations*, New York, Meredith/Appleton-Century Crofts : 33–39.

the Brahmaputra basin in India and the Irrawady basin in Burma. Rivers here are the Irrawady, the Chindwin, the Mekong, the Menam, and the Salween. In Arakan tributaries of the Salween, the Kaladan and the Lemro, rise from east Tibet. South East Asia is important not only for agriculture (its rivers, coasts, silt enriched river valleys, volcanic ash areas of Java, provide a striking contrast to the landscape of the western Indian Ocean) but also for forestry and fishing. Natural forest covers accounts for 60% coverage in South East Asia[152]. Deciduous trees such as teak is very important for commerce; something that will crop up time and again when discussing medieval Bengal's trade history. Rice, forestry and fishing enter into the commerce of the countries of southeast Asia.

This comparative survey of states in the western and eastern Indian Oceans hopes to show that the centrality of agricultural states in pre modern commercial networks cannot always be taken for granted. States that were situated at strategic points along the oceans and seas and who based their political economy on commerce could bypass the stage of extensive agricultural growth and yet retain strength and vigour over centuries. But this division between commercial states and inland agrarian state became blurred by the sixteenth century as all states along the Indian Ocean were drawn into a global exchange (Bing Wong 2002).

The Geography of Trade and Religion

Other than the state promoting trade, religion and the creation of an attendant sacred geography, also furthered trade. Religion, creation of a sacred space, the ranking of rivers in terms of purity, the construction of a pilgrimage circuit with gateway towns and with attendant rules, regulations and rituals for enjoyment, penance and slavation, all these were constructed by agencies other than the state in South Asia[153].

We know that pilgrimage facilitates trade across all cultures. Ganga, Prayag, Kası, Ayodhya were part of the Hindu circuit; Rajgir, Nalanda, Paharpur, Mainamati-Lalmai, Mahastan in eastern India did the same for Buddhism. The shrines that sprang up around the cults of pirs and Sufis in South Asia saw travellers (and trade) converging at these points. Promotion of pilgrimage/tirtha, settlement of Brahmans/sufis and construction of temples/mosques/shrines as well as other public utility

---

152 *Ibid.*: 364–5.

153 Mukherjee, Rila, 2004, 'Contested Authenticities', *Rethinking History*, Routledge, Vol. 8, 3: 459–63 and Mukherjee, Rila, 2004, 'The Vitality of Sacred Spaces' in Gopal Krishan (ed). *The Vitality of India*, Chandigarh, CRRID :173–186. See too, Mukherjee, Rila, 2005, 'Pilgrimage as Bridge', *Man and Development* XXVII, 4, December : 87–108.

monuments and buildings were not only articulations of royal power. They could help expand commerce very significantly.

Frequently, commercial imperatives cut across religious divisions. Hardwar, a sacred Hindu pilgrimage gateway, was also a horse market established by the Rohillas in the eighteenth century. The cattle fair at Bajowra in Kulu, the horse market not far from Kamakhya in Kamrup, or the camel fair at Pushkar, underscore the symbiosis between pilgrimage and trade.

How did far did religion impact on the state? One can see how *bera bhasan* became a state festival in medieval Bengal. A similar occurrence is noted for the early history of Bengal. In this land famous for its river deities, Ganga was usually depicted riding a *makar* or dolphin and Yamuna as riding a *kurma* or tortoise. In the statues excavated from North Bengal and Monghyr (in Bihar) Ganga and Yamuna are usually shown as consorts of Visnu. This is the norm in western Bengal. Significantly, in statues excavated from Bangladesh (Dhaka, Barisal, Vikrampur, Bakargunj and Rampal districts), Ganga is shown as *nagin* (with a snake canopy). Ganga as *nagin* is not a consort of Visnu, as was the case in north Bengal and Bihar, but of Siva[154]. We may suppose that Ganga's representation as a snake goddess pre dated her representation as a pure riverine goddess by virtue of the fact that in the former she is shown as a consort of Siva. It is well known that Saivism, the cult preferred by the Senas, predated Vaishnavism in South Asia. Significantly, statues of Ganga as *nagin* have come to us only from eastern Bengal, which is mainly a littoral region. These date from the eleventh and twelfth centuries. Can one then say that Ganga as snake was later transformed into Ganga with dolphin to accommodate the more refined Vaishnav cult?

Yet another example of a marine goddess being transformed into a territorial one comes to us from Java around the same time (that is, eleventh century). Lara Kidul, the cult goddess of Mataram Java, was originally a serpent deity. Other than being a royal cult Lara Kidul continues even today as a fertility goddess as well as the patron saint of fishermen in Java.

One should note that trade contacts between eastern Bengal and Java mounted from the tenth century. An immense cultural area spanning from Bodh Gaya and the Buddhist shrines of eastern Bengal (Paharpur,

[154] Bhattacharya, Gouriswar, July 2003, *Ganga-Visnupadi-Nagini*, 1st Kumar Sarat Kumar Roy Memorial Lecture, Centre for Archaeological Studies and Training, Eastern India. See pp.11–13.

Mainamati-Lalmai, Mahastan among others) radiated through Pagan (north Burma) towards China in the north and the Java Seas to the south. This was a symbiotic cultural space where both Buddhism and Hinduism supported each other in state formation. Pamela Gutman tells us that although the Chandra kings of Arakan were Buddhists they claimed descent through Siva, an early tribal god in eastern India. Ananda Chandra of Arakan, who we know reigned at Dhanyawadi in 729 AD, had as his grandfather Vajrasakti–both resolutely Sanskritised names. They were both Buddhist and Hindu and Ananda Chandra built four temples to support Brahmans[155].

Anthropologists have drawn parallels between Lara Kidul and Durga of Bengal. Durga was worshipped as Dewi Sri in Java, the fertility (harvest) goddess. But it is significant that before making the transition to land, Lara Kidul was a marine goddess and a serpent deity[156]. Jordaan writes: 'in the present state of research it is still an unresolved debate whether the snake-worship is fully derived from examples from India…We do know that the snake-cult became an integrated element of Sivaism, which was dominant in Southeast Asia. This is probably related to the fact that Siva, also by his affinity to the Vedic god Rudra, was closely connected with the worship of demonic powers of the underworld, which include the *Naga*'[157]. When the successive sultanates of Surakarta and Yogjakarta came to power in Java Lara Kidul continued as the royal cult. But now her serpent origins were obscured.

To draw a linear association between agriculture–birth of state–rise of towns–flourishing commerce is not always tenable. Similarly there could be commercial networks that cut across state boundaries and which dispensed with state patronage. Such networks functioned along pilgrimage routes; a good case is the Buddhist nework in Bihar (Bodh Gaya)–Bengal–Kamrup–Pagan–Ceylon–China–Java. Seen this way, the eastern Indian Ocean forms a distinct 'culture area' over which a functionally coherent way of life dominated an area with an exclusive core, a dominant domain and a distinctive realm (Baker 2003; 165–7). We have yet to investigate Bengal's place here.

---

155 Gutman, Pamela, 2001, *Burma's Lost Kingdoms: The Splendours of Arakan:* 41–2.

156 Jordaan, Roy E., 1984, 'The Mystery of Nyai Lara Kidul, Goddess of the Southern Ocean', *Archipel 28*, Paris, EHESS: 99–116.

157 *Ibid.*: 109.

3

Key Issues: Bengal

'A great empire which marches with the Kingdomes of Delhi, Ceylon, Cathay and Vijayanagar' (Roger Barlow, *A Briefe Summe of Geographie*, F.G.R.Taylor ed. Series II, V.69, London, The Hakluyt Society, 1929–32).

The 'Primacy' of Bengal?

From the historical accounts to academic works even today Bengal's inarguably large productive potential is taken to be an indicator of its primacy in business within South Asia and beyond. Its productive capacity is confused with the actual management of its resources and its weak commercial system. By commercial system is meant a system of controlling and diversifying production, dictating the quality of commodities and prices, a knowledge of transport networks and markets outside Bengal, and independent access to markets. Bengal's production system was agrarian-based and therefore doubly vulnerable to the vicissitudes of nature and the fluctuations in international trade. One tends to ignore these in favour of arguments highlighting the immense productivity capacity of Bengal in agriculture and crafts.

These accounts ignore the fact that despite its prodigious production, no independent mercantile activity on a large scale is noted for Bengal, after the first half of the seventeenth century. Thereafter, prominent merchants of Bengal functioned as *dadni* merchants, that is, as intermediaries between buyer and seller within Bengal, and rarely undertook commerce outside Bengal on their own initiative. Bengal merchants did not organise themselves into a trading combine vis-à-vis other 'national merchants' as did the Coromandel merchants from the seventeenth century. There were no local merchant-shipowners in eighteenth century Bengal on a scale that is noted for Surat in the same century[158]. Bengal, despite being a littoral society with a riverine network perhaps unequalled in the world has documented, to the best of our knowledge, only three major boatyards[159]. Therefore prodigious production is mistaken for commercial control.

Yet it is known that Bengal's productive base was no less than that of Surat and certainly greater than that of the Coromandel. The province was a fabled producer of cotton textiles from very early times; it was equally famous for its low prices, local spices, oils, sugar, copious grain and dairy products. From the seventeenth century it became one of the leading producers of silk in the world. In other words Bengal produced items of bulk (local), ordinary (regional) and luxury (long distance) trade. But while it was a considerable producing region the *trade* in its products was controlled by extra-regional forces from early times. From the seventeenth century merchants from Gujarat, who had a closer tie with the Mughals by virtue of the Mughal dependence on the port of Surat, controlled textile exports from Bengal. By the seventeenth century Gujarati merchants settled in Bengal. Bengal merchants rarely traded directly with Surat.

This impression of commercial passivity is reinforced through received history. Tome Pires mentioned that Bengali merchants did not venture abroad. Sixteenth century travellers made much of the fabled wealth of Bengali merchants; but Bengali merchants and shipowners rarely travelled on their ships, leaving the business of buying and selling to their *nakhodas* or captains. This was certainly the practice of the Mughal *subahdars* who frequently consigned their wares to the *nakhodas* in the seventeenth century but was not always the case. The traditional practice for local Bengali merchants in the medieval age was to sail their own ships. For example, the *Mangal Kavyas* are rife with instances of merchant-princes from Bengal sailing their own ships to ports on the Coromandel coast and to Ceylon to trade there. It therefore seems likely that the medieval period was a significant watershed in Bengal's trade.

---

158 See Ashin Das Gupta's classic study of the mercantile-shipowning class of Surat in *Indian Merchants and the Decline of Surat 1700–1750*, 1979, Wiesbaden, Franz Steiner Verlag.

159 Swarup Bhattacharya, private communication and Swarup Bhattacharya, 2000, 'Biswakarmas, of boat and their traditional knowledge of boat building in different environments with special reference to West Bengal', *Journal of the Department of Anthropology,* University of Calcutta,: 117–124. Also Swarup Bhattacharya and Lotika Varadarajan, 2000, 'Patia of Eastern India, Vestiges of a Reverse Clinker Tradition', *Techniques and Culture*, 35–36, Paris: 417–444.

The sixteenth century westward shift in trade within South Asia, which has to be seen mostly as a response to changing conditions in the Islamic world (the emergence of the Ottoman, Mughal, and Safavid states and consequent new networks) disadvantaged Bengal in two ways. First, because now ports on the westward side of Bengal such as Saptagram and Hugli became more prominent, mercantile activities in the east lost their independent momentum. Mercantile cities in the eastern part of Bengal lost control over their own networks to the east and north as now the western ports began to import eastern goods (from Kamrup, Assam and Ava) directly. Second, trade from Bengal ports now inserted itself into networks run from other ports-Cambay for example. Prodigious production did not translate into indigenous, or Bengali, commercial control over the Bengal trade.

The failure to develop an external Bengal trade dominated by indigenous Bengali merchants was due-to many reasons.

The chequered history of Bengal's ruling classes and varying ethnic compositions among them dictated fragile trade links. There was no one single controlling force that facilitated movements of goods, dictated prices and framed fiscal policies over any length of time. In the absence of a single political force Bengal's trading community was subject to multiple impulses that ultimately proved harmful to its progress.

The constant political tussle between east and west in medieval Bengal-resulted in uneven mercantile developments within Bengal. Mercantile activity in the eastern part is noted earlier than in the west. The Bengal-Arakan-China trade was carried on from the east. But mercantile management in eastern Bengal did not correspond always to the political realities in that region. States in this part of Bengal were small and fragmented. Their resource base was limited. Mercantile growth in western Bengal was more recent, more subject to political management by states with a large agrarian base and therefore weak. Lack of, or excessive, state guidance–both of these were harmful to indigenous mercantile interests in the long run, and there was, consequently,

A failure of local mercantile elites to emerge. After the Buddhists it could only be the Bengali Muslims who could effect the symbiosis between the agricultural and mercantile domains. Unfortunately, the Bengali-Muslims remained a marginal economic category, partly due to the limited cultural area of Bengali-Muslim littoral society. It has long been recognised that mercantile activities take place within a well-defined cultural zone. This cultural-commercial participation was not possible in medieval Bengal.

The overland Buddhist network which ran from Bengal, through the north-east and into Tibet and China, was on the wane by the fourteenth century. The next network in which Bengal could participate was the Islamic network. But this was geared towards the west, and not east, and *ashrafi* Muslims dominated this network. A mercantile culture, dominated by Bengali-Muslim mores, could only expand north-east of the Bay-through Arakan into the borders of Siam. This was only a small area with trade routes that were marginal to the greater Bay of Bengal-Indian Ocean trading networks. An expansive Bengali-Islamic culture could only have a limited impact; and this was confined to littoral societies along the Bay. Moreover this littoral area came under ecological pressure from the fourteenth and fifteenth centuries due to riverine shifts from *east to west* in the *thirteenth and fourteenth centuries*. When Ali Mardan settled at Lakhnawati in the thirteenth century the Ganga ran on its east side. From the 1340s the Ganga was reported to have flooded the capital. People abandoned Lakhnawati and a new capital was established at Firuzabad to the northwest. At the new settlement the Ganga still flowed on the eastern side. Jalal-ud-Din shifted back to Lakhnawati-a new city that is almost identifiable with the second city of Gaur of the city. Now the river flowed on its *western* side. This *east to west shift* is significant but it is not known how far it impacted on mercantile developments in the region. Eaton has emphasised the *sixteenth to the eighteenth centuries west to east shifts*, but archaeological and remote sensing data from research undertaken by the Centre for Archaeological Studies and Training, Eastern India, Government of West Bengal, (henceforth CASTEI) present an altogether different picture of riverine shifts in Bengal for the period immediately prior to the sixteenth century[160].

In any case these shifts seriously hampered commercial development at least in the west and the instability of rivers in Bengal also affected port growth. Rivers in Bengal were much more volatile than those on the west coast of South Asia. While we have no data as yet on port life cycles in the thirteenth and fourteenth centuries, we do know that the *west to east* riverine shifts of the sixteenth century actually slowed down commercial

[160] Personal communication from Sri Pratip Mitra, Keeper, State Archaeological Museum, Kolkata, at the offices of CASTEI on August 5 2005 regarding the thirteenth and fourteenth century riverine changes. For the sixteenth to the eighteenth century shifts see Richard Eaton's two books: Eaton, 1993, *The Rise of Islam and the Bengal Frontier 1204–1760*, California, Berkeley and L.A. and 2002, *Essays on Islam and Indian History*, Oxford University Press.

development in the east since independent commercial activity there was now hitched to the western channels through new channels; the shift also meant the financial ruin of the merchants who had hitherto concentrated on the east.

Further pressure mounted with riverine shifts further eastward in the eighteenth century which introduced six new rivers into Bengal and rendered the western delta 'moribund' and the eastern delta 'active'[161] at a time when all trade was being conducted from the western delta. Independent trade through the Meghna-Brahmaputra to the North-East, Arakan, Ava and China ceased to exist. Bengal's 'eastern' commodities could now be accessed by the 'western' ports through the 'new' rivers and the eastern routes fell into disuse. The east now became the grain belt for Bengal, and an unequal relationship between west and east Bengal commenced from this time. Various social and economic changes in Bay littoral societies resulted from these shifts. For example, riverine changes affected the rice growing areas of the delta and these in turn affected the agricultural base. The agricultural base was vital for all producing classes, even for those involved in commerce. In Bengal particularly, both merchant and weaver rested on this base. In terms of social mobility, moving from the littoral to the interior, a new type of vaishnav merchant failed to emerge in sixteenth century Bengal because of the social constraints imposed by Hinduism[162]. Moreover, although the Bengal-Arakan trade sector was immensely beneficial to the Bay trade in general and to eastern Bengal in particular, Arakan seems to have degenerated from a maritime state to a pirate state by the second half of the seventeenth century. All the sources affirm that Arakanese-Portuguese slave raids extended as far as Hugli and Pipli by the seventeenth century. It also seems that the Arakan border was an 'expanding frontier' that divided *samatata* into Bengal and Arakan around Sagor at this time. Streynsham Master wrote on September 7, 1676, going up from Hugli to Kasimbazar: 'This morning we came faire by the Arracan shore…and came to an anchor at the mouth of the River near the Ile of Coxes…(Sagor)' and added on September 8: 'This day we passed by the River which goes to Chittygom and Dacca, which the

[161] Marshall, P.J., 1987, *Bengal: The British Bridgehead, Eastern India 1740–1828,* NCHI, Cambridge, University Press,India, Orient Longman. This edition O.L.: 4.See also Eaton, Richard, 2002, *Essays on Islam and Indian History* Delhi, Oxford University Press: 262.

[162] See Sanyal, Hitesranjan, 1981, *Social Mobility in Bengal,* Calcutta, Papyrus later.

English call the River of Rogues, by reason the Arracaners used to come out there to Rob...'[163]. A maritime society had become a pirate and slave-raiding society. Bowrey, Master's contemporary in Bengal, noted: 'Many Isles there be in the mouth of the Ganges, not inhabited more than with wild beasts...the Natives much dreadinge to dwell there, being timorous of the Arrackaners with their Gylars who many times have come through the Rivers and carried away captive many poore families of the Orixa folks'[164]. He added that many pirate ships of Arakan, manned by the Arakanese and Portuguese, also infested the waters around Dhaka[165]. Yet another contemporary, Bernier, wrote that 'They scoured the neighbouring seas in light galleys, called galleasses, entered the numerous arms and branches of the Ganges, ravaged the islands of Lower Bengal, and often penetrating forty or fifty leagues up the country, surprised and carried away the entire population of villages on market days...(or) a marriage. The intruders made slaves of their unhappy captives'[166]. William Hedges, who succeeded Master as English agent in Bengal, does not mention Arakanese depredations directly; nevertheless he too makes an oblique reference to the decay of trade in *samatata* in the seventeenth century[167]. Bernier noted the depopulation of Lower Bengal in the middle of the seventeenth century[168]; more than a century later this was not reversed. Lower Bengal, once famed for trade with countries along the northern Bay of Bengal, had become a marginal land by the seventeenth century. The age of the delta ports was over. Rennell marked the Sunderbans as 'Country Depopulated by the Muggs' in *A Bengal Atlas* in the 1780s. This area was never to recover.

---

163 Temple, R.C.Temple (ed). 1911, *The Diaries of Streynsham Master 1675–1680 And Other Contemporary Papers Relating Thereto*, London, John Murray, Indian Records Series, 2 Vols., Vol. 1: 321.

164 Temple, R.C. (ed). M D CCCC V, *Thomas Bowrey, A Geographical Account of the Countries Around The Bay of Bengal 1669–1679*, Cambridge, Hakluyt Society, 211–12.

165 *Ibid.*: 140–141.

166 Francois Bernier, *Travels in the Mogul Empire*, revised Vincent A.Smith, Reprint, Delhi, 1989: 175.

167 Henry Yule and R.Barlow (Eds). , M D CCC LXXX, *Diary of William Hedges During His Agency in Bengal 1681–87*, London, Hakluyt Society, 2 vols. Vol.1: 152.

168 'It is owing to these repeated depredation (of the Maghs) that we see so many fine islands at the mouth of the Ganges, formerly thickly peopled, now entirely deserted by human beings, and become the desolate lairs of tigers and other wild beasts'. Bernier, *Travels* op.cit. 174–75.

The chief commodity of this region was timber and the dynamics of piracy and the slave trade on the east coast of South Asia (from the Arakan to the Coromandel ports) impacted adversely on Bengal's balance of trade in the first half of the seventeenth century. A triangular trade developed between Jakarta, Mrauk-U and Pulicat. This route bypassed Bengal.

The scarcity of timber for shipbuilding may be taken as yet another reason why even the Mughal *subahdars* in Bengal withdrew from trade at the end of the seventeenth century. Referring to Sagor, which may be taken as the dividing line between Arakan and Bengal Hedges wrote on December 15 1684 that until the 1640s Sagor was inhabited and the 'Raja' (*subahdar*?) got an annual rent of Rs. 26 lakhs from Sagor. The enormity of this figure can be understood if we note that the yearly rent from dominions between the River 'of Rungapula' to the River of Rajmahal was Rs. 45 lakhs[169]. Sagor's importance lay in the supply of timber to build ships. With Sagor under Arakan Bengal was effectively rendered without a supply of timber which came historically from this area running eastwards into Arakan.

Also, the agrarian base of the merchant in Bengal, while initially sustaining him, ultimately worked against an indigenous mercantile growth. In Cambay and Surat, for example, the merchant rested on a purely urban base. His urban base enabled the Cambay Gujarati-Muslim merchant to expand towards the ports of the Malabar (towards Calicut, for example)[170]. But urbanisation along the Hugli, or in *samatata* in medieval times[171], was essentially of an agrarian-mercantile nature, dominated by the great markets of the area and held together by a string of smaller *golas*, which were, in turn, nourished by the village *haats*. As part of his profits came from agriculture the merchant used that as capital to plough back into commerce and so the capital kept circulating in an endless circle without any radical breakthrough in production.

[169] Diary of William Hedges, op. cit.

[170] Duarte Barbosa (*The Book of Duarte Barbosa*, M.L.Dames, London, Hakluyt Society) mentions how the ports of the Malabar were coming under the domination of Cambay and Surat at the beginning of the sixteenth century. It seems that a hierarchy of ports had developed on the west coast. The Gujarat ports, with Cambay at the top, dominated the Malabar ports, of whom Calicut was the most important: 5–150, 183–85. Ray, Haraprasad, 2003, *Trade and Trade Routes between India and China*, Calcutta, Progressive, mentions how the west coast Arabs from Gujarat threw out the Chinese from Calicut in the middle of the fifteenth century: 206–08.

[171] See the chapters on Ports and Their Hinterland in Bengal and Markets in Bengal later.

Tarafdar notes that the Bengali-Muslim agriculturist could not make the leap from weaver and small holder to owner; either as merchant or as landlord. The same holds for the Bengali Hindu cultivator. Sanyal writes: 'the essentially agriculture-based economy of Bengal and the essentially rural character of the culture of the Begalis....failed to develop into a lever of social movement aimed at structural change'[172]. Other than hampering social change, dependence on agriculture also impeded industrial development and the consequent rise of a vigorous merchant class with clearly defined class interests. In a society centred on agricultural production, labour was cheap and abundant. Wages remained low. Urban industrial workers could draw for part of their subsistence on their villages, where, since women remained tied to the land, labour for agricultural work was cheap. There was thus little incentive to sustain technological breakthroughs[173]. This led to what Mark Elvin calls a 'high level equilibrium trap'[174] or a situation where labour intensive production led to economic expansion which in turn resulted in population growth and even institutional change. All this led to a state of affairs where the normal accumulation of capital culminated at a point of diminishing returns. So not stagnation, but rather its opposites, led to a situation where ultimately there was no breakthrough in production and distribution of goods. Such conditions certainly existed in Bengal in the seventeenth century.

Thus, *both* merchants and artisans of Bengal rested on an agrarian base. Serious disruption followed if the agrarian base collapsed; this happened either due to uncertain monsoons which resulted in famine (as in 1752) or because of battles and invasions (such as those which ravaged western Bengal from 1740). Independent mercantile activity was difficult to sustain under such circumstances; moreover the uncertainties caused by the river changes from the thirteenth century onwards may be yet another reason for agrarian uncertainty and a reason why independent large-scale mercantile activity tapers off during the course of the seventeenth century in Bengal. It seems the western delta did became

[172] Sanyal, Hiresranjan, 1981, *Social Mobility in Bengal*, Papyrus, Calcutta: 64.

[173] Goldstone, Pomeranz and Frank put forward similar arguments for China. See Jack A.Goldstone, 1996, 'Gender, Work and Culture : Why the Industrial Revolution Came Early to England but Late to China', *Sociological Perspectives*, 39, 1: 1–21; For Kenneth Pomeranz and Frank see Frank, A.G., 2005, 'Eurocentrism in Historiographic Tradition' in Mukherjee, Rila and Chattopadhyay, Kunal eds. *Europe in the Second Millennium: A Hegemony Achieved?*, Kolkata, Progressive Publishers: 73–114. See Tarafdar, M.R., 1995, *Trade, Technology and Society in Medieval Bengal*, ICBS, Dhaka, Bangladesh : 69–107.

[174] Elvin, Mark, 1973, *The Pattern of the Chinese Past*, Stanford, Stanford Press.

'moribund' as Eaton claims[175]; and the waning of the 'west' may have been expressed though lack of agricultural acivity. Does this decline of agriculture (between 1595 and 1654 the rate of growth for the west was only 20% compared to the east's 107%) explain why the western delta became a notorious area for slave ports while the more fertile eastern delta became an area for slave-raiding and piracy?

Many of these factors could well have impeded the functioning of the Gujarati merchants who were prominent in Bengal, but they seem not to have had a similarly adverse effect[176]. First of all, as mentioned before, Gujarati merchants were not tied to the agrarian base of Bengal. Their world of circulation was independent of the productive world of Bengal. Times of scarcity were possibly offset by the infusion of fresh funds from Gujarat. Secondly, historically the Gujarati merchants had not concentrated on the east-as the Bengali merchants did in the early medieval period-and thus they had less to lose when trade shifted westwards. Third, capital formation in the case of the Gujarati merchants was markedly different. The Gujarati merchants, unlike their Bengali counterparts, were not so dependent on the agrarian base of their home state. From the middle of the fifteenth century Gujarati merchants had acquired a substantial capital base. This enabled them to radiate out from Gujarat into other areas. They were active in Calicut at the end of the century[177] and they arrived in Bengal soon after[178]. They were thus in a position to sustain trade in difficult times, something the Bengali merchant was unable to do. The commercial space vacated by the merchants of Bengal was filled in by the Mughal *subahdars* who were posted to Bengal.

The commercial history of eighteenth century Bengal is the story of a takeover by the Europeans in the absence of a vigorous mercantile

---

[175] Eaton, Richard, 1993, *The Rise of Islam and the Bengal Frontier 1204–1760,* California, Berkeley and *L.A.* and 2002, *Essays on Islam and Indian History*, Oxford, University Press. That the western delta became a 'moribund delta' due to riverine shifts and that the eastern delta-the 'active' one-helped Islamic expansion to the east through superior agricultural skills is the main thrust of his argument. How far this actually happenned has recently been questioned.

[176] Memoire Generale du Commerce que la Cie. des Indes peut faire dans ses etablissements en Inde tant pour l'Europe que les autres parties de l'Inde by Jacques Vincens, A.N.Colonies C2 197 ff. 1.18/C256 ff.22–44 at Aix mentions that the Bengal-Surat run was completely in the hands of the Muslim merchants and Hindu banyans of Surat in the 1730s. See *Merchants and Companies* for more on this.

[177] Ray, Haraprasad, 2003.

[178] See later.

policy on the part of the Bengal Nawabs. This takeover happened in a vacuum for Mughal participation in trade and shipowning ceased at the end of the seventeenth century[179]. Late seventeenth century records and testimonies underline the fact that independent commercial activity had ceased to exist in Bengal.

Archetypes in Bengal's Mercantile History

Having delineated some of the probable reasons for our 'big' theme of the failure of local big merchants to emerge, other themes that mark the mercantile history of Bengal are discussed here. These themes have exercised considerable influence on the historiography of Bengal from the eleventh to the sixteenth centuries.

One such theme is the eleventh century 'trade revolution' in the Indian Ocean. It is argued here that the legacy of the eleventh century trade revolution in the Bay of Bengal was responsible for Bengal's asymmetrical development as a maritime state. The notion of a 'trade revolution' was first articulated by K.N.Chaudhuri[180] and later developed by Hermann Kulke[181], Denys Lombard[182] and Jan Wisseman Christie[183]. Kulke noted that the expansion of Chola power in the Bay of Bengal led to a 'trade revolution' in the Bay of Bengal[184]. The Chola invasion against the Sailendras (who had taken over the Srivijaya empire in the ninth century and thereby moved from Java to Sumatra[185]) and Chinese help to the Sailendras against the Mataram state in Java has to be seen

[179] Much has been written about this withdrawal; for reasons for this withdrawal see later.

[180] Chaudhuri, K.N., 1985, *Trade and Civilisation in the Indian Ocean: An Economic History from the Rise of Islam to 1750,* Cambridge, University Press.

[181] Kulke, Hermann, 1999, '*Rivalry and Competition in the Bay of Bengal in the Eleventh Century and its bearing on Indian Ocean Studies*', in Om Prakash and Denys Lombard eds. *Commerce and Culture in the Bay of Bengal 1500–1800*, New Delhi, Manohar/ ICHR: 17–35.

[182] Lombard, Denys, 1990, *Le Carrefour Javanais: Essai d'histoire Globale,* III, *L'Heritage des Royaumes Concentriques*, Paris, Editions E.H.E.S.S.

[183] Christie, Jan Wisseman, 1999, '*Asian Sea Trade between the Tenth and Thirteenth Centuries and Its Impact on the States of Java and Bali*' in Himanshu Prabha Ray ed. *Archaeology of Seafaring: The Indian Ocean in the Ancient Period*, ICHR Monograph Series 1, New Delhi, Pragati: 221–270.

[184] Kulke, H, 1999, op. cit. 17–35: 33.

[185] Quayle, G. Robina 1966, *Eastern Civilisations*, New York, Meredith/Appleton-Century Crofts: 370–72.

in this context[186]. I would go further and claim that the Cholas did not initiate the 'trade revolution', they were in fact attempting to access the benefits of the results of long term cycles of expansion in the eastern Indian Ocean. Christie noted that between the tenth and thirteenth centuries[187]:

> Different sectors of the Asian waters tended to be affected by separate regional economic cycles. However when two or more of these regional cycles coincided, the effects upon trade could be particularly dramatic. Such a convergence of regional sea cycles appears to have occurred during the period between the early tenth and mid thirteenth centuries. During these centuries several states in maritime Southeast Asia benefited from an economic boom that affected sea trade both in the Indian Ocean and the South China Sea. The Malay trading state federation or 'empire' of Srivijaya that dominated the Malacca Straits is one well-known beneficiary of this increase in sea trade. In many ways, however, the major states of Java and Bali gained more from this expansion in sea trade…

The Javanese state of Mataram pioneered this economic boom in the Malacca and Sunda Straits and the South China Sea. Cash crops rose in Java (mainly black pepper and safflower dyes) in response to Chinese demand. Early in the ninth century it minted South East Asia's first indigenous standardised coins of gold and a silver-copper alloy based on eastern Indian units and on the *prakrit-nagari* script that had come into use in north east Bengal in the eighth century[188]. Interestingly enough, the mainstream *kawi* script of Java was not used on these coins that were used for a variety of transactions : payment of taxes, tithes and fines, settlement of debts, purchase of labour and market commodities, lands and buildings. The *kawi* script had evolved from the Pallava script of South India. This dependence on the *prakrit nagari* script on the Mataram coins in preference to the *pallava* script is indeed striking when we bear in mind that conventional history tells another story. That it were the Coromandel ports, and not the Bengal ones, that carried on the most trade with South East Asia during this period. The use of an eastern *prakrit nagari* indicates

---

186 *Ibid.*: 371.

187 Christie, op.cit.: 222.

188 Christie, op.cit.: 230.

that we need to revise our ideas about the relative roles of the Bengal and south Indian ports in eastern trade.

Mataram gold and silver coinage became the norm in the trade triangle of Sumatra in the west to Bali in the east and Luzon in the north. More and more Javanese ports were annexed by Mataram. Trade with South Asian ports is attested to by the fact religious teachers from Gujarat, Sri Lanka and Gaur visited Java in the ninth and tenth centuries. Local statuary was influenced by the Pala style. Mataram and the Sailendras positioned themselves as middlemen in the trade between South Asia and China and trade in the South China Sea was dominated by Mataram and Sailendra shipping in the eleventh century.

Two events occurred in the eastern Indian Ocean in the eleventh century. First, the Chinese government now encouraged its merchants to carry their trade abroad rather than depend on South East Asian intermediaries. In 1023 the Chinese emperor urged the Arab envoys to shift their trade from the Silk Route and trade with China by sea. This suited the Cholas who were seeking to bypass the South East Asian states and trade directly with China. The chief items in this trade were black pepper and safflower, both originally south Indian cultivars, which the Javanese had taken to growing as cash crops for the Chinese market and thus displaced the south Indian commodities. Second, K.N. Chaudhuri commented on the distinctiveness of commerce in the Indian Ocean in the eleventh century; according to him there was a changeover from trans-continental (say, a direct sailing from West Asia to China) trade to shorter routes punctutated with port-cities[189]. This was known as emporia trading and rose in response to the rise of two empires in east and west in the tenth century, the Songs in China (960 AD) and the Fatimids in Egypt (967). To these Kulke adds the emergence of the Cholas in 985 AD[190]. A direct consequence of the rise of these three empires and the change in the nature of routes was that more and more ports sprang up all long the coasts as more and more regional economies participated in maritime trade.

So when the Cholas attempted to wrest control of maritime routes from the Sailendras they were not really initiating a 'trade revolution'; rather they were participating in one that was already in place. In 1006 the Sailendras successfully destroyed the Javanese state of Mataram which

[189] Chaudhuri, K.N., 1985, op. cit. 39, 49.

[190] Kulke, 1999: 20.

was challenging its maritime hegemony. In 1025, the same year as Mahmud of Ghazni raided Somnath on India's west coast, the Cholas too sought to make history by removing the Sailendra hegemony in the eastern Indian Ocean by successfully raiding their capital.

Chola maritime policy directly benefited the Coromandel ports (the various trade routes that emanated from the Coromandel used the southern Bay of Bengal. This was because the northern Bay was susceptible to cyclones, which discouraged active long distance sailings) but this trade revolution also helped generate a smaller sector trade in the northern Bay, notably between Bengal and Arakan. From the middle of the eleventh century another 'imperial kigdom' and important competitor rose in the northern Bay of Bengal area. This was Pagan[191]. Pagan linked the maritime trade of the Bay of Bengal with that of China through its access to the land route through Ava to Yunnan.

Pagan united Burma and contained the ports of Lower Burma within it. By contrast Arakan lay on an inhospitable shore and was not of much commercial importance. Yet because of its proximity to Bengal Arakan rose as a commercial power in the eleventh century. This was no accident and it is certainly also no accident that from this time the names of Sripur, Bakla, Sandwip and Sagor, deltaic ports on the Bengal coast begin to appear in records. An active Bengal-Arakan coastal trade dates from this period. After the decline of Pagan Arakan emerged as a considerable religious force. By reason of its patronage of Buddhism it linked the pilgrim circuit of Bengal and Bodh Gaya with that of Ceylon. This greatly enhanced trade in the Bay. In the fifteenth century this small sector trade route was further enhanced with the addition of the direct Bengal-China trade.

I argue that the great trading pedigree of the eastern sector was largely killed off when the Husain Shahis encouraged trade in the western sector in the next century. Owing to the eastward shift of the rivers in this century, the Husain Shahi sultans preferred to develop the western delta. They encouraged the development of Saptagram to the detriment of the deltaic ports. This caused an assymetrical mercantile development within Bengal because Saptagram could never participate in an independent economic and cultural zone as had the eastern ports in centuries earlier.

In the sixteenth century the Bengal-China trade tapered off. This accelerated the mercantile decline further. It is notable that Duarte Barbosa,

---

191 See *ibid*: 21.

who draws for us an excellent picture of trade links and port hierarchies on the west coast-Cambay as chief port and Calicut as subsidiary port for example-hardly mentions the Bengal-China trade, except for a stray reference to ships similar to Chinese junks at Chattagram, and to Arakan dealing in China goods[192]. This trading route was dominated by Arab and later Persian merchants, and not by Bengali-Muslims. Unlike ports of the west coast, or those of the Coromandel, no great trading networks intersected at Bengal. There was, consequently, little impetus to the development of an indigenous mercantile group.

Yet another theme that marks the history of Bengal is the impact of the Portuguese presence in Bengal. The conventional view is that Portuguese presence on Bengal's eastern shores, and their monitoring over trade and shipping in this part of the Bay was another factor that may have impeded in the long run the growth of an indigenous mercantile community. It seems that they were active in inland trade in western Bengal as well by the end of the sixteenth century[193]. Earlier writings focussed on the 'hegemony' of the Portuguese in the Indian Ocean and while it is recognised that 'the Portuguese have the dubious distinction of being the people who introduced politics into the ocean'[194] recent research however suggests that far from hindering local growth the Portuguese may actually have helped foster the older eastward trading networks in the Indian Ocean by enlarging the volume of trade. Certainly this seems to be the case in the Bay. Portuguese control over the Bay was small; at any one time the 'semi official' Portuguese control was effected through a handful of forces (de Brito's control over Syriam was limited to 250 men at most). Their control over trade and trade routes was never absolute[195]. Pearson makes this point about western India[196]:

> In a nutshell, then, most members of the Gujarati elite were unaffected by the Portuguese presence, or ignored them. Those who were affected resisted, but usually were defeated… . Portuguese policy, and local Indian responses to it (makes)

[192] Henry E.J. Stanley (tr). , M D CCC LXVI, Duarte Barbosa, *A Description of the Coasts of East Africa and Malabar in the Beginning of the Sixteenth Century*, London, Hakluyt Society: 178–79.

[193] Subrahmanyam, S., 1990: 113.

[194] Pearson, M.N., *The Portuguese in India*, NCHI, 1.1, Cambridge, University Press, 1987, Indian edition, Orient Longman : 29.

[195] *Ibid.* in the case of pepper and spices on the west coast throughout the sixteenth century: 43–44.

[196] *Ibid.* 55, 61, 77–8.

> clear how variegated was the official Portuguese impact:…in particular places, massive, more often nugatory…Even in the areas where some of Portugal's aims were achieved, one must recognize that this did not lead to a substantial change in existing patterns. Rather this was a redistributive empire, where the Portuguese skimmed off a layer of profits for themselves, but were not able to affect radical changes in routes, products or productive techniques at any level. In its simplest terms, the Portuguese system did nothing except divert trade in some goods, and force some Asian traders to pay extra customs duties. At most they manipulated, but did not transform.

This seems to hold for the east coast as well where the Portuguese presence was limited to negotiations with local rulers over trade and settlement, some kind of accommodation in commerce and commercial rights, and a speedy exodus if things became too hot to handle. For example, a combination of local politics, commercial factors and riverine transformations after the 1530s led the Portuguese to move out of eastern *samatata* in Bengal to both the west (Gaur, Saptagram and then Hugli) and further east to Dianga. When they were chased out of these places in the seventeenth century (1632 in the case of Hugli and 1607 in the case of Dianga) the Portuguese simply went down the coast and relocated themselves at Pipli (south-west on the present Bengal-Orissa border) and at Arakan and then Syriam (in the east). It therefore remains to be seen how far local merchants lost out with the Portuguese presence in eastern Bengal.

From the sixteenth century Bengal's riverine system had been moving east. By the end of the eighteenth century six new rivers had been added to the riverscape of Bengal. The west was deemed an 'unproductive' area. Yet the EEIC established itself (along with other European companies) on an insignificant channel-the Bhagirathi-in a 'moribund' delta. The English East India Company's increasing control over the riverine network in Bengal from the 1730s ensured that English merchant capital was able to reach internal markets and influence production patterns in the *arangs* long before the agency system was introduced in 1754. From the 1740s a new factor entered this chaotic arena–the Marathas. Their raids continued until 1751 and substantively destroyed the economy of Bengal.

Yet another theme that marks the medieval history of Bengal is that of 'magh raids'. Accounts of the Arakanese-Portuguese intervention, commonly dismissed as 'magh raids' over Bengal, gloss over the fact that this shadowy area to Bengal's south-east dictated historical events in medieval Bengal to a very great extent. Arakan was important to Bengal politics since much of southeastern Bengal was under its control from the sixteenth to the eighteenth centuries. In fact as we shall see later, Chattagram, which was possibly created and settled by the Arabs and the Arakanese from the tenth century, was treated by them as a frontier post and Feni, the river of Jugdia, was deemed the boundary between Bengal and Arakan. By British times the Naaf river, and not the Feni, was deemed the border between the two regions and the history of this expanding frontier is rife with the exploits of the 'marauding' Arakanese, freebooting Portuguese and fierce Muslim and Hindu rajas. This area was indeed the 'last frontier' of Bengal. Since no history of Bengal is complete without reference to the Arakanese intervention an attempt has been made to reconstruct the story of eastern Bengal's unwilling tryst with its eastern partner as much as the sources allow us[197].

The magh raids are inextricably linked with the slave trade in Bengal and late medieval Bengali history is also rife with instances of piracy and slavery. Historical and literary accounts of 'magh depredations' in seventeenth century Bengal; and folk tales of Portuguese 'harmads' along the creeks, rivers and islands of deltaic Bengal underscore the destructive effects of piracy in Lower Bengal[198]. Not only the boats of local merchants and dealers but also those of the European countries were attacked. There are similar tales of captivity and slavery in these accounts.

Accounts of the siege of Hugli by Shah Jahan's forces in 1632 and the anti Portuguese accounts of Lahori and Khafi Khan have been taken to be expressions of Mughal condemnations of slavery[199]. We have to ask ourselves two questions here. First, did the Mughals universally condemn slavery as a practice? If this was not the case, then why was the Portuguese trade in slaves singled out? Two, are slavery and piracy antithetical to trade? Or can we argue that the slave trade was symbiotic to 'official'

---

197 In the section Politics and Trade in Bengal and in Mukherjee, Rila, *Merchants and Companies* etc.

198 See Sen, D.C., 1932, *Eastern Bengal Ballads*, Calcutta, University Press.

199 This has been explored by Subrahmanyam, Sanjay, 2005, *'On Indian Views of the Portuguese in Asia'* and *'Dutch Tribulations in Seventeenth century Mrauk-U'* in *Explorations in Connected History; From The Tagus to The Ganges*, New Delhi, Oxford University Press 17–44 and 200–247, where the complexities in the Mughal condemnations are brought out.

trade in medieval Bengal; that the logic of the slave trade was allied to the logic of seventeenth century international trade?

In Lahori's description of the slave trade conducted by the Portuguese from Hugli in *dingas*, *ghrabs* and *jaliyas* we are told that[200] :

> these hateful practices were not confined to the lands they occupied but they seized and carried off every one they could lay their hands upon along the sides of the river.

Slavery was condemned but it needs to be emphasised that this condemnation was linked to the perceived Portuguese role in the decay of Saptagram consequent upon the rise of Hugli as port. The old markets lost their prosperity as business was diverted to Hugli[201].

Khafi Khan gave another reason for the Mughal attack on Hugli[202]:

> Their (the Portuguese) greatest act of tyranny is this. If a subject…dies, leaving young children, and no grown up son, the children are considered wards of state.

If Lahori emphasised the economic aspect of Portuguese presence in Bengal Khafi Khan only did so indirectly: 'They built villages and in all matters acted very kindly towards the people and did not vex them with oppressive taxes'[203] but Khafi Khan noted a more sinister aspect of the Portuguese presence in Bengal: minors were converted to Christianity, whether brahmins or sayyids, and sold into slavery[204]. In the absence of definite laws of inheritance the children became Portuguese property.

Why did the Mughal chroniclers condemn this trade? Perhaps, while the slave trade was carried on by all Islamic societies, such a trade carried on by a combination of Portuguese and Arakanese was deemed offensive to the Mughals. The slave trade was a royal trade. In contemporary Mughal perception the Arakanese were no different to animals. Jahangir noted in 1613 when some Maghs were presented to him at court: 'they are a bunch of animals that look like human beings. They eat every part of every kind of sea and land animal and in their religion nothing is forbidden'[205]. They were despised for eating raw food, and fish, drinking

[200] Abdul Hamid Lahori, *Padshah Nama* in Elliot and Dowson, V.7, L.P.P. Reprint, 1990, Delhi: 32.

[201] *Ibid*: 32-4.

[202] *Muntakhabu-l Luba'b* in *ibid*.: 344–5.

[203] *Ibid*.

[204] *Ibid*.: 211.

[205] *The Jahangir Nama*, Tr. Ed. and Ann. by Wheeler M.Thackston, Freer Gallery of Art and Sackler Gallery, Washington and New York, Oxford University Press 1999: 142.

buffalo blood and marrying their siblings. A slave trade conducted by them had corresponding sub human connotations. It was therefore an ignoble trade; not one that partook of the established Islamic networks but one that was carried on in humid galleys in swampy creeks.

A slave trade carried on by outsiders in which the ruling classes were not involved also challenged claims to sovereignty. Khafi Khan's rationale for the Mughal capture of Hugli becomes therefore the defence of subjecthood and pre modern claims to sovereignty.

The magh raids in lower Bengal were not exceptional. The descriptions of the slave raids in seventeenth century Bengal by Master, Bowrey and Bernier find an echo in similar practices along the Niger. Such raids rarely needed guns; on the contrary they had to be silent and stealthy. Fast boats like the Bengal *jaliyas* (galleasses) were essential. The Kurtey, themselves victims of Tuareg raids, became robbers of men along the Tilaberi archipelago[206]:

> Up to fifteen pirogues could sail up the river. But these raids were in no way epic: the Kurtey encountered no opposition on the river itself, which they sailed up by day, and they hid their pirogues when night fell. Then they paddled silently until they saw the tents of the cultivators on the edge of the water…The Kurtey encircled the huts in silence, then tied the unfortunate sleepers up in their own mat and took the whole lot away in their pirogues.

This was a silent trade, one where access to slaves took place through the market, and commodities (or money) had to be provided in exchange[207]:

> The market was necessarily the site both of the sale of slaves and of the purchase of their reproduction….The slave's rate of reproduction was his or her rate of amortization….The slave represented an investment, an immobilization of capital…Unlike the subsistence slave , the slave employed for profit (profit-slave) could be found only in the context of an extended market where the capturing societies could provide supplies of slaves in quantities determined by price ratios on the market.

The slave trade therefore took place within the nexus of networks of international trade.

---

206 In Meillassoux, Claude, 1991, *The Anthropolgy of Slavery: The Womb of Iron and Gold*, Chicago University Press: 155.

207 *Ibid.*: 94–5.

The early seventeenth century saw the birth of the slave trade (sixteenth century chronicles are silent on this) in Bengal. In the 1620s several thousand peasants and artisans from southeast Bengal were taken to Arakan. Hugli, Pipli and Mrauk-U became important slave marts and ports for the transhipment of slaves. Nicholas de Graaf spoke of the Dutch bringing in once forty slaves of both sexes from Patna to Hugli[208]. This trade did not hinder the 'official' trade from Bengal's ports. Bengal's case was not unique; this trade took place within international commercial circuits from the fifteenth to the nineteenth centuries in Asia, Africa and the Americas.

But there was another variant of the slave trade which was older in practice. This was the specialised trade in eunuchs. The *Hudud al Alam* (a tenth century Persian document) described the effects of this trade in the Sudan[209]:

> No region is more populated than this. The merchants steal children and take them away. They castrate them and take them to Egypt, where they sell them. Among them there are people who steal each other's children to sell them to the merchants when they come.

This was an universal practice: both the Roman and Byzantine worlds as well as T'ang China followed this custom of employing eunuchs at court and harem. It was termed as aristocratic slavery. That this too was a widespread practice in Bengal was attested to by Barbosa. Apparently Muslim merchants scoured the countryside catching and castrating young boys whom they then sold at 20 and 30 ducats each to Persians[210] who then exported them to various Islamic courts in West Asia. Sylhet in eastern Bengal specialised in this.

Jahangir condemned the practice of trade in eunuchs in 1608 and promulgated dectrees that made it punishable by execution[211]:

> In Hindustan especially in the province of Sylhet, a dependency of Bengal, it has long been the custom…to make eunuchs of some their sons and give them in lieu of taxes to

---

[208] *Voyage de Nicolas de Graaf aux Indes Orientales etc. (1639–87)*, Amsterdam, J.F. Bernard, MD CCXIX: 72.

[209] Quoted in Meillassoux 1991: 143.

[210] *The Book of Duarte Barbosa* op.cit.

[211] *The Jahangir Nama*, Tr. Ed. and Ann. by Wheeler M.Thackston, op. cit. 98.

> the rulers. Little by little this custom has infected other provinces, and every year many children are ruined and castrated as the custom has gained great currency.

Islam Khan, then subhahdar of Bengal, was directed to enforce this decree throughout Bengal.

The *Ain*, which mentioned the trade in eunuchs in Sylhet at the end of the sixteenth century had not condemned the practice. Indeed the trade from Sylhet was an old and established practice. When Jahangir condemned it he emphasised two aspects that displeased him: one, that it was cruel and two, that castration had become a currency so much so that people did this to avoid paying taxes.

But just as in Shah Jahan's conmdemnation of the slave trade from Hugli there was an implicit notion of the rights of subjecthood being violated, here too the rights of subjects is emphasised. For this practice has been termed as 'internal brigandage' by anthropologists, a practice of abducting captives from *within the same community*. In such cases the abduction and sale of captives was undertaken not by aliens as in the slave trade but by the *members of the community* itself, acting anonymously. No one was safe. *The protectors of the community were the abductors.* If the guardian became the attacker, the very notion of subjecthood was at stake.

But was the economics of the trade then impinging on the Mughal economy? And was that also why the Mughals were attempting some kind of ban on the European slave trade from Bengal? It seems that the European trade in slaves was eroding the Mughal economy in no small measure. Akbar, and after him Jahangir, attempted to put a stop to the business of selling off defaulting peasants into slavery on humane grounds, but there was also an economic reason for the condemnation of the slave trade. Slaves were used in Mughal India for both public works and private service. Most of the slaves used to come in from outside South Asia through the Central Asian or new Silk Route. Babur wrote in his *Memoirs* that "there are two trade-marts on the land-route between Hindustan and Khurasan; one is Kabul, the other, Qandahar... (the route to Kabul was from Lahore, and to Qandahar from Multan)... Down to Kabul every year ...from Hindustan, come every year caravans... bringing slaves (*barda*) and other commodities, and sell them at great profit. In Kabul can be had the products of Khurasan, Rum, Iraq and Chin (China)".

This caravan route was coming increasingly under strain throughout the seventeenth century. This was because intermediaries along this route were eliminated when the Russian and Chinese empires came into contact with each other. Muslim merchants along these routes were now absorbed within the two empires and became more active in internal trade[212]. This may have disrupted the supply of slaves. Note that revenue from Kabul (the route through which slaves were imported) in the eighteenth century dwindled to 15 76 25 380 dams as against 25 00 00 000 dams during Shah Jahan's reign[213].

Also, in the fifteenth century, the Ottoman capture of Constantinople in 1453 had diverted an immense flow of slaves from the Crimea, the Balkans and the steppes of western Asia to Islamic markets. Russian advance in this area cut off this flow. This southward expansion of Russia, culminating in the annexation of Crimea in 1783, gradually shut off the supply of white slaves to the Islamic markets.

These reinforce our impression that even while the supply of slaves reached critical dimensions in the seventeenth century; the Mughals remained anxious to import slaves from outside and not from within.

Yet another theme that dominates the medieval history of Bengal, and one that we shall examine in subsequent pages, is that of the Husain Shahi period as inaugurating the early modern period in Bengal. The Husain Shahis are regarded as the pioneer sultans of Bengal, partly because sources are plentiful for their reign. A kind of incipient Bengali nationalism imbues our reading of the Husain Shahi era, much of it rising from the fact that Bengal reached her greatest territorial extent in medieval times during their rule[214].

While the significance of this period is undeniable, an added lustre to Husain Shahi rule was the attribution by later historians of Bengali mercantile activities that the Husain Shahis promoted. The Husain Shahis were seen as the champions of a free and fair trade with which they were taken to be intimately connected. This perception has to do with our reading of sources of the period. The *Mangal Kavyas*, some of the most

---

[212] Togan, Isenbike, 1990, '*Inner Asian Muslim Merchants and the Closing of the Silk Route (Seventeenth and Eighteenth Centuries)*', UNESCO, Urumqui, August.

[213] Muhammad Sharif Hanafi's *Maja'lisu-s-Salatin* (a partial account of the reign of Shah Jahan) and Bakhtawar Khan's *Mira't-i-Alam* (account of Aurangzeb's reign) both in Elliot and Dowson, V.7, Delhi, L.P.P Reprint, 1990.

[214] Tarafdar, M.R. 1965, *Husain Shahi Bengal 1494–1538* AD*: A Socio-Political Study*, Dacca. See also Roy, A.C., 1986: 287–89 op. cit.

important literary sources of the Husain Shahi era affirm the existence of a strong mercantile economy and a vibrant merchant class in Bengal at that time. But it has been suggested that these texts were reiterating an earlier and forgotten tradition. A careful reading of these texts informs us that the existence of a commercial economy and a mercantile culture in Bengal pre-dated the sixteenth century.

We will argue here instead that we can trace the beginnings of such a culture from the seventh-eighth centuries when Bengal entered the circuits of maritime trade. We will also argue that the burgeoning early medieval commercial economy of Bengal had its roots in the south east. It was not the western part of Bengal that had the older trading lineage, but the eastern part comprising a section of *samatata*, south-east *vanga* and the whole of *harikela*, that was the true commercial heartland of Bengal in history. Tarafdas, 1995, makes the same point: 11-30.

It was therefore not, as is conventionally assumed, the Husain Shahi period and the west that saw the growth of trade in Bengal; despite sixteenth century *Mangal* and *Vaishnav* testimonies to that effect. The real growth occurred under the Chandras and the Pattikera kings in eastern Bengal and part of the reason for the success of Ilyas Shahi trading activities is because they inserted themselves into earlier networks that ran from eastern Bengal. The Husain Shahis continued the older trading practices of the east but they preferred to promote trade in the western part of Bengal. In the process of developing a westward-trade radiating from ports such as Saptagram in the western part of Bengal, the Husain Shahis destroyed the older commercial impulses that had originated in the eastern region, an impulse that had given birth to an unique mercantile culture in the eastern delta that radiated from *samatata* to *harikela*.

History neglects to mention the fact that it was the time stretching from the reign of the chandras (eighth century) to that of the Ilyas Shahi sultans (thirteenth and fourteenth centuries) when the east was still independent of Gaur, that individual mercantile activity really flourished in Bengal. Chinese sources tell us that trade continued to prosper in the fifteenth century[215]. Once the Husain Shahis hitched the eastern trade to that of the west, sponsored merchants and capital in Saptagram and promoted a westbound traffic, local inititative in trade was halted in Bengal. The initiative now came from 'up country' merchants who settled in Bengal. Table 3.2 shows this clearly.

[215] Ray, Haraprasad, 1993, 2003.

Yet this state policy of the Husain Shahis could have been successful; the west-oriented trade could have, in time, fostered the growth of a self-reliant merchant community, but events dictated otherwise. A stable Bengali Muslim middle class failed to evolve. Bengali Muslims did not make the translation into either an elite group of intellectuals or a landed middle class. Neither did they make the transition to a commercial middle class as might have been expected given their participation in Bengal's long distance trade. Arabs, Persians, Abyssinians-in short the Muslim *ashrafs*-and north Indians controlled this trade. The Bengali merchants worked as their junior partners and did not evolve into independent merchants in their own right.

There seem to have been two reasons for this failure of the Bengali Muslims to mature into a strong mercantile community. Bengali merchants depended on the agrarian base. Capital accumulated through agriculture. But the Bengali Muslims-the professional categories of weavers, spinners, dyers and carders involved in textile production-never evolved into a landed aristocracy; land remained under the control of the Hindus with whom the Husain Shahi formed a compact to govern Bengal. In the absence of a Bengali Muslim middle class the Husain Shahis, and then the Mughals, had to rely on a Hindu bureaucracy composed of Brahmans, Kayasthas and Vaidyas. Moreover, the cultural repository of Bengal remained resolutely Hindu and anti-trade. The regional distribution of Bengali Muslim writings of the time point to the limited nature of their impact. Produced mostly in south-eastern Bengal, comprising the Chattagram-Noakhali-Comilla region, this body of literature was unknown to the Muslims of West Asia, of North India, and also of North and West Bengal. It was likely that they were unknown to the Muslims of points further east, except perhaps Tripura and Arakan, both of which had become Islamicised to a certain extent[216]. This 'little' Islamic world, mainly restricted to the littoral regions of Bengal which functioned as a sub-set of the first Islamic empire in South Asia, interacted commercially and culturally with similar small, littoral Islamicised states, across the Bay. Ports and cities in South East Asia became islamicised at the beginning of the sixteenth century

[216] Allaol's writings at Arakan are perhaps the best examples of the Bengali-Islamic genre; in Tripura rent-free land grants were made to prominent Muslim subjects. See Tarafdar, M.R., 1986, 'The Bengali Muslims in the Pre Colonial Period: Problems of Conversion, Class Formation and Cultural Evolution', 92–110, in Marc Gaborieau (Ed). *Islam et Societe, en Asie du Sud,* Paris, *Purusartha*, Vol. 9: 106.

and this may have added an impetus to the islamicisation in Bengal. The medieval Bengali-Islamic 'cultural awakening' in a limited area of this region is indicative of the political independence of its rulers from the rest of Bengal. This reinforces our idea of the independent development of the 'far east' of Bengal.

But while the littoral area failed to evolve into a principal area, the mainstream area of Bengal showed a similar failure of mercantile elites to evolve. The 'cultural awakening' under the Husain Shahis, or the emerging religious identity through Gauriya Vaishnavism did not support a vigorous commercial culture. The Hindu merchant community failed to develop in Husain Shahi Bengal. Social constraints and elusive economic oppurtunities meant that the Vaishnav merchant of Bengal was reduced to making the pilgrimage from the east to Brindaban and vice versa as peddling merchants. They failed to derive any benefit to and from their journey to Brindaban. They had a much greater failure, they could not derive much benefit from the economic oppurtunities created by expansion of trade and commerce and industry and allowed these oppurtunities to pass into the hands of the outsiders, both European and Indian-runs the popular view[217].

Readings such as this underscore the durability of (probably) the most persistent theme in Bengal's history-the seeming passivity of Bengal's merchants in the early modern period. Sanyal is no exception to this verbalization that has now become almost routine, indeed successive generations of historians have been baffled by the same feature, and have expressed the same opinion, as earlier sections of *Strange Riches* demonstrate. The problem arises because of a misreading regarding our sources for Bengal. Sources have been utilised to show that commerce was plentiful in the sixteenth century, that Bengali merchants traded extensively, that trade routes and networks flourished at this time. All this is true. But it is never explained why these same merchants failed to make the leap into the seventeenth and eighteenth centuries.

Or in other words, ascribing the Husain Shahi period almost supernatural powers of expression of Bengali identity, culture etc. begs the question as to *why* commercial development was cut short soon after. For example, Sanyal notes[218]:

---

[217] Sanyal, Hitesranjan, 1981, *Social Mobility in Bengal*, Calcutta, Papyrus: 63.

[218] *Ibid.*: 55–64.

> It appears that for a great majority of the population, the peasants, artisans and merchants who were included in the lower castes, the major sources of social mobility were inaccessible...The pilgrim from Bengal to Brindaban was required to go along the main trade-route from eastern India to the north through which the products of Bengal were taken to north India...A visit to Brindaban, which was very much cherished by the Gauriya Vasihnavas, could put the trading followers of the sect in touch with the commercial centres and emporiums in north India, where the products of Bengal were taken for sale and from where these could be taken to West and Central Asia which were connected by trade rouites. By the first half of the seventeenth century, when the number of pilgrims visiting Brindaban had increased considerably, Agra had become the most important commercial city of north India..The choice of Brindaban appears to be still more significant in view of the subordinate position of the Bengali merchants in the expanding trade and commerce of Bengal....Available evidence regarding the Bengali traders indicates that for the most part they played second fiddle as middlemen in the expanding trade of Bengal and remained satisfied with minor shares of the profits which they could manage to secure at their native places...The Bengali merchants in the ports and emporiums of Bengal do not seem to have had much interest in shipping, or maintaining direct links with the markets where their products of their country were sold...To these home loving merchants a journey to Brindaban long the main trade-route from the east to the north and sojourn at that place near Agra might prove to be a source of inspiration or at least offer an opportunity to acquire experience in the field of their hereditary occupation. However, the Bengali merchants...failed to derive any benefit from their journey to and from Brindaban.

For perhaps the first time in history, pilgrimage and trade did not go together!

The fact that there was no sustained control over shipping and trade–despite a distinguished heritage in mercantile and sea-faring activity–may be ascribed to the fact that there was no one paramount political centre in Bengal after the Husain Shahis[219]. How far this hindered the development of a local mercantile class is open to question. The Afghan, and then Mughal, experiments in state-building in Bengal saw the locus of political power fluctuating between east and west between the sixteenth and the eighteenth centuries in their attempts to extend the frontiers of what had essentially become a conquest state from the very first.

The speedy succession of Turko-Afghan, Afghan (Sher Shah), Portuguese[220], Arakanese[221], Mughal and Nawabi rule in Bengal from the sixteenth to the eighteenth centuries could only mean that various *ashrafi* interest groups based on ethnicity and lineage (older Persian interests versus 'newer' Afghan interests, Portuguese interests versus Arakanese interests in the sixteenth century or the emergent Iranian interests in eighteenth century Bengal versus older Muslim interests are examples)–rather than a single commercial interest–amongst the ruling classes in Bengal had to be accommodated at any cost[222]. The Bengali Muslims were not a privileged group since they did not belong to any *ashrafi* group with a long lineage of cultural achievements to their credit. Of these groups the Arakanese, the Iranians and the Portuguese exercised the most influence on Bengal's external trade. The last two groups functioned as well-defined mercantile communities in the eastern part of Bengal from the seventeenth century.

It is noteworthy that under the Bengal Nawabs the Iranian group emerged as a considerable force in politics and trade. The first nawab of

---

[219] See Tarafdar, M.R. 1965, op. cit. 117.

[220] Portuguese 'informal rule' in Bengal was confined mainly to the deltaic region of samatata and harikela; nevertheless this 'rule' is significant in that many of the smaller ports which traded with other ports across the Bay were located in this area. One such was Sandwip at the mouth of the Meghna. This island was placed under the control of the Portuguese Carvalho by Kedar Rai of Sripur in 1602. During Shah Jahan's time Sandwip was well populated by the Portuguese (see Abdul Hamid Lahori's *Padshah Nama* in Elliot and Dowson's *History of India as Told by Its Own Historians*, Allahabad, 1969, Reprint, V. 7). Similarly Sripur came under Portuguese control at the end of the sixteenth century (*Narrative of Ralph Fitch 1583–91* in William Foster (Ed). *Early Travels in India 1583–1619*, London, 1921, Reprint, New Delhi, 1968). For more on this see Winius, George, 1983, 'The "Shadow Empire" of Goa in the Bay of Bengal', *Itinerario*, v.vii (2): 83–101.

[221] Around 1540 Arakanese expansion under Minbin (1531–53) extended as far as 'Chittagong, Dacca and the Sundarbans' (Subrahmanyam, S. 1990, *Improvising Empire: Portuguese Trade and Settlement in the Bay of Bengal 1500–1700*, New Delhi, Oxford University Press: 120).

[222] See the section Politics and Trade in Bengal.

Bengal, Murshid Quli Khan, had Iranian antecedents; the second Murshid Quli, Mirza Lutfullah of Tabriz, became governor of Orissa during Nawab Shuja's reign in Bengal. After taking over Bengal subah Alivardi Khan chased him out of Orissa. The second Murshid Quli was appointed Naib-Nazim (what the English refer to as the 'Chhuta Nawab') of Dhaka during Shuja's reign. This second Murshid Quli and his associates Mir Habibullah of Shiraz and Mir Razi of Shustar appear to have practiced a variant of state monopoly dubbed 'state mercantilism' from Dhaka[223] and in the process they built up a clique of Iranian and Central Asian traders in Bengal. This group maintained close links with Surat and Basra and there is every likelihood that a major portion of Bengal's westward trade was monopolized by this Iranian group. The illustrious Naib-*Subahdar* of Bengal Muhammad Reza Khan, who wrote in the 1760s and 1770s on the state of Bengal's manufactures, commerce and revenue, in short almost a treatise on political economy while an employee of the English Company, was of Iranian origin.

Who then exercised control over Bengal's trade in the seventeenth century? Was there an uniform Mughal economic realm operating in Bengal? The sources indicate that the contrary was the case. This is also borne out by Tarafdar, 1995: 101. Unlike the case as in Gujarat, Mughal control over trade from Hugli (despite it being dubbed a royal port) was nominal at best. And was there any dominant mercantile group that could replace this void? It seems not. There was no indigenous merchant community operating here as we find in Surat or in the Coromandel. Most overseas and inland trade seem to have been in the hands of Gujarati merchants or their representatives in Bengal[224] and at the end of the seventeenth century Bengal's long distance trade was controlled by Mughal *subahdars* only in a personal capacity. Local merchants seem to have operated along the smaller river tracts. Trading practices seem to have fragmented in this century and a two-tiered mercantile organisation, one regional and extra regional and the other local, seems to have emerged. Historically, Bengali

223 K.F.R. circa late 1740s.

224 Sanyal, Hitesranjan, 1981, *Social Mobilty in Bengal*, Calcutta, Papyrus, indicates that internal trade in Bengal in the sixteenth and seventeenth centuries was in the hands of 'traders from the northern and western parts of India', a category similar to the all encompassing one of 'up country' merchants, many of whom had settled in Bengal: 62–63. He means of course Gujaratis Jains here. The case studies of Khemchand and Chintaman Shah by Chaudhuri, Sushil, *Trade and Commercial Organisation in Bengal 1650–1720*, Calcutta, 1975, indicate that overseas trade from Hugli was also monopolized by Gujarati merchants.

merchants had always owned the crafts which they sailed to Ceylon or Java. By the seventeenth this practice was over. *Subahdars* now took over the practice of chartering ships; by the eighteenth century they too withdrew from this practice.

But despite the practice of 'state mercantilism'[225] in Bengal society at large was unable to participate in commerce. In the medieval period commerce in Bengal had enjoyed an ever widening social base[226]. In the seventeenth century it assumed increasingly elitist overtones when *subahdars* and their associates participated in commerce.

In the eighteenth century commerce in Bengal for Bengalis became a distant activity. Because of the lack of mercantile impulse in Bengali material life, European companies could fill in the gap. The settlements that arose in Bengal from the middle of the seventeenth century introduced yet another element of disarticulation into the commercial map of Bengal. These European port-towns diverted a substantial amount of commercial traffic from ports under Nawabi control despite Murshid Quli Khan's attempt to control the trade of Bengal from the Mughal port of Hugli by personally appointing the *Faujdar* there from 1711. Moreover these European ports did not need goods from the overland commercial (caravan) routes which had previously existed in symbiosis with Bengal's riverine and sea trade. Goods from overland routes provisioned Bengal's mart towns; now European commodities began to appear there, and since the European towns turned their faces resolutely towards the seas the supporting link between earlier port towns and the caravan routes was severed by the eighteenth century.

Commerce in Bengal became now increasingly remote from daily life. So what actually happened in the sixteenth century is a question that continues to perplex historians. If one turns to the east, one may get some answers.

The Importance of Bengal's Far Eastern Sector

Much of Bengal's history was forged in the east. But what did 'east' mean for Bengal in the medieval era? Traditionally, still today, Bengal's north-east remains a somewhat blurred zone. Historically, it was an area where small kingdoms were situtated. These may have been small but in terms of their riches and commercial potential, they were immensely

---

225 It should be noted that this was not mercantilism in the strict sense and referred to a loose kind of monopoly over production, distribution and trade that was practiced by Bengal's rulers from eastern Bengal.

226 The *Mangal Kavyas* and Chaitanya tracts in middle Bengali literature refer to commerce as the life blood of the native Bengali middle class.

wealthy. These small states guarded the land route to Yunnan in South China, an area that had emerged as one of the richest in China by the thirteenth century. Their rivers were rumoured to carry gold dust and the area was one of the chief producers of aloes wood which was a profitable commercial item in the middle ages. Aloes were in demand in both east and West Asia-China and countries in West Asia imported aloes from the region. It was therefore no accident that Bakhtiyar Khilji went northeast the moment he conquered Bengal in the thirteenth century.

It is only from the Persian annals, and accounts of expeditions launched in that area by the Bengal sultans, that one gets an idea of the political units in the area between the thirteenth and sixteenth centuries. Reading from left to right on an imaginary map of the region, they were first, Tirhut (Mithila) and Nepal in the north, second, the shadowy part of north Bengal leading to Tibet in the northeast and third, Arakan in the southeast. The Himalayan foothills divided the area into Koch Bihar and Koch Hajo (which merged in the sixteenth century into the Koch kingdom), Kamta and then Kamrup. Kamta became prominent as Kamrup ceased to be a political unit from the fourteenth century. But the name Kamrup was still retained, even after portions of it had been swallowed up by Assam and Bengal. Kamrup was separated from Bengal by the Teesta-Karatoya belt. Beyond Kamrup lay Assam. Beyond Assam lay the kingdom (or empire) of Pagan which broke down in the thirteenth century into Ava in the north and Pegu in the south. Ava lay north east of Kamrup and Assam and guarded the mountain route to China. Chattagram and Arakan in the southeast was the expanding maritime frontier of Bengal and could also link up with the land route through Ava into China. It is these last two zones-the northeast and the southeast-that we shall refer to as Bengal's 'far east' throughout the course of this book.

In the course of the sixteenth century the area of the Himalayan foothills underwent several changes. Kamrup declined–Assam, Koch Bihar and Koch Hajo emerged as dominant frontier forces. Tripura, under the Manikya dynasty, became the most important border kingdom for Bengal in the fifteenth and sixteenth centuries. Until its defeat at the hands of Arakan at the end of the sixteenth century, Tripura, along with Arakan and Bengal, frequently claimed the deep water port of Chattagram as its own.

The area east of Chattagram, the shadowy area leading to Arakan, was a no man's land. Buchanan Hamilton noted in his travels that this area was the borderland between Bengal and Arakan and that the area was settled by Muslim peasants and refugees from Arakan who moved in when Burma conquered Arakan in 1785[227]. It was an independent area during the eighteenth century and became known as the Chittagong Hill Tracts later. A British official commented in the nieneteenth century[228]:

> It is bounded on the south and southeast by Arracan; on the northwest the Fenny divides it from Hill Tipperah, west of it lie the swamps and plains of Chittagong while eastwards its limits are undefined. It is a country rough and primeval: the abode of nomad cultivators.

Yet echoes of its past grandeur still resonated. Of the Mainamati Lalmai range–one of the most important Buddhist complexes of ancient Bengal–Buchanan Hamilton noted: 'This was formerly the abode of a Rajah who, at the time of the Muhammedan conquest, was probably the head of all the country east from the Meghna and perhaps dependant on Arakan'[229].

But this area is neglected in history writing. While doing research on western Bengal one is struck by the fact that 'Bengal' really refers to a small portion of Bengal–the north-western part, centreing around the Malda-Rajmahal-Murshidabad axis. Despite Dhaka being a Mughal capital for much of the seventeenth century, and despite it being famous as a muslin producing area, Dhaka is effectively the final frontier of Bengal in official records.

One reason for this is of course that the eastern Indian Ocean, despite Denys Lombard's contention that the true history of the Indian Ocean lies in the east and not in the west, is less studied compared to the western Indian Ocean till today. Notwithstanding the works of Denys Lombard, Genevieve Bouchon and Luis Felipe Thomaz, studies of the Indian Ocean world–of which Bengal forms a part–remain firmly anchored in the west; in the ports of the Persian Gulf, the Red Sea and the east African coast. The statement of Auguste Toussaint, a pioneer in Indian Ocean studies, is symptomatic: '*La rive orientale du golfe du Bengale, de Chittagong jusqu'a l'extremite de la peninsule malaise, n'offrait, du point de vue commercial, rien de comparable aux productions de la cote de*

---

227 Van Schendel, Willem, 1992, *Francis Buchanan in South East Bengal (1798): His Journey to Chittagong, the Chittagong Hill Tracts, Noakhali and Comilla*, Dhaka University Press: 31.

228 Mackenzie, Alexander, 1884, *The North East Frontier of India*, Intr. by B.K. Roy Burman, New Delhi, Mittal Publications, 2005: 329.

229 Francis Buchanan in Van Schendel 1992: 131.

Coromandel ou a celles du Bengale, ni 'denrees coloniales' d'interet majeur, ni articles 'nobles'[230].

Towards the end of his life in 1992, at one of the very last public lectures that he gave, Ashin Dasgupta stressed the importance of the eastern Indian Ocean: 'There has been an unnecessary crowding of the western Indian Ocean, and the east has been neglected'[231].

Yet events on the eastern frontier dictated Bengal's fortunes at least as much as those on the western frontier. This coastal region, stretching from Arakan, though Pegu and Martaban, formed one of the principal motors for the economy, society and polity in Bengal. Historically the forests in this region, especially those of Arakan and Pegu, supplied Bengal with teak for building works and ships, commerce with these parts brought Bengal much silver, and the natural ports here frequently doubled as auxiliary ports for Bengal.

This south eastern coast has been highlighted in this volume. It was contiguous to the region that I dub the 'Far East of Bengal'. The area south-east of Chattagram (Chittagong)–the borderlands between Noakhali in present day Bangladesh and Rakhang in Myanmar–traditionally provided Bengal *subah* with teak for from its abundant forests, much silver, cotton[232] from the area between Tipperah and what later came to be called the Chittagong Hill Tracts and salt[233]. By the middle of the eighteenth century this area also provided the Bengal Nawabs with additional land for cultivation–land that was classed as *noabad*. This shadowy borderland between Bengal and Arakan also housed many of eastern Bengal's rulers and zamindars. Some of the *Baro Bhuyans* or independent chiefs of deltaic Bengal or *samatata* came from this obscure area.

---

[230] Toussaint, 1974, *L'Ocean Indien au XVIIIe Siecle*, Paris, Flammarion: 170. 'The eastern side of the Bay of Bengal, stretching from Chittagong to the Malay coast, produces nothing that is commercially comparable to the production of the Coromandel or of Bengal. It offers no item of interest-either as colonial produce or as items of 'noble' commerce.' (My translation).

[231] Dasgupta, Ashin, 1993, 'Europeans in India Before the Empire', Professor A.C. Banerjee Memorial Lecture, 1992, Calcutta, a Department of History, Jadavpur University publication.

[232] See the accounts of Cesare Frederick and Ralph Fitch and Toussaint 1974 for trade between Bengal and this region. For cotton see Serajuddin, A.M., 1971,*The Revenue Administration of the East India Company in Chittagong 1761–1785*, Chittagong, University Press: 168.

[233] Serajuddin 1971: 174.

This frontier area was the last to be administered by both the Mughals and the British. An indication of the commercial wealth of the region, and of the trading possibilities there, can be gauged by the fact that the official duty from *sarkar* Islamabad (the Mughal name for Chattagram) to the Dhaka *niabat* was Rs. 1,76,795 while the total duty (including the excess taxation levied by the faujdar there without notification to the *naib-nazim* of Dhaka) was Rs. 4,43,918 at the time when Chattagram passed under the Company's jurisdiction in 1760[234]. Yet this area is ignored in studies of Bengal. The lineages of Bengal's commercial history thus occupy an 'area of darkness' and the 'view' from Basra or Hormuz, rather than the 'view' from Pegu (or Syriam, or Malacca or Java), dominates writings on the commercial history not only of the Indian Ocean but of the Bay of Bengal itself.

Historically, it was the Portuguese, and then the French, who were the first to be aware of the commercial possibilities of this region. The Portuguese had centred themselves in the eastern delta from the beginning of the sixteenth century and their trading practices saw an amalgam of the earlier Arabo-Islamic, Arakanese and Bengali commercial interests. In short, they established themselves in that sensitive corridor between eastern Bengal on the one hand and Ava-Arakan-Pegu and southern China on the other–the heart of this commercial bloc as envisaged by Manrique lay in the border region between China and India described earlier by Marco Polo.

In the 1730s Dupleix dreamed of a great commercial complex, centered on Chattagram and stretching from Chandernagore in the west to Arakan, Pegu, and Ava in the east. The transport network for this grand project envisaged a melange of existing river routes, coastal sailings as well as the utilisation of the grand Brahmaputra-Meghna water route. Chevalier's attempts at opening up the north-east frontier in an effort to promote Franco-Assamese and Franco-Tibetan trade in the 1750s formed part of the same vision[235], but he took it even further. Chattagram was to be at the centre of a great maritime and strategic bloc linking the eighteenth century kingdoms of Bengal, Assam, Tripura, Ava, Arakan, Pegu, Mergui (Ile de Roy off the coast of Mergui was ceded to the French in Louis XIV's time), Andaman and Nicobar islands and southern

---

[234] See Mukherjee, *Merchants and Companies*, etc. (New Delhi, Pragati Publications).

[235] Deloche Jean ed., 1984, *Les Aventures de J.B. Chevalier dans l'Inde Orientale 1752–65,* Paris, EFEO Publications.

China[236]. China was the principal object of Chevalier's missions between 1752 and 1765 and he tried twice to go there (once from Katha and once from Tibet) but he failed. Access to China through Tibet and Katha was known as the Southern Silk Route that connected Yunnan and Szechwan with the Bay of Bengal ports. 'Catta' (Katha) in Burma on the western bank of the Irrawady obsessed Chevalier[237]. This was because Katha granted an easy access to China through river routes: it was bounded on the north by Szechwan province and on the south by Yunnan, China's gateway to South Asia.

Some two decades after Chevalier, when W.W.Hunter wrote a *Concise Account of the Kingdom of Pegu; The Climate, the Products, Trade and Government etc.* in the 1780s, it was clear that a radical reorganisation had taken place in the Bay-both political and commercial. Arakan ceased to exist by the 1780s. Chattagram was no longer important for the EEIC.

Yet Chattagram continued to occupy a central place in the FEIC commercial plans in the Bay. The reasons for concentrating on Chattagram were made clear by Joseph Cordier in his statistical account of Chandernagore in 1823[238]:

> Chatighan est placé a l'Est du Bengale, a l'embouchment du Bourampouter, à 310 milles de Chandernagor et à 50 milles de la mer. La Compagnie s'y etablit en 1747. Il ne fournissait que quelque garas grossiers, mais son voisinage des royaumes d'Ava, d'Arakan et de Pegou, joint a la surété de son port, le rendait l'entrepot general des produits de ces trois royaumes. Chatighan recevait beacoup de bois de construction de Pegou, ce qui fit construire des chantiers et fit la richesse du pays. Chatighan communiquait directement par mer avec des loges de Jougdya, Serampour, Dacca, le Silhet et Goualpara.

The reasons given by Cordier in favour of Chattagram were the three main ones of a good deep water port and sure harbour, its proximity to the eastern kingdoms of Arakan, Ava and Pegu which made it an entrepot of eastern goods, especially for wood for construction, and Chattagram's comparative cost advantage due to its location: it lay at the mouth of the

---

236 *Ibid.* 98–101.

237 Deloche Jean ed., 1990, *Statistiques de Chandernagor, 1823, 1827 and 1838, by Joseph Cordier and Achille Bedier*, Pondichery, Institut Francais: 22, 241.

238 *Ibid.*: 20.

fabled eastern riverine route of the Brahmaputra/Meghna by way of the Karnaphuli as well as near the sea. This meant that factories in the interior could be easily communicated with. Also coastal and riverine sailings could complement each other here too as in other parts of Bengal, but with an added advantage, that of a deep sea port.

The French rated commerce in this area, especially at Jugdia, higher than that anywhere else in Bengal[239]. In a letter dated April 9 1786, Dangereux the French chief at Chandernagore, placed Jugdia fourth in importance after Patna, Kasimbazar and Balasore. Dhaka was fifth in importance and was followed by the subordinate French settlements at Khirpaye, Karicola, Supur and Monipur (Mohanpur/Midnapore?)[240]. Mohanpur has been tentatively identified as Mohanpur in Bardhaman district, based on letters written in 1768 by a gomastha in the service of the French[241]. Jugdia's commercial potential was deemed supreme by the FEIC because it produced baftas (ordinary plain cotton), labour here was plentiful and cheap[242] and moreover because its chief trading partner was the east-Achin, Malacca, Pegu and Manila. But Jugdia also had the distinction of making up cargo for Basra, Mocha and Jedda[243]. Therefore Dupleix dreamed of a grand French trading complex in the Indian Ocean which would extend from Chattagram upto Pegu[244] and which would trade with both the eastern and the western Indian Oceans. This dream continued even after the Anglo-French wars in the Carnatic and Plassey in Bengal. After the EEIC takeover in the west after 1765 the French thought of withdrawing from Chandernagore and establishing their HQ in Chattagram[245]; this formed part of the vision of Chevalier.

Bengal's 'Far East' was the area that was potentially the wealthiest in Bengal. It was the area that had provided the impetus behind economic and social development of the rest of the province[246]. Even after the shift to the west in the sixteenth century this area continued to be important.

---

239 AE BIII 459.

240 C2 115.

241 Mukherjee, Rila, 2005, 'Bengali Letters in the French Archives', Tamluk, Pashchim Banga Itihas Sansad.

242 C_2 115.

243 Hossain, Hameeda, 1988, *The Company Weavers of Bengal: The East India Company and the Organization of Textile Production in Bengal 1750–1813,* Delhi, Oxford University Press 184.

244 C2 115.

245 Toussaint, Auguste, 1974, *L'Ocean Indien au XVIIIe siecle*, Paris, Flammarion.

246 See later and Mukherjee, *Merchants and Companies*, etc.

Small wonder, then, that Bengal's *subahdars* from Mir Jumla downwards concentrated on trade from this region and attempted their monopolies in commerce as a Persian combine from the 'Far East' of Bengal; both by sea down the Bay coast to the Siam and Malay ports and overland on the route that connected Eastern Bengal with China. Manrique noted in the seventeenth century that Persian merchants were present in large numbers at Ava: one of the great inland centres of commerce between Bengal and China and a great producer of rubies and musk[247].

The 'East' in Received History for Medieval Bengal

The east, we have seen, is neglected in historical studies of Bengal. A result of a west-centred vision of historical development is that the ascribed momentum to Bengal's commercial history is always deemed external–from 'powerful commercial economies' radiating eastwards from the west. This west-centred view results in the belief that Bengal's external activity was minimal because Bengal hardly features in the Persian Gulf or the Red Sea sailings and trade; a west-centred view leads us to suppose that what commerce there was flourished due to outsiders operating within Bengal; a west-centred view reinforces the impression that indigenous mercantile development comparable to those of Surat, the Malabar and the Coromandel had not occured in Bengal.

One example of a westward (and north Indian!) view that dominates the history of medieval Bengal is that of Eaton. Eaton comments[248]:

> Soon after the Turkish conquest of the delta in 1204, Muslim immigrants from points west settled in cities like Gaur, Pandua, Satgaon, Sonargaon, and Chittagong, principally as long distance traders, administrators, soldiers and literati. But from 1342 to 1574, under the rule of a succession of independent Muslim dynasties, Bengal became isolated from north India, and immigration from points west was largely curtailed. In the wake of the Mughal conquest of 1574, however, Muslim immigrants from north India once again settled the delta...at the very time that the region became integrated politically with the Mughal Empire–that is, from 1574–it was also becoming integrated economically with the

[247] Manrique, *Travels of Fray Sebastian Manrique*, 1629–1643, Tr. Luard, C.E., London, Hakluyt Society, 1967.

[248] Eaton, Richard, 2002, *Essays on Islam and Indian History*, Oxford, University Press: 249, 266.

> whole world, since silver originally mined in South or Central Amercica and shipped to Spain ultimately ended up fueling the eastward push of Bengal's economic frontier. This occurred when silver imported to pay for Bengal's textile exports was coined into Mughal currency and locally invested, as when Hindu financiers advanced capital to Muslim pioneers, who in turn organised local labour for cutting forested regions and founded mosques around which new agrarian communities coalesced.

And[249]:

> The implications of the Ganges' eastward migration...were far reaching. For one thing, it linked eastern Bengal's economy with wider markets since it opened up a heavily forested and formerly isolated region to direct commercial contact with Upper India…for the first time ever, eastern Bengal, formerly an underdeveloped, inaccessible and heavily forested hinterland, became the focus of concerted and rapid political and economic development.

Eaton's statement is problematic; indeed it contains three key assumptions still underlining the historiography of medieval Bengal. One, that the entire history of the Bengal Sultanate from 1338 (why 1342?) forms an empty space because the Delhi Sultanate was unable to inscribe it politically and economically. The Bengal Sultanate is thus seen as static, something that only the Mughal conquest of Bengal is able to change. If such is the case how does Eaton explain the constant interaction between Bengal and the greater Islamic world as exemplified in the establishment of Chisthi shrines in fourteenth and fifteenth century Pandua by the Kans dynasty or the reliquary of of Qadam Rasul established by Sultan Ala-al-Din Husain Shah in 1503–examples he himself quotes[250]? Other such instances of the Bengal Sultans' desire to reassert themselves in the greater Islamic world abound: consider the activities and reliquaries of the Shaikhs Jalal-ud-Din Yamani and Jalal-ud-Din Tabrizi in Sylhet and Gaur in the thirteenth century. These formed an attraction for the Islamic world by the fourteenth century[251]. Sikandar (Ilyas) Shah's claim

---

[249] *Ibid.*: 259, 262.

[250] *Ibid.*: 254.

[251] The names themselves are pointers to the origin of these holy men. Ibn Batuta himself made it a point to visit the tomb of the former.

to be the wisest and most liberal of the kings of Arabia and Persia when he constructed the Adina Mosque at Pandua (1365-1369) intended at that time to be the show piece of Islamic architecture, the patronage extended to the pigrims of the Haj by Ghiyas-al-Din (1390-1411) and the execution of charitable works, gardens, reservoirs and madrasas at Mecca and Medina (*madrasat-al-bangaliah*) through endowments and grants, Ghiyas-al-Din's interactions with the sultanate of Jaunpur and with China; all these were intended to raise the status of the Ilyas Shahis in the Islamic world. After the Ilyas Shahis Raja Kan's (Ganesha?) son Jalal-ud-Din converted to Islam and once again, like the Ilyas Shahis before him, laid claims to be recognised in the Islamic world as patron. He built a madrasa at Mecca and established diplomatic ties with the Timurid leader Shah Rukh of Herat and the Mamluk ruler of Egypt al-ashraf Barsbay. In his negotiations with the greater Islamic world Jalal-ud-Din was successful; by 1431 he was nominated as Khilafat Allah. In the sixteenth century Nusrat Shah Husain Shah's reign is reported to have welcomed into Bengal a number of Muslims from countries outside India.

Possibly the only instances when Bengal did not participate in the greater Islamic cultural network was the period between 1486–1493 which saw the end of Ilyas Shahi rule, the leadership of the Abyssinians and the transition to Husain Shahi rule and 1538–1574 which saw the demise of Husain Shahi rule in Bengal and the Afghan-Mughal contest for Bengal. What role did the Mongols play in this cultural interaction? We know that by the fourteenth century, when Islamic Bengal really took shape, the Mongol challenge to world Islam was exhausted. Mongol attempts to forge a reconciliation between Buddhism, Taoism and confucianism were not successful commercial ties, diplomatic negotiations, cultural ties went on much as before; if not more, with Baghdad, with Cairo, Damascus, Mecca and Medina. The Mongols themselves were now absorbed into the flourishing dinar economy; and the activities of the Bengal Sultans manifested clearly the same desire.

Two, the same Delhi-centric view that infuses Eaton's writings leads him to ignore the fact that integration into a world economy via the Mughal one led not only to Bengal occupying a fairly subordinate position within the Mughal economy as a whole, indeed it became a hinterland; but that eastern Bengal now became the hinterland to a hinterland once a west-oriented commercial policy was launched by the Mughals through the western port of Surat[252].

[252] See later.

Three, historically, eastern Bengal was initially hardly 'an underdeveloped' hinterland as this volume seeks to demonstrate. Eaton's eagerness to emphasise local 'Islam' through agricultural expansion, his insistence on the expanding eastern agrarian frontier in Islamic Bengal, enables him to interpret the sixteenth century riverine upheavals in Bengal merely as an 'expanding agrarian frontier' with an active south east delta where the Mughal revenue demand jumped by 117% between 1595 and 1659[253], to the exclusion of all else and to ignore the area's commercial lineage. We thus get a somewhat flawed picture of developments in eastern Bengal preceding that period. According to Tarafdar, it was not the agricultural frontier that formed the basis of Muslim expansion in Bengal but the textile industry. He tells us[254]:

> The technological innovations that were reaching the subcontinent from western Asia and Bengal's newly established links with the network of international trade seem to have considerably affected the caste system and brought the different groups of Bengali artisans and traders closer to Muslim merchants. The introduction of the spinning wheel or *charkha* and the bowstring in India in the early years of the Delhi sultanate are said to have increased skill and rapidity in the work of weaving and cotton carding which facilitated the expansion of textile industry in the coastal regions including Bengal. Increase in the quantity of cotton fabrics in these countries would be possible only when workers from a variety of professions had joined the weavers' community.

He comments further[255]:

> There was no wonder then that the people directly or indirectly connected with the textile industry were accepting Islam. They seem to have had vital links with the process of urbanisation which had started after the foundation of Muslim rule. The *Mangal* poems composed towards the end of the fifteenth century depict Muslim weavers or *jolas* as having grown into a distinct occupational group...The cloth dyers (*rang rez*) and the makers of looms (*sanakar*), as mentioned in the sixteenth century poem *Kavikankan Chandi*, belonged to the Muslim community. Muslim tailors also formed a social group of considerable importance. The cloth-dyer, the maker of looms

[253] Eaton, Richard 2002: 262.

[254] In *Purusartha*, Paris, 1986: 92–110, op. cit. See p. 94.

[255] *Ibid*: 95.

> and the cotton-carder...do not seem to have grown into distinct occupational groups in the pre-Muslim period. The ignoble nature of their social life...must have been responsible for their conversion.

Bengali commercial fortunes declined in the sixteenth century. The sixteenth century saw the demise of the first Islamic world dominated by the Africans, Egyptians, the Delhi and Bengal Sultans, and China and the birth of the second. This second world was dominated by the Mughals, the Iranians, the Turanis and the Ottomans where a dominant Bengali mercantile class failed to participate in international trade. Fragmentation and social immobility prevented the growth of a strong Bengali Muslim middle class. The Bengali Muslim merchants failed to coalesce into a dominant mercantile group[256]. By the seventeenth century Bengal formed a weak 'mercantile' zone. At this time the north Bay, and the eastern India Ocean, were both in decline. Would it not then be more accurate to view Bengal as a previous player in commercial arcs that descended southwards from China and westwards from northern South East Asia? Bengal formed the easternmost street corner of South Asia where all commercial interactions of the Bay of Bengal terminated. Once the Mughals took over, Bengal became a commercial and agrarian hinterland, despite Eatons contention that mughal rule greatly facililated trade from Bengal.

This idea of the commercial marginality of Bengal in the seventeenth century is reinforced by our received historiography that tells us that Bengal's trading community was weak by the time EEICs established themselves on Bengal's shores. Would it not be therefore more accurate to view Bengal as a somewhat marginal commercial power in the overall South Asian scenario and hence more susceptible to the EEIC takeover in the eighteenth century? Does not the very fact that European settlements rose on a comparatively neglected commercial channel–the Bhagirathi–rather than the vibrant eastern channels underscore the premise that the European companies concentrated on that area of waterways where they would be subjected to the least interference and moreover encouraged, in tune with prevailing Islamic norms, to develop commercial traffic there at their will? Or was Bengal, as the dominant received historiography leads us to believe, a major player in commercial history *prior* to the English takeover? As late as in 2006, the latter seems to be the dominant historiographical trend!

This book examines these contrasting viewpoints in light of the commercial history of Bengal. I argue that Bengal was hardly a prime

[256] *Ibid.*: 110.

region in South Asia; moreover it was an area of marginal concern to the Mughal Empire compared to Surat or the Coromandel. Bengal lay at the lower end of a relatively insignificant maritime and land bloc that moved in an arc from China towards the Bay. By virtue of this position Bengal engaged-not in grand commerce-but in a 'little' commerce that spanned the northernmost coast of the Bay, with countries such as Arakan, Ava, Pegu (grouped under Pagan until the thirteenth century and then as Burma), and Siam. This 'little' commerce was conducted under the aegis of two great ideological networks-Buddhism and Islam. Like the Malabar, the last great trading bloc of South Asia, Bengal stayed away from mainstream Mughal commercial history; unlike the Malabar Bengal did not have the advantage of an enduring commercial link–such as the link with East Africa–that lasted for that region well into the eighteenth century. It did not have the advantage of being part of the Persian-African cultural network as the Malabar was; moreover, lying strategically halfway on the major Indian Ocean routes, the Malabar participated fully in the Arab maritime world. By comparison Bengal's participation in the major Indian Ocean routes was more marginal, as I show later. The only advantage that Bengal had over the Malabar was the China link. Unfortunately for Bengal, the Bengal-Chinese link snapped frequently and therefore did not stand the test of time. And the Arakan association, initially beneficial for Bengal, turned adverse.

The East in the Ancient History of Bengal: Pundravardhana, Pattikera and their Monarchs: Sacred Regions, Littoral States or Commercial Nodes?

The East was not only important for the economy of medieval Bengal. It was the area that witnessed commerce appearing across the Bay of Bengal and spill over into neighbouring countries. And it was also one of the first areas in Bengal to take a coherent political shape. Some of the earliest states in Bengal appear to have originated from this region.

Although the history for this period is sketchy nevertheless the following kingdoms and states in the east can be isolated. The first region (also a state) of importance is undoubtedly Pundravardhana. Referred to as Pundravardhana *bhukti* this was initially an administrative division that gradually assumed territorial overtones. Niharranjan Ray tells us that during the Gupta period *vanga* and Pundravardhana were separate divisions. The two became merged from the Pala-Sena times, and the region known as *varendra* took shape from the tenth century[257].

As administrative division the original Pundravardhana was the tract between the Karatoya and Tista rivers: the area that came to be called *varendra*. Pundravardhana thus encompassed a substantial part of present day north Bengal and beyond; possibly up unto Kamrup. By the time of the Chandras and the Senas (ie. between the tenth and twelfth centuries) Pundravardhana also stretched southward (Ray, 1993, claims that the southward expansion of Pundravardhana started in the eighth century: 116). Chandradwip (Bakla in *samatata*) and *Harikela* were included as Pundravardhana in two inscriptions of Srichandra (nos. II and IV)[258].

Mahastan was probably the name of the capital of Pundravardhana. The Mahastan (Pundranagara) complex lies in present day Bangladesh's Bogra district. The long chronological span of this urban complex has recently come to light. A recent publication speculates that Mahastangarh may have been an autonomous state rather than a 'regional' capital of the Mauryas[259]. *The Imperial Gazeteer of India* (1908) asserted that Mahastan was the capital of Pundravardhana or the Pod peoples. Hsuan Tsang, in the first half of the seventh century, referred to Pundravardhana as an autonomous kingdom and mentioned the wealth of its capital. The names Mahastan and Pundravardhana were used interchangeably to denote both capital and kingdom. It was Buddhist in religion and Hsuan Tsang testified to a flourishing Buddhism being practiced there. This highlights the fact that Bengal housed many tribes, states and peoples and Mahastan may well have been the capital of one such state.

But Mahastan had other attributes as well. Being a part of the early Buddhist pilgrimage circuit it was also a well known trade centre in early times. Sandrine Gill calls Mahastan a riverine port in ancient Bengal[260]. Perhaps for this reason Mahastan was successively under Gupta, and then

---

[257] Ray, Niharranjan, 1993, *A History of the Bengali People*: *Early Period*, Calcutta, Dey's Publishing: 111, 116.

[258] Majumdar, R.C., 1943, *The History of Bengal*, V.1 *The Hindu Period*, Dacca University Press: 195–6.

[259] Salles, Jean Francois, Boussac, Marie Francoise, Breuil, Jean Yves, 2002, 'Mahasthangarh (Bangladesh) and the Ganges Valley in the Mauryan Period', in Gautam Sengupta and Sheena Panja eds., 2002, *Archaeology of Eastern India : New Perspectives*, Centre For Archaeological Studies and Training, Eastern India (CASTEI): 527–50.

[260] Gill, Sandrine, 1999, 'Mahasthangarh: A Riverine port in Ancient Bengal', in Himanshu Prabha Ray ed. *Archaeology of Seafaring: The Indian Ocean in the Ancient Period*, New Delhi, Pragati Publications: 154–172.

Chandra, Khambhoj and Pala control. But evidence of continued political patronage in the early period is yet to be substantiated for Mahastan.

It is significant that the site of Mahastan lies on the north-south axis from the Himalayas to the mouth of the Ganga. Mahastan is actually situated on the now almost 'moribund' Karatoya river (*Imperial Gazeteer of India* 1908). It lies in the area between the Padma and the Jamuna (tributary of the Brahmaputra river). In ancient and early medieval times the area around the Karatoya was a sacred region: its valley as well as its lower reaches where it ran into the sea was recognised as a sacred spot[261]. Its people, the Pundras, were recognised as Kshatriyas in the *Sabhaparvan* of the *Mahabharat*[262]. It was also a land sacred for Buddhists; Hsuang-Tsang journeyed from Pundravardhana to Kamrup in the seventh century and Kia Tan (785–805 AD), the monk from Tongkin, came into Magadha through Kamrup (by way of the Karatoya) and Pundravardhana[263].

The Karatoya was also described as a 'sea' in the *Karatoya-Mahatmyam*, and Bakhtiar Khilji sailed up this river with his ships in search of Assamese gold. Historically this part of Bengal carried on a substantial trade with her northern neighbours; as far north as Assam, Tibet, Burma and China[264]. Mahastan may well have been an important staging point on the overland/riverine route between *samatata*, through *harikela* into Tibet. Another trade route from Mahastan could have gone eastwards. Pelliot suggested that the Bengal-Burma-China trade existed as early as from the second century BC. Mahastan, along with Wari Bateswar or Wari Bator in the Padma-Meghna delta near Dhaka, would then have been a nodal centre in this trade[265]. Trade from Mahastan also went west. It is noteworthy that a mirror–an object foreign to Bengal in the early times although known in the Near East from the fourth century BC–has been found at Mahastangarh[266].

---

261 Majumdar, R.C., 1943, *The History of Bengal*, V.1 *The Hindu Period*, Dacca, University Press: 37.

262 *Ibid*. V.1: 37.

263 Kia Tan's itinerary has been well documented. See Majumdar, R.C., 1943, V.1: 62–3; Ray, Niharranjan, 1993, V.1: 94.

264 *The Periplus Maris Erythraei* (Ed. Casson, L.), 1989, Princeton, University Press: 63–65 in Alam, M. Shafiqul and Salles, Jean Francois (Eds)., April 2000, *France-Bangladesh Joint Venture Excavations at Mahastangarh. First Interim Report* 1993–1999, Dhaka. Liu, Xinru, 1988, *Ancient India and Ancient China. Trade and Religious Exchanges* AD *1–600*, Oxford.

265 In Gill 1999: 163–4.

266 Salles, Boussac and Breuil, 2002, in Sengupta and Panja Eds. 538–40.

But as to why it was located in the little known Bogra district at all, and not elsewhere, what gave it its name of Mahastan (great place), what contributed to its fame as a rich agricultural region and as a major centre in ancient history remain speculations to this day.

A joint Franco-Bangladesh archaeological team working since 1993 has opined that:[267]

a. Mahastan was an important regional Buddhist centre around the thrid/fourth century B.C. It is dated earlier than Paharpur and is deemed to be a sister centre of Maninamati further south near Dhaka-Suvarnagram and the Meghna river.

b. It appears to have continued as an important regional centre until the thirteenth century at least, for at the turn of the fourteenth century (1301) there is mention of an inscription attributed to Shams-al-Din Firuz Shah, honouring the tomb of Shah Sultan Balkhi-the Muslim saint of Mahastan. An excavated mosque at Mankalir Kunda is dated also to the fourteenth century. It is likely that this area formed part of Eaton's expanding Islamic frontier.

c. There was then a hiatus until the seventeenth century when, in 1685, this area came under a Muslim governor by virtue of a *sanad* in Arabic.

d. A Persian inscription for a mosque dated 1718 has been found. A building named Parshuramer Bari (Parshuram's Palace) has now been excavated and reconstructed by the joint venture team. It appears to have been a minor palace re-built over an earlier monument of the tenth/twelfth centuries for an Islamic (Mughal/ Afghan?) official in the eighteenth century. We thereby get an almost complete chronology of Mahastan from the third/fourth century to the eighteenth century.

What contributed to the decline of Mahastan? Alam's and Salles' findings speculate that the changing of the river courses in the eighteenth century, specifically that of the Karatoya and the Brahmaputra, may have finished off Mahastan. The Karatoya was once a mighty river, almost an ocean during the time of the Mahabharatas. The Karatoya-Tista river system facilitated journeys into sub-Himalayan north Bengal. We know that Bakhtiar Khilji used the Karatoya extensively in his abortive Assam-

---

[267] Alam, M. Shafiqul and Salles, Jean Francois (Eds)., April 2000, *France-Bangladesh Joint Venture Excavations at Mahastangarh. First Interim Report* 1993–1999, Dhaka.

Tibet expedition in 1206[268]. M. Mohar Ali describes a fleet sailing down the Karatoya as late as in the sixteenth century[269]. It was however a mere trickle by the late eighteenth century. Rennell's maps tell us that the Brahmaputra experienced a major channel shift westwards in the eighteenth century; it appears that this reduced the waters of the mighty Karatoya as well and signed the doom of Mahastan.

Pundravardhaha was without doubt one of the earliest, and most important, regional complexes in ancient Bengal. Its urban life as evinced from the ruins of Mahastan, its Buddhist monuments, its place in Hindu sacred lore and its strategic location point to its position as the political and economic heart of ancient Bengal. Straddling *varendra*, *samatata* and *harikela*, or three of the four divisions of Bengal, Pundravardhana came to embrace the entire Dhaka-Vikrampur region, as well as the Comilla-Mainamati and Pattikera regions within its territory. Pundravardhana contained rich agrarian land and by virtue of its location was able to connect the trade of the delta with that of the hill passes that ran into Kamrup, Assam and Pagan. The Chandra and Pala kings of ancient Bengal came from this region. It was the civilisational nerve centre of ancient Bengal.

Within the region of Pundravardhana, another smaller geographical unit is Comilla. This too has an ancient lineage. Comilla housed the Mainamati-Lalmai Buddhist complex and was the political nerve centre of the early and later Deva kings, as well as the Khadga and Chandra kings. The Pala kings, who later on moved on to Gaur, started their rule from this region. All were Buddhist except for the Brahmanical Bhadra kings ruling there in the first half of the seventh century. Brahmanical rule in Comilla was short lived and the Bhadras were succeeded by the Khadgas in the same century. Chinese evidence tells us that they ruled between 650 and 700 AD[270]; of this dynasty we have the names of three kings. The three kings were Buddhists and patrons of Buddhist shrines and monasteries. Their capital was in modern Bad Kamta, about twelve miles to the west of Comilla. Many Jains also lived in their domains. Their inscriptions tell us that their territory stretched from modern Badkamta in Tripura to Dhaka and Comilla and their territory probably comprised the whole of

[268] *Imperial Gazetteer*, 1908, Oxford Univeristy Press, III: *The Indian Empire-Economic*.

[269] Ali, M.M., 1985, *History of the Muslims of Bengal*, V.IB: 959, Riyadh, Imam Muhammad Ibn Sa'ud Islamic University Press, 2vs.

[270] There is a dispute about their date. Some scholars hold that the Khadgas ruled in the ninth century. See Majumdar, R.C., 1943, V.1: 86–87.

eastern and southern Bengal. D.C. Sen tells us that the Khadgas had marital relations with the kings of Arakan, especially during the reign of Lahaychandra who ascended the Arakan throne in 951 AD[271]; in that case the Khadgas ruled in Eastern Bengal as late as in the tenth century. There were commercial relations as well; the symbol on both the Arakan and Khadga coins was the bull in repose[272].

The Khadgas were replaced by the early Chandras who were already ruling in *vanga* from around the fifth to the eighth century, according to Taranath's testimony[273]. The existence of the early Chandras in Bengal is yet to be substantiated but we should note that there were also 19 Chandras ruling in Arakan at this time[274]. From the ninth to the eleventh century we have the later Chandras in Bengal; we know of at least four kings in this dynasty: Purnachandra (who is said to have come to Bengal from Rohitagiri-identified as either a sanskritised form of Lalmai or Rohtasgarh in Bihar), Suvarnachandra (who became Buddhist), Trailokyachandra (who added Chandradwip [Bakla] and *harikela* to his domains and thus laid the foundations of the greatness of the dynasty), and finally Srichandra who ruled for thirty five years and extended his dominions further. Two others–Layahachandra and Govindachandra may also have belonged to this dynasty; in that case we know of six Chandra kings.

Srichandra's capital was Vikrampur (all four of the copper plate grants during his reign were issued from there), he ruled over *samatata* and *harikela* (possibly he ruled the whole of east Bengal and the coastal regions of south Bengal) and it is very likely that he ruled a portion of north Bengal as well, as two of the inscriptions (II and IV) mention that the lands granted were situated in Pundravardhana bhukti. But the last may not be true for, as we have seen, Pundravardhana bhukti became an expanding territorial and sacred concept at this time. Other than at Vikrampur, Srichandra's other capital was near Comilla, at Pattikera.

---

[271] Sen, D.C., 1935, *Brihat Banga*, V.1, Calcutta, Dey's Publishing, 1993 reprint: 222–223. (In Bengali).

[272] *Ibid.*: 223.

[273] Taranath, *History of Buddhism*, mentions seven Chandra kings in Bengal in the early period. They were all pre-Pala kings. They are Vrikshachandra, Kamachandra, Simhachandra, Balachandra, Vimalachandra, Govichandra, Lalitachandra; they seem to have ruled over Kamrup, Mithila and Bangala. According to Taranath, Gopala succeeded these early Chandras.

[274] See A.P. Phayre's *History of Burma* and Gutman's *Burma's Lost Kingdoms: Splendours of Arakan.* The dates of the Chandra kings of Arakan vary in these two works.

Srichandra was, without doubt, a most powerful king. It is likely that he expanded commerce in the Bay of Bengal at a time when Rajendra Chola established his supremacy in the eastern Indian Ocean. A clash between the Cholas and the Chandras was inevitable and we hear of a Govindachandra of eastern Bengal being attacked by the Cholas during 1021 and 1023 AD. Who was Govindachandra? Majumdar identifies Govindachandra as the successor of Srichandra, based on the fact that he ruled immediately after Srichandra and because his territorial dimensions conformed to those of Srichandra's[275]. Others, such as R.D. Banerjee and D.C.Sen also identify Govindachandra as belonging to the Chandra dynasty[276]. The attack of Rajendra Chola and Govindachandra's alliance with the Cholas has been immortalised in folk songs[277] and it is highly probable that Govindachandra surrendered to the Palas soon after.

But the later Chandras were not the only ones ruling in eastern Bengal in the ninth and tenth centuries. Inscriptions tell us that there was a Maharajadhiraja Kantideva ruling from *Harikela* around 850–950 AD. Layahachandradeva, who may also have been a Deva king also ruled near Comilla for at least eighteen years in the tenth century. The political situation in Bengal between the eighth and tenth centuries was fluid; and the Palas emerged from the east around this time. They soon gave Bengal a semblance of unity but the east continued to be quasi-independent. During the reign of Gopala II, in the tenth century, there were at least three kingdoms in Bengal: the Chandras in the east and south, the Pala-Khamboj in the north and west, and the Palas in the centre at Gaur.

The energetic Buddhist pilgrimage network and maritime policy of the Khadgas and Chandras was somewhat reversed by the orthodox Brahmanical Varmans who succeeded the Chandras in the eleventh century in the Dhaka-Vikrampur region, but Buddhist activities from Comilla still continued. Only the religious and commercial mantle now passed to the Buddhist kingdom of Pattikera.

Pattikera was a 'country' with a king, referred to as a small kingdom, whose domains adjoined Arakan. Pattikera was in Tripura, i.e. to the north of Arakan, and extended as far as Comilla and Mainamati[278]. This

275 Majumdar, R.C., 1943, V.1: 196.

276 Sen, D.C., 1935, V.1: 275.

277 Songs from Rangpur in Sen, D.C., 1935, V.1: 275.

278 Majumdar, R.C., 1943, V.1: 258.

kingdom flourished from the eleventh to the thriteenth century and the Pagan chronicles are full of references to this kingdom, we shall see in a subsequent section. This was an independent kingdom; Ranavankamalla Sri Harikeladeva who ruled from 1204 at least until 1220 endowed a Buddhist monastery with a grant of land in the city of Pattikera. Harikeladeva's origins are obscure. We do not know whether he belonged to the old royal family of Pattikera that is referred to in the Pagan chronicles or whether his was a branch of the royal Devas who set up an independent kingdom in the same area. At any rate, soon after 1220, Harikeladeva's dominions were probably swallowed up by the expanding Deva dynasty in the region and Pattikera ceased to exist as an independent state[279]. The Devas, contemporaries of the Senas at Gaur and Hindu Vaishnavs, ruled Tripura, Noakhali, Comilla and Chattagram in the thirteenth century; long after the Islamic conquest of western Bengal. The Deva capital was at both Vikrampur and Suvarnagram.

What about the communication networks of this area? We have seen that this was an important region from which various commercial and religious networks emanated. We can isolate at least six routes from this area. One, from Pundravardhana to Pataliputra via Kamrup and *samatata*, two, from Pundravardhana to Varanasi via Mithila, Pataliputra and Bodh Gaya, three, from Pundravardhana to South China via Kamrup, four, from Pundravardhana to Afghanistan via Kamrup and Pagan, five, the land route from Pattikera to Pagan through the Lusai hills, and six, the route from Chattagram to Arakan[280]. These routes encompassed overland and riverine routes and sculpted this eastern area into an independent religio-commercial-political complex.

The foregoing presentation shows that between the eighth and eleventh centuries regional kingdoms and littoral states sprang up in *varendra*, *samatata* and *harikela*. These deltaic states were fragments of the earlier kingdom of Pundravardhana which commanded the gateway to the north east. Let us now study the states that sprang up in the north east during this period of the trade revolution in the eastern Indian Ocean.

The North East in Early Medieval History

The North East refers here to the area from Jalpaiguri, Kamrup and Assam up until Little Tibet or Chinese Turkestan in the north and to

---

[279] See *Ibid*.: 257–9.

[280] See Ray, Niharranjan, 1993: 92–96.

Yunnan in south China to the east. From the thirteenth century onwards, the Chinese diversion from the northern Mongol land route and the drive southwards to the sea had repercussions on Bengal's north eastern frontiers because towns now sprang up to connect the overland route to ports in south east Bengal.

By the thirteenth century a renewed urbanisation was seen in the region of Assam, Kamrup, Little Tibet and Chinese Turkestan. New towns sprang up as sea and land routes connected. One such was Karampatan in Chinese Turkestan which had a garrison of 50000 soldiers. This border town represented the boundary between the Bengal Sultanate and China. Karampatan lay on steppe land and is famous in history for the horse trade. It supplied both China and Lakhnauti, both horse deficient states. Minhaj Siraj (*Tabakat-i-Nasiri*) and Marco Polo (*Travels*) testified to 1500 horses being brought through the 35 mountain passes between Kamrup and Tibet into Lakhnawati.

The Chinese element was marked in these border towns. Mardhan Kot in Kamrup was built on the model of towns in Mongol China by Gurhasp Shah on his return from China[281]. The Brahmaputra, called Bangamathi by Minhaj, was the river that traversed both China and Bengal. Mardhan Kot was situated on this river. This was also a frontier town. According to Minhaj the river, when it entered Bengal, took the name of Samunder, so great was its length, breadth and width.

Ku'lam was known as 'a large city in India'[282]. It was known for its Chinese style ceramics and famed for its trade in aloes. The Ku'lam ceramics were sold in the Arab world along with Chinese ceramics, but it was generally agreed that they were inferior to the Chinese ceramics[283]. Ku'lam too became an important off shoot of the new silk route. The Chinese influence was marked here as well. Zakari'ya al-Kazwi'ni tells us that 'When their king dies they choose another from China'[284] which makes us wonder whether this town partook of South Asian political traditions at all.

---

[281] Minhaj, *Tabakat-i-Nasiri*, V.2. Raverty edition: 310.

[282] *A'sa'ru-l-Bilad* of Zakari'ya al Kazwi'ni in Elliot and Dowson, V. 1, Allahabad, Kitab Mahal, Reprint 1969: 96.

[283] 'They manufacture clay vessels, which are sold in our cities like those of China, but they are not the same, because the clay of China is harder than that of Ku'lam and bears the fire better…', *Ibid.*: 96.

[284] *Ibid.*: 96.

This unknown route was nevertheless a widely travelled one during the thirteenth and fourteenth centuries. While in the ancient period Buddhist travellers from China and Tongkin came into Bengal by way of this route, the Mongols too were reputed to be considering this route for an invasion of Bengal[285]. In the fourteenth century Florentine merchants, Italian monks and papal legatees present at the court of the Great Khan, such as John of Mariquolli, Pegolotti and the friar Odoric, knew of this route[286].

These towns on the northern frontier of Bengal, running through Kamrup and Ava into Chinese Turkestan and Tibet, were originally part of the old Buddhist network. But they also became part of an emerging Islamic network between Bengal and the neighbouring regions. They certainly introduced a new pattern of trade into Bengal by the end of the thirteenth century for Bengal's ports now began to connect with these caravan trading towns through its intricate fluvial system.

The north east area contained, we saw, the land routes connecting Bengal to China. Despite the thirteenth century Chinese southward drive to the sea land routes maintained their importance and, in some cases, competed very strongly with the sea routes. This was because while the sea route from Mekong (Gulf of Tongkin) to Bengal involved around 5300 km. of navigation, or the land and sea route between Pegu and Chattagram involved some 2000 km of land and sea travel, the overland route between Bengal and China (via Burma) was of only 1200 km.

Three such routes led from Bengal to Yung Chang Fu in Yunnan: from the Upper Brahmaputra Valley (Kamrup), across passes in the Patkai Range, through Mogaung, the Irrawady and Momien into China, from Manipur and Tripura (via the Imole Pass), through the Chindwin, Irrawady and Shweli rivers into south China, and from Chattagram, by way of Arakan, Pagan, Ava and Prome into China[287].

Rivers that were important for commerce here were the Karatoya, the Tista and the Brahmaputra. Of these the Brahmaputra formed the single most largest, and most important, conduit of trade between the eastern Himalayas and the Bay of Bengal.

---

[285] See further on.

[286] Yule, Henry, *Cathay and the Way Thither*, London, Hakluyt Society, MD CCC LXVI: 273–4, 335.

[287] Deyell, John, 1983, 'The China Connection: Problems of Silver Supply in Medieval Bengal' in J.F. Richards ed. *Precious Metals in the Later Medieval and Early Modern Worlds*, Durham, Carolina Academic Press: 207–227. See pp. 219–220. Reprinted in Sanjay Subrahmanyam ed., 1994, *Money and the Market in India 1100–1700*, Delhi, Oxford University Press: 112–136.

Trade and Politics in the Bay of Bengal

The Bay of Bengal-a subsector of the eastern Indian Ocean of which Bengal is a part-was ruled by different imperatives from those governing states in the western Indian Ocean. The Bay of Bengal was less conducive to favourable sailings than the Arabian Sea. Direct sailings either east or west were difficult to manage from the Bengal coast for three reasons.

First, the Bengal coast is a distinctive combination of rivers, estuaries and deltas crisscrossed with marshlands and quicksands until it reaches the sea. This made direct sailings difficult and uneconomical. Second, the northern Bay of Bengal is not a very welcoming sea; frequent cyclones there dictate that sailings be coastal rather than maritime in nature. This made for long periods of shipping and forced Bengali (and other) shipping to stay close to the Burma and Siam coast in history. Third, politics in the eastern Indian Ocean were different. The small kingdoms that surrounded the Bay such as Arakan, Burma and Sri Lanka were in constant flux; the only common tie that held them together was Buddhism: a religion that offered unparalleled scope for spiritual and political advancement through religious ties.

The Buddhist world came under pressure from the eleventh century when the Palas withdrew their patronage and converted to Hinduism. The islamization of Bengal in the thirteenth century and subsequently that of South East Asia in the sixteenth century furthered the crisis in this world. Islam is supposed to have shattered diplomatic and commercial links in the ancient Bay. The end of the early empires during this period–Pagan and Srivijaya at the end of the thirteenth century, Angkor at the end of the fourteenth and Majapahit at the beginning of the sixteenth century–signal the end of this ancient world. The Mongols too abandoned Buddhism and adopted Islam.

It is a paradox that at this time of the Mongol rupture, which saw the decline of the ancient world and the emergence of Islam in Asia, we find an enhanced level of trade emerging, visible in the minting of coins in the trading world of the Bay of Bengal. This vigorous minting may be explained by the fact that the first Islamic states rose in South Asia at this time.

Denys Lombard comments[288]:

---

[288] Lombard, Denys, 1988, 'Le Sultanat Malais Comme Modele Socio-Economique' in Denys Lombard and Jean Aubin (eds). *Marchands et Hommes d'Affaires Asiatiques dans l'Ocean Indien et la Mer de Chine 13e–20e siecles*, Paris, Editions E.H.E.S.S.: 117–124. See p.121.

> La frappe du metal blanc semble avoir commencé au Bengale au 13e siecle et c'est vers cette époque que commence dans le nord de Sumatra un monnayage d'or qui se maintiendra jusqu'aù 18e siecle. (The minting of white metal seems to have started in Bengal in the thirteenth century and at the same time Sumatra started minting a currency in gold which continued until the eighteenth century. (*my translation*)

This was not so surprising. The Brahmanic backlash against Buddhism that commenced from the eleventh century meant that Buddhism was continually pushed towards eastern Bengal. This meant, in effect, that between the eleventh and thirteenth centuries, east and north Bengal, Assam, Arakan and Ceylon formed a vibrant cultural and economic zone, and it is from this time that the commerce of Bengal: the Bengal-Arakan trade and the Bengal-China trade really came into its own.

In contemporary historiography Arakan's trade in the Bay was deemed neglible. However, Leider comments that there has been no proper evaluation of Bengal-Arakan trade. Arakan left a definite imprint both in the trade of the Bay of Bengal and in the eastern Indian Ocean[289]. That a Bengal-Arakan trade emerged from the fifth century is documented; this continued throughout the ancient period.

Arakan was swallowed up by the kingdom of Pagan by the twelfth century. The important thing to be noted here that Arakan's incorporation into Pagan offered Bengal an easier land route into South China (known as Daḷi until its cȯnquest by the Mongols at the end of the thirteenth ċentury). Zhou Qufei provided the earliest known Chinese reference to Pagan in 1178: that it was five days' journey from Dali[290]. Narapatisithu, the ruler of Pagan in the late twefth-early thirteenth centuries, conquered both Machhagiri (Arakan) and Pattikera and brought these kingdoms under the fold of Pagan[291].

Tilman Frasch comments on the political economy of this borderland in'Coastal Peripheries during the Pagan Period'[292]:

[289] Leider, Jacques P., 2005, 'A Short Discussion on Islamic Influence in the Mrauk-U Age', *Arakanese Research Journal*, V.III, July, Arakanese Research Society of Bangladesh, ed. Venerable U Bodhinyana: 99–134. See p. 102.

[290] Wicks, Robert S., 1992, *Money, Markets and Trade in Early South East Asia: The Development of Indigenous Monetary Systems to AD 1400*, SEAP, Cornell, Ithaca, New York: 131.

[291] *Ibid*: 131.

[292] in Jos Gommans./Jacques Leider (eds.), 2002, *The Maritime Frontier of Burma*, Amsterdam.

The Pagan Empire which covered most of what is modern Burma during the twelfth and thirteenth centuries had its centre in the agriculturally important areas of north and central Burma. By conquest, the two coastal strips of Arakan and Lower Burma had also come under the sway of Upper Burman rule...Agriculture specially the cultivation of wet rice (*padi*), was the backbone of the first Burmese empire (roughly corresponding to the eleventh to the thirteenth century), called the kingdom of Pagan after its capital, a small town in Central Burma. When the ethnic Burmese, nomadic pastoralists of Mongolian stock, migrated into the dry zone of Burma around the seventh to eighth centuries, they came into contact with the Pyu from whom they borrowed freely including rice cultivation, dwelling in cities, and perhaps Buddhism....Under irrigation, wet rice provides fairly reliable and rich harvests offering the potential to create a stable peasant society... initially the Burmese had no access to the sea, as Lower Burma was controlled by a number of Mon-dominated city states, and the Arakan coast by the Arakanese (besides this, Arakan was more or less inaccessible because of its topography). It was only after the conquests of King Anawrahta (c. 1044–1078) in the mid-eleventh century that the Mon dominance of Lower Burma was removed. Arakan, as far as we can tell, came under the influence of Pagan another century later when King Alaungsithu restored a deposed prince to the throne. The mid-twelfth century saw Lower Burma in rebellion on two or three occasions, once during the reign of King Alaungsithu and another outburst which was quelled by King Narapatisithu's army commander Thubayit (*Supharac*). In between came the Sinhalese raid on Lower Burma around 1164–5 which King Parakkama Bahu I of Polonaruwa had sent to extract revenge for insults he had suffered at the hands of the Burmese. According to the contemporary Sinhalese chronicle *Culavamsa*, the Sinhalese forces captured the two port towns of Kusumiya (Bassein) and Muttama (Martaban) as well as a third place called *Ukkama* which may be identified as Okkam, a place some twenty miles north of Rangoon.

The affinity of the region with Bengal's material culture–that o wet rice cultivation supporting small independent kingdoms based on a stable peasantry–is clear. Moreover, the cultural affinity of this coasta region of the Bay, from Ceylon, through Bengal to the Arakan based or an admixture of diplomatic ties through marriage and Buddhism and conquest, is evident. Alaungsithu had familial antecedents in Bengal notably through one King of Pattikera who helped Alaungsithu of Pagan and gave his daughter in marriage to him[293]. The Bengal-Arakan borde had little relevance in a land ruled by topographical similarities and Bengal played a leading role in the politics of both Arakan and Pagan from the eleventh century.

That Arakan had initially come under Indian influence is demonstratec by the Sanskrit inscriptions issued by the rulers of Mrohaung where a dynasty of Buddhist kings bearing names ending with Chandra flourishec between the fifth and the eighth centuries. Indeed the Chandras of Benga who ruled at the same time claimed their lineage from these monarchs of Arakan. Since about the eleventh century, this Buddhist tie between Arakan and northern India had gradually been subjected to mounting pressure. The first step was the reconversion of the later Pala kings o Bengal, who had been staunch supporters of Buddhist institutions such as Nalanda or Sompur, to Hinduism by the mid-eleventh century. The successive fall of the Palas at the end of this century and finally the Muslim conquest of Bengal at the beginning of the thirteenth century created several waves of Buddhist emigration from Northern India and Bengal tending either towards Tibet or towards southeast Bengal and Arakan. In Arakan, a number of new centres of Buddhism gradually emerged, protected and supported from various local dynasties. The most important and longest-lived centres in Bengal (in proximity to Arakan) were the towns of Comilla and Mainamati, both in the vicinity of the Lalmai range. Mainamati is very likely Patikkera, the neighbouring state to which Burmese chronicles attributed so much significance It was at that place where as late as in AD 1219–20 one of the ruler (named Ranavankamalla Sri Harikeladeva) made a donation to the monastery of the Buddhist goddess Durgottara.

Frasch continues[294]:

> ....Another peuliarity of Lower Burma was the noticeable presence of potters (*o-tein*) who occur on three occasions and potters' land. Thus, in the second half of the thirteenth century,

[293] See later.

[294] Frasch 2002.

> Queen *Acaw Min Hla,* while staying in Lower Burma, transfered thirty potters and 1000 *pay* of land suitable for potting to another royal highness, presumably her great-grand niece...More than rice, pots seem to have been a product of Lower Burma that was much in demand at Pagan. "In this place Arimaddanapura [i.e., Pagan], where water is difficult to get", as one inscription states (Pl. II 158 = OBI 2, p. 28, l. 1-2), the availability of water was fundamental to survival. Even today, big jars one metre in height and nearly two metres in circumfence are employed to store rain water and preserve it for human consumption. To the earliest Europeans arriving at Burma, these pots were known as "Martaban jars" or "Pegu jars[295]", indicating their provenance (Yule/Burnell 1886, 559, s.v. "Martaban"), and more than likely this tradition of pot making streches back to Pagan period and beyond (Luce 1985 (1), 50). As mentioned above, potters and land suitable for potting even appear in the epigraphy of Pagan. Adding substance to this, recent excavations have brought to light green-glazed and greenish-white glazed ceramic ware[296] (mainly bowls and plates) which are supposed to originate from production centres in (Lower) Burma (Hein 1996).

Frasch adds that despite the indisputable significance of pottery and the putative agricultural potential, the real economic importance of Lower Burma lay in the field of trade. The core area of the Pagan kingdom was landlocked, and although the international trade of the kingdom was limited, what there was would have been impossible without the ports of Lower Burma. The eleventh century witnessed a kind of trade revolution with regard to the increasing number of traders participating in commerce as well as in terms of the importance trade assumed as as source of state revenue. One drawback to full participation was that the Burmese coast lay partly in the cyclone zone of the Bay of Bengal so long-distance sailing routes across the Bay circumvented the area as far as possible. Ships coming from Sri Lanka and South India heading for Bengal usually hugged the east coast of India, while the traverse from Southeast Asia to

[295] Martaban Jars were sent to Persia. See Bowrey, note 301.

[296] See the section on celadon at Gaur later. Identification of this ware with the shards found at Gaur reinforce our assumption that trade and cultural negotiations with Arakan and Burma were an indispensable part of the economic life of medieval Bengal.

the ports of Sri Lanka ran further south, touching the southern tip of the Nicobar Islands. Burmese ports were mainly frequented by merchants engaged in a coastal peddling trade. Despite their comparatively low importance as destinations on direct trade routes, Burmese ports were indubitably involved in the trading network in the Bay of Bengal, which can, for example, be seen from the works of Arab geographers of the tenth and eleventh centuries who mention Samandar, Ornashin and Abina as important emporia, presumably of the eastern shores. Likewise, places such as Bassein and Martaban are mentioned in a variety of contexts showing that the international trading community was aware of their existence. Arakan was part of the trading network in the Bay of Bengal, although its share may have been small before the fourteenth century and rose in connection with the rise of Portuguese trading activities. As the few Arab sources show, the forests of Arakan offered trees suitable for a variety of purposes, including shipbuilding (al-Idrisi mentions aloes wood), and that it had the additional advantage in that most of its rivers were navigable up to the urban centres (Daw Thin Kyi 1970, 3, in Frasch). Arakan was even more affected by cyclones than Lower Burma, forcing ships from Southeast Asia heading for the Bengal ports to keep close to the shore. In fact, the Arab sources give the impression that direct trade with Arakan across the Bay was the fruit of ships blown off course rather than from intentional navigation. In sum, Frasch says that this leads him to conclude that although Arakan never played a prominent role in the trade of the Bay its trade could have contributed to the economic stability and welfare of an independent kingdom of Arakan already in the eleventh to the thirteenth centuries, but apart from this, rice cultivation should have been the fundament of this polity.

Turning to the commodities traded, Frasch goes on, the most important import wares for Burma, at least in terms of quantity, were cotton and cotton cloth, both of which are most likely originated in India where they had been grown and manufactured respectively since time immemorial. It stands to reason that Bassein, Tala, *Henbo*, and other ports of Lower Burma will therefore have served as the main gateways for textile imports.

The kingdom of Pagan ceded place to the Kingdom of Burmah' (or, Berma') in the fifteenth century. Visiting at the turn of the sixteenth century Barbosa noted that the kingdom of Berma was frequently at war with the kingdom of Pegu' and added that 'in this country there are no Moors, nor are there sea ports which can be made use of for trade in merchandise'[297]. Pegu indeed was the most vibrant trading area of the region; boasting three or four sea ports in the sixteenth century[298]. Barbosa noted its great trade by sea, mainly with Malacca and Sumatra, that was carried on by both Hindu and Muslim merchants[299].

Maritime trade routes know no borders and this entire coastal zone was engaged in a teak and ceramics trade (from points east) for cotton (from Bengal) from the early medieval period. Martaban jars were a well-known export item in this region: Barbosa noted, 'In this town of Martaban very large and beautiful vases are made...which are highly valued among the Moors'[300]. Martaban jars seem to have become regular items of trade (and diplomacy) not only in Bengal but also at points further west. When Thomas Bowrey went from Bengal to Persia a century later he carried several 'Mortavan Jarrs' of Ganga water for the Banians at Gombroon', which were eagerly accepted the moment the ship docked there[301].

Arakan was easily accessible from Bengal either by ship or by way of land routes, and in fact it is even impossible to define a clear boundary between southeast Bengal (ancient *Samatata*) and northern Arakan. In 1661 Glanius, shipwrecked off this stretch of coast, wrote in his diary[302]:

> La 8eme octobre nous fumes à la vue de la cote de Bengala, mais nous la vimes sans la connaitre, n'y aiant pas plus d'apparence que le fut celle que les Terres d'Arakan qui en font proches.

Like the Arakan coast, the Bengal coast was full of sandbanks. Glanius notes upon landing near Sandwip Island[303]:

---

297 Barbosa, 921: 181.

298 *Ibid.*: 183.

299 *Ibid.*: 183–85.

300 *Ibid.*: 185.

301 Temple, R.C. (Ed). M D CCCV, Thomas Bowrey's *A Geographical Account of the Countries Around the Bay of Bengal 1669–79,* Cambridge, The Hakluyt Society: 216.

302 Glanius, *Relation du Nauffrage d'un Vaisseau Hollandois Vers la Cote de Bengala*, 1661. Published 1682: 132–3. 'The 8th October we were at the Bengal coast, but we saw it without recognizing it, the Bengal coast being identical to the Arakan coast which was close.' (my translation).

303 *A Relation of An Unfortunate Voyage to the Kingdom of Bengala*, London, Henry Bonwick, 1682: 3–6.

> We knew that Bengala was full of rocks and dangerous shelves, whereupon several vessels had been cast away, but had not that necessary knowledge where they lay... . We ran upon a long shole, whence getting clear, we fell upon another, more dangerous than the former.

Instead of searching for a boundary, it seems preferable to regard the whole area as an arena of cultural mobility, interaction and exchange. Pottery from Burma (and China) found their way to Gaur via Arakan[304]. From Bengal went exotic items such as parrot beaks, kingfisher feathers and rhino horns. By contrast, access to Arakan from Burma was only possible across the Arakan Yoma, heavily covered with dense jungles that were difficult to penetrate even in the nineteenth century. This topographical feature not only made intervention itself a difficult task, it also held the intensity of alien rule at bay. Arakan and Lower Burma participated in the same maritime cultural zone from which Pagan was excluded and we may conclude that eastern Bengal was Arakan's foremost trading partner. Culturally too, Arakan seems to emerge as an independent force in its own right after the decline of Pagan.

Frasch then continues[305]:

> The connection with Sri Lanka is now corroborated by an independent source: a recently discovered inscription of the year AD 1256 reports that king Alomapyu visited Sri Lanka, perhaps in order to invite monks to help in purifying the *sangha* of Arakan....In conclusion, it should be added that this thirteenth century mission was one of several such contacts mentioned in the *Minyazakyi-Aye-sadan*, an eighteenth century chronicle from Arakan. This well-established relationship with Sri Lanka seems to be the reason why at the close of the seventeenth century the Sinhalese king... sent a mission to Arakan and not to the far more important Theravada kingdoms of Thailand or Burma (both Upper and Lower), in order to find monks willing to participate in a reform of the Sinhalese *sangha*.... The ports of Lower Burma not only handled the the overseas trade of Pagan, but also served as gateways to the Buddhist communities on the opposite side of the Bay of Bengal.

---

[304] See later.

[305] Frasch 2002.

> Arakan, in contrast, was more or less cut off from central Burma by the Arakan Yoma, but was in turn much more open to to Bengal. By manoeuvring between these two poles, the rulers of Arakan seemingly managed to preserve their independence to a fairly large degree. This they made manifest by issueing their own coins and by undermining the claim of Pagan to religious superiority.

Frasch adds further[306]:

> ... Most of what we know about Arakan during the Pagan period up to now comes from the Burmese chronicles, which in this particular case refers to the *Glass Palace Chronicle*.... The Twin Thin Taikwun Mahasithu, represents the heightened interest for Arakan which had just been conquered when he wrote his *New Chronicle* (*Yazawin-thit*) in the 1790s. One of his sources for the relations between Arakan and Pagan, and in particular for describing how a rightful heir was restored to the throne of Arakan by the king of Pagan, was the *Yakhaing Minthami Egyin*, a 15th century historical ballad. Working forty years later, the compilers of the *Glass Palace Chronicle* had additional texts such as a "*Chronicle of Arakan*" at their disposal from which they could draw their information, but they would of course pick out only what was important for them. In other words, they refered to "big history", political events and inter-state relations which would generally mean military contest. Accordingly, we learn about Anawrahta's struggle to obtain the Mahamuni image, the restoration of Lekya-min-nan to the throne of Arakan by King Alaungsithu along with the king's visit to Manaung Island, and, finally, the vain attempt of Macchagiri (obviously a part of or a synonym for Arakan) to regain its former independence when the Pagan kingdom began to fall apart (GPC, p. 65–67, 86, 133–4, 162 and 165–6)... . Between the lines, it also appears that Arakan was vital to the communication with Bengal and India. The most important place on the subcontinent was Bodhgaya, but closer to Burma was the neighbouring city and state of Patikkera in southeast Bengal whose ruler had found himself involved in Pagan politics on several

[306] Frasch 2002.

> occasions, once as the grandfather of King Alaungsithu and later as the assassin of King Narathu. Giving his daughter in marriage to Alaungsithu shows that the king of Pattikera at least temporarily acknowledged the suzerainity of Pagan. In this way, the authors created the impression that Arakan was a tributary state that had to send its princesses to the Pagan court as a kind of tribute or else fight for its independence... .

As far as Arakan-Bengal relations were concerned Arakan had always acted as an independent state; even when under Pagan. From the eleventh century onwards it became a formidable commercial ally of eastern Bengal. Historically speaking, Arakan partcipated more in the politics of Bengal than in those of Burma. By the sixteenth century it evolved into an independent state that formed a sensitive interface in the Bengal-Tripura contest for commercial supremacy and political control in south-eastern Bengal. This contest was for control of the riverine trade route in the north-east that sent goods both by way of sea and overland to China. The conflict was complicated by the entry of the Hindu rajas of deltaic Bengal into the struggle between the Bengal sultans, the Raja of Tripura and the Arakanese for a share of the Bay trade. The rajas of deltaic *samatata* used the Portuguese to rid themselves of the Arakanese threat; Kedar Rai 'gave' Sandwip to the Portguese in an attempt to counter growing Arakanese political power in that region. The economic aspect should not be overlooked here; in face of the growing Arakanese commercial threat the rajas of the port-towns of *samatata* preferred to strengthen commercial alliances with the Portuguese whose trade in the Bay offered vast oppurtunities for the little martime city states of deltaic Bengal[307].

In the seventeenth century, commercial parameters changed; the China trade in South Asian waters was over and the Portuguese commercial threat in the Bay worried both the Mughals and the Arakanese. Arakan became crucial to the Mughals as the latter sought to contain the growing Portuguese commercial threat to the far east'. Arakan participated increasingly in the politics of Mughal Bengal in the seventeenth century and formed a vital part in the political triangle involving the Portuguese, the Mughals and the Arakanese in Bengal. Older allies of the Portuguese, the sultans and the rajas of Bengal had been destroyed. By 1607 the

---

[307] See later and Mukherjee, Rila, *Merchants and Companies in Bengal: Kasimbazar and Jugdia in the Eighteenth Century*, New Delhi, Pragati Publications.

Portuguese were expelled from Chattagram and Dianga by the Arakanese. In 1613 de Brito, leader of the little' Portuguese commercial empire in Syriam, was killed by the Mons Burmese. The Mughals expelled the Portuguese from Hugli in 1632. It therefore seems that both the Mughals and the Arakanese perceived the Portuguese as a commercial threat in the seventeenth century Bay world simultaneously. It appears that the Mughals followed the policy of using the Arakanese against the Portuguese in an attempt to free eastern Bengal from Portuguese presence. Sandwip was liberated from the Portuguese and given over to Raja Salim of Arakan as a jagir. Indeed the *Baharistan-i-Gaybi* confirms this and tells us that the Arakanese king frequently abandoned his domains in eastern Bengal to face the threat emanating from Burma[308]. Manrique's dreams of a second Portuguese commercial empire in the Bay based on Arakan, one that would ultimately expel the Mughals from Bengal and engross all trade in the Bay, has to be seen in this context.

In the sixteenth century there was a quadrilateral conflict for power between the rulers of Bengal (the Husain Shahi sultans and then the Mughals), the local factor (the rajas), the external force (either Tripura or the Portuguese) and Arakan. For example, at the time of the Mughal conquest of Bengal, Tripura came into collision with Arakan and the Portuguese there. The collision was for the control of Chattagram. This port to the south of Tripura was an economic lifeline for the Manik dynasty of Tripura. But we have seen that Chattagarm was also a lifeline for Arakan and in 1587 Tripura was squeezed in from two sides: by the Mughals to the west and by the Arakanese to the east[309].

In the seventeenth century the local factor (indigenous rulers) and Tripura as external factor were removed, now there was a triangular conflict between the Mughals, the Portuguese and the Arakanese. At both times, the Arakanese stance assummed crucial importance.

Finally we come across an interesting nomenclature for Arakan that attests to that country's similarity with Bengal[310]:

> On the one hand there are the sources relating to the conquest of *Macchagiri* ('Fish Mountain') which probably refers to the dominion of the *Saks,* located somewhere in the northern

[308] See The Arakan Connection and the East in Mukherjee, *Merchants and Companies*, etc.

[309] Mackenzie, Alexander, 1884, *The North East Frontier of India*, Reprint, 2005, introduced by B.K. Roy Burman, New Delhi, Mittal Publications: 270.

[310] Frasch 2002.

> Arakan hills/Lower Patkai Range. Two inscriptions report the conquest of this region by King Alaungsithu presumably in the late eleventh century. Although both are copies, they seem to be corroborated by the Burmese chronicles which state that King Alaungsithu had the head of 'the Kadon, ruler of the Thets,' brought before him. A century later, King Narapatisithu in his Dhammayazika inscription listed *Macchagiri* among the places that had been "conquered" (*naing-ngan*) (Pl. I 20 = OBI 1, p. 68, l. 9; U Tin Htway 1974). The *Saks* tried to free themselves from Pagan overlordship in the last quarter of the thirteenth century, but obviously in vain.... (but) Arakan might have enjoyed much greater freedom than the Burmese chronicles would have us believe.

Fish Mountain' or Machhagiri as synonym for Arakan underscores both the economic activity of the area which was based on fishing and its material culture: a fish based diet; a habit specific to the Bay coast more than any other, especially in Bengal and Arakan. This synonym may also be a reference to the predominant economic activity in this part of the eastern Indian Ocean-sea fishing and commerce in both fresh and dried fish-that set it apart from other regions around the Bay. We shall see later that the Mughal despised this fish-eating land. This did not prevent them, however, in partakng of its material riches.

The Growing Importance of Arakan

As an independent force Arakan rises in history, we have already noted, between the fifth and eighth centuries when the Chandras ruled there. It was then absorbed into the kingdom of Pagan. While a part of Pagan, Arakan nevertheless maintained a distinct identity. Interactions with eastern Bengal were frequent. After the decline of the inland centre of Pagan at the end of the thirteenth century the kingdom of Arakan took on a more definite political shape.

In the early 1430s, when Nasir-al-Din Mahmud was reigning at Gaur, King Narameikhla established the centre and port of Mrauk-U. It is claimed that Narameikhla intended this to be more than just a symbolic gesture affirming his return from exile at Gaur. Although Narameikhla had reclaimed the throne of Arakan with Bengal's help, terrotrial struggles continued with Bengal in the west and Tripura in the north throughout the fifteenth century under the two succeeding kings, Min Khari (1434–59) and Ba Saw Phru (1459–82).

The great age of Mrauk-U started when Min Ba consolidated Mrauk-U polity in the middle of the sixteenth century (1530s and 1540s), and built an elaborate system of defences for the town[311]. While Mrauk-U now became a centre of a pure Theravada Buddhism (in which close relations with Sri Lanka, trade and pilgrimage played a role)[312], it also became a centre for Islamic–Sufi and Firdausi-practices in religion. Muslim cuisine influenced Arakan and Islamic litterateurs settled there and composed poems in Bengali. In short an enlightened zone of a high and literate Bengali Muslim culture flourished from Bengal to Arakan by the sixteenth century and the great age of Mrauk-U lasted until the reign of Sandathuhamma (1652-84). Sanjay Subrahmanyam has called this 'persianization'[313] and he has also linked the presence of Persians at Arakan to state formation through the mechanism of mercantilism[314].

Indeed the Persian influence was visible not just in cuisine, literature and politics, it was also evident in architecture. Gutman tells us that in the Htu-Kan-Thein friezes at Mrauk-U the tunics worn by the men were similar to the *kuleh* and the *qaba* worn by Persian aristocrats at the time. The Shit-Thawng shrine of Mrauk-U, known as the '80000 images' shrine and built by Min Ba in 1536, was similar in architecture to the mosques at Gaur[315]. Leider however contests the idea of an uniform and progressive Islamisation of Arakan from the fifteenth century as false. He notes that this view emanated from earlier writings such as that of Phayre and was furthered conditioned by those historians who used Persian and Bengali sources, and claims that the Islamization was superficial. Within Arakan, he says, Arakanese usage and not Islamic mores, continued to predominate[316].

---

311 Subrahmanyam,Sanjay, 2005, *Explorations in Connected History: From the Tagus to the Ganges*, New Delhi, Oxford University Press. See 'Dutch Tribulations in Seventeenth Century Mrauk-U': 200–247.

312 This affirms our position where we noted that Islam did not totally displace other religious circuits.

313 "Persianization and Mercantilism" in Bay of Bengal History, 1400–1700' in Subrahmanyam, Sanjay, 2005, *Explorations in Connected History: From the Tagus to the Ganges*, New Delhi, Oxford University Press: 45–79.

314 See Subrahmanyam, Sanjay, 1992, 'Iranians Abroad : Intra Asian Elite Migration and Early Modern State Formation', *The Journal of Asian Studies*, Vol. LI (2): 340–62.

315 Gutman, Pamela, 2001, *Burma's Lost Kingdoms: The Splendours of Arakan*. See pp. 118–19, 95.

316 Leider, 2005: 100–1, 105–6.

Arakan was a littoral society par excellence; moreover it was a littoral society on which a state based itself, totally, and uncompromisingly, in terms of its political economy. Manrique has left us this description of Mrauk-U, called frequently the 'City of Arracan'[317]:

> A large swiftly flowing river traverses the city, separating out into many branches throughout its area. Most of its streets, therefore, were navigable by large and small vessels which formed the principal means of traffic, both public and private. Along these watery roads they carried for sale every kind of substance, rice, locally made wines, meat, fish, fresh, salted and dried, ghi, vegetables, fruit and other articles of food; besides this, various articles of merchandise and of household use… . There were … many places called Bazaars, in which the same articles could be obtained.

The material culture of Arakan was conditioned by its proximity to the coast. 'The greater number of houses in the city are made of bambus, which, as I have already noted, are strong canes often of great thickness. These cane houses are covered with palm leaves, intertwined, known as olas…Not a single nail is used, strong ligatures being employed instead, formed of betas, or Bengal canes, as we call them in Portugal…A house bound together with these reed ligatures, if it has wooden supports, lasts for twelve to fifteen years'[318].

But Mrauk-U was not just a littoral city, it was also backed by mountains. Some thirty years after Manrique, Linschoten ascended the mountains behind Mrauk-U and reported that he saw the golden roofs of the palace, many pagodas, lakes, fish ponds, orchards, and country houses[319].

To take up Manrique's narrative again[320]:

> This great city stands in a lovely valley, some fifteen leagues wide, wholly enclosed by high rocky mountains, which serve as natural fortifications, making artificial defences unnecessary. The inner ranges of these mountains, wherever necessary, have been cut away to form gateways leading from their

---

[317] *Travels of Fray Sebastian Manrique 1629–1647*, Luard, C.E., London, Hakluyt Society, 1967: 205.

[318] *Ibid.*: 208–09.

[319] Linschoten, *Voyages*, ed. Tiele and Bernard, London, 1885, In 10 vols. see i: 167.

[320] Manrique: 205.

summits to the plains. Forts have been erected above them provided with artillery

Arakan's agriculture depended on the Kaladan and Lemro river systems. So did its commerce. There was a sensitive interface between the city and the river: 'This river reaches the sea at two points, at the post of Oriatan on one side and on the other at Dobazi, where there are settlements of merchants of various nationalities, most of them being Maumetans…At high tides the sea enters the city at seven gates with great force and retreats in similar fashion. The force of these tides varies with the height of the sea at full moon; at the full moon it is a sight worth seeing to watch the small boats called balones enter and leave the gates'[321].

Manrique put the population of the city at around 160000 inhabitants, excluding the foreign merchants. He noted that there were many such merchants due to its great trade with Bengal, Masulipatam, Tenasserim, Martaban, Achin and Jakarta. Portuguese, Pegus, Burmese, Japanese, Bengalis and Mughals formed the chief foreign nationalities in Mrauk-U[322].

The location of Mrauk-U was not the best. It was located on a fairly rocky and inhospitable coast, the town itself was some sixty miles away from the coast. The port and harbour were at some distance, but the town itself was also accessible to the standard ships of the day through its numerous creeks and lakes. Mrauk-U was a maritime city *par excellence*.

Until the sixteenth century Arakan exercised great influence on the politics and economy of Bengal. In the seventeenth century Arakan became particularly crucial for the commerce of Bengal as seen by Europeans, as we just noted from Manrique's testimony. There were two other states besides Arakan that also interacted with Bengal: Ava to the north east and Pegu further south. Arakan shared a very fluid border in the north with Ava and a more defined, but equally shifting, border with Pegu (or Burmah) in the south, as we have already noted before.

In the seventeenth century this area, today comprising the nation state of Myanmar, broke down. Around 1685 Ava conquered Pegu and the new empire stretched from Chattagram to China. In 1735, things changed and Pegu drove out Ava. In the same year the Ostend Company was chased out of Bankibazar and sought refuge in Pegu. In 1756–7 King Alompra of Ava

---

[321] *Ibid.*: 208.

[322] *Ibid.*: 216–17.

rebelled against Pegu and declared himself king of the region. After his death in 1760 the crown passed to his son Kandropa. In 1769, facing an uncertain future in Bengal-and seeing the writing on the wall-the FEIC considered securing trading privileges at Rangoon[323]. This was of course part of Chevalier's grand scheme which had been initiated by Dupleix a quarter of a century before. By the 1780s Arakan no longer existed. Burma had swallowed it up. Thus ended almost a thousand years of the independent existence of the kingdom of Arakan, southeast Bengal's neighbour, her old ally who had turned into her enemy.

Trade and Politics in the Eastern Indian Ocean

We saw earlier that the link between agriculture and the emergence of the state is not always self evident; nor is there any evidence to prove that only agricultural activities underpin a commercial network. Having delineated the difference in the political economies of the states in the western and eastern Indian Ocean let us see in greater detail how the policies of inland agrarian empires-for the eastern Indian Ocean had more such than the west-affected commercial networks emanating from their territories. Did the states in the eastern Indian Ocean impede or facilitate the furtherance and intensification of such networks?

Politics in the eastern Indian Ocean during our period was dominated by China. Chinese commerce, passing through the South East Asian ports, directly impacted on South Asian commerce in the Bay of Bengal. As noted earlier the early medieval period witnessed a kind of 'trade revolution' in the Bay world. As far as the interactions of China with the kingdoms in the Bay are concerned-the Cholas on the Coromandel, and states in Orissa and Bengal-one can find emporia style trading emerging from the late T'ang (ninth century) and continuing through the Song (960–1279) to peak in the Yuan (1279–1368) and early Ming (1368–1435) periods. From being a stopping point on other trade networks, Bengal initiated a direct Arakan-China-Burma-Malacca-Java trade. Bengal trade possibly expanded further; an eleventh century Bengali inscription has been found in Japan.

In the twelfth century the establishment of Mongol states in Central Asia cut off Chinese expansion landwards and forced China to conduct all cultural and commercial exchanges by sea. Around 1127 35% of tributes to China came in by land and 65% by sea. By the thirteenth century all

[323] Sonnerat, M. *Voyage Aux Indes et a la Chine*, Paris, MDCCC LXXXII: 38–44.

tributes came by sea[324]. In the Yuan period (1279–1368)–the time when Ibn Batuta visited Bengal and China-merchants in China controlled the government economy[325]. A vibrant Bengal-China trade dates from this period. We must note, however, that this China-India trade did not always partake of the old Buddhist network of tribute routes; Zheng-He was Muslim, most of the Chinese shipowners and traders too were Muslims. Indeed, in the fourteenth century Ibn Batuta left for China from Calicut in a Muslim junk manned by a Muslim crew.

But it is worth keeping in mind that the old Buddhist maritime route was adhered to largely in the Bay, even by the Chinese Muslims. Therefore the three hundred years of Islamic domination in Bengal from the thirteenth to the sixteenth centuries as well as the Islamisation of the Indonesian archipelago in the early sixteenth century, while signalling the end of the Buddhist world, nevertheless maintained to a great extent the commercial equilibrium of the Bay. Within Bengal the Ilyas Shahi sultans, in their attempts to develop the Bengal-China trade, actually fostered old Buddhist trading networks. After the Muslims came the first Europeans-the Portuguese. The Portuguese occupation of Malacca in 1511 was surely a cataclysmic event, but in the main the Portuguese maintained the commercial equilibrium of the eastern seas and even continued and developed older networks between Bengal, Ceylon and Pegu.

In the fourteenth century the trade of the Bay and of the Indian Ocean was boosted because of the Mongol and Ottoman campaigns in Central Asia. Byzantium declined and the ports on its shores suffered. The pattern of long distance trade underwent a change. Traditional overland routes between Byzantium and Central Asia declined and in their place sprang a vast maritime network that linked China directly to the markets of the Red Sea and East Africa. The ports of South Asia, especially those of the Malabar (Calicut) and the Coromandel (Nagapattinam and Kayal), now occupied a central place in this East-West trade. The world of emporia trading intensified in the Indian Ocean!

Nevertheless, the fluctuating fortunes of its great behemoth, China, dictated commercial fortunes in this region to a great extent. It seems that the circulation of goods received a boost in the eastern Indian Ocean when China actively pursued a commercial policy. While eastern India was known to the Chinese from early times (certainly by the time

[324] Ray, Haraprasad, 1993, *Trade and Diplomacy in India-China Relations-a Study of Bengal During the Fifteenth Century*, New Delhi, Radiant: 21–22.

[325] *Ibid.*: 22.

of the Mauryas)[326] a direct China-Bengal trade started only in the fifteenth century. While this took place initially through the Cheng-He voyages, a lot of the China-Bengal trade was since carried on independently thereafter[327]. Bengal occupied third place (four Chinese missions) in terms of Chinese missions after Calicut (eight Chinese missions) and Cochin (six) but it is significant that Bengal outranked all other South Asian states in terms of export items (twenty four as opposed to Calicut's twenty two) and in the number of missions (fourteen) sent to China[328]. The last is not surprising; the ports of the Malabar had already viable trading partners in the East African countries while developing the China trade-and through it a sizeable South East Asian trade-was Bengal's only hope of commercial success. This explains Bengal's active China policy.

One area where Bengal scored in exports over other regions in South Asia was in its cotton textiles. During the Ming period there was an excessive demand for cotton within China. Chinese cotton was not suitable, the Bengal *bafta* was, and the cotton textile trade developed accordingly. The major part of the demand for cotton came from the Chinese army and the Chinese government allowed its subjects to pay taxes in the form of cotton cloth. Moreover it itself undertook to pay the salaries of the troops partially in cotton which it bought against horses at the Yunnan border[329].

There was yet another reason for the encouragement of the Bengal-China trade in Bengal's polity in the fifteenth century. China was welcomed as both trading partner and political ally because at this time Bengal was isolated on its western frontiers. Threatened by the hostile Jaunpur and Delhi sultans and cut off from upper India, Bengal was left to her own devices. It was necessary to find both an active ally and new sources of revenue. Bengal's vast hinterland with its prosperous agriculture could support numerous artisans and traders. Cotton production and trade with China was thus promoted by the Ilyas Shahis to counter their isolation from the gangetic plain in the fifteenth century.

---

[326] The southern silk route through Assam and Nagaland to Yunnan via Burma.

[327] Ray, Haraprasad, 2003: 114, Ray, Haraprasad, 1999, *India SouthEast Asia and China: Some Historical Issues, Professor Adhir Chakravarty Memorial Lecture 1998*, Calcutta, Centre for Archaeological Studies and Training and Ray, Haraprasad, 1993.

[328] Ray, Haraprasad, 2003: 115.

[329] Ray, Haraprasad, 2003: 116–117.

Evidence of Indo-Chinese contacts comes from numismatic studies as well. It is striking that 'lion type' coins belonging to the period of Jalal-ud-Din have been found at Islampur in North Dinajpur in 1981. They were struck mostly at the Chattagram mint. The 'lion' on these 'lion type' coins may well have been the giraffe (kilin) presented to the Chinese emperor. It has also been suggested that the fire oozing lion may well have been a dragon. These 'lion type' coins were probably struck in honour of the Chinese emperor who allied with Bengal in the latter's struggle against Jaunpur in 1420–21. The lion motif-called the Indo Chinese motif-was also used by a previous Ilyas Shahi sultan, Ghiyath al Din Azam Shah[330].

In the fifteenth century two decisive events in the western and eastern Indian Ocean radically altered Chinese maritime and commercial policy towards India. One was that the Chinese were thrown out from the west coast of India. The second was that the Chinese now abandoned Bengal and located themselves on the Coromandel coast. The expulsion of the Chinese from Calicut around the middle of the fifteenth century (through pressure from Muslim merchants in Gujarat) indicates that Gujarat was abrogating to itself the key commercial position in western India. In its control of trading routes to Africa, the Red Sea and the Persian Gulf Gujarat brooked no competition; the ports of Malabar were henceforth supposed to function as sub-ports in the grand trading networks that emanated from Gujarat[331]. The Chinese were thus pushed back into the Bay. Their relocation to Nagapattinam on the Coromandel, their abandonment of Bengal ports, can be explained by the fact that from 1459 Chattagram, the premier port of Bengal, was no longer independent; it had been conquered by Tripura. Without disembarking at Chattagram journey into Bengal was difficult. Ma Huan tells us that from Samudra (North Sumatra) a journey to Chattagram took 20 days (1952 km) with the south westerly monsoon. From there one hired smaller boats to go to Suvarnagram which took 4 to 5 days (a distance of between 256–80 km) and thence overland to Pandua by road which took 7 days, being a distance of 320 km[332]. Historically, too, the Chinese had long associations with Nagapattinam. In the late ancient period they had built shrines and monasteries in this area.

---

330 See Sinha, Sutapa, 'Coin Hoards of the Bengal Sultans: Anatomy of the Hoards' in Gautam Sengupta ed. 1997–99, *Pratna Samiksha*, V. 6–8, Calcutta, Directorate of Archaeology and Museums: 136–242. See pp. 225–7.

331 See later.

332 Ray, Haraprasad, 1993: 48, 51.

The loss of Chattagram in the fifteenth century was catastrophic for Bengal. Bengal had no other comparable port with which to conduct a profitable trade with China. Chattagram had not only been a transhipment port; it had also integrated the regional produce of the hinterland into the Bengal-China trade[333]. It would only become a part of Bengal once more in 1516 when Ala-ud-Din Husain Shah conquered Chattagram and thus opened up Bengal's eastern outlet again. But by that time the Chinese trade had tapered off; what trade was conducted was undertaken by the ports of the Coromandel.

The sixteenth century saw the withdrawal of the Chinese from the Bay of Bengal, for reasons that are still not clear. However Angela Schottenhammer's study of medieval Zaitun suggests that although from the late T'ang period trade was considered a royal enterprise and merchants were given a corresponding status in Chinese society, politics (state maritime policies), economy (cash crop and craft production) and the individual (the merchant in this context) had not become fully integrated[334]. Indeed there can be a fundamental variance between the land bound attitude of the centralised state which sees maritime trade purely as a revenue earning exercise when needed and fails to make effective policy decisions to further it, and the attitude of the merchant who needs a facilitating environment to conduct his business. Chinese fiscal policy, its notable lack of silver, and repeated introduction of paper money in the T'ang, Song and Ming periods to combat this shortage without fixing appropriate exchage rates between it and the old metallic currency, effectively hindered trade. Agrarian and maritime interests clashed, often to the detriment of commerce.

The Islamic states around the western Indian Ocean placed a greater degree of emphasis on the urban nature of their economy. Lapidus comments[335]:

> Urbanisation, economic change and the formation of new communities in turn made available resources for the organisation of a new and powerful empire and the new elites of city and empire gave birth to new forms of Islamic religion and imperial culture.

---

[333] There seems to have been no great port in Bengal in the early medieval period other than the much debated Samandar (see later). Moreover see the section on port evolution earlier where I argue that it is necessary for a port to develop and command its hinterland sufficiently for it to evolve from a mere transhipment port in a network to one playing a more substantive role in commercial networks.

[334] 'The Maritime Trade of Quanzhou (Zaitun) from the Ninth through the Thirteenth Century' in Himanshu Prabha Ray ed. 1999, *Archaeology Of Seafaring: The Indian Ocean in the Ancient Period*, New Delhi, Pragati Publications: 271–290.

[335] Lapidus, Ira M., 1988, *A History of Islamic Societies*, Cambridge: 37.

This new imperial culture grew first around Arab garrison settlements in the conquered lands. Commercial activities were given priority. Agriculture was promoted around such areas through irrigation. Next followed city building efforts through mosques, gardens, libraries and other public monuments. The extra cash needed to finance these works came in through profits from overseas trade. Nevertheless, initial funding for the conquest states came from agricultural tax. In Basra, Kufa, Mosul and al-Wasit marshes and swamps were drained (around Kufa), irrigation was undertaken in the Upper Euphrates region, date palm forests were planted around Basra and the salt marshes east of Basra were claimed by the caliphs, nobility and Arab governors. Slaves were brought in from East Africa to undertake these works.

But we need to keep three things in mind when discussing agricultural developments in Islamic lands. (1) Agricultural development and commercial undertakings were constantly set back by pastoralism and nomadic attacks. (2) Agricultural development was undertaken selectively. It took place around the garrison towns and not everywhere. (3) Agricultural development was harnessed to the needs of the conquest states. *Iqta, timar, tuyul* and *jagir* were grants to support the ruling elite. The tax revenues of Syria and Egypt paid the salaries of the Sultan and Mamluk officials. *Kharaj* and *jizya*, the land and poll tax, as well as the endowment of *waqfs*, completed this edifice. (4) Peasants, when allowed to keep their lands, were taxed up to 50%[336]. This was indeed heavy especially since the lands around the western Indian Ocean were not always fertile, as we have seen earlier. A good example of heavy taxation was the Ottoman Empire. (5) In general agricultural development followed political expediency. The net result of Arab conquests was prosperity in Iran, a redistribution of the pattern of development in Iraq and the economic decline of Syria, Mesopotamia and Egypt.

The importance of international trade to these Islamic empires was emphasised[337].

> Despite conservative intentions, the Arab conquests…set in motion vast changes in patterns of international trade, urban commerce and agriculture.

States in the western Indian Ocean based themselves mainly, we have already seen, on transhipment trade. Nevertheless a certain amount of

---

[336] *Ibid.*: 45.

[337] *Ibid.*: 45.

agriculture was bound to enter this trade. These came mainly from North Africa, Arabia and Turkestan. In Spain, technology in Valencia's irrigation was boosted through the distribution of water by a fixed time flow. This greatly increased agricultural productivity. Similarly, Almoravid Tunisia flourished under Islamic rule until the thirteenth century. Palm, olive, date, grape and figs entered international trade. Towns emerged as centres of ceramic and textile production. Control over Sudanese gold routes and access to the trade routes of the Sahara and the Mediterranean facilitated this entry into international trade even further. Marinid Morocco presents a similar story. There was a temporary setback in the fifteenth century when its control over the southern sector of the Sahara-Sudan routes faced competition from Mali and its Mediterranean trade faced competition from the Osmanlis. In 1591 Morocco conquered Sudan and recovered temporarily. It became once again an important importer of South Asian spices.

In their nature the North African states were centralised state regimes with a sufi led rural population, much as in South Asia, basing themselves on maritime and overland trade. But in the sixteenth century the trade of the North African states suffered due to competition in international maritime trade from the Portuguese and Dutch. In general the North African states were shortlived because they were highly susceptible to changing patterns of trade and the rise of new tribal movements. Indeed they have been called 'cultural islands in a sea of Berber populations'[338].

In Turkestan (Transoxania, Khwarizm and Farghana) agriculture flourished in oasis cities such as Bukhara and Samarqand. These cities linked the commerce of China, India, Afghanistan, Iran and Russia upto the Black Sea. The Chinese exchanged tea, silk and porcelain against horses, cattle and Russian products such as furs. Here too the surplus from agriculture went into trade. Profits from trade supported the political and religious elite. The state apparatus under the Mings from 1368 to 1644 absorbed Muslims as astronomers, diviners, soothsayers, translators, sailors, postal officials and caravaners.

In East Africa the Islamic trading states of Malindi, Mombasa, Zanzibar, Sofala, Kilwa and Mogadishu rose by the thirteenth century and played a vital role in linking the maritime trade of South Asia with the interior of Africa. But this area was devastated when the Cape Route to

---

[338] *Ibid.*: 376.

Asia was discovered by the Portuguese in 1498. Kilwa, the most prominent trading city, surrendered to d'Almeida in 1505. By 1530 the Portuguese controlled the East African coast. There was a temporary revival of Asian traffic in 1650 when Oman expelled the Portuguese from the Persian Gulf region, attacked Pemba and Zanzibar in 1652 and took Mombasa in 1696. There was a corresponding revival in trade between the Persian Gulf, East Africa and South Asia at the end of the seventeenth century[339] and we are tempted to relate this trade revival with the Mughal desire to revive Lahori Bandar as a Mughal port at the same time.

States in the eastern Indian Ocean had less of a similar heritage of the combination of agrarian and commercial economic bases as in the western Indian Ocean. When the Portuguese captured Malacca in 1511 there was a network shift to Samudra, then Achin and Patani. The western Indian Ocean was dominated at this time by the mighty ports of Aden, Mogadishu, Malindi, Hormuz, Aleppo, Alexandria, Damascus, Amman, Beirut, Cairo, Dhofar, Calicut, Cochin and Mecca-all of which had a considerable stake in long distance trade. In contrast, the eastern Indian Ocean was dominated by inland agrarian economies such as China, Ava, Vijaynagar and Pagan as well as by the ports of Arakan, Pegu, Bengal, Champa, Java, Malacca, Ceylon, Samudra, Palembang, and Pahang-all of whom had less stake in long distance trade than the port-towns of the western Indian Ocean.

In the east, agriculture was more important in the economy than in the case of states in the west. Also certain other factors may have hindered a development of a fully commercialised economy as in the west. The main one, of course, was the fact that agrarian and mercantile interests were equally matched in the eastern region. Because both interests were in equilibrium, no one dominant interest could emerge that would lead to the intensification of maritime activities beyond a certain point. There was no steadfast commitment to the development, continuance and furthering of mercantile networks as in the cases of states in the western Indian Ocean. Again, islamization occurred late in South East Asia. The Malay and Indonesian states only converted to Islam in early sixteenth century. China was never an Islamic state although it drew upon the expertise of Muslims in seamanship and navigation. Further investigation is needed to see whether this impeded the development of mercantile networks, however the cases of Srivijaya and then Malacca in history suggest intense participation in both Buddhist and Islamic networks. But both Srivijaya

[339] *Ibid.*: 530.

and Malacca had limited hinterlands and could not transform themselves into ports that drew the regional produce of their own hinterland into maritime trade. Yet again, these states, called the Indo-Malay states, were never as islamicised as the states of the western Indian Ocean. They functioned with earlier vestiges of tribalism, Buddhism and Hinduism. While Islam was woven into the state fabric the symbols of state authority and legitimacy depended still on the heritage of Buddhist and Hindu concepts. One has to remember that states in South East Asia were never conquered by Islamic tribal peoples and that their ethos was fundamentally different to the mercantile ethos of rulers in states of the western Indian Ocean.

Finally, political fragmentation rather than imperial unity, was the rule in the eastern Indian Ocean. A certain amount of unity, either in terms of intensification or in terms of a long span over time, as in the case of the Cholas, could help maritime expansion. The one exception was China which had a maritime vision. This was visible in maritime activities during the T'ang, Han, Song, Yuan and Ming periods.

Sun[340] records three periods of particularly active trade in the eastern Indian Ocean, specially between Burma and China. The first occurred after the Yuan conquest at the end of the thirteenth century. The second occurred in late fourteenth and early fifteenth century. The third phase, which does not concern us here, occurred at the end of the eighteenth century. We should note that the first two phases coincide with the increased trade that we noted for the Bay of Bengal in the early medieval period. Contacts between Bengal and Arakan and then between Bengal-Ava-Arakan-Lower Burma-China by land and sea route intensified between the thirteenth to the fifteenth centuries.

These trading cycles reflect the commercialisation of the economy that was taking place all over the eastern Indian Ocean. From the tenth century, increasing trade between ports had led to a portion of local produce from the hinterlands of each of the ports supplementing luxury trade items. As the 'trade revolution' grew in scope along the eastern Indian Ocean, more and more regional production was drawn into international trade. With the result that there soon emerged deficit areas within each regional economy. This meant, in effect, that regional trade routes now supplemented long distance trading networks. Intense commercialisation dotted the landscape in the countries of the eastern

[340] Quoted in Frank, A.G., 1998, *ReOrient: Global Economy in the Asian Age*, University of California Press and Sage/Vistaar: 102.

Indian Ocean. Lands were turned over for cash crop cultivation. Wang Ta Yuan, visiting Bengal in 1349, noticed extensive reclamation of land for farming[341]. Indeed we have evidence of markets being established in agricultural produce in Bengal from the fifth century. In the early eleventh century a 'Cambojan' bazaar (staffed by Khmer prisoners of war) was established at Lakhiyapura, on the west bank of the Rangoon River. This river flowed directly into the Bay of Bengal and was an important trade conduit. The bazaar was known as *psa krom*-the word *psa* an indication of the impact of Arab trade in south Pagan[342]. A Mon inscription of 1102 stated unequivocally that a market economy was emerging in Pagan[343]:

> Poor people who find it hard to get rice and clothing shall wear gold ornaments and fine apparel….Always the paddy shall be full in the ear. There shall be plenty of elephants, horses, water-buffaloes, cattle, pigs, goats and fowls. His majesty shall enrich every one…Poor old women who sell pots and pot lids, shall get high prices and become rich. Those who lack slaves shall have plenty of slaves. Those who lack cattle shall have plenty of cattle. Farmers who excel in planting and harrowing, shall fill their barns and granaries with paddy, millet and all manner of grain.

Anthony Reid notes for South East Asia[344]:

> The entire period 1400–1630 was one of rapid monetization and commercialization of the economy, with the most rapid expansion in the period 1570–1630. A large proportion of the population, by any contemporary standard, was drawn into production and marketing for the world economy and came to rely on long distance imports for such everyday items of consumption such as cloth, ceramics, utensils and coinage. Trade occupied a relatively high share…of Southeast Asian national income and made possible a degree of urbanization probably higher than was achieved again before the twentieth century. Within these cities were communities that devoted themselves wholly to trade and commerce…..

---

341 Bagchi, P.C., 1945, 'The Political Relations Between Bengal and China in the Pathan Period', *Viswa Bharati Annals*, I: 96–134.

342 Wicks, 1992: 124.

343 *Ibid.*: 125.

344 Reid, Anthony, 1993, *Southeast Asia in the Age of Commerce 1450–1680*. V. 2: Expansion and Crisis, New Haven, Yale Press: 129.

The spice trade was of course very important in the eastern Indian Ocean. Both Anthony Reid[345] and Ashin Das Gupta[346] have testified to the importance of this trade in maintaining the Indonesian economy in medieval times. In its turn the spice trade encouraged import of cloths from India, silver from the Amercias and Japan and copper-cash, silks and ceramics from China. The spice trade was fundamental to the commercial economy of the eastern Indian Ocean.

At the very eastern end, the economy of the Indian Ocean was held together by China. Marks says for early modern China[347]:

> Commercialization of the economy was a powerful force remaking the landscape. Not only did peasant farmers in the Pearl River delta dig up rice paddies to make way for fish ponds and mulberry tree embankments…but their consequent need for food transformed much of the agricultural land in the rest of Lingan into monocropping, export oriented rice regions…..The peasant farmers of the Pearl River delta grew non-food crops, pushing rice production into the river valleys. There, peasant farmers subsisted on sweet potatoes and maize grown on more marginal lands in the hills, shipping rice grown in paddies downstream to the Pearl River delta [However] the system as a whole was not sustainable without greater and greater inputs from outside.

Bin Wong tells us that[348]:

> The broad features of increased cash cropping, handicrafts and trade are well known in Chinese and Japanese literature…Most famous are the expanding cotton and silk industries of the Lower Yangzi region near Shanghai, the two principal handicraft industries that join rice and other cash crops to create China's richest regional economy. To feed the population of this area, rice grown in the upstream provinces of Anhui, Jianzxi, Hubei and especially Hunan and Sichuan

[345] *Ibid.*: 23.

[346] Das Gupta, Ashin and Pearson M.N. eds. 1987, *India and the Indian Ocean 1500–1800*, Oxford University Press: 243.

[347] Marks, Robert B., 1996, 'Commercialization Without Capitalism. Processes of Environmental Change in South China 1550-1850' in *Environmental History*, I, no.1: 56–82. See page 76.

[348] Wong, R. Bin, 1997, *China Transformed: Historical Change and the Limits of European Experience,* Ithaca, Cornell Press.

> moves down the Yagtzi River. Other cash crops and handicrafts, like cotton, indigo, tobacco, pottery and paper, emerge in parts of these provinces as market expansion connects increasing numbers of locales.
>
> Market expansion was most salient along the Yangzi River, but hardly limited to this vast area. In south and southeast China, cash crops and handicrafts expanded in several areas. The Pearl River delta in Guangdong produced sugar cane, fruits, silk, cotton, ironware, and oils from sesame and tung plants. Along the southeast coast, sixteenth century foreign trade ties stimulated cash crop production in tea and sugar.

This area of South China, famous for its abundant rainfall as already noted, was the earliest area to introduce commercial agriculture. It was also the natural trading partner of Bengal from very early times. But commercialisation of the economy also implies the availability of sufficient reserves of metals to undertake the monetisation that occurs sooner or later in both international commerce and regional trade. China had one major drawback in this respect. The trade of the western Indian Ocean was carried on through the gold *dinar* and the silver *dirham*. China had very little silver. The role played by metals in powering a financial revolution during this period in the Bay of Bengal is discussed in the following pages.

The World of Finance in the Bay

From the eleventh to the sixteenth centuries, the financial realm in the Bay of Bengal comprised the circulation of two types of coinage. These were Islamic and regional. The Islamic silver *dirham* spanned a vast mercantile area throughout the western Indian Ocean and was the coinage of international trade also in the east. In the east local coinages of copper, silver and gold struggled, and at times succeeded, in achieving iconic mercantile status. This depended on the fortuitous control of maritime routes under their control. But since no one region in the eastern Indian Ocean exercised maritime hegemony over any length of time, and since none of these regions had a political and religious affiliation to a single currency as in the case of the states to the west, no comparable single currency of international trade emerged in the east.

In the ninth and tenth centuries Arab travellers attested to the *dirham* being the coinage of trade on the west coast of South Asia. The *Ashka'lu-l Bila'd* or the *Kita'bu-l Masa'lik Wa-l Mama'lik* of Ibn Haukal and the *Nizhatu-l Mushtak* of al-Idrisi refer to *dinars*, *dirhams* as well as *tatari* coins circulating in twelfth century Sindh[349]. In fact Sindh and Gujarat are reputed to have stopped producing indigenous coinage and to have depended solely on the *dinar* and the *dirham*[350].

There are indications that as early as in ninth century the *tatariya* dirhams had penetrated the eastern Indian Ocean and were active in the Malay archipelago[351]. For the same century it was noted that Ruhmi, which has been identified as the Dhaka-Arakan region[352], traded in *cauris* although it possessed more troops that Gujarat as well as aloes wood, fine textiles, gold and silver and rhinos in plenty[353]. It is striking that in this testimony, despite possessing such an abundance of commercial items, eastern Bengal had not moved to a metallic currency; but this was frequently the norm in most Asian states as Wicks points out[354] Yet there is evidence of a *prakrit nagari* coin circulating in north and east Bengal in the eighth century; this coin influenced Mataram's gold and billion coinage in the ninth century[355].

Mataram was a trading empire that rose in central Java that successfully displaced Srivijaya's maritime hegemony in the Straits of Malacca. Therefore any coinage that Mataram adopted was bound to have a hegemonic value and circulate in zones beyond its natural frontiers. Conventionally, the Coromandel's links with Java have been more emphasised in history; in such a case it is surely curious that Mataram adopted a northeast Bengal style *prakrit nagari* coin as well as the mainstream *kawi* coin in use also in Java. The latter was derived from the south Indian *pallava* script[356].

---

349 Ibn Haukal: 34 and al-Idrisi: 78, Elliot and Dowson, V.1, Allahabad, Kitab Mahal, 1969 reprint.

350 Schottenhammer 1999: 277.

351 *Salsilatu-t Tawarikh* of Suleiman: 3–4, Elliot and Dowson, V.1, Allahabad, Kitab Mahal.

352 *Ibid*. Appendix A: 361.

353 Suleiman op.cit.: 5.

354 Wicks, Robert, S., 1992, op. cit.

355 Christie, 1999: 230.

356 For an extended discussion on Javanese coinage see *Ibid*: 229–39.

Denys Lombard commented[357]:

> La frappe du metal blanc semble avoir commence au Bengale au 13e siecle et c'est vers cette époque que commence dans le nord de Sumatra un monnayage d'or qui se maintiendra jusqu'au 18e siecle.
>
> (The minting of white metal seems to have started in Bengal in the thirteenth century and at the same time Sumatra started minting a currency in gold which continued until the eighteenth century, [my translation]).

By the middle of the fifteenth century, when Min Sowa Mun or Narameikhla won back the throne of Arakan with sultan Jalal ud Din's help, mint production in Bengal had advanced sufficiently. Narameikhla was accompanied by mint experts from Bengal who helped devise standardised coins for Arakan. These coins were a combination of the Islamic style prevalent in Bengal (the Kalima and the Muslim name of the Arakan king in either Persian , Arabic or Bengali was inscribed on one side) and the Buddhist (the obverse was marked with the Buddhist name of the ruler in local script). The Arakan coins issued after 1432 were mainly silver alloy coins.

On the basis of Deyell's computation of bullion trends for Bengal from the thirteenth to the sixteenth centuries[358] one can note the following:

Table 3.1 Bengal: Bullion Trends

Years	*Deyell's comments*	*Comments*
1218–1290	Exhaustion of original silver stocks. Sporadic importation of bullion	Understandable as this is the period when both the Delhi and Bengal sultanates are established. Military campaigns depleted stocks. Importation was yet to start off on a regular basis.

Contd...

[357] Lombard, Denys, 1988, 'Le Sultanat Malais Comme Modele Socio-Economique' in Denys Lombard and Jean Aubin (eds). *Marchands et Hommes d'Affaires Asiatiques dans l'Ocean Indien et la Mer de Chine 13e-20e siecles*, Paris, Editions E.H.E.S.S.: 117–124. See p.121.

[358] Deyell 1983: 213–4.

Years	*Deyell's comments*	*Comments*
1291–1357	Large inflow on regular basis. Much greater than in the thirteenth century	Period of political turmoil. Balbani rulers are succeeded by the Tughlaks in Bengal. Trade gets underway in the Bay of Bengal. East Bengal, including Dhaka, Sylhet and Maimensigh, is brought under Bengal's control. The Ilyas Shahi sultanate is established in 1339.
1358–1366	Net outflow from Bengal	Why? Zenith of Ilyas Shahi rule in Bengal; Sikandar Shah 1358-1391. No more Tughlak rule in Bengal. Sikandar issues coins from Kamrup.
1367–1390	Moderate importation sufficient to off set attrition losses	The outflow is reversed. Silver from Kamrup coming in? Sikandar Shah rules until 1391.
1390–1415	Heavy inflow, but disturbed supply. Sharp fluctuations year to year	Ghiyath-al-Din Ilyas Shah in Bengal, 1390-1411. Early period of Chinese trade. Silver coming in. Chattagarm lost for part of the time to Tripura and Arakan
1416–1429	Net outflow from Bengal	Intensive trade with China. Does this lead to a drain of silver from Bengal? Tangled status in ownership of Chattagram. Are importations affected?
1430–1492	Moderate inflow, but sporadic	Chattagram under Bengal part of the time. But also under Tripura's control, and

Contd...

Years	*Deyell's comments*	*Comments*
		this may explain the moderate inflow of specie. But the fact that specie comes in at all may be ascribed to the vitality of the overland routes from China through Ava into Bengal. Also there is increased trade and diplomacy with Arakan; this brought in silver through trade. Mint experts from Bengal develop Arakan coinage. After 1432 the new Arakan coins struck are mostly silver alloys.
1493–1533	Steady inceasing inflow of silver on a very regular basis	Period of increased westward trade from Bengal. Much trade with Malwa and Gujarat. Links with Mewar. All three had silver supplies. Moreover Chattagram is conquered by Husain Shah in 1516. The southeastern border is secured for the time being until 1538. This brought in silver through maritime trade.

One can see from the trend of bullion flows that the eastern land and sea routes were vital for the importation of bullion into Bengal. Hence control of Chattagram was crucial for the Bengal Sultanate.

The importance of the land route that led from Yung Chang Fu in Yunnan into Bengal has already been delineated. While this was vital for commerce, Deyell opines that this route was equally important for the importation of silver into Bengal.

There was no silver stock in Bengal and silver had to be imported from the only area with known bullion supplies contiguous to Bengal:

there were Kamta and Kamrup, areas that led through Burma into China. This explains Sikandar Shah's initial coinage of 1358 with the inscription that it issued from Kamrup; the accessional issue of Husain Shah mentions likewise that he was the conqueror of Kamrup and Kamta[359]. As noted; the known bullion supply to the east explains the Bengal's sultans' obsession with the eastern frontier.

That silver supplies were plentiful in this region is attested to by the fact that soon after the establishment of the Bengal Sultanate the frontier states to the north east established their own silver currencies: Tripura (1464), Ahom (1543), Koch (Kamta Kingdom, 1555), Kachar (1583) and Jaintia (1670). Nicholas Rhoades tells us in *The Coinage of Cooch Bihar* that the silver Narayani coins of Cooch Bihar were also struck at this time.

Deyell adds that not only was eastern Bengal a transmission point for bullion movement; it was also close to bullion supplies other than Assam gold and Kamrup silver. There was in the Yunnan/Burma border a known source of silver as well as knowledge of smelting and refining (metallurgy techniques were known to the Pyus of Pagan and the Nan Chao peoples of Yunnan as early as in the ninth century), and moreover there was an agent of transmission, the Tai peoples (Shans in Burma and Nan Chao in Yunnan) who controlled the route between Burma and China by virtue of their control over silver deposits (Bawdwingyi north of Ava and the silver mines north of Yung Chang Fu and Tali Fu in the Yunnan)[360]. Therefore the east, rather than North and West India, was more important to Bengal for bullion supplies. Here the overland and maritime routes from Bengal as well as the trade of the Bay acquires added significance.

We already noted that some form of political authority was necessary to establish mints, issue coins and generally organise trade. Frequently however, this was not possible; yet trade continued, especially in littoral regions. How was such a trade organised? The evidence from the littoral zone of south east Bengal–the zone that connected with the trade routes of Pundravardhana to the north and north east is discussed as follows.

After Sasanka's reign coin production fell of sharply in north eastern India. Imitation Gupta gold coins have been found exclusively in southeastern Bengal in the seventh century; in Mainamati (Comilla

---

[359] *Ibid.* 215.

[360] *Ibid.* 216–217, 220–24.

belonging to the Khadga and Deva periods. Some imitation Gupta coins have been found at Assam, on the south bank of the Brahmaputra[361]. These coins were issued by local kings who wished to continue the Gupta financial realm and utilise the name.

But the situation changes soon after. Between the seventh and tenth centuries '*Harikela*' coins were found at places as diverse as Sandoway (Arakan) and Sylhet, leading to the supposition that by that time the term '*harikela*' did not just signify the eastern most boundary of India but a whole maritime trading zone that embraced Arakan, southeast Bengal, northeast Bengal (Sylhet) and south Tripura. It is significant that for the most part the names of rulers of the region during this period is not known. These coins, called '*harikelā*' because they do not contain the name of a ruler but of a constantly growing region, are testimony to the expanding commercial frontiers of Bengal between the seventh and the tenth centuries[362].

What happened if there was no political authority to issue coinage? The answer to this comes from the trade coinage of the Chattagram area during 1538 and 1575 when there was no one effective political power in the region[363]. Deyell writes[364]:

> An unusual 'trade coinage' imitating the money of Bengal was produced in the Chittagong region throughout this period. Local agents, either officials, bankers or traders, maintained a silver currency in circulation in the area, apparently without formal political sanction from nominal suzerains. This coinage served to convert silver bullion from Burma into a currency acceptable both in local coastal trade and in Bengal proper. Production of this coinage stopped when the Arakan rajas established their own mint at Chittagong around 1575.

The other remarkable feature of the Chattagram trade coins is that they maintained the obsolete (in the sixteenth century) *tanka* weight standard rather than the new *rupiya* or rupee standard that was increasingly adopted all over Hindustan at this time.

---

361 Wicks, 1992: 76–7.

362 Wicks, 1992: 90–92. See Sharma, R.S., 2001: 128–129. Sharma extends their circulation until the thirteenth century. See too, Tarafdas 1995 : 31–56.

363 This was the period of interregnum between Husain Shahi and Mughal rule in Bengal. Bengal was under Sher Shah's and the Karrani Afghans' rule during this period. The Portuguese also 'captured' Chattagram after Sher Shah Sur.

364 Deyell, John, 1995, 'The Trade Coinage of Chittagong Region in the Mid Sixteenth Century', *J.Asiat. Soc. Bangladesh, Hum. Vol. 40, No. 2, December*: 1–29. See p.1.

Although Deyell opines that these coins were reliable as tender but 'spurious' as a message bearing medium (p.23) it is interesting that these trade coins were struck in the names of all the contending powers in the region : ranging from Sher Shah (Plate 1), Islam Shah Sur (Plate 2), Adam Humayun (Plate 9, the Arakanese governor of Ramu under Sikandar Shah of Arakan), Jalaluddin Akbar (Plate 6), Sikandar Shah (plate 18, in Bengali, Arabic and Arakanese) and so forth.

So there are two remarkable features of these coins. One, that they were not formal coins but trade coins struck to maintain trade in an area without political sanction. This underscores the importance of the commerce of this area and the strong commercial interests in the region which transcended Husain Shahi, Afghan and Suri affiliations. Two, they were struck in the outmoded *tanka* fashion rather than the new *rupiya* style prevalent in sixteenth century Hindustan. The Arakan and Tripura rulers also followed the *tanka* weight. The *tanka* continued to be the coinage of the north Bay.

This affirms our view that Chattagram was indeed the final frontier of Bengal. It was the richest of the Bengali cities in terms of revenue paying capacity. The following table gives us an idea of the revenue capacity of Chattagram.

Table 3.2 Revenues of Sixteenth Century Port Cities in Bengal[365]

City	*Dam*	*Rupiya*	*Tanka*
Chattagram	6, 649, 410	166, 235	178, 781
Suvarnagram	459, 532	11, 488	12, 355
Fathabad (Faridpur)	902, 662	22, 567	24, 270
Saptagram	234, 890	5, 872	6, 315
Tanda	4, 326, 102	108,153	116, 315

The figures are striking. At the end of the sixteenth century, Chattagram still paid the highest revenue, followed by Tanda (Gaur). The next highest revenue paying city was Fathabad, the original seat of Husain Shahi power, also on the Ganges. Suvarnagram also paid a large revenue, but most of its former glory seems to have been lost. Saptagram was the lowest revenue paying city. The 'far east' was indeed the richest area of Bengal.

[365] Calculated from *Ain-i-Akbari* in Deyell 1995: 18.

Table 3.2 also supports the view that south eastern Bengal participated in a trade of the Bay that looked more to China and Burma rather than the middle gangetic plain. Despite Portuguese presence, it was still the richest coastal region in Bengal. As referred to earlier, Sun's estimation of two very active trade cycles between China and Burma; one at the end of the thirteenth century and another in the fourteenth and fifteenth centuries is borne out by these revenue figures. Marks, Bin Wong and Reid, quoted in the preceding section, referred to the process of agricultural commercialisation occurring intensively in China and South East Asia at this time and this must have accelerated trade further.

The east, and not the north, was the decisive factor for Bengal's commerce even during this criticial period from 1538 to 1575, long after the Husain Shahis had initiated the westward shift that the Mughals were to further after 1575. By that time, of course, Chattagram was lost to Bengal.

Further east in the Indian Ocean copper coins circulated both in the Malay and Chinese worlds. In Java (and Vietnam too) copper cash was imported from China[366]. The Zaitun records mention copper as one of the principal exports[367].

But by the end of the end of the eleventh century Chinese officials noted in alarm the size and outflow of copper to overseas markets, primarily in South East Asia[368]. By the thirteenth century export of copper was first banned and then abandoned because China switched to a paper currency during the Yuan period[369].

As regards its international trade in the eastern Indian Ocean China used a bronze currency derived from the later T'angs until the tenth century[370], But trade with the western Indian Ocean was different. As early as in the twelfth century al-Idrisi named Broach on the west coast of India as the port of Chinese shipping[371]. Every time China attempted to break into the trade of the Indian Ocean she was confronted by the *dirham* which was the currency of the trading world of the western Indian Ocean.

China had a chronic shortage of silver; despite the Yunnan deposits. To offset this shortage China was forced to import silver from both the

---

366 Christie, 1999: 238. Majapahit Java adopted Chinese copper cash in late thirteenth century (wicks, 1992: 243)

367 Schottenhammer, 1999: 276.

368 Christie, 1999: 238.

369 Christie, 1999: 238.

370 Schottenhammer, 1999: 277.

371 *Nizhatu-l Mushtak* in Elliot and Dowson, V.1 , Allahabad, Kitab Mahal 1969: 87.

Arab world and Japan[372]. This was not enough, and in T'ang, Song and Yuan times China introduced a paper currency. But Ming China was increasingly monetised on a silver standard and expanded rapidly until the 1620s. But a financial system based on the silver standard was untenable given China's silver shortage (the local coinage was copper) and the Mings considered introducing a paper currency once again in 1643. This was rejected as it would aid inflation but the Manchus did introduce a limited amount of paper currency between 1650 and 1662. Introduction of a paper currency was never truly successful because inflation and counterfeiting continued in China throughout the fourteenth to the seventeenth centuries and because standardisation with international currencies and equivalence with local currencies was never worked out.

But in the course of the tribute missions from Bengal to China and the reverse throughout the fifteenth century, the Mings always sent silks, embroideries, brocades, porcelain and *paper money* to the Bengal sultans. Paper money is mentioned in the return missions of 1409, 1420, 1421, 1438, 1439[373]. Were the Chinese thereby hoping to wean other states away from a silver standard and introduce a different financial realm in the Bay of Bengal? Was silver already difficult to access?

Yet, by the sixteenth century all trade in Ming China was conducted in silver, which in turn circulated throughout the province[374]. South China was totally transformed as it exported more and more silk for silver. Rice paddies were transformed into silk growing lands to meet the growing demand for silver[375]. The situation is analogous to the process I have described elsewhere for silk production in Bengal from the sixteenth century[376]. Mulberry cultivation was introduced into Bengal

---

[372] Japanese silver exports to China were on an average seven times greater than American silver arriving by way of the Pacific (Frank, A,G., 1998, *ReOrient: Global Economy in the Asian Age*, California Press and Sage/Vistaar: 146.)

[373] Church, Sally K., 2004, '*The Giraffe of Bengal : A Medieval Encounter in Ming China*', *MHJ*, 1, January-June: 1–37. See 10, 12, 27, 28, 30.

[374] Marks, Robert B., 1997, *Tigers Rice Silk and Silt: Environment and Economy in Late Imperial South China*, New York, Cambridge University Press.

[375] *Ibid.* and also Marks Robert B. 1996, 'Commercialisation Without Capitalism. Processes of Environmental Change in South China 1550–1850' in *Environmental History*, no.1, January: 56–82.

[376] Mukherjee, Rila, *Merchants and Companies in Bengal: Kasimbazar and Jugdia in the Eighteenth Century*, New Delhi, Pragati Publications.

to bring in coinage, and as silver circulation became more intense, more and more paddy fields were converted to mulberry lands. Frank comments[377]:

> Thus, in South China the process (of commercialisation) was analogous to that in Bengal. The agricultural and settlement frontiers expanded along with their commercialization, stimulated by demand from the outside which also generated local demand-and supply-and which were financed by the inflow of new money from abroad.

This rapid commercialisation explains the Bengal nawabs' preoccupation with the import of specie as an indicator of the wellbeing of the body politic in the eighteenth century. The proper circulation of specie was likened to that of blood in the human body. Without this circulation the organism would die. Commercialisation was deemed vital to all countries of the eastern Indian Ocean by the seventeenth century. But while this commercialisation advanced rapidly, many areas in Bengal were still left without a metallic currency. Glanius mentioned the use of *cauris* ('little shells which is the money of that country') at Sandwip in 1661, when the local official changed their money[378]. Therefore the statement of the *Ain-i-Akbari*, that peasants in Bengal paid the land revenue in currency while those in Orissa paid in *cauris*, should not be taken as evidence of a uniform agrarian commercialisation all over Bengal in the seventeenth century. Indeed the southeastern part of Bengal, the area that had seen intense mercantile activities from the late ancient period, seemed a financial wasteland by the seventeenth century.

A Shortage of Silver in the North Bay:The Arakan Slave Trade in the Seventeenth Century

As early as in 1518 Min Raza, king of Arakan, offered the first official Portuguese mission under Silveira 'many goods' if the Portuguese would base their eastern Bay of Bengal trade at the ports of Arakan and not at Chattagram. This offer is evidence of the desire of the Arakan kings to develop Mrauk-U as a centre for international trade, but Arakan, essentially a landlocked country with an inhospitable shore to the south, had little interest for Europeans in the sixteenth century. The Arakanese

---

[377] Frank A.G. 1998, *ReOrient: Global Economy in the Asian Age*, California Press and Sage/Vistaar: 162.

[378] Glanius, 1682, *A Relation of an Unfortunate Voyage to the Kingdom of Bengala*, London, Henry Bonwick: 125.

were not more successful a hundred years on. In 1623 Thirithudhamma invited the Dutch to set up a factory in Arakan. The Dutch refused.

Commerce became vital for Arakan in the seventeenth century. This increased trade was an expression of the intense commercialisation that had already taken place in South East Asia and South China (see the references to Reid, Marks, Bin Wong and Frank in an earlier section). If Arakan was to derive benefits from this increased trade in the Bay of Bengal it had to pursue an aggressive mercantile policy like the rest.

In order for it to survive Arakan had to undergo agricultural commercialisation which would bring in the much needed silver it needed to pay for the goods imported from Bengal and the Coromandel in South Asia, for the commodities merchants brought in from South East Asia and for the ceramics and silk it needed from China. The consumption of imported textiles from South East Asia, iron, steel, tobacco and Chinese wares was increasing among the Arakan elite. Traders from the Coromandel, Muslim merchants, and the powerful Persian community of Masulipatnam were bringing in textiles, yarn, iron and tobacco to Mrauk-U. The Arakan rulers and the nobles were themselves drawn into this trade. If trade was to prosper, if the lovely port of Mrauk-U was to thrive, and if its merchants were to survive, some item of export had to be found.

Other than the commercial imperatives of the Bay, there was also another reason as to why Arakan needed foreign goods. Between 1599 and 1610 the Arakan state undertook its greatest territorial expansion with Portuguese help. This expansion went two ways : into the north into the Ganges-Brahmaputra delta under the control of Bengal, and into the south into the lower Irrawady delta under the control of the Toungoo rulers of Lower Burma. The Arakanese expansion brought it into direct conflict with both the Mughals and the Toungoos in the seventeenth century. Arakan became ruled by a war economy in the early seventeenth century. Guns were imported in increasingly large numbers. By 1614 when the Toungoos reconsolidated their position Arakan was pushed on the defensive. The treasury was exhausted and alternative sources of finance had to be tapped.

Apart from elephants from the interior and rice from the coastal plains, Arakan had no trading items to offer. Moreover the rice supply was uncertain due to the frequent flooding of the Kaladan and Lemro river basins. At this point entered a new item of trade-slaves. The catchment area was southeast Bengal, contiguous to Arakan and an area over which the Arakanese had considerable influence.

Arakan was thus propelled into the slave trade due to external compulsions (participation in international trade) and internal pressures (consequences of expansionary wars) in the seventeenth century. By 1620 Portuguese and Dutch demand for slaves meant that Hugli, Pipli, Chattagram-Dianga and Mrauk-U became slave ports supplying slaves to far away markets such as Batavia in the east and Goa in the west.

There was yet another reason as to why the Arakanese entered the slave trade. This was because of the chronic shortage of manpower within Arakan. Slaves were increasingly used as craftsmen. They were also used to clear jungles for cultivation in Arakan as the Arakan state fought in vain to remake their agrarian landscape on terms we have noted already for western Bengal, South East Asia, and southern China.

Finally slavery was not only necessary for solving the manpower shortage within Arakanese society. Slave ownership became a mark of status within Arakanese society. In the second half of the seventeenth century the Arakan state introduced a new variant of the slave trade. Under the new system the Arakanese nobles now claimed slaves as captured booty directly[379]. Similarly, instead of a poll tax on imported slaves the king claimed a share of the imported slaves directly. To explain this changeover it may be useful to look at Black-Michaud's typology of scarcity in feuding societies[380].

Black-Michaud divided scarcity into two types : material or that which is perceived and moral or that which is felt. A situation of 'total' scarcity-material, institutional and moral-exists in societies that shows a combination of these types of scarcities. In such societies feud (or slave raiding as in the case of Arakan) arises in response to conditions of total scarcity. It can also be a surrogate social system of its own that is conceived to make good a variety of institutional deficiencies[381]. Feud can also be a means of social control, a means of communication and a new language of dominance-submission[382]. In societies that do not evolve beyond

[379] In Subrahmanyam, Sanjay, 2005, 'Dutch Tribulations in Seventeenth Century Mrauk-U' in *Explorations in Connected History*, From the Tagus to the Ganges. A Balasore based Armenian merchant's crew was captured and distributed as slaves in the Arakan court. Dutch letter of October 30 1643: 222–3.

[380] Black-Michaud, Jacob, 1975, *Feuding Societies*, Oxford, Basil Blackwell.

[381] *Ibid.*: 159–160.

[382] *Ibid.*: 172.

a certain point raiding can be a very effective means of managing within institutional constraints.

In his study of feuding societies in the Middle East Black-Michaud noted that there was a marked difference between sedentary agricultural societies and nomadic pastoral groups as regarded both the frequency and the intensity of feuds[383]. Fighting among pastoralists was less intensive in the hostile dry seasons because then they were fully occupied by the struggle for subsistence. Similarly, in Arakan all available manpower was harnessed to agricultural needs in the spring, autumn and winter months. During the rainy season this manpower was idle. Slave raids into southeast Bengal took place mainly during the monsoons when people were not needed to work on the fields.

In the seventeenth century Arakan was not the only centre of the slave trade in the eastern Indian Ocean. Other states too participated in this trade. Towards the end of the seventeenth century, Bowrey noted, ships from Bengal arrived at Achin with slave boys and girls[384]. Achin, the city state administered by a 'Virgin Queen'[385], became a premier trade mart in the seventeenth century, with ships from Borneo and Macassar also bringing slaves there[386]. In the seventeenth century therefore a necklace of slave ports radiated over the Bay of Bengal from Pipli, Sagor, Sandwip and Chattagram in Bengal towards Achin, Kedah and Johor in South East Asia.

This trade was geared both eastwards and westwards. It was supplemented with more traditional goods such as long pepper, which was deemed better than the Kedah pepper[387], rice, oil, wheat, butter, sugar, stick lac, and textiles such as *cambayas*, *ellachas*, *rumals*, *malmals* from Bengal[388].

The slave trade was short lived. It continued throughout the seventeenth century. But in 1682 Speelman decided that the VOC would pull out of the slave trade from Arakan as there were no more slaves[389]. While

---

383 *Ibid.*: 191, 197.

384 Bowrey.: 288–9.

385 *Ibid.*: 324–5.

386 *Ibid.*: 291.

387 *Ibid.*: 277.

388 *Ibid.*: 288–9.

389 Subrahmanyam, Sanjay, 2005, 'Dutch Tribulations etc.', 242.

the Europeans pulled out of the trade at the end of the seventeenth century slave raiding was reported in southeast Bengal as late as in the beginning of the eighteenth century, but this practice was now sporadic.

Finally Meillasoux's typology of the slave catchment area as a geographically blurred zone while both the marauder area and the ultimate slave owning society acquired distinct political and geographic features[390] raises the question as to why the original cordial relation between Arakan and southeastern Bengal soured in the seventeenth century. An answer to this has been attempted at the end of this volume.

The Land and the New State in the Eighteenth Century

The foregoing presentation of the littoral history around Bengal has made evident that Bengal participated in not the 'big' histories, but in a 'little' history of the Bay. This interaction set it apart from other regions in South Asia and determined the future shape of its history. Mughal policy and then European demand rewrote Bengal's history of the later medieval period. This 'making' of Bengal was made easier by virtue of Mughal efforts at 'unmaking' Bengal, of breaking up the spatial unity of the Bay in the seventeenth century so as to hitch Bengal to the Surat-Persian Gulf bandwagon[391]. In the same century the EEIC moved westwards from Surat, through Patna, to Bengal. By the next century Company trade was firmly entrenched in Bengal and Company demand determined the 'primacy' of Bengal (and its history) in eighteenth century South Asia. In the wake of political conquests in the middle of the eighteenth century, when the British attempted to redraft the history of Bengal, the idea of the 'primacy' of Bengal was firmly established in their minds.

So far a skewed perception of Bengal and how this resulted in the idea of 'primacy' in the seventeenth and eighteenth centuries has been discussed. But what was actually happening within Bengal at this time? In 1704 an energetic new state was established. This new state firmly underscored the westward shift; its founder, Murshid Quli Khan, quietly broke away from Dhaka, which was then the capital of Mughal Bengal.

---

390 Meillassoux, Claude, 1991, *The Anthropology of Slavery: The Womb of Iron and Gold*, Chicago, University Press.

391 See Mukherjee, Rila, *Merchants and Companies* etc.(New Delhi, Pragati Publications).

Dhaka as Mughal provincial capital was emblematic of the Mughal desire to secure the 'Far Eastern' frontier and tap the commercial possibilities still existent there. Murshid Quli's shift to the west, on the other hand, was symptomatic of the desire to manage the agrarian economy of his new state based on Murshidabad and to further the Bengal-Surat trade established by the Mughals a century earlier. Murshidabad was as far away from Dhaka as possible. Old Mughal interests still predominated there. Murshidabad, on the other hand, was new territory, free from older entrenched interests. Here Murshid would have a free hand with his policies. Moreover, Murshid's shift may also have been motivated by the desire to check out the activities of the Europeans there. This area had been neglected politically in the seventeenth century. Since Gaur there had ben no capital here and Murshid faced an uphill task trying to chart out an economic policy for his new state.

Bengal, was an amorphous political entity with hazy frontiers to the east (Arakan) and north (Tirhut or Mithila). Only in the west–cut off as Bengal was from the rest of the middle gangetic plain by the Teliagarhi Pass in the north or the forests of Jharkhand in the south–and to the south itself–where Jajnagar marked the boundary between Bengal and Kalinga–was it possible to say that there was a distinct physical frontier. The frontiers to the west and south formed initially the boundaries of Murshid's new state. Bengal's fuzzy topography, its self-contained physical character amplifed further by its notoriously unstable rivers and unique delta culture, left its imprint on societal development and identity. The distinctive topography of coastal Bengal–with its rivers, deltas and marshes on the path to the sea–make it a fascinating area for maritime historians for the history of Bengal's shipping shows an intriguing mix of littoral, (riverine and coastal) and maritime activity; but it is doubtful whether it proved as alluring to a ruling class trying to impose its control on a band of recalcitrant chiefs.

Precisely because of the imprecise nature of its boundaries the local ruling class in Bengal displayed noticeably autonomous features from the very start. The Bengal zamindars' quasi-independent status and their management of the economy (frequently evinced in their control over local bazaars) had frustrated attempts on the part of the Mughals to redefine the state's relationship with both the agrarian economy and commerce in the seventeenth century[392]. More than the faujdars, it was the zamindars who collected revenue, maintained law and order, and functioned as intermediaries between the general populace and the state. It was within their domains that artisans lived and merchants worked; zamindars in Bengal occupied that grey area between actual ownership and the post of tax-collector. The zamindar now became a crucial element in the transfer of rural surplus in the form of cash to the court.

In the eighteenth century a change took place in the composition of zamindars. Instead of assessing and collecting taxes from a great number of small and scattered zamindars Murshid Quli Khan initiated the practice of contracts with a small number of very large ones for the same purpose. This meant in turn that smaller zamindaries were swallowed up under the mantle of a few big zamindaries such as Nadia, Burdwan, Rajshahi and Dinajpur which were created in the seventeenth and eighteenth centuries. Other than these four two older zamindaries weathered the transition: these were the zamindaries of Vishupur and Birbhum-the latter known generally as the Afghan zamindari. There was also a change in the nature

---

[392] The commercialization of agriculture in the late seventeenth century led to a growing assertiveness of local zaminadars and chiefs. There are indications that the Bengal nawabs tried to bypass the traditional haats and bazaars (semi-regular markets) established and controlled by the zamindars by putting up golas (wholesale markets) such as Bhagwangola in Murshidabad. This happened mainly in the western part of Bengal however. In the east, this process had been evident from the sixteenth century (see later). The delta towns of samatata showed an intriguing mix of agrarian and commercial economies intertwined in the exercise of military valour and political authority. All of them-Bakla, Sripur, Sandwip-established marts in their ports.Control over these market places amplified the zamindars' and chiefs' political power which the Mughals and then the Bengal nawabs tried to curb. See later.

Evidence from (Azamgarh) Bihar in Muzaffar Alam's 'Aspects of Agrarian Uprisings in North India in the early Early Eighteenth Century' (reprinted in Alavi, Seema, 2002, *The Eighteenth Century in India,* New Delhi, Oxford University Press: 84–112) points to a number of bazaars and ganjs established in the middle gangetic plain by the sons and successors of the Gautam Rajputs A'zam and Azmat Khan in the early eighteenth century. These 'neo-Muslim Rajput zamindaris' built about seven ganjs. Zamindari centers such asAzamgarh and Azmatgarh evolved into district (chakla) headquarters by 1720 with a string of subsidiary market towns attached to them. We have a list of ganjs in Bihar from Yang, Anand A., 1998, *Bazaar India: Markets, Society and the Colonial State in Bihar,* California Press: 99. All were established in the early eighteenth centuryand became a new feature in the urban landscape. These new market towns were engaged in the sale of food grains.

Similar urbanization took place in the Bhadohi region with the founding of bazaars such as Bazaar Salabat Khan, Bazaar Rustam Khan, Bazaar Ahmadganj and Katra (market-place) Rusukhiat Khan between 1712 and 1737. Similarly for Mirzapur: (Yang) 94–96.

of zamindari; by the creation of a section of a large, loyal zamindar section who would collect taxes for the state, Murshid Quli sought to redefine the relations between agrarian property, the emerging capitalist agriculture, commerce and political power in Bengal.

Greater administrative and judicial responsibilities now devolved on the zamindaries. More than before, the zamindars oversaw all commercial activity within their domains by administering arangs, tolls, and mart-towns; they played a vital part in the state's fiscal policy by collecting dues from market places and through imposing tolls on trade. The fifteen zamindaries or so created by Murshid Quli Khan provided 60% of Bengal's revenue in the eighteenth century; Burdwan and Rajshahi alone accounted for a quarter of the nominal revenue of Bengal. Previously zamindari might had rested on lineage which was defined by valour, military prowess and maritime trade; now, by the creation of a formidable power bloc in Bengal, Murshid Quli introduced an element of stratification among the landed classes in Bengal. Power now meant economic power.

Taxes, Trade and Traders

In his publication of 1983 Bayly pointed to the importance of revenue for trade (what may be called the taxes for trade link). Taxation stimulated trade. Peasants and zamindars needed to sell more and more of their crops on the market in order to get the cash to pay rent and revenue. We will note later the presence of moneychangers' booths and cauri stalls at village markets which enabled peasants and farmers to convert their produce into ready cash. But while revenue demand stimulated trade, the reverse was also true. As Bayly commented[393]:

> The flow of coin from one area to another dried up unless trade gave to the periphery the coin with which to pay the centre…Bengal and Gujarat had to sell more of their goods to the centre in order to 'buy back' the bullion that was flowing there as tribute. Otherwise a continual outflow of bullion would soon have made it impossible for the outlying provinces to pay the revenue at all.

We see therefore two levels of mercantile activity. At the primary level the local merchant played an essential role in the transfer of the

[393] Bayly, C.A., 1983, *Rulers, Townsmen and Bazaars: North Indian society in the Age of British Expansion, 1770–1870*, Cambridge: 63–64.

rural surplus (as rent and revenue in cash) to the court at Mushidabad. At another level regional merchants played a crucial role in the transfer of the Bengal revenue to Delhi through treasure, commodities and bills of exchange (hundis). In the case of Bengal it was the Gujarati, and not Bengali merchant, who performed this second task. The Bengal merchant was unable to make the qualitative leap from local to regional merchant.

Therefore the local merchant who, along with the state, the zamindar and the banker played such a vital role in the burgeoning cash economy of Bengal, was yet to come into his own. Preoccupied with securing agrarian resources, the Bengal Nawabs intitally paid less attention to commerce. Their commercial policy was, predictably, one of 'impact and response'; faced with numerous European companies operating along the Bhagirathi, the Bengal Nawabs deliberated on how best to tap them. There was little intiative initially, under such circumstances, to develop an indigenous commercial elite. Documentary evidence on monopolies and patronage from Murshidabad and Dhaka suggest that the new state was trying to create a class of powerful merchants who would oppose European interests and thereby operate in a combination of lucrative deals for private gain and take measures that would enrich the new state by mid-century[394]. But until Plassey this new category of merchants was dominated by the courtier-merchants described earlier.

The very factors that made Bengal's costs competitive (and low) turned out in the long run to be Bengal's blight. Low costs, the remoteness of the producing areas, and cheap transport by Bengal's famous waterways inhibited the producer from interacting directly with the market and gave rise to a class of seemingly freeloading merchants–the *dadni* merchants–who were chiefly procurers and who supplied Bengal goods for both the regional and international markets. Some *dadni* merchants now worked with support from the courts at Murshidabad and Dhaka but they remained, in the last analysis, merely brokers[395].

Recent research however focuses on the positive role played by the brokers. The broker as middleman was neither passive nor a parasite. The broker played an important role in the local economy-i.e.at the primary level. In Bengal both merchant and artisan rested on an agrarian base that was under the control of a zamindar. The entire economy came under strain if the agrarian base collapsed as it did in times of famine (1752) or invasions (1740–51). Agriculture and textile production were intimately

[394] See Mukherjee, Rila, *Merchants and Companies*, etc.

[395] *Ibid.*

linked. Since the weaver was also a cultivator it was the advances the merchant made to him to buy seeds that enabled the cultivator to devote a part of his time to weaving. It was the purchase of his product by the merchant that enabled the peasant to pay his land revenue in cash. In Bengal the peasant paid his rent in three instalments corresponding to the three harvests of *aman*, *aus* and *boro* (in order of commercial viability). Commercial activity was closely linked to the harvest cycle; when the broker advanced money to the peasant he became tied to the agricultural rhythm determined by the cycle. If one of the cycles malfunctioned the entire agrarian and commercial enterprise collapsed.

The very richest of the merchants may not have depended totally on the countryside; they were bankers and shipowners as well as dealers in fine quality textiles which had a high mark-up. But the lesser merchants did. These were dealers in single items such as saltpetre, sugar, salt, grain and textiles. They played therefore a very important role in the revenue compact that the state had initiated with the zamindars; for they were the agency through whom the agrarian surplus was transformed into cash for revenue payments to the state, and they were, likewise, the medium through which a large section of the revenue was ploughed back into the countryside when the Murshidabad and Dhaka courts shopped at the mart-towns and arangs powered by them. In Murshidabad district a village market in the 1770s had three stalls dealing in cauries and two moneychangers' booths among thirteen or so shops[396]! The broker, therefore, formed a vital link between town and country and stimulated the growing of more and more cash crops in the villages of Bengal.

Brokers did not only power the village haats and mart-towns; they were also the medium through which foreign demand stimulated cash crops such as mulberry in interior Bengal and whereby European specie was brought into Bengal from the seventeenth century. Just as they operated from the haats and bazaars, so too at the arangs merchants were the intermediaries between the weaver in the village and the buyers at the port-towns and factories of Bengal. The *dadni* merchants therefore played a crucial role in the circulation of specie in Bengal; and since the Mughal economy was hugely dependent on the import of specie (Bengal was no exception; Dupleix once thought that starving Bengal of foreign specie in the 1730s was enough to bring the Nawab down on his knees) we can go so far as to call him an agent of change.

---

[396] Mohsin, K.M., 1973, *A Bengal District in Transition: Murshidabad (1765–93)*, Dacca: 20.

While an agent of change, the *dadni* merchant was also a transitory phenomenon. He only connected the seller with the buyer; he rarely intervened in the world of production, and when he did, it was not to bring about a qualitative change. This was because of the historical state of the productive forces. Rising population as compared to that of Europe within South Asia, and relatively low costs meant there was little innovation in production, and less inclination to invest in new technologies and skilled labour beyond a certain point.

Since Bengal cottons and silk had an almost complete monopoly on the world market there was little impetus to technological innovation on the part of both manufacturer and merchant. Insufficient technological change meant that there was little technological input into production; this in turn meant that there existed a 'glass ceiling' beyond which production simply could not outpace demand. The conjunction of these factors made for a high level equilibrium trap in Bengal[397]. Eventually there was stagnation in production which the *dadni* merchants tried to overcome by bringing ever-widening areas of procurement under their control. The *dadni* merchants were also bringing under their control the final aspects of textile production such as washing by the middle of the eighteenth century[398]. The production process was getting fragmented under the aegis of merchant capital. But it was not enough. In a situation very akin to proto-industrialisation in sixteenth and seventeenth century Europe[399] intermediate commercial activity ultimately spelt the end of the *dadni* merchant; merchant capital could not triumph over peasant household economic priorities.

There was no uniform economic realm within which the *dadni* merchant could negotitate. The world of indigenous merchant capital was not fully in command in eighteenth century Bengal. Apart from this primary historical condition the *dadni* merchant's condition was made worse by an external agent; his economic situation was further complicated by his increasingly precarious realationship with foreign capital in the eighteenth century.

---

397 Frank, A.G., 1998, *ReOrient: Global Economy in the Asian Age*, California Press and Sage/Vistaar Publications: 309.

398 See Mukherjee, Rila, *Merchants and Companies* etc., New Delhi, Pragati Publications.

399 Kriedte, Medick and Schlumbohm's proto-industrialisation thesis in their *Industrialisation before Industrialisation,* Cambridge, 1981; this debate is summed up in Mukherjee, Rila, 2003, *Europe Transformed 1350–1789*, Kolkata, Progressive.

Apart from unstable political conditions, reorientations in commercial policy and investor-unfriendly economic policies also spelt the end of the independent merchant. Geographical vagaries too played a major part in determining his commercial fortunes. The instability of Bengal's rivers contributed to transitory ports so much so that there was never one major port on the Bengal coast that could perform as an outlet[400]. The changes in the major eastern riverine courses at the end of the sixteenth century introduced new rivers into the landscape, broke up *samatata* and dislocated ports. The rivers of Bengal–traditionally referred to as Bengal's fortune–therefore turned out to be Bengal's curse as well[401].

Finally the capital that was necessary to withstand such vagaries of nature did not accumulate after the sixteenth century. From the seventeenth century whatever capital was generated within Bengal was diverted to meet the needs of the Mughal economy and the pan-Asian caravan trade through Lahore and the sea trade through Surat[402]. Moreover Bengal goods frequently had to make up the bulk of the goods, not as commodities for trade but frequently as freight in the Surat trade[403]. For the Mughal at least, the independent existence and circulation of Bengal's commodities had to end.

Our Critique of Received History

We see therefore that our received history for Bengal in the eighteenth century is inadequate. A sensitive reading of the sources brings out the definite mood of the period: its fragile politics, unstable mercantilism, its chief players and, always, the spirit of the rivers in the background. Available information for the period throw up questions which I have tried to answer here.

The first is the perplexing question of why, despite its fabled wealth and expertise, was Bengal never able to make the leap from being a mere supplier to one dominating the trade of the eastern seas? The Bengal presence at Malacca in the sixteenth century was never as prominent as that of the south; the trade to the east was always dominated by the Coromandel merchants who were active as far up as the present-day Gopalpur coast (the *klings* refererred to in the *Suma Oriental* have been translated as *kaling* [Kalinga?]).[404] *Kaling* referred to merchants from the present day Andhra-Orissa coast.

[400] See the section, on Routes, Ports and Trading Networks in Bengal.

[401] See the section, Rivers in Bengal.

[402] Mukherjee, Rila, *Merchants and Companies* etc.

[403] Gokhale, B.G., 1979, *Surat in the Seventeenth Century,* Bombay, Popular Prakashan.

Why were Bengal merchants content to be mere suppliers (*dadni* merchants or *dalals*)? We have few references to major Bengali merchants. The section on Politics and Trade attempts to sketch reasons why this might have been so but we need more data on specific epochs.

Why were most 'indigenised' merchants (either dadni or dalal) either of Gujarati and/or of upcountry origin? The list of merchants from Kasimbazar reveals mostly non-Bengali names such as Katma (Cotma) while the few names we have from Dhaka/Jugdia contain more Bengali names[405]. But these lists are by no means exhaustive and we need a factory by factory analysis of the names appearing in European company investment lists to see how prominent Bengalis were in trade.

How far did the Iranian group actually control Bengal's external trade? Until what time? How far can we dub this 'state mercantilism'? Which other groups were active in Bengal's trade? Also why do academic studies still tend to concentrate on the 'big' merchants at port-towns and ignore the fact that the major part of merchants operating in Bengal operated along the riverine tracts in small mart-towns? It is likely that these were indigenous merchants.

Bengal had a surplus silk and deficient cotton production. Since the sources tell us that unfinished silk was sent to Gujarat (Broach) to be embroidered and that excess cotton found its way from Gujarat to Bengal two assumptions may be considered. One, that Bengal had a silk production that it never exploited fully and to whose enormous potential it woke up only in the seventeenth century after the 1620-25 Hughes and Parker mission to Patna wrote back to Surat about the suitability of Kasimbazar silk for the European market and two, that its concentration on exclusive cotton production (Dhaka muslin among others) for the Mughal court elite led to an excessive dependance on Gujarat (and Burhanpur) cotton and the overland route to Gujarat. This facilitated the entry of Gujarati *banyas* into Bengal as traders. The Bengal cotton crop was augmented only in the eighteenth century when Jalal Khan, chief of the independent hill tribes of 'Tipperah and Chittagong' (later designated as the Chittagong Hill Tracts) agreed with the Mughals to pay a fixed annual cotton tribute to Murshidabad. This settlement[406] became known in the Mughal

[404] Tome Pires' *Suma Oriental 1512–1515* (Armand Cortesao edition, London, Hakluyt Society, 1944).

[405] Mukherjee Rila, *Merchants and Companies,* New Delhi, Pragati Publications.

[406] Serajuddin 1971: 168–69.

(Nawabi in the case of Bengal) revenue settlement as the *kapas mahal*.

This border area of the hill tribes had both local and Arakanese overlords who settled the terms of tribute and who had converted to Islam—another instance that it was this motor area that supplied Bengal with the raw material for one of its much valued exports-cotton fabrics. This was an overland trade and taxed through the *dallahs* or hill-passes bordering eastern Bengal[407]. Items in this 'hill trade' were exotic: crane heads, kingfisher and crow tails, dried fish, parrot beaks, rhino horns and hill ponies formed the bulk of the trade conducted through the hill passes of eastern Bengal, Arakan, Ava and Southern China[408]. The extent to which this trade was integrated with the sea trade at Bengal's ports has yet to be investigated.

Sources for the seventeenth and eighteenth centuries are the diaries/ reports of officials such as Hughes and Parker, Streynsham Master, Hedges, Bowrey, and Luillier[409], travellers' accounts such as those of Robert Challes, Francois Bernier and Jean Baptiste Tavernier and factory records of the European companies; sources which are curiously silent about other themes that mark the history of eighteenth century Bengal. We can isolate the following themes under the banners of:

Politics: (1) the rise, efflorescence and twilight of one dynasty (Murshid Quli Khan's) in 1739–40, (2) the arrival and dominance in Bengal politics of the Patna clique in the shape of Alivardi Khan's entourage from 1740; (3) challenges to the new order; (4) increasing warfare within and without.

Economy: (1) the existence of emporia trading in Bengal in the seventeenth and eighteenth centuries; and its fragmentation into lesser markets (2) The division of the market in the Mughal port of Hugli into emporium (containing goods brought down from the interior of Bengal and destined for foreign merchants) and *bazaar* (holding items of everyday use for locals)[410] mentioned in passing by both Challes and Luillier

[407] See for marts and market towns: Markets in Bengal.

[408] Ray, Haraprasad, 2003, *Trade and Trade Routes Between India and China c. 140 BC-AD 1500*, Kolkata, Progressive Publishers: 95, 193–6.

[409] *Voyage du Sieur Luillier* etc(circa 1701) *Voyage du Sieur Luillier aux Indes Orientales Avec une instruction pour le commerce des Indes Orientales*, 1705, Paris, Claude Cellier. Also *Voyages du Sieur Luillier dans des grandes Indes Orientales*, 1726, Rotterdam.

[410] Challes, Robert, 1690–1691, *Journal d'Un Voyage fait aux Indes Orientales*, Paris, Mercure de France, 1983 edition, 2 Vols. and Luillier op.cit .

(3) the subsequent morphing of the emporia market of Hugli and everyday day markets and a consequent change in the nature of the market and distributive patterns by the early decades of the eighteenth century; (4) the emergence of a new clientele, both regional and European; (5) the attempts of the Bengal Nawabs to establish wholesale markets or *golas* (such as Bhagwan Gola in Murshidabad by Murshid Quli Khan) to centralize distribution and enable uniform prices as well as to bypass the *haats* and *bazaars* from which the older gentry derived tolls; (6) the reordering of the revenue resources of Bengal through the *mal zamini* system of Murshid Quli Khan which created a new substantial zamindari class by destroying the older zaminadaries, and the resumption of *jagirdari* lands as *khalsa* lands (crown lands) by creating Orissa as a backyard of Bengal; (7) the growing control of the English over inland waterways upto Patna by the 1730s; (8) the gradual prominence of the Patna market and merchants over the Kasimbazar—Murshidabad area from the late 1740s; (9) economic dislocation, if any, arising out of these changes; (10) consequent emergence of a new type of market; the dynamics between the new market and the *arang* (interior manufactories), the consolidation of the emporia with the *arang* immediately after penetration of European capital by mid-century; (11) the consequent displacement of textiles from European trade in the 1740–1750 period and the sudden shift to the more lucrative commodities of salt petre and opium in the wake of the collapse of silk production from the 1740s; (12) the growing demand for salt-petre by the European companies and the subsequent tapping of the salt-petre/opium market by the English in Bihar.

Social: (1) the fight over resources between the new rulers and the old and dispossessed indigenous gentry; (2) scramble for market control within the ruling coterie; (3) consequent new patronage patterns and (4) the multiple roles of the elite—as official, as local gentry, as trader and later as Company servant.

New Urban Patterns: While Bengal had always had 'lost towns'[411] it was under the EEIC that the ephemerality of the Bengal town was accelerated. Port-towns appeared on the commercial map of the EEIC that

---

[411] Perhaps most visible in the deltaic area. Blochmann suggests that the towns of Pacauli, Cuipitavaz, Noldy, Dipuria and Tiparia, marked in the sixteenth century maps of de Barros, de Blaev and Van den Brouke represent lost towns [*Contributions to the History and Geography of Bengal* (*Muhammedan Period*), Calcutta, AsiaticSociety, 1968]. Rennell (*A Bengal Atlas* 1780, 1781), added that Bengal's fast-flowing rivers made and unmade towns from the sixteenth to the eighteenth centuries.

owed no lineage to the Mughal economic map. Market-condsiderations led them to establish market towns to rival older Mughal marts and these appeared and disappeared along with the fluctuating fortunes of the EEIC even before they acquired zamindari rights in Bengal. Lakhipur, or Lakshmipur, in the extreme east of the province is a good example. A booming cotton-mart town created to rival Jugdia and Kalindi (older 'market towns') after the EEIC faced difficulties there, Lakshmipur dominated the commercial map of eighteenth century Bengal. Once the exigencies of the Bengal-Britain cotton trade was over, once the Industrial Revolution established itself in Britain permanently, such towns were no longer necessary to British interests in Bengal. So Lakshmipur fell off the map. By the nineteenth century it was reported that it no longer existed[412]. Moreover the British practice of classifying towns such as 'market' etc and imposing their own hierarchisation meant that older nomenclatures were frequently obscured; the very act of reordering the urban space meant that earlier categorisations were often overridden. Hugli and Pipli were referred to in British records as mere slave-marts at a time when they were known urban centres.

Financial: the links between tribute and revenue, actual modes of revenue extraction, the rise and expenditure pattern of the service gentry, traders as service gentry, the role of the state, circulation of capital are yet to be investigated. Note that from the time that Chattagram and the hill areas were acceded to the Bengal Nawabs (eighteenth century) the revenue of the *kapas mahal* (cotton areas) was paid in kind—in cotton—through revenue gentry who functioned also as traders. These gentry-traders borrowed money from the Murshidabad treasury to buy goods for trade in the hill tracts, in return for which trade they received, not cash, but cotton[413]. Part of this cotton was repaid back to the treasury; the rest was defrayed by these service gentry-traders to contract with the cotton weavers. In a situation akin to the merchants of financial centres in sixteenth century Europe (the merchants and financiers of Antwerp are good examples of the financial linkages between the Burgundian Court, in whose regions Antwerp was situated, and the Spanish Crown to which Antwerp was subject) the Bengal merchant now emerged as the crucial link in revenue collection and trade in distant areas. In time these service gentry-traders also became local zamindars: witness the case of Brajaballabh

[412] For more on Lakshmipur, and its short life, see Mukherjee, *Merchants and Companies* etc. (New Delhi, Pragati Publications).

[413] Serajuddin 1971: 168.

who, although in arrears as zamindar, escaped Company punishment because he was also the Company's *dalal* at the lucrative cotton producing Lakhipur factory[414].

Cultural: eastern Bengal was a country apart. Research can focus on (1) how far did the eastern side really differ from the rest of Bengal? And (2) was this difference resolved in the eighteenth century under the twin aegis of Nawabi decrees and European capital?

As we conduct further research into these themes we should remember that Bengal enjoyed two distinctions in the eighteenth century. It was the first 'successor state' to be established (1704–5) and the first to be taken over-economically and politically-by the English East India Company. Moreover its transition from Mughal rule to Nawabi rule was peaceful; the picture of political confusion and unrest associated with imperial decline in the first half of the eighteenth century is not applicable to Bengal.

Bengal enjoyed yet another advantage–that of low prices. Its cheap standard of living and hence the comparative cost advantage, despite having risen somewhat from the seventeenth century, ensured that its products easily reached markets in Asia, Africa and Europe. This enabled the primacy of Bengal goods in South Asia's export trade although we should keep in mind that Bengal produced mainly fine, and consequently, expensive textiles unlike Surat and the Coromandel which produced coarser and mainly cheaper textiles. Its production base, too, continued unchanged from the seventeenth century. Merchants had already begun to have a say in production itself through the system of dadan. Merchants were also active–and later instrumental–in a particular stage of the production process; that of finishing. Most stages of finishing were in the hands of merchants in the eighteenth century; these merchants employed scores of washers, dyers etc. in the form of wage labourers.

The first crack in this state of affairs came in the 1740s with the Maratha raids. This was the first marker of decline. Indeed Marshall labels the entire period from 1740–1765 as 'The Crisis of Empire'[415]. The Maratha raids destroyed the productive base of the western part of the province; they led to a scarcity of grain since the paddy lands in the west were seriously affected, a capital shrinkage, rising taxation by the nawabs to finance wars, a shortage of labour and rising costs. Moreover textile procurements were seriously affected: there were constant shortfalls

414 *Ibid*: 48.

415 Marshall, P.J., 1987, *Bengal: The British Bridgehead Eastern India 1740–1828*, NCHI II. 2, Cambridge and Orient Longman: 70–92.

in supply and quality. The social canvas of Bengal was shattered by the Maratha raids. A direct link can be established between the devastation wrought by the raids and Bengal's productive sphere; the 'crisis' in the supply areas led the English Company to do away with the dadan system of procurement and explore new methods. I have shown this to be the case for the English Company in Kasimbazar. Om Prakash gives similar evidence for the Dutch Company in the Dhaka region (Shantipur)[416].

So when did the 'pre-colonial' end for Bengal? What is the definitive indicator? Was it in 1754 with the changeover in procurement? Was it in 1757 (Plassey) and 1764 (Buxar) signifying political victory? Or should we take 1765 (Diwani) as the date for the economic control over Bengal's revenues? Or 1793 (Permanent Settlement) when the structure of landholdings and revenue extraction was re-ordered in Bengal? As we know there can never be a definitive indicator for the passage of the pre-colonial; unfortunately since Bengal first experienced colonial hegemony in full such indicators that exist are both varied and diverse. It is this that has led to the inconclusive eighteenth century debate for historians naturally use the indicator of their choice to explain changes, breaks or continuities. Further research on the themes outlined above may clarify our ideas on Bengali history. And, having underlined the key issues in a history of Bengal, let us move on to the state as it appeared by the eighteenth century.

---

[416] 'Trade and Politics in Eighteenth Century Bengal' in Alavi, Seema, 2002 *The Eighteenth Century in India*, Delhi, Oxford University Press: 136–164. 'In 1744…it was believed that the fortunes of several of the merchants supplying textiles to the Dutch Company were under strain. These suspicions were confirmed in 1746 when it was learnt that four important merchants operating in the major textile centre of Shantipur near Dhaka–Hinkar Chaudhary, Jag Bhusan, Gokul Chand and Bhagwan Gopi Chand–together with their associates, Radhamohun Chaudhary and Radhakant Chand, had been financially ruined. The Company suffered considerable losses…But the local sarrafs and bankers, who would have been acceptable to the Company as guarantors, flatly refused, saying it (providing the merchants' sureties) was too risky a proposition': 143.

4

Introducing Bengal

Various Bengals and their Coalescence into Subah Bangla in the Eighteenth Century

'Les Khorasan l'appellent Douzakhast...ce qui signifie en arabe un enfer rempli des biens'

(The Khorasans call it [Bengal] in Arabic 'a hell full of abundance') Ibn Batuta, *Voyages*, Tome III, (Tr). Defremery, E.C., Sanguinetty, B.R., 1982, Paris, Maspero. (My translation).

The idea of Bengal, as a hell full of good things, took root from the fourteenth century. The statement above, attributed to Ibn Batuta the famous Maghrebian voyager who visted Bengal in the first half of the fourteenth century, has also been attributed to other travellers who have left behind accounts of Bengal; most notably Francois Bernier and Robert Challes, both of whom visisted Bengal in the seventeenth century. This was echoed as late as in the eighteenth century when the *Riyas-us-Salatin* stated this same sentiment unambiguously.

The flag of dissidence was frequently raised from Bengal. In 1579 Abu'l-Fazl called Bengal *bulghak-khana* or a 'house of turbulence'[417]. In Mughal times a posting to Bengal was deemed a demotion away from the corridors of power at Delhi, Agra or Lahore; yet it was emphasised that fortunes awaited those *subahdars* who braved this unsavoury posting. In travel accounts Bengal is portrayed as a frontier land, a place unknown, yet a country where fortunes could be made.

---

[417] Beveridge, H. (Tr). *The Akbar Nama of Abul-Fazl*, 3 vols., Delhi, Ess Ess Puiblications (2nd reprint,1977), V 3: 290.

Bengal's frontier culture was unfamiliar to the north. A fish-eating land, its culture was perceived as alien by the Mughal *ashrafi* culture of north India. Bengalis were dismissed as 'bands of fishermen'–a culture that the Mughals despised[418]. Given this unsavoury reputation of Bengal what could be called the distinguishing feature of Bengal that set it apart from the rest of the South Asian sub-continent? Was it its distant location, its abundant economy or its distinct frontier culture? What are its chief characteristics? Are they its trans-border affiliations, its riverine topography, or its distinct material culture? Or in other words what forms the identity of Bengal? And, is there one Bengal, or have there been many Bengals in its turbulent history?

In earlier times Bengal was an amorphous zone which contained within it various Bengals. In time the various Bengal coalesced into two Bengals: the one centreing around Lakhnawati–Gaur (west) and the other around Dhaka-Vikrampur (east). These divisions, called Lakhnawati and Bangalah, continued into the eighteenth century and their different policies–ruled by external agencies–determined economic life to a great extent. This is what the sources tell us and which we shall see in subsequent pages.

If we look back in time we see that of the many Bengals in history there was colonial Bengal in the recent past, there was Muslim (Nawabi, Mughal and Sultani) Bengal in the distant past and there was the multi-faceted *Vanga* or non aryanised Bengal in the very remote past. In recent history Bengal was the arena of British imperialism; further back Bengal was in the vortex of Muslim expansion and European discovery; and yet further back Bengal–the eastern heartland of the Gangetic plain–was part of the kingdoms of Sasanka, the Palas, the Varmans, the Chandras and the Senas. Bengal therefore has made the journey from ancient *Vanga*, via medieval Bengalla and subah Bangla, to modern Bengal in history.

Bengal's geographical boundaries have fluctuated over time; the large subah Bangalah incorporating Bihar and a part of Orissa of the eighteenth century is not the Bengal we know today. Its eastern frontier was substantially reduced after 1947 when eastern Bengal became East Pakistan (and then Bangladesh in 1971).

Bengal is a frontier zone of India even today: both locationally and culturally. Geographically speaking Bengal is a zone with fluid boundaries to the north, east and south. Its northern frontier was historically dictated

[418] Mirza Nathan, *Baharistan-i-Ghaybi*, 2: 650–51.

by its relationship with Tirhut (Mithila), and beyond; its eastern frontier depended on interactions with Tripura, Koch, Kamta and Kamrup; its southern frontier at Jajnagar at least demarcated Bengal from the mainly southernised Orissa to the south. The incorporation of Bengal into mainstream middle Gangetic culture was achieved by constantly pushing forward the various frontiers within a given period: the agrarian frontier, the political frontier, the cultural frontier, the religious frontier and the demographic frontier. In the process Bengal's story has not been simply one of integration (or incorporation) with dominant state powers emanating from the gangetic heartland but also one whereby the ascendant state power and political ideologies of any given moment have been, time and again, forced to come to terms with Bengal's unique frontier culture.

The earliest annals do not refer directly to Bengal–it was only when the frontiers of *aryabharta* were consistently pushed outwards in the aftermath of the Gupta epoch that Bengal assummed its own identity. Kulke remarks[419]:

> After the decline of the Gupta Empire and of the 'transient' successor state under King Harsa in the early seventh century, the overwhelming majority of the early medieval states of India emerged from a process of continuous agrarian expansion and political integration...this development took place mainly in those areas of the South Asian subcontinent which had lain at *the periphery or even outside the core areas of ancient state formations. This process started from local nuclei of early socio-economic and political development and increasingly came to include their hinterlands.*(my emphasis)

This passage implies the following schema for Bengal: (1) that although both the earliest centralised states in India were located in the east (viz. the Mauryas and the Guptas), Bengal lay outside their core areas, (2) the expansion of these two early centralised states was directed towards the west and not east and therefore Bengal did not form even the periphery of these states, (3) it was between the fifth and the seventh centuries that the first states appeared in Bengal[420], (4) the dynamic of state formation started from numerous 'local nuclei' of growth, and

[419] 'The Early and the Imperial Kingdom: A Processural Model of Integrative State Formation in Early Medieval India' in Herman Kulke (Ed)., 1995, *The State in India 1000–1700*, New Delhi, Oxford University Press: 233–262, see p. 233.

[420] This supposition is borne out by the archaeological evidence I discuss in the section Politics and Trade in Bengal.

(5) these local nuclei in their turn evolved into states by incorporating their hinterlands. It is therefore clear that not one, but various, states emerged from the post-Gupta phase in Bengal.

Therefore, there was never *one* Bengal even in the ancient period. Just as there have been many 'Bengals' in recorded history there have been, within each of them, 'diverse' Bengals. The area we refer to as Bengal today comprised various small states (in the order north to south) in ancient times known as Pundra, *Varendra*, Rarh and Vardhamana in the west and *Harikela* and *Samatata* in the east. The dividing line between the two regions was Pundravardhana which comprised within it the area called *Vanga* (Banga). In very early times *Vanga* was the political and social frontier of Bengal and beyond it lay unknown lands peopled by strange peoples with fanciful names. These distinct geographical and political units, inhabited by particular peoples with specific tribal attributes and social attitudes, were therefore designated within a particular place/time context that varied over time[421].

With time the different political and ethnic nomenclatures of Bengal[422] finally coalesced into *three* Bengals–*Varendra* or the political heartland, *Vanga*, its economic and cultural unit which became synonymous with the province and the often neglected *Samatata* (or the political 'other' of *Varendra*) with its autonomous economic heartland in *Harikela*.[423] These divisions were clear by the seventh century. During T'ang rule in China the monk Wu-hing arrived at '*Harikela* which is the eastern limit of Eastern India and Jambudvipa'[424].

---

[421] For more divisions within Bengal see Paul, Pramode Lal, 1939, *The Early History of Bengal*, Calcutta, Indian Research Institute and Morrison, Barrie M., 1970, *Political Centers and Cultural Regions in Early Bengal*, The Association for Asian Studies, University of Arizona Press.

[422] Bengal was variously referred to as Rarh, Varendra, Vanga, Samatata, Pundravardhana, Harikela, names that changed over time according to the changing political frontiers and the relative weight of the ethnic composition of people dominating a particular area.

[423] Two authors who also work with this divide in mind are Marshall, Peter J., 1987, *Bengal: The British Bridgehead, Eastern India 1740–1828,* The New Cambridge History of India, II, 2, Cambridge University Press and Eaton, Richard, 1993, *The Rise of Islam and the Bengal Frontier 1204–1760*, Berkeley, University Press.

[424] Chavannes, Edouard, 1894, *Memoire Compose a l'epoque de la grande dynastie T'ang sur les Religieux Eminents...par I-tsing*, Paris, in Frasch, Tilman, 2001, 'The Buddhist Connection: Sinhalese-Burmese Intercourse in the Middle Ages' in Georg Breemer, Tilman Frasch,Hermann Kulke and Jurgen Lutt (eds). *Explorations in the History of South Asia* (Festschrift Rothermund), Delhi, Manohar, 85–97: 88.

The peoples of Bengal, the Prasoi, the Pundras, the Radhs, the Suhmas, the *Vangas* and the Gaudiyas along with the cities and ports of Kotivarsam, Tamralipta and Ganga, are first attested to variously in the *Aitareya Brahman*, and the *Aitareya Aranyaka*; somewhat later they are referred to in the *Arthasastra* and in the texts of Strabo, Diodorus ,Plutarch and Pliny[425]; and they are also referred to in contemporary Jain and Buddhist texts.

States within Bengal were equally diverse. That the entire area was undergoing an almost continuous process of state formation(s) was seen in the birth of ever new names for kingdoms, cities and peoples: from later Vedic literature which mention the peoples of Anga, *Vanga* Pundra,Tamraliptaka, Suhma and Radh; from the writings of Diodorus, Curtius, Pliny and Plutarch who mention the mighty kingdoms of the Gangarides and the Prasoi (their military might, their ferocious tigers, and the splendid emporiums of Ganga in the Gangarides kingdom [both Plutarch and the anonymous *The Periplus of the Erythraean Sea* mention this]) we glean an idea of the wealth of this frontier land; and from the *Sabhaparvan* of the *Mahabharata* and the *Ayodhya Kanda* of the *Ramayana* which mention the Suhma, Prasuhma, *Vanga*, Tamralipta, and Pracya as independent kingdoms we get an idea of the diverse peoples in the region. The Jain and Buddhist inscriptions similarly attest to the existence of numerous states in ancient Bengal.

Bengal has been, through history, a cosmopolitan melting-pot. It is possible, by going through a detailed chronological study of the inscriptions and manuscripts, to discern the main lines of Bengal's early civilization from circa 2000 B.C. to the fourth century AD[426] The excavations of Pandu Rajar Dhibi prove that at least 2000 years before the beginning of the Gregorian calendar Bengal possessed a definite non-Aryan culture, based on the use of iron implements, specific black and red ware and some wet rice cultivation along with contact with overseas cultures. The find of a seal at Pandu Rajar Dhibi similar to the Minoan seals of Knossos has led many to speculate that the coastal regions of eastern India may have established contact with the Minoan civilization of Crete.

---

425 See Majumdar, R.C., 1960, *The Classical Accounts of India*, Calcutta, Firma K.L.Mukhopadhyay.

426 Roy Choudhuri, Bani, 1990, *The Political History of Bengal to the Rise of the Pala Dynasty*, Calcutta, Sanskrit Pustak Bhandar, provides much information on a neglected period in Bengal's early history; see also Majumdar R.C., 1971, *History of Bengal*, Calcutta, G. Bharadwaj vol.1 *The Ancient Period* for a reconstruction of the history of the same epoch.

It seems likely that the tribal peoples of the various parts of eastern India were slowly coming into contact with the Vedic civilization emanating from the upper Gangetic plain. The eastern limits of *madhyadesa* were constantly pushed outwards as Vedic culture changed its perception of the tribals from *rakshasas* to *mlechhas*, that is from *monsters* to *unclean* peoples, who might, at a later stage, be co opted into the Vedic hierarchy. Reading from left to right *madhyadesha's* frontiers shifted from Uttar Pradesh to Bihar and then to Bengal. By the time of the writing of the *Manava Dharmasastra* (2nd B.C.) the eastern limit of *madhyadesa* had moved to Prayag in present day Uttar Pradesh. It was now only a matter of time before Magadh (in present day Bihar state) too became a part of *aryabharta* or *madhyadesa*.

The early Jain and Buddhist texts and inscriptions also offer us a glimpse of the expanding frontiers of a hegemonic culture. Early Buddhist texts such as *Anguttara*, *Mahavastu*, *Vinaya* and *Niddesa* do not include any of the Bengal kingdoms mentioned among the sixteen great republics but the Jain *Bhagavati-Sutra* includes Anga, *Vanga* and Magadha in its list of the sixteen great countries of India. Bengal was now therefore only a step away from this radical 'colonization'; this happened under Gupta aegis around fourth century A.D. in *Vanga* but this colonization was achieved only partially. The eastern section of the gangetic delta remained outside the orbit of direct Gupta control. *Harikela* or the easternmost area became an addendum to *Samatata* and its history is neglected to this day for the most part. This area's turbulent history remains outside the ambit of historical research even today.

With time *Vanga* assummed dominant status–at least iconographically–over other states in Bengal. The reasons for the hegemony of *Vanga* is not known but it seems likely that its fame as the most productive region within Bengal as well as its proximity to *Varendra* (Gaur) or the political nerve centre was responsible for its new status. From Maurya times the region of *Vanga* or the western part of the lower gangetic delta, co-terminous with the ancient kingdom of Gangarides and wealthy in terms of natural and material resources, claimed dominance over the regions of Pundra, Radh and *Varendra* in the western half. By the time of Samudragupta the entire area was conquered and reunified as *Vanga*.

By the time the Guptas consolidated their empire in eastern India the great 'eastward migration' of the *aryas* had reached the last frontier. Rabid brahmanism under Gupta aegis combined with existing social and cultural norms to produce an *unique form of aryanisation* in Bengal.

Aryan ideals slowly permeated political and military norms. As 'aryanisation' proceeded hand in hand with expanding wet rice cultivation it became ever more imperative to find rulers of either lowly origin, or outside the Aryan fold, a place within the new social pyramid that was becoming generic throughout the upper and middle gangetic plain. Those who declined, or were considered unfit of being co opted into the new order, were banished to forests and mountains as waves of 'civilization' swelled in magnitude. Where such rulers continued in power in defiance of Aryan norms they were marginalised and referred to either as 'kings of the mountains' or 'of the forests'. The term '*Vanga*' became a general noun describing the entire state of Bengal except its eastern part–*Samatata*. Only parts of *Harikela* (north of *Samatata* and contiguous with Cooch Bihar and Tripura), *Samatata* and Kamrup remained to be aryanised.

This civilizing wave gained momentum when, around the fifth century A.D., new administrative and agrarian patterns came into being. These necessitated a new social framework. More *jatis* were born. In other parts of South Asia it was from this time that the temple and the ideological position of the Brahman became the loci from which hegemony was articulated. It was also from this time that previously obscure rulers came to the political forefront and turned to Brahmans to legitimise their lineages. Many claimed *kshatriya* status and sought fictitious genealogies linking them to the cardinal *suryavamsi* and *candravamsi* lineages of the Puranas. The Pundras, for example, inhabitants of Pundravardhaha, were described as Kshatriyas. In some cases dynasties traced their descent from powerful Brahmans. In either case these were tools exercised for assimmilating non *aryas* within the dominant ideological fold. Hinduism, as Kulke points out[427], was the most adaptive religious and social system that was open to aspects of 'localisation' or 'indigenisation'. The new model of *varna-jati* whose two criteria of *difference* were language and the observance of codes regarding the organisation of society (*varnasramadharma*) and *not* either race or economic superiority, thus offered a superb exemplar of social advancement and political authority not just within India but in neighbouring regions as well.

In Bengal, however, Buddhism was the dominant vehicle through which kingship and state formation was articulated, except in the case of the somewhat enigmatic Sasanka. The early aryanised states in Bengal offered its neighbours a novel and flexible model of political rule based on social division, equilibrium and an amalgam of Hindu practices and

---

[427] Kulke H., 1993, *Kings and Cults: State Formation and Legitimation in South East Asia*, New Delhi, Manohar: 273–274.

Buddhist ideals. Legitimation was not the only attraction for tribal leaders. It has been pointed out by Wolters that the magico-religious component of *tapasya* inherent in Hinduism was particularly attractive for tribal leaders who sought to move from a pre state to state stage[428]. Soon this model sought to replicate itself across its natural frontiers–in the case of Bengal this was naturally in the countries of northern-South East Asia. The small, scattered 'countries' and empires of south east Asia–tribal in polity and social organisation–offered an ideal terrain for this penultimate wave of 'aryanisation'. This was particularly visible in the case of the early Pyu states (Burma/Myanmar) and especially Arakan with whom Bengal shared a common cultural and economic zone[429].

However from the tenth/eleventh centuries Hinduism outpaced Buddhism in Bengal. The expanding nature of the society and economy of *vanga* is evident from the names of offices and functionaries that are mentioned in inscriptions[430]. They indicate a highly complex and sophisticated culture based on the effective appropriation of natural wealth and regulated by a strong ideological/religious system. There are separate terms for centre and district (*Adhikarana* and *Adhisthana*), mention of various taxes, names of functionaries in charge of specific manufactures, designations of supervisors of public and religious edifices (*Avasathika*) and special officers (*Devadroni-Sambaddha*) charged with the maintenance of temples and sacred water tanks. The inscriptions also mention various categories of administrative officials, numerous classes of citizens and their ocupations[431]. The variegated functions quoted above may be taken as being indicative of segregated tribal kingdoms coming under an unified political umbrella in the transition from isolationism to actual 'empire building' in ancient Bengal. The designations and offices prove that Bengal's was, then, primarily an agricultural economy. Agrarian surplus, and not profits from trade, supported the emergent state.

The brahmanisation of Bengal in the eleventh century coincided with the trade revolution that happened in the Indian Ocean at this time. Under

---

428 *Ibid*: 274.

429 Mukherjee, Rila, 2006 *Merchants and Companies* etc. (Pragati Publications, New Delhi).

430 See Morrison's data mentioned later.

431 In Bani Roy Chowdhuri 1990 op.cit. See also the categories of functionaries and citizens in the contemporaneous Varman kingdom in *samatata-harikela* in Majumdar N.G. 1929 (ed. with tr. and notes), *Inscriptions of Bengal,* Rajshahi, Varendra Research Society, Volume 3 *Containing the Inscriptions of the Chandras, the Varmans and the Senas and of Isvaraghosa and Damodara*: 4–24.

the Cholas the eastern Indian Ocean and the Bay of Bengal exploded into a hub of commercial and religious activity.

It was first George Coedes, and subsequently Quatrich-Wales, Denys Lombard and K.N.Chaudhuri (among others) who pointed out the topographical similarities between Bengal and South East Asia[432]. Such similarities contributed to the distinctive material culture of this predominantly riverine, rice-culture dominated zone and led to the formation of agrarian, rice based, empires and states in the littoral region surrounding the Bay of Bengal and the Java Sea.

Historically speaking the successful articulation of political power in this region has always based itself on two stark realities-control over surplus grain and control over the waterways[433]. This articulation of political power was effected through specific ideological structures peculiar to the eastern coast of India and south east Asia. However such a sophisticated articulation of power and its concommitant ideology was beyond the scope of warring tribes and could only come about when one tribe imposed its power over all others in the region. A degree of centralised rule, along with appropriate religio-political ideology, was therefore essential in the transformation of tribal zones into states capable of tapping the vast agrarian and natural resources at their command. With time therefore the flat riverine plains of Bengal (and South East Asia subsequently) saw the rise of a divine political economy and validating philosophy in this distinct topographic zone–what Denys Lombard calls a 'rice culture of divine right'[434] based on the successful appropriation of legitimising models for lineage construction and the economic control of the area. Such a model had to operate within societies that were organised *hierarchically* (and not *spatially* as had been tribal societies) on the basis of *varna*, with *jati* being used as a mechanism of incorporating newly conquered peoples[435].

---

[432] Kulke, H., 1993 *Kings and Cults: State Formation and Legitimation in South East Asia*, New Delhi, Manohar: 273-274, 260–261, 264–269.Quaritch-Wales, H.G., 1961, *The Making of Greater India*, London , B. Quaritch-Wales, second edition and Quatrich-Wales, 1957, *Pre History and Religion in South East Asia,* London, B.Quaritch-Wales. For the other references cited see later.The concepts of 'indianisation' and of 'agrarian empires' has been questioned by Wink, A., 1984, in 'Asian Studies: Agrarian History and Orientalism' in *Itinerario* vol.VIII, no.2.

[433] See the section, Rivers in Bengal.

[434] Lombard, Denys,1990, *Le Carrefour Javanais: Essai d'histoire Globale*, III, *L'Heritage des Royaumes Concentriques*, Paris, Editions E.H.E.S.S.: 15–54.

[435] Thapar, Romila, 1975, *Time as a Metaphor for History*, Calcutta, K.P. Bagchi: 31–33; Lombard, Denys, 1990, III: 55–56; Coedes, George, 1964, *Les Etats Hindouises d'Indochine et d'Indonesie*, Paris, Boccard: 51–53.

In Bengal from the time of the Guptas up until the time of the Senas–epochs for which we have somewhat comprehensive records–we see that major activities consisted of continually expanding the political and cultural frontiers of civilization, instituting rice culture as the dominant economy of the region and settling Brahmans in the forested lands of the eastern margin (*samatata*) to popularise wet rice cultivation in the east. In the process the tribal culture of Bengal with its *jhum* cultivation was overshadowed by emerging Brahmanical expertise based on superior agricultural skills.

Along with subordination to a vastly superior technique for expanding cultivation the tribal peoples of Bengal were subject to the hegemony of Vedic civilization as embodied in the four fold *varna* scheme. From the time of the Guptas until the rise of the Palas this process continued inexorably. More and more of the eastern part was brought under cultivation. The frontier now extended beyond *Samatata* to Kamrup and the hostile territory outside it.

Between the seventh to the ninth centuries (that is the period between Sasanka's rule and the advent of the Palas) western Bengal or *vanga* became synonymous with Gaur as the seat of the mighty empire of Sasanka. The eastern deltaic region or *samatata* remained geographically and culturally a distinct zone and often challenged Gaur's political hegemony. The questionable political allegiances of the eastern parts became evident after the downfall of Sasanka's state. Successive rulers of Bengal from the time of Sasanka tried to subdue *Samatata* and Kamrup and enrol them as feudatories but were not successful. In spite of hosting the dynamic Bhadra, Khadga and Chandra dynasties *samatata/harikela* remained a frontier region with politically suspect affiliations.

The Chandras and later the Varmans, it seems from extant inscriptions, reigned as political rivals of the Senas who succeeded the Palas in the western delta. *Samatata* continued to be, until the nineteenth century, outside the pale of *vanga's* dominion. By then of course *vanga* had metamorphosed into colonial Bengal.

From the thirteenth century, when the Bengal Sultanate established itself at Lakhnawati, this multifaceted region experienced yet another ontological shift. The establishment of Islamic rule in Bengal saw the region incorporated into a complex political/religious/diplomatic/mercantile network that stretched from China to southern Spain, Maghreb and Ifriqiya. The Islamic reign in Bengal that lasted from the thirteenth to the sixteenth centuries produced repercussions within: by the beginning of the fourteenth century the many miens of Bengal, the different names/places/cultures that we mentioned, had coalesced into the three principal areas of Gauda-Pandua-Firuzabad-Lakhnawati (the older *varendra* or the political heartland), Saptagram-Hugli-Tribeni (the old *vanga* or the cultural and economic pulse) and the Dhaka-Suvarnagram region or the old *samatata*. A new name for the eastern region had also emerged—Bangalah[436]. Only the last frontier remained to be subdued, that of *harikela* with its difficult terrain, suspect loyalties and the magnificent port of Chattagram at its southern tip; this was only partially achieved by the quasi-independent Mughal *subahdar* Shaista Khan at the end of the seventeenth century.

This is not the place to the detail the successful (and unsuccessful) attempts at expansion beyond Bengal by the Bengal sultans. However under the Ilyas Shahis, throughout the fourteenth century, attempts were made to extend hegemony over Kamrup, Kamta, Tirhut and Nepal to the north and the powerful Ganga state (medieval north Orissa) to the south. Inscriptions found in Kamrup indicate that a portion of Assam at least was brought under Muslim control by the time Sikandar Ilyas Shah and Ghiyas-al-Din Ilyas Shah were on the throne of Lakhnawati.

At the end of the fifteenth century Vipradas described the mercantile dynamism of Saptagram. It was peopled by Hindus, Mughals and Pathans; it contained a dazzling array of houses and conducted trade with Ceylon (Sarandib) and Orissa. Since the Arakan trade was not mentioned it seems likely that Arakanese disturbances in eastern Bengal had interrupted this trade. Possibly Chattagram, or Xatigam as it was called in the local dialect, conducted what little trade continued to exist with Arakan[437]. Now the Husain Shahis sought to enhance trade within their own domains by connecting Triveni (in the older *vanga* which had evolved into the cultural and economic heartland of *varendra*) with *vanga's* chief port Saptagram by way of a bridge in 1506. This bridge connected Saptagram and Triveni with the main channel of the Bhagirathi because the Saraswati had dried up. This endeavour is the east to west shift under Husain Shahi leadership that I described before.

---

436 See Ibn Batutah op.cit. Bangalah has been taken to be Dhaka. This confusion was compounded by Portuguese refernces to a 'City of Bengalla' in the sixteenth century. Bangala was actually the name of the eastern part of Bengal.

437 Ray, Aniruddha, 1997, 'Middle Bengali Literature: A Source for the Study of Bengal in the Age of Akbar' in Habib, Irfan, *Akbar and His India*, New Delhi, Oxford University Press: 229–233, traces urbanization and trade for this neglected period of Bengal's history.

Under Husain Shahi aegis a new urban complex emerged in Bengal. Gaur was the capital, Saptagram its port, Triveni its religious hinterland and Nabadwip its cultural centre. *Vanga* thus saw a new phase of urbanization. Nabadwip attracted immigrants from Sylhet (a well known intellectual centre of *harikela*) and Chattagram and soon evolved into the scholars' centre of *vanga*. By 1560 Nabadwip had evolved into a well-known market town as well; merchants were settling there and selling goods from locations as far off as Kashmir in the north to Kanchipuram in the extreme south.

From this time on textiles (mainly cottons and some silk piece goods) began to be manufactured in the towns along the lower Bhagirathi. These supplied the market towns along the Bhagirathi and provisioned the trade conducted from Saptagram. Saptagram ceased to function as a port with the establishment of Hugli as the chief port on the Bhagirathi in 1580. However the impetus of urbanization in this region continued unabated and Hugli took over the functions of Saptagram by connecting long distance trade with the hinterland.

Now Bengal came to be integrated more closely with northern India through yet anothet endeavour–Sher Shah Sur's efforts–to reorient the trade of Bengal from the east to the west. This meant that Bengal had another outlet for its manufactures apart from its riverine/oceanic trade. The construction of the Grand Trunk Road–which exists to this day–ensured that Bengal would no longer remain a marginal sultanate. The Mughals enhanced further the east-west shift. The Grand Trunk Road which was built by Sher Shah (1538–45) and finished by Akbar connected Bengal permanently with Delhi via Allahabad, Benares and Awadh.

That Bengal was in effect two states, under two sets of rulers, for much of the period under study here is therefore unquestionable. Ibn Batuta had noted this in the fourteenth century[438]. Edward Terry had commented on this when he visited Bengal in the seventeenth century[439].

Eastern and western Bengal were frequently at war. In the fourteenth century Ibn Batuta referred to the fact that the ruler of Bangalah (or *samatata/harikela* in whose dominions lay Chattagram and which Ibn Batuta visited) was frequently at war with the ruler of Lakhnawati. Ibn Batutah thus followed the accepted practice of distinguishing between Bangalah and Lakhnawati. It seems, in contemporary perception, that

438 *Voyages*, op.cit.

439 Terry, *Voyage of*, op.cit.

the ancient *vanga* or the west had become synonymous with Bangalah of the east in the fourteenth century; Lakhnawati further north was the focus of political might (and power tussles with the rest of the gangetic plain) and was regarded as a country apart, in fact as the *new-fashioned state*.[440]

The Dhaka-Vikrampur area was host to the Buddhist kings of eastern Bengal in history and displayed a markedly different political culture: witness the Chandra and Varman kings who ruled quasi-independently from the region as we have already seen. In the wake of the ferment produced by the takeover of Lakhnawati the last Sena king, Lakshman, ran away to this area; later in the post-Mughal ferment of the take-over of Gaur dispossessed Afghan/Turk adventurers also fled there.

From the end of the sixteenth century a new factor entered this area in the shape of piracy and slave-raiding under Arakan-Portuguese pressure. In the seventeenth century, therefore, the eastern frontier was blocked at Sagor under Arakanese and Portuguese compulsion. The frontier to the east was always flexible. The Bengal Nawabs in the eighteenth century transferred their less fortunate officers there. In time the Dhaka-Vikrampur region ceased to be a separate political unit and became instead an extension of Nawabi Bengal but the region still retained its separate identity.

Eastern Bengal was always the last frontier aka Eaton[441] but this frontier was repeated endlessly throughout the early history of Bengal as well. Militant sufis, radical rulers, Portuguese adventurers and Arakanese raiders did not create this Turnerian frontier; this frontier was a more gradual creation under the twin impulses of statecraft and religion from the time of the spread of Buddhism in the early centuries of the first milllenium and fashioned further by Brahmins who brought to the area superior agrarian management skills. But it was pushed forward relentlessly nevertheless throughout the centuries until Mughal regulation of this frontier put a stop to this from the seventeenth century. Separate faiths, different religious affiliations and the prevalence of many tongues and races still mark the east from the rest in Bengal. By the eighteenth century, when our story ends, Assam (Kamrup) and Koch (Cooch Bihar) delineated the final frontier of Bengal.

---

440 See Ibn Batutah and a more recent evaluation of Ibn Batutah's passages on Bengal in Muhammad Mohar Ali, 1985, *History of the Muslims of Bengal,* vol. 1A, Muslim Rule in Bengal 1203–1757 , Riyadh, Imam Muhammad, Ibn Saud Islamic University: 124–132.

441 Eaton, Richard, 1993, op.cit.

In conclusion we can assert that just prior to the eighteenth century the various Bengals through history that we noted had combined into the two Bengals that still exist today: the one situated around the heartland of Gaur, functioning through its port of Sapatagram; the other situated around Dhaka, functioning through Chattagram. While the Gaur-Pandua-Lakhnawati-Murshidabad bloc housed Bengal's western capitals, the Dhaka-Vikrampur-Suvarnagram axis had functioned as a separate capital so much in history that we can even assert that there still were also two *states* in Bengal. (It is of course significant that the borders of the present nation of Bangladesh corresponds to the old division of *samatata* and *harikela* as well as a section of *varendra*).

These two main regions of Bengal–dominated not just by political and linguistic differences that continue till today, but differing norms, economic ideas and cultural expressions that have shaped Bengal's early history–form the thrust of this book.

Capitals, Cities and Towns in Bengal

'Instability of the monuments of human grandeur cannot in any region of the globe, I apprehend, be more faithfully or grievously exemplified than at Rajmahal' (Forster, George, 1798, *A Journey from Bengal to England*. London, vols. 1 and 2. Letter 1 *On Ganges*).

Bengal has had various capital-complexes through its history. The two most enduring ones have been, of course, Gaur/Pandua/Tanda/Firuzabad/Lakhnawati in the west and Dhaka/Vikrampur in the east. While the location of the Dhaka-Vikrampur complex has been fairly stable, that of Gaur-Lakhnawati has varied over time. Nothing today is left of the first city of Gaur that was there from the eleventh to the thirteenth centuries. Scholars, when they talk of the location of Gaur, refer to the second city of Gaur that existed from the fifteenth to the sixteenth centuries[442].

The Lakhnawati of the thirteenth century, settled by Ali Mardan, was to the north of the second city of Gaur. The Ganga flowed on its eastern side. But from the thirteenth century the east to west Gangetic shift necessitated the abandonment of Lakhnawati and the move to Firuzabad to the north west. It was Jalal-ud-Din, sons of Raja Ganesa, who shifted

[442] The results of the reconnaissance survey at the second city of Gaur, undertaken by the West Bengal Directorate of Archaeology and the Centre for Archaeological Studies and Training, Eastern India, should be available by 2006.

back to a new Lakhnawati in the fifteenth century to take advantage of the Ganga now flowing past it once again. This city was also called Nasirabad, Shamsabad and Barbakabad after the various Bengal sultans, and in time this metamorphosed into the second city of Gaur. The Ganga now flowed to the west of the city[443].

Other capitals in history have been Nadia (Lakshman Sena in the thirteenth century), Suvarnagram (Ilyas Shahis in the fourteenth century), Ekdala, the capital of Ala-ud-Din Husain Shah in the early sixteenth century, and Rajmahal, Burdwan, Murshidabad, Patna and briefly, in the time of the semi-dependent nawab Mir Kasim, Munger (Monghyr in Bihar) in the seventeenth and eighteenth centuries. The historical trajectory of Bengal's capitals has always been in either a north-western or an eastern arc. Capital cities were shortlived in Bengal: apart from the Lakhnawati and Dhaka axes capitals were transient and dependent on riverine vagaries, economic impetus or the political compulsions of the age.

The seventeenth century in Bengal was a restless age as far as capital cities were concerned: this century–corresponding to the shortlived Mughal Bengal–saw the capital shifting from Rajmahal to Dhaka (1608 by Islam Khan, this move was consolidated by stationing the Nawara fleet there and renaming Dhaka Jehangirnagar), back to Rajmahal (under Prince Shuja from 1639), to Dhaka again when the river at Rajmahal changed its course (under Shaista Khan in the period 1662-89), Burdwan temporarily (Azim-us-Shan in the 1690s), back to Dhaka (Azim-us-Shan declared the city his official residence in 1696), and then to Murshidabad (circa 1705).

We know that from the sixteenth century urban momentum swung back in favour of *vanga*. This was mostly due to the fact that the Ganga now merged with the Brahmaputra by way of the Padma-Meghna. This meant that eastern and western Bengal were no longer geographically separated. From the time the Mughals conquered Bengal in 1576 it was natural that the western part of the delta–which now had as its hinterland a vastly productive agrarian base–should now become the heartland of empire. This was for locational and strategic advantages: western Bengal was closer to Mughal upper India by way of the Ganga which ran through Patna, Prayag and Benares. This urban momentum continued, except for an interlude in the seventeenth century when political compulsions dictated that Dhaka should be the provincial headquarters. By the eighteehth century

443 Personal communication from Mr. Pratip Kumar Mitra, Keeper, State Archaeological Museum, Kolkata, on August 5 2005.

the urban concentration was firmly fixed on *vanga*; the seventeenth century was therefore, to paraphrase Braudel, the last great age of *samatata*.

Samatata contained, in history, some of the most important urban complexes in Bengal. One such is Buddhist Paharpur, patronized mainly by the Palas. Dating from the eighth century, its monuments display a structural and architectural similarity with monuments in Pagan and Java[444].

The best known urban node in the east is the Mainamati-Lalmai Buddhist complex which was patronized by the Palas and the kings of Pattikera and probably served by Bakla/Chandradwip port. More than 350 coins of the Pala period have been found there which leads us to conclude that it comprised an active trading zone[445]. Commercial activity may have been accelerated further by the decline of the ports of *vanga*–Tamralipta and Gangabandar–from the eighth century[446].

Abu Imam comments that 'Mainamati is the greatest single discovery of historical importance in Bangladesh since Paharpur'[447]. The site, of eighteenth kilometres length and five kilometres width, was a predominantly Buddhist site with about 700 years of continuous occupation. Mainamati has been likened to the last outpost of Indian Buddhism with trade links to Arakan and South East Asia. Whether it was a capital city, a political centre, a military centre or a 'fort' city is not certain. What is clear is that Mainamati was also patronised by the Khadgas and the Devas of *samatata*.

Mahastan, already mentioned, was another ancient urban complex in *samatata*, first 'discovered' by Cunningham in 1879. This was a Hindu sacred place, a place for Buddhist pilgrimage, and later on, it was inhabited by Muslim chiefs.

---

444 Majumdar, R.C, 1943, *The History of Bengal*, V.1 *The Hindu Period*, Dacca, University Press: 511.

445 Kosambhi, D.D., 1956, *An Introduction to the Study of Indian History, Bombay*, Sharma, R.S., 1965, *Indian Feudalism: 300–1200*, Calcutta, University Press, Ray, Niharranjan, 1949, *Bangalir Itihas*, Calcutta (in Bengali) present a picture of urban and commercial decay following the fall in Roman trade. Rashid, M. Harunur, 1975, '*The Mainamati Gold Coins*' in *Bangladesh Lalit Kala*, I, 1and Khan, F.A., 1963, *Mainamati*, Karachi modify this schema and throw light on the persistence of commercial activity in the Harikela/Samatata division.

446 Tarafdar, M.R., 1978, 'Trade and Society in Early Medieval Bengal', *The Indian Historical Review,* January, 4, no. 2, New Delhi.

447 Imam, Abu, 2002, 'Samatata, Mainamati: Some Observations' in Gautam Sengupta and Sheena Panja (Eds). *Archaeology of Eastern India: New Perspectives*, Calcutta, Centre for Archaeological Studies and Training, Eastern India: 613–623.

Suvarnagram shares almost the same chronology as Mahastan. Its origin appears to have been an island at the mouth of the delta. Ancient Roman sources speak eloquently of its fine cottons. Ptolemy referred to it as Sonagura[448]. Suvarnagram was the capital of the Bengal sultans in eastern Bengal in the fourteenth century and under Shams-ud-din Ilyas Shah it was the capital of the whole of Bengal as well[449]. Suvarnagram's active trade may explain the continuing importance of Mahastan as well. Suvarnagram exported surplus rice to Pegu and Sumatra[450]. In the fourteenth century Ibn Batuta commented that it traded with Java[451]. At the height of its fame the city was full of palaces, mosques and forts. During the time of Sher Shah a road linked it to the Punjab. This prominence was eclipsed by the transfer of the capital to Dhaka in 1608.

It has been speculated that Dhaka has a much more recent origin because it does not feature in the *Ain*. It is about 12 kilometres from Suvarnagram and it is likely that it functioned as a satellite of that town in ancient history. By all accounts it seems however that Dhaka was a substantial township long before the Mughal conquest of Bengal in 1575 despite not figuring in the Ain's records. Dhaka shot into prominence when Islam Khan, the Mughal *subahdar* of Bengal, transferred the capital of Bengal from Rajmahal to Dhaka in 1608. Islam Khan built a fortified palace, augmented the artillery and built up the Nawara fleet to combat the Maghs (Arakanese-Portuguese freebooters under Sebastian Gonzales). Between 1662-89 Shaista Khan also chose Dhaka as his capital. Again in 1696 Azim-us-Shan made Dhaka his official residence. Suvarnagram's political importance was thereby eclipsed; it remained a manufacturing centre while Dhaka developed into a bazaar town much like its counterpart Hugli in the west.

It was said that Dhaka contained fifty-two markets and fifty-three streets[452]. The river here was also navigable; it could receive boats of

---

448 McCrindle, J.W., *Ptolemy's Geography* in Majumdar, R.C., 1960, *Classical Accounts of India*, Calcutta.

449 See Ray, Swarup Chandra, 1891, *An Ancient and Modern History of Sonargang*, Calcutta, Sakha Press (in Bengali).

450 *Ibid.*

451 Vol. 3 of Ibn Batuta op.cit.

452 Hamilton, Alexander, 1727, *A New Account of the East Indies 1688–1723,* 2 vols., Edinburgh, Hamilton, Walter, 1828, *East India Gazeteer*, 2 vs., London; Taylor, James, 1840, *A Sketch of the Topography and Statistics of Dacca.*

upto 600 tons. Bowrey went so far as to call it the principal city of Bengal[453]. It evolved into a cosmopolitan town-Greeks, Armenians, and Portuguese rubbed shoulders with Hindus and Muslims. The French, Dutch and the British established factories here. Greeks, Armenians and the Portuguese were already settled here. In the eighteenth century Rennell estimated the population of Dhaka to be around 450 000 (in 1765)[454].

In earlier times Chattagram (called variously Xatigam, Xatigao, Chatighan and Chittagong; the different spellings of the place name betray the languages of the scores of people who settled there), belonged probably to the autonomous kingdom of Tipperah (Tripura in *harikela*) for it hardly features in Bengal's ancient history. Ibn Batuta has left us a detailed account of this port en route to China in the beginning of the fourteenth century. His comment that the King of Bangalah (in whose domains lay Chattagram) was frequently at war with the king of Lakhnawati bears out that it was not a part of Bengal and probably formed the nucleus of another, maritime, state. Chattagram was annexed to Bengal only at the beginning of the sixteenth century. Later on in the sixteenth century it was taken over by the Arakanese[455] and was not recovered for Bengal until the late seventeenth (in 1666 by the Mughal *Subahdar* Shaista Khan) and then lost again.

Chattagram-part Buddhist, part Muslim and semi-Hindu-was the frontier region par excellence of Bengal. Chattagram also boasted a strategic importance: it was the gateway to Arakan and northern South East Asia. Chattagram was also the last commercial frontier of Bengal and was the centre of a quadrangular conflict between the Afghans, the Persians, the Portuguese and the Arakanese for control.

Its rise is attributed to the tenth century[456]. Joao de Barros in *Decadas da Asia* remarked that it was a large city but that it was badly fortified[457]. It was renamed Islamabad by its Mughal victors. French sources devote a lot of space to 'Chatighan'[458]. In 1750 Alivardi Khan was claimed to have given it to the French in exchange for 12 500

[453] Bowrey, Thomas, op. cit.

[454] *Memoirs of a Map of Hindustan or the Mogul's Empire,* London, 2nd ed. Also his *A Bengal Atlas*, 1780.

[455] See later.

[456] Ali, M.M., 1985 V. 1A: 37–39.

[457] In Sen, Surendranath, 1938, 'An Early Portuguese Account of Bengal' in *Calcutta Review*, January issue.

[458] Especially the voluminious C2 115, A.N., Paris, now at Aix.

francs (livres?)[459]. In 1760 it was given to the English. Be what it may, European interest in Chattagram continued to mount until the middle of the eighteenth century despite the fact that Chattagram had lost much of its former importance by that time[460]. By the 1730s Chattagram had lost its former strategic importance. Hamilton commented[461]:

> Xatigam is a Town that borders on Bengal and Arackan and its Poverty makes it a matter of indifference whom it belongs to…It is not so fertile in Corn as Bengal and has but few cotton manufactures but it affords the best Timber for building, of any Place about it.

By the end of the eighteenth century Chattagram became a poor revenue paying area.

Much has been written on this and many debates centre even today on the possible location of the 'City of Bengalla' that the Portuguese encountered and wrote about in the sixteenth century. It was the Portuguese name 'Bengalla' for *vanga* that made Bengal synonymous with the opulence of eastern empires. 'Bengalla' enjoyed the same position in the world-theatre as the 'Mogul'. The 'City of Bengalla' has been identified successively with Gaur, Chattagram, Saptagram, Suvarnagram and even with Rajmahal and Dhaka! K.K.Datta took it to be Chattagram following Barbosa. In 1518 Barbosa mentioned that the port of Chattagram, which he called 'Bengalla', was peopled by rich Muslim merchants from Arabia, Persia and Abyssinia, owning large ships and exporting cottons from Bengal to the Coromandel, Malabar, Cambay, Ceylon and to South East Asia[462]. Aniruddha Ray[463] identifies this, however, with the city of Gaur (ancient Lakhnawati) in the west. However none of the identifications are completely satisfactory since the accounts and cartography frequently do not tally. It has also been suggested that the fabled 'City of Bengalla' referred to whichever city was the most prominent in Bengal at the time[464]. It is also well possible that the 'City of Bengalla' did not owe

---

459 *Ibid.*

460 Alexander Hamilton (1727) spoke of its poverty, its anarchy, its decline in fertility and grain production compared to the rest of Bengal and the degradation of its once famed harbour in *A New Account of the East Indies* etc., London, MD CC XLIVII, V.1.

461 *Ibid.* 25.

462 Barbosa, Hakluyt, II: 144–145.

463 Ray, Aniruddha, 1986, Introduction, Abid Ali Khan's *Memoirs of Gaur and Pandua*, West Bengal Directorate of Archaeology, Calcutta.

464 See the Preface of Armand Cortesao to Tome Pires' *Suma Oriental 1512–1515* (London, Hakluyt Society, 1944) where he locates it at Gaur; see also Ray, Aniruddha, 1986.

its existence to any physical city–it was a fanciful representation of the province–a metaphor for its myriad treasures. In fact a French geographer went so far as to call it an imaginary city of the medieval era.

From the seventh to the sixteenth century Gaur (synonymous with Pandua, Tanda, Lakhnawati and Firuzabad) was the capital of western Bengal or *varendra*. This political heartland functioned with *vanga* as its economic heart. Gaur was built at the junction of the Ganga and the Mahananda. The second Gaur (dating from the fifteenth century) contained four recognizable areas: the Royal centre, the Nobles quarter, the Urban core, the Garrison area and possibly a fringe area. It was filled with magnificent palaces, lakes, forts and houses[465].

During the course of the fifteenth century Chinese visitors spoke of the splendour of the court at Gaur[466]. At the turn of the sixteenth century Portuguese visitors spoke of its opulence; they noted with awe Gaur's various gates each guarded by one hundred and fifty eunuchs, the esplanade 'as vast as one and a half arena', its buildings mounted with golden domes, the stables with four thousand five hundred horses and nine hundred and fourteen elephants kept in readiness for war, the harems with two thousand and five hundred royal wives and three thousand dependents, streets paved as in Lisbon and filled with polo playing horsemen and platoons of one thousand five hundred men who marched in columns with their own standards. Not only was the opulence restricted to the royalty and nobility. The Portuguese noted that Nusrat Shah distributed one hundred and fifty cartloads of cooked rice, bread and fruits and fifty cartloads of beef, mutton and fish, as well as the equivalent of 600000 tankas in Portuguese currency in one day in memory of his mother, the wife of Husain Shah[467].

Gaur was not just a maritime city; it was also a maritime capital. But its proximity to the river (and the changing course of the Ganga that we have already referred to) spelt its doom. By the seventeenth century the city was ruined through repeated floods. Yet Manrique commented on its great wall (six *kos* or two leagues), the decorations on the gateway to the

---

[465] See Sinha, Sutapa, 2002, 'Archaeology of the Medieval City of Gaur' in Sengupta and Panja eds. 2002: 329–356.

[466] See the accounts of the Chinese voyagers in Bagchi, P.C.ed., 1945, *Visvabharati Annals,* I, see also Ma Huan's account in Mills, J.V.G., 1970, *The Overall Survey of the Ocean's Shores,* London, Hakluyt Society.

[467] *Voyage dans le Deltas du Gange et l'Irraouady*, 1521, Anon. Presented and edited by Genevieve Bouchon and Luis Filipe Thomaz, Fondation Calouste Gulbenkian, Paris, 1988: 320–7.

city, and the fine gardens containing reservoirs of water[468]. Hedges wrote that the palace was 'considerably bigger and more beautiful than the Grand Seignor's seraglio at Constantinople or any other palace that I have seen'[469].

Under Husain Shahi aegis, we saw, a quadrilateral urban complex emerged in Bengal. After Ekdala Gaur was the capital, Saptagram its port, Triveni its religious hinterland and Nabadwip its cultural centre. Nabadwip attracted immigrants from Sylhet (a well known intellectual centre of *harikela*) and Chattagram and soon evolved into the scholars' centre of *vanga*. *Vanga* thus saw a new phase of urbanization.

Hugli, founded by the Portuguese in 1580[470], evolved into a great urban complex in the seventeenth century. The Portuguese invited their compatriots to settle there for they had been granted religious freedom at Hugli. A church was built and when Bernier visited it he estimated 8000-9000 Christians there[471]. Bowrey spoke of the opulence of Hugli, and of the English and Dutch establishments there[472]. Master called it the 'key or seale of Bengala'[473]. Linschoten spoke of its fine paved roads, well-stocked shops, the emporia-style market, and the fine cloths available there[474]. The city, built along the river, had fine walks, magnificent gardens and grand houses.

Rajmahal was another important city in the seventeenth century. It became the capital of Bengal as Akbarnagar in 1639 and was significant as the provincial mint town. It was situated on the Ganga. It was a princely city; located on superb hunting grounds. Manrique tells us that its splendour was enhanced by the fact that when Shuja Khan held court

---

468 Manrique in *The Travels of Fray Sebastian Manrique, 1629–1643,* Luard, C.E., (Tr), 1926, 1927, London, Hakluyt Society. 2 vols.

469 Hedges, William, *The Diary of...During His Agency In Bengal 1681–87.* Transcribed and illustrated R. Barlow and H.. Yule , London, Hakluyt, MDCCC LXXXVII V.1: 88.

470 We accept this date because the *Chandi* of 1577 docs not mention it by name but Fitch, visiting in 1588, does so.

471 Bernier was told so by the Augustines and Jesuits. See Francois Bernier, *Travels in the Mogul Empire,* 1656–1668, Archibald Constable (Tr). 1891, 2nd edition, Humphrey Milford, Oxford University Press, 1914.

472 Bowrey, 1905.

473 Temple, R.C.(Ed). 1911, *The Diaries of Streynsham Master 1675–80 And Other Contemporary Papers Relating Thereto,* London, John Murray, Indian Records Series, 2 Vols. V.1: 37.

474 Linschoten, *Voyages* op. cit.

there two thousand rowing boats were anchored around the city[475]. Tavernier tells us that the approach to the city was paved, so were the streets inside[476]. Between 1668 and 1672, when Marshall visited the city, the city was in decline[477], its splendid streets broken in places and Forster had difficulty believing that it had been one of the premier cities of Bengal[478].

Rajmahal possessed two palaces; one for recreational purposes along the river the other, situated among splendid gardens, functioning as the court of Shah Shuja. They were reputed to have cost 2 500 000 rupees (or 281 250 pounds sterling) at the time[479]. The plumbing of the palaces is a matter of wonder today, and even more so in the seventeenth century as this statement testfies: 'At the outside of the garden South is a place behind the King's sonn's seat to convey up water into a cistern, from which all the pipes are supplied with water, which in some Banqueting Rooms is conveyed to the second storey high'[480].

Graaf described the garden as being[481]:

> square. Two sides are on the river and two look out over the countryside…it is surrounded by a great wall ornamented with little towers…there are splendid buildings inside… with columns made of wood, stone and even of copper. Each smaller garden has fountains…of marble or alabaster, or of white and blue stone, decorated with figurines of bronze such as lions, dragons and other animals. In a word, this garden is a wonder and should definitely be seen.

Murshidabad was the capital of eighteenth century Bengal. The city probably owed its origins to the sixteenth century since it started off as a market town producing 'aftabas', 'chellamanches' and belts[482]. Its

---

[475] *The Travels of Fray Sebastaian Manrique, 1629–1643*, Luard, C.E., (Tr), 1926, 1927, London, Hakluyt Society. 2 vols.

[476] Tavernier, Jean Baptiste, *Travels in India* (Tr). Ball and Crooke, 1925, 2 vols., Oxford University Press, 2nd edition.

[477] Shafaat Ahmad, 1927, (Ed). *John Marshall in India, Notes and Observations in Bengal 1668–1672,* London, Oxford University Press.

[478] Forster, as before.

[479] John Marshall op.cit.

[480] *Ibid.*

[481] In Bernouilli, 1788, *L'Inde: Description Hisrorique et Geographique de l'Inde qui presente en trios volumes et enrichis de 64 cartes,* II, Berlin.

[482] John Marshall op.cit.

population was estimated at 1500 000[483]. It lay among mango orchards at the heart of the silk growing region of Bengal and was situated along the banks of the Ganga. It was 5 miles long and about 3 miles wide. Its twin city was Mahinagar on the opposite side. Filled with beautiful buildings the city boasted many palaces–the chief one was on the river, while the country palace, or Motijheel, was in the middle of a lake. Yet another was Hirajheel on the opposite side of the river from the main palace. There was a great oval shaped market place called the *chowk* which contained many shops[484].

The city was originally called Maksudabad but when Murshid Quli chose it as his capital he changed the name to Murshidabad. As a burgeoning provincial capital, soon to be the capital of the *nizamat* of Bengal, it assumed the trappings of an imperial city. As Ghulam Husain Salim said: 'It (was) a beautiful city. Its inhabitants in the society of the *Subahdars*, being thrown into contact with the people of Delhi, in point of refinement of manners and conversation, resemble the people of Hindustan unlike those of the other parts of Bengal[485].'

Markets in Bengal

'At this market were also many kinds of cotton goods, drugs, tobacco and opium…the eyes were attracted by the sight of such superabaundance of many things in one city.' (Manrique..*The Travels of Fray Sebastian Manrique 1629–1643*, Luard, C.E. (Tr). 2 vols. London, Hakluyt Society 1926–27.)

In the seventeenth century there were several cotton mart-towns in western Bengal. Malda was described as 'the centre of cotton goods' and Shantipur the 'chief depot for malmals'[486]. Kasimbazar evolved into a mart-town for silks. Hugli was a big market town for Bengal produce. There were similar such mart towns in eastern Bengal in the seventeenth century, Dhaka was very likely one such; but we have no specific data for the others.

More important were the grain marts. It seems that a regional grain market had appeared in eighteenth century Bengal[487]. This regional market

[483] Father Georgi in Bernouilli's *L'Inde.* op.cit.

[484] Federbe, Louis Laurent de, Comte de Modave, *Le Voyage en Inde de…etc. 1773–1776. Nouveaux Memoires sur l'Etat actuel du Bengale et de l'Indoustan* (Tr.and Ed). Jean Deloche, 1971, Paris, Ecole Francaise d'Extreme Orient.

[485] *Riyas-us-Salatin,* Tr. Maulavi Abdus, 1902, Calcutta, Asiatic Society.

[486] Master, V.1: 26, 39.

[487] D.L.Curley in Marshall, P.J., 1987, *Bengal The British Bridgehead: Eastern India 1740–1828*, Cambridge, Orient Longman: 14.

manifested itself in the stability of prices; such uniformity prevailed however only in the vicinity of large towns and along the navigable rivers. The most striking feature of urbanisation in eighteenth century Bengal was the development of market-towns based on whole sale markets (*golas*) as opposed to semi-regular *haats*. Great wholesale markets were established at strategic points along the rivers-such as Bhagwangola on the Ganga near Murshidabad, Narayanganj near Dhaka and Bakarganj on the Padma estuary. These three market towns were the great collecting points for surplus rice throughout the region. By the middle of the eighteenth century the rice supply in Bengal was controlled by Bhagwangola in the west and Bakarganj in the east and it was noted in the Fort William-India House Correspondence of 1754 that Calcutta would be reduced to misery if the rice market at Bakarganj was closed[488].

Golas as mart had their antecedents in the seventeenth century. But the term *gola* was used for warehouses even earlier. The commercialization of agriculture in the late seventeenth century led to a growing assertiveness of local zaminadars and chiefs. The Bengal nawabs tried to bypass the traditional *haats* (semi-regular markets) established and controlled by the zamindars by putting up *golas* (wholesale markets) such as Bhagwangola in Murshidabad as well as their own *ganjs*[489]. *Ganjs* or regular markets also dotted the agrarian landscape of Bengal now; these were smaller than *golas*.

While the pre-colonial market place is known today by the fashionable sobriquet of 'bazaar' we should note that in pre-colonial Bengal the term 'bazaar' was rarely used. The terms then current were *ganj* and *gola*. These *bazaars* (*ganjs* or *golas* or *haats*) were established on rent-free lands by permission (*sanad*) from the ruler. Obviously such permission was only given to favourite courtiers, close relatives or important merchants with a presence at court. Sometimes the markets were owned by the nawab or held in the name of one of his family. Ownership of these *bazaars* indicated a certain status, a certain proximity to polical power. It was also profitable for it was hereditary. Ownership could be transferred or sold as an asset. Nishatganj, established by Shahamat Jung before 1730 was given to his sister Rabia Begum who in turn presented it to Muzaffar Jung when he married her daughter. Nishatganj, in effect, was treated as part of dowry and Muzaffar Jung renamed it Bairamganj[490]. Finally a

488 Marshall, 1987: 22.

489 See later.

490 In Sen, Sudipta, 1998, *Empire of Free Trade, The East India Company and the Making of the Colonial Marketplace*, Philadelphia,University of Penn Press: 43.

bazaar/haat was also a charitable institution, used to provide pension for the families of indigent nobles. Muhammad Reza Khan granted the revenues of three *haats* near Chattagram in 1759 for the maintenace of the families of Ali Asgar, Syed Rahmatullah and Muhammad Taher[491]. The *sanad* to Ali Asgar is instructive. It stated that:[492]

> Be it known to the officers and servants of the sayer mahls in the vicinity of the town of Islamabad that whereas Sayeed Alee Asgur has represented that he is burdened with a large family and many dependants and that he hath no means of providing for their support...(he) prays that a pension be settled on him by sunnud from the produce of the haut Meeteemundy to the end that his family be herewith maintained...the sum of one anna per diem is accordingly settled on him for his maintetance.

The state took a leading role in establishing these new markets but it has been suggested by Sen (1998) that we should not read too much into the pre-colonial South Asian states' role in establishing the *bazaar* as an arena of economic activity. According to Sen the pre-colonial marketplace–collectively called the *bazaar*–was an ephemeral phenomenon; dependent on the whimsy of the monarch. *Bazaars* in Mughal India were more of a spectacle for the display of social prestige and power than an expression of an economic realm. Bazaars vanished or appeared at the will of the monarch[493]. According to this reading the true market place could only come into being with colonial reordering of the economic realm; a reordering that Sen calls a 'permanent settlement of marketplaces'[494].

Sen's assertion, that only decisive state intervention can create a market, derives from his adherence to the ideas of eighteenth century English political economy. Classical political economy as it developed in England through the writings of Smith, Hume, Ricardo and Mill proposed two distinct objects: one was to provide the state with a public revenue and the other was to provide a plentiful revenue or subsistence to the people; or to enable them to provide such a revenue or subsistence for themselves. Authors differed as to which produced wealth: land or labour.

Similarly the *bazaar* was an unit for the Mughal economy that produced revenue. But unlike eighteenth century English political economy

---

491 Serajuddin, 1971: 153–4.

492 *Ibid.*: 153–4.

493 Sen, 1998: 19.

494 *Ibid.*: 120–143.

that based itself on labour and property as indicators of productiveness and wealth Mughal political economy stayed within the broad definition of political economy that we have seen above and based itself on a complex of rights, possession and forms of property that was central to the Mughal economy. This complex rested on two basic supports: the status of persons and the disposition of rights over land. Value in pre-industrial political economies was thus differently determined.

But this is not to say that the Mughal state (and the regional states after it) had no conception of political economy at all. Like all states the Mughal (and post-Mughal states) sought to enrich both itself and its subjects. Therefore here too, as elsewhere, economic policies were pursued that safeguarded the prosperity of the political realm. *Bazaars* in Mughal India evolved naturally out of the economic demands of the state: they developed further with the growth of trade and a money economy within South Asia; they flourished due to policies of the regional as well as the Mughal state. We have already referred to the taxes and trade link that the *bazaars* furnished[495]. Finally the *bazaar* satsfied the social demands of all strata of the population. This is evident from even a cursory reading of South Asian history. That the Mughal and the post-Mughal state was the guiding spirit behind the foundation of *bazaars* and the ultimate owner was made clear by the fact that often, if the owner owed moneys to the state, his *bazaar* was seized by the government[496]. But in the final analysis ownership of a *bazaar* was subordinated to the wider social relations of superiority and subordination that the Mughal order generated. The *bazaar* was an expression of Mughal property just as the complex of rights, possession etc.were essential to the Mughal economy. If we go through the *bazaar* rents we find that the 'rent' had little to do with the volume of sales that the particular *bazaar* generated. Value (prestige) and actual wealth thus occupied different domains in Mughal political economy. Thus, in Mughal economic thought, ownership, rent and value occupied different meanings. *Bazaars* in pre-colonial South Asia were not only sites for the demonstration of social power; they were equally sites where various economic relations could be observed at play[497].

---

495 See earlier.

496 Karim, Abdul, 1964, *Dacca The Mughal Capital*, Dacca, Asiatic Society of Pakistan: 112–113.

497 For an idea of the 'coming into being' of classical political economy see Keith Tribe, 1978, *Land, Labour and Economic Discourse*, London, RKP.

In eighteenth century South Asia this complex of rights, possessions and forms of property underwent a subtle change. This occurred with the intensive commercialization of agriculture in the seventeenth century. *Bazaars* now became a form of property in their own right and not subordinated so much to wider social relations. Value acquired a monetary meaning although here too the leadership came from the political elite.

When *ganjs* sprang up in eighteenth century Bengal and became a new feature in the urban landscape they frequently combatted the role of the older urban complexes. Evidence from (Azamgarh) Bihar in Muzaffar Alam's 'Aspects of Agrarian Uprisings in North India in the Early Eighteenth Century'[498] points to a number of *bazaars* and *ganjs* established by the sons and successors of the Gautam Rajputs A'zam and Azmat Khan in the early eighteenth century. These 'neo-Muslim Rajput zamindaris' built about seven *ganjs*. Zamindari centers such as Azamgarh and Azmatgarh evolved into district (*chakla*) headquarters by 1720 with a string of subsidiary market towns attached to them-Kopaganj, Iradatganj, Sufiganj, Husainganj, Jahangirganj among others. It was evident that these Gautam Rajputs were trying to control the resources of the area by channelling the produce of the countryside into the network of markets established by them. This idea of a major market controlling a string of subsidiary markets has led scholars like Yang (1998) to apply Walter Christaller's central place theory (of a major node controlling subsidiary networks) to markets in Bihar.

There is a list of *ganjs* established in Bihar in the eighteenth century[499]. They are Murtuzaganj, Qazibagh, Kabutrah Khana, Alabakspur, Masallapur, Hakimganj, Dandunmandi, Arafabad, Rasulpur, Khamepur, Mandi Begumpur all established in the early eighteenth century. Others were Hindiganj (est. 1721), Begumganj (est.1724), and Hajiganj.

Similar urbanization took place in the Bhadohi region with the founding of bazaars such as Bazaar Salabat Khan, Bazaar Rustam Khan, Bazaar Ahmadganj and Katra (market-place) Rusukhiat Khan between 1712 and 1737. We have similar data for Mirzapur[500].

---

[498] Reprinted in Alavi, Seema, 2002, *The Eighteenth Century in India,* New Delhi, Oxford University Press: 84–112.

[499] From Yang, Anand A., 1998, *Bazaar India: Markets, Society and the Colonial State in Bihar,* California Press: 99.

[500] *Ibid*: 94–96.

Again a similar situation prevailed in Dhaka where the Mughal conquest in the seventeenth century saw the establishment of *bazaars* by ruling *subahdars*. This practice continued into the eighteenth century with the nawabs and their favourites controlling these mart-towns based on rent-free lands. For Dhaka's markets we have the following data[501]: In the seventeenth century Ibrahim Khan, the Mughal *subahdar*, established the *bazaar* of Rehmat Gunge. For the eighteenth century there are Burran Gunge established by Jesarat Khan the Naib Nazim, Emam Gunge belonging to the same family, Bazar Kartalab Khan established by Murshid Quli Khan, the first Nawab of Bengal, and Narain Gunge and Lakhi Gunge established by Benur Thakur during Muhammad Reza Khan's tenure.

Establishing *bazaars* was profitable and continued throughout the eighteenth century. *Bazaars* Jupsah, Colipara and Motibari were established before 1765; *haats* Sowapur and Burnah in the same period. Unfortunately we have no data as to the names of their founders or the dates of their establishment except that they were founded before the Diwani of 1765.

In Chattagram, as in other parts of the country, *haats* were of two kinds: zamindari and those owned by the state. Of the former we find Kumira, Kadam Rasul, Udaliya, Bhutpora, Julda, Mekhal, Durung, Jagdish Roy, Garangia, Sam Chowdhury, Karianagar, and Khandokia existing in the eighteenth century. Dates of their foundation are not given but it seems here that, in the absence of a strong political presence, local elites took the lead in establishing markets. Obviously Jagdish Roy and Shyam Chowdhury were such local elites. The state *haats* were the sair *haats* situtated on lands belonging to the state: Mirganj, Ramram, Oberam (Abhayram), Pukuria and Qutubganj. As mentioned earlier the state received no rent from them and levied a duty on goods brought there for sale[502].

For Murshidabad we have the following data on *bazaars* for our period: J'afar Ganj established by J'afar Ali Khan in 1708, Maqbara Ganj established by Kasim Ali Khan the same year, Bibi Ganj established by Majum-ud-Daula in 1749 as well as the Hat Sripur established by Mughal *subahdars* in 1700[503].

---

501 From Karim, Abdul, 1964, *Dacca The Mughal Capital*, Dacca, Asiatic Society of Pakistan: 111–113.

502 Serajuddin 1971: 150–52.

503 From Sen, 1998: 44.

It is clear therefore that from the seventeenth century there was an explosion of market-towns on the urban landscape. The process gathered momentum in the eighteenth century when the Bengal Nawabs attempted a monopoly on agrarian resources; more market-towns with bazaars came up concentrated around urban nodes such as Murshidabad and Dhaka. This is a description of the market town of Musumabazar, situated on the Hugli opposite Baliaghata that Manrique has left us[504]:

> Here there was an abundance of everything one could require, especially of eatables and of household necessities, such as corn, rice, vegetable, sugar cane, oil and many kinds of milk products. From each of these articles several vessels could have been loaded.

Manrique's keen commercial eye, the line 'from each of these articles several vessels could have been loaded', is testimony to the commercial prosperity of Bengal's market towns in the seventeenth century. All these market towns were engaged in the sale of food grains. Manrique, Bowrey, Tieffanthaler and de Gennes de la Chanceliere assert that the banks of the Bhagirathi and its tributaries were filled with market-towns[505]. Urbanisation along the Hugli, as also along the Padma-Meghna, was dominated by the great grain marts of the area, held together by a network of smaller *golas* and semi-regular *haats.*

Urbanisation along rivers also signalled the entry of a cash economy into the villages of Bengal. It was stated that in the Murshidabad district in the 1770s there were three stalls dealing in *cauris* and two moneychanger's booths: these cambios or bureaus de change were a measure of how far monetisation had penetrated into the countryside[506]!

Finally, we have a poetic description of the market-town of Burdwan in western Bengal. It was an important producer of coarse cloths (*garas* and *dusutties*) in the eighteenth century:[507]

> Beyond...the poet saw the king's market with thousands of foreign merchants sitting there. There were hundreds of traders and shopkeepers and countless gems, pearls and rubies. There were various kinds of fine and beautiful cloth such as Vanat (felt cloth), makhmal (velvet), pattu, bhunai, batadara, maldai

---

[504] Manrique (Luard), as before.

[505] Especially Bowrey: 212.

[506] Mohsin, K.M., 1973, *A Bengal District in Transition; Murshidabad 1765–93*, Dacca.

[507] From Dimock, E.C. and Gupta, Pratul Chandra (Tr.and Eds)., 1965, *Maharashtra Purana: An Eighteenth Century Bengali Text*, Honolulu, East West Center Press.

> (from Malda), daccaia (from the Dacca region), and various other kinds liked by the Amirs (nobles). There were many bilati (foreign) articles of fancy price or of fashionable designs, which were, however, heaped together for want of customers.

This description, although fanciful, is important for it indicates that European goods had penetrated the interior by 1750.

Checkpoints and Fiscal Policies in Bengal

'Le vrai tresor des Princes est le commerce, etabli sur l'exploitation des terres, les manufactures, les arts.' (The real treasure of princes lies in the exploitation of the soil, the manufactures and crafts) from Bernouilli, 1788, *L'Inde: Description Hisrorique et Geographique de l'Inde qui presente en trios volumes et enrichis de 64 cartes,* II, Berlin. (*my translation*).

Other than *ganjs*, *golas* and *haats* there existed also *chowkis* (check points for transit dues) as a fiscal category in Mughal and Nawabi Bengal. More than the *bazaars*, the establishment and functioning of the *chowkis* give an idea of the thriving commercialisation in pre-colonial Bengal. Unlike *bazaars chowkis* were not sites for the play of status, charity or power. Management of the *chowki* was essentially all about assertion of economic strength and power and consequently *chowkis* were sites where physical force found its fullest expression.

Chowkis were both zamindari and state managed. Zaminadar *chowkis* were held on payment of fixed revenues to the state. But while revenue from the state *chowkis* was classed as *sair* those collected under zamindari aegis were classed under land revenue. This meant, in practice since land revenues were fixed in advance, that zamindari *chowkis* were at liberty to increase their tolls unlike the state *chowkis*; and this was something they did frequently. Apart from official zamindari *chowkis* (both *ghats* and *dallahs*) there were also a number of semi-authorised *chowkis* established by zamindars on goods passing through their regions. These 'unofficial' *chowkis* were established through private initiative and functioned without sanction from the state. In actual fact they functioned as semi-official checkposts. While described as 'illegal' and 'sources of oppression' such semi-official *chowkis* point to the commercialisation of the economy, the increasing volume of goods for the market and the desire of both the ordinary people and the local ruling classes to participate in the burgeoning economy. Also, while the *chowkis* initially designated specific places where dues and tolls were collected, these transit points gradually evolved into semi-official markets.

Chowkis were subdivided into *ghats* (river toll posts), and *dallahs* (road duty check point at the entrance to hill passes). For the Chattagram region we have the following data on *ghats*[508]: Feni Ghat on the Feni and Patharghat on the Karnaphuli were the principal state managed *ghats* in the Chattagram region, others on the Feni were Hingoli Ghat, Suipura Ghat, Burburia Ghat, Baghkhali Ghat and Domekhali Ghat; whereas Kentigia, Angarkhali, Pukuria, Batalia, Sirmai, Mutimahanagar and Bakalia *ghats* were zamindar owned.

As for *dallahs* there were eleven in Chattagram[509]: Dallahs Fatikchari, Andharmanik, Baghpur, Haralchari, Udaliya, Karnal, Dolonia, Sagar Katra, Barakumir, Chotokumir and Phohania. Note that Sagar Katra was obviously a market.

Unlike as is the case with many *bazaars* we do not have foundation dates for the *chowkis*. But fortunately we have more data on the transit dues levied at these posts. At both *ghats* and *dallahs* tolls varied according to the commodity and the type of passenger. Commodities were charged either by weight or at the rate of per rupee of the sale value: tobacco and chillies were therefore charged at the rate of 1 *anna*, 15 gandas and 2 *cowris* per *man* while pepper, cotton, cloth, sugar, ghee and coconuts were charged at 17 *gandas* and 3 *cowris* per rupee of the sale value[510]. An ordinary passenger crossing was charged 4 *gandas* and 1 *cowra*, a passenger crossing in a palanquin was charged 2 *annas*, 13 *gandas*, 1 *cowra*, a bride and groom were charged Rs. 2[511]. It is therefore obvious that the tolls were managed on a fairly sophisticated fiscal basis, manned by financial expertise and knowhow of market rates of commodities. Interestingly the projected and actual toll collections also give us a picture of how the various social categories in rural Bengal were viewed in the eighteenth century, more, the rates testify to the fact that more and more people, of all shades and hues, travelled throughout the region.

The following table gives a glimpse of transit dues for people:

---

[508] Searuddin, 1971: 154–8.

[509] *Ibid.*: 155.

[510] *Ibid.*: 155–56. The data refers to tolls on Feni Ghat in 1780–81. These were supposedly the same as those in 1775–76.

[511] *Ibid.*: 155–56.

Table 4.1 Passenger Tolls on the Feni River in 1780–81[512]

Category	*Toll:Rs.*	*Anna*	*Ganda*	*Cauri*
Ordinary Passenger			4	1
Passenger in palanquin			13	1
Gangajatri (pilgrim)			17	3
Sivajatri (pilgrim)			8	
Bride and Groom		2		
Brasssmith			17	2

Table 4.2 Tolls for Commodities on the Feni 1780–81[513]

Category	*Toll by Weight (per man)*				*Toll per rupee of sale value*			
	Rs.	*Anna*	*Ganda*	*Cauri*	*Rs.*	*Anna*	*Ganda*	*Cauri*
Animals: Buffalo, Cow, Goat, Horse and sheep							17	3
Brass and Copper							17	3
Pepper, Cotton, Cloth, Sugar, Ghee and Coconuts							17	3
Tobacco and Chillies		1	15	2				
Hemp, Oil, Betelnut, Garlic and Onion			15	2				
Gram and Lentil		1	1	2				
Wood		1	1	2				
Bamboo		1	6					
Boats	Rs. 2 to 1 (depending on quality)							

[512] Compiled from *Ibid.*

[513] Compiled from *Ibid.*

Tolls were usually customary for a particular ghat. They were not, however, uniform even throught the same region. During the same period (that is 1775–1780) crossings on the Karnaphuli (or the river of Chattagram) through Patharghat cost less than crossings through Feni Ghat on the Feni. Ordinary passenger crossings cost 3 *gandas* 1 *cauri*, a buffalo 10 *gandas* and a cow 8 *gandas* and 1 *cauri*[514]. Were lower transit costs a reflection of the greater traffic that passed through the Karnaphuli river?

In contrast to this tolls collected at *dallahs* were not regulated by either customary or prescribed rates, at both zamindar and state managed *dallahs*. This was probably because much of the *dallah* rates could not be imposed. Bengal is surrounded by hills on three sides–to the south-west, to the north and to the north-east. Historically the northern and the north-eastern borders have always been contested lands and the Bengal Sultans' and later the Mughal's campaigns towards the north and the east were dictated as much by the need to secure the state against intruders as by the desire to participate in the wealth of the hills peoples. This was the route that conducted the traditional hill trade between the hills peoples of northern and eastern Bengal, Bhutan, Arakan, Ava and Southern China-Yunnan with items such as aloes wood, medicinal plants, aromatics, herbs and spices, parrot beaks, rhino horns, hill ponies, mules, crane heads, kingfisher and crow feathers forming the major bulk[515].

The admistration of the *chowkis* testify to the fact that, like the *bazaar* in eighteenth century Bengal, more and more *chowkis* were being now established, more people travelled, more and more mercantile acitivity was taking place within Bengal, and commodities were circulating over ever-widening areas. The movement of peoples and goods is testimony to the commercialisation that pervaded rural Bengal.

Ports and Their Hinterlands in Bengal

'Here I leave this, and pass from the great Bay of Bengalla and river Ganges ... which was the theatre wherein the Portuguese possessed so much of substance...coming to possess very substantial lands that might be equated to large kingdoms, there were in them populous cities and sumptuous churches...' (Antonio Bocarro, Livro das Plantas: Descriptions of Nagapattinam and Sao Thome in the early 1630s). From Subrahmanyam, S., 1990, Appendix: 262.

---

514 *Ibid.*: 156.

515 Ray, Haraprasad, 2003: 95, 193–196.

We have more information on ports and port-towns in Bengal. Most except for Chattagram in the east, the *samatata* ports in the centre and Tamralipta in the west, had short lives. This was mainly due to river siltation, as Bengal had no proper sea port apart from Chattagram. Ports in littoral societies act as engines of change, but if the engine is primed, not with the oil of commerce but with the saline water of rapid riverine changes, ports choke and die. This happened frequently thoughout the commercial history of Bengal.

The life of ports was also affected due to the massive riverine shifts between the sixteenth and eighteenth centuries. Prime deltaic regions were overflooded and abandoned. New ports rose in response to this emergency situtation but they themselves were frequently subject to siltation and decay. Finally, the transformation of the maritime state of Arakan into a rogue pirate state in the seventeen century meant that many former ports of Bengal, such as Pipli, Sagor and Sandwip, now became infamous nodes in the slave raiding/piracy network. Many such ports now became known as slave marts. Merchants and commerce avoided these ports.

The capital of eastern Bengal–Suvarnagram–was an important port as the early history of Bengal tells us. In the fourteenth century Ibn Batuta spoke of it as a great commercial centre and port with boats destined for Java. By the sixteenth century it appears to have been less of a port and capital city and more of a manufacturing city; both the *Ain* and Ralph Fitch enumerate the cotton products of Suvarnagram. Dhaka now rose as the Mughal port in the east.

In the western part of Bengal one port stands out from the post-Maurya period. This is Tamralipta. It was the chief western port of Bengal until about the eighth century. While not directly participating in the Roman trade network[516] Tamralipta was active in coastal trade around the Bay of Bengal from the fifth century. It also commenced direct sailings to Ceylon at this time. Fa-Hien embarked from Tamralipta for Ceylon.

The most important port of Bengal in medieval times was Chattagrama, referred to as Xatigam by the Portuguese and as Chatighan by the French. Between the time of the eclipse of Suvarnagram and the rise of Dhaka Chattagram emerged as the frontier port of Bengal. Located at the far east of *samatata/harikela* Chattagram lay at the mouth of the Karnaphuli river and connected two routes for merchandise: it was an entrepot for the goods of Dhaka-Suvarnagram-Jugdia to its west as well as for the goods

[516] See Politics and Trade in Bengal for a detailed discussion on Tamralipta's position in Roman trade.

that came down from Assam and other parts of *harikela* to its north. The Karnaphuli made for a safe harbour. The Karnaphuli was navigable from the middle of October until the end of April and communicated with Dhaka, Jugda and Linepur[517].

When did Chattagram come into existence as a port? Its origins are obscure but it seems likely that it emerged as a port under Arakanese aegis. Some Arab merchants were settled near Chattagram in the period 780 to 810 A.D.. In 957 A.D. Chattagram came under Arakanese domination; it was referred to as Tset-ta-going by the Arakanese and as Shati-al-ganga by the Arabs. In time this became Xatigaon, Xatigam, Chatigham or Sadkawan and, later, the English Chittagong[518]. So we may assume that by the eleventh century Chattagram had evolved into a full-fledged port, probably under Arakanese control.

Facing the east rather than west, Chattagram traditional trading partners were Arakan and the countries beyond. Direct sailings from Bengal to the west coast were rare but surprisingly Chattagram seems to have traded with the Malabar. At the turn of the seventeenth century Pyrard de Laval remarked that he found there a ship from Calicut[519].

In between the time when Tamralipta declined and Chattagram became the paramount port of Bengal, ie. from the 7th to the 11th centuries, we get mentions of the mysterious port of Samandar, yet to be identified conclusively. Samandar was the chief port of Bengal, at least in the eyes of its visitors, and we are told that it was the principal market and port on the Ganges delta, inhabited by wealthy merchants from all over the world , the centrepoint of trade with Assam and Ceylon, the great rice-port of Bengal and a trader in aloes-wood (for which there was a great demand in the ancient and medieval Mediterranean world) brought down from Assam[520]. Samandar was definitely in existence for three hundred years between the ninth century (Ibn Khurdadhbih) and the twelfth century (al-Idrisi) as these sources tell us.

---

[517] C2 115, A.N., Paris and Hamilton, Walter, 1828, *East India Gazeteer*, 2 vols., 2nd ed., London.

[518] Ali, Muhammad Mohar,1985, *History of the Muslims of Bengal*, V.1A Muslim Rule in Bengal 1203–1757, Saudi Arabia, Ibn Saud Islamic University Publications: 37–39.

[519] Francois Pyrard de Laval, 1887–1890, *The Voyage of ...to the East Indies, the Maldives, the Moluccas and Brazil 1601–1611*, 3 vols. (Tr). Albert Gray, London, Hakluyt Society.

[520] Ali, Muhammad Mohar, 1985: V. 1A: 30–31. See ibn Khurdadbih's and al-Idrisi's accounts in Elliot and Dowson, V.1. op. cit.

But where was Samandar situtated? There is a controversy about this since the references to its location and character are diverse. We are told that: (1) it was dependent on Kanauj, king of the country[521], (2) it was situated on an inlet which came from Kashmir[522], (3) it was built on a stream of the fragrant Musala[523], and (4) it was near to Kamru from where aloes wood–its chief item of trade–was brought down by way of a 15 to 20 day journey through sweet water[524]. We know that Kanauj, the imperial capital, had come into Pala possession in the 9th century, and therefore Samandar could justifiably be described as being part of Kanauj's (Pala) dominions. Samandar was likely to have been situated in the south-eastern delta since both ibn Khurdadbih and al-Idrisi harp its proximity to Kamrup/Sylhet (famed for aloes wood), it was probably situated on the Meghna (the Musala) for the Meghna-Brahmaputra waterway was the only large inland ('sweet water') navigable channel in that part of Bengal, and the reference to Samandar being on 'an inlet that came from Kashmir' may be explained by the fact that al-Idrisi confused the eastern Himalayas (Kailash) from where the Brahmaputra rises with the northern Himalayas (Kashmir).

While this identification of the location of Samandar seems definitive, the report of ibn Khurdadbih[525] also states that Samandar was thirty miles north of Ganjam (somewhere between Bengal and inland Assam?) which has led Ahmad to identify Samandar with Suvarnagram and Tarafdar to identify it with Gangabandar[526].

It is likely that Samandar may have been an earlier port in the Suvarnagrama region; in that case however it cannot be thirty miles north of Ganjam. Was it then in the area around Saptagram? Samandar can then be identified with Gangabandar/Tamralipta. We know that Muhammad Mohar Ali places Samandar at/around Sandwip island since al-Idrisi mentions it was one day's sail from Samandar[527]. According to al-Idrisi Samandar was near the confluence of the Meghna and the Brahmaputra near the present

[521] al-Idrisi (1164) in Muhammed Mohar Ali V. 1A: 30.

[522] *Ibid.*: 30

[523] *Ibid.*: 30

[524] ibn Khurdadbih, al-Idrisi in *Ibid.*: 30.

[525] See Ahmad, S.Maqbul, 1989, *Arabic Classical Accounts of India and China*, Shimla, Indian Institute of Advanced Study (ninth century) .

[526] Samandar has been identified with Suvarnagram by Ahmad, 1989: 24–5. However it could equally be Gangabandar in the region of the ancient port of Bengal, Tamralipta (see Tarafdar, M.R., 1978, 'Trade and Society in Early Medieval Bengal' in *The Indian Historical Review*, January, IV, 2).

[527] Ali, Muhammad Mohar (1985) V. 1A: 32–33.

port town of Chandpur in Bangladesh. Since al-Idrisi wrote in the twelfth century we know that Samandar functioned as a port from the ninth century (Ibn Khurdadhbih) for at least three hundred years. Samandar was situated on the Meghna-identified by al-Idrisi as Musala or the 'river of perfumes'. Riverine changes may have silted this port up so much so after this time that the next great port was destined to be Chattagram on the Karnaphuli further east. If Samandar is indeed Sandwip then the island enjoyed a distinguished trading lineage. It was mentioned in the *Periplus of the Erythraean Sea* as Chryse which Bhattasali interprets as Sandwip[528]. Sagor's name has also been proposed as an interim port. Both Sagor and Bakla in the Sundarbans area were functioning as ports from the twelfth century and, if Bakla is identified as Chandradwip, possibly even earlier.

These conflicting identifications of Samandar as being located in the west (Gangabandar), the east (on the Meghna) and in the centre of *samatata* (Sagor) add further to our confusion regarding the lineages of a commercial history of Bengal. It should be obvious that if the interim port of Bengal–which is assumed to have been Samandar–is located in western Bengal many of our assumptions, as regards the east being the heart of the commercial economy of medieval Bengal, have to be revised. This however is not very likely given the present state of scholarship on Samandar, which inclines to the east.

Soon after Chattagram rose into prominence there was also a minor westward shift in trade; this was visible in the establishment of ports to the west of Chattagram in the delta region. The deltaic zone of eastern *samatata* contained Bengal's chief ports from the twelfth to the sixteenth centuries. These market and port towns in Bengal flourished in medieval Bengal; however, most of these had decayed by the eighteenth century. These towns-Bakla, Chandikan (or Sagor), Sandwip and Sripur-were located in the deltaic zone which, we noted earlier, had experienced considerable urbanization in the early medieval period. Some had older lineages. The rule of the Chandras from Vikrampur, their commercial interests and their Arakanese lineage contributed to a new explosion of eastern trade from the eleventh century[529]. They used the port of Chandradwip; this is the

528 Bhattasali, N.K., 1946, 'New Light on the History of Assam' in *Indian Historical Quarterly*, 22: 250–52.

529 This explosion of trade in Bengal in the eleventh century may link up with Kulke's assertion that there was a trade revolution in the Indian Ocean at this time. See Kulke, Herman, 1999, 'Rivalry and Competition in the Bay of Bengal in the Eleventh Century and its bearing on Indian Ocean Studies' in Om Prakash and Denys Lombard (eds). *Commerce and Culture in the Bay of Bengal 1500–1800*, New Delhi, ICHR, Manohar: 17–35. See pp. 27–8.

medieval Bakla. The vehicle of the trade revolution in the northern Bay were the ports in the deltaic region of Bengal.

The towns of Bakla, Chandikan or Sagor, Sandwip and Sripur-some bases of autonomous Hindu chiefs (*baro bhuinyas*) who offered resistance to the Muslims, others well-known market and port towns-were known as naval centres, lying at the heart of celebrated producing regions. These were market towns and vibrant ports that carried on trade with Arakan and beyond[530].

These deltaic towns flowered from the early period until the seventeenth century. Factors leading to their growth may be summed up as follows. These port towns probably arose as a result of the commercial policy of the kings of Pattikera and those of Dhaka-Vikrampur. Their further development was carried on by the independent port administrations of the *baro bhuinyas*. The further evolution of these ports should be seen within the context of the eleventh century when three factors coincided: the Chola commercial resurgence further south, the 'trade revolution' in the eastern Indian Ocean, and the rise of the kingdom of Arakan. All three took place in the same century.

The Buddhist settlements in the Dhaka-Comilla region maintained close ties with Arakan and Pagan. The kings of southeastern Bengal functioned under the aegis of Vikrampur and ruled more or less independently of Lakhnawati. These kings–known to Ibn Batuta as the kings of Bangalah (as opposed to Lakhnawati)–based their regime on commercial activities. At a time when the economy of Gaur was land-based and there was a shrinking of coinage, coins found in this coastal area indicate that commerce was flourishing in the eastern part of Bengal. But the Khadgas, Chandras of Dhaka-Vikrampur and the Pattikera kings were rulers of a marginal area and therefore did not enjoy the same advantages that accrued to the rulers of Lakhnawati in terms of a well-demarcated territory, a substantial tax base and an agrarian core that was focussed to meet the needs of the middle gangetic plain, as we noted. Moreover the Chandras were succeeded by the Varmans who were orthodox Brahmans. Like their western counterparts, the Senas, the Varmans sought to regulate society on conventional hinduised lines. Agriculture and land based activities were therefore promoted. Commercial activities took a back-seat.

The disappearance of these small port towns from the political and commercial map of Bengal may be ascribed to the following factors:

---

530 See the section on Routes, Ports and Trading Networks in Bengal.

(1) Commercial growth was halted after a certain point because the commerce of this deltaic area experienced various significant shifts during its existence. These were:

A: The ports of *samatata* were the inheritors of the early Buddhist network in the Bay. The ninth century rule of Sasanka was a watershed in Bengal in that his anti-Buddhist policies actually sculpted Bengal into two distinct entities in east and west. The east remained Buddhist, while the west converted to Hinduism.The east now continued the seafaring heritage of Tamralipta, the west became largely agrarian. Note that Mohar Ali says that Samandar was probably situtated in the east. From the eleventh century Buddhism declined in Bengal when the Palas reconverted to Hinduism. However,

B: This decline was offset by a resurgence of Buddhism (and trade) in Arakan and Ceylon from the eleventh century. This was because Buddhists from Bengal and Bihar now went north to Tibet or east to Arakan. From the twelfth to the fourteenth centuries therefore these ports participated in a new Buddhist religio/political/commercial network straddling the northern Bay of Bengal of which Arakan was the most important.

C: Surprisingly, even with the foundation of the Bengal Sultanate, the eastward trade continued to prosper. Arakan was still a priority area.

D: The Ilyas Shahis in the fifteenth century started developing the China trade. Embassies from Bengal to China were sent in 1405, 1408, 1409, 1412, 1414 and 1438-39. This concentration on the China route may have disturbed the older trading networks of the region as it meant that sailings were now diverted southward in the Bay (see the section on Routes Ports and Networks in Bengal).

E: Husain Shahi policy in the fifteenth and sixteenth centuries cut short this network. Significantly there were no more state sponsored sailings to China; shipping lanes had to relocate themselves once again. But Ray maintains that trade to China continued in the sixteenth century[531]. Moreover,

F: The Chinese withdrew from trade in the Bay and the Indian Ocean. In the middle of the fifteenth century they left

[531] Ray, Haraprasad 2003: 213–215.

Calicut and concentrated on Nagapattinam. After the death of Cheng He there were no more official sailings.

G: Portuguese hegemony in this region meant that from the sixteenth century trade was diverted southward to the Coromandel and Ceylon and eastward to Malacca.

H: The Arakanese asserted their dominion over this area and captured Chattagram, the chief port in the east, by mid-century. This meant, to all intents and purposes, that Bengal was bereft of its major eastern outlet of trade.

I: In the seventeenth century the world of Bay trade broke down with the decline of the Portuguese and the transformation of Arakan into a pirate state. It became more over a slave trade, first with Portuguese help (utilising Portuguese networks along the Bengal and Coromandel coasts) and then with Dutch help (the Malacca-Batavia network). This meant that Bengal could not participate in this trade any longer.

J: In the seventeenth century the produce of Bengal were diverted to serve the trading needs of the overland and maritime trade of the Mughal world economy spanning Turan and Iran.

K: In the eighteenth century English shipping took over where the Portuguese had left off. Devastated by Portuguese-Arakanese conflict for much of the sixteenth and seventeenth centuries and mauled by Mughal attacks on their sovereignty the ports of the Pratapadityas and Kedar Rais had little part to play in these new trade networks[532].

(2) The great riverine changes of the second half of the sixteenth century meant that new rivers such as the Bhairab, the Matabhanga, the Garai-Madhumati, the Arial Kha now linked western Bengal and the Ganga through the Padma-Meghna which in turn linked up wiith the Brahmaputra. This meant that east Bengal ceased to be a remote region. Through the Padma-Meghna system Dhaka could now connect up with the Saptagram-Hugli ports. This meant that north-east riverine sailings up the Brahmaputra to connect up with the older northern route to Upper India were no longer necessary. The drying up of the mighty Karatoya at the end of the

---

[532] See *Merchants and Companies in Bengal: Kasimbazar and Jugdia in the Eighteenth Century* (Pragati Publications, New Delhi).

sixteenth century was symptomatic of the end of the last great age of connectivity of medieval Bengali ports with the great silk route that ran from China to the west. Eastern goods now found an outlet through the western ports of Bengal. Chattagram became isolated; its claim to Porto Grande status of Bengal diminished. Within western Bengal this change meant the dislocation of ports such as Saptagram (which 'dried' up; from the east bank Saptagram now moved to the west bank), introduction of new rivers and the fragmentation of *samatata*. The trade channels of the deltaic ports could not constantly readjust to new routes deriving from variable economic, political and ecological compulsions and were thus effectively destroyed.

(3) The Arakanese (Magh) 'depredations' in this area. From the fifteenth to the eighteenth century these port-towns were fought over by Tripura, Arakan and Bengal. When the Arakanese could not retain hegemony over these tracts permanently they led frequent raids against this area which ruined its economy.

(4) The Portuguese factor. The Portuguese controlled much of the delta–either informally or by means of direct political control from the sixteenth century. The fortunes of these port towns declined with the fall in Portuguese fortunes in Bengal and in South East Asia in the seventeenth century[533].

(5) It is yet to be seen whether the conversion of this area into a slave raiding area hampered the evolution of port towns in this region.

The history of these ports is illuminating. The sovereigns of Bakla were known as the rajas of Chandradwip. We have sources affirming to the existence of Bakla from the twelfth century. But Chandradwip existed earlier[534]. The *Ain* mentions Bakla in its catalogue of important towns in Bengal, so does Ralph Fitch[535]. Manrique commented that the city contributed to the wealth of Dhaka[536]. By the mid-seventeenth century Bakla was in decline.

Chandikan or Sagor, was the most important maritime power of the region. Its importance at the beginning of the seventeenth century was

533 See Routes, Ports and Trading Networks in Bengal.

534 See earlier section on the east in ancient Bengal. Chandradwip was under the Chandra kings.

535 Allami, Abul Fazl, *Ain-I-Akbari* (Tr.Jarrett and Sarkar), v. 2: 147; Fitch, Ralph, Ed. Foster, William, *Early Travels in India 1583–1619*, London, 1921.

536 Manrique, op.cit.

immense, as we know from Roe and Monserrate[537]. It was the principality of Pratapaditya who built up a strong navy and constructed ship-building yards at Dadkhah, Jahajghata and Chakvasi. This fleet became known as the Nawara fleet, later used by the Mughals to repel the Maghs; however, we have no documentation as to whether the kings of Chandikan were then co-opted into the Mughal ruling hierarchy[538]. Chandikan was reputed to be a great commercial centre and in time became an important centre for Portuguese commercial operations as well. The Jesuits built their first church here.

Findings from coastal archaeology tells us that Chandikan was also a temple town. Archaeological artefacts and statues have been found here dating from the third century BC. These are Hindu, Buddhist and Jain in origin and traverse the Maurya-Sunga period until the Sena period.[539] Chandikan formed part of the ancient and sacred Pundravardhana and its other name, Sagor, is symbolic. Sagor is the final resting point of the Ganga before it merges into the Bay of Bengal.

However by mid seventeenth century the island's coasts were menaced by the Maghs as Manrique tells us[540] but it still retained its religious importance and attracted thousands of pilgrims. It contained reservoirs of fresh water (Manrique)–a bonus in deltaic regions–and fish products were cheap and plentiful[541]. At the end of the seventeenth century Master and Bowrey commented that it had become a depot for Arakanese raids[542]. Yet it was still a deep water port[543] but because of Arakanese raids it was unpopulated. By the eighteenth century it, too, was abandoned.

---

537 Foster, W., (Ed). 1926, *Sir Thomas Roe: His Embassy to the Court of the Great Moghul 1615–1619*, London; Father Hosten, (Ed). Monserrate, *Mongolicae Legationis Commentarius*, 1590, Memoirs of the Asiatic Society of Bengal, v. 3, No. 9.

538 Pratapaditya was defeated in 1612 by one of Islam Khan's generals–Ghias Khan. It has been speculated that the Nadia Rajas assisted the Mughal general and in so doing consolidated their position in Saptagram as *qanungo*-a fact which later led to their confirmation as the Rajas of Nadia (Curley, David L., 2002, '*Maharaja Krisnacandra, Hinduism and Kingship in the Contact Zone of Bengal*' in Richard B. Barnett (Ed) *Rethinking Early Modern India*, New Delhi, Manohar: 88–89).

539 Chattopadhyay, Sagar, 2005, *Dakshin Chabbish Porgona Jelar Purakirti*, Kolkata, W B. State Archaeological Museum, Publication: 279 (in Bengali).

540 Manrique, op.cit.

541 Master, Streynsham, *Diaries 1675–80* (September 5, 1676) 2 vols.(Ed). R.C.Temple London, John Murray, 1911.

542 *Ibid.*; Bowrey: 211–12.

543 Bowrey: 209.

Cesare Frederici visited Sandwip in 1569. At the start of the seventeenth century it was under the rule of Kedar Rai. In 1602 he 'liberated' Sandwip from the Mughals and placed it under Carvalho. Lahori tells us that there was a substantial Portuguese colony there during the seventeenth century. Later in the seventeenth century the Mughal *subahdar* of Dhaka 'liberated' it from the Portuguese Gonzales and gave it to Arakan as *jagir*. Hamilton attests to its cheap prices (of rice, eggs and poultry) in the eighteenth century[544].

Sripur was also a well-known port. Sripur came under Portuguese control by the end of the sixteenth century. It was celebrated as one of the most powerful towns of Bengal. By the eighteenth century it too had fallen off the map.

These little capital towns, centers of autonomous chiefdoms were, as we saw, substantial ports. It was but natural that they evolved into market towns as well. Bakla was a great entrepot of rice, cottons and silk cloths[545]. Sripur was well known for its cotton goods. As well as these items the deltaic ports carried on commerce in grain, oilseeds and dairy products with their neighbours.

In the sixteenth century the economic impetus swung in favour of *Vanga* by way of political and geographical imperatives. In 1506 Ala-ud-Din Husain Shah built a bridge connecting Triveni/Nabadwip with Saptagram, then the chief port in the west. By 1560 Nabadwip had evolved into a well-known market town; merchants were settling there and selling goods from locations as far off as Kashmir in the north to Kanchipuram in the extreme south. Saptagram silted up by 1560 and contributed mightily to the decline of Gaur.

From the seventeenth century, with the Mughal conquest of Bengal, we get information on the administration of the port-towns. By the time the Bengal Nawabs ruled Bengal four main ports were administered by them: of them three were in Bengal and one in Bihar. They were Murshidabad under the Pachotra Bandar or Daroga as he is referred to in English records, Hugli under the Baksh Bandar and Dhaka under the Shah Bandar. The first controlled the imperial dues coming into the capital, the second dues from overseas trade and the third collected duties arising out of the trade of the eastern districts. The Budrekha Bandar of Patna controlled the duties from trade with the middle and upper gangetic plain.

[544] Hamilton, Alexander, *A New Account Etc.*

[545] Varthema, Ludovico, *The Itinerary of...*(Tr. R.C. Temple), London, Hakluyt, 1928.

Saptagram was replaced by Hugli as chief port and mart-town of Bengal in 1580. We do not have exact dates of the establishment of port administration in Hugli as opposed to its foundation as port town. It was probably from the time of Shah Jahan's expulsion of the Portuguese from Hugli in 1632 that port administration in Hugli started in earnest. Manrique tells us of his visit there in the seventeenth century: it appears that the town was initially founded as a mart by the Portuguese. Big '*golas*' containing trade items were divided into rudimentary rooms. They soon evolved into a permanent structure and Hugli became an emporia town. To distinguish this market from smaller markets it was called the 'great' or 'public' bazaar. This corresponds to Luillier's observations about Hugli at the turn of the eighteenth century. There were also smaller markets which sold daily provisions, cottons and coarse cloth.[546] It seems that Hugli had evolved naturally into a mercantile city par excellence; it had the best caravanserai in the province, many rich muslim merchants lived here and moreover stuff from all corners of Mughal India were available here. It was a Mughal port dominated by Persians, Armenians, Turks, Kashmiris and merchants from Central Asia; despite being expelled from there by Shah Jahan in 1632 Portuguese presence in Hugli was still major in the seventeenth century.

Rajmahal was another important seventeenth century market-town and port but with a difference. It connected the markets of Bihar with those of Bengal and especially those of Patna with Malda. Moreover a portion of Agra goods which came down the river to Patna were shipped onto Bengal via Rajmahal. Rajmahal therefore connected not only the markets of Bengal and Bihar through the Ganga-Yamuna riverine system but was also an important riverine port in the North India-Eastern India trade. It was also a producing centre for textiles for we have evidence of a Mughal *karkhana* there[547]. Trade must have been brisk for Tieffanthaler has spoken of the caravanserai here. One found in its markets all the produce of the interior (Rajmahal was between Bengal and Bihar). Manrique noted that prices here were cheap[548].

The date of origin of Dhaka as Mughal port is also obscure but it probably evolved into an imperial port with proper administration after

---

546 Bowrey, op.cit.: 170.

547 Karim, Khondkar Mahibubul, 1974, *The Provinces of Bihar and Bengal Under Shah Jahan*, Daaca, Asiatic Society of Bangladesh: 32. However he seems to confuse Akbarnagar (Rajmahal) with Gaur: 39.

548 Manrique.

the Mughal conquest of Bengal. Though an important Mughal port in the seventeenth century, the jurisdiction of the Shah Bandar of Dhaka declined with the transfer of the diwani to Murshidabad and the establishment of the office of the Pachotra Bandar there.

Kasimbazar, the chief port of Murshidabad, the base of the Pachotra Bandar's operations rose into prominence with the shift of capital in the eighteenth century. It became the most important market-town for textiles in eighteenth century Bengal and was important enough to give its name to the Bhagirathi that flowed past its banks[549]. Originally a seventeenth century mart-town famed for its silk mix cloths, Kasimbazar formed an island bound by the Bhagirathi, the Jalangi and the Padma and this island was covered with mulberry trees[550]. It was this that contributed to the celebrity of Kasimbazar for it was the centre of silk production in Bengal as well as the centre of all commerce in Bengal[551].

As port Kasimbazar experienced a riverine traffic during the monsoon whose importance and variety has been called unique in the world[552]. As the centre for commerce in all Bengal it housed the English factory (established 1658–9), the factories of the Dutch and the French (at Kalikapur) and the Armenian settlement at Saidapur at a distance.

It seems that commercial possibilities in Kasimbazar were so extensive that foreign merchants such as Kashmiris, Gujaratis, Persians and Turks had permanent residences there. Kasimbazar's location was strategic; its proximity to the court at Murshidabad was another atrraction for foreign merchants for they could then petition the court for grievances if any. These merchants built beautiful buildings along the river for Kasimbazar was also known for its salubrious climate in the eighteenth century.

In 1813 this magnificent city, emblematic of thriving commerce and sumptous silk, died out. The changing of the course of the Bhagirathi resulted in the city being transformed into a unhealthy swamp. Like Ashin Das Gupta's Malabar this area too hides under its marshes the vanished history of a million secrets and magnificent palaces.

The origin of Patna as Mughal port under the Bengal Nawabs is obscure but it probably dated from the time of commercial decline of Rajmahal due to a change in the course of the Ganga.

[549] It was frequently called the Kasimbazar river by Europeans in the eighteenth century.

[550] Modave op.cit.

[551] Hamilton, Walter op.cit. Also *The Imperial Gazeteer*, 1908, vol. XI. See also Hamilton, Alexander op. cit and Bowrey op. cit.: 213.

[552] Hamilton, Walter op. cit.

European Settlements along the Bhagirathi

'Pour ce qui va dans l'Inde, militaire,medecin, missionaire, homme de letters, est marchand comme le marin, l'employe, le simple negociant.'

(Whoever goes to India–soldier, doctor, missionary or scholar–is a merchant like the sailor, the company employee or the ordinary seller) Tieffanthaler (but also attributed to Anquetil Duperron) in Bernouilli, 1788, *L'Inde*, III, Berlin. (*My translation*).

There was a new spurt of urbanization along the Bhagirathi belt at the end of the seventeenth century as European companies left Hugli and founded their own settlements. It is to be noted that all these urban clusters were port-settlements giving on to the Bhagirathi, the chief channel of western Bengal. This urbanization was different in nature, for reasons that are spelt out below. These settlements–in order of ascent–were Calcutta (English), Baranagar (a subsidiary Dutch settlement) both on the right bank, Srirampur (Danish) on the left bank, Barrackpur on the right bank, Bankibazar also on the right (Belgians), and then Chandernagar (French), Chinsura or Chunchura (Dutch), Hugli, Bandel (Portuguese) on the right bank leading to the defunct Saptagram. These European settlements, which grew into substantial townships in the eighteenth century, exercised a different relationship with the countryside from the towns that we have already noted.

First of all, the economic morphology of these settlements dictated their relationship with the surrounding area. They exercised no symbiotic relationship with the country around them, while situated within the countryside this countryside was an area to be exploited for purposes of trade. The countryside therefore became a productive hinterland for these townships.

Second, these townships were artificial townships in that they were not the natural outcomes of urban growth but alien intrusions into a foreign body. Peopled almost entirely by their own nationals these European townships soon attracted a dependent indigenous population as satellites. Driven by different compulsions, these European townships' attempts at fortification, their hostilities with their neighbours, their demands for minting rights, their usage of the river as a shipping highway to distant lands and their extractive role with the countryside, meant that they were viewed with suspicion (and resentment) by the ruling class from Murshidabad.

Third, these townships combined all urban functions within their walls. They were port-town and market town in one, they generated a different way of life by the very virtue of their origin, they exercised independent jusrisdiction within their environs and were territorially sovereign, and furthermore they were nodal points in a commercial atlas which bore little relationship to the mercantile map we have so far described because the span of their operations, and the implications of it, were so huge.

Finally, there is historic evidence of one disjuncture that these alien port-towns caused in the commercial map of Bengal. For long port-towns had existed in an organic symbiosis with land (caravan) routes so much so that the Indian Ocean maritime trade and the continental overland trade were mirror images of one another. These overland caravan routes were the Bengal-Bihar-Nepal-Tibet route and the Bengal-Assam-China routes among others. Murshidabad-Rajmahal-Patna for the former .and Dhaka-Chattagram for the latter were therefore important port towns that linked up with these caravan routes. The statement that the price of silk at Kasimbazar was linked to the prices set by the Agra market points to the linking of maritime, riverine and overland trade[553].

A section of the earlier route went further north-west to join the Silk Route through Central Asia[554]. From Central Asia this route joined up with the great caravan routes linking Bengal with West Asia[555]. These routes now fell into disuse as more and more taffic was diverted to the sea route for trade with Europe under the aegis of European capital and shipping.

In earlier sections we had stressed repeatedly that the economy of Bengal–and therefore of its towns and villages–were part of a larger network of religio-political compulsions. Commerce had flowed naturally from such integrations: be it towards Buddhist lands to the east or Islamic lands to the west. Now for the first time the towns and villages of Bengal were being slowly integrated into a *commercial* network that was truly global in scope and in which they would play henceforth a subsidiary role based on a fundamentally unequal relationship.

Rivers in Bengal

> Unchecked, untramelled, the river slips by laughing as if with joy to be free....on these same banks for centuries it has watched men come and go. It has seen great kingdoms rise

[553] 'According as this silk sells in Agra, so the price of silk in Kasimbazar riseth or falleth' in Chaudhuri, K.N., 1978, *The Trading World of Asia and the English East India Company 1660–1760*, Cambridge University Press: 354.

[554] See section titled Was there Ever an 'Indian' Trade?.

[555] See section on Routes, Ports and Trading Networks in Bengal

> and fall...That wonderful brief hush that come before the dawn enfold(s) the world...the sun arises like a giant refreshed with sleep...the river is alive with craft...On either hand it is historic ground. Hidden, forgotten in the noise and stir of this busy mart, memories still cling thick round these lower reaches of the Lakhiya, close by where the great rivers meet. But just below the Megna, the Ganges, the Brahmaputra, the Dullasery and the Ichamati all unite (at) this meeting place of the giant watercourses...Slowly it draws to evening...a single sail chasing the setting sun glides on till it loses itself in the golden crest...Across the water, soft and low, there comes the call to prayer from the mosque beyond the trees...Throughout the East, the wonderful mystic East, throbbing with the hopes and fears of its countless people...The sun sinks low. Focussed until now in one great ball of fire, it breaks suddenly, spread left and right in a blaze of colour over the west. Sapphire and topaz and pearl, opal and amethyst and onyx it blends them all in a glorious blaze of light . Faithfully the river mirrors them back. One moment a shimmer of gold, the next a leaping column of fire, it pales at last to orange and mauve and grey. The river itself grows almost still[556].

These lines, so evocative of the swampy, almost Conradesque waterscape of Bengal were written by an English civil servant named Bradley in the nineteenth century. The passage captures the spirit of the land–a land carved by turbulent water courses and marked by rivers. Bound by mountains to the north, west and east, Bengal has always been a plains land of rivers, marshes and deltas. Bengal is largely a littoral country, particularly in its east, now Bangladesh.

The riverine tracts described here refer to eastern Bengal; more specifically to the area around Jugdia. Rivers near this deltaic part of Bengal are swift, fast-flowing and vicious; they mark their passage by frequently demolishing villages and port-towns on their course. By contrast rivers to the west are more placid; even the now-forgotten Jalangi near Kasimbazar never followed the reckless routes of her eastern sisters.

Touring Bengal from 1669–1679, Thomas Bowrey wrote of the Ganges, the principal river of Bengal[557]:

[556] Bradley F.B. (circa 1905) *The Romance of an Eastern Capital* published 1975, Delhi, Metropolitan, Indian edition:. 318–19, 323–24, 337–39.

[557] Bowrey: 210–11.

> the Great River Ganges that Alexander the Great sailed downe in time of his great conquests in Asia...It disperseth its streams through many spacious deserts and multitudes of Kingdoms and is known to be of great breadth in many places Up in the Countrey of Pattana...

The intricate riverine system of Bengal, to which English cartographers such as Rennell[558] devoted so much time, is infinitely easier to comprehend if divided it into the regional blocs of *Vanga-Samatata* (west-east) on the one side and *Harikela-Varendra* (east-north) on the other. West to east, therefore, the main rivers, with their channels, are the Rupnarayan, Damodar, Bhagirathi, Bidyadhari, Jalangi, Mathabhanga, Piyali, Jamuna, Karatoya, Matla, Saraswati, Ichamati, Gaureshwar and Kalindi among others. Lesser rivers here are Ajoy, Mayurakshi, Brahmani, Kunur, Banka, Kahari, Behula, Gangur, Saraswati, Kunti, Dwarekeshwar, Mundeswari, Kasai, Silai and several other rivers that have died out today, but are attested to by travellers.

Bidyadhari seems to have been, in early times, the chief channel of the Hugli (Bhagirathi) and housed the site of Chandraketugarh on its shores. The Jamuna, in the seventeenth century, probably functioned as a port as well, for we get references to Pratapaditya of Jessore's war-ships being moored there at Chandikan. From late sixteenth century this area saw a triangular tussle for control between Bengali chiefs, Portuguese freebooters and Magh (Arakanese) raiders. This contested territory carried on a brisk trade with Arakan, China and South East Asia.

The mangrove swamp between the Hugli and the Meghna (still in *samatata*) is known as the Sundarbans and houses some of the fastest-flowing rivers of the region such as Piyali, Bidyadhari, Matla, Baleswar, Madhumati, ArialKha, Tarki, Lakhiya, Nayabaghini, GourNadi, Bhairab, Shibsa–the list is endless. On the west these small rivers are fed by the Hugli/Bhagirathi/Ganga and by the Meghna/Padma/Brahmaputra on the east. While not geographically significant, these miniature riverine systems are vital in that they provide Sundarban's main source of sustenance and communication. Small maritime states with unpretentious bazaars and transient ports were housed on their banks: we can think of Bakla, Sripur, Chandikan which carried on a thriving trade in cottons and food-grain with their eastern neighbours across the Bay of Bengal. Indeed Bakla's (or Bakergunge) mercantile antecedents go back to the twelfth century[559]. As Chandradwip its commercial acvities go back even further.

---

[558] *A Bengal Atlas,* London, 1780, 1781.

[559] Ray, Aniruddha, 1997: 227.

In the east of the province the main rivers are the eastern Ganga or the Padma, the Meghna and the Brahmaputra; these waters of *harikela* linked up with the Mahananda in *varendra* (Gaur region) and provided *varendra* with a link to *harikela* and thereby to *samatata/vanga* as well. In this way it was possible to circumnavigate Bengal by its complex inland watersystem.

It has been remarked that, seen from above, Bengal's river-network resembles a spider's web. But it must be remembered that this web was also a very high tension web for apart from these wilful rivers cutting their course through the plains of Bengal to the Bay (and destroying anything that came into their path) any attempt to interfere with their course by cutting channels to facilitate communication and trade frequently led to their drying up and the consequent depopulation of their villages. In the sixteenth century Sultan Ala-ud-Din Husain Shah built a bridge linking Triveni with Saptagram (the Portuguese Porto Pequeno) on the Saraswati to facilitate trade. Within fifty years the Saraswati dried up. Later on, in 1750, Nawab Alivardi Khan had a channel dug to connect the Ganga with the Sarawati; the consequence was that the old bed of the Ganga (Adi Ganga) practically dried up as well. Riverine valleys in Bengal– and their habitation–are therefore notoriously unstable; old towns and villages are liable to disappear overnight.

Bengal, unlike any other region of India, is therefore first and foremost a land made by rivers. Rivers are the source of sustenance, travel, trade in Bengal. The culture of its people is inextricably bound up with its rivers. In its topography Bengal shares many characteristics with the countries of south east Asia. Both regions are predominantly *riverine* areas with flat plains and marshy lands interspersed with estuaries which determine their distinct bio social character. Both have two major zones– one coastal (marked by extensive trade) and the other composed of river valleys (fertile and thereby the main source of sustenance of both their peoples and political power). Both form baskets of some of the best riceculture the world has known. The two zones–coastal and inland–are linked by the piowerful river systems which connect coastal and internal trade. This part of the globe is dominated by powerful rivers such as the Irrawady (Ava and Pegu or Hamsavati), the Chindwin (Pagan or Arimaddhanapura), the Salwin (Thaton), the Menam (Ayuthia), the Mekong (Sudhammavati or present day Laos), the Red River (Champa, Panduranga, Vijaya and Amaravati in present Vietnam), and the Padma/Meghna, the Bhagirathi and the Brahmaputra with their infinite tributaries (Bengal).

All these rivers perform the binary functions of being the chief source of sustenance and the principal channel for communcation as we shall see in the section on Politics and Trade in Bengal.

Control over its produce–the surplus grain–and control over waterways formed the basis of the successful articulation of political power in Bengal. This region followed a system of agriculture that amounted to the age-old custom of a rice culture of divine right in South East Asia[560]. Grain, chiefly rice, is the chief produce of the entire Bengal and south east Asian belt and forms the main part of the diet of the people. From very early times there has been a brisk riverine trade in grain. The produce of the rivers–fish and crustacaeans–provide another portion of the diet of the peoples of these regions. Coconut trees dot the coastal plains and their fruits are used in cuisines in a variety of innovative ways–from sauces to desserts. Cowries form the medium of everyday exchange all along this eastern seaboard: from Orissa and Bengal upto China.

Therefore, in its physical landscape Bengal is distinctive. Its physical geography is very different from that of the Indian heartland. Its topographical distinctiveness is accentuated by the Teliagarhi pass on its western frontiers which forms a natural barrier against upper India. This barrier is further underlined by the Ekdala fort which was the fortified zone of defence against invaders–from the very earliest times to the Muslim period. Since Bengal lies at one corner of the peninsula it faces the southeast rather than the middle gangetic plain of India. Accidents of topography have made it almost inaccessible from upper India: the instability of its rivers and the formidable Teliagarhi pass on its western frontier have proved formidable barriers throughout time. Perhaps because of this topographic isolation Bengal has always been aloof from major currents and upheavals in north Indian history; historically its links–cultural, commercial and political–have been forged with the countries bordering the sea to which it gives its name. Classically its social structures and corresponding cultures have found an echo in the riverine states of south east Asia. These states, notably those countries around the Bay of Bengal and the Indonesian Sea, are closer to Bengal even today in terms of material culture. Along with topographical parallelism geological similarities too have played a substantial role in determining the social structures, culture, political forms and ideologies of this region.

Like the peoples of Bengal those of the entire south east Asian belt too are tribal of origin and late to adapt to 'civilising' norms. They are

560 Lombard, Denys, 1990, III.

peoples with little pretension to either divine knowledge or 'high' culture. This cultural affinity–and trade zone–was shattered to a great extent when, in the 1520s Ala ud din Husain Shah attempted to integrate Bengal's economy with that of the middle Gangetic plain. When, in the 1540s, Sher Shah Sur built a highway from Suvarnagram in eastern Bengal to North India (the Grand Trunk Road) Bengal's economic orientation turned decisively westward. Some decades later, when the Mughals conquered Bengal, this east to west shift was finally complete. From then on Bengal's economic landscape became west-looking and north-oriented; the cultural and commercial linkages that Bengal had historically built up in its 'far east' from the eighth century withered. It was in the sixteenth century that the foundations for the unequal exchange between western and eastern Bengal that prevail today were laid. Developments in the seventeenth century furthered this process as a maritime and littoral society was integrated into a land based one and the historical inequalities were even more accentuated in the eighteenth century.

Routes, Ports and Trading Networks in Bengal

'La navigation y est bien dangereuse; autrement le Bengale serait la region la plus belle, fertile et profitable dans le monde'

(If the navigation had not been so dangerous here Bengal would have been the most beautiful, the most wealthy and the most abundant region in the world) Pyrard de Laval *The Voyage of...to the East Indies, the Maldives, the Moluccas, and Brazil 1601–1611*, 1887, 1888, 1890, Albert Gray, London, Hakluyt Society (My translation).

The main problem of maritime navigation in Bengal was that Bengal had no deep sea port. The only one which could take in large ships was Chattagram; this was the reason why the trade of medieval Bengal was concentrated at Chattagram. We saw in the preceding section that attempts were underway to connect Bengal with the land-routes crisscrossing the Gangetic plain. From the sixteenth century, therefore, riverine and sea routes were not the only means of Bengal's communication with the outside world. Sources[561] tell us of two main land routes linking Bengal with the rest of the sub-continent in the eighteenth century.

[561] From Rennell, James, 1793, *Memoir of a Map of Hindoostan or the Mogul Empire*, London, Editions Indian, 1976; Gole, Susan, 1988, *Maps of Mughal India* contains maps of d' Anville's *Carte de l'Inde,* 1752, and Gentil, 1770, New Delhi, Manohar. Rennell acknowledges his debt to d'Anville in *Memoir* etc.; however he is curiously silent about Gentil's contribution to cartography. Habib, Irfan, 1982, *An Atlas of the Mughal Empire*, New Delhi, Oxford; Jarrett, H.S. (Tr). *The Ain-I-Akbari By Abul Fazl Allami*, Jadunath Sarkar annotated 2nd edition, Oriental Books, New Delhi, 1978.

The first was the main caravan route that linked eighteenth century Bengal with Gujarat through Agra, Malwa and Khandesh. The chief entrepot and capital of Khandesh, Burhanpur, not only linked North and South India but was also the point where the route forked off north-west to the marts of Gujarat and its sea ports of Surat/Lahori Bandar and south-west towards Pune-Mumbai. While not an important staging-point in the land route connecting Bengal to western India, Burhanpur may have occasionally functioned as a relay centre in the transhipment of Bengal goods to points further south-west in India. The city developed into an important market for textiles[562]. At any rate a Bengal-Burhanpur trade developed in the seventeenth century via Agra whereby chintz and red cloth (*salu*) as well raw cotton was imported into Bengal from there[563].

The second was the caravan route that ran from China-Tibet into Bengal/Bihar through Suvarnagram-Rajmahal-Patna-Benares-Prayag upto Agra where it connected with Kabul or Multan which in their turn connected up with the new (Mongol) silk route in operation from the sixteenth century[564].

Of the riverine routes the fabled Bengal-North India water route upto Allahabad/Faizabad through the Ganga gained prominence from the sixteenth century. This enabled access to both North India as well as Nepal and Bhutan through Patna. The second was the old Meghna/Padma/Brahmaputra water route linking Cooch Behar and Rangamati/Goalpara in Assam. One could then travel further east onto Arakan or north into Tibet. This route was initially used to connect up with the second caravan route towards north India; this was no longer used after the riverine changes of the sixteenth century linked east and west Bengal once the Ganga joined up with the Brahmaputra via the Padma-Meghna and a host of smaller rivers[565].

As for sea routes Kenneth McPherson points out that the Bay of Bengal trading system was based on two older systems, one that linked Ceylon, eastern India, Bengal and Arakan and the other that linked China

562 Gordon, Stewart, 1994, *Marathas, Marauders and State Formation in Eighteenth Century India*, Delhi, Oxford University Press, 'Burhanpur: Entrepot and Hinterland 1650–1750': 163–181.

563 Raychaudhuri, Tapan, 1982, Chapter XI, 'Inland Trade' in Tapan Raychaudhuri and Irfan Habib (Eds). *The Cambridge Economic History of India*, I, Cambridge/Orient Longman: 332.

564 See the section Was there ever an 'Indian' Trade?

565 See before.

and South East Asia with eastern India[566]. The first sea route was therefore the coastal route linking Bengal with the Coromandel coast and Ceylon (present Sri Lanka). The second sea route is the little-explored Ava/Pegu/South East Asia/Malacca/ Junk Ceylon/China route that radiated from little deltaic ports such as Sripur and Bakla in *samatata*. This route, given the frontier nature of a region manifesting such intense cultural contacts transcending political borders, was as cosmopolitan as the south-bound Arakan/Bengal/Coromandel/Ceylon route. Unfortunately as seen in preceding sections historical scholarship has neglected *samatata*; consequently routes emanating from there have attracted limited scholarly attention.

The second sea route contained a number of feeder routes. One principal route was of course the route to China. We can glean an idea of this latter route from Arabic and Chinese sources spanning the ninth to the fifteenth centuries[567]. This route seems to have been popular for both trade and diplomatic missions to and from China and was also explored frequently by Arabic travellers. In Bengal Chattagram was the chief port for the China trade in the fifteenth century. The Chinese also disembarked at Chattagram and then went inland by river. Ports on the eastern route were Nagapattinam (called Bullin by the Arabs), Ganjam (Kanja) and Chilka, and possibly Gopalpur in present day Orissa, the unidentified Samandar thirty miles north of Ganjam[568], Nicobar Islands, Kedah , Java and Khmer and this was the preferred route from the eastern sea board to China according to the ninth century *Al-Masalik wa'l Mamalik* of Ibn Khurdadhbih[569].

The second subsidiary route within this network was the coastal route that connected Bengal with Arakan, Pegu and Mergui. Robert Challes has

---

566 'Trade and Traders in the Bay of Bengal: Fifteenth to Nineteenth Centuries' in R.Mukherjee and L. Subramanian (Eds). 1998, *Politics and Trade in the Indian Ocean World: Essays in Honour of Ashin Das Gupta*, Delhi, Oxford.

567 See Ahmad, S. Maqbul, 1989, *Arabic Classical Accounts of India and China*, Shimla, Indian Institute of Advanced Study (ninth century); *Voyages of Ibn Batutah* (fourteenth century); Mills, J.V.G., 1970, *The Overall Survey of the Ocean's Shores* (An Account of Ma Huan's voyage to Bengal), London, Hakluyt Society; Bagchi P.C., 1945, (ed). *'Political Relations Between Bengal and China in the Pathan Period' Visva Bharati Annals*, vol 1, Cheena Bhavan. (for the fifteenth century).

568 Samandar has been identified with Suvarnagram by Ahmad, 1989: 24–5. However it could equally be Gangabandar in the region of the ancient port of Bengal, Tamralipta (see Tarafdar, M.R., 1978, 'Trade and Society in Early Medieval Bengal' in *The Indian Historical Review*, January, IV, 2). See later on in this volume.

569 In Ahmad, 1989: 5.

left us a description of this short and well travelled route[570]. Within Pegu there were three important ports-Martaban, Dagon and Cosmin: among these Cosmin was the principal port in the sixteenth century and welcomed four or five boats (*naus*) from Bengal bringing *sinabaf* and other textiles[571] The third route connected Bengal to the Nicobar Islands and Java.

It is striking that there is no mention of Chattagram, the great eastern port, in the ninth century account; however by the time of Ibn Batutah's voyages in the fourteenth century Chattagram had emerged as the greatest port on the eastern sea board after the Coromandel ports. The flourishing production and foreign trade centred on the Chattagram-Suvarnagram complex was described by Chinese visitors as well as in the Chaitanya Mangala of Jayananda[572]. In the interim period some other port in the region probably served as port for both the Dhaka-Suvarnagram production complex as well as for the Buddhist complexes in the region[573]. The Lalmai, Paharpur and Mahastan complex had ties with Buddhist centers in South East Asia. The importance of this deltaic region is underscored by the fact that the Arabic name for the Bay of Bengal–Sea of Harkhand– was derived from Harikelya or the eastern part of Bengal[574].

What then was the chief port of Bengal in the interim period? It is likely to be Samandar for we are told that it was the principal market and port on the Ganges delta, inhabited by wealthy merchants from all over the world, the centrepoint of trade with Assam and Ceylon and trader in aloes-wood (for which there was a great demand) brought down from Assam[575]. Samandar was definitely in existence for three hundred years between the ninth century (Ibn Khurdadhbih) and the twelfth century (al-Idrisi) as sources tell us. It is likely that Samandar may have been an earlier port in the Suvarnagrama region; in that case however it cannot be thirty miles north of Ganjam. Was it then in the area around Saptagram? Samandar can then be identified with Gangabandar/Tamralipta (see previous note).

---

570 Challes, Robert, 1690–1691, *Journal d'Un Voyage fait aux Indes Orientales*, Paris, Mercure de France, 2 vs. 1983 edition, Volume II: 41–100.

571 Subrahmanyam, S. 1990: 101–2.

572 Bagchi, P.C., 1945; Jayananda, *Chaitanya Mangala*, Calcutta, 1971: 10–11; also Vrindaban Das, *Chaitanya Bhagavat*, Nabadwip, 3rd ed.: 161 (in Ray, Anirudhha, 1997, 'Middle Bengali Literature: A Source for the Study of Bengal in the Age of Akbar' in Habib, Irfan (ed). 1997, *Akbar and His India*, Delhi, Oxford).

573 See before.

574 Ahmad, 1989: 59.

575 *Ibid.*: 24.

Muhammad Mohar Ali, we saw before, places Samandar at/around Sandwip island[576]. According to al-Idrisi Samandar was near the confluence of the Meghna and the Brahmaputra. Ali identifies Samandar as being near the present port town of Chandpur in Bangladesh. Since al-Idrisi wrote in the twelfth century we know that Samandar functioned as a port from the ninth century (Ibn Khurdadhbih's testimony) for at least three hundred years.

Samandar was situated on the Meghna. Riverine changes may have silted this port up so much so after this time that the next great port was Chattagram on the Karnaphuli further east. Sagor's name has also been proposed as an interim port. Known as the Isle of Cox (or Cocks) Sagor was in existence from the twelfth century and was a deep sea port as late as in the seventeenth century. It is being considered today, in the twenty first century, as a sea port for Bengal once again. Bowrey mentioned of Sagor towards the end of the seventeenth century: 'The River of Ganges is of large and wonderful extent. Once I went through a small rivolet of it called Dobra within the Isla of Cocks, and came into the Great River, which rather deserves to be called the Sea of Ganges…about forty miles from Ganga Sagar'[577].

Bakla in the Sundarbans area was also a functioning port from the twelfth century. We also have shadowy references to Dianga port in the Chattagram region by the seventeenth century. It was known a Feringhjibazaar or Feringhibandar and functioned as a subsidiary port of Chattagram. It was given by Shaista Khan to the Portuguese in the seventeenth century[578].

From the middle of the sixteenth century the Bhagirathi route was more used, possibly due to Arakan depredations in the Chattagram region and even more due to the riverine changes that came soon after. Intense urbanization along the Bhagirathi river under Husain Shahi aegis, the growth of Nabadwip and Triveni and the linking of Triveni by a bridge to *vanga's* chief port Saptagram in 1506 indicated that the economic focus was shifting back to *vanga* once again. Temples, study centers and brick-built houses were signs of this new urbanization. Textile manufacturing centers sprang up around these towns[579].

---

[576] Mohar Ali, Muhammad, 1985, *History of the Muslims of Bengal*, V.1A *Muslim Rule in Bengal 1203–1757*, Saudi Arabia, Ibn Saud Islamic University Publications: 30–34.

[577] Bowrey: 209.

[578] Dianga was described as a suburb of Chattagram in the sixteenth century, Subrahmanyam, 1990: 121.

[579] Ray, Aniruddha, 1997: 229–233.

By the seventeenth century the chief port of Bengal was Hugli (official foundation circa 1580, although in use even earlier), with Balasore (foundation 1640) serving as a secondary port. Both ports were founded by the Portuguese who seem to have abandoned *samatata* in favour of *vanga*. In the eighteenth century *vanga* dictated the economic pulse of Bengal. The focus had shifted from *samatata* to *vanga*.[580]

It is worth noting that despite the names of 'Harkhand' and 'Bengal' to denote the Bay of Bengal, the Coromandel, by the eighteenth century, enjoyed a more privileged position as regards trade and influence in this sea space. This affirms our position that the primacy of Bengal in this zone was derived from the earlier period of contacts with South East Asia in ancient times; this primacy was reinforced subsequently in the Islamic period when the ports of *harikela* dominated the eastbound coastal trade. This was lost in the course of the seventeenth century when the focus shifted to the *vanga* ports. The Coromandel ports with their robust merchant and ship owning class could from then on offer better advantages in direct sailings to the eastern waters.

Bengal's shipowning class declined dramatically from the late seventeenth century[581], moreover by the eighteenth century eastward sailings from Bengal were almost nil while the Coromandel routes continued to thrive[582]. The chapter called Politics and Trade in Bengal attempts to explain why Bengal's external trade was cut short time and time again.

The Structure of Trade in Medieval Bengal

Formerly yea not many years agoe, the inhabitants of the Northern parts of Bengala trained up their children…to eat raw fish and flesh and when growne up sent them…to discover the great Ganges to find out the garden of Eden (by order of theire kings) but few or none ever made returne. (Thomas Bowrey: 211)

This passage shows very clearly the limited geographical knowledge Europeans had of the north east when they first set foot in Bengal. It echoes also the Mughal prejudice of the east (Bengal and Arakan)

[580] Challes (1690–91) op.cit., Luillier (circa 1701) *Voyage du Sieur Luillier aux Indes Orientales Avec une instruction pour le commerce des Indes Orientales*, 1705, Paris, Claude Cellier. Also *Voyages du Sieur Luillier dans des grandes Indes Orientales,* 1726, Rotterdam.

[581] Das Gupta, Ashin, 1989, *Bangoposagor* (in Bengali). Also his '*Trade and Politics in Eighteenth Century India*' 1970, 1998: 387–88.

[582] *Ibid*. Also McPherson, 1998: 197 and Arasaratnam, S., 1998, '*The Eastward Trade of India in the Eighteenth Century*' in Mukherjee and Subramanian 1998: 216.

being *terra incognita*, a place where the raw was preferred over the cooked.

But Bengal seemed a mythic place to seventeenth century Europeans as well. The passage refers also to an area supposedly inhabited by primitive tribes in search of paradise. This was north Bengal and the north eastern parts of South Asia. The sacredness of the area was enhanced by the fact of its proximity to Tibet; the area supposed by medieval travellers to be the source of the Ganges.

The supposed sanctity conferred on this space a certain haziness, an ambiguity that was enhanced by objective conditions. Until the end of the eighteenth century there were no precise geographical coordinates fixed for the region. This area was therefore perceived as vile, mythic, sacred and yet hazy, all at the same time.

But this ambiguous area, stretching upwards from the Brahmaputra, was the old area that was the lifeblood for the commerce of Bengal. This was the old Pundravardhana that led on to Kamrup and beyond. What is mentioned here clearly refers to the borderlands between Bengal and China, the corridor that was crucial for the preservation of Bengal's medieval overland trade. This was an ancient trade that existed for millennia, a trade which was furthered by the Buddhist network and later greatly expanded by its proximity to the Southern Silk Route during the early Islamic period. This space had no precise geographical boundaries; consequently myths abounded about this region stretching from north Bengal, through Kamrup, Assam, Ava into Tibet, Turkestan and China. Strabo noted[583]:

> certain mouthless people were brought to him (Sandrocottus, king of Palibothra and of the Prasoi peoples), a gentle folk; and they live round the sources of the Ganges; and they sustain themselves by means of vapours from roasted meat and odours from fruits and flowers, since instead of mouths they have only breathing orifices; and they suffer pain when they breathe bad odours…

Bengal's maritime trade does not have such hazy contours. Here we can isolate the following phases that determined Bengal's commercial record in medieval times. First, we have already referred to the early medieval trade revolution where there was a changeover from trans-

[583] In Majumdar, R.C., 1960, *The Classical Accounts of India*, Calcutta, Firma K.L. Mukhopadhyay: *Geography of Strabo*, 272.

continental (direct sailings from West Asia to China, for example) trade to shorter routes punctutated with port-cities[584]. This was known as emporia trading. K.N. Chaudhuri tells us that at this time the nature of trade routes experienced a fundamental shift–instead of long-distance sailings shorter sailings became the norm–but it is not quite clear why this should have happened. It is possible that as Islam united the seas more items entered world commerce. Segmented trade offered greater scope for profits not only for merchants but also for indicvidual political units. More and more port-towns now became necessary to service international trade.

New ports consequently sprang up. The coastal regions of South Asia gained in this shift. Ports on the Bengal and Orissa coasts and the Coromandel and Ceylon emerged in the Bay; likewise Cambay and Diu in the Saurashtra Peninsula and Calicut, Cochin and Quilon on the Malabar coast appeared as important ports in the Arabian Sea.

This commercial distinctiveness was termed the eleventh century trade revolution. Herman Kulke noted that it happened in the eastern Indian Ocean under the aegis of the Chola and that the expansion of Chola power in the Bay of Bengal led to this 'trade revolution' in the Bay of Bengal[585]. While this directly benefited the Coromandel ports (the various trade routes that emanated from the Coromandel used the southern Bay of Bengal since the northern Bay was susceptible to cyclones, which discouraged active long distance sailings from Bengal) this trade revolution also helped generate trade in the northern Bay, notably from Bengal and Arakan to South East Asia and China. In the eastern Indian Ocean, Christie tells us, such a 'trade revolution' was visible from as early as the tenth century[586]. The states around the Bay of Bengal thus participated in a more extensive commerce from this time.

It is no accident that Arakan rose as a maritime state soon after this time, and this is also the period from when we can date the enhanced importance of ports such as Samandar, Sripur, Bakla, Sandwip and Sagor on the Bengal coast. An active Bengal-Arakan coastal trade dates from this period.

---

584 Chaudhuri, K.N., 1985: 39, 49.

585 Kulke, H, 1999 op. cit. 17–35: 33.

586 Christie, Jan Wisseman, 1999, op. cit. 221–270.

In the fifteenth century this trade route was further enhanced with the addition of the Bengal-China trade. This trading route was dominated by Arab and later Persian merchants, and not by Bengali-Muslims. But the port towns in the Bay faced a disadvantage with their counterparts in the Arabian Sea. The latter had enduring links with countries west of the Arabian Sea. The port-towns of the Saurashtra Peninsula had long and time tested trading links with the Persian and Ottoman domains by both land and sea. The port-towns of the Malabar had emerged in response to the trading needs of sailings from the East African coast. The Bay of Bengal ports had no such enduring link. Their sailings were in three directions: to China, to South East Asia and to Ceylon and the Maldives. Of these, the China link was probably the oldest but ultimately it too did not stand the test of time.

Second, in the fourteen century Mongol disturbances in Central Asia and Asia Minor meant the importance of the emerging maritime routes over land routes. Here too the ports of the western coast profited more than the Bay coast. By the fifteenth century Calicut was deemed an international port where Arabs from the western seas and the Chinese from the eastern seas traded. Chattagram enjoyed no such distinction.

In the sixteenth and seventeenth centuries the Coromandel ports gained a further advantage over the Bengal ports. One chief reason was that the Coromandel ports were deep water ports, unlike the Bengal ports which were essentially estuarine in nature. Another reason was that growing Portuguese control over the Gujarat, Goa and Malabar coasts diverted traditional Islamic shipping to the Coromandel coasts which were a short distance away. No such short term shift advantaged the Bengal ports; indeed events from the fifteenth to the seventeenth centuries effectively sealed the fate of Bengal's ports[587].

Reconstructing the medieval Bay of Bengal trade with China it appears that China traditionally had cultural and commercial dealings with the Coromandel, Orissa and Bengal coasts from very early times[588]. In the

---

[587] The Chinese switchover to Nagapattinam as the premier port for the China-Bay trade in the late fifteenth century disadvantaged Bengal; moreover the troubles in sixteenth century Bengal between various ruling groups, the Portuguese and Arakanese made the Bengal coast subject to piracy. By the seventeenth century, the Portuguese, who could have weathered this crisis and thereby helped Bengal's trade to maintain the status quo, were effectively decimated.

[588] Ray, Haraprasad, 2003, see chapters 1, 6 and 7.

tenth century Chinese ships traded at Broach. But in the first half of the fifteenth century the Chinese missions and official trade touched two points in India: Bengal and the Malabar. Calicut was favoured over Bengal since it was an international sea port. By contrast Bengal had only Chattagram; from there to travel into Bengal the Chinese had to depend on riverine routes. That Calicut was important to Chinese trade is vouched for in the number of Chinese missions there as opposed to those to Bengal. We may conclude that the Chinese were more interested in breaking into the Red Sea and Persian Gulf trade than in the trade to states around the Bay where they already played a substantial role from the Song period.

But trade at Calicut posed difficulties for the Chinese. This was because the Gujarati and Malabar merchants wanted to reserve the lucrative trade of the western Indian Ocean for themselves. Trade at Calicut-lying as it did at the junction of some of the great routes of the western Indian Ocean-was vital to the merchants of western India and the Chinese were forced to abandon Calicut. In the second half of the fifteenth century rivalry from Gujarati-Arab merchants who controlled the Mogadishu-Malindi-Mecca trade at Malabar forced the Chinese to withdraw from Calicut and concentrate on Nagapattinam instead[589]. Trade under private initiative between Bengal and China continued but the Chinese did not officially come back to Bengal.

Now the Coromandel-South East Asia-Malacca-China trade route started floursishing. Bengal was left out from this trade. But interestingly enough exports from Bengal to China were the largest; with Calicut lying second[590]. This may be because only Bengal in South Asia supplied China with a coveted item: horses[591]. Marco Polo had referred to the great horse marts in Bengal. In 1420 Sultan Jalal ud Din sent an envoy to China to present famous breeds of horses[592]. The Chinese were always short of horses: these were supplied only by Hormuz and Bengal[593].

The sixteenth century, we noted, saw the redirection of Bengal's commerce towards the west. The Portuguese and the Arakanese, in combination with Bengali rulers and merchants, dominated this century. Yet it was also a turbulent century; the Husain Shahis developed their

---

[589] *Ibid.*

[590] *Ibid.*

[591] *Ibid.*

[592] Ming Tai zong shi-lu 2229 (230.1a) in Church 2004: 27.

[593] Ray, Haraprasad, 2003.

western ports in Bengal to the detriment of the eastern ports. The eastward shift of the rivers started towards the end of the century and contributed to the economic desolation of eastern Bengal. Dhaka was left as the only port of any consequence.

The early years of the EEIC in the Bay tell us that Bengal was under the agency of the Company on the Coromandel coast; it was only after Master (1675–1680) and during the tenure of Hedges, that is from the period 1681–1687, that the EEIC established an independent commercial presence in Bengal[594]. By the early eighteenth century the importance of the Coromandel coast over the Bengal coast-in terms of locational advantage as regards trade routes-was unquestioned. Bengal only became primary to the EEIC insofar as it was the first territory to be acquired by them.

The early years of the EEIC in seventeenth century Bengal give us a clear picture of how trade was organised in Bengal. Trade was conducted mainly from the northern part of Bengal, through the Murshidabad-Malda-Rajmahal-Patna route, and this sector was well organized with a mint, shroffs and substantial merchants. Hugli was still the major 'sea port'; Bowrey noted[595]:

> The Towne is not very uniforme but is a very good and pleasant place, inhabited with some of the Richest Merchants of the Kingdome, and all sorts of Commodities that Orixa, Bengala and Pattana doe afford are here dayly to be bought and sold in the publicke Bazaar, commonly called the Great Bazar, by reason there are many where only cotton, coarse calicoes, provisions etc. are to be sold.

The subsidiary ports of Hugli were first Harispur and then Balasore and Pipli. In the absence of a viable port on the Orissa coast[596] these ports were now becoming increasingly important for Bengal. The produce of the southern coasts were brought into these ports and shipped to Hugli from where they were sent upriver to Patna-the great emporia between Bengal and Orissa and the north.

The EEIC concentrated on the western part of the province where a commercial realm was yet to emerge. The EEIC wanted to conduct trade

594 See Temple, R.C. (ed) 1911, *The Diaries of Streynsham Master 1675–80 and Other Contemporary Papers Relating Thereto*, London, John Murray (Indian Records Series, 2 Vols.) and Barlow, R. and Yule, H. (M DCCC LXXX VII), *Diary of William Hedges During His Agency in Bengal 1681–1687*, London, Hakluyt Society, 2 Vols.

595 Bowrey: 167–168.

596 See below.

at the different textile mart-towns of Bengal. Waldegrave, the EEIC agent in Bengal, had 'lost' EEIC trading rights in Bengal in 1654. EEIC trade was in a mess and the Bengal trade was run from the Coromandel. DEIC trade in Bengal, run from Chinsura, was flourishing. Dutch ships of six or seven hundred tons were sailing up the Hughly and the EEIC wished to develop trade of a similar magnitude in Bengal[597]. When Master came to put EEIC trade with Bengal on a firm footing during 1675-80, he commissioned a number of reports. On the basis of Edwardes' report Malda was declared a 'centre of cotton goods' and Shantipur the 'chief depot of malmals'[598].

The next thing to do was to choose a port for operations. In the middle of the seventeenth century Harispur (or Hariharpur in Orissa) was the EEIC port of choice. In the 1670s it could only accommodate ships of 200 tons[599]. Interestingly enough, the EEIC never considered Pipli, possibly because it was a thriving Arakanese-Portuguese slave mart at this time[600]. When Harispur silted up Balasore was chosen, but soon after Master decided to concentrate all EEIC operations at Hugli, it being the 'key or seale of Bengala'[601].

As for finance, the money market was concentrated in the north and east of the province. Financial management was centred around Dhaka, the present capital, and Rajmahal, the former capital. The mint was located at Rajmahal and because of its location the Bengal-Patna trade was flourishing. Bowrey noted that[602]:

> Pattana (is) a very large and potent Kingdom...This is a Countrey of Very Greate Trafficke and Commerce and is really the great Gate that Openeth into Bengala and Orixa, and soe consequently into most parts of India, Vizt. from the Northerne Kingdomes or Empires (by land), namely Persia, Carmania, Georgia, Tartaria...

Patna accessed all the textiles of Bengal; *cossaes* from Dhaka and raw and wrought silks with gold and silver stripes from Kasimbazar[603].

---

597 Master V.1: 53.

598 *Ibid.*: 26, 37.

599 Bowrey: 129.

600 Master, V. 2: 66; Bernier too attests to Pipli as a thriving slave mart in the seventeenth century .

601 *Ibid.* V.1: 37.

602 Bowrey: 225.

603 *Ibid.*: 230.

Sanas, ginghams, *rumalls* and cotton yarn from Hugli and Balasore also found their way to Patna[604]. Patna was truly the inland emporia of eastern goods and this account reinforces two points that I made before.

One, that the trade of Bengal had completely reoriented itself towards the west in the seventeenth century. The Bengal-North India trade was evidently primed from Rajmahal, south of the border from Patna. Malda was the closest textile mart and it had a thriving trade in *khasas*, *alachas* and *malmals* with merchants from Agra, Benares and Gujarat active in this trade. These merchants sent their boats to transport the goods to North India, but goods were also conveyed by land to North India[605]. Second, we had noted that port towns existed in pre-modern South Asia in a close symbiosis with the caravan routes; the account reinforces this point. Once these trade routes declined the symbiosis between the various port-towns and caravan points collapsed.

As for merchants and trade it appears that the Mughals were conscious of maintaining the commercial equilibrium of the region. Mughal intervention took place in the shape of the exercise of monopolies, granting of rights to salt-farms to favourites and the appointment of officers who were deeply suspicious of European motives. There were certain royal monopolies in force in Bengal and Bihar. Referred to as 'Mughal monopolies' they were administered by the representatives of the Mughal *subahdar*. These were: beeswax at Patna[606], lead at Patna[607], and beeswax and salt in Bengal[608]. These were farmed out: the salt trade was farmed out to the Portuguese Nicolao De Parteca for Rs. 100 000 per annum[609]. Obviously the Portuguese were no longer considered Europeans but as subjects of the Mughal. Bowrey commented that[610]:

> A Great Multitude of Portugals inhabit the Kingdome of Bengala Especially in Hugli and some Other Creeks or Rivolets of the River Thereto….

He added that the Portuguese received favoured treatement over other European nations; they could live anywhere in Bengal and while they had

---

604 *Ibid.* 231–32.

605 Master, V.1: 26.

606 Bowrey: 225.

607 Master V.1: 55.

608 *Ibid.* V.1: 321.

609 *Ibid.* V.2: 81.

610 Bowrey: 191.

to pay customs dues they were not subject to 'exactions laid on Gentue and Banjan merchants'[611].

The interventions of Mughal officers, commonly interpreted by the EICs as 'harrassment' were actually expressive of their aim to conduct the political ecomony of commerce according to Mughal norms of equity. I am not talking here of the struggle for trading rights or the fight for mint privileges. My point is that stories of 'extortion' and 'bribes' can also be interpreted quite differently. Case histories from Murshidabad and Hugli illustrate this.

The two main actors at the end of the seventeenth century in western Bengal, with whom the EEIC clashed, were Bal Chand the 'Governor' (Kotwal?) of Murshidabad[612], and Malik Beg, the Faujdar of Hugli for twenty years (1647–1667). The latter was succeeded by Malik Kasim as the Faujdar of Hugli and Balasore[613]. Bal Chand was the judge and arbiter in all matters pertaining to the Indian servants of the EEIC such as the case of the EEIC *poddar* Raghu who died mysteriously. The faujdars, especially Malik Kasim along with his son Malik Zindi, who effectively controlled all commercial traffic out of Bengal's two premier ports of Balasore and Hugli for almost fifteen years (1668-1681), were in effect the 'kings' of Bengal, with Mir Jumla, the actual Mughal *subahdar*, far away in his seat at Dhaka-the regional capital. Malik Zindi deputized for Malik Kasim at Hugli and Balasore and was probably a ship owner himself[614]. The faujdar's power derived from the fact that the upper echelons of the ruling class left day to day affairs of ports and shipping to the faujdar. Bowrey comments: 'The Prince now (neither did the Nabob before him) not in the least concern themselves with their ships'[615]. Interestingly enough, although Pipli is referred to by Master and Bernier as an Arakanese 'slave mart' Bowrey, Master's contemporary, noted extensive trade at Hugli, Balasore and also at Pipli: 'The Nabob and some Merchants here (Hugli) and in Ballasore and Pipli have about twenty saile of ships of considerable burthen that annually trade to Sea, some to Ceylone, Some to Tannassaree…[616]. These fetched elephants while others,

[611] *Ibid.*: 194.

[612] Master, V.1: 143–48, in the case of Raghu the EEIC's Poddar's 'suicide', or 'murder' for which the English factors Hall, Smith, Clavell, Marshall and Vincent were deemed culpable. Hedges, V.1: 33–4 refers to Bal Chand stopping EEIC trade.

[613] Master, V.1: 99.

[614] Master V.1: 44–47.

[615] Bowrey: 180.

[616] Bowrey: 179.

some six or seven ships, went to the Maldives for cauris which was very profitable[617]. This is of course not so surprising, the slave trade frequently complemented 'respectable' trade.

As noted earlier, the money market in western Bengal was not uniform and somewhat unregulated. This made trade a risky affair for strangers. Balasore, one of the important ports of the seventeenth century, had no coined money as the EEIC factors noted[618]. This bears out the assertion made earlier that the west was a marginal area to the Mughals, still awaiting regulation. The east-with Dhaka as Mughal capital-and the north-with Rajmahal as the former capital-were the focal points of Mughal presence at the end of the seventeenth century. A commercial zone, extending from Balasore and Pipli in the south, through Hugli in the centre to Kasimbazar in the north was coming into being only now, and largely through European intervention.

Balasore's principal merchants were mentioned as 'Chimchamsaw' and 'Chittamundsaw'[619], 'Chittermull' of Kasimbazar was the principal shroff[620] who converted the EEIC's bullion (reals of eight, Mexico and Pilar Dollars, gold 'pistolls') into rupees[621]. Another such was Mathura Shahoo (Muttrasaw) of Hugli, referred to as 'banker and trader' who converted English bullion[622]. Chittermull was also referred to as 'merchant'[623]. Obviously bankers and traders were indistinguishable in Bengal at this time; this was a trait that we find continuing into the middle of the eighteenth century. Some were also royal courtiers; Mathuradas, a substantial merchant, was Paramsurdas' 'servant'. Paramsurdas in turn was Bal Chand, the 'governor' of Murshidabad's 'servant'[624] These were the merchants 'endorsed' by the government at the ports of Hugli, Balasore, Kasimbazar, Malda and Dhaka.

The EEIC, early on, took the decision to not concentrate on any one particular merchant and to contract with a number of smaller merchants. The EEIC was always on guard against the machinations and monopolizing

---

617 *Ibid.*: 179–180.

618 Master V.1: 53–54.

619 Master,V.2: 222. Bowrey: 156.

620 Master,V.1: 99. V.2:´303, 305, 309. Hedges, Diary: V.1: 75 however refers to ChittarmullSaw as a 'merchant of this place' and in 121 as a 'Cossimbazar' merchant.

621 Master V.2: 307.

622 Hedges V.1: 74.

623 *Ibid.* V.1: 75.

624 *Ibid.* V.1: 33–34.

habits of Mathuradas; yet the Court of Directors instructed the Bengal Council to hold 'a fair correspondence...we being well assured, that he is able cunning fellow, competently rich, and that his masters in Dhaka are men of very great Estates...moneyed men...'[625].

Chaudhuri mentions that there were two categories of merchants in Bengal, one rich and operating competently on a large scale with a substantial dealer network, the other composed of smaller merchants, operating on commissions, and adds further that the EEIC and the DEIC preferred to deal with the first group in the early eighteenth century[626]. But there are indications that the EEIC, at least, were already beginning to consider the second group as a viable alternative to the first from the 1670s. On December 15 1676 Clavell (in Master's council) referred to this as the 'practice of contracting with the Town Merchants'[627] and in this way the EICs created a whole new group of contract-merchants. When Hedges succeeded Master a new category of merchants was in place: 'Horkissincotma'[628], 'Muttrasaw', 'Rupsuliman','Rogoodee', 'Giachundsaw', 'Rogonaut', 'Ramchandparamanick', 'Ramnarain', 'Mudducawn' were the 'Hugli merchants'[629]. But other groups of merchants were also eager to deal as Hedges' consultations at Hugli reveal[630]:

> Yesterday a certain number of Merchants came to me and offered to undertake ye providing what goods we shall have occasion for this year, to be paid for when said Goods were brought in, and at as cheap rates as if money were given out beforehand...

The passage suggests that this latter group was the first group of substantial merchants with enough capital to sustain trade and with their own dealer network. It also suggests that the practice of giving out Investment beforehand was not yet an established norm in Hugli at least at the end of the seventeenth century. But more importantly perhaps, it also suggests that different merchant groups were jockeying for the prestige of furnishing large investments; this itself being indicative of the fact that a mercantile stratification had already occurred within Bengal.

---

625 Chaudhuri, 1978: 147.

626 *Ibid.*: 148–149.

627 Master V.2: 86.

628 For the future activities of the Katmas see Mukherjee, Rila, 1994, 'The Story of Kasimbazar', *REVIEW*. The Katmas ultimately abandoned the silk trade at Kasimbazar and moved to Calcutta to live under British protection in the 1740s. See also Mukherjee, Rila, 2006, *Merchants and Companies in Bengal*, etc.

629 Hedges V.1: 73.

630 Hedges V.1: 76.

EEIC business practice tells us that there were three ways of procuring goods: (1) procurement through ready money sales was in practice in emporia towns such as Hugli and Patna-this practice was not favoured by the EICs and was never pursued once the EEIC had gripped the market as excessive demand in a particular year could push up prices and throw all budgets out of gear (2) the practice of procuring goods through investment whereby upto 80% was paid beforehand to merchants of good standing and security-this was favoured by all EICs since supply was assured through 'captive' merchants who had already accepted advances. Here the chief surety of the merchant was his reputation in the mercantile community as well as his networking with the court, and (3) a combination of the first two, as Hedges' consultations reveal.

The EEIC decision to not deal with 'prominent merchants' but rather to create a 'merchant' category of their own, who would essentially be suppliers to the English and none else, least of all to the Dutch and certainly not to the North Indian and other traditional big buyers of Bengal goods, was mostly prompted by the desire to escape excessive government interference in their trade; just as the EICs had decided earlier to concentrate on a relatively marginal riverine channel-the Bhagirathi-now too they decided to bypass traditional merchants and to contract with new merchants both as broker and supplier. A statement by Hedges is illustrative of the mistrust of 'traditional' merchants[631]:

> This day Five dellolls, or Brokers, of Dhaka, after they had been with me, went to Mr.Beard's Chamber to pay their respects to him, taking with them James Price, ye Vekeel. Mr. Beard demanded, 'who they were?' James answered, 'the Dellolls of Dacca'. Mr. Beard replied I know their business very well, I know what they come for. Mr. Frenchfield…said 'I am sorry these men have found ye way to Hugly: this will spoil the Co's business'; and soe ye men were dismist. (July 25 1684)

The oft repeated lament that a particular town had no substantial merchants (and therefore, by implication, no trade!) has to be re-read in this context.

In Balasore, where Mughal control was particularly severe, it was decided not to contract with any one merchant[632]. For Dhaka and Malda it was noted that there were 'no leading merchants' to act as the EEIC's

631 *Ibid*.V.1: 152.

632 Master V.1: 54.

broker and that one had to depend on small merchants and petty brokers[633] Hervy's report on Dhaka of October 16 1676 noted that brokers gave money to *pykars* who went from town to town delivering it to weavers. Hervy's report suggested that the EEIC find 'responsible merchants' at Dhaka as it had done at Balasore and Hugli[634] and added that[635]:

> Delolls or Brokers accustomed with, and appointed by the Government to the business of Cloth, take four month's time for its delivery...the said Broakers, having tooke money, deliver it to the picars...

This statement leads us to suppose that there were no substantial merchants at Dhaka but Hervy goes on to say that if the *dalals* were unsatisfactory '...a Merchant of the Citty is by Joynt consent chosen and desired to determine therein...'[636]. But the *dalals* of Dhaka were not always insignificant creatures; 'Raynund deloll' was actually Rai Nanda Lal, the Nawab of Dhaka's diwan[637].

Unconsciously perhaps, but clearly, company records reveal that they were not merely attempting to create a subservient category of merchants as suppliers and brokers in Bengal. They were also attempting, even at this early stage, to 'tie' merchants to their investments, just as the EEIC was to do later with the weavers in Bengal[638]. The problem was to find merchants who were subservient, because only the insignificant could be 'lesser', and therefore subservient, merchants. But investments dictated that the same subservient category be merchants of professional integrity, of good standing with peers, and with sufficient networking ability at court to resolve trade blockages. And this is where European mercantilism clashed with the political economy of the Mughal.

Politics and Trade in Bengal

'The sea-borne trade of Bengal had completely gone out of the reach of local traders and...was...controlled by the Arab and Persian merchants who (enjoyed) a complete monopoly in the navigation of the Eastern seas. These traders (maintained) oceanic communication between Bengal and the Persian Gulf area and...China...Arabia and Abyssinia' M.R. Tarafdar,

---

633 Master V.1: 136.

634 Master , V.1: 42

635 Master, V.2: 16.

636 Master V.2: 15.

637 Master V.2: 73.

638 See Mukherjee, Rila, 1994, 'The Story Of Kasimbazar', *Review,* N.Y.

Husain Shahi Bengal: 1494–1538 A.D. A Socio-Political Study, Asiatic Society of Pakistan, Dacca, 1965: 146.

We suggested earlier that despite sporadic practices of state mercantilism there was no sustained local control over trade in Bengal. Commercial activity in Bengal seemed to be ruled by external factors and agents. Om Prakash (1998, NCHI, II. 5) writes: 'The accounts of Tome Pires and Barbosa also enable one to decipher the principal components of the mercantile community operating from Bengal. The indigenous merchants of Bengal are described as "merchants with great fortunes" and were as important constituent of the trading community. But a large part of the trade would seem to have been controlled either by merchants based at the partner ports or by foreign merchant groups settled in the Bengal ports. Thus the trade with Malacca was dominated by the keling merchants settled there. The pepper trade with Pasai and Pidia was carried on by Persian merchants settled at the port of Chattagram. This last mentioned group would seem also to have dominated the trade to the Indian Ocean ports, though the traders on these routes also included Turks, Arabs, Rumis, Abyssimans and merchants from Chaul, Dabhol and Goa' (pp. 21–22) Received history tells us that Roman trade, Buddhist expansion, resurgent Hinduism, incoming Islam and a renewed China trade shaped mercantile policy between the early years of the Christian Era until the fifteenth century where the majority of players were external to Bengal.

How far these stimuli actually determined the material life of the people of Bengal is open to question. However it is undeniable that the three religions had, to a great extent, integrated Bengal within a larger framework of exchange in the Indian Ocean. A closer examination of Bengal's place in the networks they generated, each of which succeeded the other, will help us reconstruct a picture of Bengal's position in the maritime world of the Bay of Bengal[639].

It is now accepted that direct Roman trade trade with Bengal has been greatly exaggerated. Romanis and Tchernia, in their survey of Mediterrannean contacts with India, make no reference to Roman trade with Bengal[640]. Ray observes[641]:

639 See Mukherjee, Rila, 2004, 'Rice Culture of Divine Right in a Celestially Ordered Zone: A Case Study of South Asian and South East Ideologies and Hegemonies from c. 2000 BC to c. 1800 AD with Specific Reference to Bengal', *Campus Social,* Lisbon,.

640 *Crossings: Early Mediterrannean Contacts with India*, F.de Romanis and A. Tchernia (Eds)., 1997, Delhi, A Manohar-CSH-Italian Embassy Cultural Centre Publication.

641 Ray, Himanshu Prabha, 1994, *The Winds of Change, Buddhism and the Maritime Links of Early South Asia,* Delhi; Oxford University Press: 5.

> the Early Historical levels are far richer in material remains than those of the previous periods...A major issue that confronts ancient Indian historiography is to what extent can this prosperity be attributed to the expansion of external trade contacts, particularly the so-called Roman contacts in the early centuries of the Christian era? Or has the impact of Roman trade been exaggerated?

Sengupta observes that the 2nd century BC to the 2nd century AD marks the most active phase in the economic life of coastal Bengal (Chandraketugarh/Tamralipta) but concedes that the Bengal coast has not 'yielded even a single Roman coin'[642].

It follows that the historical reputation of Tamralipta as a port conducting direct Roman trade is inflated. Roman trade with coastal Bengal was conducted through the medium of the Coromandel ports such as Arikamedu. Was Tamralipta then merely a regional port conducting trade with coastal Coromandel and beyond? Archaeological evidence points to this latter premise. The Bengal ports emerged onto the historical stage with the Coromandel dominated Buddhist network in the Bay from the fifth century. It was within this network that Tamralipta achieved fame as port. This is corroborated by the fact that Tamralipta started direct sailings to Ceylon in the 5th century AD. Fa-Hien, the Buddhist monk from China, embarked at Tamralipta for Ceylon.

Ray continues[643]:

> In fact the beginnings of change in the centuries prior to the Christian era was the result of a series of socio-economic developments in the Ganga valley that led to the emergence of centralized polities...and especially to the rise of Magadha in the 3rd century BC...Another factor that contributed in no small way was the institutionalisation of the Buddhist Sangha...(they were) able to provide (a) cohesiveness to trading groups. It is the internal dynamics which led to an expansion of maritime networks in the post Mauryan period...

There was a substantial Buddhist network that passed overland through North India. Maurice Lombard tells us of the Buddhist network of trade through Turkestan which joined India and China through mountain passes

642 Sengupta, Gautam, 1996, 'Archaelogy of Coastal Bengal' in *Tradition and Archaelogy: Early Maritime Contacts in The Indian Ocean*, (Eds). Himanshu Prabha Ray and Jean Francois Salles, New Delhi, Manohar: 115–128. See pp. 120–121.

643 Ray, 1994: 5.

of the Hindu Kush and Central Asia. The Buddhist network actually made use of an earlier network that had been in existence. This was the old land route through the mountain passes of north east India that linked the mountainous countries of north Bengal, Bhutan, Tibet, Sikkim with south China through Ava.

This was also a massive conduit for trade. Cotton went from India to China in the sixth century through this route[644]; By the ninth century cotton had reached Japan[645]. Chaudhuri opines however that cotton cultivation really expanded in China in the post Song period in the eleventh century[646] and Haraprasad Ray affirms that this increased in the Yuan and Ming periods.

The Buddhist network was a bond that greatly expanded the maritime trade from Bengal. The one emanating from Bengal dominated the northern Bay of Bengal while the Coromandel ports concentrated on the southern Bay of Bengal world. Leaving aside the issues of 'colonisation', 'brahmanisation', 'indigenisation' or 'acculteration' that have been raised by R.C.Majumdar, Nilkantha Sastri, George Coedes, Kulke and Quatrich-Wales[647], it was clear that a new maritime space had come into being in the Bay. How was this effected?

From the seventh century onwards the decline in Roman trade was apparent. Arab trade now provided the impetus behind external trade. Unlike the case with Roman trade, here Bengal played an increasingly important role. Mohar Ali points to three Abbasid coins that were found at the Buddhist settlements of Paharpur and Mainamati as indicative of growing Islamic trade in eastern *samatata* in the eighth/ninth centuries[648]. Growing Islamic presence in the Chattagram/Arakan area during this time indicate that this part of Bengal was becoming integrated into the growing Islamic trading network[649]. The culture of cotton cultivation spread from India to Mesopotamia and the Mediterannean world (Syria, Aleppo, the

---

644 Lombard, Maurice, 1971, *L'Islam dans sa Premiere Grandeur, VIIIe-XIe siecles,* Paris, Flammarion: 201.

645 Mookerji, Radha Kumud, 1962: 122–123.

646 Chaudhuri, K.N., 1990, *Asia Before Europe: Economy And Civilisation of the Indian Ocean From the Rise of Islam to 1750*, Cambridge: 107.

647 Kulke H., 1993, *Kings and Cults: State Formation and Legitimation in South East Asia*, New Delhi, Manohar: 273–274. Quaritch-Wales H.G., 1961, *The Making of Greater India*, London , B. Quaritch-Wales, second edition and also B.Quaritch-Wales, 1957, *Pre History and Religion in South East Asia*, London.

648 Ali, M.M., 1985 V. 1A: 35–36.

649 *Ibid.*: 37–40.

shores of the Dead Sea, Damascus and Cilisia) by the seventh century[650]. It is likely that some of the cotton that found its way both east (China) and west (Mesopotamia/Mediterrannean region) originated from the Bengal trade. Some cotton went to South East Asia from Bengal by way of the Bay.

The important trading network that developed at this time was the Buddhist network. Studies in coastal archaeology reveals that the Bengal-Orissa coast (Sisupalgarh/Tamralipta) traded with Burma, Thailand and Malaysia; what is pertinent to Bengal's maritime links with the world of the northern Bay is that of these the site of Beikthano on the Irrawady in Central Burma, which experienced considerable trade with Bengal (on the basis of Rouletted Ware findings), was occupied until the eighth century AD[651].

The evidence from Beikthano is particularly important in light of the thesis we are developing about Bengal's commercial contacts with Arakan. Beikthano was populated by the Pyus. The state of Arakan that rose in the eleventh century was Pyu in origin. While it now seems evident that the growing Arab presence in the Bay was responsible for the decay of the ancient maritime sites in the Bay of Bengal, a Buddhist network continued to exist in the northern Bay until at least the fourteenth century. This linkage between the Bengal and Burma coasts continued well beyond the eleventh century when the greater Buddhist network was extended in the north Bay with the emergence of the states of Pagan and Arakan. Bengal and Burma, with their fluid borders, extensive riverine and coastal networks and a shared material culture continued to experience commercial ties until the conclusive Mughal orientation of Bengal's trade westward broke up this 'little' trade that encompassed the Padma, Meghna, Brahmaputra and Irrawady valleys and the numerous creeks that acted as outlets to the Bay.

Bengal played a part therefore within a regional economic bloc; this was oriented towards the eastern seas until at least the fifteenth century. However trade cannot sustain itself for long without some amount of control over production and the market. This was not made possible under Sena rule and the early Islamic 'conquest' states that followed them. It was made possible in the fifteenth century when Bengal was under Ilyas Shahi rule. From the sixteenth century (the time of Husain Shahi rule) there is evidence of a regional market centreing around the Nabadwip-Saptagram-Tribeni axis coming into being in western Bengal.

---

650 Lombard, Maurice, 1971: 201.

651 Glover, Ian C., 1996, 'Recent Archaeological Evidence for Early Maritime Contacts Between India and South-East Asia', in Ray and Salles (eds). 1996: 129–158. See p. 136.

There is, therefore, a gap in our historical knowledge of Bengal and the evolution of its market between the thirteenth to the sixteenth centuries. Dynastic histories are insufficient for our purposes here. The Husain Shahi market initiative was cut short by the political turmoil that followed Husain Shahi collapse in the sixteenth century. In the seventeenth century the regional market was centred around Dhaka which became the seat of Mughal administration for most of the century.

There exists an abundance of data for the eighteenth century in Bengal yet the eighteenth century debate is difficult to apply to Bengal because there is no historical continuity from the sixteenth century. Data is scanty; we are forced to depend on European travel accounts for the economy of Bengal in this period. We can assume however that the political flux in Bengal from the post Husain Shahi period uptil the eighteenth century inhibited further development of the regional market. Middle Bengali literature tells us that after Husain Shahi times trade ceased to be an indispensable part of material life and culture in Bengal. This fact impacted on Bengal's extra-regional markets and consequently on control of foreign trade in Bengal.

It seems evident from what we discussed in earlier sections that we have to turn to events in south eastern Bengal to reconstruct a picture of the economic developments in Bengal. We have seen that the most active commercial area in Bengal comprised the deltaic belt upto Chattagram. This area corresponds to the traditional *samatata-harikela* division. In this area lay the vibrant ports of Sripur, Bakla, Sandwip and Sagor; and the most flourishing port in this area was Chattagram. This delta area linked up with the mart towns in the north east, running on the arc from Bengal to Little Tibet and Chinese Turkestan, that we referred to.

What of trade and politics of this area in history? While there is scanty data regarding trade and polity in early medieval Bengal let us recapitulate what is known of the political history of Bengal.

1. Buddhist Bengal and overseas trade

The post-Sasanka and pre Pala period (eighth-ninth centuries) is traditionally described as the period of *matsya-nyaya* or interregnum in Bengal. But a closer investigation of the period under review shows that this was essentially a Gaur (or west) centred view of politics in Bengal. While political authority may have declined from Gaur in the post-Sasanka period the region of *samatata* or the south eastern portion of the delta seem to have emerged as a distinct economic region. It manifested considerable political and economic vigour as evidenced from the verve of so called 'minor' dynasties there: the Bhadras, the Khadgas, the Chandras, the Varmans and the Devas who continued to rule as independent kings up until the time of the Sena conquest of the twelth century. After Sasanka, therefore, there emerged two centers of poltical authority in Bengal: Gaur and Vikrampur.

What seems certain is that Brahmanical and Buddhist 'colonisation' in Bengal, far from unifying the region, had actually sculpted it into two distinct political entities. One was Gaur from where the dominant political discourse was articulated. The other was the Dhaka-Vikrampur region which enunciated a different rhetoric–one that frequently challenged Gaur.

Morrison's analysis of inscriptions from land grants suggests that far from being an alternative capital Vikrampur may have been the only capital in the delta that was the administrative centre for the whole of Bengal. Note that Vikrampur lay in a strategic position at the joining of the Meghna and the Padma, an area with an ancient commercial lineage.

It was placed in a supreme position for putting the goods of the north-east through the Brahmaputra in touch with the goods of the west through the Ganga-Padma. Plates of property transfers from Vikrampur from the tenth to the thirteenth centuries suggest that it was the only capital that had the power to issue proclamations for the whole of Bengal[652]. Moreover land grants from *samatata* exhibit a different character from those elsewhere in the delta. This area recorded the highest number of land grants and property transfers to collectives rather than individuals- such as monasteries and shrines. The plates from *samatata* are markedly pro-Buddhist (six out of seventeen inscriptions) unlike those of *varendra* which are pro-brahman in character. It is clear that *samatata*, bound by the three large river systems of the Ganga/Padma, the Meghna and the Brahmaputra, was the political and economic nerve centre of the region from where the Chandras, the Varmans and the Senas ruled Bengal. The large grants to institutions, the concentration of major building sites (Lalmai/ Paharpur) and the existence of a silver currency in *samatata* suggest its rulers were wealthier and more able to offer a stable administrative system than their contemporaries in the west[653]. Inscriptional evidence from *samatata* therefore modifies considerably the received history about Gaur as the only durable capital of an unified Bengal.

The region of Vikrampur manifested considerable economic vitality. At a time when the Palas used cowrie shells as currency in Gaur their

---

[652] Morrison, Barrie M., 1970, *Political Centers and Cultural Regions in Early Bengal*, The Association for Asian Studies, University of Arizona Press: 57, 153.

[653] *Ibid.*: 101, 107,115, 119, 124–5, 152-3.

rivals, the Chandras, used a silver currency in the east. The Chandras were Buddhists from Rohtasgarh in Bihar. More significant, they were an offshoot of the royal house of Arakan which is further proof of the very fluid borders that existed between Bengal and upper south east Asia. The dynasty, by reason of its proximity to the sea and by virtue of its considerable international trade, maintained a large fleet. It is said that the Varmans defeated the Chandras in a sea battle where the last Chandra king went down in his ship. This ended Buddhist rule in the east. Similarly the Buddhist Palas of Gaur were defeated by another band of military adventurers from outside (Senas) which professed srtong Brahmanical loyalties.

Moreover since the Chandras were supposed to be of Arakanese lineage this fact helped cement Bengal's traditional commercial links further with Arakan from the eleventh century[654]. The usage of a medium of international trade points to the area's enduring ties with northern south east Asia at a time when trade possibilities radiating from Gaur towards the middle gangetic plain were shrinking. The rise of Chattagram as the premier port of the region dates from this period.

Bengal then continued to have two distinct centres of political authority: one drawing upon the resources of the Bhagirathi-Hugli basin and basing itself on paddy cultivation, the other relying upon the Padma-Meghna delta and participating in international trade. Inscriptions of the Chandras and the Varmans from their capital at Vikrampur illustrate the measures that these dynasties were taking to strengthen their empire in the *harikela-samatata* region. The Rampal and Kedarpur copper plates of Srichandra and the Belava copper plate of Bhojavarman clearly articulate an alternate discourse of kingship from Pala to Sena times in eastern Bengal[655].

This is what the Belava copper plate says of Bhojavarman's rule[656]:

> He spread his paramount sovereignty by... extending his dominion over the Angas, by humiliating the dignity of Kamarupa, by bringing to disgrace the strength of the arms of Divya (the Kaivartya leader), by damaging the fortunes of Govarddhana and by vesting wealth in Brahmans versed in the Vedas.(verse 8) [and] Now from the illustrious camp of victory

654 For more on this see Paul, Pramode Lal, 1939: 78.

655 See Majumdar N.G., 1929, op.cit: 3–13; see also Majumdar R.C. *History of Ancient Bengal* op.cit.: 198–212. Majumdar however identifies the plate with Jatavarman: 198.

656 *Ibid.*

situated at Vikramapura the devout worshipper of Visnu, the Parameswara (etc.) the illustrious Bhojavarman duly... commands all those that are present namely the rajas, the rajanayakas, the queen, the Ranakas, the Rajaputras, the prime minister, the priest, the Pithikavitta, Mahadhamadhyaksha Mahasandhivigrahika, Mahasenapati, Mahamudradhikrita, Antananga-brihaduparika, Mahakshapatavika, Mahapratihara, Mahabhogika, Mahavyuhapati, Mahapilupati, Mahaganastha, Daussadhika, Chauroddhanavika and all officers in charge of the fleet and infantry, elephants, horses, cows, buffaloes, goats, sheep etc., the Gaulmikas, Dandapasikas, Dandanayakas, Vishayapatis and others ... depending on the king...' (verse 15 Ll.24-37).

From the eleventh century the social map of Bengal underwent a radical transformation; one that was in keeping with the political tune of the times. Bengal was progressively 'hinduised'. The Palas converted to Hinduism. This hinduisation had repercussions on Bengal's international trade. Trade was no longer promoted as the dominant official activity. From as early as the ninth century Bengal's contacts with south east Asia were on the wane and Buddhism thus lost one of its major *raison d'etre*. It was no longer required as a vessel for 'exporting' Indian social and political culture overseas.

Table 4.3 shows that *samatatà* or eastern Bengal was still fighting a losing war against the encroachment of Brahmanism. The region's adherence to Buddhism has already been explained by the area's economic and cultural ties with South East Asia, with the resurgence of the Bay trade in the eleventh century and the rise of the state of Arakan, as we noted. There was a migration of Buddhists from Bengal to Arakan. A new Buddhist cultural and commercial network was forged between eastern Bengal, Ceylon and Arakan.

But the old order was breaking up. Buddhism was perceived as inadequate as a state religion at a time when rapidly expanding states needed new integrative mechanisms for order and rule. It is no coincidence that both Buddhist dynasties–the Palas in Gaur and the Chandras in Vikrampur–were succeeded by the two orthodox Brahmanical dynasties of Sena and Varman respectively. By the eleventh century then, Buddhism, was under attack. Table 4.3 offers a glimpse of this changeover.

Table 4.3 Relative Strengths of Buddhism and Brahmanism in Bengal: fifth to seventh centuries

Period	*Place*	*No. of monasteries*	*No. of temples*
Early fifth century	Tamralipta	22	not available
Seventh century	Tamralipta	10	50
End seventh century	Tamralipta	6	not available
Seventh century	*Varendra*	20	100
Seventh century	*Samatata*	30	100

The eleventh century, then, was a century that ended the isolation of Bengal from the rest of the sub continent and brought it in line with developments on the mainland. From this century the great northward push of adventurers of the Karnate (the Senas) and of Kalinga (the Varmans) arrived in Bengal and based themselves at Gaur and Vikrampur respectively. This consolidated the brahmanical reconstruction in Bengal which was already underway from the tenth century. It is therefore no coincidence that the Varmans, and later the Devas, were devout followers of Visnu in keeping with ideological changes in the countries eastward of the Bay while the Senas initially started off as devout saivites and adopted vaisnavism subsequently.

2. *Brahmanised Bengal and the development of regionalism*

The eleventh to the thirteenth centuries was a period of flux. Bengal was progressively 'brahmanised'. The Buddhist network of the Bay lost some of its earlier vigour. There was a silent economic tussle underway in Bengal. What was to be the key note of the state-Hinduism and a predominantly agrarian economy or Buddhism and a mercantile world? At the same time there occurred the Islamic invasion and the establishment of the Bengal Sultanate which placed Bengal in a network straddling three continents: Africa, Europe and Asia. We should remember however that Bakhtiyar Khalji's defeat of Lakshman Sena did not herald the end of Sena rule immediately; it meant only that the Senas were displaced from Gaur/Nadia. The Senas still ruled from *samatata* and the Sena dynasty continued with Lakshman's sons and successors at Dhaka-Vikrampur for another century. This period also saw a new pattern of migration in Bengal; Brahmans fled south to Jajnagar on the Bengal-Orissa border while Buddhists went further east to Arakan and north to Tibet.

3. *The Mongol network and Bengal*

Early raids against Kamrup, Kamta, Nepal and Tibet (from the time of Bakhtiyar Khilji until the early Ilyas Shahis)[657] tells us that the Ilyas Shahis were obsessed with their eastern frontier. A desire to participate in the Mongol caravan trade which spanned China from the east, through Tibet, Afghanistan, Arabia upto Iraq and Persia may have been the reason. We have seen already that the Mongol putsch southwards impacted on Bengal in two ways. On land new town sprang up in Kamrup and beyond which traded with Bengal, such as Karampatan. On sea, the Mongols destroyed both Pagan and Srivijaya by the 1290s. This made for new possibilities in the trade of the Bay. Ilyas Shahi perceived the need to safeguard this area from Mongol attack. Later on they negotiated with Ming China which was seeking an alternative route through Central Asia for its caravan trade. Ilyas Shahi Bengal maintained close relations with both Yuan (Mongol) and Ming China; its most celebrated visitor in mid-fourteenth century, Ibn Batuta, exited Bengal from Chattagram en route to China. This is testimony to the commercial importance of eastern Bengal which was seen both as a gateway to sea trade with the Arakan and the archipelago as well as an entrepot that connected with caravan routes going both west to Afghanistan and east to China. For until the riverine changes of the late sixteenth century the Brahmaputra water route and the Mongol caravan trade route were the only routes by which eastern Bengal's goods could go north, east and west.

There developed a cotton-for silk exchange whereby trade was undertaken not only in the above items but the crops themselves were exchanged between Bengal and China. We have seen that cotton was introduced from Bengal into China from the seventh century onward. It was in the Yuan period (late thirteenth century and after) that cotton cultivation, spinning and weaving really took off in China[658]. In the early fifteenth century Ghiyath-al-Din Azam Shah opened diplomatic relations with Ming China directly. It was during this century that the Chinese method of silk cultivation (*harir sini*) was introduced into Bengal[659].

The China that Bengal intitally came into direct contact with was Mongol China, carved out by Chingiz Khan in the middle years of the thirteenth century. Chingiz Khan's partiality towards traders and his fondness

[657] See Mohar Ali, 1985, op. cit. for more on this, V 1A.

[658] Chaudhuri, K.N., 1990: 107.

[659] See Mukherjee, Rila, *Merchants and Companies* etc. (New Delhi, Pragati Publications).

for trade is brought out by Minhaj-ud-Din Siraj[660] who is otherwise hostile to the entire Mongol agenda. This agenda, Minhaj felt, threatened to overthrow the nascent Islamic regimes in South Asia[661] and indeed all over the Euro-Asian world.

The successors of Chingiz Khan dreamt of a vast Mongol empire spanning the continents of Asia and Europe which would, in turn, challenge the Islamic trading empire straddlling three continents (Asia, Africa and Europe) with success. In 1237 Fra Julian warned Europe that the Mongols sought world domination. In 1241 Pope Gregory IX sought to raise an abortive crusade against the Mongols. To this end various Italian monks, friars and merchants were sent to the Mongol court. But unlike what has been conventionally portrayed, Chingiz Khan was not a plunderer. For him trade brought in condiderable benefits and augmented the wealth of nations. To that end, maintainenance of towns and *serais* on the Silk Route and the continuation and expansion of the caravan trade was a matter of the utmost concern to the Mongols.

The Mongol putsch therefore impacted on Bengal in the form of a renewed Bengal-China trade. After the death of Kubla'i Khan in 1294 however, trade declined. The descendants of Chingiz converted to Islam; there now developed a hostility between them and the Chinese. Central Asia fell into disarray as horde after horde of Mongols now converted to Islam; this also meant the forging of new commercial alliances as well as confrontations between Mongol rulers and Muslim merchants as they fought over the same commercial space in Central Asia. As conditions in Central Asia became more uncertain the sea routes became more important.

In 1395 Tamerlane planned to re-establish the old Mongol Empire and between 1395 and 1405 he decided to invade China. In light of these events the emperors Hongwu and Yongle initiated a policy of trade and diplomacy in the Indian Ocean. Therefore the contacts between the Ilyas Shahis and the Mings should be seen not merely as commercial undertakings but as diplomatic missions as well, as the Chinese searched for allies across the seas to take off the pressure from the Mongols on their northern borders[662].

---

660 'Khwarazm Shah..Muhammad the Aghri (robber)…was not a monarch: he was a robber. Had he been a monarch he would not have slain my envoys and traders…for kings should not slay ambassadors', attributed to Chingiz Khan in Minhaj-ud-Din Abu Umar-I-Usman's *Tabakat-I-Nasiri: A General History of the Muhammadan Dynasties of Asia from 810 AD to 1260 AD and the Irruption of the Infidel Mughals into Islam* (Tr). Raverty, H.G.1881, Reprint ,New Delhi, Oriental Books Corporation, 1970: 1041.

661 The *Tabakat-I-Nasiri* is littered with references to infidels from hell etc.

662 Ray, Haraprasad, 2003: 182–184.

4. *Ilyas Shahi Bengal and the Islamic network*

The disintegration of the Tughlak Sultanate saw independent regional kingdoms coming into being in Bengal, Gujarat, the Deccan, Jaunpur and Malwa. Bengal under Ilyas Shahi rule now participated in the Islamic trading network; this participation was made obvious by the fact that Ibn Batuta, in his travels from the Maghreb, through Byzantium and Persia, made a stop in the newly islamicised states of Delhi and Bengal on his way to China. The route of Ibn Batuta therefore gives us an indication of the Islamic political and commercial networks that existed in the fourteenth century. The Ilyas Shahis participated in the greater Islamic trade routes spanning Africa and the Middle East. They continued the older legacy of supporting networks in the eastern seas; but they added to trade with south east Asia a new dimension: trade and diplomatic negotiations were established with China. The contact with the Yuans and the Mings has been seen in the context of an alternative caravan route the Mings were attempting to sponsor; in an attempt to byass the newly established Mongol routes. When the Mongols converted to Islam the problem of trade routes was solved. This was the economic zone that Ibn Batuta travelled through; he even went to China in a Chinese boat manned by Chinese Muslims.

An Africa-Malabar-Bengal-China trade developed and a giraffe from Africa was sent from Bengal to China[663]. The Chinese had an acute interest in Natural History; apart from horses, other animals that they imported from the Indian Ocean countries were camels, donkeys, mules, oxen, goats as well as exotic animals such as lions, zebra, golden spotted leopards, ostriches and white pigeons[664].

In return, silk cultivation was introduced into Bengal from China and with this valuable commodity Bengal participated in the dinar economy[665]. The Ilyas Shahi period furthered the creation of a vibrant mercantile economy in Bengal. It is not yet known how far riverine shifts from east to west impacted on Bengal's rice growing lands during this period. It is also not known how far port evolution was affected by fluvial changes during this period.

5. *Husain Shahi Bengal and the consolidation of regionalism*

This phase of Sultani Bengal saw a reversal of earlier policies. There was a mercantile swing from the east that went fully in favour of the

663 Filesi, Teobaldo, 1972, *China and Africa in the Middle Ages*, London.
664 Ray, Haraprasad, 2003: 195–196.
665 See Mukherjee, Rila, *Merchants and Companies* etc.

west. This was partly due to the massive riverine changes of the sixteenth century which made for a west to east shift. The fragmentation of the delta meant that new channels (rivers) and new outlets (ports) were introduced into western Bengal. Trade and alliance with Ming China was no longer pursued. The Husain Shahis on the other hand redirected trade and diplomacy away from Bengal's eastern frontiers and concentrated instead on the west: both within India and the Middle East. The Husain Shahis developed the western port of Saptagram from 1506 by linking it to its productive hinterland by way of a bridge. They got back Chattagram in 1516 from Tripura in a bid to control Bengal's premier easternmost port. In the west Bengal suffered no more invasions either from Delhi or Jaunpur[666]. The Sayyids and Lodis of Delhi abandoned the imperial dreams of their predecessors and Bengal was left free to pursue an independent course.

It has been suggested that because the Husain Shahis did not enjoy good relations with their neighbours to the north-west (Tirhut/Mithila), north-east (Kamrup, Tripura) and south (Orissa) they abandoned land routes and the caravan trade and concentrated on sea trade instead[667]. This sea trade spanned the Islamic shipping lanes in the Indian Ocean (Africa) and the Arabian Sea/Persian Gulf/Red Sea. The sea routes described in the section Routes and Ports in Bengal were routes developed and patronized by the Husain Shahis. It has also been suggested that to shake off undue Abyssinian influence on court politics in Bengal the Husain Shahis wooed local elements into politics and administration (see later) and they coopted the Portuguese into sharing in the economic life at Saptagram and Chattagram.

The Husain Shahis offered Bengal a stable leadership and a concerted economic policy after centuries. Their policies saw the emergence of a regional market; moreover this new market was oriented southward and westward through Husain Shahi strategy. The Husain Shahi rule therefore is a significant marker in the mercantile history of Bengal.

An abundance of silver coins of their reign suggests that there was a great increase in the volume of foreign trade at this time[668]. Husain

---

[666] Roy, N.B., 1958, *Niamatullah's History of the Afghans or Makhzan-I-Afghani*, Santiniketan Press, West Bengal.

[667] Tarafdar 1965: 144. Expeditions against these areas were as much to secure Bengal's frontiers as to attempt to access the northern trade of Tibet whose route ran through North Bengal and Kamrup.

[668] Copper coins were absent during Husain Shahi rule. They were probably represented by *cauris*. Silver coins were of three types in the ratio of 4: 2: 1. Two gold coins have also been discovered. Tarafdar 1965: 152–155.

Shahi economic policy was not one of state mercantilism; rather it was one of an open market policy. It was through their policies that the ports of Saptagram, Suvarnagram and Chattagram and a host of smaller ports became integral to the economic life of Bengal. This proved immensely beneficial to the economic life of Bengal; witness the many faceted commercial and urban life in sixteenth century Bengal that we referred to earlier. Port revenues coupled with the revenues from Husain Shahi mint-towns such as Lakhnawati, Suvarnagram, Husainabad (Gaur?), Saptagram, Chattagram, Pandua/Firuzabad and Mahmudabad added to the material wealth of Bengal. This radical commercial policy was cut short by two factors: the loss of Chattagram to the Arakanese and the silting up of Saptagram from the middle of the sixteenth century. Bengal was thus left without a port until the rise of Hugli in the 1580s.

The second half of the sixteenth century was also a period of anarchy for Bengal. Bengal experienced disturbances in both east and west. In the east the Husain Shahis had brought a major part of *samatata* and *harikela* in line with developments within *vanga*. Their political and cultural influence had spread as far as Arakan. This expansive rule was interrupted in the 1540s by two factors: the increasingly overpowering Portuguese presence in the deltaic area and the progressively disturbing Arakanese expansion through Chattagram and Dhaka upto the portion of the delta known as the Sundarbans. In the west the silting up of Saptagram and the Afghan conquest signaled the fall of Gaur.

6. *The first Europeans and maritime trade*

The Portuguese carved out an independent trading space for themselves in eastern Bengal in the sixteenth century. Winius has pointed out[669] that the Portuguese 'empire' in the east was an informal one based on alliances with local powers and frequently at variance with official Portuguese rule emanating from Goa. Subrahmanyam modifies this thesis by pointing out that despite variance with the 'official' empire of the Estado da India Portuguese private trade in the Bay attempted an accommodation with official trade. This led to a reorientation of trade routes emanating from Bengal[670]. Arakanese trade was no longer the chief priority–the three principal official routes were (1) to Malacca (2) to Ceylon through Nagapattinam and (3) to Hormuz.

---

669 Winius, 1983 op. cit.

670 Subrahmanyam, S., 1990; see also Subrahmanyam, S., 1993, *The Portuguese Empire in Asia 1500–1700*, Longman, London/N.Y.

The Portuguese carved out an autonomous area for themselves in the fluid *samatata/harikela* area. Sripur came under Portuguese control at the end of the sixteenth century. Sandwip at the mouth of the Meghna river was officially placed under Portuguese control in 1602. The seventeenth century saw a growing Portuguese population there. Both the ports formed part of that intensely mercantile area that traded with Arakan in textiles (cottons and increasingly from the end of the sixteenth century in silk goods) and grain. This Bengal-Arakan trade to as conducted mainly by the 'unofficial' Portuguese use.

The most important port of this region, we know, was Chattagram. Chattagram was a frontier port and was fought over in the early sixteenth century by the Husain Shahis and the kingdom of Tripura, and in the latter part of the sixteenth century, by the Portuguese and the Arakanese. It belonged initially to Tripura and was only added to Bengal by Rukn-ud-Din Barbak (1459–74). In early sixteenth century it was taken back by Tripura and Chattagram was formally incorporated into Bengal only in 1516 and was a part of Bengal till 1538 when it was taken over by the Arakanese.

The position of Chattagram as the primary port of the region is uncontested from the fourteenth century. In the sixteenth century Chattagram controlled the lion's share of the trade of Bengal and was consequently the largest revenue earning district within the state. The groups controlling trade from Chattagram in the sixteenth century were 'Rumis', Turks, Arabs, Abyssinians as well as merchants from west India[671]. Among them the Portuguese and a group of Persian merchants seem to have been the most prominent in Bengal trade.

Unfortunately, there are no precise statistics for Chattagram; but despite the westward shift it was intimately linked to Husain Shahi polity and was even then the chief port of Gaur. Tarafdar tells us that it contributed greatly to the material wealth of Bengal. With the fall of Gaur to Sher Shah's army in the 1530s Chattagram fell prey to a dual conflict between the Arakanese and the Portuguese. For much of the sixteenth century Chattagram lay at the heart of that disputed area in *harikela* to which both Bengal and Arakan laid claims. Finally Chattagram was claimed by Arakan and was lost to Bengal for much of the sixteenth century. The Portuguese too were expelled from Chattagram and with this expulsion died hopes of the last great revival of trade in eastern Bengal. Most of eastern Bengal

[671] Tome Pires, *Suma Oriental* (Ed). Armand Cortesao, Coimbra edition, 1978; Duarte Barbosa, *The Book of* etc. 1518, 2 vols. Tr. and Ed. M.L.Dames, 1918–1921, London.

was taken over by Min Bin's armies and Arakanese influence extended as far west as Dhaka and the Sunderbans. In the seventeenth century the Portuguese were thrown out of Dianga where they had relocated after being displaced from Chattagram. The Portuguese concentrated therefore more on the western ports of Saptagram and Pipli from the mid-sixteenth century.

Finally, it seems that despite earlier hostilities between the Portuguese and the Husain Shahis some sort of accommodation had been reached at the very end of Husain Shahi rule in Bengal. When Sher Shah appeared before the Teliagarhi Pass in 1536 Portuguese soldiers assisted the Husain Shahi garrisons. It is no coincidence that Martim Afonzo da Mello was given the right to build factories in Chattagram and Saptagram and to control the customs houses of the two ports the same year, probably as reward by Ghiyath-ud-Din Mahmud Shah III[672]. The Mughal policy of alienating a portion of maritime wealth to Europeans was started by the Husain Shahis.

7. *Arakanese Bengal and the Politics of Samatata/Harikela*

A major player in this area were the Arakanese. Not such is known about them but it is certain that they claimed a large portion of *samatata* as their own for reasons of ethnicity, culture, and sheer economics. Relations between Bengal and Arakan were cordial initially; in the early part of the fifteenth century the Arakanese king Narameikhla spent his exile from Arakan at Gaur and later regained his throne with help of the Ilyas Shahi sultan. Narameikhla's successors used Muslim designations and titles and issued Islamic style coins[673]. There are similar records for Matak Rai who was given asylum at Dhaka[674].

It is noteworthy that the resurgence of Arakan is intimately linked to the fortunes of the Husain Shahis. Under Ilyas Shahi rule Arakan had come into the political and cultural fold of Bengal. In the Husain Shahi period contacts between the two countries expanded. In the post-Husain Shahi period the Arakan kings (who had already adopted Muslim names) claimed succession to the rulers of Gaur (possibly through their ancient lineage with the Chandras), expanded into eastern Bengal and developed the port of Mrauk U in the Arakan to rival Chattagram. There was no such close relationship during the Mughal tenure in Bengal in the seventeenth century. Throughout this period relationships deteriorated.

[672] Tarafdar 1965: 86, 146.

[673] In *Ibid.*: 122.

[674] See later.

The early history of Arakan is obscure as we saw. It really comes to the forefront of Bay history with the rise of Burma (Pegu) as its political other in the sixteenth century. The Toungoo dynasty built up a strong maritime state with Pegu (and then Syriam) as rivals to Arakan which was then the strongest maritime state in the north Bay. The Toungoos wished to capture Siam and thereby control the ports of Martaban, Moulmein, Tavoy, Mergui and Tenasserim. The last three ports lay in the hazy frontier area between Burma and Siam and both countries sought to control them as a pathway to maritime wealth. Campaigns undertaken by Burma towards Siam produced no permanent results; on the contrary the Thai offensive against Pegu at the end of the sixteenth century, combined with the Arakanese-Portuguese assault upon Burma at the same time left the Irrawady delta in ruins. De Brito founded a maritime state based on Syriam in 1600 while King Naresuen of Siam annexed southern Burma upto Martaban. By the end of the sixteenth century Burma declined, to the advantage of Arakan.

What were the territorial boundaries of the state of Arakan; a state that functioned as Bengal's political monster for much of the medieval period? In the seventeenth century Arakan's western frontier was Chattagram-Jugdia, its northern frontier was Tripura, its southern frontier Pegu under the King of Burma and Syriam under the Portuguese and its eastern frontier was Siam. But in the seventeenth century there was a brief revival in the Irrawady delta under the leadership of Burma and Arakan was attacked repeatedly[675]. This southern offensive against Arakan impacted on the history of Bengal since the only alternative open to Arakan, in the face of a political reassertion by Burma, was to defend its chief maritime port through eastward expansion into Bengal by way of Chattagram-Jugdia.

The commercial promise of the Irrawady delta was abortive. Between 1629 and 1648, the period coinciding with Manrique's visit to Bengal and Arakan, King Thalun abandoned Pegu and concentrated on inland Ava instead. Manrique's Portuguese policy for Arakan, and Portuguese were dreams of a commercial empire in the Bay, has to be seen in light of the breakdown of Arakanese-Portuguese relations in the early seventeenth century, the gradual expansion of Mughal power in the east, the frustration of the Portuguese after their expulsion from Hugli in 1632 by the Mughals and the gradual development of a Thai commercial policy along the ports of the isthmus under kings Naresuen, Songtham and Prasart Thong from

[675] *Baharistan-I-Ghaybi.* See later.

the 1590s to the 1650s which effectively challenged Arakan's commercial domination of the north Bay.

Contacts between Arakan and Bengal are significant to the history of Bengal because a part of medieval Bengal, namely the Chattagram-Jugdia area, lay within Arakanese territory for much of their histories. The hazy boundaries to Arakan's west comprise today's Bangladesh; the part of Bengal that withstood Arakanese territorial ambitions through the sixteenth and seventeenth centuries. Bhalwa (in Noakhali district in Bangladesh) was the shadowy area through which Arakanese forces approached Bengal. Bhalwa's zamindar in the early seventeenth century, Ananta Manik, shared a common surname with the Tripura and Arakanese kings; *Manik* was a honorific title frequently bestowed on the Tripura and Arakanese royal families. And not just a name, the three dynasties also shared a common geographical and political space.

Between the fifteenth and eighteenth centuries the Chattagram-Jugdia area was fought over by the kings of Arakan, Tripura and Bengal[676]. A new dimension was added to this conflict when the Mughal made Bengal a Mughal province. Ananta Manik of Bhalwa frequently enlisted Arakanese help to retain his zamindari in the face of the Mughal threat emanating from Bengal. This fight was complicated by the Portuguese presence in the area. The latter frequently acted as mercenaries in the countries of the Bay and were utilized as such by local rulers in their wars against each other.

The early history of Chattagram, which concerns us here, is therefore shadowy despite Bengali historiography to the contrary. This is the political chronology that we have been able to piece together for Chattagram and its environs:

1. Fourteenth century: Chattagram part of Bengal according to Ibn Batutah's testimony.
2. 1459–82 King Basawpyn (Kalim Shah) occupies Chattagram. But also occupied by Tripura and Bengal (Rukhud-Din Barbak)
3. 1516–Bengal gets back Chattagram from Tripura. A triumph for Ala-ud-Din Husain Shah. Obviously the Arakanese lost Chattagram to Tripura in the interim.
4. 1540s–Arakan reconquers Chattagram. With the fall of Gaur to Sher Shah's army in the 1530s eastern Bengal and Tripura upto the Meghna-especially the Chattagram area-fell prey to conflicts between the Arakanese and the Portuguese. For much of the sixteenth and seventeenth centuries Chattagram lay at the heart of

676 Chattagram was regained from Tripura in 1516.

that disputed area in *harikela* to which both Bengal and Arakan laid claims. Finally, Chattagram was claimed by Arakan and was lost to Bengal for much of the sixteenth century. The Portuguese were expelled from Chattagram soon after 1540. Most of eastern Bengal was taken over by Min Bin's armies and Arakanese influence extended as far west as Dhaka and the Sunderbans.

5. Qasim Khan leads an expedition against Arakan in early seventeenth century. This is abortive and Chattagram's fate is not settled in favour of Bengal[677].
6. Arakanese hold on to Chattagram until 1666.
7. 1666–Mughals (Shaista Khan) conquer Chattagram and annex it to Bengal.
8. 1729–Bengal Nawabs reconquer Chattagram. In the interim Chattagram may have been regained by Arakan?

Chattagram, historically regarded as the economic nerve-centre of medieval Bengal was, we thus see, only notionally a part of Bengal: in the fourteenth century (Ilyas Shahi period), then again from 1516 to 1538 (Husain Shahi period), for some time after 1666 (Mughal period in Bengal) and then again after 1729 (during Shuja's nawabship in Bengal).

Yet relations between Arakan and Bengal were also cordial; Bengal seems to have been a favourite place of refuge for Arakanese kings.It was the Portuguese presence that often complicated matters; coupled with both Bengal's and Arakan's territorial ambitions over the no-man's land of Chattagram-Tripura-Bhalwa. Chattagram was the solution to Arakan's tactical interest in east South Asia. Arakan was frequently attacked by its immediate southern neighbour, the king of Barhama (Burmah or Burma)[678] and these attacks foretell the rise of Arakan's political other-Pegu.

The only solution, for Arakan, was to go west. Arakan was a militarized country with a strong navy. Mirza Nathan noted the military might of Arakan: 10 000 war boats, 1500 elephants and 1 000 000 infantry[679]. But it had no comparable deep water port. It is here that Chattagram assumed significance for the Arakanese.The Arakanese kept 2 000 jaliyas there against the Mughals' 30 or so war boats[680].

677 Mirza Nathan, V.I: 404–08.

678 Mirza Nathan, V.II: 641.

679 *Ibid.* V.II: 710. Talish also speaks of the might of the Arakanese navy which he deemed superior to that of the Mughals in *Fathiya-I-Ibriya*.

680 *Ibid.* V. II: 629–30

Chattagram therefore became a lifeline for Arakan. Shihabuddin Talish noted that the King of Arakan maintained a viceroy/governor there[681]. This post was entrusted to a relative. Fortifications were erected at Chattagram. The governor issued gold coins from Chattagram in the Raja's name. The king also sent to Chattagram each year a hundred boats full of soldiers and artillery. When Qasim Khan attacked Arakan they built a new fort at Kathgarh/ Sitakunda (in Bangladesh) in the Chattagram district. The Arakanese also sent 100 000 infantry, 1 000 war boats and 400 elephants to Kathgarh. It was a strategic point in Arakanese defence against Bengal. Indeed the western frontier was so important to Arakan that the king himself came to Chattagram with 10 000 horsemen, 300 000 infantry and a great number of elephants and boats to repel Qasim Khan. Cannons, guns, rockets, stones and bows and arrows were used against the Mughal army[682]. In face of these priorities Arakan entered into an uneasy alliance with the Portuguese and employed them as mercenaries in return for which the Portuguese were allowed to live and trade from Chattagram and Dianga.

This Arakanese-Portuguese entente was soon shattered; and the policy doomed for the Portuguese were massacred and expelled from Dianga in 1607. King Thiri Thudhamma thereafter sent Shah Jahan a mission at Dhaka during the latter's revolt in Bengal in the 1620s. The mission presented Shah Jahan with gifts worth Rs. 100 000 in return for which Shah Jahan recognized Arakan's sovereignty[683]. The Portuguese also abandoned their imperial ambitions in Arakan; after the grant of 'Portuguese' Sandwip (Gonzales) as jagir by Islam Khan to Salim of Arakan they lived as Arakanese subjects and relocated their commercial operations to the west to Hugli. It is to be noted that the Mughals used the Arakanese to break the Portuguese stranglehold in east Bengal; this strategy was repeated again through the expulsion of the Portuguese from Hugli in 1632.

Manrique was instrumental in forging another Portuguese-Arakan alliance in the 1630s; after the expulsion of the Portuguese from Hugli in 1632 he advised Thiri Thudamma, the king of Arakan, as part of official Portuguese policy, to enlist Portuguese aid once again to repel Mughal expansion in the east. But it was too late; the glory days of both

---

681 *Fathiya-I-Ibriya.*

682 Mirza Nathan, V.I: 405–08.

683 For opinions on this controversial mission see Karim, Kondkar Mahbubul, 1974, *The Provinces of Bihar and Bengal under Shahjahan*, Dacca, The Asiatic Society of Bangladesh: 114–15 and Mirza Nathan, V.II: 710–11.

the Arakanese and the Portuguese on the coast were over. Henceforth Mughal policy determined the politics of the eastern frontier. Yet the Dutch attempted to take over where the Portuguese had left off[684].

Chattagram was also the key to Arakan's commercial dominance on the coast. We do not know much about the Arakan-Bengal trade; however we do know that the Arakanese traded not only through Chattagram but at Hugli as well. The most lucrative commodity were slaves. This was a three-way trade. The Arakanese brought in their prisoners to be sold as slaves to the Portuguese at Hugli in the seventeenth century. Moreover they–along with the Portuguese–conducted slave-hunting raids along the coast in Chattagram, Jessore, Bakla, Bakergunge, Hijli and Orissa and sold their booty at the principal slave marts of Hugli, Tamralipta, Pipli, St.Thome, Goa, Surat and Ceylon[685] so much so that deltaic Sunderbans was depopulated in the seventeenth century[686]. The Arakanese also imported slaves from Bengal. Manrique tells us that in the middle of the seventeenth century the Arakanese brought 18 000 slaves in five years from Bengal to Arakan (Dianga and Angarcale). The Arakanese sought to develop their own port of Mrauk U after their failure to hold permanently onto Chattagram. This was a short-lived port in history; its trade and traffic was soon eclipsed by Pegu.

8. *Many Islams*

While the Arakan-Portuguese-Bengal drama was played out in south eastren Bengal, Muslims other than the ruling class, peopled the region. These were mainly merchants, but there were also dispossessed landlords, chiefs and former rulers. Bengal's trade history is littered with references to Arabs, Pathans, Afghans, Turks, Tajiks and Mughals. While this is undoubtedly confusing for the student of history it is clear that these ethnic designations emanated from four political blocs as we know them today: the Middle East (which exported a vast amount of Arabic speaking merchants to India's shores), Afghanistan which provided South Asia with the Ghaznavid and Ghurid kings (the Pathans came from the same area),

---

684 Sanjay Subrahmanyam tells us that the VOC powered the slave trade from Jakarta and Pulicat via Arakan. See '*Dutch Tribulations in Seventeenth Century Mrauk U*' in *Explorations in Connected History: From the Tagus to the Ganges*, 2005, Oxford University Press.

685 Barbosa: 363; Pyrard, I: 322 and Ain, II: 122 (Jarrett, account of Bengal), Bernier: 174–175.

686 Shah Jahan retaliated by sending the entire Portuguese population of Hugli as slaves to Agra in 1629.

Turkestan or that vast area between China and Russia which comprised the Mongol khanate and included Turks as both Tatars and Mongols (Mughals) and Tajiks from the eastern reaches of Persia contiguous with Turkestan.

In other words both the Mughals and the Turko-Afghan sultans of India were Turks but the former were Mongol while the latter were Tatars and traditional enemies of the Mongols. And the Tajiks were also Turks but from a different area. While all these ethnic groups were 'Muslim' by the sixteenth century their political affiliations, arising out of their area of origin, dictated the commercial partiality of each of these groups[687].

9. *Afghan and Mughal Bengal*

In the west Husain Shahi stability was destroyed with the Afghan victory in Bengal in the 1530s. This shortlived triumph was shattered once again with the Mughal victory (albeit nominal at that time) in 1576. The Mughal decree of 1580 to the Portuguese Pedro Tavares to establish a port at Hugli signaled the passing away of Husain Shahi mercantile policy; from now on lower Bengal and not the Saptagram-Triveni-Nabadwip complex would dictate Bengal's mercantile history. The changes in the river system ensured that the ports of western Bengal would now conduct overseas commerce by linking the coast with the produce of the interior. Goods on the Padma-Meghna-Brahmaputra waterway now communicated directly with Hugli in the west through the Ganga.

10. *'Persianised' Bengal and Its Politics*

In the last analysis the only trading combine that showed staying power in the eastern side were the Persians. The Gromalles and the Khwajas of early Portuguese documents exhibited remarkable staying power in the sixteenth century; in the seventeenth century we have Muhammad Sayyid (the infamous Mir Jumla of Persian origin) as *subahdar* and monopolist in Bengal and the extensive Shi'a migration from Persia into Bengal during Prince Shuja's subahdarship from 1639–60; and in the eighteenth century we get a group of wealthy Persian merchants/officials dominating trade from Dhaka.

The second Murshid Quli, Mirza Lutfullah of Tabriz, became governor of Orissa during Nawab Shuja's reign in Bengal. Subrahmanyam (1992)

---

[687] See Khondkar Fuzli Rubbee, 1895, *The Origin of the Musalmans of Bengal being a Translation of Haqiqate Musalman-I-Bengalah*, Calcutta, Thacker and Spink and Co. for the diverse Islamic groups in Bengal.

says that the second Murshud Quli weathered the storm of the 1739–40 succession dispute and was appointed Naib-Nazim (what the English refer to as the 'Chhota Nawab') of Dhaka during Alivardi's reign[688]; this however is incorrect[689]. This second Murshid Quli and his associates Mir Habibullah of Shiraz and Mir Razi of Shustar appear to have practiced a minor variant of state mercantilism from Dhaka[690] and in the process built up a clique of Iranian and Central Asian traders in Bengal. Mir Habib had previously been a 'broker' at Hugli and he now advised Murshid Quli Khan II on economic matters[691]. Mir Habibullah's most notable achievement was the conquest of Tripura which brought to Bengal much booty and elephants. The conquest of Tripura was the final card in the control of Bengal's far eastern frontier. The decline of Arakan at this time may be seen as indicative of the economic and cultural decline that this zone was experiencing. This decline was to the benefit of the Persian merchants.

They dealt mainly in monopolies of lucrative items for trade from Dhaka; we do not know what these commodities were but cottons, dairy products, sugar and grain probably were probably the chief commodities. This group also maintained close links with Surat and Basra and there is every likelihood that a major portion of Bengal's westward trade was monopolized by this Iranian group.

What made Persians move to Bengal? They seem to have come initially mostly from the Deccan where they migrated as merchants, religious leaders and men of letters from as early as the fourteenth century[692], and in the sixteenth century, from Delhi as well. They then metamorphosed into a court elite in the numerous Islamic courts of South Asia and in so doing moved onto the east as well. In Bengal they seem to have been mostly traders; lured there by the rich pickings that trade offered.

What were the reasons behind this Persians exodus to South Asia in such huge numbers? While this has been discussed in greater detail in my *Merchants and Companies* etc. we may present a brief account here. The conventional reasons are one, disturbances in the Central Asian world

[688] Subrahmanyam, S., 1992, 'Iranians Abroad: Intra-Asian Elite Migration and Early Modern State Formation' in *The Journal of Asian Studies*, 51, 2, May: 340–63.

[689] Karim, Abdul, 1964, *Dacca The Mughal Capital*, Dacca, Asiatic Society of Pakistan however puts his tenure at Dhaka as Naib Nazim from 1728–34: 26. Mohar Ali agrees: V. 1A 585–7.

[690] K.F.R. circa late 1740s.

[691] Mohar Ali, V. 1A: 585.

[692] Subrahmanyam, S., 1992, *Journal of Asian Studies*: 340–63.

which made Muslims view South Asia as the custodian of Islam, and two, the diplomatic ties established by Akbar with the Safavid Empire. These were furthered by Jahangir's identification with Persian kingship and his alliance with Shah Abbas in the seventeenth century. However a recent book[693] suggests that more fundamental causes were at work behind the migration of the Persians from Persia.

The Safavids converted to Islam in 1500. Persia therefore became a nodal point in the vast Islamic network of trade and politics that spanned continents. The mercantilist and statist polcies of Shah Abbas I at the start of the seventeenth century were aimed to put Persia on the world map of Islam. Shah Abbas' policies resulted in the resettlement of the Armenians in New Julfa as part of Shah Abbas' strategy to counter the economic might of the Tajiks in Persia (who now migrated to South Asia in large numbers), an exploitation of the Armenian overseas trade network and consequently increased trade with South Asia (since the Armenians were long settled there) and the attempt to control all trade within Persia, especially that of silk, to the profit of the Safavid state. The Persia of Shah Abbas was essentially a mercantilist state and his silk policy was one whereby he attempted to counter the Ottoman domination of the European market for silk.

Persian-Mughal relations became more genial when Jahangir became emperor. In his bid to assume the title of ruler of the world Jahangir entered into a friendly competition with Shah Abbas[694]. During Jahangir's reign a Persian embassy toured all provinces of the Mughal empire to see the fresh conquests. In keeping with the diplomatic/commercial network favoured by Shah Abbas this mission visted Bengal in the 1620s as well. This happened during Islam Khan's tenure and the mission was royally entertained at the Mughal provincial court at Dhaka[695].

The Persians who settled in the numerous states around the Bay in Eastern South Asia were soon made aware of the trading possibilities of the region. In the sixteenth century the major Deccani sultanates-Bijapur, Golconda and Ahmadnagar-boasted Iranian antecedents or links[696]. Trade

693 McCabe, Ina B., 1999, *The Shah's Silk for Europe's Silver: The Eurasian Trade of the Julfa Armenians in Safavid Iran and India 1530–1750* (Armenian Texts and Studies, 150), Georgia, Scholars Press.

694 See Mughal miniatures depicting both Jahangir and Shah Abbas standing, facing one another, on a globe; indicating clearly their equal status as world-rulers, at least of the Islamic realm.

695 Mirza Nathan, *Baharistan-I-Ghaybi*, V.I: 212.

696 Subrahmanyam, S., 1992: 343–44.

with Arakan became a favourite; in time Persian migrants settled at the Arakanese court of Mrauk U persianised the Arakanese court in terms of rituals and commerce. The Htu-Kan-Thein shrine built by Min Phalaung in 1571 showed men dressed in the *kuleh* and *qaba* of the time. These were the favoured Persianate style dress favoured by the Persian aristocracy[697]. By the seventeenth century Persians were present in Thailand as well-notably in Mergui and Auythia where they exercised considerable power. It is claimed that Thai royal dishes were persianised[698]. Religious dissidents from Persia also found their way to South Asia which, by virtue of its numerous and flourishing Islamic states was seen as the guardian of Islam. By the seventeenth century many more such Persian elite were founding states in South Asia; the founder of the Bengal *nizamat* of the eighteenth century, Murshid Quli Khan for example, had a Persian background. Many more such nobles such as the second Murshid Quli followed and set up secure mercantile bases in eastern Bengal.

There may be another reason for this intensive commercial contact between Bengal and Persia. It seems that as in Bengal Persian overland and maritime trade was more complementary than competitive and the caravan trade between South Asia and Persia enjoyed a long lineage. The overland route flourished throughout the eighteenth century and carried as much merchandise as the sea route. Moreover not just cargo but merchants kept in close touch with Persia. It was reported[699] that in the middle of the fifteenth century there arrived in Hormuz merchants from foreign territories such as Egypt, Syria, Anatolia, Turkestan, Russia, China, Java and Bengal , Siam, Tenasserim, Bijapur, Malabar, Cambay, Arabia and Yemen–in short the entire trading world of medieval times was present in Hormuz long before the Portuguese arrival. Persia's neighbouring state, Uzbeg Turan, housed textile merchants from Bengal in December 1557[700].

Mohar Ali claims however that a section of Persians, known as Tajiks, had visited eastern *samatata* even earlier and takes an inscription of Ratnapala (ninth/tenth century) to suggest that some may actually have settled in the region of Chattagram/Arakan from those times. Similar evidence comes from the Buddhist site of Paharpur (in Rajshahi district

697 Gutman, Pamela, 2001, *Burma's Lost Kingdoms: Splendours of Arakan*, CT, Weatherhill, and Bangkok, Orchid Press: 118–9.

698 Subrahmanyam, S. 1992, *Journal of Asian Studies*: 348–350.

699 In Frank, A.G., 1998: *Re Orient: Global Economy in the Asian Age*, University of California/Sage-Vistaar.

700 Jenkinson, Anthony, *Early Voyages and Travels to Russia and Persia,* Delmar Morgan and C.H. Coote (Eds)., 1886, Volume II, London, Hakluyt Society: 87.

just across the river from Murshidabad) where a coin from the Abbasid Caliph Harun-al-Rashid has been found[701]. That Persia had a long lineage of contact with Bengal is now corroborated by other scholars.

So southeastern Bengal was known to the Persians from very early times. Minhaj-I-Siraj who accompanied Bakhtiar Khalji on his north-eastern campaign in Bengal was Persian. His *Tabaqat-I-Nasiri* may have served as a practical guide for eastern India just as it does for historians today. This long history of interaction between Bengal and Persia has attracted little attention in historical research[702] and the ship-owning/ mercantile activities of Persian merchants and officials offers substantial scope for historical research in early medieval Bengal.

The End of 'Noble Trade' in the 'Far East'

'Adieu to ye Bay of Bengal, ye Best Flower in ye Company's Garden and all India' (Hedges, *Diary*, 1683, I, 117)

While Persian *subahdars* and their friends were trading from Dhaka in the east a wind of change had blown in from the west. The emotional statement of Hedges is indicative of the fact that the EEIC now saw its trade in the Coromandel and the Bay as the most important in Asia. Moreover, Hedges made the statement at the time when the Bengal factories were made independent of the Coromandel. Bengal now became the prime area of activity for the EEIC. But the theatre of this activity was the west, and not eastern Bengal with its older commercial lineage, and trade routes radiating from the east declined in consequence.

Historically, after Asians, it was the Portuguese and then the French who were the first to be aware of the commercial possibilities of the 'Far East'. The Portuguese centred themselves in the eastern delta from the beguinning of the sixteenth century and their trading practices saw an amalgam of the earlier Arabo-Islamic, Persian, Arakanese and Bengali commercial interests. In short, they established themselves in that sensitive corridor between eastern Bengal on the one hand and Ava-Arakan-Pegu and southern China on the other–the heart of this commercial bloc as envisaged by Manrique lay in the border region between China and India described earlier by Marco Polo. At the beginning of the sixteenth century

[701] Ali, M.M., 1985, V. 1A: 36–38.

[702] Muzaffar Alam, Francoise 'Nalini' Delvoye and Marc Gaborieu (Eds)., 2000, *The Making of Indo-Persian Culture*, New Delhi, Manohar has not even one article on Bengal. We can refer to Tarafdar's thesis of the limited output and area of Bengali-Muslim culture, *Purusartha*, Paris, 1986, in this context.

Duarte Barbosa noted that Ere Can Guy (Arakan) was filled with gentiles and contained twelve towns within the kingdon which brought Chinese goods, lac and musk (presumably by the overland-riverine route through Ava and Yunnan just described) to Pegu[703]. He added 'This King (of Ere Can Guy) is very rich in money, and powerful from the number of his men at arms; he is often at war with his neighbours, and some of them obey him against their wills and render him tribute'[704].

Eastern and Northern Bengal-Arakan-Ava formed a distinct cultural zone. Aloes-wood, the great export item of the sixteenth century, madly coveted in the Indian Ocean world, was found in the hilly and riverine area of Bengal-Arakan-Ava[705] The merchandise of Bengal-Arakan-Ava found a natural outlet through the ports of Pegu; Barbosa noted that Ava was 'a very great and opulent city…a place of rich merchants…'[706], a statement that testifies to the great trade that this landlocked kingdom carried out with its neighbours in rubies and musk, its chief exports, and also in Chinese goods from its border with Yunnan[707].

The failure of the Portuguese policy was apparent by the 1630s. The next European company to take up the project was not the English, but the French. In the 1730s Dupleix dreamed of a great commercial complex, centreing on Chattagram and stretching from Chandernagore in the west to Arakan, Pegu, and Ava in the east. The transport network for this grand project envisaged a melange of existing river routes, coastal sailings as well as the utilisation of the grand Brahmaputra-Meghna water route. Chevalier's attempts at opening up the north-east frontier in an effort to promote Franco-Assamese and Franco-Tibetan trade in the 1750s formed part of the same vision[708], but he took it even further. Chattagram was to be at the centre of a great maritime and strategic bloc linking the eighteenth century kingdoms of Bengal, Assam, Tripura, Ava, Arakan, Pegu, Mergui (Ile de Roy off the coast of Mergui was ceded to the French in Louis XIV's time), Andaman and Nicobar islands and southern China[709]. Ile de Roy opposite the port of Mergui with its deep harbour

[703] Barbosa: 182.

[704] *Ibid.*: 182.

[705] Varthema: 234–237.

[706] Barbosa: 186.

[707] *Ibid.*: 186, 184.

[708] Deloche Jean (Ed). 1984, *Les Aventures de J.B.Chevalier dans l'Inde Orientale 1752–65,* Paris, EFEO Publications.

[709] *Ibid.* 98–101.

was central to this scheme and Chevalier wrote a note on it after his visit there in July 1765[710]. After the loss of Bengal to the EEIC he suggested that the FEIC develop this port as a French port and colony. Being just across the Bay from Pondichery it assured the FEIC a military and strategic location in eastern Bay of Bengal[711]. The development of Ile de Roy as port, and the conquest of the Andaman and Nicobar islands, would patrol the entry of all vessels into the Bay of Bengal and effectively hamper EEIC rule in Bengal. Unfortunately this suggestion was not acted upon in Paris[712].

China was the principal object of Chevalier's missions between 1752 and 1765 and he tried twice to go there (once from Katha and once from Tibet) but he failed. Access to China through Tibet and Katha was known as the Southern Silk Route that connected Yunnan and Szechwan with the Bay of Bengal ports. 'Catta' (Katha) in Burma on the western bank of the Irrawady haunted Chevalier[713]. This was because Katha granted an easy access to China through river routes: it was bounded on the north by Szechwan province and on the south by Yunnan, China's gateway to South Asia.

What were the items that would feature in this trading zone? Historically the route between Bengal and China through Assam and the north east carried textiles such as *muslins*, *saklats*, *sof* and *baftas*, pearls, horses, saddles with gold/silver embroidery, rhino horns, crane heads, kingfisher feathers, sugar crystals, parrots and parrot beak, rhubarb, lignum aloes, sesame, catechu, ebony and areca-nut as exports from Bengal and the north east, and gold, silver, satin, taffetas, blue and white porcelain ware, copper coin, musk, vermilion, quick silver and grassmats as imports from China into Bengal[714]. Yunnan produced gold, Chinese green tea, silk, many medicinal plants and precious stones[715]. At the end of the sixteenth century, long after the China-Bengal missions stopped, Bengal carried on the South East Asia-China trade. Bengal exported pepper, catechu, *baftas*, ivory, crowns of cranes, glazed vases, blue glazed and patterned brush

[710] *Ibid.*: 91.

[711] *Ibid.*: 99.

[712] *Ibid.* 101.

[713] Deloche Jean Ed. 1990, *Statistiques de Chandernagor , 1823, 1827 and 1838, by Joseph Cordier and Achille Bedier*, Pondichery, Institut Francais: 22, 241.

[714] Ray, Haraprasad, 2003, *Trade and Trade Routes Between India and China c. 140 B.C.–1500 A.D.*, Kolkata, Progressive Publishers: 124.

[715] *Ibid*: 22.

pots, white glazed cups, horse tails, horse, tiger, leopard and ox skins, cloaks or wraps, 'western ocean' fabrics, linseed, paper and cotton velvet[716].

In this zone these were deemed items of 'noble commerce' and in 1755 Chevalier thought to augment this trade with ivory, pepper, lacquer, gold, wood for construction, cottons and other textiles (possibly wild silk for which Chevalier noted there was great demand in the Mughal Empire, Tartary, Persia and Arabia) against French textiles and other European articles for which there was a demand in Asian countries[717]. He wrote of Assam: 'La proximité avec la Chine, le Tibet, le royaume d'Ava et tous les pays adjacents ouvroient un debouche immense aux manufactures…de France'[718]. Chevalier thus dreamed of reviving the old Bengal-China trade through the Mongol (overland) route, much as Marco Polo had written about five hundred years before him. Chattagram was the key to this grand design and in 1786 a small portion of Ava passed into French hands[719] but nothing really came of this plan.

Some three decades after Chevalier, when W.W.Hunter wrote *A Concise Account of the Kingdom of Pegu: The Climate, the Products, Trade and Government etc.* in the 1780s, a radical reorganisation had taken place in the Bay world-both politically and commercially. Arakan ceased to exist by the 1780s. The China trade through India's north-east was no longer a prime concern; instead Hunter suggested that trade with Pegu by sea was the future of the Bengal-Pegu-China trade[720]. The 'little noble trade' described above was no longer a matter of interest; the EEIC had already redefined the commercial map of the Bay and Hunter suggested that the Bengal-Pegu-China trade be financed through opium grown in Bengal[721]. Pegu's wood was still important, but so was its honey, areca nut, cachow, rice, cloth 'like tartan' and horses[722]. Pegu also produced minerals and metals in abundance. The wealth of this land was evident by the fact that the people used silver as their currency, but not as coins but by weight. One *tycal* of 25% silver was equivalent to 1Sicca Rupee of Bengal[723]. It

---

716 *Ibid.*: 142.

717 Deloche, 1984: 23.

718 *Ibid.*: 23.

719 *Ibid*: 239.

720 Hunter, W.W., 1785, Calcutta, John Hay: 93.

721 *Ibid*: 94.

722 *Ibid*: 72, 81, 83–4.

723 *Ibid*: 85.

had gold in abundance; the EEIC eyed this supply since their only source was the Malay coast, but Pegu forbade its export[724]. It also had tin in abundance[725]. Commerce was obviously important to Pegu; Hunter wrote that of its four 'magistrates' the *meoon* presided over the council, the *reoon* over justice, the *shahbunder* (a Persian term) over trade and the *cheekaw* over other matters[726].

As regards the wood, Hunter wrote that the abundant supply of teak in Pegu made it the only source in the Bay and vital for the construction of warships[727]. The only other similar source was in the area around Bombay. He added[728]:

> (Pegu's wood is vital) in the construction of ships; and it has this advantage over every kind of wood–that it is much less corruptible in water.

Pegu, or Burma which had swallowed up Arakan, was now a dependency of Ava. In this new political climate Hunter wrote[729]:

> The trade to Pegu has never been esteemed a national concern; ...carried on by a few private adventurers who were, in general, such as had not capital sufficient to begin any other branch of commerce. Any man who could find money enough to purchase a small vessel, on the coast of the Coromandel, might, by carrying a little tobacco, some blue cloth, and a few iron nails, to the island of Carnicobar, get, in exchange for these articles, which had cost him almost nothing, a ship load of cocoa nuts; for these he could procure, at Pegu, a cargo of wood, which he afterwards sold, to great advantage, either on the coast, or in Bengal.

The old and 'noble' trade, carried on historically from Bengal, had now become a petty trade, carried on by private European adventurers. With the old overland-riverine-coastal route in disarray the launching pad for this trade had moved away from Bengal to the Coromandel. *The Accompt of the Trade of Metchlepatam* in Master's *Diary* noted in 1675 that ships belonging to natives were constantly employed on voyages to

---

[724] *Ibid*: 93.

[725] *Ibid.*: 93.

[726] *Ibid.*: 51–53.

[727] *Ibid.*: 91.

[728] *Ibid.*: 81.

[729] *Ibid.*: viii–ix.

Arakan, Pegu and Tenasserim[730]. 'Native' trade on this route from Bengal was no more. Because of the realignment of routes Carnicobar had emerged as a vial point in the Coromandel-South Asia-South East Asia trade; and it was from here, for a 'ship load of cocoa nuts', that trade in the formerly patrician items that Pegu produced could be financed.

And what was the fate of the old river and land route through Bengal and Assam into China? Welsh's *Report on Assam* stated in 1794 that of the items to be procured from Assam sugar cane, poppy, pepper, indigo, mustard seed, tobacco, supari, ginger, rice were important. Others were gold, iron, salt petre, lac, *muga* silk, rhino horn, elephants' tusks, buffalo hide and deer skin[731]. Aloes wood from this area, which had supplied the Indian Ocean world was not mentioned. Henceforth new items were to determine the trading fortunes of Bengal and eastern India.

---

730 Master, V2: 113.

731 In Mackenzie, Alexander, 1884, *The North East Frontier of India,* Intr.by B.K. Roy Burman, New Delhi; Mittal Publications, 2005: 387–89.

5

The Debated Century

'Bengal is an extensive country and fertile, and produces a large revenue. The climate however is very damp, on account of the quantity of rain that falls and its proximity to the salt sea' (Khwaja Abdul Karim Khan, *Baya'n-i-Waki*, Elliot and Dowson, V.8: 130).

The Eighteenth Century and Bengal – The Foundations

A major component of the eighteenth century debate is the received idea of Bengal's primacy. This book has questioned the notion of the 'primacy' of Bengal in the previous chapters. The story narrated in this book ends in the eighteenth century. The eighteenth century was crucial for Bengal for it experienced all three of the themes that distinguishes the eighteenth century from others: it saw the formal distintegration of Mughal administration in Bengal, it experienced the rise of a regional power (the Murshidabad *nizamat*), and faced the domination of foreign capital on its shores, rivers, inland markets and manufactures.

Because of these three markers the importance of the eighteenth century continues unabated in South Asian history; but it is important to keep in mind that in Bengal the eighteenth century brought with it yet another dimension. From then on, the economic and political focus was finally concentrated on the west (*vanga*). The east or *samatata* became a marginal land.

The eighteenth century–a century of change–is now itself the subject of a debate[732]. It hinges around three themes: the decline of imperial

[732] The most recent overview of the debate is found in Marshall, P.J., (Ed). 2003, *The Eighteenth Century in Indian History: Evolution or Revolution*?, New Delhi, Oxford University Press.

power, the emergence of regional powers, and the rise of European economic and political power. The eighteenth century debate originated from the idea that the fragmentation of the Mughal Empire in the post-Aurangzeb era brought forth an era of decay in the sub-continent. In 1700 the Mughals ruled from Kashmir to Assam in the North and their rule extended to almost what is today Tamil Nadu in the south. By 1765 this vast empire had shrunk to territories around Delhi in the wake of the Afghan invasions of Nadir Shah (1739–40) and Ahmad Shah Abdali (1761). By 1720 a new political power emerged in the shape of the Marathas who overran much of central, southern and eastern parts of South Asia. Between 1757 and 1765 another political power emerged; the English East India Company (EEIC) won a political victory in Bengal (Plassey in 1757), repulsed the Marathas (the third battle of Panipat in 1761) and resumed the rights of revenue collection (Diwani) in Bengal *suba* in 1765. Between 1765 and 1813 the EEIC marched up the middle gangetic plain; by 1856 a major part of the sub-continent was under its rule. The emperor at Delhi had been reduced to the status of a shadow emperor.

English historiography referred to the events at Plassey as a 'revolution'; successive victories that consolidated their territorial power only reinforced the idea of Plassey as a revolution. This 'revolution' was of course possible because of the decline of the later Mughals ; an idea that was emphasized in the writings of Irvine (*Later Mughals*, Calcutta, 1922) and Jadunath Sarkar (*History of Aurangzeb, The Fall of the Mughal Empire,* and *History of Bengal: The Muslim Period 1200–1757*).

Herman Goetz (*The Crisis of Indian Civilisation in the Eighteenth and early Nineteenth Centuries: The Genesis of Indo-Muslim Civilisation*, Calcutta, 1938) and Philip Calkins (1970, 'The Formation of a Regionally-oriented Ruling Group in Bengal 1700–1740', *Journal of Asian Studies,* 29, 4: 799–806) moved away from the idea of political decline and drew attention to the fact that a new cultural revolution was underway in the states that emerged in the wake of the Mughal decline. In fact Calkins went so far as to emphasize the links between the new state, the merchants, *zamindars* and the financiers; a point that was made by C.A. Bayly (1983, *Rulers Townsmen and Bazaars: North Indian Society in the Age of British Expansion*, 1770–1870, Cambridge and 1987, The New Cambridge History of India, 1, *Indian Society and the Making of the British Empire*, Cambridge). Bernard Cohn (1962, 'Political Systems in Eighteenth Century India: The Banaras Region', *Journal of the American Oriental Society*, lxxxii, July–Sept: 312–19 and 'The Initial British Impact on India: A Case Study of the Banaras Region' in *An Anthropologist Among The*

Historians and Other Essays, OUP, 1987) emphasized new political systems that were emerging in eighteenth century India. The emphasis therefore moved away from the eighteenth century decline in the centre and towards the cultural and political vigour of the new states that arose in the wake of the Mughal disintegration.

The eighteenth century debate, therefore is inextricably bound up with reasons for the decline of the Mughal state and, in recent times, with the nature of the Mughal state itself. Despite alternative explanations emphasizing the vigour of regional political systems, and because of the rise of British power in Bengal in the eighteenth century, the idea of decline has been paramount in debates on the eighteenth century in India. Along with the theme of territorial decline the eighteenth century debate underscores another decline; that of indigenous trade. In subsequent pages we shall see how effective indigenous trade was in Bengal in the eighteenth century.

The Foundations-The Decline School: Territory

The dominant set of explanations of the decline of the Mughal state was provided by the Aligarh school. Irfan Habib stressed the unequal tax burden that put an intolerable strain on the peasant and ultimately fragmented the empire[733] and Satish Chandra stressed prevailing expenditure norms among the Mughal elite which became too hard to sustain after 1707 and thereby caused the crash of the Mughals[734]. Chandra thus opened up the debate to the question of the 'jagirdari crisis'. Crisis in governance led to speculations in terms of the level of assimilation of the Deccani jagirdars into the empire, which further exacerbated the political and economic crisis[735]. There was also speculation that the withdrawal of banking support may have contributed to the fall of the Mughals[736]. The reasons for decline were, in this set of explanations, sought either in the extractive character of the Mughal state, spendthrift elites, or loss of confidence in the imperial system.

Athar Ali moved away from the territorial entity of the Mughal Empire and sought reasons for its decline in the overall Islamic world. He drew attention to the cultural and economic decline in the Safavid-Ottoman-

[733] *The Agrarian System of Mughal India, 1556–1707*, Bombay, 1963.

[734] *Parties and Politics at the Mughal Court 1707–40*, 3rd ed. Delhi, 1982; see also his *Medieval India: Society, the Jagirdari Crisis and the Village*, Macmillan, 1982.

[735] Richards, J.F. '*The Imperial Crisis in The Deccan*', *Journal of Asian Studies*, XXXV, 2: 237–256.

[736] Leonard, Karen, 1979, 'The "Great Firm" Theory of the Decline of the Mughal Empire', *Comparative Studies in Society and History*, 21, 2: 151–167.

Mughal world from the late seventeenth century owing to the diversification of trade routes under the impetus of European trade. He argued that the 'rise of the west' followed immediately after the 'decline of the east'[737] and suggested we seek a connection between these two events which henceforth dictated the directions of Asian (and European) histories. The most important point made by Athar Ali was that of a cultural inability to adapt to new norms and a consequent technological decline in the Islamic world[738]. These main lines of the 'decline' argument from the Aligarh school have the merit of providing explanations from the vantage point of production, circulation of wealth, technology and material culture.

The Aligarh school continued, however, to believe in the Mughal system as a closely–knit empire. This myth of Mughal governance as a closely integrated empire resting on a uniform system of rule was first blown apart by J.F. Richards[739] and then by Muzaffar Alam and Sanjay Subrahmanyam who emphasized that the Empire was always a 'patchwork quilt' of areas over which imperial control operated at uneven levels[740]. Others who attacked the omnipotence of the Mughal state in the 1970s and 1980s were Pearson and Blake[741]. Pearson, and then Blake, suggested that the patrimonial model of empire was one best suited to the Mughal.

737 'The Eighteenth Century: An Interpretation', *The Indian Historical Review*, v, 1978–9: 175–186: see 175–76.

738 Ali, 1978–79; 'Recent Theories of Eighteenth Century India', *The Indian Historical Review*, xiii, 1986–87: 102–110; 'The Passing of Empire: The Mughal Case', *Modern Asian Studies*, ix, 1975: 385–96.

739 where Richards argues that failure to assimilate the Deccani nobles into the Mughal administrative apparatus was largely responsible for the Mughal decline : 'The explanation advanced herein for the descent of imperial authority and power in the south has been offered as an alternative to that now accepted by many historians. Rather than a failure of resources for jagirs, incomplete administrative and political consolidation in Bijapur and Golconda after 1686–87 and commitment of the best military and administrative resources of the empire to continued expansion in the south brought about a crisis of public order and public confidence': *Journal of Asian Studies*, 255.

740 *The Mughal State 1526–1750*, Delhi, Oxford University Press, 1998.

741 See M.N. Pearson, 1976, 'Shivaji and the Decline of the Mughal Empire', *Journal of Asian Studies*, XXXV, 2: 221–35. See Stephen P. Blake, 1979, 'The Patrimonial-Bureaucratic Empire of the Mughals', *The Journal of Asian Studies*, XXXIX, 1: 77–94. See also Blake, 1991, *Shahajanabad: The Sovereign City in Mughal India 1639–1739,* Cambridge University Press. For a critique of Streusand's and Blake's positions, see Subrahmanyam, Sanjay, 1988, 'State Formation and Transformation in Early Modern India and South East Asia', *Itinerario*,: 98 and Subrahmanyam, 1992, 'The Mughal State-Structure or Process? Reflections on Recent Western Historiography', *The Indian Economic and Social History Review*, 29, 3: 291–321.

Blake called it the 'bureaucratic-patrimonial' model. Both Pearson and Richards focussed on the relations of the Mughal with the aristocratic patrimonies it sought to absorb in the Deccan. Muzaffar Alam focussed on the zamindari uprisings in Bihar and Awadh[742].

The third set of explanations focus on the on the nature of the Mughal state itself, its sources of social power and on the Central Asian Islamic tradition of kingship itself. While these do not directly throw light on the eighteenth century decline; the distinct nature of Central Asian origin myths, the lineage of the Mughal state, and thereby its distinctive character may provide alternative explanations of the spectacular end of the Mughal Empire[743].

The Foundations–The Decline School: Plassey and the Trading World

The nationalist and Marxist schools of historiography held growing European trade along with territorial fragmentation responsible for the decline of South Asian fortunes. While this is undeniable some have gone on to label this changeover as one from 'prosperity to decline'. This school takes 1757 (Battle of Plassey) as the marker for the slide from prosperity to decline. This issue now finds few takers.

We have to remember however that while it is true that the date 1757 still dominates history books and to historians accustomed to working with linear time it is a convenient date to signal the long-term process of the British conquest of India, yet at the time 1757 was only relevant for Bengal because, seen in retrospect, *Palashi* (Plassey) was a local war with a limited engagement. 1757 was not relevant for South Asia as a whole.

But it is also a significant date because, though apparently random, its long term consequences have spanned centuries until today. The consequences of *Palashi* were enormous: it paved the way for the establishment of British hegemony in Bengal and subsequently over India. But this happened in the nineteenth, and not in the eighteenth, century.

742 Alam, Muzaffar, 1986, *The Crisis of Empire in Mughal North India*, New Delhi, Oxford University Press.

743 See Hintze, Andrea, 1997, *The Mughal Empire and Its Decline: An Interpretation of the Sources of Social Power*, Aldershot ; Streusand, Douglas, E., 1989, *The Formation of the Mughal Empire*, Delhi. On the origins of the Timurid state, and its departures from the Chingiz Khanid model, see Jamaluddin S., 1995, *The State under Timur*, New Delhi, Har Anand. For a critique of Streusand's position, see Subrahmanyam, Sanjay, 1992, 'The Mughal State-Structure or Process? Reflections on Recent Western Historiography', *The Indian Economic and Social History Review*, 29, 3: 291–321.

Sources indicate however that commercial and economic decline within Bengal started prior to *Palashi*[744]. Production and trade flows were diverted to meet European needs from the 1720s; and by the 1730s the EEIC had started controlling the riverine network in Bengal. From the 1740s it was clear that the entire production process-spinning, carding, weaving and finishing-was increasingly geared to meet EEIC investment needs. This resulted in diminished production for the Asian market; moreover the increased commercialisation of the landscape led to frequent rice shortages in Bengal from this time. Finally, production for the European markets entered a phase of crisis from the 1740s; Mukherjee (1990–91 and 1994) shows that production simply could not keep pace with European demand[745]. 1757 was not the date signalling the decline of the maritime world; this started long before.

As for trade, there are two sets of narratives for the European presence in the eighteenth century Bengal. The first runs thus:

1. Mr. X, the English Company servant arrives in Hugli, exclaims at the variety of merchandise available for trade, moves on to settle Calcutta, conducts a thriving trade in textiles, penetrates inland into the countryside by the 1730s, seizes control of the waterways, clashes with the nawab's court at Murshidabad, is harassed by the moneylender Jagat Seth and his ilk, is forever milked by local officials, and is helpless in dealings with the dadni merchants with whom he contracts for textile supply. His trade, which his company's Court of Directors in London forever urge him to expand, is at an all time low. To counter these annoyances Mr.X seeks control of the region by the 'revolution of 1757' with the help of traitorous nawabs and villainous financiers. Mr. X (and the EEIC) thus lead the onward march of English power in India by mid-century.

The second account is even more naive and its argument is:

2. Since records claim that Bengal was prosperous in the seventeenth century and that its merchants carried on a thriving trade in textiles

[744] Das Gupta, 1970, 1998: 388. Mukherjee, Rila, 1990–91, 'The French East India Company's Trade in East Bengal From 1750–1753: A Look at the Chandernagore-Jugdia Letters', *Indian Historical Review*, XVII, nos.1–2, 122–135; Mukherjee, Rila, 1994, 'The Story of Kasimbazar: Silk Merchants and Commerce in Eighteenth Century India', *Review*, XVII, 4, Fall Issue, Fernand Braudel Center, New York.

[745] Similar references to a crisis in the textile industry on the Coromandel can be found from the Pondichery correspondence with other factories. See papers in Bibliotheque R.R., Pondi.

(silk and cotton stuffs as well as raw silk) and food stuffs (sugar, ghee, rice) this prosperity attracted foreign predators.

This point of view owes much to Bernier's comments in this period about the fabled wealth of Bengal[746]. Bernier likened Bengal to a siren and went on to add that there were many doors to enter Bengal but none to depart. This ambiguous statement may be taken in two ways. The 'prosperity to decline' brigade means Bengal supplied all that one could desire. According to this camp Bengal thus slides from 'prosperity to decline' with the arrival of the Europeans and colonial India is born.

Actually the inherent ambiguity in Bernier was an acho of the Mughal feeling towards Bengal in the seventeenth century. The *Riyas-us-Salatin* and the narrative of Robert Challes[747] tells us that while Bengal was rumoured to be a place where fortunes could be readily made, Mughal *mansabdars* also regarded a posting to the province as sheer hell because of its unfavourable climes. Another reason for the antipathy towards Bengal was its remote location.

This same remoteness from Delhi also made for the attraction of Bengal. It was easy for ambitious *subahdars* with dynastic ambitions to raise the flag of revolt from Delhi (witness the case of Mir Jumla; in his second tenure in Bengal he made his dynastic ambitions so manifest that Bernier tells us that Aurangzeb took the precaution of dispatching him from Delhi while keeping on Mir Jumla's wife and family at court)[748].

Actually, the marginality of Bengal, and its cheap production costs, and not its prosperity, was the attraction of Bengal for the EICs. It were internal factors, and not external causes, that determined initially European penetration into Bengal. Once they were inside Bengal, so to speak, Europeans knew they were on to a good thing! But Bengal's slide from prosperity to decline is discussed in the light of external factors (EIC penetration, Maratha raids, EEIC legislation) much like the Pirenne thesis that marked the Dobb-Sweezy debate of the coming of capitalism to Europe[749]. But these were not determing factors, they came later and completed a process of decline that had started for centuries prior to *Palashi*.

---

[746] Bernier.

[747] Challes, Robert, 1690–91.

[748] Bernier.

[749] Chaudhuri, Sushil, 1995, *From Prosperity to Decline: Bengal in the Eighteenth Century*, New Delhi, Manohar Publications.

The Foundations–Was there ever an 'Indian' Trade?

While subscribing to the decline theory, Ashin Das Gupta's position was somewhat different from those mentioned earlier. He attempted to weld together the pictures of territorial and maritime decline into a single canvas that would explain the instability of the Indian Ocean world. His impassioned plea to reconsider trade in eighteenth century India remains significant and unchallenged to this day[750].

The term 'Indian trade' encompasses two trades in reality. On the one hand it refers to sea trade; 'Indian trade' could therefore be seen as a number of port towns in a necklace stretching from Malacca, Achin and Canton in the east through Hugli, Masulipatam, Surat/Cambay in South Asia, to Hormuz, Gombroon, Bandar Abbas, Basra on the Persian Gulf and Aden, Mocha and Jedda on the Red Sea. On the other hand 'Indian trade' also partook in an overland trade; here there were two routes. One was the old silk route which ran from Ying in China through Succur, Khotan, Yarkand and Kashgar (Turkestan) to Bukhara from where it connected with Astrakhan in Rus and another from Ying in China through Succur, Khotan, Yarkand and Kashgar where it went southwest to Kabul, Balkh, Kandahar, Herat, Yezd, Ispahan and Tabriz. This was the new variation introduced by Chingiz Khan on the old silk route, and after him, Tamerlane[751]. At Tabriz it split into three subsidiary, but nonetheless important, routes. The first went onto the right to Trebizond, the second turned off on the left to Aleppo/Damascus/Cairo/Alexandria and the third one went staright onto Bursa near Constantinople.

Within India a wide caravan network connected both these trans-continental caravan networks to the Mughal port cities of Cambay/Surat, Masulipattinam and Hugli. These were:

1. Eastern Bengal (Suvarnagram/Sripur/Dhaka) and western Bengal (Hugli)-to Akbarnagar (Rajmahal)-Patna-Benares-Prayag-Agra-Delhi-Lahore. This then connected up with the 'new' silk route established by the Mongols.
2. From Lahore there were three routes. One went to Kabul, another to Multan and Kandahar (both part of the Mongol 'new' route) and the third to Lahori Bandar which faced the Gulf of Oman and from where the ports of the Persian Gulf such as Hormuz, Gombroon (Bandar Abbas) and Basra were only a short sail away.

---

[750] 'Trade and Politics in Eighteenth Century India' in Richards, D.S., 1970, *Islam and the Trade of Asia,* Philadelphia, reprinted in Alam, M. and Subrahmanyam, S. 1998, *The Mughal State 1526–1750*, New Delhi, Oxford University Press: 364.

[751] See the section titled The Mongol Rupture and Bengal.

3. The Surat-Agra caravan route on the west connecting the great seventeenth century Mughal port with the great inland mart of North India.
4. The Surat-Goa-Masulipatam route.

But 'Indian trade' went beyond territorial blocs. The two coastal regions–west and east–and their subsequent sub-divisions into Gujarat/Malabar in the west and Coromandel/Bengal in the east displayed distinct cross-border affilations. It is no accident that as early as in the thirteenth century both Montecorvino and Marco Polo spoke of 'three Indias': western India or India Major extended upto a part of today's Middle East and East Africa, Middle India or India proper contained mainland India and India Minor consisted of Bengal and eastern India upto South East Asia. This view of India, echoed in subsequent travel literature as late as in the fifteenth century, reveals that the outsider's perception of India was ruled, not by the land-based economy of the sub-continent, but by its commercial and cultural links beyond frontiers.

Trade, consequently, was influenced by the dominant regional coalitions of these areas: in the case of Gujarat, the orientation was towards the Persian Gulf, the Red Sea and East Africa; for the Malabar it was East Africa again; for the Coromandel it was southern South East Asia comprising the islands of the Indonesian archipelago, Malacca, and China; for Bengal it was northern South East Asia comprising Arakan, Ava, Pegu, Syriam, Champa (Cambodia). The ebb and flow of trade, and trading fortunes of the Indian merchant, was influenced to a great extent by the political and economic fortunes of their corresponding regional blocs[752]. This world collapsed after 1700 as Surat started to decay[753].

Moreover the poltical and economic fortunes of the four regions was so very different that it is almost impossible to develop a typology of 'Indian trade' in the eighteenth century[754]. Therefore, Das Gupta summed up that it is doubtful whether we can speak of an 'Indian trade' in the eighteenth century.

[752] Athar Ali, 1975, 1978–9.

[753] Das Gupta, Ashin, *Indian Merchants and the Decline of Surat,* Wiesbaden, Academie Verlag; Furber, Holden, *Rival Empires of Trade in the Orient,* Delhi, Oxford University Press.

[754] Alam, M. and Subrahmanyam, S. 1998, *The Mughal State 1526–1750,* New Delhi, Oxford University Press: 370–97.

For the same reason Ashin Das Gupta felt that it may be immature to speak of 'India' in the political sense in the eighteenth century. In Aurangzeb's time the acquisition of Bijapur and Golconda marked the outermost limits of the empire; in a loose sense we can then speak of an India stretching from Gujarat in the west to Bengal in the east, and Kashmir in the north to the Deccani sultanates in the south. But parts of Tamil Nadu and the whole of Malabar was not a part of it. Moreover this unfinished 'India' was rendered even more partial with the onset of Maratha expansion from the beginning of the eighteenth century.

The Departures – The 'Community/Ethnic School'

It should be clear by now that no single marker can be found to denote the eighteenth century in South Asia. For this reason the 'Cambridge School' talks of a long eighteenth century which ended only in the early parts of the nineteenth century. Yet, in today's academic climate in South Asia, to deny the thesis of the eighteenth century anarchy and decline is tantamount to an apology for the 'British' India that rose in the eighteenth century.

Alam and Subrahmanyam point out however that this idea of decline is a double-edged sword for just as South Asian intellectuals and literati use the idea of the eighteenth century decline to pinpoint the actual moment of colonial drain in the same way 'imperial' historians and apologists of the British Empire use the thesis of the eighteenth anarchy as a convenient justification for imposition of colonial rule'[755].

For Alam and Subrahmanyam the eighteenth century's chief marker is not the regional state but the 'ethnic' state such as those of the Jats, Marathas, Sikhs and Rohillas who built states over much of what had been previously the Mughal Empire[756]. Rather than adhering too firmly to a single logic of decline they assert that unlike regional successor states such as Awadh or Hyderabad (which had themselves been recognized as regional states in the immediate pre-Mughal period) other states with a relatively recent lineage and original character emerged in the eighteenth century by virtue of unique regional experiences. The states of the Marathas, the Jats and the Sikhs had no real precedent in medieval South Asian history.

---

[755] *Ibid.*: 70.
[756] *Ibid.*: 68.

If we accept the notion of communities being at the base of much of state formation in the eighteenth century South Asia then we have the added advantage of moving away from the 'successor state' concept which is limited as we saw, for it glosses over the many state forms that appeared in the wake of the Mughal collapse, and of moving forward with new motions for our understanding of state formation in eighteenth century South Asia mentioned as early as 1962 by Cohn.

While the notion of the ethnic state, in vogue from the last decade, is undoubtedly attractive and calls for a return to the regions (and away from the Mughal behemoth), it is clearly untenable for regional states such as Hyderabad and Awadh. Bengal still remains, in this formulation, a case apart.

The Departures – The Continuity School

The Cambridge school whose chief exponents are Marshall, Bayly, Washbrook and Stein (and the early Subrahmanyam) stress continuities of the epoch. In their view the 'long eighteenth century' in South Asia contained characteristics (a dynamic economy, intensification of money use, new economic relations, investment of capital from new sources, the domination of tax-farmers and monopoly contractors, a commercialization of rights that were previously outside the commercial nexus, et cetera) that were eradicated only after British conquest of upper India in early nineteenth century (circa 1830). A unifying political system and total English management of the South Asian economy is their main criterion in identifying the end-point of the eighteenth century. Reliance on Indian agents (fiscal and commercial) stopped only after the 1830s. Therefore the changeover in economic management from the 1760s is not, according to the Cambridge School, the chief marker of the eighteenth century. According to Bayly, economic losses in one region were recouped by another throughout the eighteenth century[757]. The inherent spirit, indeed the boom, of the eighteenth century continued unabated.

Marshall comments[758]:

> Contemporary Englishmen sometimes described the changes that took place in the middle of the eighteenth century in Bengal as a 'revolution', and later generations of historians

---

[757] Bayly, C.A., 1983.

[758] Marshall, P.J., 1987, *Bengal The British Bridgehead: Eastern India 1740–1828*, Cambridge and Orient Longman: 1–2.

> tended to agree with them..The change from Mughal to British rule has commonly been seen as the beginning of a 'modern era'…For very good reasons, what happened in Bengal during the early years of British rule has become one of the classic case studies for those concerned with assessing the impact of foreign rule on conquered societies.
>
> In recent years, however, the revolutionary consequences of the establishment of colonial rule have been called into question for many different parts of the world… . Colonial rule, with its vast detritus of written records easily accessible to historians, and the growth of international trade which usually accompanied it, may look like the most formidable agents of change, but in many cases they can be shown to be only one part of a complex pattern of developments, other processes working at quite different speeds but often ultimately with mich greater effect. A chronology which is determined by the rise and firm establishment of a colonial regime may thus prove to be a somewhat misleading one.
>
> Such an approach to the modern history of eastern India has much to commend it. Whatever the ultimate significance of their rule, the British were by no means the only agents of change…In the history of eastern India the fall of the Mughals and the coming of the British are only episodes in a much longer play whose principal actors inevitably remain anonymous: pioneers who settled new lands, merchants who organized handicrafts, Vaishnavite teachers, guardians of Muslim shrines and even the rivers and the *Anopheles* mosquito.

However since it is undeniable that both economic control (manifested in disruption of overseas trade, production and internal trade, interference in the internal market) and political supremacy of the English East India Company manifested themselves first in Bengal the 'long eighteenth century' thesis is clearly inappropriate for Bengal. Marshall himself concedes that the British introduced new elements into the economy of Bengal: filatures for silk, indigo factories, sugar plantations and opium and salt monopolies[759]. To this list we can add increased salt–petre exports.

[759] *Ibid.*: 107–112.

Arasaratnam and Das Gupta show that Bengal's shipping and overseas trade were the first to be affected; similarly production and the market were diverted to meet British demands[760].

From the 1770s onwards the Company preoccupied itself increasingly with the question of ensuring a stable land revenue. This saw fruition in the establishment of the Permanent Settlement of 1793. The Company as trader as well as ruler pursued policies of 'improvement' in Bengal to the ultimate benefit of the British Government.Therefore the notion of 'evolution' rather than revolution is untenable for the eighteenth century Bengal.

How did contemporaries view the eighteenth century? Did the mid-century rupture translate into a definite break with earlier times? The author of *Syer-ul-Mutakherin*, Ghulam Husain Tabatabhai, certainly thought so; for him British rule was 'alien', the new regime was one of Hat Wearers, their ways of raising tribute, estimating revenues or gathering tax different[761]. It is noteworthy that for Ghulam Husain the coming of the British signalled the passing away of the old and the coming of the new, or 'modern', times. Shah Ayatulla Jauhari's and Ghulam Ali Rasikh's laments (poems written in circa mid-century) point to changing times. Jauhari wrote in *Shahr-i-Ashob* that 'times are changing...worthy men, good fortune, prosperity...all are gone from this world. Friendship and love have dwindled, and beastly avarice has increased'[762]. Rasikh lamented

[760] Arasaratnam,S., 1998 in Mukherjee and Subramanian 1998; Das Gupta, Ashin, 1970, 'Trade and Politics in Eighteenth Century India' from Richards, D.S. (Ed). *Islam and the Trade of Asia*, Philadelphia reprinted in Alam, M. amd Subrahmanyam, S. (Eds)., 1998, *The Mughal State 1526–1750*, New Delhi, Oxford University Press: 387–88. Om Prakash 1998, 'European Corporate Enterprises and the Politics of Trade in India, 1600–1800' in *ibid*; See also Mukherjee, Rila, 1990–91, 1994. Om Prakash states categorically: 'It was, however, in Bengal, where the Company first obtained formal diwani rights in 1765, that the full impact of the Company's new status was in evidence....Gross abuse of the newly found political power available to the English factors turned this relationship (between the Company, the intermediary merchant and the artisan) into one of widespread coercion...A rough idea of what the Company subjected the weavers to can be formed by the fact that pieces classified as third quality would gladly have been accepted by the Dutch Company as first quality at a considerably higher price': 177–78. My evidence on producing areas around Kasimbazar and Jugdia supports this (see Mukherjee, Rila, 1990–1991 and 1994. See also *Merchants and Companies* etc.)

[761] Syed Ghulam Husain Khan, *The Seir Mutaqherin or View of Modern Times Being an History of India from the Year 1181 to the Year 1194,* (tr). Nota Manus, 4 vols., Calcutta, T.D. Chatterjee, 1902: V.3–162, V.2–155, 231.

[762] Quoted in Yang, Anand A. 1998, *Bazaar India: Markets, Society and the Colonial State in Bihar*, Berkeley and L.A., California Press: 62.

similarly in a narrative poem *Description of the Times of Upheaval and Lamentation to Heaven* etc. *of the Inhabitants of the Town of Azimabad* of cholera, corruption and ruin[763]. All three authors lament the passing of the old order; in a way this change *was* a social revolution.

The Departures – The Eighteenth Century as an Unit of Historical Analysis

The historiography of the eighteenth century, we noted, is marked by three themes–central decline, the rise of regional powers and the control of foreign trade by European powers. All three factors were present, at some time or the other, throughout the history of South Asia. What makes us, then, single out the eighteenth century for special treatment?

It has become increasingly clear that the category of the eighteenth century as a unit of historical analysis is now questioned. The thesis of decline has been successfully contested. Seen from the centre the eighteenth century is certainly a period of decline. Seen from the regions the picture is different. Also as Alam and Subrahmanyam[764] point out, no single chronology of prosperity and decline is likely to fit all the regions of India in this century. As I have also shown, the trajectory of the regions was mixed. Regarding the coastal regions Gujarat and the Malabar collapsed from the 1700s[765]; this collapse was evident in Bengal only from the 1740s[766] and in Coromandel even later. As for inland formations in the first half of the century Bengal, Hyderabad, Jaipur and to a great extent Awadh, showed continuous expansion. Mysore and the Punjab bloomed briefly only in the latter half of the century.

The fact of the rise of regional powers is uncontested, but as a thesis it remains incomplete in the absence of a single explanation of the rise of these powers except the obvious one of political fragmentation at the centre. As Pearson points out, the premise of the regional states system depends on the nature of their base: Ashin Das Gupta's merchants, Karen Leonard's clerks (*daftardars*), Bernard Cohn's lineages or Philip Calkin's bankers. We can add to this list Bayly and Subrahmanyam's 'portfolio capitalists'–those who made a packet out of a combination of revenue rights, trading, moneylending and war financing[767]. A similar case for

[763] *Ibid*: 62–66.

[764] *The Mughal State 1526–1750*, Introduction: 69.

[765] Das Gupta, 1970, 1998, in *Ibid*.: 372–87.

[766] Mukherjee, Rila, 1990–91 and 1994.

[767] Portfolio Capitalists and the Political Economy of Early Modern India' in *The Indian Economic and Social History Review*, 25, 4, 1988: 401–24.

political participation can be made out, as Pearson argues, for the Mughal state itself[768]. The only single uncontested thesis of the eighteenth century seems to be the monopoly of external trade by European powers.

Alavi (2002) has modified this schema somewhat[769]. For her growth of European trade is only a sub-theme. Her markers for the eighteenth century are 'two critical transitions which changed the structure of power and initiated important social and economic reconfigurations. The first was the transition in the first half of the century from the Mughal political economy to regional political orders. The second was the transition in the period following the battles of Palashi (1757) and Buxar (1764) in 'polity, society and economy as the English East india Company steered its way to a position of political prominence in north India'.

For Alavi the notion of century as an unitary category persists despite Habib's cautionary note in the same volume that 'A century is only a convenient period of time: even with the most approximate limits it remains an unsuitable pigeon-hole for most historical phenomena'[770] witness her mid-century division of the political and the economic. In this division English control over foreign trade is assigned a secondary place and that too after the mid-century break despite recent scholarship to the contrary.

A reading of South Asian history in the eighteenth century shows us that the 'eighteenth century crisis' worked at different levels at different places. The literature of the past few years leads us to constitute a partial and impressionistic picture rather than one based on a single, central, motor. A new study of this category–the eighteenth century material transition in Mughal India–requires a return to the regions and to the regional data found there.

The delineation of the century and the continuities/breaks ascribed to it depends on the markers we choose. In terms of the economy (both commercial and agrarian) there was a radical break by the end of the century. In terms of politics the 'long' eighteenth century continued at least until the second Anglo Maratha War of 1805. In terms of cultural vigour similar processes were seen at work as late as in the nineteenth century. In terms of regional political dynamism there was no chronological

768 Pearson, M.N., 1972, 'Political Participation in Mughal India' in *The Indian Economic and Social History Review*, IX, 2: 113–131.

769 Alavi, Seema, 2002, *The Eighteenth Century in India,* New Delhi, Oxford University Press, Introduction: 1-56.

770 The Eighteenth Century in Indian Economic History' p. 57 in *Ibid.*: 57–83. Also in P.J. Marshall, 2003: 100–119.

consistency. Seen this way the pre-colonial and the colonial merge at times; at others there is a sharp disjuncture between the two. The concept of the eighteenth century is thus chronologically inconsistent, thematically inadequate and spatially insufficient. If we cannot find a single distinguishing marker for the eighteenth century–either chronological or thematic–then the foregoing formulations of the eighteenth century itself–excepting that which ceded way to foreign rule, colonial tribute and the drain of wealth-is open to question.

The Departures – A Gentle Evolution Rather than Revolution?

The invention of a particular historiographical tradition for South Asian economies that we are fighting even today follows logically from those ideological assumptions mentioned at the start of this essay. It is undeniable that as Cohn (1962) pointed out that the eighteenth century in India is dominated by three themes: the dissolution of the Mughal political order, attempts by some regional powers to expand their system into imperial states, and the British success in becoming the heirs of the Mughal Empire[771].

But it is also noteworthy that, as Stein points out[772], the notion of a dark century or a fractured century is rooted historically in a monolithically constructed nationalism that rejects everything to the primary contradiction of foreign rule. This supposed disjuncture is a weak one because it begets the question whether India had the capacity to commence a process leading to capitalism fom its Mughal base. We have discussed this. The Cambridge School rejects the 'increasingly questionable characterizations' of the Mughal state and economy; it prefers to 'abandon this weak counterfactual formulation and adopt a view for which there is considerable evidence about economic and administrative changes over an extended eighteenth century'[773].

Because of the contested terrain that the eighteenth century debate has come to occupy recent works tend to emphasise, not political/economic continuities/discontinuities but rather peoples' perceptions of the eighteenth century, notions of identity, models of lineage formation and genres of

---

[771] Cohn, Bernard S., 1962, 'Political Systems in Eighteenth Century India: The Banaras Region' referred before. Also in Marshall, 2003: 123–136.

[772] Stein, B., 1989. 'Eighteenth Century India : Another view', in Marshall 2003.

[773] *Ibid.* In Marshall, 2003: 87.

family histories. A recent addition to the eighteenth century debate is the volume edited by Richard B. Barnett[774] which claims:

> Thus early modern India's revisionists are not laying out a theory of Mughal decline at all. They are responding to growing evidence of continuity rather than discontinuity, of local and regional economic growth, of ecological pragmatism and political realism ... of entrepreneurial activity indigenous to India and not imported from outside. The new impetus of eighteenth and early nineteenth century research is free from Eurocentric, dogmatic, prefiguring, Mughal-centric, and essentialist viewpoints, and increasingly concerned with actual indigenous Indian pragmatism and realism from the ground up...We revisionists ... acknowledge the immortality of Mughal accomplishments, but instead of obsessing about the loss of empire, we seek to appreciate the emergence of a rich variety of highly pragmatic social and political formations... .[775]

Iqbal Ghani Khan's illuminating look at technological interventions of the Rohilla rulers in North India (Rohilkand) tells us that elite assimilation of scientific ideas and technological intervention continued even after imperial decline[776]. This essay is important especially in light of the idea of intellectual decay we ascribe to the Islamic world in the eighteenth century–a barrenness heightened by a resistance to new technologies emanating from Europe in the Ottoman, Safavid and Mughal worlds[777]. Technological experiments–what Ghani Khan calls intervention–went on in the military, agrarian and craft sectors in the Rohilla cities. Workshops (*karkhanas*) flourished, building works were commissioned. As Ghani Khan rightly points out the prevalence of scientific interest throughout the eighteenth century in India (albeit in certain parts) does not make for a persuasive argument in favour of intellectual decline.

Recent French research into library holdings in the Ottoman world and in the collections of the rulers of Rajput states and the Banaras Rajas

---

[774] *Rethinking Early Modern India*, 2002, New Delhi, Manohar.

[775] *Ibid*, Introduction: 21–22.

[776] 'Technology and the Question of Elite Intervention in Eighteenth Century North India' in *Ibid.*: 257–288.

[777] Athar Ali The Eighteenth Century: An Interpretation', *The Indian Historical Review,* v, 1978–9: 175–186: see 175–76; 'Recent Theories of Eighteenth Century India', *The Indian Historical Review*, xiii, 1986–87: 102–110; 'The Passing of Empire: The Mughal Case', *Modern Asian Studies*, ix, 1975: 385–96.

reinforce Ghani Khan's thesis and demonstrate that scientific interest was not flagging in the Indo-Islamic world; indeed the Ottomans played a pivotal role in the transmission of European ideas on technology, history and politics to the South Asian world in the eighteenth century.

It is to this question of intellectual decline ascribed to the eighteenth century that we should address ourselves, for an over-emphasis on mere political or economic decline masks the reality of eighteenth century Bengal: the fact a new political and economic system replaced the older system. As Habib noted: 'The extraction of…tribute was what colonialism in its eighteenth century phase…was about'[778].

But this took place only in Bengal in the eighteenth century and, as discussed in the previous pages, Bengal was really a case apart. This reinforces my argument that EEIC insistence on Bengal as an important political arena of Company activity, the constant harping on the economy of Bengal as a synonym for the entire South Asian economy meant that the British facilitated their entry into Bengal as emblematic of an entry into South Asia as a whole into European historical consciousness from the very start.

Events in Bengal were unique. The roots of British colonialism in South Asia were laid in Bengal. Political control and economic hegemony over the rest of South Asia were achieved only in the nineteenth century. The importance of Bengal in Company affairs meant a highlighting of Bengal affairs to the exclusion of all else in official correspondence to England throughout the eighteenth and the nineteenth centuries.

In their apology for the establishment of British rule, Company officials were at pains to highlight the misrule of the Nawabs which necessitated EEIC intervention and benefits that would accrue to the English Crown if Parliament accepted Company rule in Bengal. The 'riches' of Bengal were thus inordinately emphasised without an examination of how these had come about historically, therefore our contention that the EEIC 'made' Bengal in the eighteenth century.

While the interpretations of the loosely termed Cambridge School[779] have gained currency in academic circles and many now think of the eighteenth century in South Asia as showing more signs of continuity than change, it is a fact that events in eighteenth century Bengal showed a violent break with the past. Colonial extraction was a fundamental and

[778] 'The Eighteenth Century in Indian Economic History' in Alavi 2002: 71.

[779] C.A. Bayly's, *Rulers, Townsmen and Bazaars* is still the most influential book from the school.

significant change that was introduced into the economic landscape of Bengal in the eighteenth century. In 1757 the EEIC 'acquired' 150 000 square miles or 388 500 square kilometres of Indian (Bengal's) territory; by 1857 this had expanded into a million square miles comprising 63% of the territory and 78% of the population. In other words the English East India Company annexed, on an average, some 27 square miles of Indian territory per day over the century from 1757. Whether a transition continued into the nineteenth century is irrelevant in this context for Bengal; the violent break had occurred by mid-century.

The Cambridge Schools' formulation that the business class helped the English achieve power is clearly unacceptable; this has however led one historian off the archival track with his insistence that there was no crisis either in the body politic or the economy of Bengal in the eighteenth century and to overturn received history on its head[780]. In his eagerness to disprove the Bayly thesis of a collaboration between the ruling classes and the agrarian and financial interests, Sushil Chaudhury claims that 'historians rely too much on contemporary Bengali literature and Persian chronicles to corroborate the disastrous effects of the Maratha invasions...That these are mostly exaggerated accounts is clear from the very nature of the evidence'[781]. The evidences cited are 'Bengali' authors such as Gangaram (Maharashtra Purana), Bharatchandra and 'Persian' sources such as the *Riyas us Salatin*. But French sources such as de Gennes de la Chanceliere noted in his voyage from Chandernagore upto Kasimbazar in 1743, at the height of the Maratha raids[782]:

> It (Shantipur) seemed to have been totally destroyed the year before by the Marathas...one comes across the village of Nodia (whose) Raja Quisim-Cha (Krisna Candra) has escaped being pillaged by the Marathas by paying two lacs of roupies...It is a pity that all this land, fine and fertile by itself was sacked by the Marathas...The country is still smouldering from the fires and damages which these barbarians have inflicted to the areas round the Ganges from which they have taken

[780] Chaudhury, Sushil, 2002, 'Was There a Crisis in Mid-Eighteenth Century Bengal?' in Barnett op.cit.: 129–152.

[781] *Ibid.*: 135.

[782] Subramanian, L. (Ed)., 1999, *The French East India Company and the Trade of the Indian Ocean: A Collection of Essays by Indrani Ray*, CSSSC, Munshiram Manoharlal. See Chapter 7 'Journey to Cassimbazar and Murshidabad: Observations of a French Visitor to Bengal in 1743': 155, 156, 161, 162, 170.

> contributions…This has led to the near complete ruin of the inhabitants of these fertile regions…On approaching Cassenbazar and Moxudabad, the famous capital of the kingdom of Bengal, the country seems to have suffered a little less of pillage…there was at that time (in Murshidabad) a camp of six thousand cavalrymen in order to oppose the insult of the Marathas who had thought of taking the town last year.

The description is typical of those of both contemporaries and later historians of Bengal, the list of whom is large to mention here, but Chaudhury seeks to ignore this by affirming that:[783]

> There is no denying the fact that they (the Maratha raids) resulted in serious dislocation in the economy of some areas in Bengal, but the impact has been greatly exaggerated. The Marathas caused destruction generally along the line of their march, leaving the remaining part of the country more or less unaffected. Even in the affected areas…Richard Becher…pointed out the Marathas were obliged to return home at the approach of the rainy season, and the inhabitants were again safe till the following January.

This twisting of Becher's statement of fact about the duration of Maratha raids into a vindication of his thesis that the Maratha invasions did not devastate the economy of Bengal is patently obvious as is Chaudhury's contention that merchants were not affected, that prices did not rise and that investments from Bengal continued unaffected. The K.F.R on May 15,1745 noted that the dadni merchants had withdrawn all *garas* (coarse cloths) from their *arangs* (warehouses) in fear of the Marathas. The *garas* came from the Bardhaman area which was regularly overrun by the Marathas. On April 3 1746 K.F.R. noted that the price of raw silk was high because the Marathas had passed through the *patni* (silk thread) making areas and destroyed most of it. What *patni* there remained had already been bought up by the Armenians and Gujarati merchants but that too at a higher price. Similar apprehensions were expressed on June 13, 22 and August 12,1746 and on January 27,1748[784].

That prices *did* continue to rise, that merchants *were* affected and that European investments *were* disturbed was borne out by the data from Kasimbazar already published[785]. Despite Chaudhury's table on Garah prices

[783] Chaudhury 2002: 134.

[784] K.F.R. now in King's Cross (Previously IOLR) in London.

[785] Mukherjee 1994.

(Table 7 p.147 in Barnett 2002) the Court of Directors in London reprimanded the Kasimbazar factory in their *gara* investments in 1749 and stressed that *garas* were becoming unprofitable trade items because their price kept rising[786].

Finally we should note that most of Chaudhury's 'new evidence' comes from the Dhaka region which was mostly unaffected by the Maratha raids and which he then uses to justify his views on the Maratha raids *which affected western Bengal* and he concludes[787]:

> Thus the thesis of the crisis in mid-eighteenth century Bengal crumbles under close scrutiny. Indeed it was not because of any internal crisis in Bengal that the British had to intervene; it was because of the private trade-interests of the Company servants. This was the motivating force behind the conquest. The golden days of British private trade began to decline from the late 1730s; it was facing a severe crisis in the late 1740s and early 1750s because of a substantial increase in French private trade.

The conspiracy theory of 'private' trade versus 'official' trade influencing East India Company policy arising out of the fact that English private trade declined from the 1730s and the fact that French trade boomed in the 1740s are generalizations that have a long lineage. Much of the conspiracy theory does not stand up either under scrutiny or in light of archival sources: be they 'Persian and Bengali' or French and English records as is argued below.

There are three sets of explanations for the annexation policies of the English East India Company. The first is the moral and patriotic explanation, offered often by contemporaries, that the 'conquest' of Bengal was but a natural progression of British triumphs at home. Such a conquest, they felt, was natural, adding as it did to the already existing, and various, *glories* of the British. Morerover the 'conquests' would *civilize* the natives.

The second set of explanations focussed on the political aspects of the annexation policies of the EEIC in India in general. According to this view the Company felt it was advisable to take political control rather than be faced with the hostility and political instability of Indian states which would *engender their trade interests.*

786 *Ibid.*: 534. See Mukherjee, Rila, *Merchants and Companies*, etc.

787 Chaudhury 2002: 149.

The third set of explanations is the most cogent and well-reasoned. Ramakrishna Mukherjee pointed out in the 1950s that it was in the inherently mercantilist nature of the EEIC to seek conquest as a legitimate means of safeguarding its commercial interests in Bengal[788]. While the Court of Directors in London, and indeed the English Parliament, viewed Palashi with disquiet, reminding the EEIC that they were in India as traders and not as empirebuilders, the EEIC in Bengal had no such qualms. They were convinced that the 'conquest' of Bengal would lead to greater trade for the EEIC. Consider the following letter of Clive to Pitt on January 7, 1759, that is after the 'annexation' of Bengal[789]:

> The close attention you bestow on the affairs of the British nation…has induced me to trouble you with a few particulars relative to India, and lay before you an exact account of the revenues of this country … . The great revolution that has been effected here by the success of the English arms, and the vast advantages gained to the Company (is evident and will) enable them to embrace the first opportunity of further aggrandizing themselves; … (if) the Company (is allowed) to take the sovereignty (of Bengal) upon themselves … . But so large a sovereignty may possibly be an object too extensive for a mercantile Company … without the nation's assistance. I have therefore presumed, Sir, to represent this matter to you … whether the execution of (such) a design … be worthy of the Government's taking it into hand … there will be little or no difficulty in obtaining the absolute possession of these rich kingdoms … . Now I leave it to you to judge, whether an income yearly of two millions sterling, with the possession of three provinces abounding in the most valuable productions of nature and art, be an object deserving the public attention; and whether it be worth the nation's while to take the proper measures to secure such an acquisition (which) … would prove a source of immense wealth to the kingdom, and might in time be appropriated in part as a fund towards diminishing the heavy load of debt under which we presently labour. Add to these advantages the influence

788 *The Rise and Fall of the English East India Company: A Sociological Appraisal*, Second edition, Berlin, Verlag der Wissenschaft, 1957.

789 In Fisher, Michael, H., 1993, *The Politics of the British Annexation of India 1757–1857*, Delhi, Oxford University Press: 60–64.

> we shall thereby acquire over the several European nations engaged in the commerce here...It is well worthy of consideration, that this project may be brought about without draining the mother country, as has been too much the case with our possessions in America.

The letter contains two themes: the mercantile interests of the EEIC are to be safeguarded while the advantages that such an acquistion would bring to the British nation both politically (in terms of acquiring an ascendancy over other European powers)[790] and economically (in terms of lessenning the National Debt) are enumerated. Note that it is essentially pragmatic in tone; no appeals are made to British glory except indirectly, note too that the 'conquest' is clearly labelled as 'design' and the annexation as 'project'. Finally the acquisition of Bengal, Bihar and Orissa is clearly attributed to the EEIC and not to the British nation. Mercantilist interests were to be protected at all costs.

In the Fort William Correspondence of 1756 there is a letter from the Court of Directors dated January 31 1755 to the Kasimbazar factors (and not private traders !) which says[791]:

> The bad circumstances of the generality of the merchants employed in the providing of your Investments...have for a long time been so notorious that other measures were absolutely necessary to be taken....the laying you under the necessity of making the Investment in a new method...has been already a great advantage in point of profit and will, we are satisfied, be productive of much greater if pursued with zeal and vigour and conducted with integrity.

Within the behemoth that was the EEIC it was all but natural that faced with lucrative trade opportunities, company servants would ask for a share of the pie, and when it was denied officially, carry on clandestine private trade. But we have to remember that unlike the 'interlopers' private traders were not a distinct group. Most, if not all, private traders were company servants. Historians have long puzzled over the fact that just prior to the 'annexation' of 1757 the volume of English Company trade in Bengal was shrinking. English trade in raw silk dropped from 784–690 lbs. in 1733–1737 to 183–212 lbs. in 1753–1757[792].

---

[790] Note that at this time the British and French were fighting in Europe as well in the Seven Years' War.

[791] Mukherjee 1994: 540. (HMS 804 and BPC Feb. 25 1747/8 to Dec. 9 1761).

[792] Fisher, 1993: 68.

By the 1750s the EEIC` also faced stiff competition from the Dutch and French in Bengal in furnishing its investments. It was therefore in its own mercantilist interests that the EEIC 'annexed' Bengal. The collusions of private traders and the 'Hindu' business class existed not separately and as distinct from Company interests but within the general framework of a mercantilist 'project' in Bengal.

The trade interests of the EEIC also led it to finance costly wars on the Indian sub-continent. Hastings' *Memoirs Relative to the State of India*[793], written in 1785 from his retirement (and exile) at Bath, attempts to defend this drain on the Bengal Treasury by pointing out the benefits accruing from the defeat of the Marathas, Hyder Ali and the French. In the last analysis it were the trade interests of the EEIC that dictated the course of Brirtish conquests in India.

Historians working on Bengal have tended to focus more on the political and the economic aspects; however it is also high time we took stock of the history of eighteenth century South Asia and the pathetic treatment the history of eastern India has received so far. The story of Kasimbazar narrated elsewhere[794] shows the implications of the Maratha raids on the economy of Bengal and their impact on prices, merchants' fortunes and on European investments. The stories of Kasimbazar and Jugdia taken together demonstrate how absolute the British hold over the inland waterways and interior markets had become by mid-century; abortive French demands for investment in Jugdia show a definite disjunction between production and market in eighteenth century Bengal[795]. English domination over the production process, procurement and the internal market was absolute before Plassey. But the 'official' stories of Kasimbazar and Jugdia also have an 'unofficial' theme: the story of their Bengali protagonists. There is no doubt that one order had passed and another was coming into being.

The Departures – Cartography as a Tool for 'Knowing India' in the Eighteenth Century

The introduction of route surveys as an early form of colonial control over terrain by the English East India Company and the subsequent mapping

[793] Warren Hastings, London, 1786, Indian Edition July, 1978, Calcutta, M.L.Ghosh, Distributor K.P. Bagchi.

[794] Mukherjee, Rila, 1994; and *Merchants and Companies* (New Delhi, Pragati Publications).

[795] Mukherjee, Rila, 1990–91.

of Bengal by the colonial state reinforces the strongest arguments in favour of 'revolution' rather than 'evolution' in the eighteenth century India. There was nothing gentle about the colonial intrusion into Bengal; the process of conquest and economic domination was accompanied by the practice of 'knowing' India. In this exercise cartography emerged as the handmaiden of empire in Bengal in the last quarter of the eighteenth century.

The eighteenth century rupture in Bengal can be examined not merely in terms of a political change or economic rule but also in terms of a physical reordering of space. James Rennell's *A Bengal Atlas Containing Maps of the Theatre of War and Commerce on that Side of Hindoostan* published from London in 1780 and 1781 is a living testimony to the radical break brought about by EEIC intrusion into Bengal in the eighteenth century[796]. Published soon after the actual 'conquest' and 'annexation' the series of maps in the *Atlas* on Bengal's land routes and waterways express the desire of the British to open up the region to colonial rule. *A Bengal Atlas* was designed to serve as a handbook to facilitate the penetration of British capital into Bengal Subah as well as to provide the framework for the subsequent imposition of a uniform economic realm over Bengal, Bihar and Orissa.

The meticulous cartography as evidenced in *A Bengal Atlas* with its extensive mapping of the terrain, the obsessive preoccupation with riverine courses and their changes over time, the detailed attention paid to the *Brahmaputra* to ascertain whether it actually flowed into the Bay, were animated not by geographical curiosity alone but also by a desire to provide the Company with a blueprint to aid the extraction of Bengal's land and commercial revenues. In the process this historical space was transformed not only into a place–a 'theatre of war and commerce'–but also into a territory, that of the British in India. Murshidabad–the capital of independent Subah Bangalah and indeed the living symbol of independent Bengal–was effaced from the Map of Cossimbazar Island (Plate XI). In this way a new sense of history was created; this 'history' was deemed to have started with the 'dawn' of British power over Bengal. No sense of the 'pre-colonial' lingers in these maps; the 'pre-British' is conveniently erased. There is also no dynamic of urban history in the Map of Cossimbazar Island. While Calcutta, the capital, is prominently displayed, its precursor–Murshidabad, is conveniently ignored.

[796] See also Barrow, Ian, J., 2003, *Making History Drawing Territory: British Mapping In India c. 1756–1905*, New Delhi, Oxford University Press. See particularly Chapter One 'Sentimental Conquests and Evocative Histories in an Atlas of Bengal': 50–59.

Nowhere is the reodering of space more evident than in the Map of Cossimbazar Island. In the process of Rennell's map-making a *historically insignificant* portion of Bengal was given a centrality through the politics of nomenclature while the capital of the region itself–the political heart of the region–was passed over. This politics of nomenclature points to the essentially mercantilist nature of the EEIC's annexations: Kasimbazar, although not historically noteworthy was commercially nevertheless the most important place after Dhaka in Bengal. Therefore what at first sight seems to be the geographical study of an obscure island is transformed by Rennell into the theatre of war; a theatre that tells of a political 'revolution'. Just as in its contents, in the deliberate omissions and the silences, so also in the actual mapping itself the dramatic rise of a new power is told: Barrow points out that by centreing the map's prime meridian on Calcutta the insignificance of Murshidabad is again underscored[797].

Finally this territorial possession was ascribed, not to the Company, but to the British 'nation' whose triumph at the battle of Plassey was highlighted and *A Bengal Atlas* thus foretold the rise of the British Empire in India. While the nature of the history was deemed 'national'. Rennell also noted that the British nation owed the sovereignty of Bengal to Robert Clive. Thus was Company rule highlighted; it was made clear that while the 'conquest' was British , the 'revolution' effected at Plaseey was more than a simple act of conquest. It was the start of a long-term administration of territory and only Company rule in Bengal could bring about the sort of changes and profits that were to be expected[798].

The OSM Debate – Frank, De Sousa, Baily, Hodgson, Subrahmanyam and others

Recently the various positions (and the ideological implications for those studying the pre colonial South Asian economy) was summed up by Frank[799]. He pointed out that a narrative of the story of the pre-colonial south Asian economy is incomplete without referring to contacts between the four empires of the Ottomans, the Safavids, the Mughals and the Chinese (with various points in between such as the northern Mediterrannean, northern and eastern Africa and the Indonesian archipelago).

---

[797] *Ibid.*: 57.

[798] See Clive's letter to Pitt where the same themes are repeated.

[799] Frank, A.G., 1998. *ReOrient: Global Economy in the Asian Age*, California Press and Sage/Vistaar Publications.

Frank said in *ReOrient* that a history of trade, finance and price movements, as well as population, money and commodity flows, necessitates a new world history from a 'globological' perspective. Eurocentric history and social theory are inadequate to explain the 'rise of the west' between 1400–1800. Unfortunately this was not how maritime trade is constructed by economic and maritime historians. A reconstruction of South Asian (and Bengal's) maritime history has to take in long-term cycles of expansion and decline in the world economy in the period from 1400 to 1800. Such a reading will show that regional 'hegemons' such as the Ottoman, Persian, Central Asian, South Asian, the Javan-Sumatran and the Chinese were far more influential in determining trends than a relatively insignificant region such as the European.

The Ottoman-Safavid-Mughal (OSM) debate has so far centred around the themes of technological decline in the Islamic world[800], inability to adopt to new commercial systems, the dissonance between the productive base, elite aspiration and expansion/contraction of the limits of empire and consequently insufficient mobilisation of resources in the OSM world. This attempt to see the OSM world as an integrated political/religious/economic/fiscal bloc has also been extended to the cultural domain.

Recently the cultural unity of this bloc has been given an added nuance by considering the whole region as one harbouring millenarian aspirations that found their echo in the Judaeo-Christian world as well and thus extended from the Tagus to the Ganges[801]. Cornell Fleischer has argued that the northern and southern shores of the Mediterrannean were linked not only by climate, geography, economic forces and political rivalry, but also by certain common cultural traits including a shared sense of millenarian expectation from the sixteenth century[802]. Fleischer argued that the Ottoman Empire partook of this space and thus shared in the millenarian expectation, Subrahmanyam however argues that such millenarian expectations also issued from Safavid Persia, Mughal India and the Deccan, and opines that by bringing together such 'connected histories' ('as a way of bringing together historical phenomena that have all too often been artificially separated by historical convention') we can

[800] See Athar Ali, 1975, 1978–1979, 1986–1987.

[801] Subrahmayam, Sanjay, 2003, 'Turning the Stones Over: Sixteenth century Millenarianism From the Tagus to the Ganges' in *Indian Economic and Social History Review*, XL, 2 , April–June: 129–161. Now as Chapter 5 'Sixteenth Century Millenarianism from The Tagus to the Ganges' in *Explorations in Connected History: From the Tagus to the Ganges*, New Delhi, Oxford University Press, 2005.

[802] In *Ibid*: 135.

bridge the gap between grand narratives of comparative history or micro studies that insist on the specificity of a region[803].

The power of synchronism was significant in the sixteenth century. As Columbus and Cabral went westward, as Vasco da Gama went east, as the Ottomans consolidated their rule between Basra and Morocco, as Magellan circumnavigated the globe, as the Safavids interacted with the Deccan Sultanates, possibilities were opened up in which cultural and material processes could find a different synergy. Subrahmanyam begins and ends with a quote from the Sibylline Prophecy at Sintra of 1499[804]:

> The stones shall turn and the letters fall straight and in order
>
> When you O Occident, see the riches of the Orient
>
> The Ganges, Indus and Tagus shall be a sight marvellous to behold
>
> For each shall exchange its goods with the other.

Historians however continue to discover other 'synergies' and comparative histories of the OSM formations continue to be written till today. It was Marshall Hodgson first who attempted a theory of the simultaneous rise and fall of what he termed 'gunpowder empires'. Recently Rohan D' Souza and Bayly and others[805] have propounded alternate theories of the decline of the OSM states.

For D'Souza the decline is found in an almost simultaneous inability to expand the frontier and effect fiscal policies to increase revenue. In the Mughal case the frontier was rendered inelastic; moreover the blunting of the traditional Mughal advantage in heavy cavalry-based warfare underlined the contradictions and limits of empire[806]. D'Souza adds[807]: 'The drive to secure agrarian surpluses, tribute and war plunder, through a decentralised military and fiscal system which in turn, was regulated by a significant imperial administration, generated several tensions that were specific to such a structure of rule' and 'In effect, the moment cavalry warfare, the principal fighting strategy of the OSM, was no longer able to deliver

803 *Ibid*: 130.

804 *Ibid*: 129, 161.

805 D'Souza, Rohan 2002, 'Crisis Before the Fall: Some Speculations on the Decline of the Ottomans, Safavids and Mughals', *Social Scientist*, 30, 9–10, September-October: 3–30 and Bayly and others in *The Medieval History Journal, Special Issue Tributary Empires in History: Comparative Perspectives from Antiquity to the Late Medieval*, 6, 2, July–December 2003. Guest Editors: C.A.Bayly and P.F. Bang.

806 D'Souza, Rohan, 2002: See 7, 9–10, 20.

807 *Ibid*: 11, 13.

military success or expand the frontiers, these empires were plunged into a 'staggered crisis' that characterised their period of slide and inevitable eclipse. The OSM's respective trajectories of decline, however, were broken by a variety of political initiatives and responses, which account for the differences in the velocity and rate of collapse'. In other words, the same things happened, but not all at the same time. It is also not clear why the OSM states lost the capacity to conduct military warfare, and why cavalry warfare lost its edge.

Bayly located the crisis of the OSM states in a scenario where new agrarian and commercial interests collided with the overarching frame of empire[808]. The relative peace and stability provided by the OSM states led to a deepening of commercial networks, rapid urbanisation and a new crystallisation of landed elites. A combination of attempts to accommodate 'indigenous capitalism' and the prevailing fiscal emaciation caused the unsettling of the gargantuan centralised bureaucracies of the OSM states. The OSM states were shattered by an aggregation of political tremors which originated from within the folds of empire. The emphasis therefore moves away from the themes of cultural stagnation, military decline or spendthrift elites.

In *MHJ* the articles edited by Bayly and Bang seek to locate trajectories and points of decline in pre-modern empires throughout Asian history: in the Roman Empire, T'ang and Ming China, Ottoman Turkey and Mughal India. The justification for undertaking a comparative study is that all these empires were, for most of the time at least, tributary empires. They were all, in the last analysis, patrimonial empires[809]. The mechanism of extraction of tribute (revenue) and the fiscal changes they gencrated form the chief themes of this collection.

Earlier the Mughal state was known as patrimonial-bureaucratic; problems with this formulation led historians to adopt only the patrimonial/tributary model. But within the tributary/patrimonial model–after all this is a character of all largc, multi ethnic empires–what was the sepecificity of the Mughal case? Various labels such as 'agrarian', 'universal', 'pre-modern', 'early modern' or 'archaic' have their limitations. Ultimately, however, the modernising approach to complex agrarian societies outside early modern Europe remains unsatisfactory.

---

[808] Bayly, C.A, 1989, *Imperial Meridian: The British Empire and the World 1780–1830*, London, Longman: 16–73, see p. 35.

[809] Bang, P.F., 2003, 'Rome and the Comparative Study of Tributary Empires, *MHJ*: 189–216. See p. 208.

Bang writes[810]:

> During the 1960s and 1970s, the school of 'Aligarh' historians pioneered research into the governing institutional mechanisms and social processes behind the political history of the Mughal empire…They convey an image of a strong state based on a vast, expansive administrative apparatus and an elaborate bureaucratic hierarchy able to impose a strict level of control on the numerous villages…In the 1970s and 1980s, however, doubts began to surface about the underlying reality of this seemingly omnipotent state…J.F.Richards, Michael Pearson and Muzaffar Alam [had] begun to voice considerable concerns about the effective reach of Mughal bureaucratic administration…the bureaucratic model of the Mughal state has therefore come under considerable pressure and the patrimonial aspects of imperial power have received greater attention. Michael Pearson opened the debate…In his view the Mughal state should be perceived as identical with the network of aristocratic patrimonies in the service of the emperor…Stephen Blake introduced Weber's model of patrimonial bureaucratic empires to account for the functioning of the Mughal state…Behind the bureaucratic façade, a system begins to appear, based on an imperial aristocracy governed not by detailed bureaucratic regulations but by a system of intertwining cultural norms. The debate on how the different aspects of the Mughal state should be assessed is still undecided… . A recent contribution to the debate by S.Subrahmanyam and M.Alam is symptomatic of our present problems in conceptualising traditional imperial state formations.

Certain themes are highlighted in the *MHJ*. One is the promotion of differences among subjects. Bayly and Bang comment[811]:

> imperial power very often cherished and promoted 'difference' rather than struggling with it and merely accommodating it…Ideological power within the old states was as segmented and complex as political power and often intertwined with it.

---

810 *Ibid.*: 196–99.

811 Bayly, C.A., and Bang, P.F., 2003, 'Introduction: Comparing Pre-Modern Empires' in *MHJ* op.cit: 169–187. See 175–76.

> The cult of the Roman emperor, for instance, covered a wide diversity of religious notions and practices shaped by differing political statuses and local traditions. It was a multifaceted, not a unitary phenomenon...The Muslim Mughal emperor, regent of God on earth..., regularly cast his blessed gaze over the hordes of naked Hindu holy men who gathered on the River Jumna...It was in the emperor's armies that were firmed up once shifting social categories such as 'Rajputs', 'Mughals', 'Turks' and 'Persians'.

Thus Akbar, as Khalifa, was also equated with Ram.

Yet another theme highlighted in the *MHJ* collection is the sequencing of their development, or in other words, tracing the trajectories of decline. Bayly and Bang point to the central states' inability to raise the land tax and to share in the fruits of agrarian expansion in the eighteenth century Ottoman and Mughal states[812] and suggest comparative studies of institutional processes. They sum up the attributes of pre-modern empires by pointing out that the universal empires' claim to rule was based on a cultural heterogeneity which ultimately led to decline. Instead of concentration of rule the administration of the universal empire led to an aristocratic provincialisation ['These 'archaic' empires did not 'set in motion a process of steadily deepening bureaucratisation; their servants continuously transformed political offices into agglomerations of semi-independent rurally entrenched power networks. The basic order of society remained aristocratic'[813]] and the capitalist world system that engulfed these empires represented a very different system of resource mobilisation than that generated by the tributary states' system of resource mobilisation from the agrarian surplus. Rajat Datta writes of eighteenth century India[814]:

> Thus the eighteenth century witnessed some crucial changes in the fiscal matrices of the state compared to the revenue-based orientation of the Mughal state. One major change was the mode of fiscal management in the new regional polities..While the central financial prop of these regimes was the assessment and collection of the land tax in cash, the

[812] *Ibid*: 178–79.

[813] *Ibid*: 181.

[814] 'Commercialisation, Tribute and the Transition from Late Mughal to Early Colonial in India' in *Ibid*: 259–291. See 262.

> management and its execution was given over to revenue farmers (ijaradar). The practice of ijaradari...exploded all over India in the eighteenth century.

In the *Birth of the Modern World, 1780–1914: Global Connections and Comparisons*, Blackwell, 2004, Bayly characterises the eighteenth century in south Asia, along with East and Central Asia and Africa, as the century that saw the final end of old regimes and 'archaic globalizations' (see pp. 29–90). From 1780 these societies participated in a modernity that emanated from Europe. 1780, according to Bayly, signalled the birth of the modern world.

This volume seeks to locate the roots of the eighteenth century crisis for Bengal in terms of long waves of expansion and contraction in the eastern Indian Ocean, more specifically in the Bay of Bengal.

6

Networks and States in South Asia

Bengal in the Islamic Network and the Rise of the Early Modern States System

Chingiz Khan sent a great number of rareties and offerings with us for presentation to Sultan Muhammad, Khwarazm Shah, and said–"Say ye unto Khwarazm Shah, I am the sovereign of the sunrise and thou the sovereign of the sunset"', on the occasion of his march from China (Tibet) towards Persia, in Minhaj-ud-Din Abu Umar-I-Usman's *Tabakat-I-Nasiri: A General History of the Muhammadan Dynasties of Asia from 810* AD *to 1260* AD *and the Irruption of the Infidel Mughals into Islam* (Tr). Raverty, H.G.1881, Reprint, New Delhi, Oriental Books Corporation, 1970: 966.

If structural changes in the Islamic and Christian worlds signalled the ending of the ancient world by the early medieval period in South Asia the Mongols too paved the way for the ending of the ancient world in Asia in the thirteenth century. Paradoxically this was also the century when Islam formally entered Bengal and the first ever Islamic state was established there.

What was the nature of this new Islamic state? Do we merely designate it as a 'conquest' state with a dynamism directed towards events within South Asia or do we seek to integrate the inherent dynamism of this new state within the larger framework of Islamic states that stretched across the civilised world in the thirteenth century? In other words can we establish a typology for this new state form that arose in South Asia and thereby move away from the 'Islamic' label? Can we call the state forms of this time precursors of the early modern state? Here, we run into a conceptual problem that has baffled historians of the state in South Asia.

The eighties and the nineties of the twentieth century saw an intense debate on the processes underlying the rise of the early modern state (henceforth EMS) and the specific attributes of such states. This happenned both in the west and in India. However, in locational and ideological terms this debate has been primarily concerned with the rise of the EMS within Europe. This emphasis on Christian and Islamic worlds is understandable given the preoccupation of western historians and sociologists to demarcate successive stages in the development of Europe; it is also understandable given the enormous corpus of literature on law, polity, culture and religion which throw light on stages in history available there. The greatest body of work has been done on the rise of the state in Europe and the enormous amount of literature recovered by European historians has made it all the easier to speak of definite periods and state forms in European history–the period of empire, state forms of the middle ages, the rise of national monarchies, the feudal state, the late medieval state (or the EMS of the thirteenth to fifteenth centuries), the transitional Renaissance state of the sixteenth century Europe, the absolutist (and quasi-absolutist) states of the seventeenth century, the weak state forms of central and eastern Europe, the mercantilist state, the liberal state, the democratic state and the various state forms of the twentieth century–the capitalist state, the welfare state, the fascist state, the totalitarian state, the communist state among others.

In sociological parlance the debate has traced stages of evolution between the sovereign state, the national state and the nation-state. Ideologically speaking this bias is understandable given that much of historiography, even in the twenty-first century, remains the domain of the west.

In India too historians and anthropologists have examined the attributes of the South Asian state in history but here the attempts have been directed more towards a comparison of the South Asian experience with developments in European history. In consequence Indian historians have always searched for labels that would place the South Asian state in the larger context of European models of the rise of the state. The debate on the emergence of the state in South Asia has become further complicated with contradictory models such as the Asiatic (Marx), the unitary (Aligarh School), the feudal (Mukhia), the segmentary (Aidan Southall, Stein), the patrimonial-bureaucratic (Blake) and the 'patchwork quilt' (Alam and Subrahmanyam)[815]. This obsession with labels, and the absence of data in general on the South Asian state, has prevented the emergence of a typology of the state that has a certain synchrononity in terms of grand phases as we find in the case of states in the Christian and Islamic worlds. This non-synchronicity is inevitable in a large land mass such as South Asia where there were noticeably differential levels of development in history; so much so that we find often that when *samantaisation* occurs at one place tribalism rules in another.

It is for reasons such as this that typologies of the state in the early history of South Asia revolve around spatial concepts such as 'local' and 'regional' or around expansive notions such as 'early' and 'imperial' kingdoms that talk of the transition to empire through an examination of the administrative apparatus of 'nucleus', expansionist and imperial states. The result has been an over emphasis on administrative history.

For Guenee, the early modern states system originated in Europe from the late twelfth century; for Maurice Lombard the early modern states system originated in the Islamic world by the eleventh century[816]. Less attention has been paid to the rise of the early modern states system in other parts of the world; however it is accepted that the early modern states system originated for the Central Asian world with the rise of the Mongols in the thirteenth century.

For our purposes here, the appearance of the states system in the Islamic and Mongol worlds is the most important. By the eleventh century there was in place an Islamic network of trade, dominated by an urban network, mediated by the dinar economy, that stretched through the ancient zones of civilisation of the Indian Ocean and the Mediterranean. This Islamic network covered two areas: the maritime world of the seas and oceans and the great continental land routes stretching from the steppes, through the deserts and oases of Central Asia upto western Africa. This Islamic network mediated not only with the older networks set in place by China, India and Byzantium, but also included those set in place by

[815] See the Introduction in Alam and Subrahmanyam's *The Mughal State 1526–1750*, Delhi, Oxford University Press, 1998, Hermann Kulke's Introduction in Kulke (ed). *The State in India 1000–1700*, Delhi, 1995 and Panda, Sisir Kumar, 1995, *The State and Statecraft in Medieval Orissa Under the Later Eastern Gangas (AD 1038–1434)* Calcutta.

[816] Guenee, Bernard, 1985, *States and Rulers in Later Medieval Europe*, Oxford University Press, Blackwell. Lombard, Maurice, 1971, *L'Islam dans Sa Premiere Grandeur, VIIIe a XI siecles*, Paris, Flammarion.

the Turkish steppesmen, the Berbers of sub-saharan Africa, the Christians of the Occident, the Russians of Rus, the Buddhists in South Asia and the Arabs of Mesopotamia and Iberia.

Ibn Khurdadbih noted that this urban network was so linked with other parts of the world through the medium of exchange that a cash economy had penetrated the most remote regions of the Islamic world. Muslim merchants dominated this trade network; but they had also incorporated older mercantile networks. The most important of these mercantile sub-stratas incorporated within the Islamic network were the Radanite Jews expelled from Byzantium and especially from Alexandria. These traded through Syria, Armenia, the Caspian Sea and the Indian Ocean in the eleventh century[817]. The newly reconstituted Islamic network of the early medieval world traded in wood, steel, iron, textiles, slaves, writing materials and medicinal products that spanned a vast area stretching from China in the east to Spain in the west.

At the Patiala Session of the Indian History Congress Nihar Ranjan Ray attempted to trace a chronological basis for the early modern states system in South Asian History. He demarcated specific phases with an underlying coherence that made up the 'medieval phase' in Indian history. He located three such phases:

a. from the seventh to the twelfth centuries,

b. from the twelfth century to the early sixteenth century, and

c. from the sixteenth to the eighteenth centuries.

He cited here the following characteristics for the first phase: ruling dynasties became regional and followed paths similar to that of early modern states in Europe following the breakup of the Empire, the economy reverted to a 'natural' economy much like that of medieval Europe and a social crystallisation of a regional character now took place which displayed itself in art, language and the proliferation of religious sects. This social crystallisation finally resulted in the formation of regional identities (such as Sena, Pallava, Chola).

In 1990, Wink followed this schema and laid bare the political *conjonctures* that shaped South Asian history from the seventh century onwards and which paved the way for both the Mongol rupture and the thirteenth century crisis (or changeover to Islamic rule) in South Asia. He noted the following factors that went to make up medieval Bengal:

---

[817] Lombard, Maurice, 1971: 223–230.

i. The focus of political power moved from Magadh to Kanauj which now became the spiritual/imperial capital. The monarch controlling Kanauj commanded upper India.

ii. The Palas, especially Dharmapala and Devapala, controlled Kanauj and so maintained their north Indian hegemony. This hegemony was reinforced by alliances with Lalitaditya and Jayapida of Kashmir.

iii. From the eighth century Kanauj and the control of northern India became the bone of contention between three new regional powers– the Palas, the Gurjara-Pratiharas and the Rashtrakutas. By the tenth century the Palas lost Kanauj. The Palas retreated leaving north India to the Gurjaras and Rashtrakutas[818].

Brajadulal Chattopadhyay suggested that the essence of the economic process lay in the horizontal spread of rural agrarian settlements despite the accent on urban economy and money economy even in early South Asian history[819]. Both Chattopadhyay and Kulke emphasised the role of religious cults in the formation of the state and the articulation of royal authority[820]. The difference lies in the extent of emphasis; for Kulke the role of cults is more important in the extension of royal power while Chattopadhyay insists more on the interlinkage between local state polities and supra-local polities. This, he feels, may be more fruitful in assessing the nature of the state rather than viewing structures in terms of a 'perennial oscillation between forces of centralization and decentralization'[821]. Both Chattopadhyaya and Kulke insist that the nuclear zone, from which political expansion and ideological impulses radiated, may not be in zones of intensive cultivation (river basins/doab) or originating from earlier political centres[822]. This schema is clearly applicable to early Bengal.

For the pre Pala period we have already located the following phases:

i. An early phase of small states in south eastern Bengal, displaying marked cross border affiliations and trade contacts, such as the

[818] Wink, Andre, 1990, *Al-Hind*, I, New Delhi, Oxford University Press: 267, 277.

[819] Brajadulal Chattopadhyay, 1995, 'Political Processes and the Structure of Polity in Early Medieval India' in Kulke (ed). 1995: 195–232. See 213–214.

[820] Chattopadhyay, 1995: 214, Kulke, 1995, 'The Early and the Imperial Kingdom: A Processural Model of Integrative State Formation in Early Medieval India': 233–262. See: 237–8, 259–262 in Kulke (ed) 1995.

[821] Chattopadhyay, 1995: 215.

[822] Chattopadhyay, 1995: 221–2. Kulke 1995: 235.

Chandras and the Khadgas around Dhaka-Vikrampur and Comilla from the fourth century onwards.

ii. A similar phenomenon centreing around Mahastan (in Bogra district in Bangladesh) in Pundravardhana which maintained links with South China and Cambodia through the overland mountain route at around the same time.

iii. This early trade network linking the delta with the mountain passes within Bengal coalesces into a stronger trading bloc with growing interaction with Pagan in the tenth and eleventh centuries.

iv. This interaction is furthered despite the fall of Pagan at the end of the thirteenth century; independent contacts resume between Pattikera and Arakan in the south east as also between Pundravardhana and Ava in the north east.

v. Despite the Islamic invasion of western Bengal, Buddhist ties and the commercial dynamism of the eastern sector continue to prosper.

We can also underline the following developments in the post Pala period regarding western Bengal.

i. The 'officialdom' of Brahmanism of the Guptas and Palas had hardened into a conservative Brahmanical aristocracy by the time of the Senas in twelfth century Bengal. The fact that the political centre moved away from eastern (Bengal/Bihar under the Guptas) to upper India (from Magadh to Kanauj) is further indicative of intensive aryanisation and the growing ascendancy and religious/temporal power of the priestly cult.

ii. Along with the conservative backlash under Sena rule there was a corresponding 'closing' of frontiers; Bengal under the Senas became more inward looking, more interior based unlike the earlier 'expansive' empires.

iii. This conservative crystallisation under Sena rule has to be seen in the context of reactions that were appearing all over India from the ninth century–starting from Sankaracarya in the south to Medhatithi in the north. What we witness of eastern India from the eleventh century is a society withering away on the tree of orthodoxy[823].

iv. By the end of the tenth century many merchants in western Bengal were converting back from Buddhism to Hinduism once again.

[823] I am indebted to Prof. Prabhati Mukherjee for information on Brahmanical orthodoxy.

But note that this picture is mainly applicable to western Bengal. In southeastern Bengal trade and transborder affiliations continued long after as we have seen. Therefore we see that the thirteenth century crisis was not an accidental event; the ground for the rupture was prepared long before. Yet this 'crisis' paved the way for new state forms to emerge in South Asia. There is a consensus among historians that by the end of the thirteenth century Islamic states, based on invasive agrarian practices, had consolidated themselves in both Delhi and Bengal. The Khaljis at Delhi and the Ilyas Shahis in Bengal in the fourteenth century strengthened their tax base through an intensive assessment of the revenue potential, expanded their domains to incorporate ever more new areas into the core state and promoted a trade that transcended South Asian borders.

But the Islamic invasion was more than a turning point in the history of Bengal; it was far more than the incorporation of Bengal into an Islamic network of trade and culture. It also paved the way for the emergence of a regional identity. The expression of this regional identity–based on a syncretic mix of Hindu and Muslim culture–formed the basis of the early modern state in Bengal.

Apart from a consciously demarcated territory and a centralized administrative apparatus emanating from Gaur/Lakhnawati the attempts of the Ilyas Shahis to open an official dialogue with Yuan and Ming China and the ending of this fruitful dialogue by the Husain Shahis probably with their attempts to control the *tangan* horse trade to the detriment of Chinese interests point to different political interests. A different border policy was articulated by the Bengal Sultans in the sixteenth century. Expanding agriculture, increasing trade, the growth of towns and the emergence of an intensely urban economy marked this new state. An emergence of a definite north-east frontier policy and expeditions against the Koch and Kamta kingdoms were visible attempts to control and expand the resources of the new state. Control over the north-east border states became the determinant of the early modern state's success or failure as an integrative mechanism. Here Bengal faced a formidable frontier indeed; and it was one where the Mongol sub-clans were dominant. We shall study this in greater detail in the next section.

The Mongol Rupture and Bengal

'The turban is part of the costume of the merchants…the turban is the crown and diadem of the Arab…Muhammad…was a turban-wearer…The interpretation is this, that the kingdoms of Islam will come into thy possession' on Chingiz Khan's dream, in Minhaj-ud-Din Abu Umar-I-Usman's *Tabakat-I-Nasiri: A General History of the Muhammadan Dynasties of Asia from 810 AD to 1260 AD and the Irruption of the Infidel Mughals into Islam* (Tr). Raverty, H.G.1881, Reprint, New Delhi, Oriental Books Corporation, 1970: 975.

Minhaj's *Tabakat-i-Nasiri* bewails the catastrophic effects of the Mongol putsch towards the west on the Delhi Sultanate. As an eyewitness account of the thirteenth century crisis, it is unrivalled for the scope of its tales of plunder, devastation and conquest of political orders in regions immediately to the north and east of South Asia such as Afghanistan, Persia and China. Readers of the *Tabakat-I-Nasiri* relive the days of uncertainty that the Mongol dream of world domination brought in its wake; the overthrowing of established political orders meant the loosening of political, diplomatic and economic ties that kept the South Asian world going. The dream turned into the reality of nightmare for north India with the Mongol defeat of Khwarizim (Persia) in 1218–19. This was perceived as a defeat for world Islam.

If Minhaj gives an eyewitness account of the rise of the Mongols from the political point of view (and his meeting with the world-conqueror Chingiz Khan), Ibn Khaldun gives us a sociological explanation for the decline of the Islamic states (which belief was reinforced after his meeting with the emperor Taimur). Ibn Khaldun was from a trading empire that connected the Mediterrannean with northern Africa and the Far East through the Red Sea. Travelling in the fourteenth century, Ibn Khaldun traversed lands previously under Islamic sway but now overrun by Mongol armies. From the Danube to Annam, Mongol and post-Mongol states ruled. Christian or Islamic states were no alternatives to the great states established by the Mongols. Regions previously at the heart of the Muslim world were now a former shadow of themselves–a state that Ibn Khaldun attributed to the weakening of *asabiya* or community spirit that had reinforced Islamic communities through centuries. Contrast Ibn Khaldun's experience with that of Ibn Khurdadbih earlier. Ibn Khurdadbih had experienced, with amazement, a flourishing Islamic economy and culture that spanned continents and integrated remote zones into a trading network[824]. This world collapsed with the fall of Baghdad to the Mongols in 1258. The destruction of Baghdad and the Caliphate signalled a crisis in the early medieval Islamic order. The three hundred years from the thirteenth to the

[824] See before, also Maurice Lombard, 1971.

sixteenth centuries saw therefore not just an end of the old order but the birth of a new world for both Europe and Asia.

Islamic states adhered to two models. The Umayyads and the Abbassids adopted the Roman/Byzantine agricultural-estate system but in North Africa, where Byzantium's influence was minimal, states arose which exercised,as the basis of their prosperity, control over the caravans traversing the gold routes of the Sudan: these states consequently redrew the map of North Africa and Iberia with the most intensive surge of urbanisation known in those parts. These were the Fatimids of the tenth century who became so powerful that they conquered Egypt and founded Cairo (973 AD), the Almoravids who ruled between the tenth and twelfth centuries and who conquered Morocco, founded Marrakesh and captured Spain, the Almohads who followed the Almoravids in the twelfth century, and the Marinids who presided over the ruins of empire of Spain, Maghreb and Ifriqiyah.

What was the state form that the Mongols espoused? Evidence leads us to assume that the Mongols adopted the Islamic model of a commercial network of states. They therefore attempted, in China, Iran, Turan, Rus and later in South Asia to take over the existing Islamic networks of trade. Recent research reveals that all three founding fathers (Chingiz, Kubla'i and Taimur) believed in the beneficial powers of trade and believed that a flourishing commerce lay at the base of the prosperity of nations. In his collection of poems *Kutadgu Bilik*, Chingiz held up merchants as models to be as emulated as warriors. Like these North African states the strength of the Mongol empire depended on trade. The Mongol political machine based itself on its control over trade routes to both east and west and the alliance of Chingiz Khan with merchants has to be seen in this light. This trade, like the Maghrebian states, was a caravan trade.

What then was the political economy of the Mongol empire? Conventional historiography tells us that it was based on plunder and anarchy. This notion derives from the fact that Chingiz Khan's army of about 200 000 marched on Khwarazm-Shah of Samarkhand and destroyed some of the greatest Islamic cities: Herat, Balkh, Merv and Nishapur before devastating Iran. It has been estimated that 2,000,000 plus people were massacred[825]. To the civilised world of Islam in India the Mongol eruption was viewed as an act of punishment from God.

Recent research, we see, reveals that the Mongols believed that a flourishing trade lay behind the 'wealth of nations'. It is significant that

825 Chaudhuri, K.N., 1990, *Asia Before Europe: Economy and Civilisation of the Indian Ocean From the Rise of Islam to 1750*, Cambridge: 274–5.

Chingiz started his dream of world domination with the conquest of China and then moved on to Persia. It was within these two countries that the majority of caravan routes plied in a east-west trade. The Mongols built bridges, posting-roads, and serais and cut through rocks to make passes traversable all over Russia, Persia, Turkestan and China. There were 10 000 posting stations with over 300 000 horses to serve for mercantile traffic between China and Persia. Similar facilities were established for communications from post to post and it has been remarked 'What European technique has only of late achieved in the matter of annihilating space was already effected in the thirteenth century…by the savage energy of Chingiz Khan, and the last touches of perfection to the organization were given by Kublai'[826]. Mongol trade routes were overland routes; the seas were left to the Europeans in the fifteenth century such as the Venetians in Aleppo (the eastern Mediterrannean), the Spaniards in the Americas (the Atlantic) and the Portuguese in Calicut (the Indian Ocean).

The Mongols were not only concerned with establishing new trade routes within their domains; they also participated in an industrial relocation and a re-distribution of skills. The silk and cotton weavers of Samarkhand were pressed into the service of Chingiz' military followers, Taimur imported Indian stonemasons, arguably the best in Asia at the time, into Samarkhand, Chinese craftsmen were re-settled in Trans-Oxania; all these are proof that the Mongols were attempting to supplement their 'new' silk route through Trans-Oxania with industrial production.

These prime movers, the Mongols, who were responsible for the breakup of the ancient world order initially impacted only marginally on Bengal. The Mongols originated from Central Asia. Originally steppesmen from Mongolia, their various branches fanned out east and west in the thirteenth century under Chingiz Khan.The split of the Mongolian Horde into its eastern and western branches and their subsequent march southwards and westwards subverted older state forms in both Asia and Europe. The westward Mongol putsch has attracted more attention in historical scholarship.

The western branch, swelled by Turkish hordes, consolidated itself into a powerful bloc. It soon confronted the old European Mediterranean order. It battered Byzantium from the eleventh century onwards. In 1241 at the time of the Polos' visit to the Great Khan at Khanbalik in Central Asia, the Mongols invaded Hungary and Poland. This order finally culminated in the mighty Ottoman Empire in eastern Europe in 1453.

[826] Prawdin, Michael, 1940, *The Mongol Empire: Its Rise and Legacy*, London, Allen and Unwin: 330.

The Mongols also went westward from Tibet towards Afghanistan where they combatted the predecessors of Taimur, the Central Asian Ghaznavids and Ghorids who were already established on India's north west frontiers from the eleventh century. A sub-branch of the Ghorids had arrived in India by the turn of the thirteenth century. Here they inaugurated the Delhi and Bengal Sultanates and the political and economic repercussions of the Mongol putsch over their original homelands was felt keenly by them, as Minhaj tells us.

The eastern branch became subdivided into the two central Asian houses of Chingiz Khan and Taimur, the latter the ancestor of the Mughals. The eastern branch fanned out from Tibet in two directions. It went eastward to establish itself in China; a move that was to have enormous repercussions for Bengal[827], for this meant that the Mongols sought to keep the eastern gates of Kamrup, Koch and Kamta open for their expansion. Kubla'i, grandson of Chingiz Khan, founded the Yuan dynasty in 1260, transferred the capital in 1264 from Karakorum to Peking, sought the submission of China, and swept down to south east Asia. In his wake came the T'ais who carved out principalities on Bengal's eastern frontiers as close as Assam. It is said that Kubla'i explored the feasibility of launching an invasion of Bengal through the present Bhutan-Jalpaiguri area (the Dooars)[828].

Some historians have also referred to a Mongol invasion of Bengal by Chingiz Khan in 1244. Apparently he attacked Bengal with 30 000 soldiers. Most now dismiss this as a myth[829] but we should remember that this area–*varendra*–was like *harikela* one frontier that was always open to regulation. Karampattan in Chinese Turkestan had a garrison of 50 000 soldiers. It is therefore not unlikely that a border dispute took place as two expanding powers, the Mongols and the Turko Afghans, met. This explains the Bengal Sultanates' obsession with the north eastern portals of their state; for it was through this region that they interacted with north India as well as points both west and east. The Mongol rupture of the thirteenth century, while not directly impacting on Bengal, nevertheless left a permanent imprint on the Bengal sultanate's north-east border policy.

---

[827] See section on Politics and Trade before.

[828] For more on this see Petech, Luciano, 1990, *Central Tibet and the Mongols–The Yuan-sa-Skya Period of Tibetan History*, Rome, Serie Orientale Roma, Instituto Italiano Per Il Medio ed Estremo Oriente: 24.

[829] Roy, Atul Chandra, 1986, *History of Bengal: Turko Afghan Period*, New Delhi and Ludhiana, Kalyani Publishers: 71–72.

We know that this contained the land route from Bengal to China from ancient times. Buddhist pilgrims made use of this route frequently[830]. The route led from Pundravardhana (north Bengal) up the Karatoya into Kamrup and then through the Brahmaputra towards Little Tibet, Turkestan, and China. In the thirteenth century Odoric mentioned this same route[831], only now this route also went either to Afghanistan or through Ava under the Mongols into Yunnan in South China. This seems to be a frontier country; Minhaj mentioned in the *Tabaqat-i-Nasiri* that Karampattan was a garrison town with 50 000 Turkic soldiers. It was also a horse mart. Fifteen hundred horses a day were sold there, Minhaj says. Marco Polo repeats this and adds that these horses were destined for Gaur.

In succeeding centuries when the Bengal-China (Yuan and Ming) trade was given an official standing, the Mongol domination of China formed a distant memory. Yet the renewed efforts of Tamerlane at the end of the fourteenth century to invade China once again not only shaped Ming foreign policy to the extent that trade and diplomatic missions were sent to foreign lands, Bengal among them; also Mongol invasions in Central Asia disturbed land routes and thus gave a fillip to maritime routes from which Bengal profited to a great extent.

What did the Mongol world order dream of? Certainly it dreamt of political conquest, of making their civilization the centre of the world to rival Rome or Constantinople. But it also dreamt of economic hegemony, of controlling a trans-Asian/European trade that spanned continents, of being a second Baghdad or Damascus. Possessing neither the refinement and economic strength of the Islamic order nor the strong theological/liturgical base of the Byzantine/Latin order, the Mongol-mega machine was powered by ruthless ambition and driven by insatiability. But Chingiz Khan did not only dream of plunder on a mega-scale, being an ambassador he also advocated trade between empires, and he established diplomatic relations (based on tribute and fiefdom!) with states he conquered[832]. From the end of the thirteenth century Venetian, Pisan and Genoese merchants acted as the Khan's diplomatic messengers in an attempt to open trade with the west through South Asia, Central Asia, southern Russia and Iran[833]. Under Kubla'i Khan, China became a great trading

---

[830] Ray, Nihar Ranjan, 1993, *Bangalir Itihas*, Adiparba, Calcutta, Dey's Publishing: 94–95; Sen, Dinesh Chandra, *Brihat Banga*, V.I: 28–29 (both in Bengali).

[831] Yule, Henry, *Cathay and the Way Thither*, V.II, London, Hakluyt Society, MCCCC LXVI: 273–4.

[832] *Tabaqat-I-Nasiri*: 961, 1041.

[833] Mukherjee, Rila, 2003, *The Lost Worlds of Europe*, Kolkata, Progressive: chs. VI and IX.

nation. Similarly Taimur wrote to all kings and princes not subject to him, urging them to send merchants since 'trade makes for prosperity'[834].

This was a Central Asian world order incorporating Rus, Iran, China, South East Asia, Tibet and a part of Central Asia[835]. A smaller Mongol world order incorporating China, north Bengal, the T'ai Ahom kingdom of Assam, Shan Ava, Tibet, and Chinese Turkestan was born by the end of the thirteenth century. It subverted the caravan routes on which the known world depended: Baghdad was replaced by Tabriz in the fourteenth century as the emporia city in the west-east trade. Tabriz was replaced in its turn by Samarkhand through Taimur's conquests for he blocked the caravan routes running from the Black Sea to China and opened instead a new route passing though his dominions: Transoxania.

The Mongol mercantile world now confronted the Mediterrannean Islamic world order. In 1258 it sacked Baghdad and in 1260 the Mongols occupied Aleppo and Damascus: meeting-ground of Christian-Islamic trade. It is precisely because of the uncertainity caused in the old commercial cities of Asia that the nascent Bengal Sultanate could not form a successful commercial policy in the thirteenth century. Things settled down in the fourteenth century. It is only from the early Ilyas Shahi period, at the time Ibn Batuta visited Bengal, that we find commerce thriving in Bengal once again.

But the Mongol dream of economic domination was abortive. Despite the Khanate's desire to ally itself with the Papacy and combat Islam[836] in the Holy Land this was not achieved. In both east and west robust Islamic empires carried on their political/diplomatic/economic functions much as they had done before the Mongol interregnum. After wreaking untold havoc in Asia and Europe the Central Asian order became integrated into the much older and commercially vibrant Islamic world order. Most Mongol chiefs converted to Islam. By the sixteenth century the descendants of the Mongols, the Mughals, were established at Delhi as Islamic potentates. They never came to Bengal as Mongols again.

Bengal: An Early Modern State

'When we arrived within the boundaries of Tamghaj...a high white mound appeared in sight...We...supposed that that white eminence was perhaps a hill of snow, and we made enquiries of the guides...and they

---

[834] Prawdin, 1940: 475.

[835] Petech, Luciano, 1990.

[836] See Mukherjee, Rila 2003, *The Lost Worlds of Europe*, chapter VI: 156–157.

replied "The whole of it is the bones of men slain" in Minhaj-ud-Din Abu Umar-I-Usman's *Tabakat-I-Nasiri: A General History of the Muhammadan Dynasties of Asia from 810* AD *to 1260* AD *and the Irruption of the Infidel Mughals into Islam* (Tr). Raverty, H.G. 1881, Reprint, New Delhi, Oriental Books Corporation, 1970: 965.

Coinciding with the Mongol phenomenon there was now the birth of new states stretching from South East Asia, through the Indian subcontinent, Central Asia, into Europe. The twelfth-thirteenth century birth of new states in Europe and the Middle East through the reordering of older ones, the fragmentation of Byzantium, and the split of the Islam world into emirates, empires and monarchies at this time is well known.

Some of these state forms soon moved on to form territorial units by a series of conquests in South Asia, witness the Tughlaks at Delhi or the Ilyas Shahis in Bengal, or indeed the Gujarati sultanate. Later the expansive character of these early states gave way to a consolidational phase: witness the 'new' regionalized Delhi Sultanate of the Sayyids and Lodhis and the Bengal Sultanate of the Husain Shahis. The nascent Islamic states of the fourteenth and the fifteenth century Bengal that mediated with the Mongol world contained within themselves many of the traits we associate with the early modern state[837].

It is the last three criteria of the early modern state, the consolidation of a definite regional culture and consciousness that nurtured the first tentative articulation of a composite 'Bengali' identity according to Eaton, that was most visible in the early modern state of Bengal. The name that the Sultans gave to Bengal–'Bangal'–may be indicatory of an attempt at reconciling in the 'Banga' of ancient times with the 'al' that denotes patrimony[838].

---

837 Any state that displays at least the following characteristics fulfill the criteria demanded by what historians and sociologists call the EMS in Europe. They are a consciously demarcated territory with the gradual emergence of a fixed capital, a coherent economic policy to regulate the flow of internal resources, a tangible polity that is articulated at all levels of inter-state contact, attempts to centralise the administrative apparatus and effect unified rule, the proliferation of bureaucratisation, espionage and diplomacy to achieve this end, deliberate attempts to redefine the parameters of both language and culture which culminate in the establishment of the state's hegemony in extra economic and political domains through manipulations and (ab)uses of history, myths and legends to create the illusion of 'national' feeling, conscious invocations of the ideals of *loyalty, patriotism and the sense of a nation* and finally as a result of these factors a constant attempt to either win over minorities or marginalise them with social and religious sanctions.

838 Khandkar Muzammil Haq pp.59–76 in *Bangla Akademi Patrika* Dacca, vol. 38 No.3 1993. The *Ain* however is of the opinion that the word *al* was a local word signifying an embankment.

During the reign of the Husain Shahis a closer integration with 'local' elements was seen. Much has been written about the roles the celebrated Rup and Sanatan played in the political administration in Husain Shahi Bengal–one as Sarkar Malik the other as Dabir-i-Khas. But there were also other 'local recruits': Jagai and Madhai as *kotwals*, Gopinath Basu as minister, Ramchandra Khan as border officer, Mukunda Das as royal physician, Keshav Chattri as chief royal bodyguard, Gaur Mallick as army commander, and Anup as mint-officer. This integration paved the way for a definite articulation of Bengal's polity as an Islamic state.

Of all the Bengal Sultans it was the first Husain Shah–Ala-al-Din–who openly championed the cause of Islam as his state policy. Ala al Din sought legitimacy by declaring himself the descendant of Muhammad at the time of his conquest of Bengal in 1494 both in the Deopara inscription and in two gold and silver coins dated 1494. As he embarked upon his conquests in the eastern region he proclaimed himself the champion and defender of Islam, and often as the Messenger, the Fighter, the Imam and Khalifa of Muhammad. He described himself in several inscriptions as the champion and advocate of Islam. In keeping with this self styled image as the defender of the true faith he endowed several institutions and built at the very least eight mosques in Bengal. Finally he built a madrassa at Gaur in 1502 for the specific purpose of 'teaching the sciences of religion and imparting instructions in the injunctions of the faith'[839] Such a close identification of polity with religion undermines Tarafdar's claim that Ala-al-Din Husain Shah dissociated religion from politics[840].

It is therefore clear that Ala-al-din was the first Muslim ruler who attempted to transform Islam from a marginal and 'frontier' religion in Bengal into a dominant ideology that was closely linked with polity and expansion of empire. It is noteworthy that he was the first Sultan to successfully attempt to bring the periphery of Bengal (Kamrup, Tripura, Chattagram and Orissa) under Islamic hegemony. It is also clear that a consolidated Muslim identity took shape in Bengal during Husain Shahi rule. A distinct Muslim consciousness began to express itself in literature. This new Bengali Muslim literature was an admixture of the tenets of Islam, *baul* songs, vaisnavite *bhakti* and the influence of heterodox sects in which *sufi* philosophy predominated. Vernacular Muslim literature

[839] Quoted in Mohar Ali, vol 1A: 208–209.
[840] *Husain Shahi Bengal*, 1965: 67.

culminated in the *RasulVijaya* of the poet Shaikh Chand in Eastern Bengal (1650–1725)[841]. Apart from Muslim writings in the vernacular writings in Arabic and Persian were common. What is noteworthy is that language was not made a criterion of differentiation among religious communities in Bengal. Muslims wrote in Bengali; Hindus–especially those in administration–mastered Arabic and Persian. In legal writings too we find the existence of two distinct domains–the one governed with political sanction and the other governed according to legal codes which had stood the test of time. The two separate realms of Islamic law and Hindu law moved in two distinct arenas over the population of Bengal[842].

The vaisnavite movement in sixteenth century Bengal has to be seen more in the context of a fear at the policy of integration with 'local' elements that the Husain Shahis consciously promoted than the unease felt at the full expression of a growingly assertive Muslim identity in Bengal. It is perhaps in reaction to this burgeoning of an Islamic identity, as much as to Brahmanical orthodoxy, that Chaitanya's popular vaisnavite movement gained momentum in Bengal. Chaitanya's movement can be regarded as the expression of a nascent yet complete *Bengali* (but Hindu) identity. It has already been noted in previous sections that popular vaisnavism offered a greater scope of social integration than other cults. It was a potent force for it combined under its umbrella all the folk/tribal elements, brought them within the Puranic fold and presented them to people. Popular vaisnavism thus offered an effective ideological reply to Brahmanical hierarchism as well as challenging Islamic hegemony in Bengal. It rallied effectively under its banner those orders which had converted to Islam[843].

Chaitanya's message was not for the political or religious elite–popular vaisnavism's message was for the economically mobile who now aspired social and political recognition. His mission was directed not towards the population in the larger towns in Bengal, but for those in the *bazaars*, *ganjs*, *mandis* and *ghats* of semi-rural Bengal. His *method* of preaching–derived from the ancient tradition of *kirtan, kathakata* and *pancalika* of

[841] For more information on popular culture and new trends see Bashir Al Helal in *Uttaradhikar*, Bangla Akademi, Dhaka, July-September 1995; Khandkar Muzammil Haq, A.K.M.Shahnawaz in *Bangla Akedemi Patrika*, Dhaka, vol. 38 No. 3 1993; Mafidul Haq in *Theatre*, Dhaka, October 1995; Karunamoy Goswami in *Bangla Akademi Patrika* vol. 33 No. 4 1900.

[842] As late as in the 14th century redefinitions of the Dharmasastras were still attempted. Kullukabhakta commented on the Laws of Manu from Bengal in the 14th century.

[843] For more on Vaishnavism in Bengal see Chakravarti, Ramakanta, 1985, *Vaishnavism in Bengal 1486–1900*, Calcutta, Sanskrit Pustak Bhandar.

Bengal–was through a mixture of *nagar-sankirtana*, *krsnalila* and *krsnakirtana* whose idiom was widely acceptable. His message was welcoming for all.

The outcome of Chaitanya's movement was a tremendous development of vernacular (as distinct from the old sanskritised) literature in Bengali. The resurgence of middle Bengali literature during this time–especially the *mangalkavyas* which told us so much about trade, routes and ports in Bengal–mirror accurately Chaitanya's agenda. Tribal deities and cult shakti figures that still lingered in Bengal were now incorporated within the Puranic mantle; elements of the old tribal/shakti cult such as Manasa, Kali and Chandi were given centre stage where they waged a vengeful war for legitimisation.

Apart from the *mangalkavyas*, the various biographies of Chaitanya written during this period, the translations of epics such as the Mahabharata (first done in Bengal at the end of the thirteenth century) and the rise of a class of courtier/litterateurs who produced secular literature at the courts of Gaur and Arakan are living testimony to the efflorescence of Bengali consciousness in the sixteenth and seventeenth centuries. Alaol composed his *Padmavati* at the Arakan court; this was indicative of a desire to integrate the culture of the frontier region with that of the gangetic plain. The elevation of individual writers such as Jaidev, Mukunda Chakravarty, Babu Chandidas and Bidyapati to cult status is indicative of the surge in creative activity in Chaitanya's Bengal.

By the sixteenth century the map of the world was substantially changed. There were now two key world orders: the emergent European and the older Islamic. Both fought for hegemony in the same space. In the east the older eastern Mongol order had merged itself with the Chinese. Part of the western Mongol order merged with the Islamic. Within South Asia descendants of the Mongols–the Mughals–were firmly established.

At the very time that a definite regional consciousness emerged in Bengal a new order based on greater dialogue and exchange, new identities and new zonal economies began to take shape. Interactions between the two 'mongol' empires, the Mughal and the Ottoman, became common. Early modern or proto-modern state forms sprang up in various parts of Asia. Bengal was conquered by the Mughals and redirected into a trade network that spanned seas and lands in the former Mongol lands. It was therefore inevitable that Bengal underwent a significant change in this process. From the seventeenth century, Bengal occupied but a subordinate place in trade routes and commercial networks now developed by the Mughals, the successors of Chingiz Khan and Taimur.

The Mughal World and Bengal's Place in an Asian Economy

'In the Beginning of the month of Day (October 1615) merchants came from Persia and brought pomegranates from Yazd and melons from Kariz, which are the best of the Khurasan melons' (Jahangir, *Tuzuk-I-Jahangiri*, I, 270).

The War of the Melons: Shah Jahan prohibited all caravans from Persia from entering Mughal territory because Iranian officials had not exported any of the Kariz melons (kharbuzah-i-kariz). These 'unfriendly proceedings' almost escalated into a trade war; however Iran informed Shah Jahan that only a poor melon harvest had interrupted its export that year (1641 or 1642). Shah Jahan relented and allowed the caravan traffic to resume. (In Dale, Stephen, F., 1994, *Indian Merchants and Eurasian Trade 1600–1750*, Cambridge, University Press: 22).

These passages express the Mughal nostalgia for their ancestral homeland. This nostalgia was summed up in the Mughal craving for fruits which the tended gardens of Farghana once provided Babur. More importantly for us, the two passages evoke the commercial landscape of the Mughals and give an idea of the mighty caravan trade that spanned the Safavid and Mughal domains in the seventeenth century.

Yet we tend to ignore this commerce when we discuss the Mughal economy. Received historiography tells us that the Mughals favoured a land based economy for South Asia; and since they extracted their surplus from agriculture they had little interest in trade. Mughal commercial policy is seen primarily as response to European impact.

A disdain of trade and traders, indifference to other traders within its realms, the fact that the economy of the Mughal empire was primarily based on land revenue and not on receipts from trade; all these factors have gone on to reinforce the assumption that the Mughal's interest in external trade was marginal.

But how are we then to explain the booming commercial economies of sixteenth and seventeenth century Mughal India, the existence of urban centres specialising in crafts all over India and the launch of the Mecca sailings by Akbar which increasingly transformed themselves into diplomatic and commercial missions to the Islamic 'centre of the world'? For these indicate that the Mughals were not so impervious to trade as has been suggested.

Records tell us that there was substantial trade carried on between the Mughal and the contiguous Safavid and Turan (Uzbeg) worlds both by land and sea. Cotton textiles worth one million rupees was shipped from Surat to Iran in 1661. The entire amount was not destined for the Persian market; some of this was sent up north-eastwards to Turan via the caravan route and a portion went westward to the Ottoman cities. More than half of Mughal India's cloth exports was destined for the traditional markets in Iran, Turan and the Ottoman empire in the seventeenth century. This commerce has been neglected in modern historical scholarship on 'Asian Trade'.

It is my contention that European and Mughal views on commerce were essentially at variance. Within Europe commercial activity had gained respectability after a long and bloody battle with entrenched agrarian interests. Trading rights and political influence had been achieved by aggressively regulated companies formed by royal charter that gradually saw themselves as an alternative to the feudal economy in Europe.

The Mughal world view was fundamentally different. Heirs to the Timurid tradition, which in turn owed its lineage to the Chingiz Khanid model, Mughal political economy combined agrarian activity with commercial pursuits that transcended the known Islamic world. All merchants were deemed equal and the Mughals envisioned a free flow of goods and people between political boundaries.

The European notion that the Mughals were anti-trade, or at least indifferent to trade, stems from the sixteenth century European amazement that the Mughals did not safeguard the resources of the state through the same kind of mercantilism as was being practised in Europe (in England, France, Spain and Holland). Bullion (specie) was seen in the Mughal tradition as a means of maintaining the equilibrium of the body politic and not as an end in itself, as was the case in Europe. Therefore, all who brought in specie were welcome. This view of bullion as health (and not wealth) and traders as benefactors explains the inexplicable fact (to both Europeans as well as Indians today!) that the Mughals actually welcomed Europeans on their shores more and more from the seventeenth century. Despite occasional skirmishes with regional powers and the Mughal-Portuguese and Mughal-English hostilities at Hugli and Surat, Europeans were generally left alone in the seventeenth century. The income they generated in their trade with South Asia was seen as an extra financial benefit for the Mughal and local rulers. Europeans, the Mughals felt, were like other merchants; their trade on South Asian shores would bring only prosperity to the realm. Despite the fact that the latter engrossed much of the economy by the eighteenth century we have no evidence that Aurangzeb and the later Mughals engaged in trade wars with Europeans.

This idea of the Mughal's anti-trade attitude colours historical scholarship even today. More important, the fact that this notion also serves as a justification for the imposition of British rule in India, is ignored by the academy. But how exactly was the Mughal anti-trade? Was it because his trade interests did not necessarily embrace the seas?

Political boundaries in the Mughal world were naturally land-based (and not sea-based) entities. The Mongol and Mughal notion of space was, through necessity and historical experience, land based. The prime movers of Mongol history, politics and economy came from land based empires running from China to Iran. Mongol history had been forged on the dusty steppes of Central Asia, through the mountains of north India, and on the plains of China. The Caspian Sea, the Bay of Bengal, and the Arabian Sea were seen as limits of empire and not zones to be transcended. Most Mughals had never seen the sea despite ruling over an empire bound by seas on three sides. The Khyber Pass and not the Indian Ocean was more integral to the Mughal commercial world.

If we look at primate cities in the Indian Ocean world we find them frequently to be port cities: long distance trade in the whole of the Indian Ocean and the Mediterrannean was held together by a string of cities running from east to west such as Hangchow, Canton, Malacca, Calicut, Cambay, Hormuz, Basra, Aden, Alexandria, Aleppo and Venice. The political world of the Indian Ocean however was land based and was held together by 'primate' cities such as Peking, Delhi, Agra, Baghdad, Damascus, Cairo, Isfahan and Constantinople; similarly the religious world of the Indian Ocean was held together by Jerusalem, Mecca, Medina, Damascus, Baghdad and Istanbul.

Note now that within the historical geography of the Mughal Empire, imperial control drived from the cities of Kabul, Kandahar, Lahore, Delhi, Agra, Patna, Burhanpur and Ahmedabad. The control of these eight capital cities signified the possession of the peacock throne, which was the true sign of the Padshah of Hindustan. None of these cities are, we should note, maritime cities–Surat, Masulipatnam and Hugli do not feature on the list; nor does a provincial Mughal capital such as Dhaka. The coastal world of South Asia remained completely outside the vision of Mughal sovereignty and the Mughal vision of space was therefore of necessity a territorial one in contrast to those of European states whose destinies were as much determined by winds of change blowing in from oceans as by events shaped on terra firma[844].

The Mughal world interacted commercially and diplomatically with the three other worlds of the Ottomans, the Safavids and the Uzbegs and all four, taken in conjunction, formed an Asian economy that straddled the continents of Asia and Europe. This world owed its administrative and cultural lineage to the Mongol world economy described in earlier pages for all four polities traced their genealogy to the Timurid tradition[845].

Indeed it may not be an exaggeration to say that the four empires formed an intergrated regional market with an emergent 'international'credit system facilitating trade. Of these Shah Abbas' Iran and Jahangir's India formed the most integrated bloc. Persian mercantilist policies after 1500 mixed with the more powerful laissez-faire Mughal economy and its free trade economic policy. The increasingly closer links with north, east, west and south-east Mughal India that Iran initiated were efforts at instituting an uniform credit/banking system to facilitate trade between the two empires. By contrast trade with the Uzbeg states and Rus seems less integrated from the point of view of India. Likewise with the Ottoman Empire; but here strong religious ties, reinforced by the regular Haj sailings to Mecca from Akbar's time, constituted a powerful argument for commerce. But we find no similar financial and economic policies with the Ottomans as was the case with the Safavids; perhaps because here the Armenians, and not local merchants, controlled the external trade.

Indeed Safavid Persia played a key role in determining Mughal relations with the world of Islam. It certainly played a key role in determining Mughal-Ottoman relations, for it controlled the land (caravan) routes between the two empires. We have already noted the presence of South Asian merchants from as far away as Bengal present at both Hormuz and Bukhara in the fifteenth century, selling cotton textiles at local markets[846]. The Ottoman bloc, with which the Mughals had political and commercial ties, was nurtured through trade and diplomatic missions that passed mainly through Iran. In short Iran guarded the key to the trade with Ottoman Turkey and Rus while Uzbeg Turan controlled the routes to Rus.

---

[844] For more on the European view of space see Mukherjee, Rila, 2003, *Europe Transformed* and *The Lost Worlds of Europe*, Kolkata, both from Progressive Publishers.

[845] Dale, Stephen, F., 1994, *Indian Merchants and Eurasian Trade 1600–1750*, Cambridge University Press: 5, 7.

[846] As before. See the f.n. for Anthony Jenkinson.

The Mughals, the Safavids and the Ottomans established an effective pax Islamica through the traditional trading states of Asia. From the sixteenth century the rulers of these three dynasties implemented political and economic policies designed to stimulate regional markets within their domains and to foster external trade. Chingiz Khan had welcomed caravans between countries as a measure of the wealth of nations. Heirs to that tradition, the Mughals, along with their political counterparts in Ottoman Turkey, Uzbeg Turan and Safavid Iran, envisioned a similar world economy. Akbar himself built a chain of caravanserais along the Attock-Kabul route after the border with Turan had been made secure after 1587. For the first time ever the Khyber Pass became the most important conduit between north-west India and Kabul; similar measures were undertaken on the south-western routes to Afghanistan after the conquest of Sind in 1590. Additional bridges and caravanserais were built along the Khyber route by Shah Jahan.

Indeed Safavid Basra, Baghdad and Bandar Abbas, Turan Bukhara, Herat and Samarkhand, Rus Astrakhan and Kazan were integrated into the Mughal world through Thatta (Lahori Bandar), Lahore and Agra. In the Ottoman world Damascus and Mecca were important market towns as well as civilisational sites which Indian merchants had penetrated. The three most famous Ottoman ports were Istanbul, Cairo and Aleppo; in the last Tavernier noted the presence of Indians at the end of the seventeenth century. His citing of the commerce of the Turks, Persians and Indians at Aleppo in the same breath indicates that he regarded them as part of the same world economy[847]. There can be no doubt therefore that a mighty regional economy had come into being in the seventeenth century.

It is therefore a contention that the Mughals were not anti-trade as has been asummed; it was just that they were inclined to leave the seas more open for what they considered to be *parvenu* merchants while concentrating on the ancient and lucrative (and prestigious!) caravan trade that spanned the Mongol heartlands and Turan and that which they conducted with Iran and Rus through the riverine port of Thatta (Sind). It was in this region (Sind) that the key to the South Asian commercial economy of the early medieval period lay: the port of Lahori Bandar connected to its hinterland of Multan by the Indus.

The region of Sind, the town of Multan and the port of Lahori Bandar are neglected in historical writings on 'Asian Trade' in South

[847] Tavernier, Jean-Baptiste, (Intr). Yerasimos, S., 1981, *Les Six Voyages en Turquie et en Perse*, I, Paris, Maspero: 213.

Asia. While Lahori Bandar features in A.H. Dani's *Thatta: A District in Sindh* and J.N. Sarkar's *History Of Aurangzeb* within the parameters of a regional political and economic history, this port is treated as incidental to the trade history of South Asia. One exception is Stephen Frederic Dale whose *Indian Merchants and Eurasian Trade 1600–1750* focusses on this port, and the economies radiating from it, in great detail[848].

Lahori Bandar featured in Arab writings from the ninth century. Ibn Khurdadbih, Ibn Hauqal, al-Biruni, al-Idrisi and Ibn Batuta have left us accounts of the flourishing trade carried on from this port[849]. Indeed we can say that Lahori Bandar was the most famous port of the Delhi sultans; it directly faced Hormuz for it lay at the mouth of the Arabian Sea and the Persian Gulf. While Thatta, the riverine port, was the starting point for the despatch of goods to Turan, Rus or Ottoman lands, Lahori Bandar was the natural, and strategic, choice for trade with the ports of the Gulf. The advantage of the Thatta/Lahori Bandar routes was that riverine and sea routes were faster, cheaper and safer. Hence, the prominence of Lahori Bandar.

The importance of Lahori Bandar can be gauged further when we remember that although the commerce with the Turan/Ottoman domains yielded necessary staples, the trade with the Gulf had a different dimension given the religious significance of the area, its proximity to Mecca and the value that the Mughals placed on diplomatic and religious missions with Safavid Iran. In addition, the trade of the Gulf was a high-value luxury trade; of prancing horses and lustrous pearls, indeed the stuff of fables. Received historiography tells us that Surat was the most important port of the Mughal, we should note that this importance derived primarily from Surat's trade with the Gulf. In this Lahori Bandar was the precursor of Surat (and indeed of other western ports such as Cambay and Diu). Lahori Bandar's continuing importance can be judged by the fact that Aurangzeb tried to revive it at the end of the seventeenth century; an indication that the last grand Mughal was trying to keep alive the heritage of the trans-continental caravan trade and also, possibly, to escape the English stranglehold at the port of Surat.

Until the rise of Surat from the 1620s Lahori Bandar was the only great Mughal port in the west other than Cambay. It was deemed to carry the greatest amount of traffic in the Indies. Whittington visited it in the early part of that century when the Portuguese presence was powerful in

848 See also Kevran 1999 further on.

849 In Elliot and Dowson, V.1.

that port and left us an account of his experiences at that port[850]. Tavernier, Thevenot and Manucci left accounts of its flourishing commerce and its position as the gateway to the Persian Gulf. The existence of caravan (3000 camel loads passed a year in the early sixteenth century and more later between the Mughal dominions and the other two empires), riverine (this took four to five months by barge from Lahore to Ispahan via the Indus and the Arabian Sea and was very economical), and sea routes (this was the fastest taking two to three weeks from Lahori Bandar to Bandar Abbas with the north-east monsoon from December to March) in this part of the Mughal empire brought down costs and made for a speedy despatch of goods to Iran and Turan and subsequently to Rus in the north and the Ottoman empire to the west. Moreover the interchangeability of sea and land routes made commerce less of a headache in these parts. Last but not least, goods supplied from Multan, which was itself a great production centre of cottons and some raw silk as well as an important commercial and political centre throughout medieval times, augmented the freight in both land and sea trade and cut down transhipment costs of goods from other parts of the Mughal empire. Multani goods were prominent in the external trade that we just described; moreover the advantage of having such a production centre at the confluence of land, river and sea routes (Multan is located at the crossroads of the overland and riverine/sea routes that connected north India with Afghanistan, Iran and the Arabian Sea and retained much of its importance even after the opening of the Khyber Pass) meant that Multani goods could provide additional freight if the distant dominions of the Mughal in the east or south were racked by warfare and were therefore unable to despatch goods to Thatta or Lahori Bandar.

We have noted that because Lahori Bandar faced the Persian Gulf it was the prime conduit of trade between the Mughals and the Safavids. A conjuncture of commercial and strategic factors in the Indian Ocean and in Sind made the Mughal trade with Safavid Persia profitable. Jean Aubin points to the simultaneous disappearance of the Red Sea Karimi group of merchants (which controlled the spice trade between Mamluk Egypt and Calicut) and the Persian Gulf Kazaruni merchants (who controlled the trade between the Ottoman Empire and the East) by early

[850] Foster, W., 1921, 1985, *Early Travels in India*, Reprint, Oriental Books Corporation, New Delhi: 208–209, 212, 217–218 (Nicholas Whittington 1612–16). 'As regards Sind…any other city does not have…in India a more superior commercial activity than that of Thatta and its principal port Lowri Bandar three days of journey from there; a good harbour at the mouth of the river.'

sixteenth century[851]. The Kazaruni had established a trading zone based on caravanserais and an uniform banking system running from Ottoman Turkey to Asia. The Shi'ite persecution of the Sunni Kazarunis by Shah Ismael of Iran in 1504 destroyed this network. The commerce between Ottoman Turkey and Iran now passed into the hands of the Armenians; and flourished more so after the Armenians were established at New Julfa by Shah Abbas after 1500. Persian merchant-adventurers now moved into India; witness the Nematollah order which counted as their disciple Ahmad Shah Bahmani in the Dakhin[852]. This Persian diaspora then moved eastwards towards Bengal, Arakan and Siam[853].

But the original Kazaruni trading and financial network was taken over by the Safavids and the Mughals who now integrated the two empires into a strong regional economy. Persian caravan convoys sometimes joined Indian ones[854]. For reasons of unstable politics and tribalism, Persian merchants were unable to form great urban concentrations as was the case in Ottoman Turkey and India. Persian merchants operated in the smaller towns of north-west Iran, around the sericultures of Gilan. In Iran the towns of Herat, Shiraz and Tabriz always played an inferior role compared to the Ottoman towns of Aleppo, Damascus, Cairo and Mecca or the Indian centres of Agra, Lahore and Multan. In consequence, Persian merchants concentrated on their home market; and the lucrative India-Persia trade was controlled by Indians. As early as in the fourteenth century, Barani commented on Multan's leading postion in India's external trade[855]; this pre-eminent position was maintained in the seventeenth century by Mughal traffic to Iran through Lahori Bandar (and then Surat).

The merchants who engaged in trade with Persia from Lahori Bandar and Surat in the seventeenth century were mostly Indians as opposed to the Mughal-Ottoman trade which was controlled by Armenians[856] or the Mughal-Bay of Bengal trade which was dominated by Persians[857].

851 Aubin, Jean, 1988, 'Marchands de Mer Rouge et du Golfe Persique au tournant des 15e et 16e siecles' in Denys and Aubin, Jean (Eds). *Marchands et Hommes d'Affaires Asiatiques dans l'Ocean Indien et la Mer de Chine, 13e a 20e siecles*, Paris, Publications E.H.E.S.S.: 83–90.

852 *Ibid.*: 86–87.

853 See before.

854 In Dale, 1994: 55.

855 Ziauddin Barani (1357), *Tarikh-I-Firuz Shahi,* (Ed). S.A.Khan, Calcutta, Bibliotheca India, 1860–2. See also Habib, 1982, in *CEHI*, I, 'Non Agricultural Production and Urban Economy': 85.

856 Ahgassian, Michel and Kevonian, Keram, 1988, 'Le Commerce Armenien dans l'Ocean Indien aux 17e et 18e siecles' in Jean Aubin and Denys Lombard eds. 1988: 155–181.

857 See before.

But Lahori Bandar's greatest days were over by the seventeenth century. After the Portuguese attack on the port, the revenue of the region (Sind, Multan, Thatta) dwindled to 40 00 00 000 dams[858]. At the turn of the eighteenth century the revenues of the region dwindled further to 24 53 18 575 dams[859]. Thatta, the district where Lahori Bandar was situated, accounted for only 5 74 98 690 dams.

Yet even at this late time Lahori Bandar was emblematic of wealth and opulence to Mughal political economy. Distances in the Mughal Empire were given with Lahori Bandar as the westernmost point: 'The length of the daily increasing empire, from the port of Lahori, province of Thatta, to the *thana* of Bindasar in Bengal is 994 royal *kos*, 1740 common *kos*', ran Bakhtawar Khan's *Mira't-i-Alam*[860]. Even Alexander Hamilton who visited Lahori Bandar at the turn of the eighteenth century and left us a largely negative impression of the port (political uncertainty, robberies, houses built of straw and mud etc.) spoke of Thatta still being a very large emporium of all goods, and how the area was connected by the Indus to Kashmir, through the west to Kabul and by the east to Lahore and Multan: 'And indeed in all my travels I never saw better conveniences for travel by Water'[861].

There was a temporary revival of Asian traffic in 1650 when Oman expelled the Portuguese from the Persian Gulf region, attacked Pemba and Zanzibar in 1652 and took Mombasa in 1696. There was a corresponding revival in trade between the Persian Gulf, East Africa and South Asia at the end of the seventeenth century[862] and we may relate this trade revival with the Mughal desire to revive Lahori Bandar as a Mughal port at the same time. But it was then too late. At the end of the seventeenth century, in 1698, when two great sedentary empires, Russia and China converged at Turkestan and merchants began to exchange goods directly, the great caravan route that ran through this region and 'fed' the port of Lahori Bandar, broke down. Merchants of the two empires became more interested in internal trade. For example the merchants of Bukhara now became active in the trade of the Russian Empire.

---

858 Muhammad Sharif Hanafi's *Maja'lisu-s-Salatin* written during Shah Jahan's reign and printed in Elliot and Dowson V. 7 op. cit.

859 Bakhtawar Khan's *Mira't-i-Alam* written during Aurangzeb's reign in *Ibid.*

860 *Ibid.*: 162–3.

861 Hamilton, Alexander, *A New Account of the East Indies*, V.1 London, MD CC XLIVII: 124.

862 Lapidus 1988: 530.

Yet Lahori Bandar continued to be emblematic of a glorious past. As late as in 1739 Nadir Shah's treaty with the Mughals attest to the importance of Lahori Bandar to the empire[863]:

> The fortress and the city of Lahori Bandar as also those lying in the vicinity of it to the east of the river Attock, the waters of Sind and the Nala Sankra will belong as in the past to the empire of Hindustan.

Bengal had no such comparable port. At the height of the first Islamic world economy, when Lahori Bandar controlled all traffic from the west, we have no mention of a similar port dominating traffic from the east[864], with the exception of Chattagram. But Chattagram was frequently lost to Bengal. Samandar could well have been such a port, but its location is yet to be identified conclusively, and anyway it did not have an enduring presence through centuries as Lahori Bandar.

Moreover, no Bengal port had such a vital trading network radiating from it as Lahori Bandar. We have already seen from the *Ain-i-Akbari* that maritime wages in Bengal were lower than on the west coast. These wages were determined by the cost of living at the port itself as well as the profitability of the commercial networks that radiated from it. The length of the sea voyage was also a factor in determining wages. We have seen that vessels from the Bengal ports conducted short voyages.

Finally we can only say that it was an accident of history that the merger of the Ganga with the Padma (and the linking of the eastern and western parts of Bengal) happened at the same time that Bengal was absorbed into one of the largest imperial systems to be seen in South Asia. From then on Bengal's primate economic zone–the east–was destined to be a hinterland to western Bengal–which became in its turn a zone of marginal importance to the Mughal economy as a whole.

When the English achieved primacy in Nawabi Bengal, in a state that had become a shadow of its former self, the last nawabs of Bengal carried on the Mughal tradition of hospitability to traders. The man who would

---

863 In Kevran, Monique, 1999, 'Multiple Ports at the Mouth of the River Indus: Barbarike, Deb, Daybul, Lahori Bandar, Diul Sinde' in Ray, Himanshu Prabha ed. *Archaeology of Seafaring: The Indian Ocean in the Ancient Period*, New Delhi, Pragati Publications: 70–153. See p. 98.

864 See the debate on the port of Samandar that follows later.

be known to students of imperial history as Clive of India was still welcomed at the court of Murshidabad, but with a new name. Henceforth, he was to be known as Sabut Jang[865]. In the perception of the nawabs, Plassey had changed nothing; Clive the Conqueror was still Clive the Trader, a man to be welcomed and cherished for the manifold riches his nation brought into Bengal. Clive was thus absorbed into Mughal court etiquette as an honoured courtier. And this speaks eloquently of the commercial world of the Mughal; the fact that hegemony at sea was not perceived as a threat. Instead of the merchant capturing the state, the state had absorbed the merchant.

[865] See Khan, Abdul Majed, 1969, *The Transition in Bengal 1756–1775: A Study of Saiyid Muhammad Reya Khan*, Cambridge University Press for names given to other 'favourites'.

7

Unities of Time and Space in Bengal

'The ground is rich in everything although the waters are bad because the area is entirely covered in swampland. Very long crescent shaped lakes stretch between the palm groves, and all along the shores of these lakes there are houses whose doors open onto the water' Bouchon, Genevieve and Thomaz, Luis Filipe, '*Voyage dans les deltas du Gange et de l'Irraoaddy 1521*', Fondation Calouste Gulbenkian, Paris, 1988: 316)

Unities of Time and Space: The Place of Bengal in the History of South Asia

This passage evokes the sense of a littoral land, something we discussed right at the beginning. A land of marshes, salt seas and swamps; Bengal's topography is unique in South Asia. We have already underlined the distinctiveness of her landscape.

We examined the place of Bengal within the overall debate on the eighteenth century in South Asia, and noted that the eighteenth century debate has concerned itself mainly with territorial South Asia. While Bengal's primacy in the eighteenth century is unquestioned readings of the commercial history of Bengal in earlier periods suggest a different engagement with the major trade networks emanating from the ancient period.

How then, did Bengal achieve this pre-eminent economic postion in the eighteenth century? Part of this has already been answered. It was its cheap prices and lack of control over its own resources. But what facilitated the entry of the Europeans into Bengal? I have argued that, one, it was the very marginality of Bengal in the greater Indian Ocean trade, and two, its increasingly subordinate position within the greater Mughal commercial networks from the seventeenth century onwards that ended the commercial vitality of Bengal even within the Bay of Bengal from this time.

We have already seen that within the world of the Bay of Bengal trade, Bengal had manifested considerable commercial vitality between the fourth to the fifteenth centuries. This commercial vitality was visible in the east (Dhaka/Chattagram) and in the centre (the deltaic ports of Sripur, Bakla, Chandikan/Sagar and Sandwip) and initially concerned the Buddhist lands to the north and east of Bengal. Later the trading empires of the Maghreb, of South East Asia and of China[866] became part of this network. At the end of the sixteenth century this vitality was cut short. Bengal therefore occupied a more important position in the first Islamic network than in the second one.

We saw that in the sixteenth century the political and economic centre of Bengal swung towards the west. With the westward shift to Saptagram under the Husain Shahis the commercial vitality of the east was killed to a great extent. This westward shift of the sixteenth century has to be seen in the light of political and economic decline in the Maghreb-Red Sea-Delhi-Bengal-China world; what is called the first Islamic trading network. By the next century the great Islamic empires of the Ottomans, the Safavids, the Mughals and the Uzbegs comprised an even greater Islamic commercial network; what is referred to as the second Islamic commercial network. Bengal now occupied a subordinate position within this network. The Coromandel emerged as the economic motor in the Bay world of South Asia from this time.

The secondary position of Bengal from the seventeenth century has to be regarded not merely in terms of the westward shift but also in terms of the instability in the Bay world from the sixteenth century. The Arakanese and Portuguese presence in Bengal and in the trade of the Bay were major

[866] Lombard, Maurice, 1971, *l'Islam dans sa Premiere Grandeur, VIIIe-XIe siecle*, Paris, Flammarion: 19. In English as *The Golden Age Of Islam*, (Tr). J. Spencer, Amsterdam, 1975 . Ahmad, S. Maqbul, 1989, *Arabic Classical Accounts of India and China*, Indian Institute for Advanced Study, Shimla.Ibn Batuta, *Voyages*, II, Paris, Maspero, 1982 (as before), Defremery, C. and Sanguinetti, B.R. (trs). See the introduction and notes of Stephane Yerasimos. See also Lombard, Denys, 1990, for an excellent interpretation of al-Idrisi's accounts of India and China and of Ibn Batuta's travels in *Le Carrefour Javanais*, II, Les Reseaux Asiatiques. All these works give us an excellent idea of the early Islamic network that stretched from China to North Africa.

factors here. Moreover, the practical closure of the north Bay commercial world (the disturbances in Arakan, Pegu and Siam, the withdrawal of the Chinese and the practical eviction of the Portuguese) signalled the end of the Arakan-Siam-China trade on which Bengal depended.

Third, the secondary position of Bengal in South Asian trade networks can also be seen by the fact that from this time Bengal became largely an area of raw and finished materials for the Mughal world. This becomes apparent if we study the revenue figures for the sixteenth, seventeenth and eighteenth centuries in Table 7.1.

Table 7.1 Revenue figures (in *dams*) for Mughal India and Bengal: sixteenth to eighteenth Centuries

Provinces or Subahs	*Ain-i-Akbari* by Abul Fazl (Akbar's regin)[867]	*Maja'lisu-s Salatin* by Muhammad (Shah Jahan's region)[868]	*Mira't-Alam* by Bakhtawar Khan (Aurangzeb's regin)[869]
Delhi	60 16 15 555	65 61 00 000	Not available
Agra	54 62 50 304	82 25 00 000	1 05 17 09 283
Lahore	55 94 58 423	82 50 00 000	90 70 16 125
Kabul	80 507 465 of which Kashmir accounts for 62 113 040.5 *dams*. That is Kabul accounts for 18000000 *dams* + approximately	25 00 00 000	15 76 25 380
Dakhin	Not Available	28 35 00 000	Not Available
Khandesh Berar	45 52 94 232 (Khandesh) + 64 26 03 272 (Berar) =1 09 78 97 504	87 32 00 000	Not Available

[867] From *Ain-i-Akbari*, Tr.Col.H.S. Jarrett and forward by Sir J.N. Sarkar, First ed. 1891, second ed (by J.N.Sarkar) 1949. Reprint 1988, New Delhi, Crown Publications, V. 2.

[868] Elliot and Dowson,V.7, L.P.P. Reprint, New Delhi, 1990.

[869] *Ibid.*

Malwa	24 06 95 052	28 00 00 000	42 54 76 670
Gujarat	43 68 22 301	50 64 00 000	Not Available
Bihar	22 19 19 404.5	31 27 00 000	Not Available
Oudh	20 17 58 172	23 22 00 000	32 00 72 193
Ajmer	28 84 01 557	42 05 00 000	63 68 94 882
Allahabad	21 14 17 819	30 70 00 000	43 66 88 072
Sindh, Multan, Thatta (Including Lahori Bandar)	15 14 03 619 (only Multan)	40 00 00 000	24 53 18 575 of which Thatta accounts for 5 74 98 690
Bengal	59 84 59 319	50 00 00 000	52 37 39 110

For the first period, that is between the sixteenth to the seventeenth centuries (between Akbar's and Shah Jahan's reign), the provinces that show a steady rise in revenue assessment are, in descending order of importance: Agra, Lahore, Ajmer, Bihar, Allahabad and Gujarat. More important, the decrease in revenue from Khandesh/Berar is very apparent.

In the seventeenth to the eighteenth centuries the two provinces that show the maximum increase in revenue were Malwa and Ajmer; two provinces that show the most decline are, not surprisingly, Kabul and Sindh. In fact Kabul's figures indicate the area's decay except during the reign of Shah Jahan when the Mughal-Uzbeg trade was at its height. Likewise Lahori Bandar remained important during Shah Jahan's time but during Aurangzeb's reign the decrease in revenue from this area is striking and is a proof that all traffic on the west coast was going through Surat.

For all three centuries taken together the *subahs* that show a steady rise in a descending order of importance are: Agra at number one, then Lahore, Ajmer, Allahabad, Malwa and Oudh. Bengal shows a decline during all three centuries, despite a very minor recovery at the end of the seventeenth-beginning of the eighteenth century.

Granted that these figures are approximate, and that statistical data is always suspect, the figures for Bengal show nevertheless that first, agricultural growth was largely static for Bengal for the period from the sixteenth to the eighteenth centuries and two, that Bengal's projected revenue was in any case much lower than that of the other subahs in the seventeenth-early eighteenth century, that is, during the reigns of Shah Jahan and Aurangzeb.

But more important, the revenue for Bengal at the time of Akbar, that is at the time of its incorporation into the Mughal economy, was high in comparison to those for other *subahs.* Bengal was truly a land of riches for the Mughal at this time. In descending order, the revenue assessment during Akbar's reign stood at 60 crore dams plus for Delhi, 59 plus for Bengal, 55 plus for Lahore, 54 plus for Agra and 43 plus for Gujarat. These figures may have also contributed to the notion of the 'primacy' of Bengal as late as in the seventeenth and eighteenth centuries.

But this was an abortive promise and this growth could not sustain itself in the following centuries. The *subahs* that registered much lower revenue demands in Akbar's time (Ajmer at 28 crore *dams* plus, Malwa at 24 plus, Bihar at 22 plus, Allahabad at 21 plus and Oudh at 20 plus), experienced steadier growth, although only Ajmer surpassed Bengal at 63 plus in Aurangzeb's time. Agra maintained its lead from Akbar's time and registered 1 05 17 09 283 *dams* at the time of Aurangzeb's reign, almost double that of Bengal.

In the sixteenth century, when Bengal was conquered by the Mughals, it was one of the richest provinces in the land. But from the seventeenth century Bengal entered into a dependent relationship with the Mughal at Agra. The *subah* now became a raw material and agricultural cash crop supplier for the Mughal; this factor accounted for its still high revenue assessment at 50 crore dams. Bengal agricultural produce fed other, and deficit, parts of the Mughal's empire throughout the seventeenth century. Sugar, and not textiles, were shipped from Bengal as freight to Surat. Bengal had become a land of marginal economic importance for Mughal trade, but it now acquired a new importance in the eighteenth century. Once trade declined in the western Indian Ocean, Bengal sugar and Bengal grains were used to provision the internal market of the Mughal. The 'primacy' of Bengal, then, was not so much in trade, but in supplying regions with deficit production.

The point of issue here is of course how we view a region and a regional economy. Between the thirteenth and eighteenth centuries eight regional economies were visible. Eight mutually overlapping regional ellipses were regions centred on Europe, the Mediterranean, the Red Sea, the Persian Gulf, the Arabian Sea, the Bay of Bengal, the South China sea and Inner Asia. Despite the addition of an Atlantic ellipse in the sixteenth century these regions continued to play major, although not equal, roles in world trade until the eighteenth century.

Within these eight (or nine) regional economies the role of the Asian economies, especially that of China, was spectacular. China's great productivity in agriculture, industry, and water transport was reflected in her favourable balance of trade despite a chronic shortage of silver. Other than China, India was also central to the world economy. Because, if we visualise China's position in the world in terms of concentric circles, China would be at the centre, Japan, Korea, Central and South East Asia in the next circle and South Asia in the third circle. We have already seen that Bengal lay to one side of the South Asian economy centred on the western Indian Ocean. It also occupied a marginal position in the Sinic economy centred on the South China Sea and partially on the Bay of Bengal. So, within South Asia, Bengal would form a very small (in terms of importance) regional economy. And the produce of this regional economy was used by the Mughal to supply the economies centred on the Red Sea and the Persian Gulf. Once trade tapered off in the Arabian Sea the agricultural produce of Bengal supplied the marts of South Asia.

Developments in the seventeenth century were, therefore, crucial for the emergence of a new dependent Bengal. Events on land do not completely explain this new aspect of Bengal. Therefore, the first point I would make in this section is the suggestion that we move the eighteenth century debate away from territorial South Asia and into the greater world of the Indian Ocean states. This shift will yield a different picture for Bengal.

The second point that I make is that the Husain Shahis initiated a radical break in the trading world of the Bay of Bengal which the Mughals furthered (by hijacking the Bay's vibrant commercial networks into their westward trade through Surat). We have, in the preceding pages traced the reasons why they did so. The European companies, then, may not have been the first to do so in the seventeenth century; the process may already have been initiated earlier.

The third point elaborated in this volume is the suggestion that we view the lineages of the eighteenth century break within the greater world of the Indian Ocean, and its eight seas[870]. This suggestion has of course been made earlier, as we have seen in the section on the debate on the eighteenth century, but the emphasis in this volume has been on Bengal's place in trade and politics of the eastern Indian Ocean.

One last point. We may have to revise our notions of the Portuguese impact on Bengal. However negative this may have been, the Portuguese continued the early Islamic network in the Bay for yet another century; however the disturbances of the seventeenth century put paid to that

[870] The Persian Gulf, the Red Sea, the Arabian Sea, the Bay of Bengal, the Gulf of Siam, the Straits of Malacca, the Java Sea and the China Seas are the major divisions.

network once and for all. With the demise of the early Islamic network ended Bengal's median position in the Bay commerce.

Unities of Time and Space: The Place of Bengal in the World of the Indian Ocean

When we discussed the eighteenth century in Bengal from the point of view of South Asian history we suffered from two conceptual limitations. We examined only our own chronological spans and areas of interest. The limitations of this vision has been addressed throughout this volume.

As South Asian historians we seem also more prone to comparing our experiences with Europe rather than with other regions of Asia. In this volume an attempt has been made to redress this imbalance by moving the discussion on Bengal away from the territorial identity of the middle Gangetic plain and re-orienting it more towards the countries of the northern Bay of Bengal. By doing so I hoped to show that the mercantile experience of Bengal was not unique; there was a structural totality of economic and social life specific to the eastern Indian Ocean world that we often ignore[871].

Moreover the discussions in the foregoing pages show that Bengal's contribution to the main streams of South Asian history was minimal. If we accept then that Bengal participated more in the winds of change blowing in from the Bay of Bengal let us now relocate ourselves and look at Bengal from the perspective of the Indian Ocean.

But here too one is in for a surprise. Bengal occupied a very secondary position, both chronologically and locationally, in the Indian Ocean world. As with its engagement with the territorial history of South Asia here too the rhythm of its lifestyle, the cadence of its production, the tempo of its history, was equally trivial to the pulse of the Indian Ocean world.

The Indian Ocean world was not just one made up of eight seas. It was a terrestrial world made up of cultures and empires spanning Asia, Africa, the Middle East, and the Mediterranean. In this terrestrial world of the Indian Ocean, of which Bengal is a part, there are certain dates that impose a unity in terms of historical time. For historians accustomed to working with linear time the following dates share a common attribute: at first sight they appear random but actually have the capacity to signal long term movements lasting centuries.

---

[871] Chaudhuri, K.N., 1990: 33. Also see the section Introducing Bengal.

The most explosive event in the history of the Indian Ocean was the birth of Islam and its expansion until 1750. Within this broad span from 630 to 1750 three sub-sets of waves that influenced Asian history can be perceived: the unification of China by the Tangs in 618 and the expansion of Chinese civilisation into Central and South East Asia, the southward, eastward and westward migration of nomadic steppes people in the shape of the Turks, Mongols, Mughals and Manchus lasting from the thirteenth to the seventeenth centuries and their transformation into a sedentary culture that gave birth to great empires, and finally the eruption of Europeans into Asian waters from the fifteenth century that subsequently paved the way for colonialism. The first two of these, we have seen, impacted on Bengal very marginally; it is then all the more surprising that the last, English rule in South Asia, was visible first in Bengal.

Let us now look at important dates in the history of the Indian Ocean.

The first millennium saw the birth and putsch of Islam. Significant dates are 641 AD, the capture of Alexandria by the Arabs; 712 AD, the Islamic conquest of Sind; 749 AD, the Abbassid revolution in Iraq; 750 AD, fall of Umayyad Damascus to the Abbassids; 960 AD, the accession of the Songs in China; 969 AD, the Fatimid conquest of Egypt; 973 AD, the birth of Cairo 985 AD the rise of cholas and 1071 AD, fall of Jerusalem to the Seljuk Turks. Bengal is untouched by these events. Moreover Bengal's history in the first millennium is shrouded in obscurity. We can therefore say that no such momentous dates are available for Bengal.

The second millennium saw the further expansion of Islam but also the Mongol challenge to Islamic lands : Islam enters into India in 1192; during 1203-1206, the Delhi and Bengal Sultanates are established in South Asia; there is a setback for Islam when Baghdad is sacked by the Mongols in 1258; in 1279, the Mongols conquer China; 1368 sees the accession of the Mings in China; in 1398, Delhi is attacked by Taimur; in 1453, Constantinople is taken by the Turks and renamed Istanbul–this ends the brilliant one thousand year old Byzantine civilisation; in 1492, Islam is finally displaced from Iberia after over 700 years of dominance and there is a Muslim exodus eastwards to Istanbul; 1492, heralds the 'discovery' of America which leads in turn to the exploration of the Pacific upto China, Japan and the Phillipines and the circumnavigation of the world; in 1498, the Portuguese, in the shape of Vasco da Gama, arrive at Calicut and this heralds a violent transformation of the Indian Ocean;

in 1526, the Mughals arrive in North India; in 1644, the Mings are overthrown by the Manchus in China; in 1722, the Safavids fall in Iran; and in 1739, Delhi is sacked by Nadir Shah. Note that Bengal remains aloof from these key dates in Asian history until 1576 (when the Mughals conquer a part of Bengal) and 1757, when we see the rise of British power in Bengal. Bengal, therefore, enters into the main currents of history only in the last two hundred years of this time line–i.e. from 1576 to 1757.

Unities of Time and Space: The Place of Bengal in the Terrestrial World of the Indian Ocean

The Indian Ocean is as we just noted, one ocean comprising eight seas. It comprised the Persian Gulf, the Red Sea, the Arabian Sea, the Bay of Bengal, the Straits of Malacca, the Gulf of Siam, the Java Seas and the South China Sea. Dates in this maritime (as opposed to the terrestrial) world of the Indian Ocean are also seemingly random but have a similar long term significance. Here, too, the position of Bengal in the overall scheme of things is marginal at best. In the ancient world Roman trade concentrated on the west coast of India. The ports of Barygaza and Sopara in western India feature in the manuals of Roman trade with India. Bengal ports did not participate directly in Roman trade. The classical accounts of Roman trade with India–*Periplus Maris Erythraei*, Strabo's *Geography*, Pliny's *Natural History* and Ptolemy's *Geography* refer to ports and routes in western India[872]. In the period of Buddhism received history tells us that it was the ports of the Coromandel, and not Bengal, that dominated the trade of the Bay. Bengal occupied a sub-stratum in the Buddhist north Bay of Bengal network[873].

After Islam irrupted into Asian waters the commercial arc ran from Zaitun in the east to Sofala, Kilwa, and Zanzibar in the west. Within this network the trading states of Mombasa, Mogadishu and Malindi had achieved great status by the end of the thirteenth century. In the period following the Mongol invasion, the economy of Asia was held together by cities such as Karakorum, Peking, Kashgar, Herat, Mashad, Tabriz, Isfahan and Astrakhan. In the later Islamic period long distance trade in the whole

---

872 F.de Romanis and A. Tchernia, (Eds). 1997, *Crossings: Early Mediterrannean Contacts with India*, New Delhi, CSH-Manohar Publication in Association with Italian Embassy Cultural Centre. See the Introduction by Romila Thapar: 11–40.

873 Ray, H.P., 1994, *The Winds of Change, Buddhism and the Maritime Links of Early South Asia*, New Delhi, OUP and Mukherjee, Rila, *Merchants and Companies in Bengal: Kasimbazar and Jugdia in the Eighteenth Century* op. cit.

of the Indian Ocean and the Mediterrannean was held together by a string of cities running from east to west: Hangchow, Canton, Malacca, Calicut, Cambay, Hormuz, Basra, Aden, Alexandria, Aleppo and Venice. No such commercial city emerged in Bengal that could feature in either of these networks.

The political world of the Indian Ocean was held together by 'primate' cities such as Peking, Delhi, Agra, Lahore, Baghdad, Damascus, Fustat-Cairo, Isfahan and Constantinople; the religious world was held together by Jerusalem, Mecca, Medina, Damascus, Baghdad, Nalanda, Varanasi and Istanbul; within the historical geography of the Mughal Empire however imperial control derived only from the inland cities of Kabul, Kandahar, Lahore, Delhi, Agra, Patna, Burhanpur and Ahmedabad. The control of these eight capital cities signified the possession of the peacock throne, the true sign of the Padshah of Hindustan.

Note that none of the cities of Bengal figure in this list of primate Mughal cities; note too that the dates of the origin of Dhaka, Patna Murshidabad and Kasimbazar–'primate' cities within Bengal–are obscure. We have yet to identify the mysterious Samandar of the early Arab accounts in Bengal. We are told for the capital of Nawabi Bengal only that Maksudabad was renamed Murshidabad by Murshid Quli Khan with the shift of the capital there; even this date, 1704/5 or 1708, is contested. Kasimbazar's origins are unclear, we know only that it was a mart town established by one Kasim Khan in the seventeenth century. The cities of the 'far east' had lost their dynamism by this time and do not merit a mention in historical annals.

Let us recapitulate some median dates in the maritime history of the Indian Ocean: in the 1420s, the inexplicable Ming abandonment of an energetic maritime policy and withdrawal from the Indian Ocean heralds a major closure of Bengal's eastern trade. This has some impact on Ilyas Shahi commercial and diplomatic policy as we have seen. In 1510, the Portuguese capture of Goa from Bijapur and in 1511 the Portuguese occupation of Malacca, herald the Portuguese domination of the Indian Ocean; in 1515, the Portuguese attempt to gain a foothold in the Western Indian Ocean by controlling Hormuz; in 1538, the Ottoman Turks secure Aden at the mouth of the Red Sea and in 1546, the Ottomans conquer Basra from the Safavids: these two dates signify Islamic domination of the Red Sea and the Persian Gulf and thereby of the Western Indian Ocean.

This Persian resurgence continues into the 1620s, with the establishment of Bandar Abbas by the Safavids in an attempt to divert trade from Portuguese

Hormuz; in 1632, the Portuguese are expelled from Hugli by the Mughals–this 'liberates' Bengal's trade to a great extent and Hugli evolves into the 'Mughal' port of Bengal; in 1641, the Portuguese are expelled from Malacca by the Dutch; in 1644, a Persian-British initiative expels the Portuguese from Hormuz; in 1650, the fall of Muscat to the Yarubis effectively ends Portuguese domination of the Indian Ocean.

Portuguese settlements in western India are now attacked: Bombay in 1661–1662, Diu in 1668 and 1676, and Bassein in 1674. In the east a similar situation prevails. There are four significant events of the early seventeenth century that impact on the world of the Bay trade: the massacre of the Portuguese by the Arakanese at Dianga in 1607 soon after the latter had thrown out the Portuguese from Chattagram, then the execution of de Brito, the 'independent' Portuguese ruler of Syriam by the Mons-Burmese in 1613, followed by the defeat of the Portuguese by the Kandy forces in Ceylon in August 1630, and finally the fall of Acheh in 1636 in the wake of Dutch conquests in the Indonesian archipelago. These dates signify the collapse of the Portuguese network of trade in the Bay of Bengal. Ashin Das Gupta comments: 'The Portuguese challenge in the eastern Indian Ocean, even in its semi-official form, was now finally over'[874].

From the second half of the seventeenth century the decay of the Indian Ocean world was visible. In the eastern Indian Ocean insecurity at sea probably resulted in the Manchu interdiction of all foreign trade in 1655. The China-Indian Ocean trade tapered off. The Bugi network of ports and merchants spanning the Java sea declined. In the western Indian Ocean the Safavids descended into decline from the late seventeenth century, and finally folded up in 1722. By the beginning of the eighteenth century the great Indian Ocean empires too were in decline. Surat crashed soon after 1700[875] and by the 1740s, in contemporary European perception, trade at Surat was deemed to have 'declined'.

There was a similar decline in inland states: Turan folded up after the death of Abd Allah in the eighteenth century. Land communications between Sindh, Kabul and the Uzbeg states deteriorated. In Ottoman and Persian lands foreign trade stagnated as a whole. In Persia political troubles were accompanied by a shrinking agricultural base. Ports in the Persian Gulf came increasingly under British and Dutch control. The Ottoman

874 *'Introduction II : The Story'* in DasGupta, Ashin and Pearson, M.N. (Eds) , 1987, *India and The Indian Ocean 1500–1800*, Delhi, Oxford University Press: 37.

875 Das Gupta, Ashin, 1979, *Indian Merchants and the Decline of Surat c. 1700–1750*, Wiesbaden, Franz Steiner Verlag and Furber, Holden, 1990, *Rival Empires of Trade in the Orient 1600–1800*, Delhi, Oxford University Press.

economic decline accelerated after 1760. More and more agricultural land, held by the elite, were declared tax exempt. The consequence was tax farming; this increased the burden on the rural poor. The result was rural-urban migration. By the end of the eighteenth century, North American cotton replaced Anatolian cotton and Carribbean coffee replaced Arabian coffee exported through Cairo.

With the decline of Surat and the uncertainities in the western Indian Ocean, Mughal trade with Persia and the Ottoman domains tapered off. East Africa was held by the Portuguese despite temporary revival in Oman. Here, too Mughal trade declined. In the east disturbances in Arakan, Ava and Pegu led to the northern Bay ports losing much of their commercial dynamism. Arakan became a rogue state and decimated most of south eastern Bengal. Chattagram was lost to the Mughals and Dhaka became the final frontier in the east. Within Mughal domains similar disturbances were noticed for the east and the south. Textile production and trade in Bengal and in the Coromandel entered a phase of crisis from this time from which they never recovered[876].

Unities of Time and Space: The Place of Bengal in the Commercial History of the Bay of Bengal

Bengal's Central Position in the Bay World Until the Mid Fifteenth Century

It is by now abundantly clear that it was the eastern part of the delta, and the ports there, that carried on the major part of Bengal's commerce. The western channel–the Bhagirathi (Hugli and the older Saraswati)–was relatively neglected; it played a subordinate role until the sixteenth century and only shot into prominence in the seventeenth century with the establishment of European settlements along its river banks. But it was this western channel (and not the eastern rivers of the Padma and the Meghna) that determined Bengal's prominent place in the commercial annals of eighteenth century South Asia.

Within this spectrum of 'grand' dates mentioned earlier there are some lesser dates and phases that give us some pointers into the trading world of the Bay of Bengal. We find, not surprisingly, that coastal southeastern Bengal–and not the inland state of Gaur, plays a focal role within this substrata of dates, ruled mostly through its interactions with the northern Bay world via the Pyus of Arakan/Central Burma from the

876 Mukherjee, Rila, 1990–1991 and 1994. Also in Frank, A.G., *ReOrient* op.cit: 268.

eighth century (see the mention of Beikthano earlier). This was the Buddhist world, over which Bengal steadily expanded her influence.

In the period from the fourth to the seventh century the Buddhist Chandra dynasty ruled in both southeastern Bengal and Arakan. We do not know much about the early Chandras, but it seems that they might have continued to rule in Bengal even after the Arakan branch died out. For there was also a later Chandra dynasty in Bengal in the tenth and the eleventh centuries. Set against the backdrop of the early medieval trade revolution in the Bay of Bengal the rule of the Chandras from Vikrampur, with their commercial interests and their Arakanese lineage, acquires a new significance for the mercantile history of Bengal.

Nor was Bengal's influence confined to Arakan. Around the middle of the ninth century a Srivijaya emperor asked Devapala's permission to establish a monastery for Javanese students at Nalanda[877].

By the tenth century a north east (probably from Sylhet) *prakrit-nagari* style coin circulated in the Java Seas when the kingdom of Mataram adopted this as a medium of trade. Mataram was the first state in South East Asia to produce a standardised indigenous system of coinage. Note that Sylhet lay within Pundravardhana, an area that was known for trade with the Buddhist world from early times. It is particularly significant that Mataram adopted this style and not the pallava style *kawi* script that circulated in the Bay from the Coromandel region. Christie comments that[878]:

> the script used on these coins was the *nagari* script that was just coming into use in northeast India during the eighth century. The use of *nagari* script on Javanese coins is interesting, particularly given that the fact that the script was otherwise rarely used in Java, the mainstream *kawi* script of the island having been developed out of the South Indian Pallava script.

As Mataram was an important commercial power at this time, this type of 'sandalwood flower' coin became a trade coin in the eastern Indian Ocean during the tenth and eleventh centuries. Although received history tells us that the Coromandel-South East Asia commercial link was more vibrant, the circulation of Bengal *nagari* coins in South East Asia is significant.

What was the areal extent of this circulation? Christie adds[879]:

---

877 Nalanda copper plate of 849 AD. The Srivijaya king was Balaputradeva (Mookerji, R.K., 1962: 123).

878 Christie, 1999: 230.

879 Christie, 1999: 222–223.

> By the late ninth century, the state of Mataram had expanded eastwards…As Mataram expanded, its coinage was carried eastwards…this process of annexing ports continued…As the Asian trade boom gathered pace in the tenth century…Mataram's regional economic influence grew. Mataram played a key role in moulding maritime Southeast Asia's shared economic culture…By this time, coins derived from both the gold and silver coinages of Mataram and based on the same system of weights and values were beginning to be minted across the maritime region, from Sumatra…in the west, to Bali in the east, and…Luzon in the north….Before the end of the eleventh century…trade in the South China Sea appears to have been dominated by Southeast Asian shipping, much of it from Java and Srivijaya.

The Chandras seem to have benefited from this new explosion of eastern trade from the tenth century. The Chandras' issue of silver coins is testimony to their commercial strength. This is significant for this happenened at a time when the more 'regional' Palas in the west had no currency and little trade. The commercial activities of the kings based at Dhaka-Vikrampur furthered new commercial trends. At a time when the economy of Gaur was land-based and there was a shrinking of coinage, coins found in this coastal area indicate that commerce was flourishing in the eastern part of Bengal. This trade was carried by the ports in the deltaic region of Bengal. But in the eleventh century this world came under pressure.

Mataram now challenged Srivijaya's commercial stranglehold in the Malacca Straits. In 1006 the Sailendras of Srivijaya successfully destroyed this state which was challenging its maritime hegemony. The Chinese refused to support them against Srivijaya. But soon after, in 1025, the Cholas attacked Srivijaya[880]. A Chola general also invaded Bengal and possibly defeated the last Chandra king. With the decline of Mataram and Srivijaya and the rise of Chola power in the eastern Indian Ocean, a radical reorganisation of politics and trade now took place in this region. Bengal did not participate in the politics of this new maritime world.

After the eleventh century reshuffle, Mongol invasions in the thirteenth century resulted in new commercial configurations in the Bay world.

[880] Quayle, Robina G., 1966, *Eastern Civilisations*, New York, Meredith/Appleton-Century-Crofts: 370–1.

First, the diminution of Srivijaya authority in the Malay Peninsula when, in 1286, the new Singhasari rulers of Java no longer acknowledged Srivijaya's authority, meant that smaller trading empires could now bypass the Srivijaya stranglehold in the Straits of Malacca and directly trade eastwards. Second, Srivijaya's decline and the establishment of Majapahit in Java in 1293, furthered this trend and third, the disintegration of Pagan and its fragmentation into Ava and Pegu meant that Arakan now emerged as a fully independent force. All three events had considerable impact on southeastern Bengal.

But from the twelfth century onwards Bengal concentrated increasingly on internal affairs. She refrained from politics in the north Bay and worked on reestablishing her ties with Arakan. Until the thirteenth century this took place through Pagan, and after the fall of Pagan, continued independently. Although Arakan turned into a terror for Bengal in late medieval times, initially the Arakan-Bengal interaction was beneficial for Bengal. But in the late medieval period this interaction with Arakan was not always fortuitious; and Bengal-Arakan relations deteriorated after the sixteenth century. Locked into the power struggles of Upper and Lower Burma the Arakanese frequently expanded their dominions north towards Tripura or west towards Bengal in the sixteenth and seventeenth centuries, as we have already seen[881].

The Delta Ports of Bengal as Successors of the Ancient Bay World

The ports participating in the Bay commerce were the deltaic port towns which really flowered in early medieval Bengal. It is by now certain that these towns arose as a result of the early medieval trade revolution in the Bay of Bengal, but Bakla was under Chandra control and known as Chandradwip even earlier. These deltaic towns experienced further growth during the Ilyas Shahi reign in Bengal of the fourteenth and the fifteenth century. By the sixteenth century they had evolved into distinct political entities occupying the middle ground between the polities of Gaur and Bangalah. The rulers of the delta towns employed more and more Portuguese in their armies and navies and sought to lay the foundations

---

[881] See Duarte Barbosa *A Description of the Coasts of East Africa and Malabar in the Beginningof the Sixteenth Century*, Tr. Henry E.J. Stanley, London, Hakluyt Society, M D CCC LXVI: 181 for the sixteenth century power struggles between Arakan and Burma and *Baharistan-I-Ghaybi* for Arakan-Burma relations in the seventeenth century.

of their rule on a combination of political expediency, naval strength and commercial acumen. We saw in the section Maritime Cities, Harbours and Ports how these ports constantly jockeyed for favourable terms of trade, how they attempted to draw in foreign trade at their ports and thereby secure trading privileges to both the eastern and western Indian Oceans.

The market and port towns of Bakla, Chandikan or Sagor, Sandwip and Sripur became bases of autonomous chiefs, known as the *baro bhuiyas*, who offered resistance to the Mughals at the beginning of the seventeenth century. As they were well known market and port towns, and also known as naval centres, lying at the heart of celebrated producing regions of cottons and rice, they became a prize that was fought over by the Mughals, the Portuguese and the Arakanese in the seventeenth century. We have already spoken of this in detail.

In the sixteenth century the *Ain* mentioned Bakla in its catalogue of important towns in Bengal, so did Ralph Fitch[882]. In the seventeenth century Manrique commented that the city contributed to the wealth of Dhaka[883]. But by the mid-seventeenth century Bakla was in decline.

Chandikan or Sagor was the most important maritime power of the region. Its importance at the beginning of the seventeenth century was immense, as we know from Roe and Monserrate[884]. It was the principality of Pratapaditya who built up a strong navy and constructed ship-building yards at Dadkhah, Jahajghata and Chakvasi. This fleet became known as the Nawara fleet, later used by the Mughals to repel the Maghs. By the mid-seventeenth century the island's coasts were menaced by the maghs as Manrique tells us[885] but it still retained its religious importance and attracted thousands of pilgrims. But by the end of the seventeenth century, Master and Bowrey tell us that the island was practically desterted[886]. By the eighteenth century it was abandoned.

Sandwip, at the mouth of the Meghna and possibly the famed Samandar of the tenth century as Mohar Ali claims, was under the rule of Kedar Rai at the end of the sixteenth century. In 1602 he 'liberated' Sandwip from the Mughals and placed it under the Portuguese Carvalho. It merited

[882] Allami, Abul Fazl, *Ain-I-Akbari* (Tr.Jarrett and Sarkar), V.2: 147; Fitch, Ralph, 1583–91, in William Foster ed. *Early Travels in India 1583–1619*, New Delhi, Oriental Books Reprint Corporation, 1985: 27–8.

[883] Manrique op. cit.

[884] Roe and Monserrate op. cit.

[885] Manriquc op.cit.

[886] Master op.cit ; Bowrey op. cit.

a place on every travellers' itinerary in the sixteenth century and Cesare Frederici visited Sandwip in 1569. Lahori tells us that there was a substantial Portuguese colony there during the seventeenth century. Later in the seventeenth century the Mughal *subahdar* of Dhaka 'liberated' it from the Portuguese Gonzales and gave it to Arakan as *jagir*. Sandwip therefore was a 'frontier' port and shifted its alliances accordingly. We also do not know how far its trade was affected as a consequence.

Sripur was also a well known port. Sripur too came under Portuguese control by the end of the sixteenth century. It was celebrated as one of the most powerful towns of Bengal. By the eighteenth century it too had fallen off the map.

Fitch's testimony of the deltaic towns is particularly important for he visited the area soon after Akbar conquered Bengal. He therefore gives us a view of the commerce as it must have been before the Mughals, and after them the Arakanese, destroyed this area for good. The commercial space of the delta towns were, he tells us, 'India, Ceilon, Pegu, Malacca, Sumatra and many other places'[887].

Why and how did this vibrant commercial world die out? An ultimate lack of resources may have been a factor in their decline. While the initial impetus behind the founding of many of these towns in deltaic *samatata* may have come from the littoral kings we should note that such rulers did not have the resources to pursue a wide-ranging commercial policy. The Khadgas and Chandras for example were rulers of a marginal area and therefore did not enjoy the same advantages that accrued to the rulers of Lakhnawati in terms of a well-demarcated territory, a substantial tax base and an agrarian core that was focussed to meet the needs of the middle gangetic plain.

Moreover the Chandras were succeeded by the Varmans who were orthodox Brahmans. Like their western counterparts, the Senas, the Varmans sought to regulate society on conventional hinduised lines. Agriculture and land based activities were therefore promoted. It was only under the Ilyas Shahis again that commercial activities in this area received a boost. There was thus no sustained commercial policy in this region.

Also as we saw before, the commerce of this deltaic area experienced various crucial shifts during its existence. These are, to recapitulate:

One, from very early times until at least the fourteenth century these towns were part of a Buddhist religio/political/commercial network straddling the northern Bay of Bengal of which Pagan was the most important.

---

[887] In Foster op. cit: 28.

This network radiated eastwards from southeastern Bengal and passed through Kamrup-Ava and then north into Yunnan and south into Arakan, Pegu and Ceylon. The Buddhist network was on the decline by the fourteenth century, as we have seen.

Two, from the fourteenth century the commerce of these towns was increasingly re-directed westward with the foundation of the Bengal Sultanate. Arakan however was still a priority area. Silver flowed in from the east.

Three, the Ilyas Shahis in the fifteenth century started developing the China trade. Bengal's eastern ports became important once again. Embassies from Bengal to China were sent in 1405, 1408, 1409, 1412, 1414 and 1438–1939. Chinese missions to Bengal were in 1409, 1413, 1415, possibly 1419, circa 1421, and around 1431. This concentration on the China route may have disturbed the older trading networks of the region as it meant that sailings were now diverted southward in the Bay (see the section on Routes, Ports and Trading Networks in Bengal).

Four, Husain Shahi policy in the sixteenth century initiated a westward trade. Ports in the western part of Bengal were now developed. This policy cut short the China network (significantly there were no more trade and diplomatic sailings to China) and although traffic on the Bengal-China route continued, it was significantly diminished. Shipping lanes had to relocate themselves once again.

Five, at the beginning of the sixteenth century Bengal's premier exports of sugar and textiles suffered due to the oppressive Portuguese presence on the Gujarat and Malabar coasts. Muslim shipping from the western Indian Ocean concentrated on the Coromandel ports to bypass the Portuguese presence at Gujarat and Malabar, but they did not come as far as Bengal. In the absence of effective political power in the east the Portuguese entrenched themselves in the *samatata* ports.

Moreover, six, Portuguese hegemony in the eastern region meant that from the sixteenth century trade was diverted southward to the Coromandel and Ceylon and eastward to Malacca; Arakan thus was no longer a priority area.

Seven, the Arakanese asserted their dominion over *harikela* and a major part of *samatata* between the sixteenth and the eighteenth centuries and captured Chattagram, the chief port in the east, by the middle of the sixteenth century. This meant, to all intents, that Bengal was bereft of its major eastern outlet of trade.

Eight, the Persian diaspora, entrenched at Chattagram and points further east on the Bay, continued the slave trade; significantly this trade was augmented in the seventeenth century when Arakan turned into a pirate state. In the wake of decline of the Arakanese state and Portuguese fortunes in the seventeenth century these two powers now turned into slave-rainding powers.

Nine, in the seventeenth century this fragile world of Bay trade broke down. So did Portuguese networks of sea trade in this world. South east Bengal became a no man's land. It became a slave raiding zone. Ports in the area were devastated.

Ten, in the seventeenth century the produce of Bengal was diverted to serve the trading needs of the overland and sea trade of the Mughal world economy spanning Turan and Iran.

Eleven, in the eighteenth century English shipping took partly over where the Portuguese had left off. Devastated by Portuguese-Arakanese conflict for much of the sixteenth and seventeenth centuries and mauled by Mughal attacks on their sovereignty the *samatata* ports of the Pratapadityas and Kedar Rais had little part to play in these new trade networks[888].

The life of these ports finally ended in the seventeenth century when magh depredations destroyed this area. But there may also have been another reason. Mughal coastal presence, in the efforts to combat the Maghs, turned this area into a war zone. In the 1630s, during the tenure of Fidai Khan, practically no revenue was remitted to Delhi, as *jagirs* on the coast were given out to protect the area. By the time Shuja took over as *subahdar* many of the coastal jagirdars were impoverished. In the 1650s and 1660s Mir Jumla spent a lot of money for the construction of forts and roads in the region, as well as building up the depleted nawara fleet. After Mir Jumla Shaista Khan redoubled efforts to build up the fleet; to this end all wood and carpenters were seized by bailiffs from villages in the regions and taken to Dhaka to build the new fleet[889]. Mughal administration of the delta region was conducted on a war footing throughout the seventeenth century. Under such conditions it was difficult for ports and commerce to flourish in southeast Bengal.

The Mystery of Samandar

But were there other ports? We have already noted that between the decline of Tamralipta in the seventh century and the rise of Chattagram

---

[888] See Mukherjee, Rila, *Merchants and Companies In Bengal: Kasimbazar and Jugdia in the Eighteenth Century*, New Delhi, Pragati Publications.

[889] Mookerji, R.K., 1962: 161–3.

from the thirteenth century, recorded ports in Bengal, other than the shadowy Samandar, do not exist[890]. Ports on the eastern route were Nagapattinam (called Bullin by the Arabs), Ganjam (Kanja) in present day Orissa, the unidentified Samandar[891] thirty miles north of Ganjam (somewhere between Bengal and inland Assam?)[892], Nicobar Islands, Kedah, Java and Khmer and this was the preferred route from the eastern sea board to China according to the ninth century *Al-Masalik wa'l Mamalik* of Ibn Khurdadhbih.

It is striking that there is no mention of Chattagram, the great eastern port, in the ninth century account; however by the time of Ibn Batutah's voyages in the fourteenth century Chattagram had emerged as the greatest port on the eastern sea board after the Coromandel ports. It probably dated from the tenth century as discussed earlier. The flourishing production and foreign trade centred on the Chatagram-Suvarnagram complex was described by Chinese visitors as well as in the Chaitanya Mangala of Jayananda[893]. What then seved as port for the Dhaka-Suvarnagram production complex as well as for the Buddhist Mainamati-Lalmai complex in the region? What was the chief port of Bengal in this period? It is likely to be Samandar for we are told that it was the principal market and port on the Ganges delta, inhabited by wealthy merchants from all over the world , the centrepoint of trade with Assam and Ceylon and trader in aloes-wood (for which there was a great demand, especially in China) brought down from Assam[894].

Samandar was definitely in existence for three hundred years between the ninth century (Ibn Khurdadhbih) and the twelfth century (al-Idrisi) as sources tell us. It is likely that Samandar may have been an earlier port in the Suvarnagrama region; in that case however it cannot be thirty miles

[890] See the section on Routes, Ports and Trading Networks in Bengal.

[891] Samandar has been identified with Suvarnagram by Ahmad, 1989: 24–25. However it could equally be Gangabandar in the region of the ancient port of Bengal, Tamralipta (see Tarafdar, M.R., 1978, 'Trade and Society in Early Medieval Bengal' in *The Indian Historical Review*, January, IV, 2).

[892] In Ahmad, 1989: 5.

[893] Bagchi, P.C., 1945; Jayananda, *Chaitanya Mangala*, Calcutta, 1971: 10–11; also Vrindaban Das, *Chaitanya Bhagavat*, Nabadwip, 3rd ed.: 161 (in Ray, Aniruddha, 1997, 'Middle Bengali Literature: A Source for the Study of Bengal in the Age of Akbar' in Habib, Irfan (ed). 1997, *Akbar and His India*, Delhi, Oxford University Press.

[894] Elliot and Dowson, V.1. Also Mohar Ali Muhammad, 1985, *History of the Muslims of Bengal*, V.1A Muslim Rule in Bengal 1203–1757, Saudi Arabia, Ibn Saud Islamic University Publications: 24.

north of Ganjam. Was it then in the area around Saptagram? Samandar can then be identified with Gangabandar/Tamralipta (see previous note). If Samandar is identified to be in the west we may have to revise our ideas about the commercial importance of the east in the early medieval period.

Muhammad Mohar Ali places Samandar at/around Sandwip island[895] According to al-Idrisi Samandar was near the confluence of the Meghna and the Brahmaputra near the present port town of Chandpur in Bangladesh. Since al-Idrisi wrote in the twelfth century we know that Samandar functioned as a port from the ninth century (Ibn Khurdadhbih) for at least three hundred years. Samandar was situated on the Meghna. Riverine changes may have silted this port up so much so after this time that the next great port was destined to be Chattagram on the Karnaphuli further east.

But apart from the confusion regarding Samandar's location within Bengal, there is also a doubt whether Samandar was situated in Bengal at all. For there are certain problems with Mohar Ali's identification. Al-Idrisi wrote[896]:

> Samandar is a large town, commercial and rich, where there are good profits to be made. It is a port dependant upon Kanauj, King of this country. It stands upon a river which comes from the country of Kashmir...Aloes wood is brought hither from the country of Karmut fifteen day's distance by a river of which the waters are sweet. The aloes wood which comes from this country is of a superior quality and of a delicious perfume. It grows in the mountains of Karan....to the north at seven day's distance from Samandar, is the city of Kashmir the inner, celebrated throughout India, which is under the rule of Kanauj...This is a fine commercial city which gives its name to the King of the country (Kanauj). It is built upon the banks of a large river which falls into the Musala...the River of Perfumes. It rises in the mountains of Karan...and at length falls into the sea.

Mohar Ali's identification of Samandar as a port in eastern Bengal hinges on three key facts. First, the identification of Karmut/ Karan with

[895] Mohar Ali 1985, V. 1A: 30–34.

[896] Nizhatu-l Mushtak of al-Idrisi in Elliot and Dowson, *The History of India as Told by its Own Historians: The Muhammadan Period*, V.1, Allahabad, Kitab Mahal: 74–93. See pp. 90–91.

Kamrup, the legendary producer of aloes wood; second, with the identification of Musala as the Meghna and third, as being the premier port for receiving and exporting aloes wood in the east. But how do we reconcile this identification with other facets of al-Idrisi's description: that the river (Musala) comes from Kashmir and that 'the city of Kashmir the inner' is at seven day's distance from Samandar?

Indeed there is a confusion about the name Samandar. Samandar could be in peninsular South Asia as well. The *Jamiu-t Tawarikh* of Rashi'du-d D'in of the early fourteenth century (1310) mentions Duru Samundar (Dwara Samudra) 'adjoining M'abar Island'[897]. But it could equally be located on the west coast, in Sindh province, in the Multan and Kandahar/Kabul area which also produced aloes[898]. In such a case, the reputedly sweet and perfumed waters of the Musala, which Mohar Ali takes to be the Meghna on account of the trade in perfumed aloes-could apply equally to the Mihran (Indus). The twelfth century account of ibn Haukal tells us that the waters of the Sandaruz (Sind-rud) whose waters were 'sweet and abundant' joined the Mihran above Basmad[899]. And there was a Samandar on the Mihran. The book of Abu Ishak al Istakhri, composed aound the mid-tenth century, tells us that Samand 'is a small city situated like Multan on the east of the river Mihran' and adds that the distance between Multan and Samand was 2 parasangs (roughly eleven miles). According to Abu Ishak it was also called Samundur[900].

There are also Basmand, and Basmat in Sindh as well as Sandur, 'situated on the banks of a river which falls into the Mihran (Indus) above Samand'. There is no mention of aloes but al-Idrisi mentions its wealth and commerce[901]; and this may well be the Samandar taken by Mohar Ali to be in eastern Bengal.

Therefore, all indications point to Samandar being situtated in Sindh. But the identification of Samandar hinges on its association with aloes. Was this region a producer of aloes wood? Yes. We have already seen that Multan in Sindh province as well as the Kabul/Kandahar region produced aloes in plenty[902]. Moreover this seems to have been the chief source of revenue to the rulers of Multan; and a brisk trade in aloes wood was

---

897 In *ibid*.: 73.

898 Al-Idrisi in *ibid*.: 91–2.

899 Ibn Haukal, *Ashka'lu-l Bila'd* or the *Kita'bu-l Masa'lik Wa-l Mama'lik*, in *Ibid*.: 40.

900 *Kita'bu-l Aka'li'm* in *ibid*.: 28, 30.

901 Al-Idrisi in *ibid*.: 83.

902 Al-Idrisi, op.cit.: 91–2.

carried on by pilgrim merchants when they visited the temple at Multan. We do not know what idol the temple housed as it is referred to as the 'idol' of Multan, or occasionally as 'Multan' as well. This is what the tenth century Muslim travellers had to say about it:[903]

> The idol called Multan is situated in the environs of Mansura (in Sindh), and people come on pilgrimage to it...They bring thither the Indian aloes called al-kamrun from Kamrun the name of the country where it grows. These aloes are of the finest quality. They are given to the ministers of the temple for use as incense...Merchants buy them of the ministers of the temple.

And[904],

> 'the greatest part of the revenues of the Kingdom of Multan is derived from the rich presents brought to the idol of the pure aloes wood of Kumar...and one *man* of which is worth 200 dinars.

So where was the kingdom of Kumar/Kamrun located? According to Mohar Ali this was Kamrup, but again, there are problems in reaching this conclusion. Abu Zaidu-l Hasan tells us that the kingdom of Kumar 'which produces the aloes known as kumari' was situated 'on that side that faces the country of the Arabs', that is, the western side of South Asia[905]. But Ibn Khurdadbih tells us that Kamrun was 'contiguous to China'[906] which exported 'aloes to Kilkan, Luan and Kanja by the freshwater route in fifteen days'[907]. Kanja is probably Ganjam (Orissa), so a fifteen days river journey is likely from Bengal down there. Moreover, Ibn Khurdadbih wrote that the distance between Samandar and Urashir was twelve pharasangs[908]. Twelve pharasangs is roughly a distance of 70 miles. If Urashir is Orissa, as seems likely, then Samandar was situated on the west Bengal coast, and not on the Meghna, as Mohar Ali claims. Al Idrisi noted that Samandar was situtated thirty miles north of Ganjam[909].

---

[903] The additions of Abu Zaidu-l Hasan of Siraf in the 'Salsilatu-l Tawarikh' of the Merchant Suleiman in Elliot and Dowson, V.1, op.cit.: 11.

[904] Al Masudi, Muru'ju-l Zahal in *Ibid.*: 23.

[905] As before: 8.

[906] 'Kitabu-l Masalik Wa-l Mamalik' by Ibn Khurdadbih in Elliot and Dowson, V.1, op.cit: 14.

[907] *Ibid.*: 16.

[908] *Ibid.*: 16.

[909] Al Idrisi, op.cit.: 90.

If that is the case then Samandar may well be identified with Gangabandar as Tarafdar claimed[910].

Other than Kumar, there was also the Kingdom of Kaman in the east which, al-Masudi tells us, was next to the kingdom of Rahma[911].

Is Kaman then Kamrup? If so, where is Rahma? Rahma (or ruhmi) was the name given to that part of Bengal that bordered the Arakan region, that is, the easternmost part of the province. Elliot and Dowson tell us that ruhmi or rahma referred to the Dhaka-Arakan region[912]. Suleiman tells us that Ruhmi possessed more troops that Gujarat, it was a producer of fine textiles, it traded through cauris and had gold, silver, rhinos and aloes in plenty[913]. So in reality, there may have been two regions producing aloes: Kumar in the west and Kaman in the east.

Mohar Ali depends largely on al-Idrisi's text for his identification of Samandar. But al-Idrisi's text is inconclusive; rather it is only Ibn Khurdadbih's text that contains all three key indicators: aloes, Kamrun as next to China, and the existence of a port called Samandar there. All other texts that have been referred to; those of Abu Zaidu-l Hasan, al-Masudi, Abu Ishak, Ibn Haukal–mention some, but not all of the key facts as just mentioned.

Samandar could be a generic name such as Bandel (a Portuguese corruption of Bandar or port) was to prove two centuries later. Or it could also refer to any port on a wide river. Minhaj tells us that Mardhan Kot in Kamrud (Kamrup) was situated on the banks of the Bangamathi or Brahmaputra. 'When it (the Bangamathi) enters the country of Hindustan it receives in the hindustani language the name of Samundar. In length, breadth and depth, it is three times greater than the Ganges'[914].

Finally, it is indeed unlikely that there was an active Bengal-Multan trade in aloes as early as in the tenth century; it is therefore more probable that the aloes brought to the temple at Multans came from a source near it. We should also note that while six sources spanning three hundred years, Abu Zaidu-l of Siraf, Al Masudi, Abu Ishak (tenth century), Ibn Haukal, al Idrisi (twelfth century) and Zakari'ya al Kazwi'ni (thirteenth century), mention the idol of Multan and its worship in detail, only two

---

910 Tarafdar, 1978, op.cit.

911 Al Masudi, op. cit. 'the kingdom of Rahma is bounded by an inland state called the Kingdom of Kaman': 25.

912 Elliot and Dowson, V.1 op.cit., Appendix A: 361.

913 'Salsilatu-t Tawarikh', op.cit.: 5.

914 *Tabaqat-i-Nasiri*, V.2: 310.

tenth century sources, those of Abu Zaidu-l and al Masudi, mention the trade in aloes at the Multan temple[915]. Had the trade in aloes at Multan died out after that time? This seems unlikely, given the tremendous demand for aloes in West Asia. Had an alternative centre been established on the west coast for the aloes trade? This seems more likely. The trade at Multan declined possibly after the Ghaznavid attacks in the region in the eleventh century. The aloes trade probably moved out of the confines of the pilgrimage circuit and entered the commercial realm at that time.

Sagor's name has also been proposed as an interim port as alternative to Samandar. Both Sagor and Bakla in the Sundarbans area were functioning as ports from the twelfth century. We also have shadowy references to Dianga port in the Chattagram region by the seventeenth century. It was known as Feringhjibazaar or Feringhibandar and functioned as a suburb of Chattagram. It was given by Shaista Khan to the Portuguese in the seventeenth century[916]. We do not know if it also functioned as an interim port-town in the period between the decline of Tamralipta and the rise of Chattagram. Thus we have a very hazy picture of mercantile activities from Bengal in the early medieval period.

The Husain Shahi Divide

We therefore see that our received history on the world of the northern Bay trade is vague. Moreover, this world was in constant flux, and this has added to our confusion. Note that there are no dates in this picture of Bengal trade given above; the changes enumerated above seem to have occurred on an atemporal surface. For western Bengal however, we do find some median dates for politics and commerce.

In the sixteenth century, when the economic impetus swung in favour of *Vanga*, the following dates acquired prominence: in 1506, Ala-ud-Din Husain Shah builds a bridge connecting Triveni/Nabadwip with Saptagram, then the chief port in the west. In 1516, the Husain Shahis wrest Chattagram from Tripura and this is celebrated as a great victory. This again heralds the reputation of Chattagram as the premier port of Bengal. By 1560 Nabadwip evolves into a well-known market town; merchants were settling there and selling goods from locations as far off as Kashmir in the north to Kanchipuram in the extreme south. Saptagram silts up by 1560 and contributes to the decline of Gaur.

---

[915] Conclusion reached after an examination of these sources in Elliot and Dowson, V.1, op.cit.

[916] Dianga was described as a suburb of Chattagram in the sixteenth century, Subrahmanyam, 1990: 121.

Husain Shahi radical commercial policy is cut short by three factors: 1536, the fall of Husain Shahi Bengal to Sher Shah, 1538, the loss of Chattagram to the Arakanese and the silting up of Saptagram from the middle of the sixteenth century. Bengal is thus left without a port until the rise of Hugli in the 1580s. In 1576, Bengal is conquered by the Mughals. And in 1580, Hugli is settled by the Portuguese by virtue of an imperial *farman* from Akbar. Sandwip at the mouth of the Meghna river is officially placed under Portuguese control in 1602. These two ports, in west and east both under the Portuguese, could have finthered the maritime lineage of the delta ports.

Trade Cycles in Medieval Bengal

We had seen before that two great trade cycles emanating from China impacted on south eastern Bengal and Burma in the medieval period[917]. They were visible in the active trade between Burma and China after the Yuan conquest in the late thirteenth century, and again in the late fourteenth and early fifteenth century along with the expansion of production and trade all over the eastern Indian Ocean around 1400. These trade cycles fit in well with the observations we have made about Bengal's commercial evolution; the thirteenth century saw a renewed urbanisation along the north eastern frontiers of Bengal, and these towns linked up with the new silk route through Turkestan that the Mongols established in the thirteenth century. The fifteenth century saw increased trade between Bengal and China in the Bay; this fits in with the fact that now the Chinese were attemting to move away from Mongol control of overland commercial routes and conduct all trade by sea. Therefore there seems to have been an explosion of trade by both land and sea during the period from the late thirteenth to the mid fifteenth century.

The beneficiaries of the second trade cycle were of course the deltaic ports of Bengal. This world, fought over by independent Bengali princes, peripatetic Islamic rulers, emergent Mughals, the Portuguese and the Arakanese, testify to the fact that this was the most vibrant economic region of the province. The political economy of this area reached such lucrative heights that from the fifteenth to the eighteenth centuries the port-towns of eastern *samatata* and *harikela* were fought over by Tripura, Arakan, the Portuguese and the Sultans and Mughals of Bengal. When the Arakanese could not retain hegemony over these tracts permanently they led frequent raids against this area.

[917] Sun Laichen quoted in Frank, A.G., 1998, *ReOrient*: 102.

The Portuguese controlled much of the delta, either informally or by means of direct political control, from the sixteenth century. The fortunes of these port towns finally declined with the fall in Portuguese fortunes in the seventeenth century in Bengal and in South East Asia[918]. They could not always readjust to new trade channels and routes that rose from economic and political compulsions. They were effectively destroyed. Portuguese-Arakan (*Magh*) raids, and Portuguese piracy (*harmad*) were other factors. The seventeenth century was the last great age of the eastern ports.

From then on, the east becomes a marginal land in Bengal's history. Part of the reason for this is political (Husain Shahi policy) as we saw, part of the reason was economic by virtue of the fact that Arakanese raids were reputed to have killed off the area. The history of this land now lives on only in folk tales that bewail the ruinous effects of *magh* slave raids and *harmad* piracy.

K.N.Chaudhuri, in his last major work, *Asia Before Europe*, summed up the marginality of Bengal succinctly. In four maps of 3D images centred on the world from four points: Mecca, Delhi, Jakarta and Peking, he noted a peculiarity. Bengal's marginality from all four centres of politics and commerce came out in these computer generated maps[919].

---

918 See before in this volume.

919 *Asia Before Europe: Economy and Civilisation of the Indian Ocean From the Rise of Islam to 1750*, Cambridge University Press, 1990: 32–35.

8

Bengal in the Indian Ocean Centred World Economy

'Early modern history was shaped by a long since operational world economy and not just by the expansion of a European world system' (A.G.Frank, 1998, *Re Orient: Global Economy in an Asian Age*, University of California Press and Sage/Vistaar: 327)

We have spoken this far of the 'world empires' of the Mings (1368), Ottomans (1453), the Mughals (1526) and the Safavids (1600) who participated in the politics and trade of this world. Let us now speak of 'world economies'. World empires can exist as sub-sets within a single world economy and the world economy ultimately creates a world system with a hierarchical ordering of spatial units articulated to the structure of the state that is central to it[920]. We saw that the Indian Ocean was a world system motored by a world economy that was constituted by the world empires that participated in its economic life.

So what denotes a world economy? It denotes, firstly, a spatial physical territory centred around an intital process of state formation and its outward projections over space and time. The two main markers of a world economy are its durability over time and its capacity to govern economic activities from its peripheries to the advantage of its core area. Secondly, a world economy, when it has retained its hegemony over surrounding regions for a long enough time, transforms itself into a world system where the dominant positions of power may not always be expressed through economic relationships. These can be political, cultural, religious, and linguistic.

---

[920] Wallerstein, Immanuel, *The Modern World System* I (1974), II (1980) and III (1989), New York, Academic Books/Academic Press. See also Wallerstein's 'World System versus World Systems: A Critique when we referred to the territorial and maritime world of the Indian Ocean, in *Critique of Anthropology*, II, 2, 1991.

It is therefore, evident that the Islamic empires had managed to coalesce into an Islamic world economy and ultimately an Islamic world system by the tenth century. This came about when the core of the Muslim world–bound on the east by the Red Sea and the Persian Gulf, on the north by the Caspian and Black Seas and on the west by the Mediterranean–placed itself at the intersection of two great economic units: the Indian Ocean area and the Mediterrannean area[921]. This aided its subsequent expansion east into India and China, south into Ifriquiya and west into Iberia. This core area that had been one in Hellenistic times but had split into two hostile units, the Roman/Byzantine and the Parthian/ Sassanian, was now united together once again through the Islamic conquest. This area experienced capitalistic activity from very early times: the signs of incipent capialism were intense urbanisation, the rise of regional empires, the growth of international trade, emergence of a labour market, the birth of a cash economy, the invention of a paper money and so on[922]. Within this world functioned the world empires of the Turko-Afghans and the Mongols of the thirteenth century; these in turn were absorbed into the greater world empires of the sixteenth century–the Ottomans, the Safavids, the Mughals and the Chinese.

The period from the time of the travels of Ibn Khurdadbih (ninth century) to those of Ibn Batuta and Ibn Khaldun (fourteenth century) was the period of an early Islamic world economy. All three witnessed the economic impact of the explosion of Islam on the map of the world. Ibn Khurdadbih, geographer and traveller, who revised Ptolemy's *Geographia*, left an account of roads and kingdoms in all lands that Islam had touched. Bengal was sufficiently important to the Islamic world to have featured in his *al-Masalik Wa'l Mamalik* (or Account of Roads and Kingdoms)[923]. Yet another work, the *Akhbar Al-Sin Wa'l Hind* compiled in 851 AD, which was the work of Sulayman al-Tajit and other merchants and travellers who visited India and China, referred to routes and ports in Bengal. Therefore, eastern Bengal was sufficiently important to the Islamic world economy as early as the ninth–tenth centuries.

In the 1330s, Ibn Batuta undertook his long journey from Mecca to the Russian steppes by way of the Red Sea, the Yemen, the Hadramaut,

[921] Lombard, Maurice, 1971, *l'Islam dans sa Premiere Grandeur, VIIIe–XIe siecle*, Paris, Flammarion: 19. In English as *The Golden Age Of Islam,* (Tr). J. Spencer, Amsterdam, 1975: 9–10.

[922] Braudel, Fernand, 1984, *Civilization and Capitalism , III, The Perspective of the World* (Tr). S.Reynolds, London: 21–22.

[923] Ahmad, 1989.

Constantinople, Anatolia, the newly conquered Ottoman territories in Asia Minor, and through Delhi, Bengal and China. A third of his account is devoted to India; this was testimony to South Asia's place in the growing Islamic world economy of the fourteenth century stretching from the Maghreb to China[924]. In this network, Delhi occupied a primate position; Bengal's position was defined, as we saw before in Ibn Khurdadbih's and Sulayman al-Tajit's works, by its relation to the China trade which was occupying an increasingly important place in the Islamic network.

This Bengal-China trade has a social dimension which is yet to be worked on. Recent publications on Gaur tell us that Chinese ceramics were not only present at sites in Gaur and Pandua but Chinese ceramics were also used as part of the built environment as in glazed tiles and bricks[925]. More important, Sinha (2002) tells us that Chinese influenced glazed bricks and tiles decorated not only the royal quarters at Gaur but also the nobles' area and the urban heart of the city[926]; an indication that the practice of using Chinese style bricks and tiles was not confined to royal consumption alone but was a widespread urban practice at Gaur[927].

The porcelain and ceramic shards found at Gaur have been designated 'pre-Ming'[928]. There has been, to date, no Ming porcelain found for the period that Gaur was inhabited. What is important to note is that apart from the usual blue ware (Song or Yuan?) a great amount of celadon ware was found at Gaur.

Celadon is a glaze that was developed from the tenth to the fourteenth century in North China. It achieved world recognition due to Song mercantile practices. Celadon, along with silk, was used as a tool of diplomacy (trade as tribute) by the Songs. While ceramic production was traditionally concentrated in the north[929], under the Songs the focus of

---

924 Ibn Batuta, *Voyages*, II, Paris, Maspero, 1982 (as before). Defremery, C. and Sanguinetti, B.R. (trs). See the introduction and notes of Stephane Yerasimos. See also Lombard, Denys, 1990, for an excellent interpretation of Ibn Batuta's travels. *Le Carrefour Javanais*, II, 'Les Reseaux Asiatiques': 33.

925 Mitra, Pratip Kumar, 2002, 'Source Material on the Medieval Cities of Gaur and Pandua in the the British Public Collections': 277–328 and Sinha, Sutapa, 2002, 'Archaeology of the Medieval City of Gaur': 329–356 in Sengupta and Panja eds. 2002. See pages 302–3, and Figures 19, 21 and 22 in Mitra, 2002, and Sinha, 2002, 333–5, which clearly point to Chinese influences in tile and brick glazing in the royal apartments at Gaur, notably in the *khas* and *zenana mahals* of the Royal Quarters.

926 Sinha, 2002, 334–339.

927 *Ibid.*: 335.

928 Mitra, 2002.

929 There is actually a Northern Celadon. See Medley, Margaret, 1976, *The Chinese Potter: A Practical History of Chinese Ceramics*, Oxford, Phaidon Press:115–18, 129.

economic wealth was centred on the south. Hangchew in south China became the Song capital after 1127. Trade, as far as ceramics was concerned, moved away from the Central Asian land routes and concentrated towards the ports of south-eastern China. Wen-chou in Chekiang became the imperial port, close to the Song capital at Hangchew; nevertheless Canton continued to be a favourite for trade. Imperial superintendents to oversee trade were posted at both Wen-chou and Canton by the Songs. The port that achieved the most phenomenal growth under the Songs was the port of Ch'uan-chou or Quanzhou (northern Fukien), which is known to the students of history as Marco Polo's Zaitun. From the beginning of the fourteenth century until the middle of the fifteenth century this was the greatest mercantile city in East Asia.

In response to the new maritime trade routes ceramic production, too, moved south and received imperial patronage from the late twelfth and the thirteenth centuries. To ward off the threat from the north excess revenue was essential and the Songs did much to encourage foreign trade. Foreign merchants contracted with the southern potteries as ceramics, after silk, was the most valuable Chinese export. During the Song period the kiln at Guangxi, near Zaitun, produced ceramics with a green glaze similar to the northern celadon in appearance[930]. Another of the southern kilns, Lung-Ch'uan, started celadon production. This ware enjoyed great popularity until the middle of the fourteenth century, and Lung-Ch'uan celadon imitations continued to be made until the end of that century.

Potteries underwent a change from casual to systematic organisation in Song times and their output was sent to the Phillipines, south East Asia, Indonesia, South Asia, the Near East, to the ports on the Persian Gulf and the Red Sea as far as Cairo. This practice was then continued by the Y'uans. It is likely that the celadon found at Gaur was Lung-Ch'uang celadon or Guangxi green glazes. Since the excavations at the second city of Gaur fix habitation there from the fifteenth century until the late sixteenth century; it is apparent that the Yuans (Mongols) had continued the Song practice of exporting celadonware.

But blue and white ware too was found in plenty at Gaur. Other than in the Song period, a certain amount of blue and white ware was produced

---

[930] See Scott, Rosemary, 1995, 'Southern Chinese Provincial Kilns : Their Importance and Possible Influence on South East Asian Ceramics' in Rosemary Scott and John Guy eds. *South East Asia and China: Art, Interaction and Commerce*, London, Percival David Foundation: 187–204. See p. 194.

during the Yuan period[931] and this may have found its way to Gaur. In South East Asia too the first Islamic states were beginning to appear from this time and they continued the old tradition of importing Chinese ceramic ware.

When Ibn Batuta moved away from the Persian Gulf towards the eastern seas he found the local Islamic states and the Chinese reinforcing their commercial positions. Within the Chinese commercial strategy Muslims played an important role: Cheng He the famous admiral who commanded the fleet to Ceylon, Quilon, Cochin, Calicut, Hormuz, Jedda, Mogadishu and Malindi was a Muslim and the son of a Haji from Yunnan. Ibn Batuta himself left Calicut on a Chinese junk whose pilot was Muslim named Suleiman; he mentioned, moreover, that the cabins were rented by Chinese Muslim merchants returning to Zaitun[932]. Ch'uan-chou or Zaitun was truly an Islamic mercantile city; peopled by Persian, Arab, Syrian and Chinese Muslim traders. When he returned to India, on a ship belonging to the King of Zahir, Ibn Batuta noted that the crew was entirely Muslim[933].

A few years later, also in the fourteenth century, Ibn Khaldun drew the contemporary world's notice to the flourishing 'dinar economy' that propelled the societies of the Islamic lands he traversed from the Maghreb to the Middle East; unfortunately for the students of historical geography Ibn Khaldun confronted Tamerlane at the gates of Baghdad and did not proceed further east. Instead he devoted the *Muqadammiya* (or world history) to the reason of the vulnerability of Islamic states to the Mongols. While he did not visit Bengal his accounts of other islamicised lands give us a vivid picture of the Islamic world economy that encircled the world.

What would be the position of Bengal in this network? In the tenth century *nagari* style coins from Bengal and not *pallava* style coins from Southern India were in circulation in Mataram Java. In the fourteenth century merchants from 'Goda' (Gaur) were mentioned at Majapahit Java[934]. It is noticeable that merchants from Bengal were singled out from those from the rest of India–merchants from India, Cambodia, China,

[931] See Beamish, Jane, 1995, 'The Significance of Yuan Blue and White Exported to South East Asia' in Rosemary Scott and John Guy eds. *South East Asia and China: Art, Interaction and Commerce*, London, Percival David Foundation: 225–251. See p. 228.

[932] Lombard, 1990, II, 'Les Reseaux Asiatiques': 33.

[933] *Ibid.*

[934] *Ibid*: 33.

Vietnam, Campa, Karnataka, Bengal and Siam were named[935]. Tome Pires mentioned Bengali merchants at Java and Malacca in the sixteenth century[936]. Early on in the seventeenth century (1609) Pyrard de Laval noted that there were merchants from Bengal at Banten[937] and later in the same century Bengali ships were mentioned at Kedah and Achin[938].

But Bengal did not possess a primate position in this network. There were three preconditions that argue for a primate position within such a network: first, if the locale was part of a centralised political empire, it was axiomatic that the imperial capital would serve as a model for locating power, second, active long-distance trade and a primary role played by merchants and bankers into turning rural production into disposable state finance strengthened the position of central places, third, a strong association between religion, cultural life and towns produced similar results. Bengal, we saw, possessed none of these criteria in history.

The social dimensions of urban settlements were linked to those of space through the need for centrality. There were no such central places within Bengal. Control over urban space as an attribute of power was slow to emerge in Bengal–Gaur, Dhaka and Murshidabad are ephemeral examples. While Agra, Lahore and Delhi have survived in history, Bengal's only primate city that survives today–Calcutta–was a creation of the British. If al-Muqaddasi described capitals as kings, provincial capitals as chamberlains, ordinary towns as cavalrymen and villages as foot-soldiers[939] then from the seventeenth century Bengal essentially supplied men who marched to the imperial drum beating from Delhi.

Port evolution in Bengal mirrors this pattern. In her study of the famous port of Quanzhou Schottenhammer demonstrates clearly that a port has to evolve from being a transhipment point for commodities to one that involved the shipment of the produce of an ever expanding hinterland if it was to earn the status of a 'great' port[940]. Hegemony over

---

[935] Jamdudwipa, Khamboja, Cina, Yawana, Len, Champa, Kharnnatakadi, Goda etc. mentioned in the 'Nagar Kertagama' of Majapahit Java in Lombard, 1990, II: 325.

[936] *Suma Oriental*, (Ed). A. Cortesao.

[937] Albert Gray edition op.cit.

[938] Bowrey: 272, 288–9.

[939] al-Muqaddasi, *Ahsanu-t-Taqasim fi Ma'rifati-l-aqalim*, (Eng.Tr. G.S.A. Ranking and R.F.Azoo, Calcutta, 1901) quoted in K.N.Chaudhuri, 1990: 354.

[940] Scottenhammer, Angela, 1999, 'The Maritime Trade of Quanzhou (Zaitun) from the Ninth through the Thirteenth Century' in Himanshu Prabha Ray ed. *Archaeology of Seafaring: The Indian Ocean in the Ancient Period*, New Delhi, Pragati Publications: 271–290.

the hinterland was necessary for a port to evolve. Political stability in a hinterland linked to a centralised regime that distributed rural and commercial surplus to the advantage of both the core and peripheral areas was therefore crucial. This did not happen in Bengal.

The rich merchants that we find described in fourteenth century Chattagram, or sixteenth century Gaur, or seventeenth century Hugli, were merchants involved essentially in the transhipment of goods. Entrepot functions ruled Bengal's coast but as Bengal's involvement in major maritime networks was minimal, ports (and merchants) could not grow beyond a certain point. With the glass ceiling reached, Bengal's merchants had no option but to turn into brokers. Here they played an important role in transforming the rural surplus into disposable cash. Wealth from trade remained confined to coastal areas and translated into tangible power only in the eighteenth century when the merchant became indispensable for the tax-trade nexus to function.

This early Islamic world economy broke down in the fifteenth century. Throughout Asia the Mongols were busy diverting trade routes through their domains. In the Mediterranean the Christian onslaught on Ceuta in 1415 ended the Maghrebian domination of the trans-saharan trade. The Spanish now took over Granada, unified Spain and attempted to control the southern Mediterranean trade. The Almohad empire of the Maghreb collapsed. Soon after the Ottoman Turks overran this Islamic world of flourishing little states and emirates. The commercial network that this early Islamic world spanned was the one that the Ilyas Shahis had negotiated with in the fifteenth century where they occupied a primate position between the Chinese and Maghrebian trade. By the 1430s this network had collapsed. The eastern Indian Ocean entered a period of flux from this time. Bengal's commerce had to readjust to new impetuses. In 1453, the Turks conquered Constantinople and announced the coming of the next Islamic world system.

The second Islamic world economy appeared the sixteenth century–one dominated by the mighty empires of the Ottomans, the Mughals and the Persians. Turkic military groups formed these three mighty empires that stretched from the Balkans into the Bay of Bengal. Unlike the first Islamic world economy of volatile mercantile states this second Islamic world economy was founded by military aristocracies and 'noble' bureaucracies that were based, in their turn, on agrarian surplus, tribute and war plunder. In a word, the cavalry and effective fiscal policies were the blocs on which the entire edifice rested.

This world was ruled by three major monarchs, whose reigns taken together span over a century: Suleyman the Magnificent the Ottoman (1521–1566), Akbar the Mughal (1556–1605) and Shah Abbas the Persian (1588–1629) managed an integrated world economy in the sixteenth and the seventeenth centuries. We have already studied the fiscal policies undertaken by these monarches to underpin an integrated fiscal, commercial and political Islamic economy in the sixteenth century.

The Mings withdrew from this world; with this withdrawal, Bengal's trade went into decline. From 1506, the Husain Shahis worked at reorienting Bengal's trade to the west and not the east. In the 1560s, the Venetian Cesare Frederici praised the great port of Saptagram–emblematic of the sixteenth century shift from east to west within Bengal.

Barbosa and Varthema, who visited this world in the very beginning of the sixteenth century, have left us a fascinating account of the port-cities of the Indian Ocean. We note from their accounts that the position of the Bay ports was already marginal to this world.

There were three sets of ports in the western Indian Ocean. The first were the east African ports of Sofala, Malindi, Kilwa, Mombasa, Zanzibar and Mogadishu. These ports were important as sources of gold and for the route into Africa. The second lot were Aden and the ports of the Hadramaut that guarded the entrance to the Red Sea. This route was important for the horse trade and for religious missions as the holy towns of Mecca and Medina were accessed by this route. The third set of ports were the Persian Gulf ports, dominated by Hormuz, from whence came bullion (silver) and horses. These ports were also important as they, along with the Hadramaut ports, formed the pathway to the Ottoman ports of Alexandria and Aleppo. Gold, silver and horses dominated the trade of the western Indian Ocean. By contrast, the eastern Indian Ocean did not contain such items of 'noble' trade; it offered rice, textiles, spices, dyes and teak in exchange.

South Asia's first port city, wielding indisputed influence over the entire Arabian Sea and the Indian Ocean in the sixteenth century, was Cambay. The opulence and wealth of Cambay was well known by the beginning of the sixteenth century[941]. It traded with the entire world of the Western Indian Ocean–with Sofala, Malindi, Kilwa, Mombasa, Mogadishu and Angoy[942]. Of these the trade with Kilwa was vital; Kilwa's gold was sent all over Arabia Felix and a portion of it also found its way to Cambay.

---

[941] *The Travels of Ludovico di Varthema in Egypt, Syria, Arabia Deserta and Arabia Felix, in Persia, India and Ethiopia* AD *1503–1508.* (Tr). J.W. John, (Ed). G.P. Badger, London, Hakluyt Society, M D CCC XIII: 111.

[942] Duarte Barbosa (Tr. Henry E.J.Stanley): 4–16.

While these 'primate' ports were mainly dominated by Cambay merchants with their ships, ports after Mogadishu such as Cape Guardafun were visited also by ships from the other Gujarat ports-such as Chaul and Dabhol[943]. This was because Cape Guardafun was not just an Indian Ocean port-Cape Guardafun also guarded the entrance to the Red Sea.

From Cape Guardafun it was possible to enter the Red Sea ports of Mecca (Jedda) and Barbera[944]. Cambay ships bringing spices carried away gold from Barbera[945]; but it seemed that Calicut now competed against Cambay to send spices directly to Mecca through Cape Guardafun[946].

In the Indian Ocean, Aden was the great port and emporium that connected ships from west (Hormuz) and east (Cambay, Chaul, Dabhol, Calicut) with the Red Sea ports[947]. The Calicut merchants were well established at Aden. Varthema referred to Aden as the rendez-vous 'for all the ships which come from India Major and Minor, from Ethiopia and Persia. All the ships which are bound for Mecca put in here'[948]. Cotton goods, apart from spices, formed Indian exports to Aden. Ships from Jedda, Zeyla and Barbera carried away Cambay goods[949]. Barbosa commented; 'And these ships of Cambay are so many and so large, and with so much merchandise, that it is a terrible thing to think of so great an expenditure of cotton stuffs as they bring'[950].

Xeher, the sea port of the Hadramaut, functioned as a subsidiary of Aden. All ships from India which were delayed for the Red Sea, sold their stuff here. This was an important port; it was a horses for cotton and rice trade that was carried on here. It was visited mainly by ships from the Gujarat coast, from Cambay, Chaul and Dabhol[951].

Hormuz was of course the 'primate' port city on the Persian Gulf; it was not only an emporia for ships from Cambay, Chaul and Dabhol in the east and Alexandria and Cairo on the west but also for ships coming from further afield-from Bengal, China and Cathay[952].

---

943 *Ibid.*: 16–17.

944 Badger identifies Berbera with Mosullon of the *Periplus* (Varthema, notes: 89.)

945 Barbosa: 17.

946 *Ibid.*: 23–24.

947 *Ibid.*: 27–28.

948 Varthema: 60.

949 Barbosa: 27.

950 *Ibid.*: 28.

951 *Ibid.*: 30–31.

952 *Ibid.*: 42.

It seems, reading Barbosa, that there was a clearly defined hierarchy of ports in the western Indian Ocean, Aden was the chief entrepot of the Indian Ocean, Xeher functioned as its subsidiary. Apart from ships from the Gujarati ports and from Calicut that we have already mentioned, Aden was visited by ships from Bengal, Sumatra and Malacca[953]. Kilwa was important for gold and for access to sub-saharan and trans-saharan Africa. Cape Guardafun guarded the entry into the Red Sea. Apart from ships from Cambay, Chaul, Dabhol, and the Malabar, it was the one port that was visited *regularly* by ships from the eastern Indian Ocean ports: Ceylon, Coromandel, Bengal, Sumatra, Pegu, Tenasserim, Malacca and China and 'from here they all enter the Red Sea and Mecca'[954]. Obviously the islamisation of the eastern Indian Ocean had a lot to do with this shipping vigour. Religion and trade went hand in hand. On the Indian side the Gujarat ports (mainly Cambay) were the undisputed leaders in the western Indian Ocean trade at the beginning of the sixteenth century, but the Malabar ports (Calicut) were already coming a close second.

Of the Gujarati ports Cambay was the most active, with Dabhol[955] (emporia between Malabar and Cambay and Diu as well as between Malabar and Mecca, Aden, and Hormuz) and Chaul[956] (emporia between the Malabar ports and Cambay) coming as the second and the third. The last two were dominated, according to Varthema, by 'Moorish merchants'[957]. Cost consciousness and profit motives determined that Cambay did not trade with Calicut; this was left to the 'smaller' Gujarat ports of Dabhol and Chaul. Apart from the western Indian Ocean ports Cambay ships went to ports in the Malabar and the Coromandel for Ceylon elephants and pearls[958] and to Pegu as well for elephants[959]. But Barbosa mentions no direct Cambay-Ceylon trade.

But Calicut was beginning to outpace Cambay as the most active South Asian port in the western Indian Ocean in the beginning of the sixteenth century. Already established at Aden, its merchants were trying to break into the lucrative Red Sea Trade and had established trading links with the other Indian ports of Diu, Surat, Dabhol, Mangalore and

953 *Ibid.*: 28.

954 *Ibid.*: 16–17.

955 *Ibid.* : 71–72.

956 *Ibid.*: 69–70.

957 Varthema: 114–115.

958 Barbosa: 167.

959 *Ibid.*: 183–185.

Chaul in an effort to access the goods of their hinterlands[960]. Chaul was the emporia between Malabar and Cambay[961], but Malabar ships were becoming increasingly visible at Dabhol as well[962]. The Malabar vessels collected *bairams* from Chaul and Dabhol and sold these and their own spices at Diu[963]. Barbosa noted the boom of Calicut's trade; Arabs, Persians, Gujarati, Khorasani and *dakhini* merchants at Calicut sent ten to twelve ships a year (in February) to the Red Sea and Aden from whence other merchants transported the goods to Turkey, Suez, Cairo and Alexandria[964]. This must have been the trade route that the Chinese were attempting to access first from Broach in the twelfth century[965] and then from Calicut in the fifteenth century[966].

The Malabar ports were also acting as intermediaries in the East-West trade; Ravel (unidentified) traded with Malacca, Bengal, Tenasserim, Pegu, Martaban and Sumatra from where they accessed Chinese silk and porcelain, possibly for re-export westwards to the Indian Ocean ports[967]. This seems to bear out the impression that the Chinese had left the western Indian Ocean for good[968].

Other than Calicut and Ravel the ports of the Malabar next in importance were Cananore (trading with Hormuz, Cambay, Banda, Ceylon and the Maldives)[969] and Kollam (Quilon) which produced pepper in abundance and traded with the Coromandel, Ceylon, Bengal, Malacca, Sumatra and Pegu and 'these do not trade with Cambay'[970]. Obviously the trade with Cambay had to be run through Cananore, and this fact may explain the traditional hostility between Calicut and Cananore.

---

960 *Ibid*.: 59, 63.

961 *Ibid*.: 69–70.

962 *Ibid*.: 71-2.

963 *Ibid*.: 60.

964 *Ibid*.: 147.

965 'Nizhatu-l Mushtak' of al-Idrisi in Elliot and Dowson, V.1, Allahabad, Kitab Mahal edition: 74–93. see p.87.

966 Ray, Haraprasad, 2003.

967 Barbosa: 67.

968 Ray, Haraprasad 2003, says that the Chinese left the trade at Calicut after they were thrown out in mid-fifteenth century, but they shifted their southern Indian base to Nagapattinam (Coromandel): 206–09, but it seems from Barbosa's account that Malabar now dominated the China-Western Indian Ocean trade. Nagapattinam continued active in the eastern Indian Ocean trade with South East Asia and China.

969 Barbosa: 150.

970 *Ibid*.: 157–58.

Pulicat on the Coromandel coast was the primate port-city of the sixteenth century in the Bay. It traded west with Muslim ships from the western Indian Ocean ports and east with Pegu for elephants[971]. Pulicat flourished because Muslim ships diverted their shipping from the Gujarat and Malabar ports and picked up stuffs from the Malabar, China and Bengal there. This diversion was due to the Portuguese trading presence on the Gujarat and Malabar coasts; and Barbosa's statement seems to endorse the conventional view that the Portuguese did initially make an impact on the trading system of the Indian Ocean[972].

If Portuguese depredations on the west coast resulted in Muslim shipping being diverted to the Coromandel ports to Coromandel's gain, Bengal, situated further north in the Bay, had no such luck. Indeed it was said that its premier products–sugar and textiles, fetched lower prices and that the Portuguese presence in Gujarat and the Malabar ports greatly hampered Bengal's trade[973]. But its trade with the Coromandel, Maldives, Cambay, Pegu, Tenasserim, Sumatra, Ceylon , Malabar and Malacca still continued in 'Mecca ships' and 'Chinese junks'[974]. This trade from Chattagram-'with a very good harbour'-was conducted, not by native Bengali merchants, but by Arab, Persian, Abyssinian and 'Indian' merchants[975]. It is somewhat strange that Barbosa gives us this somewhat negative pcture of Bengal's ports and trade, when his contemporary Varthema notes of Gaur: 'And here there are the richest merchants I ever met with'[976]. Fifty ships a year were despatched from Gaur to ports east and west.

In the sixteenth century Pulicat and Pegu were the two great ports in the Bay of Bengal which connected to the Far Eastern trade through Malacca. Pegu possessed four ports by the turn of the sixteenth century, Moorish and Gentoo merchants fuelled this trade[977]. One aspect of Pegu's trade that has been overlooked is its overland trade; Barbosa noted that Chinese goods also came to Pegu's ports through the landlocked kingdom of Ava[978].

The Persian motif is stressed by Barbosa when talking of Bengal's trade[979]. Shah Ismael, the Persian king had then been defeated by Selim

---

971 *Ibid.*: 183–85.

972 *Ibid.*: 174, 177.

973 *Ibid.*: 179.

974 *Ibid.*: 179.

975 *Ibid.*; 178–179.

976 Varthema: 212.

977 Barbosa: 183.

978 *Ibid.*: 186.

979 Barbosa: 180.

of Turkey but was perceived as a 'king (who) ruled over a part of Babilonia, and Armenia, and Persia and a large part of Arabia, and of India near to the Kingdom of Cambay'[980]. This vision of west India as a part of Persia is not unusual when we remember that Arab accounts of the tenth to the twelfth centuries had mentioned Sindh as a part of Persia[981]. Marco Polo, Montecorvino and Nicolo da Conti had divided India into India Major (Gujarat and the east coast of Africa), Middle India (or India proper) and India Minor (upto South East Asia). Varthema, Barbosa's contemporary, referred to India Major and India Minor[982].

While Varthema's opinion evidently stemmed from the trading affiliations of the three blocs it is indeed striking that Barbosa abandoned this later, and by now conventional, view of India and saw western India as an appendage of Persia instead; a testimony to Sindh once being part of Persia. It was also a portent for the future; the trade between Mughal and Safavid Persia would soon take off. As late as in 1699 Alexander Hamilton mentioned Lahori Bandar as lawless; being a region where two legal domains, the Persian and the Mughal, held sway. To this end Barbosa also divided India into three Indias; but with a difference. The first India had the Indus, the second the Ganges and the third Malacca[983]. Barbosa therefore saw the Bengal ports as appendages to the Malacca-Sumatra trade that was conducted from Pegu.

We have no accounts of the eastern Indian Ocean ports to rival those of Barbosa and Varthema. But we know that the Bengal ports attempted another trade which would grant them a primate place within the trade of the Bay and the Java Seas. This was the slave trade, but we do not know how far Bengali merchants participated in it. Because 'Bengal' does not mean, necessarily, 'Bengali' merchants; and there has not been, to date, no definition of the 'Bengali' merchant. Yet the tragic history of Arakan and the helplessness of southeast Bengal in the seventeenth century tells us that this area was inexorably drawn into the orbit of international trade, not through cash crops, but through humans as commodities. Why was this so?

At the beginning of the sixteenth century, with the South East Asian states turning to Islam, there occurred a great demand for natural eunuchs and castrated slaves all over the Bay of Bengal. The trade involvement of

980 *Ibid.*: 39–40.

981 See the accounts of Ibn Khurdadbih, al Masudi, Ibn Haukal, al Idrisi, amomg others, in Elliot and Dowson, V.1.

982 Varthema: 60.

983 Barbosa: 40–41, 178.

Bengal with Persia has been documented. Bengal supplied castrated and natural born eunuchs as slaves to the Persians 'who value them as guards to their wives and houses'[984]. This slave trade was historically conducted by Persians, Arabs and Abyssinians based at Chattagram.

Therefore, slaves seem to have been traditionally an export of Bengal, initially geared towards the west to Persia. These were eunuchs, but in the seventeenth century this trade was expanded to embrace other categories of free born men as well. The Portuguese conducted this trade through the Coromnadel ports to Goa.

This trade was now also geared eastwards, mainly by the Dutch at Pulicat through Mrauk-U towards Batavia from the 1620s, and supplemented with more traditional goods such as long pepper, which was deemed better than the Kedah pepper[985], rice, oil, wheat, butter, sugar, stick lac, and textiles such as *cambayas, ellachas, rumals, malmals*[986].

Towards the end of the seventeenth century, Bowrey noted, ships from Bengal arrived at Achin with slave boys and girls[987]. Achin, the city state administered by a Virgin Queen[988], seems to have been a premier trade mart in the seventeenth century, with ships from Borneo and Macassar also bringing slaves there[989]. Alexander Hamilton wrote that the Queen of Achin was sent a letter and some brass guns by Queen Elizabeth of England and that the high regard the two queens evinced for each other was manifested in the indulgences the Achinese queen showed to the English Company at Achin[990]. But 'Bengali' shipowners and merchants seem not to have been active in this trade in the Bay; the initiative had clearly passed to European merchants.

In the seventeenth century a necklace of slave ports radiated from Pipli, Sagor, Sandwip and Chattagram in Bengal towards Mrauk-U in Arakan, and Achin, Kedah and Johor in South East Asia.The economics of slave ports dictated a different relation with the hinterland: instead of a close symbiosis between caravan and sea routes, slave ports needed a

---

[984] Barbosa: 180.

[985] Bowrey: 277.

[986] *Ibid.*: 288–289.

[987] *Ibid.*: 288–289.

[988] *Ibid.*: 324–325.

[989] *Ibid.*: 291.

[990] Hamilton, Alexander, *A New Account of the East Indies*, London, MDCC XLIVII, V.II: 100–1. This seems unlikely as Hamilton was writing in 1699 and the Achinese queen died in 1700. Either an earlier Achinese queen is meant, or it is possible that Hamilton meant Queen Anne of England.

'raiding region' in deltas infested with creeks through which boats could sneak up and carry off unsuspecting villagers. A slave could be sold for between 10 and 40 tankas (the price depended on age and gender); this low price meant that ever newer regions (and peoples) had to be brought into the radius of the slave trade. Slave ports acted as focal points of the marauding regions; they were the zones of housing and transhipment of slaves. By definition, dealing with a perishable commodity such as human life, moreover a commodity whose supply had to be renewed constantly meant, in effect, that when the Portuguese and Arakanese moved out of the slave trade in the seventeenth century a large part of the delta was left devastated.

In tradition and in history (although the two are frequently the same), Bengal was neither an aristocratic slave/eunuch owning society, nor was it a military slaving society. Aristocratic slavery was introduced into Bengal when the Islamic conquest state was established and the Bengal nawabs imported slaves for court, harem and military duties. It never became a military slave society. But the slavery that was introduced into Bengal in the seventeenth century was neither aristocratic, nor military; it was fundamentally different. It was merchant slavery, where the slave trade existed along with conventional trade and it was a system where the relations between the raiding peoples and those who were raided were made even more unequal, brutal, discontinuous and circumstantial.

Such a system normally gives rise to two distinctions. While the locus of the raiding state remained fixed, that of the raided region expands constantly. Moreover, it was a *hazy*, blurry zone that included *nameless* victims. In other words, geographical distance laid the basis for social distance. This geographical space of slavery within which humans were moulded into merchandise was structured, organised and articulated for this purpose. It was not an ordered and institutionalised economic system.

On the one hand was the slave raiding society which was historically identifiable and geographically defined, politically, militarily and commercially organised, on the other was the indistinct zone that supplied slaves. Meillassoux writes for Africa[991]:

> (These) were nameless and distant populations, scattered, often little known to the above societies and seen as part of a vague and unorganised set of savages. There was no formal relation between the two, no link other than the raw violence

[991] Meillassoux, Claude, 1991, *The Anthropology of Slavery: The Womb of Iron and Gold*, Chicago University Press: 73–4.

> imposed by one of the parties where neither war nor peace was ever declared or concluded.The apparatuses established to link slave-owning societies and societies which produced slaves-the army or the pillaging band-did not, by their very nature, allow mutual political recognition.

Moreover, the mostly overseas society for whom slaves were destined was also identifiable and defined; both in locational and historical terms. This classic account of how slavery functioned in African societies is not really useful for our purposes here. Because, in a majority of cases from the mid seventeenth century, the Arakanese claimed the captives for their own. A slave market had grown up *within* Arakan as well.

The account above does not also explain the strained relationship between Arakan and southeastern Bengal in the seventeenth century. Why did this historical ally turn into a foe? How did this contiguous land (southeastern Bengal) turn into a 'distant' land, an indistinct area that supplied nameless slaves? The answer may lie in the radical political reorganisation set in motion in the area once the Mughals established their sovereignty at Dhaka. The attempts from the time of *subahdar* Islam Khan to govern the area, the decimation of the independent chiefs of the delta area, and Shah Jahan's assertion of power at Dhaka must have changed, in Arakanese perception, established power relations between Gaur and Mrauk-U. It is noticeable that the friendly relations between the two states, as exemplified in the adoption of Islamic names and coinage from the fifteenth century, were radically altered after 1622. At the height of their power, at a time when the Islamic cultural influence was supposed to be most visible at the Arakan court, the Arakanese monarchs no longer felt it necessary to use Islamic names to proclaim their might. From 1634, the old practice of minting coins in three languages; Bengali, Persian and Arakanese was dropped. Henceforth only Arakanese was used on the coins[992]. Bangalah therefore became a distant land.

The same equations worked for the Portuguese as well. They too, once their commercial power was broken by the Dutch and the English, turned to the slave trade. We should always remember that unlike the second wave of Europeans such as the Dutch, the British and the French, the Portuguese always remained a coastal power. The power of the Portuguese derived from their control over ports, this control in turn was determined by the nature of their trade. Once they turned to the slave trade, the Portuguese 'control' over ports in Bengal became ultimately

[992] Leider, 2005: 114.

detrimental to these ports. Dealing in a persishable commodity such as human life, a make or break situtation resulted if the supply dwindled.

Slavery never created a surplus, although it did allow accumulation upto a certain point. This accumulation without surplus could only result in the decrease of the pillaged populations. In the long term, the flow of supplies to the slave markets could only dry up. In societies where the emergence of a market for land was blocked by patrimonial ownership, and where the self-sufficiency of the labourers was a fact and not fiction, the drying up of supplies of slaves meant the drying up of the market as a whole. Deprived of its pivot, trade could only involve a limited amount of exchange. Transactions became less numerous, less varied. They became limited to luxury goods. The market's lack of fluidity did not favour exchange of articles of daily use. Nor did it favour the generalised use of money.

This scenario will help us to understand as to why parts of lower Bengal were depopulated in the seventeenth century, why trade 'stopped' there and why the use of non-metallic currencies such as *cauris* became widespread again in south eastern Bengal from the middle of the seventeenth century, as Glanius' testimony tells us. Ports which had already a short life in Bengal, due to ecological reasons described earlier, were therefore now even more vulnerable. The hinterland had become perverted. This explains why Sagor, once a flourishing port of Bengal and a place of pilgrimage from the eleventh century, was abandoned at the close of the seventeenth century. So were most other ports in Lower Bengal.

Finally, it was only the 'unofficial' Portuguese who attempted to revive the Bay trade for another century. The fact that a broken Portuguese was spoken all around the Indian Ocean was testimony to the efforts of the 'private', 'unofficial' Portuguese who peopled the coast. Their objective was however not the older China-Bengal-Delhi-Red Sea network but the Malacca-Pegu-Coromandel network which brought in very cheap gold and the best rubies from Pegu. In this trade Arakan and Bengal occupied primate positions in terms of imports but not for exports. Manrique's voyage to Bengal, and his negotiations with the Arakanese king in the 1630s, is testimony to a last attempt by the Portuguese to revive this once flourishing trade. But it was too late, because the Portuguese themselves were part of the process that had rendered the area barren.

In 1612 Pegu was closed off to all trade. Also the massacre of the Portuguese by the Arakanese at Dianga in 1607 soon after the latter had thrown out the Portuguese from Chattagram, then the execution of de

Brito, the 'independent' Portuguese ruler of Syriam by the Mons-Burmese in 1613, followed by the defeat of the Portuguese by the Kandy forces in Ceylon in August 1630, and finally the fall of Acheh in 1636 in the wake of Dutch conquests in the Indonesian archipelago signified the collapse of the informal Portuguese network of trade in the Bay of Bengal. The Portuguese officially 'stayed' back only at the slave port of Pipli. Bocarro's lament of the Bay trade in the *Livro das Plantas*, in the 1630s runs thus[993]:

> the great Bay of Bengala, and Pegu, where ...we once had great settlements of Portuguese...all of them came to an end with great destruction and devastation, and hence today one only navigates to the port of Orixa in the kingdom of Bengala (Pipli), where there is a Portuguese captain appointed by the viceroy only in order to treat with the Moorish vassals of the Mogor, to whom the port belongs...but he has nothing else there, not even a house, save some made of straw....

The association between political power, long-distance trade and a high level of economic activities in cities of substantial status was taken for granted in the Islamic world economy. The historical connection between long-distance trade and the process of urbanisation was a simultaneous phenomenon; one that could make or break the port cities of the Indian Ocean world. Wholesale merchants and bankers engaged in transcontinental trade found all the supporting services at these ports. These advantages collapsed if there was political instability in the states that supported this network. The urban centres were the first to pay a heavy price for political instability or invasions. This is borne out in the case of Bengal's ports. Their instability, once the eastern Bay trade collapsed, has been documented already.

This volume suggested earlier the advantages of discussing regional histories in the world systemic perspective. If we site Bengal within the early and later Islamic world economies, then the enigma of its marginal position both in terms of the territorial history of South Asia and of the maritime world of the Indian Ocean can be transcended. In the eighteenth century, not just Bengal but the whole region from Iran to South East Asia was undergoing internal decline. Political vigour was flagging, once flourishing towns and their urban economies were lagging behind. Indeed this whole area, and not just Bengal, was reeling from European attacks on their economy, sovereignty and way

[993] Subrahmanyam,S., 1990, Appendix: 261.

of life. While the very marginality of Bengal, both in the Mughal political world and in the trading life of the Indian Ocean after the sixteenth century, enabled English commercial dominance in the eighteenth century, paradoxically it were English annals that celebrated the 'primacy' of Bengal. Because what we have at work is the notion of two separate histories coming together: a marginal area becomes a primary area for another nation and its history. Seen this way, the inconsistencies and contradictions of the eighteenth century debate, at least as far as Bengal is concerned, can be explained away. Bengal was marginal to the rhythms of history that made up the greater history of the region, both by sea and land. The 'primacy' of Bengal, may have been a factor in the trade of the Bay a long time ago; by the eighteenth century this was at best a myth.

The Effects of Long Term Cycles of Expansion and Contraction of the Indian Ocean Economy: Bengal and South Asia

'Le relative succès des marchands europeens en Asie ne va pas de soi en effet. L'argument ideologique, insistant sur la superiorité de "l'esprit de la Renaissance"–ne convaine plus guère aujourd'hui' (Lombard, Denys, 1990, *Le Carrefour Javanais: Essai d'histoire globale*, V.II *Les Reseaux Asiatiques*, Paris, E.H.E.S.S.: 10). The relative success of the European merchants in Asia (is debated)–the idea of the superiority of the 'Renaissance spirit' hardly convinces one today.

In *Leading Sectors and World Powers* Modelski and Thomson identified nineteen Kondratieff cycles (of 50 years each) of expansion and contraction of the world economy. They identified four such cycles in Song China between 930 and 1250 AD, after which they claimed that the focus of the economy had shifted to western Europe[994]. This has recently been debated; even after 1190 (the Champagne Fairs), when Modelski and Thomson claimed that the world economy lay centred on Europe, the innovations continued to be centred on Asia related factors such as the Black Sea trade, Venetian galleys, pepper, and Indian spices until the 1570s. K13 in the seventeenth century introduced a new dimension: the Amerasian plantation economy and trade. Only in the 1760s, when Britain introduced cotton technology and transport innovations did the focus shift firmly to

[994] Modelski. George and Thomson, William, 1996, *Leading Sectors and World Powers: The Co-Evolution of Global Economics and Politics*, Columbia, South Carolina Press.

Europe. Therefore, K12 too was centred on trade growth in Asia. Since K12 focussed on the sixteenth century this validates our thesis that trade in Bengal experienced growth until the sixteenth century (the Husain Shahi Divide).

The K cycles (with K5 at 1190) underscore the economic vitality in Bengal from K2 (1030s) to K 12 (1530s). Of these K2 to K10 (around 1430) were based on south eastern Bengal. This corresponds to Sun Laichen's delineation of active trade cycles between Burma and China in the late thirteenth century (K7) and in late fourteenth/early fifteenth centuries (K9 and K10).

This economic growth was centred on the delta ports of the Bay of Bengal. This area grew slowly. Most of if faced the sea at first. It developed actively from the fourteenth to the sixteenth centuries when the riverine network shifted from east to west. Sandbars, bays and inlets were introduced into this landscape as more rivers appeared in the west to east shifts of the sixteenth to the eighteenth centuries. This delta was not only made by rivers, it was made also by humans. As more and more land rose from the bay settlements appeared, markets were set up and ports established. In a situation analogous to that described by Robert Marks (1998 : 66 – 83) for the Pearl River Delta (in which lay Zaitun and with which area Bengal's delta had topographical and commercial synergies) this delta area witnessed active urbanisation and intense commercialization in medieval times, as we noted.

In this active delta agricultural productivity jumped by 107% between 1595 and 1659, as Eaton (1993) has shown. In 1595 the productivity of the south east was only 59% of that of south west Bengal. In 1659 this productivity climbed to 84% of that of the south west.

But this growing productivity was not reflected in Bengal's revenue figures. For both 1595 and 1659 the revenue figures for the south west comprised a third of Bengal's total figures – 35% and 33% respectively. Eaton explains the contradiction by asserting that the south west had a head start in terms of agrarian development, but we can explain this anomaly by way of slave raids, piracy and depopulation in the south east in the seventeenth century.

K 11 and K 12 saw the focus shift to south west. Growth in this region was initially slower and this is reflected in Table 7.1's revenue figures for Bengal.

But growth in China continued until the end of the eighteenth century[995]. And we saw growth continued until the end of the seventeenth century for the South Asian world. By the seventeenth century Agra, Delhi and Lahore had populations over half a million, some of the port cities contained upwards of 200 000 people. Urbanisation in cities over 5 000 reached 15% of the population. A comparable development was not visible for Bengal which stopped growing after the sixteenth century.

From World Economy to World System: The case of the Indian Ocean

By the seventeenth century the Indian Ocean World had transformed itself into a new world system. Its linkages with the African and Asian worlds, its economic relations with the Mediterranean and caspian seas ensured it a leading role in the has nascent west European economy.

But in this very century, when the second wave of Europeans set foot in Asia, there were signs that the Indian Ocean system was in crisis. Growth was flagging, technology did not keep pace with changes, and the largely military empires around the Indian Ocean devoted time and money to the management of empire. The consequence was, at the end of the seventeenth century, a decline of indigenous participation in the maritime zones. Coastal areas could not sustain the same rate of growth. Under these circumstances it was easy for European capital to penetrate the fringes of empire. In the eighteenth century this became a reality in Bengal.

[995] See Frank, A.G., 2005, 'The Centrality of China and the Marginality of Europe in the World Economy' in Mukherjee Rila and Chattopadhyaya, Kunal eds. *Europe in the Second Millennium: A Hegemony Achieved*? Kolkata, Progressive Publishers: 135–192. See Appendix 3 'On Modelski and Thomson's Kondratieffs': 186–188.

9

Conclusion

'Let traders and *karwans* on both sides come and go, and let the precious products and ordinary commodities which may be in my territory be conveyed by them into thine, and those of thine, in the same manner, let them bring into mine', Chingiz Khan to Sultan Muhammad Khwarazm Shah, on the occasion of his march towards Persia (Khwarizim) through Afghanistan, in Minhaj-ud-Din Abu Umar-I-Usman's *Tabakat-I-Nasiri: A General History of the Muhammadan Dynasties of Asia from 810* AD *to 1260* AD *and the Irruption of the Infidel Mughals into Islam* (Tr). Raverty, H.G. 1881, Reprint, New Delhi, Oriental Books Corporation, 1970: 966.

There was, we know, another 'Asian Trade' in existence in South Asia: an Asian trade of caravans, mules and nomadic tribesmen who traversed mighty passes, steep ravines and inhospitable terrain in a vast trade route spanning the cities of Asia, Arabia, Mongolia and China. This 'Asian (overland) Trade' was very different from Asian trade in Asian waters; nevertheless due to accessibility of sources it has always been this latter (sea) trade that has been treated under the idiom of 'Asian Trade' for the purposes of historical research[996].

We have seen that in the eighties the frontiers of this new subject–Asian Sea Trade–were pushed ahead by the provocative works of Ashin Das Gupta on the Malabar and Surat, by Om Prakash–and to a certain degree by Sushil Chaudhuri–for Bengal, by Aniruddha Ray on Cambay, by Sinappah Arasaratnam for the Coromandel and by K.N. Chaudhuri for the whole of the Indian Ocean World.

[996] See section on 'Was There ever an 'Indian' Trade?' for more on this.

The quandary faced when dealing with this ubiquitous topic called Asian Trade–which is itself based exclusively on official European sources that are then used to reconstruct a very imperfect picture of a portion of the sub-continent's economy–had already begun to be reflected in the works of these scholars. Studies of coastal trade and long distance trade will always remain one dimensional if developments–comprising linkages, growth, ruptures, transitions and transformations–on both *land* and sea are not taken into account[997].

In the absence of prolific Asian–and Indian–records there is a massive dependence on western accounts for the reconstruction of one of the most significant centuries–the eighteenth–in Indian history. But in this dependance one is imperceptibly faced with the prejudice implicit in the western hemeneutical tradition–a prejudice that dictates the parameters within which our very own society one is seen[998].

At the same time prosaic documents such as factory records and private diaries and correspondance of European company officials threw up another picture: that of a vibrant commercial economy in Bengal; albeit one that was markedly different to commercial economies in place in the Europe of the eighteenth century. In other words what the enlightened English/European official was describing with his eighteenth century pen was the functioning of the Mughal political economy in Bengal. He was describing, in effect, the pre-modern state of Bengal–a state that relied more on pomp and outward displays of majesty rather than a state that embraced within its confines all aspects of life: the social, the religious, the moral and the economic. This implied that the commercial domain in Bengal was still unregulated, still open to intervention from forces other than from the state or the market.

Similarly another question that is pertinent even today–at the time of writing this book–is how can one reconcile ones findings with the debate on the eighteenth century? It is noted that Bengal was a case apart. That the eighteenth century debate has now exhausted itself largely due to its

---

997 This was done by Ray for Gaur and by Subrahmanyam for Arcot and the Nayaka states (Subrahmanyam, S., Schulman, D., Rao, V.N. in *Symbols of Substance* etc. New Delhi Oxford University Press 1992).

998 In my readings of official documents I encountered traces of the idea of asiatic despotism, the illiberal tradition of the orient, the lack of movement and progress, the impermanence of Asiatic cities, the poverty of society, the lack of a rule of law, the absence of a state in the occidental sense, the incomprehensible pageantry of the ruling class, the non-existence of a bourgeoisie, the mendacity of brahmans and banians, the avarice of rulers, and the laziness of natives. These were mirrored in records, travel accounts, and diaries as well as in semi-official correspondence regarding South Asia.

temporal and spatial insufficiencies has been made clear in sections preceding this.

The focus on Bengal has been retained here since it was the foremost arena of European trading activities in the eighteenth century but the study would be more fleshed out if there is a broader enquiry to look into the genealogy of a commercial economy in Bengal. Sources are plenty. Travellers' accounts–both European and Arabic–provide insights. Almost a continuous commercial history of Bengal can be found from the early fourteenth century until the late seventeenth century at which point one can switch over to factory records supplemented by a growing number of French, Dutch and English 'official' travel accounts; think of the account of Ibn Batuta for the fourteenth century, the records of the Chinese missions for the fifteenth century, witness the Mangal Kavyas, and the accounts of Barbosa and Varthema for the early sixteenth century as well as the accounts of Frederici and Fitch for the later part; similarly the seventeenth century is well covered by Laval, Bowrey and Manrique from the early to the middle period and the diaries of Master and Hedges cover twelve continuous years (1675–80 and 81–87 respectively)[999]. Only the fifteenth century stands forlorn; a century without corroborating records except Chinese sources for the first half.

In the process certain themes have been emphasized while writing this book: the Mongol rupture, the thirteenth century crisis, state formation in Bengal, the articulation of a specific polity, the formation of a composite regional identity and of course Bengal's position in the Islamic world economy. It might well be argued that a study of the eighteenth century Bengal does not merit a digression into an earlier period but I would argue that any discussion of the eighteenth century economy in Bengal would be redundant if one does not take into account the processes that the events of the thirteenth century unleashed in Bengal. I maintained that at this critical juncture for history as a discipline new doors be opened and ideas invited with tools borrowed from subjects other than conventional historiography.

This volume has surveyed the historical evolution of Bengal as a region. In the twentieth century the eastern part of Bengal, the area that has been highlighted here, was partitioned off as East Pakistan. East Pakistan split from Pakistan and the independent country of Bangladesh was created in 1971.

---

[999] See references in footnotes throughout this volume.

The trade figures between India and Bangladesh for the last decade (see Table 9.1 below) support one of the assertions made in this volume; that although this was one of the earliest regions in eastern India to show commercial vitality, the productive capacity of this area was subordinated, increasingly, to meet the demands of the Mughal home market from the seventeenth century. At the turn of the twenty first century, this region, now an independent country, is still primarily an agricultural country. Its unequal balance of trade with India shows that historically conditioned links of dependency still continue to exist between Bangladesh and India.

Table 9.1: Trade figures for India and Bangladesh: end twentieth and early twenty-first century[1000]

India	325.00	960.00	1042.00			
	1991	1995	2002	1991	1995	2002
B'desh				23.00	36.00	39.33
	B'desh	B'desh	B'desh	India	India	India

India–Bangladesh Trade matrix

(US$ million)

			Export			
			Import			
	B'desh	B'desh	B'desh	India	India	India
	1991	1995	2002	1991	1995	2002
B'desh				189.00	994.00	1145.83
India	6.00	79.00	43.00			
			Total			
	B'desh	B'desh	B'desh	India	India	India
	1991	1995	2002	1991	1995	2002
B'desh				189.00	994.00	#VALUE!
India	6.00	79.00	#VALUE!			

Tables 9.2 and 9.3 highlight this unequal balance and give us more data on imports into India and exports to Bangladesh in the last decade.

[1000] From Prabir De, Associate Fellow at Research and Information Systems, New Delhi. Source India Trade Database, CMIE.

Table 9.2 : Imports from Bangladesh[1001]

Commodity	*Rs.Lakh Cumulative 1991–1992 val*	*Rs.Lakh Cumulative 1995–1996 val*	*Rs.Lakh Cumulative 2001–2002 val*	*Rs.Lakh Cumulative 2002–2003 val*
1 Fish and crustaceans, molluscs and other aquatic invertebrates.		2719.65	2025.39	1721.88
2 Dairy produce, birds' eggs; natural honey; edible products of animal origin, not specified or included elsewhere.			9.37	
3 Products of animal origin, not specified or included elsewhere.				3.96
4 Edible vegetables and certain roots and tubers.			4.2	0.4
5 Edible fruit and nuts; peel or citrus fruit or melons.			210.31	925.06
6 Coffee, tea, mate and spices.		40.21	14.15	38.76
7 Cereals.			68.02	
8 Products of the milling industry; malt; starches; inulin; wheat gluten.			1.72	3.49
9 Oil seeds and oleaginous fruits; miscellaneous grains,				

Contd...

[1001] As before.

Commodity	*Rs.Lakh Cumulative 1991–1992 val*	*Rs.Lakh Cumulative 1995–1996 val*	*Rs.Lakh Cumulative 2001–2002 val*	*Rs.Lakh Cumulative 2002–2003 val*
seeds and fruit; industrial or medicinal plants; straw and fodder.			0.42	19.28
10 Vegetable plaiting materials; vegetable products not elsewhere specified or included.			1.11	
11 Animal or vegetable fats and oils and their cleavage products; prepared edible fats; animal or vegetable waxes.	66.69	12.29		
12 Sugars and sugar confectionery.				16.3
13 Preparations of cereals, flour, starch or milk; pastrycooks' products.			11.69	31.2
14 Preparations of vegetables, fruit, nuts or other parts of plants.			31.51	92.16
15 Miscellaneous edible preparations.			0.89	0.65
16 Beverages, spirits and vinegar.			4.98	8.01
17 Tobacco and manufactured tobacco substitutes.	8.67			

Contd...

Commodity	*Rs.Lakh Cumulative 1991–1992 val*	*Rs.Lakh Cumulative 1995–1996 val*	*Rs.Lakh Cumulative 2001–2002 val*	*Rs.Lakh Cumulative 2002–2003 val*
18 Salt; sulphur; earths and stone; plastering materials, lime and cement.		8.92		35.45
19 Ores, slag and ash.	7.44	6.02	0.88	
20 Inorganic chemicals; organic or inorganic compounds of precious metals, of rare-earth metals, or radioactive elements or of isotopes.		9354	7175.68	8110.99
21 Organic Chemicals		1.87		46.45
22 Pharmaceutical products.			0.99	
23 Fertilisers		11524.49	861.55	
24 Tanning or dyeing extracts; tannins and their derivatives; dyes, pigments and other colouring matter; paints and varnishes; putty and other mastics; inks.				23.2
25 Essential oils and resinoids; perfumery, cosmetic or toilet preparations.			5.51	2.91
26 Soap, organic surface-active agents, washing preparations, lubricating preparations, artificial waxes,				

Contd...

Commodity	*Rs.Lakh Cumulative 1991–1992 val*	*Rs.Lakh Cumulative 1995–1996 val*	*Rs.Lakh Cumulative 2001–2002 val*	*Rs.Lakh Cumulative 2002–2003 val*
prepared waxes, polishing or scouring preparations, candles and similar articles, modelling paste UNIT			49.45	2.76
27 Photographic or cinematographic goods.			0.32	
28 Miscellaneous chemical products.			11.46	
29 Plastics and articles thereof.			21.89	105.94
30 Rubber and articles thereof.		0.13	1.89	1.97
31 Raw hides and skins (other than furskins) and leather.	179.97	365.94	716.46	822.24
32 Articles of leather, saddlery and harness; travel goods, handbags and similar containers of articles of animal gut (other than silk-worm gut).				0.03
33 Pulp of wood or of other fibrous cellulosic material; waste and scrap of paper or paperboard.			3.51	
34 Paper and paperboard; articles of paper pulp, of paper or of paperboard.	411.07	0.01	7.1	8.36

Contd...

Commodity	*Rs.Lakh Cumulative 1991–1992 val*	*Rs.Lakh Cumulative 1995–1996 val*	*Rs.Lakh Cumulative 2001–2002 val*	*Rs.Lakh Cumulative 2002–2003 val*
35 Printed books, newspapers, pictures and other products of the printing industry; manuscripts, typescripts and plans.	0.89	39.57	36.7	47.09
36 Silk		1.04	151.8	0.16
37 Wool, fine or coarse animal hair; horsehair yarn and woven fabric.			5.02	6.95
38 Cotton	10.32	139.96	97.12	279.88
39 Other vegetable textile fibres; paper yarn and woven fabrics of paper yarn.	681.08	3843.4	9906.8	11468.64
40 Man-made filaments		0.38	98.62	1.03
41 Man-made staple fibres.		1.07		13.58
42 Wadding, felt and nonwovens; special yarns; twine, cordage, ropes and cables and articles thereof.		1.05	370.47	224.84
43 Carpets and other textile floor coverings.			9.23	3.49
44 Special woven fabrics; tufted textile fabrics; lace; tapestries; trimmings; embroidery.		1.14	7.95	1.21

Contd...

Commodity	*Rs.Lakh Cumulative 1991–1992 val*	*Rs.Lakh Cumulative 1995–1996 val*	*Rs.Lakh Cumulative 2001–2002 val*	*Rs.Lakh Cumulative 2002–2003 val*
45 Impregnated, coated, covered or laminated textile fabrics; textile articles of a kind suitable for industrial use.			8.91	
46 Knitted or crocheted fabrics.		9.65		0.12
47 Articles of apparel and clothing accessories, knitted or crocheted.			83.07	268.81
48 Articles of apparel and clothing accessories, not knitted or crocheted.			802	635.44
49 Other made up textile articles; sets; worn clothing and worn textile articles; rags.		0.55	4521.56	710.77
50 Prepared feathers and down and articles made of feathers or of down; artificial flowers; articles of human hair.		0.9	0.21	
51 Articles of stone, plaster, cement, asbestos, mica or similar materials.				11.63
52 Ceramic products.		0.03	80.41	63.11

Contd...

Commodity	Rs.Lakh Cumulative 1991--1992 val	Rs.Lakh Cumulative 1995–1996 val	Rs.Lakh Cumulative 2001–2002 val	Rs.Lakh Cumulative 2002–2003 val
53 Glass and glassware.		0.01		0.01
54 Natural or cultured pearls, precious or semi-precious stones, precious metals, metals clad with precious metal and articles thereof; imitation jewellery; coin.		1.69		
55 Iron and steel.		0.15	13.69	14.81
56 Articles of iron or steel.	0.08		24.05	6.06
57 Copper and articles thereof.			181.54	0.24
58 Lead and articles thereof.	Not Available	NA	NA	NA
59 Zinc and articles thereof.	NA	NA	NA	NA
60 Tools, implements, cutlery, spoons and forks, of base metal; parts thereof of base metal.	NA	NA	NA	NA
61 Miscellaneous articles of base metal.	NA	NA	NA	NA
62 Nuclear reactors, boilers, machinery and mechanical appliances; parts thereof.	NA	NA	NA	NA

Contd...

Commodity	*Rs.Lakh Cumulative 1991–1992 val*	*Rs.Lakh Cumulative 1995–1996 val*	*Rs.Lakh Cumulative 2001–2002 val*	*Rs.Lakh Cumulative 2002–2003 val*
63 Electrical machinery and equipment and parts thereof; sound recorders and reproducers, television image and sound reacorders and reproducers, and parts and accessories of articles.	NA	NA	NA	NA
64 Vehicles other than railway or tramway rolling stock, and parts and accessories thereof.	NA	NA	NA	NA
65 Aircraft, spacecraft, and parts thereof.	NA	NA	NA	NA
66 Ships, boats and floating structures.	NA	NA	NA	NA
67 Optical, photographic, cinematographic, measuring, checking, precision, medical or surgical instruments and apparatus; parts and accessories thereof.	NA	NA	NA	NA
68 Clocks and watches and parts thereof.	NA	NA	NA	NA
69 Furniture; bedding, mattresses, mattress supports, cushions and similar stuffed				

Contd...

Commodity	*Rs.Lakh Cumulative 1991–1992 val*	*Rs.Lakh Cumulative 1995–1996 val*	*Rs.Lakh Cumulative 2001–2002 val*	*Rs.Lakh Cumulative 2002–2003 val*
furnishings; lamps and lighting fittings, not elsewhere specified or included; illuminated signs, illuminated name-plate UNIT	NA	NA	NA	NA
70 Toys, games and sports requisites; parts and accessories thereof.	NA	NA	NA	NA
71 Miscellaneous manufactured articles.	NA	NA	NA	NA
72 Project Goods; some special uses.	NA	NA	NA	NA
73 Miscellaneous goods.	NA	NA	NA	NA

Table 9.3 : Indian Exports to Bangladesh[1002]

Commodities	*Rs.Lakh Cumulative 1991–1992*	*Rs.Lakh Cumulative 1995–1996*	*Rs.Lakh Cumulative 2001–2002*	*Rs.Lakh Cumulative 2002–2003*
1 Live Animals	40.07	716.99	188.9	325.81
2 Meat and edible meat offal.			1.49	10.9
3 Fish and crustaceans, molluscs and other aquatic invertebrates.		520.22	3838.26	532.08
4 Dairy produce, birds' eggs; natural honey; edible products of				

Contd...

[1002] As before.

Commodities	*Rs.Lakh Cumulative 1991–1992*	*Rs.Lakh Cumulative 1995–1996*	*Rs.Lakh Cumulative 2001–2002*	*Rs.Lakh Cumulative 2002–2003*
animal origin, not elsewhere specified or included.	607.02	587.43	5683.98	3681.61
5 Products of animal origin, not elsewhere specified or included.		4.37		10.71
6 Live trees, and other plants; bulbs, roots and the like; cut flowers and ornamental foliage.			7.25	11.06
7 Edible vegetables and certain roots and tubers.	6015.75	2169.12	18251.3	18005.3
8 Edible fruit and nuts; peel or citrus fruit or melons.	1492.62	3250.98	11754.67	5894.3
9 Coffee, tea, mate and spices.	4501.88	4147.63	5020.4	4843.13
10 Cereals.	199.14	103059.3	54813.03	90048.76
11 Products of the milling industry; malt; starches; inulin; wheat gluten.	2.48	577.97	4875.29	582.54
12 Oil seeds and oleaginous fruits; miscellaneous grains, seeds and fruit; industrial or medicinal plants; straw and fodder.	208.64	354.09	779.89	442.33
13 Lac; gums, resins and other vegetable saps and extracts.	40.2	44.04	527.54	152.27

Contd...

Commodities	*Rs.Lakh Cumulative 1991–1992*	*Rs.Lakh Cumulative 1995–1996*	*Rs.Lakh Cumulative 2001–2002*	*Rs.Lakh Cumulative 2002–2003*
14 Vegetable plaiting materials; vegetable products not elsewhere specified or included.		8.7	31.93	17.65
15 Animal or vegetable fats and oils and their cleavage products; prepared edible fats; animal or vegetable waxes.	9.25	57.14	497.45	2498.31
16 Sugars and sugar confectionery.		59.52	18431.92	29590.9
17 Cocoa and cocoa preparations.	0.1	159.76	300.82	198.14
18 Preparations of cereals, flour, starch or milk; pastrycooks' products.	187	635.24	1605.17	193.62
19 Preparations of vegetables, fruit, nuts or other parts of plants.	20.09	4.1	169.81	70.65
20 Miscellaneous edible preparations.	0.26	144.54	203.78	84.82
21 Beverages, spiris and vinegar.		2.65	80.32	125.12
22 Residues and waste from the food industries; prepared animal fodder.	44.99	493.58	21253.94	17311.03
23 Tobacco and manufactured tobacco substitutes.	271.75	2909.48	1056.42	1198.54

Contd...

Commodities	*Rs.Lakh Cumulative 1991–1992*	*Rs.Lakh Cumulative 1995–1996*	*Rs.Lakh Cumulative 2001–2002*	*Rs.Lakh Cumulative 2002–2003*
24 Salt; sulphur; earths and stone; plastering materials, lime and cement.	2807.32	13416.38	14684.74	8582.33
25 Ores, slag and ash.	33.12	2.99	994.52	1362.39
26 Mineral fuels, mineral oils and products or their distillation; bituminous substances; mineral waxes.	998.61	7893.46	20613.06	29061.49
27 Inorganic chemicals; organic or inorganic compounds of precious metals, of rare-earth metals, or radioactive elements or of isotopes.	755.73	3024.05	6568.41	4676.26
28 Organic Chemicals	726.94	3517.97	8563.62	11719.8
29 Pharmaceutical products.	2348.68	1520.01	5528.45	5958.5
30 Fertilisers	1.94	5097.61	156.66	19.82
31 Tanning or dyeing extracts; tannins and their derivatives; dyes, pigments and other colouring matter; paints and varnishes; putty and other mastics; inks.	1333.5	4193.84	8037.84	9012.88
32 Essential oils and resinoids; perfumery, cosmetic or toilet preparations.	12.18	523.35	1447.78	761.49

Contd...

Commodities	*Rs.Lakh Cumulative 1991–1992*	*Rs.Lakh Cumulative 1995–1996*	*Rs.Lakh Cumulative 2001–2002*	*Rs.Lakh Cumulative 2002–2003*
33 Soap, organic surface-active agents, washing preparations, lubricating preparations, artificial waxes, prepared waxes, polishing or scouring preparations, candles and similar articles, modelling paste UNIT	35.09	1774.14	1342.75	1005.68
34 Albuminoidal substances; modified starches; glues; enzymes.	60.48	146.36	250.26	415.74
35 Explosives; pyrotechnic products; matches; pyrophoric alloys; certain combustible preparations.		21.29	31.43	23.73
36 Photographic or cinematographic goods.	19.93	59.81	96.64	143.95
37 Miscellaneous chemical products.	360.23	1067.51	2739.89	2714.96
38 Plastics and articles thereof.	344.46	1431.38	8227.88	11759.75
39 Rubber and articles thereof.	2763.37	7265.87	7798.61	8371.08
40 Raw hides and skins (other than furskins) and leather.	18.52	15.52	187.66	48.23
41 Articles of leather, saddlery and harness; travel goods,				

Contd...

Commodities	*Rs.Lakh Cumulative 1991–1992*	*Rs.Lakh Cumulative 1995–1996*	*Rs.Lakh Cumulative 2001–2002*	*Rs.Lakh Cumulative 2002–2003*
handbags and similar containers, articles of animal gut (other than silk-worm gut).	18.42	15.03	65.52	48.85
42 Wood and articles of wood; wood charcoal.	39.3	370.74	209.9	651.4
43 Cork and articles of cork.	0.06		5.81	7.57
44 Manufacturers of straw; of esparto or of other plaiting materials; basketware and wickerwork.			1.81	3.63
45 Paper and paperboard; articles of paper pulp, of paper or of paperboard.	435.16	6562.61	12839.13	8920.37
46 Printed books, newspapers, pictures and other products of the printing industry; manuscripts, typescripts and plans.	467.99	1284.51	1507.37	1370.61
47 Silk	9.89	22.27	192.81	10.59
48 Wool, fine or coarse animal hair; horsehair yarn and woven fabric.		24.64	121.49	589.27
49 Cotton	22290.42	85308.09	77919.21	61644.13

Contd...

Commodities	*Rs.Lakh Cumulative 1991–1992*	*Rs.Lakh Cumulative 1995–1996*	*Rs.Lakh Cumulative 2001–2002*	*Rs.Lakh Cumulative 2002–2003*
50 Other vegetable textile fibres; paper yarn and woven fabrics of paper yarn.		20.47	31.85	88.8
51 Man-made filaments	3523.9	1742.97	1760.3	2424.27
52 Man-made staple fibres.	1056.8	3022.38	6158.05	9283.48
53 Wadding, felt and nonwovens; special yarns; twine, cordage, ropes and cables and articles thereof.	6.66	22.08	40.05	235.13
54 Carpets and other textile floor coverings.	9.66	28.89	45.8	112.68
55 Special woven fabrics; tufted textile fabrics; lace; tapestries; trimmings; embroidery.	71.44	78.11	586.76	476.65
56 Impregnated, coated, covered or laminated textile fabrics; textile articles of a kind suitable for industrial use.	15.7	35.27	278.38	154.48
57 Knitted or crocheted fabrics.	9158.3	7761.8	641.63	811.68
58 Articles of apparel and clothing accessories, knitted or crocheted.	218.15	92.73	183.79	1136.58
59 Articles of apparel and clothing accessories, not knitted or crocheted.	107.92	358.07	740.57	2831.47

Contd...

Commodities	*Rs.Lakh Cumulative 1991–1992*	*Rs.Lakh Cumulative 1995–1996*	*Rs.Lakh Cumulative 2001–2002*	*Rs.Lakh Cumulative 2002–2003*
60 Other made up textile articles; sets; worn clothing and worn textile articles; rags.	136.21	131.94	297.22	218.02
61 Footwear, gaiters and the like; parts of such articles.	2.98	27.83	266.7	167.64
62 Headgear and parts thereof.		1.9	5.76	75.96
63 Umbrellas, sun umbrellas, walking-sticks, seat-sticks, whips, riding-crops and parts thereof.	0.81	13.88	17.75	13.04
64 Articles of stone, plaster, cement, asbestos, mica or similar materials.	36.35	395.46	1761.56	804.9
65 Ceramic products.	51.62	218.78	567.88	240.89
66 Glass and glassware.	451.94	1715.89	1974.57	1913.45
67 Natural or cultured pearls, precious or semi-precious stones, precious metals, metals clad with precious metal and articles thereof; imitation jewellery; coin.	49.98	973.78	471.71	179.61
68 Iron and steel.	821.61	11445.1	16513.62	32627.68

Contd...

Commodities	*Rs.Lakh Cumulative 1991–1992*	*Rs.Lakh Cumulative 1995–1996*	*Rs.Lakh Cumulative 2001–2002*	*Rs.Lakh Cumulative 2002–2003*
69 Articles of iron or steel.	807.82	1566.35	10262.46	5657.87
70 Copper and articles thereof.	63.59	37.92	581.3	920.81
71 Nickel and articles thereof.		12.45		12.41
72 Aluminium and articles thereof.	1189.38	2488.94	10016.1	8175.88
73 Lead and articles thereof.	0.12	36.54	26.25	26.8
74 Zinc and articles thereof.	0.5	2.96	34.24	
75 Tin and articles thereof.	7.54	6.22	0.82	3.67
76 Other base metals; cermets; articles thereof.	4.27	43.04	225.73	185.75
77 Tools, implements, cutlery, spoons and forks, of base metal; parts thereof of base metal.	90.97	192.47	570.52	792.93
78 Miscellaneous articles of base metal.	92.78	172.82	641.73	295.56
79 Nuclear reactors, boilers, machinery and mechanical appliances; parts thereof.	6839.22	14018.82	30584.06	17371.32
80 Electrical machinery and equipment and parts thereof; sound recorders and reproducers, television				

Contd...

Commodities	*Rs.Lakh Cumulative 1991–1992*	*Rs.Lakh Cumulative 1995–1996*	*Rs.Lakh Cumulative 2001–2002*	*Rs.Lakh Cumulative 2002–2003*
image and sound recorders and reproducers, and parts and accessories of articles.	1508.33	9387.84	18176.78	14447.23
81 Railway or tramway locomotives, rolling-stock and parts thereof; railway or tramway track fixtures and fittings and parts thereof; mechanical (including electro-mechanical) traffic signalling equipment UNIT	284.9	67.6	9116.84	674.87
82 Vehicles other than railway or tramway rolling stock, and parts and accessories thereof.	2159.1	28887.54	28139.54	25872.7
83 Aircraft, spacecraft, and parts thereof.			0.23	0.17
84 Optical, photographic, cinematographic, measuring, checking, precision, medical or surgical instruments and apparatus; parts and accessories thereof.	249.89	337.01	3159.86	1381.71
85 Clocks and watches and parts thereof.	12.73		19.64	24.44

Contd...

Commodities	*Rs.Lakh Cumulative 1991–1992*	*Rs.Lakh Cumulative 1995–1996*	*Rs.Lakh Cumulative 2001–2002*	*Rs.Lakh Cumulative 2002–2003*
86 Musical instruments; parts and accessories of such articles.	2.12	0.81	1.54	8.19
87 Furniture; bedding, mattresses, mattress supports, cushions and similar stuffed furnishings; lamps and lighting fittings, not elsewhere specified or included; illuminated signs, illuminated name-plate UNIT	0.3	11.92	415.33	175.4
88 Toys, games and sports requisites; parts and accessories thereof.	12.37	74.72	207.8	269.29
89 Miscellaneous manufactured articles.	36.05	181.17	562.46	1960.98
90 Project Goods; some special uses.	935.86	645.39	8.44	30.94
91 Miscellaneous goods.	95.55	158.16	3355.56	626.95
Total (Rs. lakh)	79636	350884.3	477957.99	477426.36
Total (Rs. billion)	7.96		47.80	47.74
Total (US $)		308188854.5	992025716.1	994016989.4
Total (US$ million)	308.19		992.03	994.02

As with the unequal balance of trade, we find that imports from Bangladesh are fewer (73) than exports (91). Moreover the cumulative value of imports and exports show the differences in the economies of the two nations today. Eastern Bengal, once a cotton surplus area, imports today more cotton from India than it exports there. Its comparative advantage in the world textile market is not reflected in its export list to India. Table 9.4 highlights this.

Table 9.4 : Structure and Trend of Textile imports from India by Bangladesh (in crore *Taka*)[1003]

Item	*FY 1985*	*FY1991*	*FY 1995*	*FY 1999*
Textiles and textile articles of which	26.05	337.38	969.99	1127.6
Cotton	15.94	27.17	25.96	15.82

Only six items including Jamdani sarees, chemical fertilizers, raw jute and frozen fish accounted for almost 95% of Bangladesh's total exports to India in FY 1998[1004]. This trend continues into the twenty first century. Bangladesh's trade deficit with India stood at -35.3 (million $ US) for FY 1985; this increased to -1176 in FY 2003[1005].

Other than trade deficits, burning issues today in India and Bangladesh relations are: border issues (undemarcated boundary, illegal movements of peoples and goods etc), insurgency and transborder movements, sanctuary and training of insurgents in Bangladesh, transit/transhipment issues and issues relating to common rivers (sharing of dry season flows, flood forecasting and management, diversion of rivers etc)[1006]. Of the Ganges-Brahmaputra-Meghna waterway, Bangladesh accounts for 7% of the total catchment area, while India accounts for 63%. As Bangladesh is right at the bottom of all three river systems, it faces the twin brunt of excessive flooding as well as lean water flows throughout the year[1007].

A survey of the big issues in the evolving relationship between the two nations shows the unequal growth of the two Bengals. This growth was historically determined and culturally conditioned. Western Bengal prospered while the east became a marginal land after the sixteenth century. The long term effects of K1 to K4 generated from China lingered in this region until at least the fifteenth century; and this movement set off a boom that

[1003] From Dutta, Jyoti Prakash, 2005, 'Challenges and Prospects of Bangladesh-India Economic Cooperation: Trade and Investmernt' In Haidar, Salman, ed. *India-Bangladesh: Strengthening the Partnership*, Chandigarh, Centre for Research in Rural and Industrial Development: 34.

[1004] *Ibid*: 34.

[1005] *Ibid*: 33.

[1006] Mohammed, M.F., 2005, 'Outstanding Issues in Bangladesh-India Relations' in *Ibid*.: 1–2.

[1007] Ahmad, Q.K., 2005, 'Indo-Bangladesh Co-operation on Transboundary Rivers: Revisiting the Unrealized Oppurtunities and Unmitigated Challenges' in *Ibid*: 14.

lingered on in south east Bengal until the end of the sixteenth century. The emission of 'trade coins' from Chattagram in mid sixteenth century, at a time when the political situation was extremely fluid in Bengal-was testimony to this boom. But the later phases of Kondratieff cycles from K5 on and dealing with pepper, spices and 'Asian Trade' goods such as cotton and silk, left an impact on mainland, and not littoral, eastern South Asia. Surat on the west coast became the premier port in South Asia.

The non-commercial attitude of inland states from the sixteenth century hindered the development of a maritime ethos in Bengal: at a time when the littoral society of southeastern Bengal exhibited a commercial vitality perhaps unsurpassed at any other time in Bengal's history the Husain Shahi court was impervious to maritime concerns. In 1521 Nusrat Shah at Gaur was faced with a potential Portuguese espionage mission suspected of malafide intentions towards Bengal. Suspicion of Portuguese intents was understandable given their success at Goa in 1510 and Malacca in 1511. There was a heated argument at the mosque where the Portuguese were brought in to face trial. A section of the nobility was suspicious of Portuguese intentions; they knew fully about the latters' success in Malabar, Malacca, Goa and Hormuz. But a shipowner–unnamed but called 'Gromalle' in this account by the Portuguese–who had commanded three ships from Bengal to Malacca and knew well the changing power structure there, intervened that[1008]:

> I had already been in Malacca in your father Husain's time and in your lifetime I returned there with three ships.–If these noblemen ask Your Highness not to make peace with the Portuguese it is because they receive numerous allowances and are all counts, dukes and marquises. Above all it (Gaur) is because one hundred and fifty leagues inland they do not fear reprisals. We forget that it is the poor merchants who travel the seas who have to pay for whatever happens. Your Highness well knows that the Portuguese are so powerful here that nothing stands in their way. It would only need for the smallest of their ships to position itself at the harbour bar of Chittagong or Satgaon and no other ship would be able to leave or enter. If this were to happen, if the traders no longer sold the country's goods, if foreigners were no longer able to enter the country, the Governors would find it hard to pay the allowances that are incumbent upon them. It is

[1008] Bouchon, Genevieve and Thomaz, Luis Filipe, 1998, 'Voyage dans le delta du Gange et l'Irraouaddy, 1521', Foundation Calouste Gulbenkian, Paris: 332–3.

> sufficient to give as testimony the three ships which came to this kingdom of Your Highness against which Abbas Khan, Governor of Chittagong, fought many times with heavy losses until in the end he asked for a peace agreement–It therefore seems to me that Your Highness should offer them the peace and friendship they have come to seek. The benefit from this will outweigh any harm it might cause

The changing parameters of space in the Bay was summed up in this altercation between Nusrat Shah and the Portuguese. When the former asked why the Portuguese had seized two of the Sultan's ships valued at 250 000 cruzados, he was told by the Portuguese that[1009]:

> The King our Lord was by title, and therefore in fact, King of the sea and a large part of the land and for this reason no boat could sail without his granting it safe-conduct. That is why we stop and inspect all ships of those we consider to be our enemies when they are not known to us.

This new notion of maritime rights was indeed the result of the renaissance spirit whereby the Iberian humanists introduced the new natural law and a more focussed notion of rights into the Indian Ocean. A new maritime ethic now assumed centre stage in the Bay.

Nusrat Shah's Bengal was not the only one to incomprehend the new politics in Asian waters. The situation was the same on the west coast. Later on in the sixteenth century-in Akbar's time- we are told that[1010]:

> From the time the ships of Akbar were attacked by the Portuguese the sending of vessels to the ports of Arabia and Persia were entirely closed, not only in the Dakhin and Bengal but in other parts of Hindustan, because it was considered beneath the royal dignity to enter into treaties with the Firinghis, and to but send them (ships) without entering into any understanding was to throw lives and property into danger.

But this did not hinder trade in the western Indian Ocean. The same document tells us that the Mughal nobility made private arrangements with the Portuguese and continued sending out their own ships to Arabia and Persia. The successor state of the Husain Shahis in Bengal, the Mughals, continued this practice from Bengal in the seventeenth century. Independent mercantile intitative ceased in Bengal.

[1009] *Ibid*. 332.

[1010] Nawab Muhabbat Khan, 'Akhbar-i-Muhabbat', Elliot and Dowson, V. 8, L.P.P. Reprint, Delhi, 1990: 390.

Bibliography

I Primary Sources–Archival Material

London:

Kasimbazar Factory Records (K.F.R.) G, 23 Series, India Office Library and Records, London. Now at British Library, King's Cross, London, U.K.

Home Miscellaneous Series 804 at British Library, King's Cross, London, U.K.

Bengal Public Consultations from Feb. 25 1747/8 to Dec. 9 1761 at British Library, King's Cross, London, U.K..

France/Paris and Aix en Provence:

Entry No.2530, 22MI41 at Centre des Archives Outre Mer, Aix-en-Provence, France.

A.N.Colonies C2 197 ff. 1.18/C2 56 ff.22–44 at Aix. 'Memoire Generale du Commerce que la Cie. des Indes peut faire dans ses etablissements en Inde tant pour l'Europe que les autres parties de l'Inde' by Jacques Vincens,

Affaires Etrangeres (AE) BIII 459, of Archives Nationales, Section Outre Mer of Rue Oudinot Paris, now at Centre des Archives Outre Mer, Aix en Provence .

C2 115, 'Histoire des Etablissements Francais en Asie et Principalement Ceux du Bengale–1537–1822', by Darrac, Capitaine de la Loge de Dacca, Archives Nationales, Paris, now at Centre des Archives Outre Mer, Aix en Provence.

C2 62 'Indes Orientales: Correspondance Generale 1666–1676' at above.

C2 56 'Indes Orientales: Commerce 1686–1788' at above.

India/Pondicherry :

Coromandel entries, Correspondance between Chandernagore and Pondicherry. Unmarked and uncatalogued. Bibliotheque Romain Rolland, Pondicherry.

II Primary Soruces–Printed Materal

II.1 Oriental Travel Accounts

Abu Ishak al Ishtakhri, 'Kita'bu-l Aka'li'm' in Elliot and Dowson, *The History of India* as *Told By its Own Historians*, V.1, Allahabad, Kitab Mahal, 1969 Reprint.

Abu Zaidu-l Hasan of Siraf, the additions of, in the 'Salsilatu-l Tawarikh' of the Merchant Suleiman in Elliot and Dowson, *The History of India as Told By its Own Historians,* V.1, Allahabad, Kitab Mahal, 1969 Reprint.

Ahmad, S.Maqbul,1989, *Arabic Classical Accounts of India and China*, Shimla, Indian Institute of Advanced Study.

Al-Idrisi, 'Nizhatu-l Mushtak' in Elliot and Dowson, *The History of India as Told By its Own Historians*, V.1, Allahabad, Kitab Mahal, 1969 Reprint.

Al Masudi, 'Muru'ju-l Zahal' in Elliot and Dowson, *The History of India as Told By its Own Historians*, V.1, Allahabad, Kitab Mahal, 1969 Reprint.

Ibn Batuta, *Voyages*, 3 vols., (Tr). Defremery, E.C., Sanguinetty, B.R., 1982, Paris, Maspero.

Ibn Haukal, 'Ashka'lu-l Bila'd' or the 'Kita'bu-l Masa'lik Wa-l Mama'lik', in Elliot and Dowson, *The History of India as Told By its Own Historians*, V.1, Allahabad, Kitab Mahal, 1969 Reprint.

Ibn Khurdadba, 'Kitabu-l Masalik Wa-l Mamalik' in Elliot and Dowson, *The History of India as Told By its Own Historians*, V.1, Allahabad, Kitab Mahal, 1969 Reprint.

Ma Huan, Mills, J.V.G., 1970, *The Overall Survey of the Ocean's Shores* (An Account of Ma Huan's voyage to Bengal), London, Hakluyt Society

Rashi'du-d D'in, 'Jami'u-t Tawari'kh', in Elliot and Dowson, *The History of India as told By Its Own Historians*, V.1, Allahabad, Kitab Mahal, 1969 Reprint.

Suleiman, 'Salsilatu-t Tawarikh', in Elliot and Dowson, *The History of India as told By Its Own Historians*, V.1, Allahabad, Kitab Mahal, 1969 Reprint.

Zakari'ya al Kazwi'ni, 'A'sa'ru-l Bila'd', in Elliot and Dowson, *The History of India as told By Its Own Historians*, V.1, Allahabad, Kitab Mahal, 1969 Reprint.

II.2. European Travel Accounts

Anon. Bouchon, Genevieve and Thomaz, Luis Filipe, eds. 1988, 'Voyage Dans Les Deltas du Gange et de l'Irraouaddy 1521', Paris, Fondation Calouste Gulbenkian,

Barlow, Roger, *A Briefe Summe of Geographie*, F.G.R.Taylor ed. Series II, V.69, London, The Hakluyt Society, 1929–32.

Bernier, Francois, *Travels in the Mogul Empire*, 1656–1668, revised Vincent A. Smith, 1992 Munshiram Manoharlal Reprint, Delhi.

Bernier, Francois, *Travels in the Mogul Empire*, 1656–1668, Archibald Constable (Tr). 1891, 2nd edition, Humphrey Milford, Oxford University Press, 1914.

Bernouilli, 1788, *L'Inde: Description Hisrorique et Geographique de l'Inde qui presente en trois volumes et enrichis de 64 cartes*, 3 vols. Berlin. Contains accounts of Tieffanthaler, Rennell, Father Georgi and Anquetil-Duperron among others. I. La Geographie de l'Indoustan par le Pere Joseph Tieffanthaler, II. Des Recherches Historiques et Chronologiques sur l'Inde et la description du Cours du Gange et du Gagra avec une tres grande carte par M. Anquetil Duperron, III. La carte Generale de l'Inde, Celle du Cours du Brahmapoutre, et de la navigation interieure du Bengale, avec des Memoires Relatifs a ces cartes, par M. Jacques Rennell.

Bowrey, Thomas, *A Geographical account of the Countries Around the Bay of Bengal 1669–1679*, R.C.Temple (Ed). Cambridge, Hakluyt Society, M D CCCCV.

Challes Robert, Journal d'un Vogyae fait aux Indes Orientales, 2vs, Mercure de France, MCMLXXXIII

Chevalier, Deloche Jean (Ed). 1984, *Les Aventures de Jean Baptiste Chevalier dans l'Inde Orientale 1752–65*, Paris, EFEO Publications.

De Graaf, *Voyages de Nicolas de Graaf aux Indes Orientales* etcetera (1639–1689), Amsterdam, J.F. Bernard, MD CCXIX .

Duarte Barbosa, *The Book of Duarte Barbosa*, Tr. M.L.Dames, 1921 London, Hakluyt Society.

Duarte Barbosa, Stanley, Henry E.J. (tr)., M D CCC LXVI, *A Description of the Coasts of East Africa and Malabar in the Beginning of the Sixteenth Century*, London, Hakluyt Society.

Father Hosten, (Ed). *Monserrate, Mongolicae Legationis Commentarius*, 1590, Memoirs of the Asiatic Society of Bengal, v. 3, No. 9.

Federbe, Louis Laurent de, Comte de Modave, *Le Voyage en Inde de...etc. 1773–1776. Nouveaux Memoires sur l'Etat actuel du Bengale et de l'Indoustan* (Tr. and Ed). Jean Deloche, 1971, Paris, Ecole Francaise d'Extreme Orient.

Forster, George, 1798, *A Journey from Bengal to England*. London, 2 vols.

Foster, W., (Ed). 1926, *Sir Thomas Roe: His Embassy to the Court of the Great Moghul 1615–1619*, London.

Foster, William (Ed). 1921, *Early Travels in India 1583–1619*, London, Reprint, New Delhi, 1968.

Francois Pyrard de Laval, 1887-1890, *The Voyage of...to the East Indies, the Maldives, the Moluccas and Brazil 1601–1611*, 3 vols. (Tr). Albert Gray, London, Hakluyt Society.

Glanius, *Relation du Nauffrage d'un Vaisseau Hollandois Vers la Cote de Bengala*, 1661. Published 1682.

Glanius, *A Relation of An Unfortunate Voyage to the Kingdom of Bengala*, London, Henry Bonwick, 1682.

Hamilton, Alexander, 1727, *A New Account of the East Indies 1688–1723*, 2 vols., Edinburgh.

John Marshall, Shafaat Ahmad, 1927, (Ed). *John Marshall in India, Notes and Observations in Bengal 1668–1672*, London, Oxford University Press.

Jenkinson, Anthony, *Early Voyages and Travels to Russia and Persia*, Delmar Morgan and C.H. Coote (Eds)., 1886, 2 vols. London, Hakluyt Society.

Linschoten, *Voyages*, ed. Tiele, P.A. and Bernard, A.C., London, 1885. In 10vs.

Luiller, *Voyage du Sieur Luillier aux Grandes Indes avec une Instruction Pour le Commerce des Indes Orientales*, Paris, Claude Cellier, MC CC V.

Luillier, *Voyage du Sieur Luillier aux Indes Orientales avec une instruction pour le commerce des Indes Orientales*, 1705, Paris, Claude Cellier.

Also Luillier, *Voyages du Sieur Luillier dans des grandes Indes Orientales*, 1726, Rotterdam.

Major, R.H., (ed.)1857, *India in the Fifteenth Century, Being a Collection of Narratives of Voyages to India*, London, Hakluyt Society.

Manrique ..*The Travels of Fray Sebastian Manrique 1629–1643*, Luard, C.E. (Tr). 2 vols. London, Hakluyt Society 1926–1927.

Ralph Fitch, 'Narrative of Ralph Fitch 1583–91' in William Foster (Ed). *Early Travels in India 1583–1619*, London, 1921, Reprint, New Delhi, 1968.

Sonnerat, M. *Voyage Aux Indes et a la Chine*, Paris, MDCCC LXXXII.

Tavernier, Jean Baptiste, *Travels in India* (Tr). Ball and Crooke, 1925, 2 vols., Oxford, University Press, 2nd edition.

Tavernier, Jean-Baptiste, (Intr). Yerasimos, S., 1981, *Les Six Voyages en Turquie et en Perse*, 3 vols., Paris, Maspero.

Terry, Edward, *Voyage to East India*, London, T.Wilkes, MDCC LXXVIII.

Tome Pires, *Suma Oriental 1512–1515*, Preface, Armand Cortesao, London, Hakluyt Society, 1944.

Tome Pires, *Suma Oriental* (Ed). Armand Cortesao, Coimbra edition, 1978.

Varthema, Ludovico, *The Itinerary of*...(Tr. R.C.Temple), London, Hakluyt, 1928.

Varthema, Ludovico, *The Travels of Ludovico di Varthema in Egypt, Syria, Arabia Deserta and Arabia Felix, in Persia, India and Ethiopia* AD *1503–1508.* (Tr). J.W.John, (Ed). G.P. Badger, London, Hakluyt Society, M D CCC XIII.

Yule, Henry, *Cathay and the Way Thither*, London, Hakluyt Society, MD CCC LXVI.

II.3 Contemporary European documents other than Travel Accounts

Deloche Jean Ed. 1990, *Statistiques de Chandernagor, 1823, 1827 and 1838, by Joseph Cordier and Achille Bedier*, Pondichery, Institut Francais: 22.

Hamilton, Walter,1828, *East India Gazeteer*, 2 vols., London.

Hastings, Warren, 1786, *Memoirs Relative to the State of India*, London, Indian Edition July, 1978, Calcutta, M.L.Ghosh, Distributor K.P.Bagchi.

Hedges, William, *Diary of, During His Agency in Bengal 1681 87*, R. Barlow and H.Yule (eds). 2 vols. London, Hakluyt Society, M D CCC LXXX.

Imperial Gazetteer, 1908, Oxford University Press, III: *The Indian Empire-Economic*.

Master, Streynsham, R.C.Temple (ed). 1911, *The Diaries of Streynsham Master 1675–1680 And Other Contemporary Papers Relating Thereto*, London, John Murray, Indian Records Series, 2 Vols.

Taylor, James, 1851, *A Descriptive and Historical Account of the Cotton Manufactures of Dacca*, London.

Taylor, James, 1840, *A Sketch of the Topography and Statistics of Dacca* Calcutta.

II.4 Contemporary Oriental documents other than Travel Accounts

Abdul Hamid Lahori's 'Padshah Nama' in Elliot and Dowson's *History of India as Told by Its Own Historians*, V.7, Allahabad, Kitab Mahal. Reprint 1969.

Abdul Hamid Lahori, 'Padshah Nama' in Elliot and Dowson, *History of India as Told By its Own Historians*, V.7, L.P.P. Reprint, 1990, Delhi.

Abul Fazl, *The Ain-i-Akbari of Abul Fazl Allami'*, Translated by Col.H.S.Jarrett and forwarded by Sir Jadunath Sarkar, 1891, 2nd ed. (by J.N. Sarkar), 1949, first reprint of 1988, New Delhi, Crown Publication.

Abul Fazl, Jarrett, H.S. (Tr). *The Ain-I-Akbari By Abul Fazl Allami*, Jadunath Sarkar annotated 2nd edition, Oriental Books, New Delhi, 1978.

al-Muqaddasi, *Ahsanu-t-Taqasim fi Ma'rifati-l-aqalim*, (Eng.Tr. G.S.A. Ranking and R.F.Azoo), Calcutta, 1901.

Bakhtawar Khan's 'Mira't-i-Alam' (account of Aurangzeb's reign), Elliot and Dowson, *History of India as Told by Its Own Historians*, V.7, L.P.P Reprint, Delhi,1990.

Beveridge, H. (Tr). *The Akbar Nama of Abul-Fazl*, 3 vols., Delhi, Ess Ess Publications (2nd reprint,1977).

Ghulam Hussein Salim, *Riyas-us-Salatin*, Tr. Maulavi Abdus, 1902, Calcutta, Asiatic Society.

Jahangir, *Tuzuk-I-Jahangiri*, Tr. A. Rogers and H. Beveridge, 2 vols., London 1909–1914.

The Jahangir Nama, translated, edited and annotated by Wheeler M. Thackston, Freer Gallery of Art and Sackler Gallery, Washington and Oxford University Press, New York, Oxford, 1999.

Khafi, Khan, 'Muntakhabu-l Luba'b' in Elliot and Dowson, *History of India as Told By its Own Historians*, V.7., L.P.P. Reprint, 1990, Delhi.

Khwaja Abdul Karim Khan, 'Baya'n-i-Waki', Elliot and Dowson, *History of India as Told By its Own Historians*, V.8, L.P.P. Reprint, 1990, Delhi.

Minhaj-ud-Din Abu Umar-I-Usman's *Tabakat-I-Nasiri: A General History of the Muhammadan Dynasties of Asia from 810 AD to 1260 AD and the Irruption of the Infidel Mughals into Islam* (Tr). Raverty, H.G.1881, Reprint, New Delhi, Oriental Books Corporation, 1970.

Mirza Nathan, *Baharistan-i-Ghaybi*, 2 vols. Tr. By M. I. Borah, Government of Assam, 1936.

Muhammad Sharif Hanafi's 'Maja'lisu-s-Salatin' (a partial account of the reign of Shah Jahan), Elliot and Dowson, *History of India as Told by Its Own Historians*, V.7, L.P.P. Reprint, Delhi, 1990.

Nawab Muhabbat Khan, 'Akbar-i-Muhabbat' in Elliot and Dowson, *History of India as Told by Its Own Historians*, V.8, L.P.P. Reprint, Delhi, 1990.

Salim Allah, 1788, *Tawarikh-i-Bangalah or a Narrative of the Transactions in Bengal* (Tr.Francis Gladwin), Calcutta.

Seid Gholam Hossein Khan, *Seir Mutaqherin or View of Modern Times*, (Tr). Nota Manus, Calcutta, T.D. Chatterjee, 4 vols.

Shihabuddin Talish, *Fathiyya-i-Ibriyya*. Tr. Blochmann, J.A.S.B. 1872.

Shihabuddin Talish, *Fathiyya-i-Ibriyya*. Tr. J.N, Sarkar, J.A.S.B. 1906–07. Excerpts only.

Ziauddin Barani (1357), *Tarikh-I-Firuz Shahi*, (Ed). S.A.Khan, Calcutta, Bibliotheca India, 1860–2.

III. Secondary Sources: Books and Articles

Aghassian, Michel and Kevonian, Keram, 1988, 'Le Commerce Armenien dans l'Ocean Indien aux 17e et 18e siecles' in Lombard, Denys and Aubin, Jean (Eds). 1988, *Marchands et Hommes d'Affaires dans l'Ocean Indien et la Mer de Chine, 13e a 20e siecles*, Paris, Publications E.H.E.S.S.: 155–181.

Ahmad, Q.K., 2005, 'Indo-Bangladesh Co opration on Transboundary Rivers: Revisiting the Unrealized Oppurtunities and Unmitigated Challenges' in Haidar, Salman, ed. *India-Bangladesh: Strengthening the Partnership*, Chandigarh, Centre for Research in Rural and Industrial Development: 14–30.

Alam, Muzaffar, 2004, *The Languages of Political Islam in India c.1200–1800*. New Delhi, Permanent Black.

Alam, Muzaffar, 2002, 'Aspects of Agrarian Uprisings in North India in the Early Eighteenth Century' reprinted in Alavi, Seema, 2002,

The Eighteenth Century in India, New Delhi, Oxford University Press: 84–112.

Alam, M., Delvoye, N., and Gaborieau, M., eds. 2000 *The Making of Indo-Persian Culture*. New Delhi, Manohar and CSH.

Alam, M. and Subrahmanyam, S. 1998, *The Mughal State 1526–1750*, New Delhi, Oxford University Press.

Alam, Muzaffar, 1986, *The Crisis of Empire in Mughal North India*, New Delhi, Oxford University Press.

Alam, M.Shafiqul and Salles, Jean Francois (Eds) April 2000, *France-Bangladesh Joint Venture Excavations at Mahastangarh. First Interim Report* 1993–1999, Dhaka.

Alavi, Seema, 2002, *The Eighteenth Century in India*, Delhi, Oxford University Press.

Ali, Athar, 1978–9, 'The Eighteenth Century: An Interpretation', *The Indian Historical Review*, v: 175–186.

Ali, Athar, 1986–87, 'Recent Theories of Eighteenth Century India', *The Indian Historical Review*, xiii, reprinted in Marshall, P.J., ed. 2003, *The Eighteenth Century in Indian History: Evolution or Revolution*? New Delhi, Oxford University Press: 90–99.

Ali, Athar, 1975, 'The Passing of Empire: The Mughal Case', *Modern Asian Studies*, ix: 385–96.

Ali, M.M., 1985, *History of the Muslims of Bengal*, 2 vols, Riyadh, Imam Muhammad Ibn Sa'ud Islamic University Press.

Arakanese Research Journal of Bangladesh, 2005, Ed. U Bodhinyana. V.3, Arakanese Research Society of Bangladesh.

Arasaratnam, Sinappah, 1992, '*Pre Colonial and Early-Colonial Port Towns'* in Indu Banga ed. *Ports and Their Hinterlands in India 1700–1950*, New Delhi, Manohar: 367–374.

Arasaratnam, Sinappah, 1998, 'The Eastward Trade of India in the Eighteenth Century' in Mukherjee, R. and Subramanian, L. (Eds). 1998, *Politics and Trade in the Indian Ocean World: Essays in Honour of Ashin Das Gupta*, Delhi, Oxford University Press.

Arasaratnam, Sinappah,1986, *Merchants, Companies and Commerce on the Coromandel Coast, 1650–1740*. Delhi: Oxford University Press.

Aubin, Jean, 1988, 'Marchands de Mer rouge et du Golfe Persique au tournant des 15e et 16e siecles' in, Lombard, Denys and Aubin, Jean (Eds). *Marchands et Hommes d'Affaires Asiatiques dans l'Ocean Indien et la Mer de Chine, 13e a 20e siecles*, Paris, Publications E.H.E.S.S.: 83–90.

Aubin Jean and Lombard, Denys (eds). *Marchands et Hommes d'Affaires Asiatiques dans l'Ocean Indien et la Mer de Chine 13e–20e siecles*, Paris, Editions E.H.E.S.S.

Bagchi P.C., 1945, (ed). 'Political Relations Between Bengal and China in the Pathan Period', *Visva Bharati Annals*, vol 1, Cheena Bhavan.

Baker, Alan, R.H., 2003, *Georgraphy and History: Bridging the Divide*, Cambridge University Press.

Bang, P.F., 2003, 'Rome and the Comparative Study of Tributary Empires, *MHJ Special Issue Tributary Empires in History: Comparative Perspectives from Antiquity to the Late Medieval*, 6, 2, July–December 2003. Guest Editors: C.A.Bayly and P.F.Bang: 189–216.

Barnett, R., ed. 2002, *Rethinking Early Modern India*, New Delhi, Manohar.

Barrow, Ian, J., 2003, *Making History Drawing Territory: British Mapping In India c. 1756–1905*, New Delhi, Oxford University Press.

Bayly, C.A. 2004. *The Birth of the Modern World 1780–1914*, Blackwell.

Bayly, C.A. and Bang, P.F. Guest Editors, 2003, *The Medieval History Journal*, *Special Issue Tributary Empires in History: Comparative Perspectives from Antiquity to the Late Medieval*, 6, 2, July–December.

Bayly, C.A., and Bang, P.F., 2003, 'Introduction: Comparing Pre-Modern Empires' in *MHJ*, *Special Issue Tributary Empires in History: Comparative Perspectives from Antiquity to the Late Medieval*, 6, 2, July–December 2003. Guest Editors: C.A. Bayly and P.F. Bang: 169–187.

Bayly, C.A, 1989, *Imperial Meridian: The British Empire and the World 1780–1830*, London, Longman.

Bayly, C. A. 1983, *Rulers, Townsmen and Bazaars: North Indian society in the Age of British Expansion, 1770–1870*, Cambridge, University Press.

Beamish, Jane, 1995, 'The Significance Of Yuan Blue and White Exported to South East Asia' in Rosemary Scott and John Guy eds. *South East Asia and China: Art, Interaction and Commerce*, London, Percival David Foundation: 225–251.

Bhattacharya, Gouriswar, July 2003, *Ganga–Visnupadi-Nagini*, 1st Kumar Sarat Kumar Roy Memorial Lecture, Calcutta, Centre for Archaeological Studies and Training, Eastern India.

Bhattacharya, R.N., 2003, 'Pre Historic Stone Figurines in Eastern India', *Journal of the Asiatic Society*, XLV, 2, Calcutta: 1–52.

Bhattacharya, Swarup, 2000, 'Biswakarmas, of boat and their traditional knowledge of boat building in different environments with special reference to West Bengal', *Journal of the Department of Anthropology* University of Calcutta,: 117–124.

Bhattacharya, Swarup and Varadarajan, Lotika, 2000, 'Patia of Eastern India, Vestiges of a Reverse Clinker Tradition', *Techniques & Culture*, 35–36, Paris: 417–444.

Bhattasali, N.K., 1946, 'New Light on the History of Assam' in *Indian Historical Quarterly*, 22.

Black, Anthony, 2004, *The History of Islamic Political Thought (From the Prophet to the Present*) Oxford University Press, Pakistan.

Black-Michaud, Jacob, 1975, *Feuding Societies*, Oxford, Basil Blackwell.

Blake, Stephen P., 1991, *Shahajanabad: The Sovereign City in Mughal India 1639–1739*, Cambridge.

Blake, Stephen P., 1979, 'The Patrimonial-Bureaucratic Empire of the Mughals', *The Journal of Asian Studies*, XXXIX, 1: 77–94.

Blochmann, H., 1867,'Notes on Sirajuddaulah and the Town of Murshidabad, taken from a Persian Manuscript of the Tarikh-i-Mancuri', *Journal of the Asiatic Society*, Part I, no.II.

Blochmann, H., 1968, *Contributions to the History and Geography of Bengal (Muhammedan Period*), Calcutta, Asiatic Society, Reprint.

Bradley F.B. (circa 1905) *The Romance of an Eastern Capital*, published 1975 Delhi, Metropolitan, Indian edition.

Braudel, Fernand,1949, *La Mediterranee et le Monde Mediterraneen*, Paris, Armand Colin.

Braudel, Fernand, 1979, 1981, 1984, *Civilization and Capitalism*, 3 vols., Paris, Armand Colin.

Braudel, Fernand,1984, *Civilization and Capitalism, V. III, The Perspective of the World* (Tr). S.Reynolds, London.

Braudel, Fernand, 1996, *Autour de la Mediterranee*, Preface by Maurice Aymard. Paris, Fallois.

Broeze, Frank, 1992, 'The External Dynamics of Port City Morphology: Bombay 1815-1914' in Indu Banga ed. *Ports and Their Hinterlands in India 1700–1950*, New Delhi, Manohar: 245–272.

Bull, Hedley and Watson, Adam (eds). 1984–85, *The Expansion of International Society*, Oxford University Press, Clarendon.

Calkins, Philip,1970, 'The Formation of a Regionally-oriented Ruling Group in Bengal 1700–1740', *Journal of Asian Studies*, 29,4: 799–806.

Chakravarti, Ramakanta, 1985, *Vaishnavism in Bengal 1486–1900*, Calcutta, Sanskrit Pustak Bhandar.

Chandra, Satish, 2003, *Essays on Medieval Indian History*, New Delhi, Oxford University Press.

Chandra, Satish, 1982, *Parties and Politics at the Mughal Court 1707–40*, 3rd ed. Delhi.

Chandra, Satish, 1982, *Medieval India: Society, the Jagirdari Crisis and the Village*, Macmillan.

Charney, Michael W., 1998, 'Crisis and Reformation in a Maritime Kingdom of Southeast Asia: Forces of Instability and Political Disintegration in Western Burma (Arakan), 1603–1701, *Journal of the Economic and Social History of the Orient*, V.41: 185–219.

Chatterjee, Anjali, 1967, *Bengal in the Reign of Aurangzib 1658–1707*, Calcutta, Progressive Publishers.

Chatterjee K., 1996, *Merchants, Politics and Society in Early Modern India: Bihar 1733–1820*, E.J.Brill, Leiden.

Chattopadhyay, Brajadulal, 1995, 'Political Processes and the Structure of Polity in Early Medieval India' in Kulke (ed). 1995, *The State in India 1000–1700*, New Delhi, Oxford University Press: 195–232.

Chattopadhyay, Sagar, 2005, *Dakshin Chabbish Porgona Jelar Purakirti*, Kolkata, West Bengal State Archaeological Museum Publication (in Bengali).

Chaudhuri, K.N., 1990, *Asia Before Europe: Economy And Civilisation of the Indian Ocean From the Rise of Islam to 1750*, Cambridge University Press.

Chaudhuri, K.N., 1985, *Trade and Civilisation in the Indian Ocean : An Economic History from the Rise of Islam to 1750*, Cambridge University Press.

Chaudhuri, K.N., 1978, *The Trading World of Asia and the English East India Company 1660–1760*. Cambridge University Press.

Chaudhuri, Sushil, 2002, 'Was There a Crisis in Mid-Eighteenth Century Bengal?' in Barnett, R., ed. 2002, *Rethinking Early Modern India*, New Delhi, Manohar: 129–152.

Chaudhuri, Sushil and Morineau, Michel eds. 1999, *Merchants, Companies and Trade–Europe and Asia in the Early Modern Era*, Cambridge University Press.

Chaudhuri Sushil, 1995, *From Prosperity to Decline, Bengal in the Eighteenth Century*. New Delhi, Manohar.

Chaudhuri, Sushil, 1975, *Trade and Commercial Organisation in Bengal, 1650–1720*. Calcutta: Firma KLM.

Chavannes, Edouard, 1894, *Memoire Compose a l'epoque de la grande dynastie T'ang sur les Religieux Eminents...par I-tsing*, Paris.

Christie, Jan Wisseman, 1999, 'Asian Sea Trade between the Tenth and Thirteenth Centuries and Its Impact on the States of Java and Bali' in Himanshu Prabha Ray ed. *Archaeology of Seafaring: The Indian Ocean in the Ancient Period*, ICHR Monograph Series 1, New Delhi, Pragati Publications: 221–270.

Church, Sally, K., 2004, 'The Giraffe of Bengal: A Medieval Encounter in Ming China', *Medieval History Journal*, 7,1: 1–37.

Coedes, George, 1964, *Les Etats Hindouises d'Indochine et d'Indonesie*, Paris, Boccard.

Cohn, Bernard S., 1962, 'Political Systems in Eighteenth Century India: The Banaras Region' *Journal of the American Oriental Society*, lxxxii, July–Sept: 312-319, reprinted in Marshall, P.J., 2003, *The Eighteenth Century in Indian History: Evolution or Revolution?* New Delhi, Oxford University Press: 123–136.

Cohn, Bernard S., 1987, 'The Initial British Impact on India: A Case Study of the Banaras Region' in *An Anthropologist Among The Historians and Other Essays*, Oxford University Press.

Curley, David L., 2002, 'Maharaja Krisnacandra, Hinduism and Kingship in the Contact Zone of Bengal' in Richard B. Barnett (Ed). 2002, *Rethinking Early Modern India*, New Delhi. Manohar.

Dale, Stephen, F., 1994, *Indian Merchants and Eurasian Trade 1600–1750*, Cambridge University Press.

Das Gupta, Ashin, 1993, *Europeans in India Before the Empire*, Professor A.C.Banerjee Memorial Lecture, 1992, Calcutta, a Department of History, Jadavpur University, publication.

Das Gupta, Ashin, 1992, '*The Maritime City*' in Indu Banga ed. *Ports and Their Hinterlands in India 1700–1950*, New Delhi, Manohar: 359–365.

Das Gupta, Ashin, 1989, *Bangoposagor*, *Itihas Anusandhan* (in Bengali).

Das Gupta, Ashin, 1987, '*Introduction II: The Story*' in Das Gupta, Ashin and Pearson, M.N. Eds., 1987, *India and The Indian Ocean 1500–1800*, Calcutta, Oxford University Press.

Das Gupta, A. and Pearson, M.N.eds., 1987, *India and the Indian Ocean 1500–1800*. Calcutta: Oxford University Press.

Das Gupta, Ashin, 1979, *Indian Merchants and The Decline of Surat, 1700–1750*, Wiesbaden, Steiner Verlag.

Das Gupta, Ashin, 1970, *'Trade and Politics in Eighteenth Century India'* from Richards, D.S. (Ed). *Islam and the Trade of Asia*, Philadelphia reprinted in Alam, M. and Subrahmanyam, S. (Eds)., 1998, *The Mughal State 1526–1750*, New Delhi, Oxford University Press: 370–397.

Das Gupta, Ashin, 1967, *Malabar in Asian Trade*, Cambridge, University Press.

Das Gupta, J.N. 1914, *Bengal in the Sixteenth Century* A.D., Calcutta, Calcutta University.

Das, Vrindaban, *Chaitanya Bhagavat*, Nabadwip, 3rd ed.

Datta, Rajat, 2003, 'Commercialisation, Tribute and the Transition from the Late Mughal to the Early Colonial in India' in *The Medieval History Journal, Special Issue Tributary Empires in History: Comparative Perspectives from Antiquity to the Late Medieval*, 6, 2, July–December 2003. Guest Editors: C.A. Bayly and P.F.Bang: 259–291.

Datta, Rajat, 2000, *Society, Economy and the Market : Commercialisation in Rural Bengal c. 1760–1800*, Manohar, Delhi.

Deloche Jean, 1980, *La Circulation en Inde avant la Revolution des Transports*, 2 vols., Paris, EFEO.

Deloche Jean, 1967, *Recherches sur les Routes de l''inde au temps des Mogoles*, Paris, EFEO.

Deyell, John, 1995, 'The Trade Coinage of Chittagong Region in the Mid Sixteenth Century' in *Journal of the Asiatic Society of Bangladesh*, Vol.40, No. 2, December.

Deyell, John, 1983, 'The China Connection : Problems of Silver Supply in Medieval Bengal' in J.F. Richards ed. *Precious Metals in the Later Medieval and Early Modern Worlds*, Durham, Carolina Academic Press: 207–227. Reprinted in Subrahmanyam Sanjay ed. 1994, *Money and the Market in India 1100–1700*, Delhi, Oxford University Press: 112–136.

Dimock, E.C. and Gupta, Pratul Chandra (Tr. and Eds)., 1965, *Maharashtra Purana: An Eighteenth Century Bengali Text*, Honolulu, East West Center Press.

D'Souza, 2002, 'Crisis Before the Fall: Some Speculations on the Decline of the Ottomans, Safavids and Mughals', *Social Scientist*, 30, 9–10, September-October: 3–30.

Dutta, Jyoti Prakash, 2005, 'Challenges and Prospects of Bangladesh-India Economic Cooperation: Trade and Investment' In Haidar, Salman, ed. *India-Bangladesh: Strengthening the Partnership*, Chandigarh, Centre for Research in Rural and Industrial Development: 31–53.

Eaton, Richard, 2002, *Essays on Islam and Indian History*, Oxford University Press.

Eaton, Richard, 1993, *The Rise of Islam and the Bengal Frontier 1204-1760*, California, Berkeley and L.A.

Elvin, Mark, 1973, *The Pattern of the Chinese Past*, Stanford, Stanford Press.

Filesi, Teobaldo, 1972, *China and Africa in the Middle Ages*, London.

Fisher, Michael, H., 1993, *The Politics of the British Annexation of India 1757–1857*, Delhi, Oxford University Press.

Frank, A.G., 2005, 'Eurocentrism in Historiographic Tradition' in Mukherjee, Rila and Chattopadhyay, Kunal eds. 2005, *Europe in the Second Millennium: A Hegemony Achieved?*, Kolkata, Progressive Publishers: 73–114.

Frank, A.G., 2005, 'The Centrality of China and the Marginality of Europe in the World Economy' in Mukherjee, Rila and Chattopadhyaya, Kunal eds. 2005, *Europe in the Second Millennium: A Hegemony Achieved*? Kolkata, Progressive Publishers: 135–192.

Frank, A.G., 1998, *Reorient: Global Economy in the Asian Age*, University of California Press and Sage/Vistaar.

Frasch, Tilman, 2002, 'Coastal Peripheries during the Pagan Period' in Gommans, Jos and Leider, Jacques (eds). 2002, *The Maritime Frontier of Burma: Exploring Political, Cultural and Commercial Interaction in the Indian Ocean World, 1200–1800*, Leiden.

Frasch, Tilman, 2001, 'The Buddhist Connection: Sinhalese-Burmese Intercourse in the Middle Ages' in Georg Breemer, Tilman Frasch, Hermann Kulke and Jurgen Lutt (eds). 2001, *Explorations in the History of South Asia* (Festschrift Rothermund), Delhi, Manohar: 85–97.

Frasch, Tilman, 1998, 'A Buddhist Network in the Bay of Bengal: Relations Between Bodhgaya, Burma and Sri Lanka, c.300–1300' in Claude Guillot, Denys Lombard and Roderick Ptak (eds). 1998, *From the Mediterranean to the China Sea: Miscellaneous Notes*, Wiesbaden.

Furber, Holden, 1990, *Rival Empires of Trade in the Orient 1600–1800*, Delhi, Oxford University Press.

Furber, Holden (1951). *John Company at Work, A Study of European Expansion in India in the Eighteenth Century*. Cambridge: Harvard Press.

Ghosh, Amitava, 2005, *The Hungry Tide*, India, Harper Collins.

Ghosh, Ishani, 1997-8, 'A Folk Ritual and the Emergence of a Regional Polity: Murshid Quli Khan and local Cults in Bengal', *Journal of History*, Jadavpur University, V. XVI: 49–54.

Gill, Sandrine, 1999, 'Mahasthangarh : A Riverine port in Ancient Bengal', in Himanshu Prabha Ray ed. *Archaeology of Seafaring: The Indian Ocean in the Ancient Period*, New Delhi, Pragati Publications: 154–172.

Glamann, K., 1981, *Dutch-Asiatic Trade 1620-1740*, The Hague, Martinus Njihoff, second ed.

Glover, Ian C., 1996, 'Recent Archaeological Evidence for Early Maritime Contacts Between India and South-East Asia', in Ray, Himanshu Prabha and Salles, Jean Francois eds. 1996, *Tradition and Archaelogy: Early Maritime Contacts in The Indian Ocean*, New Delhi, Manohar: 129–158.

Goetz, Herman, 1938, *The Crisis of Indian Civilisation in the Eighteenth and early Nineteenth Centuries: The Genesis of Indo-Muslim Civilisation*, Calcutta.

Gokhale, B.G., 1979, *Surat in the Seventeenth Century*, Bombay, Popular Prakashan.

Goldstone, Jack A., 1996, 'Gender, Work and Culture: Why the Industrial Revolution Came Early to England but Late to China', *Sociological Perspectives*, 39, 1: 1–21.

Gole, Susan, 1988, *Maps of Mughal India*, New Delhi, Manohar.

Gommans, Jos and Leider, Jacques (eds.), 2002, *The Maritime Frontier of Burma, Exploring Political, Cultural and Commercial Interaction in the Indian Ocean World, 1200–1800*, Leiden.

Gordon, Stewart, 1994, *Marathas, Marauders and State Formation in Eighteenth Century India*, Delhi, Oxford University Press.

Gordon, Stewart, 1994, 'Burhanpur: Entrepot and Hinterland 1650–1750', in *Marathas, Marauders and State Formation in Eighteenth Century India*, Delhi, Oxford University Press: 163–181.

Guenee, Bernard, 1985, *States and Rulers in Later Medieval Europe*, Oxford, Blackwell.

Gutman, Pamela, 2001, *Burma's Lost Kingdoms: The Splendours of Arakan*, CT. Weatherhill and Bangkok, Orchid Press.

Habib, Irfan, 2002, '*The Eighteenth Century in Indian Economic History*' in Alavi, Seema, 2002, *The Eighteenth Century in India*, New Delhi, Oxford University Press: 57–83. Also in Marshall, P.J, 2003, *The Eighteenth Century in Indian History: Evolution or Revolution*?: 100–119.

Habib, Irfan, 1995, 'Potentialities of Capitalist Development in the Economy of Mughal India' in Habib, Irfan, 1995, *Essays in Indian History: Towards a Marxist Perception*, New Delhi: 180–232

Habib, Irfan, 1982, *An Atlas of the Mughal Empire*, New Delhi, Oxford University Press.

Habib, Irfan, 1982, 'Non Agricultural Production and Urban Economy' in Tapan Raychaudhuri and Irfan Habib (Eds). *The Cambridge Economic History of India*,V. I, Cambridge/Orient Longman.

Habib Irfan and Raychaudhuri, Tapan, (Eds). 1982, *The Cambridge Economic History of India*,V. I, Cambridge/Orient Longman.

Habib Irfan, 1963, *The Agrarian Crisis of the Mughal Empire 1556–1707*, Bombay/New York, Asia Publishing House..

Heesterman, J.C., 1980, 'Littoral etl'interieur de l'Inde', *Itinerario*, I

Hintze, Andrea, 1997, *The Mughal Empire and Its Decline: An Interpretation of the Sources of Social Power*, Aldershot.

Hossain, Hameeda, 1988, *The Company Weavers of Bengal: The East India Company and the Organization of Textile Production in Bengal 1750–1813*, Delhi, Oxford University Press.

Humphreys, R. Stephen, 2003, *Islamic History: A Framework for Inquiry* Revised Edition, Oxford University Press, Pakistan.

Hunter, W.W., 1785, A *Concise Account of the Kingdom of Pegu; The Climate. the Products, Trade and Government etc.*, Calcutta, John Hay.

Imam, Abu, 2002, 'Samatata, Mainamati: Some Observations' in Gautam Sengupta and Sheena Panja (Eds). *Archaeology of Eastern India: New Perspectives*, Calcutta, Centre for Archaeological Studies and Training, Eastern India: 613–623.

Irvine, William, 1922, *Later Mughals*, Calcutta.

Jamaluddin S., 1995, *The State under Timur*, New Delhi, Har Anand.

Jayananda, *Chaitanya Mangala*, Calcutta, 1971.

Jordaan, Roy E., 1984, 'The Mystery of Nyai Lara Kidul, Goddess of the Southern Ocean', *Archipel 28*, Paris, EHESS: 99–116.

Karim, Abdul, 1964, *Dacca The Mughal Capital*, Dacca, Asiatic Society of Pakistan.

Karim, Khondkar Mahibubul, 1974, *The Provinces of Bihar and Bengal Under Shah Jahan*, Dacca, Asiatic Society of Bangladesh.

Kervran, Monique, 1999, 'Multiple Ports at the Mouth of the River Indus: Barbarike, Deb, Daybul, Lahori Bandar, Diul Sinde' in in Himanshu Prabha Ray ed. *Archaeology of Seafaring: The Indian Ocean in the Ancient Period*, New Delhi, Pragati Publications: 70–153.

Khan, Abdul Majed, 1969, The Transition in Bengal 1756–1775 : A Case Study of Saiyid Mohammad Reza Khan, Cambridge University Press.

Khan, F.A., 1963, *Mainamati*, Karachi.

Khan, Iqbal Ghani, 'Technology and the Question of Elite Intervention in Eighteenth Century North India' in Barnett, R., ed. 2002, *Rethinking Early Modern India*, New Delhi, Manohar: 257–288.

Khondkar Fuzli Rubbee, 1895, *The Origin of the Musalmans of Bengal being a Translation of Haqiqate Musalman-I-Bengalah*, Calcutta, Thacker and Spink and Co.

Kidwai, Atiya Habeeb, 1992, 'Conceptual and Methodological Issues: Ports, Port Cities and Port Hinterlands' in Indu Banga ed. *Ports and Their Hinterlands in India 1700–1950*, New Delhi, Manohar: 7–44.

Kosambhi, D.D., 1956, *An Introduction to the Study of Indian History*, Bombay.

Kriedte, Peter, Medick, Hans and Schlumbohm, Jurgen, 1981, *Industrialisation before Industrialisation*, Cambridge, University Press.

Kulke, Herman, 1999, 'Rivalry and Competition in the Bay of Bengal in the Eleventh Century and its bearing on Indian Ocean Studies', in

Om Prakash and Denys Lombard eds. *Commerce and Culture in the Bay of Bengal 1500–1800*, New Delhi, Manohar/ICHR: 17–35.

Kulke, Herman, 1995, 'The Early and the Imperial Kingdom: A Processural Model of Integrative State Formation in Early Medieval India' in Herman Kulke (Ed). 1995, *The State in India 1000–1700*, New Delhi, Oxford University Press: 233–262.

Kulke, Herman (Ed).1995, *The State in India 1000–1700*, New Delhi, Oxford University Press.

Kulke Herman, 1993, *Kings and Cults: State Formation and Legitimation in South East Asia*, New Delhi, Manohar.

Lapidus, Ira M., 1988, *A History of Islamic Societies*, Cambridge.

Leider, Jacques P., 2005, 'A Short Discussion on Islamic Influence in the Mrauk-U Age' in *Arakanese Reseach Journal*, V. III, July, Arakanese Research Society of Bangladesh: 99–134. (Translated into Bengali).

Leonard, Karen, 1979, 'The "Great Firm" Theory of the Decline of the Mughal Empire', *Comparative Studies in Society and History*, 21, 2: 151–167.

Liu, Xinru, 1988, *Ancient India and Ancient China. Trade and Religious Exchanges AD 1–600*, New Delhi, Oxford University Press.

Lombard, Denys, 1990, *Le Carrefour Javanais: Essai d'histoire Globale*, V. II, *Les Reseaux Asiatiques*, V.III, *L'Heritage des Royaumes Concentriques*, Paris, Editions E.H.E.S.S.

Lombard, Denys, 1988, 'Le Sultanat Malais Comme Modele Socio-Economique' in Lombard, Denys and Aubin Jean (eds). *Marchands et Hommes d'Affaires Asiatiques dans l'Ocean Indien et la Mer de Chine 13e–20e siecles*, Paris, Editions E.H.E.S.S.: 117–124.

Lombard, Denys and Aubin Jean (eds). *Marchands et Hommes d'Affaires Asiatiques dans l'Ocean Indien et la Mer de Chine 13e–20e siecles*, Paris, Editions E.H.E.S.S.

Lombard, Maurice, 1971, *l'Islam dans sa Premiere Grandeur, VIIIe–XIe siecle*, Paris, Flammarion. In English as *The Golden Age Of Islam*, (Tr). J. Spencer, Amsterdam, 1975.

Mackenzie, Alexander, 1884, *The North East Frontier of India*, Intr. by B.K.Roy Burman, New Delhi, Mittal Publications, 2005.

MacPherson, Kenneth, 1998, 'Trade and Traders in the Bay of Bengal: Fifteenth to Nineteenth Centuries' in Mukherjee, R. and Subramanian,

L. (Eds). 1998, *Politics and Trade in the Indian Ocean World: Essays in Honour of Ashin Das Gupta*, Delhi, Oxford University Press.

MacPherson, Kenneth, *The Indian Ocean: A History of the People and the Sea*, 1993, New Delhi, Oxford University Press.

Majumdar N.G. 1929 (ed. with tr. and notes), *Inscriptions of Bengal*, Rajshahi, Varendra Research Society, Volume 3 *Containing the Inscriptions of the Chandras, the Varmans and the Senas and of Isvaraghosa and Damodara.*

Majumdar, R.C., 1960, *The Classical Accounts of India*, Calcutta, Firma K.L.Mukhopadhyay.

Majumdar, R.C. ed. 1943, *The History of Bengal*. V.1 *Hindu Period*, Dacca, The University of Dacca.

Marks, Robert B., 1997, *Tigers, Rice, Silk and Silt: Environment and Economy in Late Imperial South China*, New York, Cambridge University Press.

Marks, Robert B., 1996, 'Commercialization Without Capitalism. Processes of Environmental Change in South China 1550–1850' in *Environmental History*, I, No.1: 56–82.

Marshall, Peter J. (Ed). 2003, *The Eighteenth Century in Indian History: Evolution or Revolution?* Delhi, Oxford University Press.

Marshall, P.J., 1987, *Bengal: The British Bridgehead, Eastern India 1740–1828*, NCHI, Cambridge University Press, India, Orient Longman.

Marshall, Peter J., 1976, *East Indian Fortunes*, Oxford University Press.

McCrindle, J.W., *Ptolemy's Geography* in Majumdar, R.C., 1960, *Classical Accounts of India*, Calcutta.

McCabe, Ina B., 1999, *The Shah's Silk for Europe's Silver: The Eurasian Trade of the Julfa Armenians in Safavid Iran and India 1530–1750* (Armenian Texts and Studies, 150), Georgia, Scholars Press.

Medley, Margaret, 1976, *The Chinese Potter: A Practical History of Chinese Ceramics*, Oxford, Phaidon Press.

Meilink-Roelofz, M.A.P., 1962, *Asian Trade and European Influence in the Indonesian Archipelago Between 1500 and about 1630*, The Hague, Martinus Njihoff.

Meillassoux, Claude, 1991, *The Anthropolgy of Slavery: The Womb of Iron and Gold*, Chicago University Press.

Menon, Dilip, 2000, '*Houses by the Sea: State Experimentation in Malabar 1760-1800'* in Chandoke, N. (ed). *Mapping History: Essays Presented to Ravinder Kumar*, Delhi: 161–86.

Mitra, Pratip Kumar, 2002, 'Source Material on the Medieval Cities of Gaur and Pandua in the the British Public Collections', in Sengupta, Gautam and Panja, Sheena eds. *Archaeology of Eastern India: New Perspectives*, Calcutta, Centre for Archaeological Studies and Training, Eastern India: 277–328.

Modelski. George and Thomson, William, 1996, *Leading Sectors and World Powers: The Co-Evolution of Global Economics and Politics*, Columbia, South Carolina Press.

Mohammed, M.F., 2005, 'Outstanding Issues in Bangladesh-India Relations' in Haidar, Salman, ed. *India-Bangladesh: Strengthening the Partnership*, Chandigarh, Centre for Research in Rural and Industrial Development: 1–13.

Mohsin, K.M., 1973, *A Bengal District in Transition: Murshidabad (1765–93)*, Dacca.

Mookerji, Radha Kumud, 1962 (Reprint), *Indian Shipping, A History of the Sea Borne Trade and Maritime Activity of the Indians from the Earliest Times*, Allahabad, Kitab Mahal.

Moosvi, Shireen, 1992, 'The Gujarat Ports and Their Hinterland: The Economic Relationship' in Indu Banga ed. *Ports and Their Hinterlands in India 1700–1950*, New Delhi, Manohar: 121–129.

Moreland, W.H., 1929, *The Agrarian System of Moslem India*, Cambridge University Press.

Morgan, F.W., 1952, *Ports and Harbours*, London, Hutchinsons'.

Morrison, Barrie M., 1970, *Political Centers and Cultural Regions in Early Bengal*, The Association for Asian Studies, University of Arizona Press.

Mukherjee, R. and Subramanian, L. (Eds). 1998, *Politics and Trade in the Indian Ocean World: Essays in Honour of Ashin Das Gupta*, Delhi, Oxford University Press.

Mukherjee, Ramkrishna, *The Rise and Fall of the English East India Company: a Sociological Appraisal*, 2nd edition, Berlin, Verlag der Wissenschaft, 1957.

Mukherjee, Rila, 2005, 'Pilgrimage as Bridge', *Man & Development*, XXVII, 4, December: 87-108.

Mukherjee, Rila, 2004, 'Rice Culture of Divine Right in a Celestially Ordered Zone: A Case Study of South Asian and South East, Asian

Ideologies and Hegemonies from c. 2000 BC to c. 1800 AD with Specific Reference to Bengal', *Campus Social*, Lisbon,.

Mukherjee, Rila, 2004, 'Contested Authenticities', *Rethinking History*, Routledge, Vol.8, 3: 459–463.

Mukherjee, Rila, 2004, 'The Vitality of Sacred Spaces' in Gopal Krishan (ed). *The Vitality of India*, Chandigarh, Centre for Research in Rural and Industrial Development: 173–186.

Mukherjee, Rila, 2003, *Europe Transformed 1350–1789*, Kolkata, Progressive Publishers.

Mukherjee, Rila, 2003, *The Lost Worlds of Europe*, Kolkata, Progressive Publishers.

Mukherjee, Rila, 1994, 'The Story of Kasimbazar: Silk Merchants and Commerce in Eighteenth Century India', *Review*, XVII, 4, Fall Issue: 499–554.

Mukherjee, Rila, 1990–91, 'The French East India Company's Trade in East Bengal From 1750–1753: A Look at the Chandernagore-Jugdia Letters', *Indian Historical Review*, XVII, nos.1–2: 122–135.

Mukhia, Harbans. 2004, *The Mughals of India*, Blackwell Publishing.

Norton, William, 1984, *Historical Analysis in Geography*, U.K., Longman.

O'Malley, L.S.S., and Chakravarti, M., 1914, *Bengal District Gazeteer: Murshidabad*, Calcutta, Bengal Secretariat Book Depot.

Om Prakash, 2002, 'Trade and Politics in Eighteenth Century Bengal' in Alavi, Seema, 2002, *The Eighteenth Century in India*, Delhi, Oxford University Press: 136–164.

Om Prakash and Lombard, Denys (eds). 1999, *Commerce and Culture in The Bay of Bengal 1500–1800*, Delhi, ICHR/ Manohar.

Om Prakash, 1998, 'European Corporate Enterprises and the Politics of Trade in India, 1600–1800' in Alam, M. and Subrahmanyam, S. (Eds)., 1998, *The Mughal State 1526–1750*, New Delhi, Oxford University Press.

Om Prakash, 1998, European Commercial Enterprise in Pre-Colonial India, NCHI, II.5, Cambridge University Press.

Om Prakash,1986, *The Dutch East India Company and the Economy of Bengal, 1640–1720*, Princeton University Press.

Panda, Sisir Kumar, 1995, *The State and Statecraft in Medieval Orissa Under the Later Eastern Gangas (AD 1038–1434)*, Calcutta, K.P. Bagchi.

Paul, Pramode Lal, 1939, *The Early History of Bengal*, Calcutta, Indian Research Institute.

Pearson, M.N., Unpublished keynote address to the conference *'Seascapes, Littoral Cultures and Trans-oceanic Exchanges,'* sponsored by the American Historical Association, Washington DC, February 12–15, 2003.

Pearson, M.N., 1987, *The Portuguese in India*, *NCHI*, 1.1, Cambridge University Press, Indian edition, Orient Longman.

Pearson, M.N. 1976, 'Shivaji and the Decline of the Mughal Empire', Journal of Asian Studies, XXXV, 2: 221–35.

Pearson, M.N., 1972, 'Political Participation in Mughal India' in *The Indian Economic and Social History Review*, IX, 2: 113–131.

Petech, Luciano, 1990, *Central Tibet and the Mongols-The Yuan-sa-Skya Period of Tibetan History*, Rome, Serie Orientale Roma, Instituto Italiano Per Il Medio ed Estremo Oriente.

Phayre, A.P., 1884, *History of Burma*, London.

Poonawala, Ismail Kurban Husein (revised and annotated), 2004, *The Pillars of Islam*, or the *Da'a'im al-Islam* of al-Qadi al-Nu'man. Translated by Asaf A.A. Fyzee. Oxford University Press, India. 2 vols.

Prawdin, Michael, 1940, *The Mongol Empire: Its Rise and Legacy*, London, Allen and Unwin.

Quanungo, S.B., 1988, *A History of Chittagong*, V.1 *From Ancient Times Down to 1761*, Chittagong, Signet.

Quaritch-Wales, H.G., 1961, *The Making of Greater India*, London, B. Quaritch-Wales, second edition

Quatrich-Wales, H.G., 1957, *Pre History and Religion in South East Asia*, London, B.Quaritch-Wales.

Quayle, Robina G., 1966, *Eastern Civilisations*, New York, Meredith/ Appleton-Century-Crofts.

Rao, V. N. Schulman D and Subrahmanyam, S. 1992, *Symbols of Substance: Court and State in Nayaka Period Tamil Nadu*, New Delhi, Oxford University Press.

Rashid, M. Harunur, 1975, 'The Mainamati Gold Coins' in *Bangladesh Lalit Kala*, I,

Ray, Aniruddha, 2004, *The Merchant and the State: The French in India 1666–1739*, New Delhi, Munshiram Manoharlal.

Ray, Aniruddha, 1997, 'Middle Bengali Literature: A Source for the Study of Bengal in the Age of Akbar' in Habib, Irfan, *Akbar and His India*, New Delhi, Oxford University Press: 225–242.

Ray, Aniruddha, 1986, Introduction to Abid Ali Khan's *Memoirs of Gaur and Pandua*, Calcutta, West Bengal Directorate of Archaeology.

Ray, B., 1961, *West Bengal District Census Handbook: Murshidabad*, Calcutta.

Ray, Haraprasad, 2003, *Trade and Trade Routes between India and China*, Calcutta, Progressive Publishers.

Ray, Haraprasad, 1999, *India South East Asia and China: Some Historical Issues*, Professor Adhir Chakravarty Memorial Lecture 1998, Calcutta, Centre for Archaeological Studies and Training, Eastern India.

Ray, Haraprasad, 1993, *Trade and Diplomacy in India-China Relations-a Study of Bengal During the Fifteenth Century*, New Delhi, Radiant.

Ray, Himanshu Prabha, 2003, *The Archaeology Of Seafaring in Ancient South Asia*, Cambridge World Archaeology Series, Cambridge University Press.

Ray, Himanshu Prabha, 1999, *Archaeology of Seafaring: The Indian Ocean in The Ancient Period*, New Delhi, Pragati Publications.

Ray, Himanshu Prabha and Salles, Jean Francois eds. 1996, *Tradition and Archaelogy: Early Maritime Contacts in The Indian Ocean*, New Delhi, Manohar.

Ray, Himangshu Prabha, 1996, 'Sea Faring and Maritime Contacts: An Agenda for Historical Analysis', *JESHO*, 39,4.

Ray, Himanshu Prabha, 1994, *The Winds of Change, Buddhism and the Maritime LInks of Early South Asia*, New Delhi, Oxford University Press.

Ray, Niharranjan, 1993, *A History of the Bengali People*, V.1 *Early Period*, Calcutta, Dey's Publishing. In Bengali.

Ray, Swarup Chandra, 1891, *An Ancient and Modern History of Sonargang*, Calcutta, Sakha Press (in Bengali).

Raychaudhuri, Tapan, 1982, Chapter XI, 'Inland Trade' in Tapan Raychaudhuri and Irfan Habib (Eds). *The Cambridge Economic History of India*,V. I, Cambridge/Orient Longman.

Raychaudhuri, Tapan and Habib, Irfan (Eds). 1982, *The Cambridge Economic History of India*, V. I, Cambridge/Orient Longman.

Raychaudhuri, Tapan, 1969, *Bengal Under Akbar and Jahangir, An Introductory Study in Social History,* 2nd edition, Delhi, Munshiram Manoharlal.

Reid, Anthony, 1993, *Southeast Asia in the Age of Commerce 1450–1680.* 2 vols. V.2: *Expansion and Crisis*, New Haven, Yale Press.

Rennell James, 1780, 1781, *A Bengal Atlas Containing Maps of the Theatre of War and Commerce on that Side of Hindoostan*, London.

Rennell, James, 1976, *Memoirs of a Map of Hindoostan or the Mogul Empire*, Reprint, Editions Indian, Calcutta.

de Romanis, F. and Tchernia, A. (Eds). 1997, *Crossings: Early Mediterrannean Contacts with India*, New Delhi, CSH/Manohar Publication in Association with Italian Embassy Cultural Centre.

Richards, J.F. 'The Imperial Crisis in The Deccan', *Journal of Asian Studies*, XXXV, 2: 237–256.

Rimmer, P.S. 1973, 'The Search for Spatial Regularities in the Development of Australian Seaports 1861–1961/2' in B.S. Hoyle ed. *Transport and Development*, London, Macmillan: 63–86.

Rothermund, Dietmar, 1981, *Asian Trade and European Expansion in The Age of Mercantilism*, Delhi, Manohar.

Roy, Atul Chandra, 1986, *A History of Bengal: Turko-Afghan Period*, New Delhi/Ludhiana, Kalyani Publishers.

Roy Choudhuri, Bani, 1990, *The Political History of Bengal to the Rise of the Pala Dynasty*, Calcutta, Sanskrit Pustak Bhandar.

Roy, N.B., 1958, *Niamatullah's History of the Afghans or Makhzan-I-Afghani*, Santiniketan Press, West Bengal.

Salles, Jean Francois, Boussac, Marie Francoise, Breuil, Jean Yves, 2002, 'Mahasthangarh (Bangladesh) and the Ganges Valley in the Mauryan Period' in Sengupta, Gautam and Panja, Sheena eds. *Archaeology of Eastern India: New Perspectives*, Calcutta, Centre for Archaeological Studies and Training, Eastern India: 527–50.

Sanyal, Hitesranjan, 1981, *Social Mobility in Bengal*, Calcutta, Papyrus.

Sarkar, Jadunath, 1921, *History of Aurangzeb*, Calcutta.

Sarkar, Jadunath, *1912-30*, *The Fall of the Mughal Empire*, 4 vols., Calcutta.

Sarkar, Jadunath, 1973, *The History of Bengal: Muslim Period 1200–1757*, Patna, Academica Asiatica, eprint.

Sastri, Haraprasad, 1980, *Bener Meye, Collected Works*, V.1 .Calcutta, West Bengal State Book Board.

Schottenhammer, Angela, 1999, 'The Maritime Trade of Quanzhou (Zaitun) from the Ninth through the Thirteenth Century' in Himanshu Prabha Ray ed. *Archaeology of Seafaring: The Indian Ocean in The Ancient Period*, New Delhi, Pragati Publications: 271–290.

Scott, Rosemary, 1995, 'Southern Chinese Provincial Kilns: their Importance and Possible Influence on South East Asian Ceramics', in Rosemary Scott and John Guy eds. *South East Asia and China: Art, Interaction and Commerce*, London, Percival David Foundation: 187–204.

Sen, D.C., 1932, *Eastern Bengal Ballads*, Calcutta University Press.

Sen, D.C., 1935, *Brihat Banga*, V.1, Calcutta, Dey's Publishing, 1993 reprint. (In Bengali).

Sen, Sudipta, 1998, *Empire of Free Trude, The East India Company and the Making of the Colonial Marketplace*, Philadelphia, University of Pennsylvania Press.

Sen, Surendranath, 1938, 'An Early Portuguese Account of Bengal' in *Calcutta Review*, January issue.

Sengupta, Gautam and Panja, Sheena, eds. 2002, *Archaeology of Eastern India: New Perspectives*, Calcutta, Centre for Archaeological Studies and Training, Eastern India.

Sengupta, Gautam ed. 1997–99, *Pratna Samiksha*, V.6–8, Calcutta, Directorate of Archaeology and Museums

Sengupta, Gautam, 1996, 'Archaelogy of Coastal Bengal' in Ray, Himanshu Prabha and Salles, Jean Francois, (Eds). *Tradition and Archaelogy: Early Maritime Contacts in The Indian Ocean*, New Delhi, Manohar: 115–128.

Serajuddin, A.M., 1971, *The Revenue Administration of the East India Company in Chittagong 1761–1785*, Chittagong, University Press.

Sharma, R.S., 2001, *Early Medieval Indian Society: A study in Feudalisation*, Orient Longman.

Sharma, R.S., 1965, *Indian Feudalism: 300–1200*, Calcutta, University Press.

Sinha, Sutapa, 2002, '*Archaeology of the Medieval City of Gaur*' in Sengupta, Gautam and Panja, Sheena, eds. 2002, *Archaeology of Eastern India: New Perspectives*, Calcutta, Centre for Archaeological Studies and Training, Eastern India: 329–356.

Sinha, Sutapa, 1997-99, 'Coin Hoards of the Bengal Sultans: Anatomy of the Hoards' in Gautam Sengupta ed. 1997-1999, *Pratna Samiksha*, V.6–8, Calcutta, Directorate of Archaeology and Museums.

Steensgaard, N., 1974, *The Asian Trade Revolution of the Seventeenth Century*, Chicago Press.

Stein, Burton, 1989, 'Eighteenth Century India: Another View', *Studies In History*, v. reprinted in Marshall, P.J., 2003, (Ed). *The Eighteenth Century in Indian History: Evolution or Revolution?* Oxford University Press: 62–89.

Stewart, Charles, 1903, *The History of Bengal*, Calcutta, Bangabashi Press.

Streusand, Douglas, E.,1989, *The Formation of the Mughal Empire*, Oxford University Press, Delhi.

Subramanian, L. (Ed). 1999, *The French East India Company and the Trade of the Indian Ocean: A Collection of Essays by Indrani Ray*, CSSSC/ Munshiram Manoharlal.

Subramanian, L. and Mukherjee, R. (Eds). 1998, *Politics and Trade in the Indian Ocean World: Essays in Honour of Ashin Das Gupta*, Delhi, Oxford University Press.

Subrahmanyam, Sanjay, 2005, 'Dreaming an Indo-Persian Empire in South Asia: 1740–1800', in Subrahmanyam, Sanjay, 2005, *Explorations in Connected History: Mughals and Franks*, New Delhi, Oxford University Press.

Subrahmanyam, Sanjay, 2005, 'On Indian Views of the Portuguese in Asia', in Subrahmanyam,Sanjay, 2005, *Explorations in Connected History; From The Tagus to The Ganges*, New Delhi, Oxford University Press.

Subrahmanyam, Sanjay, 2005, "Persianization and Mercantilism" in Bay of Bengal History, 1400–1700' in Subrahmanyam,Sanjay, 2005, *Explorations in Connected History: From the Tagus to the Ganges*, New Delhi, Oxford University Press: 45–79.

Subrahmanyam, Sanjay, 2005,'Dutch Tribulations in Seventeenth century Mrauk-U' in Subrahmanyam,Sanjay, 2005, *Explorations in Connected History; From The Tagus to The Ganges*, New Delhi, Oxford University Press.

Subrahmayam, Sanjay, 2003, 'Turning the Stones Over: Sixteenth century Millenarianism From the Tagus to the Ganges' in *Indian Economic and Social History Review*, XL, 2, April–June: 129–161. Now as Chapter 5 'Sixteenth Century Millenarianism from The Tagus to the

Ganges' in *Explorations in Connected History: From the Tagus to the Ganges*, New Delhi, Oxford University Press, 2005.

Subrahmanyam, Sanjay ed. 1994, *Money and the Market in India 1100–1700* Delhi, Oxford University Press.

Subrahmanyam, Sanjay, 1993, *The Portuguese Empire in Asia 1500–1700*, London/New York, Longman.

Subrahmanyam, Sanjay, 1992, 'Iranians Abroad: Intra Asian Elite Migration and Early Modern State Formation', *The Journal of Asian Studies*, Vol. 51, 2: 340–63.

Subrahmanyam, 1992, 'The Mughal State-Structure or Process? Reflections on Recent Western Historiography', *The Indian Economic and Social History Review*, 29,3: 291-321.

Subrahmanyam, Sanjay, 1990, *Improvising Empire, Portuguese Trade and Settlement in the Bay of Bengal, 1500-1700*. Delhi, Oxford University Press.

Subrahmanyam Sanjay, 1990, *The Political Economy of Commerce: Southern India 1500–1650*. South Asian Studies #45, Cambridge.

Subrahmanyam, Sanjay, 1988, 'State Formation and Transformation in Early Modern India and South East Asia', *Itinerario*.

Subrahmanyam, Sanjay and Bayly, C.A. 1988, 'Portfolio Capitalists and the Political Economy of Early Modern India' in *The Indian Economic and Social History Review*, 25, 4: 401–24.

Supple, Barry B., 1970, *Commercial Crisis and Change in England 1600–1642: A Study in the Instability of a Mercantile Economy*, Cambridge University Press.

Tarafdar, M.R., 1995, Trade, Technology and Society in Medieval Bengal, ICBS, Dhaka.

Tarafdar, M.R., 1986, The Bengali Muslims in the Pre Colonial Period: Problems of Conversion, Class Formation and Cultural Evolution, 92–110, in Marc Gaborieau (Ed). *Islam et Societe en Asie du Sud*, Paris, *Purusartha*, Vol. 9.

Tarafdar, M.R., 1978, 'Trade and Society in Early Medieval Bengal', *The Indian Historical Review*, January, 4, No. 2, New Delhi.

Tarafdar, M.R., 1965, *Husain Shahi Bengal: A Socio Political Study*, Dacca, Asiatic Society of Pakistan.

Thapar, Romila, 2002, *The Penguin History of Early India, From the Origins to AD 1300*, Penguin Books, India.

Thapar, Romila, 2000, *Cultural Pasts*, New Delhi, Oxford University Press.

Thapar, Romila, 1975, *Time as a Metaphor for History*, Calcutta, K.P. Bagchi.

Togan, Isenbike, 1990, '*Inner Asian Muslim Merchants and the Closing of the Silk Route (17th and 18th Centuries)*', *UNESCO*, Urumqui, August.

Toussaint, Auguste, 1974, *L'Ocean Indien au XVIIIe Siecle*, Paris, Flammarion.

Tracy, J.D. (ed). 1990, *The Rise of the Merchant Empires : Long Distance Trade in the Early Modern World 1350–1750*, Cambridge University Press.

Tracy, J.D. (ed). 1991, *The Political Economy of Merchant Empires*, Cambridge, University Press.

Tribe, Keith, 1978, *Land, Labour and Economic Discourse*, London, RKP.

Van Leur, J.C., 1955, *Indonesian Trade and Society: Essays in Social and Economic History*, The Hague and Bandung, W. van Hoeve.

Van Schendel, Willem, 1992, *Francis Buchanan in South East Bengal (1798): His Journey to Chittagong, the Chittagong Hill Tracts, Noakhali and Comilla*, Dhaka University Press.

Wallerstein, Immanuel, 1991, 'World System versus World Systems. *A Ctitique*' in *Critique of Anthropology*, II, 2.

Wallerstein, Immanuel, 1974–1989, *The Modern World System* I (1974), II (1980) and III (1989), New York, Academic Books/Academic Press.

Wicks, Robert S., 1992, *Money, Markets and Trade in Early Southeast Asia : The Development of Indigenous Monetary Systems to AD 1400*, Cornell, Ithaca/New York.

Winius, George, 1983, 'The "Shadow Empire" of Goa in the Bay of Bengal', *Itinerario*, V.vii (2): 83–101.

Wink, Andre, 1990, *Al Hind*, V.1. New Delhi, Oxford University Press.

Wink, Andre, 1999, *Al Hind*, V.2, New Delhi, Oxford University Press.

Wink, A., 1984 'Asian Studies: Agrarian History and Orientalism' in *Itinerario*, vol.VIII, no.2.

Wong, R. Bin, 2002, The Search for European Differences and Domination in the Early Modern World : A view from Asia', in the *American Historical Review* 107, 2, April.

Wong, R. Bin, 1997, *China Transformed: Historical Change and the Limits of European Experience*, Ithaca, Cornell Press.

Yang, Anand A., 1998, *Bazaar India: Markets, Society and the Colonial State in Bihar*, Berkeley and L.A., California Press.

Index